Symmetrical and Asymmetrical Distributions in Statistics and Data Science

Symmetrical and Asymmetrical Distributions in Statistics and Data Science

Editors

Arne Johannssen
Nataliya Chukhrova
Quanxin Zhu

Basel • Beijing • Wuhan • Barcelona • Belgrade • Novi Sad • Cluj • Manchester

Editors

Arne Johannssen
Faculty of Business Studies
Harz University of
Applied Sciences
Wernigerode
Germany

Nataliya Chukhrova
Faculty of Engineering
University of Southern
Denmark
Odense
Denmark

Quanxin Zhu
School of Mathematics
and Statistics
Hunan Normal University
Changsha
China

Editorial Office
MDPI AG
Grosspeteranlage 5
4052 Basel, Switzerland

This is a reprint of articles from the Special Issue published online in the open access journal *Symmetry* (ISSN 2073-8994) (available at: https://www.mdpi.com/journal/symmetry/special_issues/Symmetrical_Asymmetrical_Distributions_Statistics_Data_Science).

For citation purposes, cite each article independently as indicated on the article page online and as indicated below:

Lastname, A.A.; Lastname, B.B. Article Title. *Journal Name* **Year**, *Volume Number*, Page Range.

ISBN 978-3-7258-2150-1 (Hbk)
ISBN 978-3-7258-2149-5 (PDF)
doi.org/10.3390/books978-3-7258-2149-5

© 2024 by the authors. Articles in this book are Open Access and distributed under the Creative Commons Attribution (CC BY) license. The book as a whole is distributed by MDPI under the terms and conditions of the Creative Commons Attribution-NonCommercial-NoDerivs (CC BY-NC-ND) license.

Contents

About the Editors vii

Arne Johannssen, Nataliya Chukhrova and Quanxin Zhu
Symmetrical and Asymmetrical Distributions in Statistics and Data Science
Reprinted from: *Symmetry* 2023, 15, 2140, doi:10.3390/sym15122140 1

Xuelong Hu, Suying Zhang, Guan Sun, Jianlan Zhong and Shu Wu
Modified One-Sided EWMA Charts without- and with Variable Sampling Intervals for
Monitoring a Normal Process
Reprinted from: *Symmetry* 2022, 14, 159, doi:10.3390/sym14010159 5

Jia-Han Shih, Yoshihiko Konno, Yuan-Tsung Chang and Takeshi Emura
Copula-Based Estimation Methods for a Common Mean Vector for Bivariate Meta-Analyses
Reprinted from: *Symmetry* 2022, 14, 186, doi:10.3390/sym14020186 20

Salem A. Alyami, Moolath Girish Babu, Ibrahim Elbatal, Naif Alotaibi and Mohammed Elgarhy
Type II Half-Logistic Odd Fréchet Class of Distributions: Statistical Theory and Applications
Reprinted from: *Symmetry* 2022, 14, 1222, doi:10.3390/sym14061222 47

Xuelong Hu, Guan Sun, Fupeng Xie and Anan Tang
Monitoring the Ratio of Two Normal Variables Based on Triple Exponentially Weighted Moving
Average Control Charts with Fixed and Variable Sampling Intervals
Reprinted from: *Symmetry* 2022, 14, 1236, doi:10.3390/sym14061236 68

Hanan Haj Ahmad and Ehab M. Almetwally
Generating Optimal Discrete Analogue of the Generalized Pareto Distribution under Bayesian
Inference with Applications
Reprinted from: *Symmetry* 2022, 14, 1457, doi:10.3390/sym14071457 90

Franz H. Harke, Miryam S. Merk and Philipp Otto
Estimation of Asymmetric Spatial Autoregressive Dependence on Irregular Lattices
Reprinted from: *Symmetry* 2022, 14, 1474, doi:10.3390/sym14071474 108

Ismailkhan Enayathulla Khan and Rajendran Paramasivam
Reduction in Waiting Time in an M/M/1/N Encouraged Arrival Queue with Feedback, Balking
and Maintaining of Reneged Customers
Reprinted from: *Symmetry* 2022, 14, 1743, doi:10.3390/sym14081743 121

Hanan Haj Ahmad, Ehab M. Almetwally, Ahmed Rabaiah and Dina A. Ramadan
Statistical Analysis of Alpha Power Inverse Weibull Distribution under Hybrid Censored
Scheme with Applications to Ball Bearings Technology and Biomedical Data
Reprinted from: *Symmetry* 2023, 15, 161, doi:10.3390/sym15010161 139

Refah Alotaibi, Hoda Rezk and Ahmed Elshahhat
Computational Analysis for Fréchet Parameters of Life from Generalized Type-II Progressive
Hybrid Censored Data with Applications in Physics and Engineering
Reprinted from: *Symmetry* 2023, 15, 348, doi:10.3390/sym15020348 168

Muhammad Arslan, Sadia Anwar, Nevine M. Gunaime, Sana Shahab, Showkat Ahmad Lone and Zahid Rasheed
An Improved Charting Scheme to Monitor the Process Mean Using Two Supplementary
Variables
Reprinted from: *Symmetry* 2023, 15, 482, doi:10.3390/sym15020482 192

Habbiburr Rehman, Navin Chandra, Takeshi Emura and Manju Pandey
Estimation of the Modified Weibull Additive Hazards Regression Model under Competing Risks
Reprinted from: *Symmetry* **2023**, *15*, 485, doi:10.3390/sym15020485 206

Hanan Haj Ahmad, Dina A. Ramadan, Mahmoud M. M. Mansour and Mohamed S. Aboshady
The Reliability of Stored Water Behind Dams Using the Multi-Component Stress-Strength System
Reprinted from: *Symmetry* **2023**, *15*, 766, doi:10.3390/sym15030766 224

Refah Alotaibi, Ehab M. Almetwally and Hoda Rezk
Reliability Analysis of Kavya Manoharan Kumaraswamy Distribution under Generalized Progressive Hybrid Data
Reprinted from: *Symmetry* **2023**, *15*, 1671, doi:10.3390/sym15091671 240

About the Editors

Arne Johannssen

Arne Johannssen holds a Master's degree in Economics and a PhD in Statistics from the University of Hamburg, Germany. He is a Professor of Statistics and Data Analytics at Harz University of Applied Sciences, Germany. His research interests are artificial intelligence, computational statistics, data science, soft computing, and statistical learning with applications in business and economics. He authored 50 publications in renowned international journals, and especially in the top-tier journals of *Artificial Intelligence* and *Statistics and Probability*. His research is funded by the German Research Foundation (DFG), among others.

Nataliya Chukhrova

Nataliya Chukhrova is an Assistant Professor in Applied AI and Data Science at the Maersk McKinney Moller Institute, Faculty of Engineering, University of Southern Denmark (SDU). Her focus in research and teaching is on computational statistics, statistical inference, statistical learning, and artificial intelligence with applications in medicine and industry. Her research is funded by the DFG and the Federal Ministry of Education and Research (BMBF), among others. Nataliya has given numerous lectures on mathematics and statistics and has been awarded the Excellence in Higher Education Award.

Quanxin Zhu

Quanxin Zhu received his Ph.D. degree from Sun Yatsen (Zhongshan) University, Guangzhou, China, in 2005. He is currently a professor at Hunan Normal University, and he has obtained the Alexander von Humboldt Foundation of Germany. Professor Zhu is distinguished professor of Furong scholars in Hunan Province, leading talent of scientific and technological innovation in Hunan Province, and deputy director of the Key Laboratory of computing and stochastic mathematics of the Ministry of Education. Professor Zhu is a highly cited scientist in the world in 2018–2023. Also, Professor Zhu is a senior member of the IEEE, and he is the Lead Guest Editor of several international journals. He is an Associate Editor of six international SCI journals, including *IEEE Transactions on Automation Science and Engineering*. He has obtained the first prize of the Hunan Natural Science Award in 2021 and the list of the top two percent scientists in 2020–2023. Professor Zhu has obtained the 2011 Annual Chinese "One Hundred The Most Influential International Academic Paper" award and has been one of the most cited Chinese researchers in 2014–2023, Elsevier. Professor Zhu is a reviewer of more than 50 other journals, and he is the author or coauthor of more than 300 journal papers. His research interests include stochastic control, stochastic differential equations, stochastic stability, stochastic nonlinear systems, Markovian jump systems, stochastic neural networks, and stochastic complex networks.

Editorial

Symmetrical and Asymmetrical Distributions in Statistics and Data Science

Arne Johannssen [1,*], Nataliya Chukhrova [1] and Quanxin Zhu [2]

1. Faculty of Business Administration, University of Hamburg, 20146 Hamburg, Germany; nataliya.chukhrova@uni-hamburg.de
2. School of Mathematical Sciences and Statistics, Hunan Normal University, Changsha 410081, China; zqx22@126.com
* Correspondence: arne.johannssen@uni-hamburg.de

Citation: Johannssen, A.; Chukhrova, N.; Zhu, Q. Symmetrical and Asymmetrical Distributions in Statistics and Data Science. *Symmetry* 2023, 15, 2140. https://doi.org/10.3390/sym15122140

Received: 5 September 2023
Accepted: 23 November 2023
Published: 1 December 2023

Copyright: © 2023 by the authors. Licensee MDPI, Basel, Switzerland. This article is an open access article distributed under the terms and conditions of the Creative Commons Attribution (CC BY) license (https://creativecommons.org/licenses/by/4.0/).

Probability distributions are a fundamental topic of Statistics and Data Science that is highly relevant in both theory and practical applications. There are numerous probability distributions that come in many shapes and with different properties. In order to identify an appropriate distribution for modeling the statistical properties of a population of interest, one should consider the shape of the distribution as a crucial factor. In particular, the symmetry or asymmetry of the distribution plays a decisive role.

The objective of this Special Issue, entitled "Symmetrical and Asymmetrical Distributions in Statistics and Data Science", is to highlight the importance of symmetrical and asymmetrical distributions in its thematic breadth and with applications in many fields. We welcomed submissions related to the latest developments in the area of symmetrical and asymmetrical distributions in Statistics and Data Science. The response from the scientific community was remarkable: 39 papers were submitted for consideration, and 13 papers were finally accepted after a rigorous peer-review process. The remainder of this editorial contains a summary of the contributions to this Special Issue, ordered by date of publication.

Hu et al. [1] study the performance of the modified one-sided Exponentially Weighted Moving Average (EWMA) $\bar{X}$ control chart for monitoring normally distributed processes that are characterized by a perfectly symmetrical shape. Using Monte Carlo simulations and a real data application in semiconductor manufacturing, the authors demonstrate the properties and features of the proposed chart. They also show that the performance of the chart can be further increased by adding the Variable Sampling Interval (VSI) feature to the monitoring procedure.

Shih et al. [2] are concerned with copulas that can be either symmetric (e.g., Gaussian copula) or asymmetric (e.g., Clayton copula). As there are only a few studies on copula-based bivariate meta-analysis, the authors develop the corresponding methodology and theory, specifically to estimate the common mean vector, in this paper. For direct implementation, the authors also provide the R package CommonMean.Copula. To illustrate the practical applicability of the proposed methods, the authors conduct two applications with real data in the educational and medical sectors.

Alyami et al. [3] present a new class of statistical distributions in their paper, the so called type II half-Logistic odd Fréchet-G class. This class contains various distributions of symmetrical or asymmetrical shapes. The authors discuss four of these specific distributions in the paper, derive their statistical properties, and conduct real-life applications using biomedical, engineering, environmental, and manufacturing data sets.

Hu et al. [4] propose a modified EWMA control chart to monitor the ratio of two normally distributed random variables. As in [1], the authors consider their chart with and without the VSI feature. Based on a simulation study and a real data application in the food industry, the authors illustrate the properties and features of the control chart. They conclude that the proposed chart (1) with VSI is superior and (2) the VSI-based chart also leads to better results than previous approaches in the literature.

Haj Ahmad and Almetwally [5] discuss three discretization methods to formulate discrete analogues of the continuous generalized Pareto distribution. The authors use Bayesian inference techniques to estimate the discrete models with different symmetric (squared error) and asymmetric (linear exponential and general entropy) loss functions. They perform a comparative analysis and find that the discretized generalized Pareto distribution is a promising alternative. The practical applications are conducted using medical data (COVID-19 daily deaths in the United States and in Italy).

Harke et al. [6] present a data-driven method to estimate the spatial autoregressive dependence on irregular lattices. As the structure of the spatial weights matrix $\mathbf{W}$ is difficult to obtain in practical applications, they introduce a method to obtain $\mathbf{W}$, whether it is symmetric or asymmetric. The authors verify their method using simulation and comparative studies. They also discuss a practical application on the evolution of sales prices for building land in Brandenburg, Germany, and conclude that this evolution and its spatial dependence are mainly driven by the orientation towards Berlin.

Khan and Paramasivam [7] explore how feedback, balking, retaining reneged clients, and the quality control technique affect the encouraged arrival queuing model. The encouraged arrival is valuable for many different businesses in terms of managing operations, deliberating, outlining, implementation, and service development. The authors derive performance measures for the expected number of units in the system, the average number of occupied services and the expected waiting time in the system as well as in the queue.

Haj Ahmad et al. [8] provide a statistical analysis of the alpha power inverse Weibull distribution under a hybrid type II censoring scheme. Their study is motivated by applications in the medical field, namely ball bearings and the resistance of guinea pigs. In these applications, type II censored schemes are recommended to minimize the experimental time and cost where the components are following the alpha power inverse Weibull distribution. The authors conclude that this distribution under a hybrid type II censoring scheme is suitable to model real biomedical data.

Alotaibi et al. [9] investigate parameter estimation, reliability, and hazard rate functions of the Fréchet distribution based on generalized type II progressive hybrid censored data. The Bayesian estimators are computed with independent gamma conjugate priors using the symmetrical squared error loss function. The authors perform comprehensive Monte Carlo simulations and discuss practical applications in physics (precipitation in Minneapolis–Saint Paul) and engineering (vehicle fatalities in South Carolina).

Arslan et al. [10] introduce a control chart for monitoring the process mean based on two supplementary variables. These variables are correlated with the study variable in the form of a regression estimator that is an efficient and unbiased estimator for the process mean. The authors state that the proposed charting scheme performs effectively when both supplementary variables are uncorrelated. The applicability of the proposed chart is shown within a real-data example based on carbon fiber manufacturing data.

Rehman et al. [11] deal with parametric regression analysis of survival data using the additive hazards model with competing risks in the presence of independent right censoring. The baseline hazard function is parameterized using a modified Weibull distribution as a lifetime model. The parameters are estimated using maximum likelihood and Bayesian methods, and the asymptotic confidence interval and the Bayes credible interval of the parameters are derived. The finite sample behavior of the estimators is investigated through simulations, and the model is applied to liver transplant data.

Haj Ahmad et al. [12] analyze a multi-component stress–strength system that provides a useful framework to evaluate the reliability of dams and their ability to cope with external influences such as water pressure, earthquake activity, and erosion. The authors suggest the Gumbel type II distribution as a suitable model for fitting related data. Both classical and Bayesian approaches are used to estimate the reliability function, and Monte Carlo simulations are employed for parameter estimation. As a real case study, the paper considers data from the Shasta reservoir in the United States.

Alotaibi et al. [13] investigate the difficulties associated with estimating the model parameters and reliability time functions of the Kavya Manoharan Kumaraswamy distribution based on generalized type II progressive hybrid censoring. Using the symmetrical squared error loss function, independent gamma conjugate priors are employed to compute the Bayesian estimators. As the Bayesian estimators cannot be derived analytically, the authors implement Markov Chain Monte Carlo (MCMC) techniques. A practical application is provided using a data set on the tensile strength of polyester fibers.

Finally, we would like to congratulate all the above authors on the acceptance of their paper(s) to this Special Issue. We hope that this Special Issue will inspire further researchers to make important discoveries and contributions in the field of "Symmetrical and Asymmetrical Distributions in Statistics and Data Science". To provide the best possible platform for further significant contributions, Volume II of this Special Issue in *Symmetry* is already established (https://www.mdpi.com/journal/symmetry/special_issues/A28X1PLF7Y).

We would therefore like to invite researchers to submit their contributions to Volume II of this Special Issue. A potential topic of interest could be the remarkable revival of the hypergeometric and the negative hypergeometric distribution in various areas such as healthcare [14], manufacturing [15], risk management [16], statistical inference [17], and beyond. We look forward to many high-quality papers and a successful second edition of this Special Issue.

Conflicts of Interest: The authors declare no conflict of interest.

References

1. Hu, X.; Zhang, S.; Sun, G.; Zhong, J.; Wu, S. Modified One-Sided EWMA Charts without- and with Variable Sampling Intervals for Monitoring a Normal Process. *Symmetry* **2022**, *14*, 159. [CrossRef]
2. Shih, J.-H.; Konno, Y.; Chang, Y.-T.; Emura, T. Copula-Based Estimation Methods for a Common Mean Vector for Bivariate Meta-Analyses. *Symmetry* **2022**, *14*, 186. [CrossRef]
3. Alyami, S.A.; Babu, M.G.; Elbatal, I.; Alotaibi, N.; Elgarhy, M. Type II Half-Logistic Odd Fréchet Class of Distributions: Statistical Theory and Applications. *Symmetry* **2022**, *14*, 1222. [CrossRef]
4. Hu, X.; Sun, G.; Xie, F.; Tang, A. Monitoring the Ratio of Two Normal Variables Based on Triple Exponentially Weighted Moving Average Control Charts with Fixed and Variable Sampling Intervals. *Symmetry* **2022**, *14*, 1236. [CrossRef]
5. Haj Ahmad, H.; Almetwally, E.M. Generating Optimal Discrete Analogue of the Generalized Pareto Distribution under Bayesian Inference with Applications. *Symmetry* **2022**, *14*, 1457. [CrossRef]
6. Harke, F.H.; Merk, M.S.; Otto, P. Estimation of Asymmetric Spatial Autoregressive Dependence on Irregular Lattices. *Symmetry* **2022**, *14*, 1474. [CrossRef]
7. Khan, I.E.; Paramasivam, R. Reduction in Waiting Time in an M/M/1/N Encouraged Arrival Queue with Feedback, Balking and Maintaining of Reneged Customers. *Symmetry* **2022**, *14*, 1743. [CrossRef]
8. Haj Ahmad, H.; Almetwally, E.M.; Rabaiah, A.; Ramadan, D.A. Statistical Analysis of Alpha Power Inverse Weibull Distribution under Hybrid Censored Scheme with Applications to Ball Bearings Technology and Biomedical Data. *Symmetry* **2023**, *15*, 161. [CrossRef]
9. Alotaibi, R.; Rezk, H.; Elshahhat, A. Computational Analysis for Fréchet Parameters of Life from Generalized Type-II Progressive Hybrid Censored Data with Applications in Physics and Engineering. *Symmetry* **2023**, *15*, 348. [CrossRef]
10. Arslan, M.; Anwar, S.; Gunaime, N.M.; Shahab, S.; Lone, S.A.; Rasheed, Z. An Improved Charting Scheme to Monitor the Process Mean Using Two Supplementary Variables. *Symmetry* **2023**, *15*, 482. [CrossRef]
11. Rehman, H.; Chandra, N.; Emura, T.; Pandey, M. Estimation of the Modified Weibull Additive Hazards Regression Model under Competing Risks. *Symmetry* **2023**, *15*, 485. [CrossRef]
12. Haj Ahmad, H.; Ramadan, D.A.; Mansour, M.M.M.; Aboshady, M.S. The Reliability of Stored Water behind Dams Using the Multi-Component Stress-Strength System. *Symmetry* **2023**, *15*, 766. [CrossRef]
13. Alotaibi, R.; Almetwally, E.M.; Rezk, H. Reliability Analysis of Kavya Manoharan Kumaraswamy Distribution under Generalized Progressive Hybrid Data. *Symmetry* **2023**, *15*, 1671. [CrossRef]
14. Chukhrova, N.; Johannssen, A. Monitoring of high-yield and periodical processes in health care. *Health Care Manag. Sci.* **2020**, *23*, 619–639. [CrossRef] [PubMed]
15. Johannssen, A.; Chukhrova, N.; Celano, G.; Castagliola, P. A number-between-events control chart for monitoring finite horizon production processes. *Qual. Reliab. Eng. Int.* **2022**, *38*, 2110–2138. [CrossRef]

16. Johannssen, A.; Chukhrova, N.; Castagliola, P. Efficient algorithms for calculating the probability distribution of the sum of hypergeometric-distributed random variables. *MethodsX* **2021**, *8*, 101507. [CrossRef] [PubMed]
17. Chukhrova, N.; Johannssen, A. Randomized vs. non-randomized hypergeometric hypothesis testing with crisp and fuzzy hypotheses. *Stat. Pap.* **2020**, *61*, 2605–2641. [CrossRef]

Disclaimer/Publisher's Note: The statements, opinions and data contained in all publications are solely those of the individual author(s) and contributor(s) and not of MDPI and/or the editor(s). MDPI and/or the editor(s) disclaim responsibility for any injury to people or property resulting from any ideas, methods, instructions or products referred to in the content.

Article

Modified One-Sided EWMA Charts without- and with Variable Sampling Intervals for Monitoring a Normal Process

Xuelong Hu [1,*], Suying Zhang [1,†], Guan Sun [1,†], Jianlan Zhong [2,†] and Shu Wu [3,†]

1. School of Management, Nanjing University of Posts and Telecommunications, No. 66, Xinmofan Road, Nanjing 210003, China; 1020112326@njupt.edu.cn (S.Z.); 1020112320@njupt.edu.cn (G.S.)
2. College of Management & College of Tourism, Fujian Agriculture and Forestry University, Fuzhou 350002, China; zhongjianlan@fafu.edu.cn
3. School of Logistics, Wuhan University of Technology, Wuhan 430063, China; wushu@whut.edu.cn
* Correspondence: hxl0419@njupt.edu.cn; Tel.: +86-159-5056-7942
† These authors contributed equally to this work.

Abstract: Much research has been conducted on two-sided Exponentially Weighted Moving Average (EWMA) control charts, while less work has been devoted to the one-sided EWMA charts. Traditional one-sided EWMA charts involve resetting the EWMA statistic to the target whenever it falls below or above the target, or truncating the observations above or below the target and further applying the EWMA statistic to the truncated samples. In order to further improve the performance of traditional one-sided EWMA mean ($\bar{X}$) charts, this paper studies the performance of the Modified One-sided EWMA (MOEWMA) $\bar{X}$ charts to monitor a normally distributed process. The Monte-Carlo simulation method is used to obtain the zero- and steady-state Run Length (RL) properties of the proposed control charts. Through extensive simulations and comparisons with other charts, it is shown that the proposed MOEWMA $\bar{X}$ charts compare favorably with some existing competing charts. Moreover, by attaching the variable sampling intervals (VSI) feature to the MOEWMA $\bar{X}$ charts, it is shown that the VSI MOEWMA charts outperform the corresponding charts without the VSI feature. Finally, a real data example from manufacturing process shows the implementation of the proposed one-sided charts.

Keywords: one-sided EWMA $\bar{X}$ charts; variable sampling interval; monte-carlo simulation; run length; zero-state; steady-state

1. Introduction

A main objective for a process is to continuously improve its quality, which can be statistically expressed as variation reduction. Chance and assignable causes exist and lead to variation in a process. The variation caused by change is unavoidable and always exists in a process, even if the operation is carried out using standardized raw material and methods. It is not practical to eliminate the chance cause technically and economically, while variation caused by assignable causes indicates that there exist some unwanted factors to be detected.

Statistical Process Monitoring (SPM) provides a large set of tools to help practitioners in monitoring manufacturing or service processes to quickly detect assignable causes. Among these, control charts are widely used online and can be implemented with a charting statistic related to the process mean or/and dispersion. The aim of a control chart is to detect abnormal changes in the process as soon as possible. Many univariate mean ($\bar{X}$) charts, such as the Shewhart $\bar{X}$ chart, Cumulative Sum (CUSUM) $\bar{X}$ chart, and Exponentially Weighted Moving Average (EWMA) $\bar{X}$ chart were investigated by researchers; see Brook and Evans [1], Nelson [2], Lucas and Saccucci [3], and Hawkins and Olwell [4]. More recent works on control charts can refer to Li et al. [5], Mukherjee and Rakitzis [6], Zwetsloot et al. [7], and Perry [8], to name a few. The Shewhart charts are known to be effective when the shift size in the process is large. For the detection of small to moderate shifts, both CUSUM and EWMA charts using the current and former samples information perform much better than Shewhart type charts, see Montgomery [9].

Since the primary works of Crowder [10], Lucas and Saccucci [3], and Domangue and Patch [11], EWMA type charts have received much attention. For example, for non-normal and autocorrelated processes, the properties of EWMA $\bar{X}$ charts were first investigated by Borror et al. [12] and Lu and Jr. [13], respectively. The performance of the EWMA $\bar{X}$ chart was investigated by Jones et al. [14] when the process parameters are estimated. Recently, Celano et al. [15], Calzada and Scariano [16], and Haq et al. [17] studied the run length performance of the EWMA t charts. To summarise, only a two-sided EWMA chart was used in the above researches. In practice, the direction of the out-of-control shift is usually known in advance, which implies that it is possible to tune the upward and downward parts of EWMA charts separately [18]. Then two separate one-sided EWMA charts were studied by some researchers. For instance, Tran et al. [19] and Tran and Knoth [20] studied the properties of two one-sided EWMA charts to monitor the ratio of two variables. Zhang et al. [21] and Muhammad et al. [22] investigated the performance of two one-sided EWMA charts for monitoring the coefficient of variation (CV).

In this paper, the work in Zhang et al. [21] is highlighted for the new resetting model of the Modified One-sided EWMA (MOEWMA) charting statistic. In the EWMA charting statistic, information of former and current samples are both used and the charting statistic is reset to the target if it is smaller than the target. While their work studied the EWMA chart for monitoring the CV, as far as we know, there is no research on the proposed scheme for monitoring the mean of a normally distributed process. In fact, a normally distributed quality characteristic usually exists in some industrial processes. To fill this gap, we investigate the properties of the MOEWMA $\bar{X}$ charts. In addition, it is known that control charts with the variable sampling interval (VSI) features are more efficient than the corresponding fixed sampling interval (FSI) charts in the detection of shifts. In the past decades, much research has been conducted on VSI control charts. For instance, Nguyen et al. [23] suggested a VSI CUSUM chart to monitor the ratio of two normal variables and showed that the proposed chart had some advantages over the corresponding FSI CUSUM chart. Using extensive Monte-Carlo simulations, Haq [24] studied the performance of the weighted adaptive multivariate CUSUM chart with VSI feature. It was shown that the proposed charts perform uniformly better than the corresponding FSI charts in terms of the ATS (Average Time to Signal) and AATS (Average Adjusted Time to Signal) performances. Coelho et al. [25] proposed a VSI nonparametric Shewhart type control chart, which was shown to be better than the existing FSI chart. For more research works, we direct readers to the works [26–31] and the references cited therein. To further increase the sensitivity of the MOEWMA $\bar{X}$ charts and gain motivation from the above works on the VSI charts, the VSI MOEWMA $\bar{X}$ charts are proposed, and it is expected that the VSI MOEWMA charts perform better than the corresponding FSI one-sided charts.

The remainder of this paper is organized as follows: Section 2 reviews several types of one-sided EWMA $\bar{X}$ charts and presents the MOEWMA $\bar{X}$ chart. The zero-state (ZS) and steady-state (SS) Average Run Length (ARL) performances of the proposed MOEWMA $\bar{X}$ charts are presented in Section 3 and are compared with other competing charts. Section 4 presents the detailed construction of the MOEWMA $\bar{X}$ charts with the VSI feature and, moreover, both the ZS and SS performances of the proposed VSI MOEWMA $\bar{X}$ charts are investigated. A real data example is used to illustrate the implementation of the MOEWMA $\bar{X}$ charts in Section 5. Finally, some conclusions and recommendations are made in the last section.

2. One-Sided EWMA Type Charts

Assume that $\{X_{t,1}, \ldots, X_{t,n}\}$, $t = 1, 2, \ldots$ is a sample of size $n \geq 1$ from an independent normal distribution, i.e., $X_t \sim N(\mu_0 + \delta\sigma_0, \sigma_0)$, where μ_0 and σ_0 are the in-control mean and standard deviation, respectively, and δ is the magnitude of the mean shift. When $\delta = 0$, the process is considered to be in-control. Otherwise, the process is out-of-control. At each sample point $t = 1, 2, \ldots$, the sample mean $\bar{X}_t = \frac{1}{n}\sum_{j=1}^{n} X_{t,j}$ is computed for the process monitoring, where $\bar{X}_t \sim N(\mu_0 + \delta\sigma_0, \frac{\sigma_0}{\sqrt{n}})$. Without loss of generality, we assume $\mu_0 = 0$ and $\sigma_0 = 1$ in this paper.

2.1. Traditional One-Sided EWMA Charts

The traditional two-sided EWMA $\bar{X}$ chart construct the monitoring statistic $Z_t = \lambda \bar{X}_t + (1-\lambda)Z_{t-1}, t = 1, 2, 3, \ldots$, with a fixed smoothing constant $\lambda \in (0, 1]$ and the initial value $Z_0 = \mu_0$. The upper (UCL) and lower (LCL) control limits of the EWMA $\bar{X}$ chart are generally selected based on the constraint of the desired in-control ARL. If $Z_t \in [LCL, UCL]$, the process is considered to be in-control. Otherwise, if $Z_t \notin [LCL, UCL]$, the process is deemed to be out-of-control. Instead of using a single two-sided EWMA $\bar{X}$ chart, when the direction of the shift is known, three types of one-sided EWMA $\bar{X}$ charts were suggested by some researchers. These charts are summarized as follows:

(1) A simple use of the one-sided EWMA $\bar{X}$ chart is to set only an upper control limit (UCL) or a lower control limit (LCL) with the traditional charting statistic $Z_t = \lambda \bar{X}_t + (1-\lambda)Z_{t-1}$ and the initial value $Z_0 = \mu_0$. This chart is denoted as SEWMA $\bar{X}$ chart. That is to say, the upper-sided SEWMA $\bar{X}$ chart declares an alarm when $Z_t > UCL$ and the lower-sided SEWMA $\bar{X}$ chart declares an alarm when $Z_t < LCL$. More details of the SEWMA $\bar{X}$ chart can be seen in Robinson and Ho [32].

(2) A second use of the one-sided EWMA $\bar{X}$ chart is to reset the traditional EWMA statistic to the target whenever it is smaller than the target (for the upper-sided chart) or whenever it is larger than the target (for the lower-sided chart). This chart is denoted as REWMA $\bar{X}$ chart. The charting statistics Z_t^+ and Z_t^- of the upper- and lower-sided REWMA $\bar{X}$ charts are given as follows,

$$Z_t^+ = \max(\mu_0, \lambda \bar{X}_t + (1-\lambda)Z_{t-1}^+), \quad (1)$$

and

$$Z_t^- = \min(\mu_0, \lambda \bar{X}_t + (1-\lambda)Z_{t-1}^-). \quad (2)$$

with the initial value $Z_0 = \mu_0$. An out-of-control signal is triggered as soon as $Z_t^+ > UCL$ (for the upper-sided REWMA $\bar{X}$ chart) or $Z_t^- < LCL$ (for the lower-sided REWMA $\bar{X}$ chart), respectively. More details of REWMA type charts can be seen in Hamilton and Crowder [33] and Gan [34].

(3) A third use of the one-sided EWMA $\bar{X}$ chart is first truncate the sample mean $\bar{X}_t$ below the target to the target value (for the upper-sided chart) or above the target to the target value (for the lower-sided chart), and then apply the EWMA recursion to these truncated values. This chart is denoted as IEWMA $\bar{X}$ chart. The charting statistic Z_t of the IEWMA chart is given as follows:

$$Z_t = \lambda W_t + (1-\lambda)Z_{t-1}, \quad (3)$$

where $W_t = \frac{W_t' - (\mu_0 + 1/\sqrt{2\pi}\sigma_0)/\sqrt{n}}{\sigma_0\sqrt{0.5 - 0.5/\pi}/\sqrt{n}}$ is the standardized value of $W_t' = \max(\mu_0, \bar{X}_t)$ (for the upper-sided chart), and $W_t = \frac{W_t' - (\mu_0 - 1/\sqrt{2\pi}\sigma_0)/\sqrt{n}}{\sigma_0\sqrt{0.5 - 0.5/\pi}/\sqrt{n}}$ is the standardized value of $W_t' = \min(\mu_0, \bar{X}_t)$ (for the lower-sided chart). The initial value Z_0 is set as 0. An out-of-control signal is given when $Z_t > UCL$ in the upper-sided chart or $Z_t < LCL$ in the lower-sided chart. More details of this chart can be seen in Shu and Jiang [35] and Shu et al. [36].

2.2. The Proposed MOEWMA $\bar{X}$ Charts

In this section, the MOEWMA $\bar{X}$ charts with a new resetting model are investigated. As it will be shown in Section 3, the proposed charts outperform the traditional one-sided EWMA $\bar{X}$ charts presented in Section 2.1.

It can be seen from Equation (1) that, when $\lambda \bar{X}_t + (1-\lambda)Z_{t-1}^+$ is smaller than μ_0, then $Z_t^+ = \mu_0$ and $Z_{t+1}^+ = \max(\mu_0, \lambda \bar{X}_{t+1} + (1-\lambda)\mu_0)$. All the samples information collected before time $t+1$ are lost. As the main advantage of EWMA type charts is to use both current and former samples information, the charting statistic of the upper-sided MOEWMA $\bar{X}$ chart is constructed as,

$$Z_t^+ = \max(\mu_0, \lambda \bar{X}_t + (1-\lambda)Z_{t-1}), \tag{4}$$

where $Z_{t-1} = \lambda \bar{X}_{t-1} + (1-\lambda)Z_{t-2}$ and the initial value $Z_0 = \mu_0$. It can be noted that the charting statistic Z_t^+ in Equation (4) uses all samples information collected before. The chart triggers an out-of-control signal if Z_t^+ is larger than the UCL. Similarly, a lower-sided MOEWMA $\bar{X}$ is suggested with the following charting statistic,

$$Z_t^- = \min(\mu_0, \lambda \bar{X}_t + (1-\lambda)Z_{t-1}), \tag{5}$$

where the initial value $Z_0 = \mu_0$. An out-of-control signal is triggered if Z_t^- is smaller than the LCL.

3. Numerical Results and Comparisons

In this section, some RL measures, including the ARL and the Standard Deviation of Run Length ($SDRL$) are used to investigate the performance of the one-sided EWMA charts in Section 2. The ARL is defined as the expected number of samples on the chart until a signal occurs. A control chart is desirable when the in-control ARL is large and at the same time, the out-of-control ARL is as small as possible. In addition, the $SDRL$ determines the variability of the RL distribution. The smaller the $SDRL$ value, the better the ARL performance of a control chart, see Haq [37]. In addition, the subscripts 0 and 1 are used with ARL and $SDRL$ to denote the in-control and out-of-control properties, respectively. To obtain these RL properties of the proposed chart, the Monte-Carlo method is adopted in this paper. Under each simulation run, 10^5 iterations of RL values are used to calculate the values of ARL and $SDRL$.

3.1. Comparisons with Some Competing Charts

In this section, to provide some direct insight into the performance of the proposed charts, the (ARL, $SDRL$) of the MOEWMA $\bar{X}$ charts are compared with the ones of the SEWMA, REWMA, and IEWMA $\bar{X}$ charts. The properties of the SEWMA, REWMA, and IEWMA $\bar{X}$ charts can be obtained using the Markov chain approach. For the EWMA type charts, values of $0.05 \leq \lambda \leq 0.25$ were recommended by Montgomery [9]. Moreover, a relatively small smoothing parameter λ is usually suggested for monitoring small shifts while larger values of λ are suggested for larger shifts. In this paper, $\lambda \in \{0.05, 0.1, 0.2, 0.25\}$ are selected for illustration and the corresponding control limits of EWMA type charts can be obtained with the constraint on the desired ARL_0. For simplicity, the ARL_0 is set to be 200. For the proposed one-sided MOEWMA $\bar{X}$ chart, a bisection algorithm similar to Dickinson et al. [38] is used to find the control limit. The algorithm stops when the in-control ARL falls within the interval $[ARL_0 - 1, ARL_0 + 1]$.

Table 1 presents the (ARL_1, $SDRL_1$) values of these EWMA control charts for different shifts δ varying from 0.1 to 3 when $n \in \{3,5\}$. It can be noted from this table that, for the upper-sided MOEWMA $\bar{X}$ chart, a small value of λ is relatively effective for small shifts δ and vice verse. For instance, when $n = 3$ and $\delta = 0.1$, the (ARL_1, $SDRL_1$) = (54.06, 45.94) of the upper-sided MOEWMA $\bar{X}$ chart when $\lambda = 0.05$ is smaller than the (ARL_1, $SDRL_1$) = (75.26, 71.98) of the chart when $\lambda = 0.25$. Compared with the competing EWMA (SEWMA, REWMA, and IEWMA) charts, some conclusions are made as follows:

- Irrespective of the values of δ and n, the ARL_1 and $SDRL_1$ values of the upper-sided MOEWMA $\bar{X}$ chart are generally smaller than the ones of the upper-sided REWMA $\bar{X}$ chart, especially for small shifts. This fact clearly demonstrates the advantage of the proposed chart. For instance, when $n = 3$, $\lambda = 0.1$, and $\delta = 0.1$, the $(ARL_1, SDRL_1) = (60.12, 54.07)$ of the upper-sided MOEWMA $\bar{X}$ chart are smaller than the $(ARL_1, SDRL_1) = (70.17, 62.84)$ of the upper-sided REWMA $\bar{X}$ chart.
- The proposed chart always has a little smaller ARL_1 value than the one of the upper-sided SEWMA $\bar{X}$ chart. For example, for the same values of n, λ and δ presented above, the $(ARL_1, SDRL_1) = (61.11, 54.11)$ of the upper-sided SEWMA $\bar{X}$ chart are close to the ones of the upper-sided MOEWMA $\bar{X}$ chart.
- Compared with the upper-sided IEWMA $\bar{X}$ chart, the proposed chart performs better for small shifts and worse for moderate to large shifts. For instance, when $n = 3$ and $\lambda = 0.1$, the upper-sided MOEWMA $\bar{X}$ chart with $(ARL_1, SDRL_1) = (60.12, 54.07)$ is better than the upper-sided IEWMA $\bar{X}$ chart with $(ARL_1, SDRL_1) = (68.17, 63.64)$ for the detection of $\delta = 0.1$. However, for the detection of $\delta = 1$, the upper-sided MOEWMA chart with $(ARL_1, SDRL_1) = (3.81, 1.29)$ is worse than the upper-sided IEWMA chart with $(ARL_1, SDRL_1) = (3.38, 1.43)$.
- For a large shift, for instance when $\delta = 3$ or larger than 3, all the charts perform similarly, as the ARL_1 is close to 1 and the $SDRL_1$ value converges to 0 with δ increasing.

Table 1. The profiles $(ARL_1, SDRL_1)$ of EWMA type charts when $ARL_0 = 200$.

n	λ	Chart	UCL	δ = 0.1		0.3		0.5		1.0		1.5		2.0		2.5		3.0	
3	0.05	SEWMA	0.1665	(54.38	45.62)	(16.09	9.28)	(8.99	3.96)	(4.34	1.29)	(2.95	0.72)	(2.28	0.48)	(1.98	0.30)	(1.78	0.42)
		IEWMA	0.3149	(60.67	54.46)	(16.89	11.53)	(8.63	4.77)	(3.61	1.41)	(2.33	0.71)	(1.78	0.52)	(1.41	0.50)	(1.13	0.34)
		REWMA	0.1979	(64.42	53.32)	(18.96	10.69)	(10.45	4.40)	(4.97	1.40)	(3.34	0.76)	(2.56	0.56)	(2.12	0.34)	(1.96	0.24)
		MOEWMA	0.1669	(54.06	45.94)	(15.76	9.21)	(8.79	3.93)	(4.24	1.28)	(2.88	0.72)	(2.23	0.46)	(1.95	0.31)	(1.72	0.45)
	0.10	SEWMA	0.2793	(61.11	54.11)	(16.71	10.94)	(8.75	4.37)	(3.98	1.31)	(2.66	0.70)	(2.09	0.43)	(1.80	0.42)	(1.48	0.50)
		IEWMA	0.5567	(68.17	63.64)	(17.95	13.64)	(8.59	5.29)	(3.38	1.43)	(2.14	0.71)	(1.60	0.54)	(1.25	0.44)	(1.06	0.24)
		REWMA	0.3133	(70.17	62.84)	(18.93	12.79)	(9.60	4.86)	(4.25	1.39)	(2.81	0.74)	(2.18	0.45)	(1.88	0.38)	(1.59	0.49)
		MOEWMA	0.2797	(60.12	54.07)	(16.26	11.02)	(8.44	4.32)	(3.81	1.29)	(2.55	0.68)	(2.02	0.43)	(1.70	0.47)	(1.36	0.48)
	0.15	SEWMA	0.3710	(66.01	61.12)	(17.15	12.62)	(8.41	4.80)	(3.59	1.33)	(2.38	0.67)	(1.87	0.48)	(1.51	0.50)	(1.20	0.40)
		IEWMA	0.7668	(74.14	70.61)	(19.30	15.70)	(8.77	5.87)	(3.26	1.48)	(2.02	0.73)	(1.49	0.54)	(1.17	0.38)	(1.04	0.18)
		REWMA	0.4059	(75.41	69.90)	(19.83	14.89)	(9.42	5.42)	(3.90	1.42)	(2.54	0.71)	(1.99	0.46)	(1.65	0.49)	(1.31	0.46)
		MOEWMA	0.3710	(65.90	61.20)	(17.06	12.65)	(8.34	4.77)	(3.56	1.32)	(2.36	0.67)	(1.85	0.49)	(1.48	0.50)	(1.18	0.39)
	0.20	SEWMA	0.4511	(70.98	67.01)	(18.23	14.36)	(8.52	5.32)	(3.44	1.37)	(2.24	0.68)	(1.72	0.52)	(1.35	0.48)	(1.11	0.31)
		IEWMA	0.9584	(79.07	76.29)	(20.72	17.70)	(9.05	6.48)	(3.18	1.53)	(1.93	0.75)	(1.41	0.52)	(1.13	0.34)	(1.02	0.15)
		REWMA	0.4867	(80.05	75.64)	(21.08	16.96)	(9.53	6.05)	(3.70	1.47)	(2.38	0.71)	(1.83	0.51)	(1.46	0.50)	(1.16	0.37)
		MOEWMA	0.4511	(70.90	67.21)	(18.26	14.54)	(8.48	5.36)	(3.40	1.36)	(2.22	0.68)	(1.71	0.53)	(1.34	0.48)	(1.10	0.30)
	0.25	SEWMA	0.5241	(75.48	72.10)	(19.52	16.12)	(8.79	5.88)	(3.36	1.43)	(2.15	0.70)	(1.62	0.54)	(1.26	0.44)	(1.07	0.25)
		IEWMA	1.1425	(83.50	81.21)	(22.29	19.70)	(9.46	7.15)	(3.14	1.61)	(1.87	0.76)	(1.36	0.51)	(1.10	0.30)	(1.02	0.13)
		REWMA	0.5602	(84.19	80.54)	(22.51	18.98)	(9.80	6.73)	(3.58	1.53)	(2.25	0.73)	(1.70	0.54)	(1.33	0.47)	(1.09	0.29)
		MOEWMA	0.5241	(75.26	71.98)	(19.38	16.13)	(8.69	5.85)	(3.31	1.42)	(2.12	0.70)	(1.59	0.54)	(1.24	0.43)	(1.06	0.23)
5	0.05	SEWMA	0.1290	(42.01	33.31)	(11.99	6.07)	(6.81	2.60)	(3.39	0.88)	(2.34	0.51)	(1.95	0.30)	(1.64	0.48)	(1.23	0.42)
		IEWMA	0.3149	(46.96	40.53)	(12.08	7.45)	(6.20	3.04)	(2.71	0.91)	(1.84	0.53)	(1.35	0.48)	(1.07	0.25)	(1.00	0.07)
		REWMA	0.1533	(50.18	39.42)	(14.02	6.85)	(7.88	2.85)	(3.86	0.95)	(2.64	0.58)	(2.08	0.30)	(1.90	0.31)	(1.56	0.50)
		MOEWMA	0.1293	(41.82	33.56)	(11.74	6.05)	(6.65	2.57)	(3.31	0.88)	(2.29	0.50)	(1.92	0.32)	(1.58	0.49)	(1.18	0.38)
	0.10	SEWMA	0.2164	(47.09	40.12)	(12.03	6.94)	(6.45	2.77)	(3.08	0.88)	(2.14	0.46)	(1.76	0.44)	(1.33	0.47)	(1.06	0.24)
		IEWMA	0.5567	(52.93	48.23)	(12.41	8.56)	(6.00	3.25)	(2.51	0.91)	(1.66	0.55)	(1.21	0.41)	(1.03	0.16)	(1.00	0.03)
		REWMA	0.2427	(54.60	47.37)	(13.40	7.91)	(7.00	3.01)	(3.26	0.92)	(2.23	0.49)	(1.84	0.39)	(1.44	0.50)	(1.10	0.30)
		MOEWMA	0.2169	(46.69	40.38)	(11.61	6.86)	(6.19	2.73)	(2.94	0.86)	(2.06	0.45)	(1.65	0.48)	(1.23	0.42)	(1.03	0.18)
	0.15	SEWMA	0.2873	(50.97	46.00)	(11.95	7.84)	(6.03	2.95)	(2.75	0.86)	(1.92	0.49)	(1.45	0.50)	(1.11	0.31)	(1.01	0.09)
		IEWMA	0.7668	(58.05	54.38)	(13.03	9.72)	(5.97	3.50)	(2.39	0.93)	(1.54	0.56)	(1.14	0.35)	(1.01	0.12)	(1.00	0.02)
		REWMA	0.3144	(59.09	53.60)	(13.61	9.08)	(6.66	3.25)	(2.96	0.92)	(2.04	0.48)	(1.59	0.50)	(1.18	0.39)	(1.02	0.15)
		MOEWMA	0.2874	(50.92	46.12)	(11.87	7.89)	(5.99	2.95)	(2.72	0.86)	(1.90	0.49)	(1.42	0.50)	(1.10	0.30)	(1.01	0.09)
	0.20	SEWMA	0.3494	(55.21	51.15)	(12.43	8.85)	(5.96	3.18)	(2.60	0.87)	(1.78	0.53)	(1.30	0.46)	(1.05	0.22)	(1.00	0.05)
		IEWMA	0.9584	(62.47	59.55)	(13.75	10.90)	(6.02	3.79)	(2.30	0.95)	(1.46	0.55)	(1.10	0.30)	(1.01	0.09)	(1.00	0.01)
		REWMA	0.3770	(63.26	58.85)	(14.15	10.30)	(6.55	3.53)	(2.77	0.92)	(1.88	0.52)	(1.40	0.49)	(1.08	0.28)	(1.01	0.08)
		MOEWMA	0.3494	(55.20	51.00)	(12.34	8.80)	(5.92	3.19)	(2.57	0.86)	(1.76	0.53)	(1.28	0.45)	(1.05	0.21)	(1.00	0.05)
	0.25	SEWMA	0.4060	(59.20	55.74)	(13.10	9.90)	(6.00	3.45)	(2.51	0.89)	(1.68	0.55)	(1.22	0.42)	(1.03	0.17)	(1.00	0.04)
		IEWMA	1.1425	(66.56	64.16)	(14.63	12.13)	(6.15	4.11)	(2.24	0.98)	(1.41	0.53)	(1.08	0.27)	(1.01	0.08)	(1.00	0.01)
		REWMA	0.4339	(67.12	63.46)	(14.90	11.55)	(6.57	3.85)	(2.64	0.94)	(1.76	0.55)	(1.28	0.45)	(1.04	0.20)	(1.00	0.05)
		MOEWMA	0.4058	(58.98	55.43)	(12.95	9.80)	(5.95	3.46)	(2.47	0.89)	(1.65	0.55)	(1.20	0.40)	(1.03	0.16)	(1.00	0.03)

As the symmetry of the normal distribution, similar conclusions are drawn for the lower-sided MOEWMA $\bar{X}$ chart. For simplicity, these results are not presented here.

3.2. Optimal Performance of the Proposed MOEWMA $\bar{X}$ Charts

The results in Section 3.1 show the advantage of the proposed chart over the SEWMA, REWMA, and IEWMA $\bar{X}$ charts. All of the simulations above are for a fixed value of λ, which is not optimal for the specified shift size δ_{opt}. To provide a fare comparison, the optimal performances of different charts for the intended shift size are compared in this section. The optimal design of the upper-sided MOEWMA $\bar{X}$ chart involves determining the chart parameters (λ, UCL) to minimize the ARL_1 at a specified mean shift δ_{opt}, at the same time, satisfying the constraint on the desired ARL_0. The procedure can be concluded as a constrained nonlinear minimization problem:

$$(\lambda^*, UCL^*) = \underset{(\lambda, UCL)}{\operatorname{argmin}} ARL_1(n, \lambda, UCL, \delta_{opt}),$$

subject to

$$ARL(n, \lambda, UCL, \delta = 0) = ARL_0.$$

By using this model, extensive computation works are then performed to numerically find the nearly optimal parameters (λ^*, UCL^*) of the upper-sided MOEWMA $\bar{X}$ chart. Table 2 presents the optimal chart parameters (λ^*, UCL^*) of the proposed chart for δ_{opt} and the $(ARL_1, SDRL_1)$ values of the chart at shift δ varying from 0.1 to 3. As a comparison, the nearly optimal parameters and performances of the REWMA, SEWMA, and IEWMA $\bar{X}$ charts are also presented. All charts are designed to maintain $ARL_0 = 200$. For example, if the specified shift size $\delta_{opt} = 0.3$, the $UCLs$ of the upper-sided MOEWMA $\bar{X}$ chart are first determined for $\lambda \in \{0.05, 0.06, ..., 0.99, 1\}$ to obtain $ARL_0 = 200$. The ARL_1 values are then computed for all the combinations of (λ, UCL). The parameters $(\lambda^*, UCL^*) = (0.05, 0.17)$ leading to the smallest $ARL_1 = 15.79$ are considered to be the nearly optimal parameters of the control chart.

It can be concluded from Table 2 that:

- If the specified shift is small ($\delta_{opt} \leq 0.5$), the optimal upper-sided MOEWMA $\bar{X}$ chart performs better than the optimal REWMA, SEWMA, and IEWMA $\bar{X}$ charts. For instance, if $\delta_{opt} = 0.3$, the optimal parameters (λ^*, UCL^*) of the upper-sided MOEWMA $\bar{X}$ chart is $(0.05, 0.17)$ and the corresponding $(ARL_1, SDRL_1) = (15.79, 9.27)$ is the smallest one among these charts.
- The upper-sided MOEWMA $\bar{X}$ chart provides a good sensitivity against shifts smaller than the specified δ_{opt} and the upper-sided IEWMA $\bar{X}$ chart performs better than other charts for shifts larger than the specified δ_{opt}. For instance, if $\delta_{opt} = 0.3$, while the actual shift size in the process is not the specified one and is $\delta = 0.1$ (smaller than $\delta_{opt} = 0.3$), the upper-sided MOEWMA $\bar{X}$ chart with $(ARL_1, SDRL_1) = (53.80, 45.49)$ is better than other charts. If the actual shift size is $\delta = 1$ (larger than $\delta_{opt} = 0.3$), the upper-sided IEWMA $\bar{X}$ chart with $(ARL_1, SDRL_1) = (3.61, 1.41)$ performs better than other charts.
- If the specified shift is moderate ($1 < \delta_{opt} \leq 2$), the upper-sided IEWMA $\bar{X}$ chart has better sensitivity than the REWMA, SEWMA, and MOEWMA $\bar{X}$ charts for all the shift sizes. For example, when $\delta_{opt} = 1.5$, the optimal $(ARL_1, SDRL_1) = (1.74, 0.87)$ of the upper-sided IEWMA $\bar{X}$ chart is smaller than the ones of these charts, and if the actual shift sizes is smaller or larger than 1.5, the upper-sided IEWMA $\bar{X}$ chart still performs better than these charts.
- If the actual shift size is large ($\delta_{opt} \geq 2.5$), the upper-sided MOEWMA $\bar{X}$ chart has the best performance among all the charts. For instance, when $\delta_{opt} = 3$, the optimal $(ARL_1, SDRL_1) = (1.00, 0.07)$ is the same for all the charts. If the actual shift size is smaller than $\delta_{opt} = 3$, it can be seen that the upper-sided MOEWMA $\bar{X}$ chart has the smallest $(ARL_1, SDRL_1)$ value among these EWMA type charts.

The above results also indicate that both the upper-sided IEWMA and MOEWMA $\bar{X}$ charts have a practical property of good performance over a wide range of shifts rather than a scheme to optimize the control charts at a specified shift δ_{opt}. This property was considered to be important, as in applications, the value of shift size is seldom known, and therefore a robust monitoring procedure that efficiently signals a range of shifts is useful [39].

Table 2. The profiles $(ARL_1, SDRL_1)$ of several optimal EWMA type charts when $ARL_0 = 200$ and $n = 3$.

		$\delta_{opt} = 0.1$					$\delta_{opt} = 0.3$			
		SEWMA	REWMA	IEWMA	MOEWMA	SEWMA	REWMA	IEWMA	MOEWMA
	λ^*	0.05	0.05	0.05	0.05	0.06	0.07	0.05	0.05
δ	UCL^*	0.17	0.20	0.31	0.17	0.19	0.25	0.31	0.17
0.1		(54.38 45.62)	(64.42 53.32)	(60.67 54.46)	(54.00 45.92)	(55.72 47.56)	(66.74 57.56)	(60.67 54.46)	(53.80 45.49)
0.3		(16.09 9.28)	(18.96 10.69)	(16.89 11.53)	(15.80 9.25)	(16.09 9.61)	(18.76 11.52)	(16.89 11.53)	(15.79 9.27)
0.5		(8.99 3.96)	(10.45 4.40)	(8.63 4.77)	(8.80 3.94)	(8.85 4.03)	(9.97 4.56)	(8.63 4.77)	(8.80 3.93)
1.0		(4.34 1.29)	(4.97 1.40)	(3.61 1.41)	(4.24 1.28)	(4.21 1.29)	(4.61 1.39)	(3.61 1.41)	(4.24 1.28)
1.5		(2.95 0.72)	(3.34 0.76)	(2.33 0.71)	(2.88 0.72)	(2.85 0.72)	(3.08 0.76)	(2.33 0.71)	(2.88 0.71)
2.0		(2.28 0.48)	(2.56 0.56)	(1.78 0.52)	(2.24 0.46)	(2.22 0.46)	(2.36 0.52)	(1.78 0.52)	(2.24 0.46)
2.5		(1.98 0.30)	(2.12 0.34)	(1.41 0.50)	(1.95 0.31)	(1.94 0.33)	(2.02 0.30)	(1.41 0.50)	(1.95 0.31)
3.0		(1.78 0.42)	(1.96 0.24)	(1.13 0.34)	(1.72 0.45)	(1.69 0.46)	(1.83 0.38)	(1.13 0.34)	(1.72 0.45)

		$\delta_{opt} = 0.5$					$\delta_{opt} = 1$			
		SEWMA	REWMA	IEWMA	MOEWMA	SEWMA	REWMA	IEWMA	MOEWMA
	λ^*	0.15	0.15	0.08	0.15	0.42	0.40	0.28	0.37
δ	UCL^*	0.37	0.41	0.47	0.37	0.75	0.76	1.25	0.68
0.1		(66.01 61.12)	(75.41 69.90)	(65.39 60.37)	(65.75 61.01)	(88.41 86.39)	(94.75 92.41)	(85.91 83.85)	(84.41 82.17)
0.3		(17.15 12.62)	(19.83 14.89)	(17.45 12.81)	(17.08 12.63)	(24.59 22.38)	(27.40 25.02)	(23.26 20.88)	(22.80 20.46)
0.5		(8.41 4.80)	(9.42 5.42)	(8.54 5.07)	(8.32 4.78)	(10.24 8.16)	(11.25 9.02)	(9.73 7.57)	(9.65 7.43)
1.0		(3.59 1.33)	(3.90 1.42)	(3.44 1.42)	(3.56 1.32)	(3.24 1.72)	(3.45 1.81)	(3.13 1.65)	(3.21 1.61)
1.5		(2.38 0.67)	(2.54 0.71)	(2.20 0.71)	(2.35 0.66)	(1.91 0.78)	(2.02 0.80)	(1.84 0.77)	(1.94 0.76)
2.0		(1.87 0.48)	(1.99 0.46)	(1.66 0.54)	(1.85 0.49)	(1.38 0.52)	(1.45 0.54)	(1.33 0.50)	(1.41 0.53)
2.5		(1.51 0.50)	(1.65 0.49)	(1.29 0.46)	(1.48 0.50)	(1.11 0.32)	(1.15 0.36)	(1.09 0.29)	(1.13 0.34)
3.0		(1.20 0.40)	(1.31 0.46)	(1.08 0.27)	(1.18 0.39)	(1.02 0.13)	(1.03 0.16)	(1.01 0.12)	(1.02 0.15)

		$\delta_{opt} = 1.5$					$\delta_{opt} = 2$			
		SEWMA	REWMA	IEWMA	MOEWMA	SEWMA	REWMA	IEWMA	MOEWMA
	λ^*	0.72	0.71	0.55	0.73	0.89	1.00	0.79	0.88
δ	UCL^*	1.11	1.13	2.15	1.12	1.33	1.49	2.97	1.32
0.1		(107.18 106.17)	(111.94 110.88)	(103.46 102.47)	(107.06 106.43)	(116.78 116.17)	(122.87 122.36)	(115.37 114.75)	(115.66 115.35)
0.3		(36.16 35.03)	(39.33 38.19)	(32.89 31.66)	(36.35 35.20)	(44.27 43.59)	(50.30 49.80)	(42.45 41.72)	(43.71 42.85)
0.5		(15.06 13.90)	(16.42 15.25)	(13.32 12.03)	(15.17 14.13)	(19.31 18.58)	(22.91 22.40)	(18.06 17.26)	(18.98 18.23)
1.0		(3.68 2.64)	(3.86 2.82)	(3.37 2.27)	(3.65 2.67)	(4.31 3.58)	(5.02 4.49)	(4.02 3.22)	(4.24 3.52)
1.5		(1.81 0.96)	(1.86 1.00)	(1.74 0.87)	(1.78 0.96)	(1.86 1.16)	(1.97 1.38)	(1.80 1.07)	(1.84 1.15)
2.0		(1.25 0.48)	(1.26 0.50)	(1.23 0.46)	(1.23 0.47)	(1.22 0.49)	(1.23 0.53)	(1.22 0.47)	(1.22 0.49)
2.5		(1.05 0.23)	(1.06 0.24)	(1.05 0.22)	(1.05 0.21)	(1.04 0.21)	(1.04 0.21)	(1.04 0.20)	(1.04 0.20)
3.0		(1.01 0.08)	(1.01 0.09)	(1.01 0.08)	(1.01 0.07)	(1.00 0.07)	(1.00 0.07)	(1.00 0.07)	(1.00 0.07)

		$\delta_{opt} = 2.5$					$\delta_{opt} = 3$			
		SEWMA	REWMA	IEWMA	MOEWMA	SEWMA	REWMA	IEWMA	MOEWMA
	λ^*	0.99	1.00	0.90	0.90	1.00	1.00	0.96	0.90
δ	UCL^*	1.47	1.49	3.40	1.34	1.49	1.49	3.58	1.34
0.1		(122.32 121.81)	(122.87 122.36)	(120.03 119.50)	(117.74 116.67)	(122.87 122.36)	(122.87 122.36)	(121.68 121.17)	(117.27 116.27)
0.3		(49.72 49.21)	(50.30 49.80)	(47.11 46.54)	(44.98 44.08)	(50.30 49.80)	(50.30 49.80)	(48.93 48.40)	(44.47 43.61)
0.5		(22.55 22.03)	(22.91 22.40)	(20.82 20.21)	(19.57 18.87)	(22.91 22.40)	(22.91 22.40)	(21.98 21.44)	(19.64 18.93)
1.0		(4.94 4.39)	(5.02 4.49)	(4.54 3.89)	(4.35 3.64)	(5.02 4.49)	(5.02 4.49)	(4.79 4.21)	(4.35 3.65)
1.5		(1.95 1.35)	(1.97 1.38)	(1.88 1.22)	(1.86 1.18)	(1.97 1.38)	(1.97 1.38)	(1.92 1.30)	(1.86 1.17)
2.0		(1.23 0.53)	(1.23 0.53)	(1.22 0.50)	(1.22 0.49)	(1.23 0.53)	(1.23 0.53)	(1.23 0.52)	(1.22 0.49)
2.5		(1.04 0.21)	(1.04 0.21)	(1.04 0.20)	(1.04 0.21)	(1.04 0.21)	(1.04 0.21)	(1.04 0.21)	(1.04 0.20)
3.0		(1.00 0.07)	(1.00 0.07)	(1.00 0.07)	(1.00 0.07)	(1.00 0.07)	(1.00 0.07)	(1.00 0.07)	(1.00 0.07)

3.3. The Steady-State Performance of the Proposed Chart

The results presented in the previous section are for the case in which the shift occurs from the beginning of the process or the charting statistic is at its initial starting value when the shift occurs. The computed ARL in this way is referred as the zero-state ARL. The steady-state ARL is based on the assumption that the process remains in-control for a long time and a shift occurs later in the process. The steady-state ARL of control chart is considered to be more realistic than the zero-state ARL, see Zwetsloot et al. [7]. For the steady-state case, 10^5 Monte-Carlo simulations are used to estimate the steady-state ARL values of control charts and the shift is assumed to happen in the process after 50 in-control samples, see Dickinson et al. [38], Xu and Jeske [40], and Haq [24].

The out-of-control steady-state ARL_1 and $SDRL_1$ of the proposed chart together with the ones of the REWMA, SEWMA, and IEWMA $\bar{X}$ charts are presented in Table 3 for different combinations of n, λ, and δ. The in-control ARL_0 is set to be 200. It can be noted from Table 3 that the steady-state performance of the upper-sided MOEWMA $\bar{X}$ chart is almost the same as the upper-sided SEWMA $\bar{X}$ chart. Moreover, for a small shift ($\delta \leq 0.3$), both the upper-sided MOEWMA $\bar{X}$ chart and the upper-sided SEWMA $\bar{X}$ chart generally perform better than the upper-sided IEWMA and REWMA $\bar{X}$ charts. For instance, when $n = 3$, $\lambda = 0.1$, and $\delta = 0.1$, the steady-state $(ARL_1, SDRL_1) = (58.66, 54.58)$ and $(ARL_1, SDRL_1) = (58.63, 54.38)$ of the upper-sided SEWMA and MOEWMA $\bar{X}$ charts are smaller than the steady-state $(ARL_1, SDRL_1) = (67.22, 63.92)$ and $(ARL_1, SDRL_1) = (65.35, 62.84)$ of the upper-sided IEWMA and REWMA $\bar{X}$ charts. Moreover, for the shifts larger than 0.5, we can note that the upper-sided IEWMA $\bar{X}$ chart generally performs best among these charts. The upper-sided REWMA $\bar{X}$ chart is preferred only when $\delta = 0.5$.

Table 3. The steady-state profiles $(ARL_1, SDRL_1)$ of EWMA type charts when $ARL_0 = 200$.

n	λ	Chart	UCL	δ = 0.1		0.3		0.5		1.0		1.5		2.0		2.5		3.0	
3	0.05	SEWMA	0.1665	(52.08	46.35)	(15.67	10.34)	(8.83	4.95)	(4.33	2.04)	(2.96	1.28)	(2.31	0.94)	(1.93	0.75)	(1.69	0.64)
		IEWMA	0.3149	(59.80	55.06)	(16.97	12.25)	(8.78	5.42)	(3.71	1.82)	(2.39	1.01)	(1.83	0.70)	(1.52	0.56)	(1.32	0.47)
		REWMA	0.1979	(57.16	53.11)	(15.43	10.90)	(8.17	4.61)	(3.80	1.62)	(2.57	0.95)	(2.00	0.68)	(1.69	0.54)	(1.49	0.50)
		MOEWMA	0.1669	(52.49	46.75)	(15.69	10.34)	(8.86	4.95)	(4.33	2.04)	(2.96	1.28)	(2.31	0.94)	(1.93	0.75)	(1.69	0.63)
	0.10	SEWMA	0.2793	(58.66	54.58)	(15.85	11.30)	(8.32	4.84)	(3.81	1.72)	(2.57	1.03)	(2.00	0.75)	(1.68	0.61)	(1.46	0.53)
		IEWMA	0.5567	(67.22	63.92)	(17.68	13.89)	(8.56	5.53)	(3.41	1.65)	(2.17	0.88)	(1.65	0.61)	(1.36	0.49)	(1.17	0.37)
		REWMA	0.3133	(65.35	62.84)	(16.52	12.86)	(8.02	4.98)	(3.44	1.51)	(2.28	0.84)	(1.78	0.59)	(1.50	0.51)	(1.27	0.44)
		MOEWMA	0.2797	(58.63	54.38)	(15.90	11.38)	(8.29	4.83)	(3.80	1.72)	(2.57	1.03)	(2.00	0.75)	(1.67	0.61)	(1.47	0.53)
	0.15	SEWMA	0.3710	(64.65	61.24)	(16.69	12.79)	(8.20	5.07)	(3.53	1.61)	(2.34	0.92)	(1.82	0.67)	(1.53	0.55)	(1.32	0.47)
		IEWMA	0.7668	(73.10	70.67)	(19.06	15.80)	(8.68	6.02)	(3.27	1.63)	(2.04	0.82)	(1.54	0.57)	(1.26	0.44)	(1.09	0.29)
		REWMA	0.4059	(71.85	69.83)	(17.93	14.92)	(8.21	5.50)	(3.26	1.49)	(2.12	0.79)	(1.65	0.57)	(1.35	0.48)	(1.14	0.35)
		MOEWMA	0.3710	(64.57	61.00)	(16.67	12.83)	(8.17	5.06)	(3.53	1.60)	(2.35	0.93)	(1.82	0.67)	(1.52	0.55)	(1.32	0.47)
	0.20	SEWMA	0.4511	(69.62	67.06)	(17.75	14.59)	(8.28	5.46)	(3.37	1.57)	(2.20	0.87)	(1.70	0.62)	(1.42	0.51)	(1.22	0.42)
		IEWMA	0.9584	(77.87	76.16)	(20.49	17.75)	(8.96	6.55)	(3.18	1.63)	(1.95	0.81)	(1.46	0.55)	(1.19	0.39)	(1.05	0.22)
		REWMA	0.4867	(77.02	75.44)	(19.47	17.00)	(8.49	6.06)	(3.17	1.53)	(2.02	0.77)	(1.54	0.56)	(1.25	0.44)	(1.08	0.27)
		MOEWMA	0.4511	(69.70	67.05)	(17.77	14.52)	(8.30	5.46)	(3.37	1.57)	(2.20	0.87)	(1.70	0.62)	(1.42	0.51)	(1.22	0.42)
	0.25	SEWMA	0.5241	(74.30	72.09)	(19.03	16.30)	(8.52	5.94)	(3.26	1.57)	(2.09	0.84)	(1.61	0.59)	(1.33	0.48)	(1.15	0.36)
		IEWMA	1.1425	(82.89	81.77)	(22.13	19.77)	(9.42	7.24)	(3.13	1.66)	(1.89	0.80)	(1.40	0.53)	(1.15	0.36)	(1.03	0.18)
		REWMA	0.5602	(82.05	80.61)	(21.21	19.07)	(8.92	6.71)	(3.13	1.57)	(1.94	0.77)	(1.47	0.55)	(1.19	0.39)	(1.05	0.21)
		MOEWMA	0.5241	(74.37	72.49)	(19.02	16.10)	(8.55	5.99)	(3.27	1.58)	(2.09	0.83)	(1.61	0.59)	(1.33	0.48)	(1.15	0.36)
5	0.05	SEWMA	0.1290	(40.36	33.99)	(11.76	7.13)	(6.72	3.51)	(3.39	1.51)	(2.37	0.97)	(1.88	0.73)	(1.60	0.60)	(1.41	0.52)
		IEWMA	0.3149	(46.55	41.45)	(12.27	8.21)	(6.36	3.60)	(2.80	1.25)	(1.88	0.73)	(1.48	0.54)	(1.25	0.43)	(1.10	0.30)
		REWMA	0.1533	(43.64	39.46)	(11.16	7.04)	(6.07	3.08)	(2.95	1.15)	(2.06	0.71)	(1.65	0.53)	(1.41	0.49)	(1.18	0.39)
		MOEWMA	0.1293	(40.53	34.19)	(11.75	7.11)	(6.75	3.53)	(3.39	1.51)	(2.38	0.97)	(1.89	0.73)	(1.60	0.60)	(1.41	0.51)
	0.10	SEWMA	0.2164	(45.12	40.43)	(11.41	7.33)	(6.13	3.20)	(2.94	1.23)	(2.05	0.78)	(1.64	0.59)	(1.39	0.50)	(1.21	0.41)
		IEWMA	0.5567	(51.61	48.00)	(12.33	8.85)	(6.01	3.52)	(2.54	1.09)	(1.70	0.63)	(1.32	0.47)	(1.11	0.31)	(1.02	0.14)
		REWMA	0.2427	(50.46	47.19)	(11.40	7.94)	(5.76	3.10)	(2.64	1.03)	(1.82	0.61)	(1.46	0.51)	(1.18	0.38)	(1.03	0.18)
		MOEWMA	0.2169	(45.27	40.64)	(11.43	7.34)	(6.14	3.22)	(2.95	1.24)	(2.06	0.77)	(1.63	0.59)	(1.39	0.50)	(1.21	0.41)
	0.15	SEWMA	0.2873	(49.61	46.09)	(11.61	8.12)	(5.89	3.21)	(2.71	1.12)	(1.87	0.69)	(1.49	0.54)	(1.25	0.43)	(1.10	0.30)
		IEWMA	0.7668	(57.42	54.58)	(12.90	9.88)	(5.95	3.67)	(2.40	1.05)	(1.59	0.59)	(1.22	0.42)	(1.05	0.21)	(1.01	0.07)
		REWMA	0.3144	(55.97	53.56)	(12.11	9.16)	(5.68	3.30)	(2.46	0.99)	(1.69	0.59)	(1.31	0.47)	(1.08	0.27)	(1.01	0.09)
		MOEWMA	0.2874	(49.90	46.16)	(11.58	8.08)	(5.88	3.21)	(2.71	1.12)	(1.87	0.69)	(1.49	0.54)	(1.25	0.44)	(1.10	0.30)
	0.20	SEWMA	0.3494	(54.33	51.41)	(12.07	8.98)	(5.81	3.37)	(2.55	1.07)	(1.75	0.64)	(1.38	0.50)	(1.16	0.36)	(1.05	0.21)
		IEWMA	0.9584	(61.58	59.19)	(13.59	10.98)	(5.97	3.88)	(2.31	1.03)	(1.51	0.57)	(1.16	0.37)	(1.03	0.16)	(1.00	0.04)
		REWMA	0.3770	(60.84	58.42)	(12.90	10.35)	(5.74	3.56)	(2.36	0.98)	(1.59	0.57)	(1.22	0.41)	(1.04	0.19)	(1.00	0.05)
		MOEWMA	0.3494	(53.88	51.17)	(12.12	9.00)	(5.80	3.36)	(2.56	1.07)	(1.75	0.65)	(1.38	0.50)	(1.16	0.37)	(1.05	0.21)
	0.25	SEWMA	0.4060	(58.34	56.16)	(12.75	10.05)	(5.83	3.58)	(2.44	1.04)	(1.65	0.61)	(1.29	0.46)	(1.10	0.30)	(1.02	0.14)
		IEWMA	1.1425	(66.01	64.36)	(14.51	12.23)	(6.12	4.19)	(2.25	1.03)	(1.45	0.56)	(1.12	0.33)	(1.02	0.12)	(1.00	0.02)
		REWMA	0.4339	(65.24	63.38)	(13.79	11.56)	(5.85	3.85)	(2.29	0.99)	(1.51	0.56)	(1.16	0.36)	(1.02	0.14)	(1.00	0.03)
		MOEWMA	0.4058	(57.74	55.66)	(12.70	9.99)	(5.81	3.55)	(2.44	1.04)	(1.66	0.62)	(1.29	0.46)	(1.10	0.30)	(1.02	0.15)

4. MOEWMA $\bar{X}$ Charts with Variable Sampling Intervals

4.1. Construction of the VSI MOEWMA $\bar{X}$ Charts

The MOEWMA $\bar{X}$ charts studied above are FSI type charts, which fixes the time intervals between samples. As suggested by Reynolds et al. [41], $\bar{X}$ chart with VSI features performed better than the corresponding FSI chart. The VSI feature allows a chart to vary the time intervals between samples depending on the value of the charting statistic. For the one-sided type charts, by adding an upper warning limit (UWL) of the upper-sided chart (or a lower warning limit (LWL) of the lower-sided chart), the in-control region of one-sided control charts are divided into a warning region and a central region. If the value of the charting statistic falls in the warning region, it is suspected that the process is at risk and the next sample should be taken after a short sampling interval h_S. If the value of the charting statistic falls in the central region, the process is deemed to be safe and the next sample could be taken after a long sampling interval h_L. Otherwise, the process is considered to be out-of-control when the value of the charting statistic falls outside the UCL the upper-sided chart (or the LCL of the lower-sided chart).

Let UWL and LWL be the warning limits of the upper-sided and lower-sided VSI MOEWMA $\bar{X}$ chart, respectively, and $h_t \in \{h_S, h_L\}$ be the sampling interval between the tth and $(t+1)$th samples. The central regions of the upper-sided and lower-sided MOEWMA $\bar{X}$ charts are $[0, UWL]$ and $[LWL, 0]$, respectively. The warning regions of the upper-sided and lower-sided MOEWMA $\bar{X}$ charts are $(UWL, UCL]$ and $[LCL, LWL)$, respectively. For the upper-sided VSI MOEWMA $\bar{X}$ chart, h_t switches as follows:

$$h_t = \begin{cases} h_S, & Z_t^+ \in [0, UWL], \\ h_L, & Z_t^+ \in (UWL, UCL]. \end{cases} \tag{6}$$

where Z_t^+ is defined in Equation (4). Similarly, the h_t of the lower-sided VSI MOEWMA $\bar{X}$ chart depends on the value of the Z_t^- defined in Equation (5). Thus, for the VSI MOEWMA $\bar{X}$ chart, the sampling intervals h_t varies as a function of the charting statistic Z_t^+ (for the upper-sided chart) or Z_t^- (for the lower-sided chart).

When the process monitoring starts at time 0, no sample information is available to select the value of h_0. It might be practical to use the short sampling interval $h_0 = h_S$ to protect against problems in the start-up period [41]. As suggested by Reynolds et al. [42], when the process is in-control, the values of sampling intervals h_S and h_L are obtained by satisfying the following constraints,

$$\begin{cases} \rho_1 h_S + \rho_2 h_L = 1, \\ \rho_1 + \rho_2 = 1, \end{cases} \tag{7}$$

where ρ_1 and ρ_2 are the long run proportions of sampling intervals that are h_S and h_L, respectively. In addition, it is noted that the charting statistics in Equation (4) is reset to 0 if it is smaller than 0. This causes the fact that nearly half values of the in-control charting statistics are always 0 and are in the safe region and the sampling interval corresponding to these values is h_L. By doing many simulations, it is then found that the value of ρ_1 and ρ_2 are always smaller and larger than 0.5, respectively. For illustration, $\rho_1 = 0.4$, $\rho_2 = 0.6$, and $(h_S, h_L) = (0.1, 1.6)$ are selected in this paper. It is noted that the value of h_S may be practically determined by the minimum time required to take a sample and h_L should not exceed the maximum time to allow the process to run without sampling. In addition, the values of ρ_1, ρ_2 and (h_S, h_L) should satisfy the constraint in Equation (7). For simplicity, the VSI MOEWMA $\bar{X}$ chart's performance for other combination of ρ_1, ρ_2, and (h_S, h_L) are not presented in this manuscript.

4.2. Comparison with the FSI MOEWMA $\bar{X}$ Charts

It is well known that the ATS, instead of ARL, was usually suggested to evaluate a VSI chart's performance. For an FSI chart, the ATS is a constant multiple of the ARL, while for a VSI chart, the ATS is no longer a constant multiple of the ARL due to the varying of sampling intervals. In this case, the ATS is defined as the expected time from the start of the process to an out-of-control signal. Similarly, if the process has been running for a long time so the EWMA statistic is in a steady-state before the shift happens, the adjusted ATS ($AATS$) is usually used to evaluate the properties of a VSI chart, see Reynolds et al. [42]. In this paper, both ATS and $AATS$ are used together to compare the performances of the FSI and VSI MOEWMA $\bar{X}$ charts. The Monte-Carlo method is also used to obtain the ATS and $AATS$ of the VSI MOEWMA $\bar{X}$ chart. The simulation settings of the VSI MOEWMA $\bar{X}$ chart is similar to those of the FSI MOEWMA charts in Section 3.3.

Tables 4 and 5 present the out-of-control ATS and $AATS$ of the FSI and VSI MOEWMA $\bar{X}$ charts for different values of λ and δ when $n \in \{3, 5\}$. In addition, the subscripts 0 and 1 are used with ATS and $AATS$ to denote the in-control and out-of-control properties of the VSI chart, respectively. For fair comparisons, the desired in-control ATS_0 of both charts are matched as 200.

Table 4. The out-of-control profiles ATS_1 of the VSI and FSI upper-sided MOEWMA $\bar{X}$ charts when $ATS_0 = 200$.

n	λ	Chart	UWL	UCL	δ							
					0.1	0.3	0.5	1.0	1.5	2.0	2.5	3.0
3	0.05	FSI	-	0.1669	54.06	15.76	8.79	4.24	2.88	2.23	1.95	1.72
		VSI	0.0078	0.1669	32.52	4.83	1.90	0.56	0.30	0.22	0.20	0.17
	0.1	FSI	-	0.2797	60.12	16.26	8.44	3.81	2.55	2.02	1.70	1.36
		VSI	0.0218	0.2797	40.62	5.60	2.06	0.54	0.28	0.20	0.17	0.14
	0.15	FSI	-	0.3710	65.90	17.06	8.34	3.56	2.36	1.85	1.48	1.18
		VSI	0.0290	0.3710	45.89	6.15	2.06	0.50	0.25	0.19	0.15	0.12
	0.2	FSI	-	0.4511	70.90	18.26	8.48	3.40	2.22	1.71	1.34	1.10
		VSI	0.0388	0.4511	51.86	7.02	2.17	0.49	0.24	0.17	0.13	0.11
	0.25	FSI	-	0.5241	75.26	19.38	8.69	3.31	2.12	1.59	1.24	1.06
		VSI	0.0491	0.5241	57.46	8.11	2.31	0.49	0.23	0.16	0.12	0.11
5	0.05	FSI	-	0.1293	41.82	11.74	6.65	3.31	2.29	1.92	1.58	1.18
		VSI	0.0061	0.1293	21.99	3.01	1.21	0.37	0.23	0.19	0.16	0.12
	0.1	FSI	-	0.2169	46.69	11.61	6.19	2.94	2.06	1.65	1.23	1.03
		VSI	0.0169	0.2169	27.96	3.37	1.25	0.34	0.21	0.16	0.12	0.10
	0.15	FSI	-	0.2874	50.92	11.87	5.99	2.72	1.90	1.42	1.10	1.01
		VSI	0.0225	0.2874	32.03	3.52	1.22	0.32	0.19	0.14	0.11	0.10
	0.2	FSI	-	0.3494	55.20	12.34	5.92	2.57	1.76	1.28	1.05	1.00
		VSI	0.0300	0.3494	36.85	3.87	1.23	0.30	0.18	0.13	0.10	0.10
	0.25	FSI	-	0.4058	58.98	12.95	5.95	2.47	1.65	1.20	1.03	1.00
		VSI	0.0380	0.4058	41.20	4.39	1.28	0.29	0.17	0.12	0.10	0.10

From these tables, it can be concluded that whether in the zero-state or steady-state, for fixed values of n, λ and δ, the VSI MOEWMA $\bar{X}$ chart has smaller ATS_1 or $AATS_1$ values than the those of the corresponding FSI chart. This fact indicates that the VSI MOEWMA $\bar{X}$ chart is substantially better than the FSI MOEWMA $\bar{X}$ chart. For example, for the zero-state case in Table 4, when $n = 3$ and $\lambda = 0.1$, the $ATS_1 = 40.62$ of the VSI MOEWMA $\bar{X}$ chart is smaller than the $ATS_1 = 60.12$ of the FSI MOEWMA $\bar{X}$ chart for $\delta = 0.1$. In addition, the VSI MOEWMA $\bar{X}$ chart with a small λ performs better than the chart with a large λ to detect small shifts in the process and viceversa. For example, if the specified shift $\delta = 0.1$, the $ATS_1 = 32.52$ of the VSI MOEWMA $\bar{X}$ chart with $\lambda = 0.05$ performs better than the $ATS_1 = 57.46$ of the chart with $\lambda = 0.25$. Furthermore, if the specified shift $\delta = 2.0$, the $ATS_1 = 0.22$ of the VSI MOEWMA $\bar{X}$ chart with $\lambda = 0.05$ is worse than the $ATS_1 = 0.16$ of the chart with $\lambda = 0.25$. As the ATS_1 or $AATS_1$ values are close to 0 for large shifts, the VSI MOEWMA $\bar{X}$ chart with a smaller λ is generally recommended in practice. Moreover, for fixed values of n, λ, and δ, the $AATS_1$ value of the VSI MOEWMA $\bar{X}$ chart is larger than the ATS_1 of the chart. For example, when $n = 3$, $\lambda = 0.1$, and $\delta = 0.1$, the $AATS_1 = 47.35$ (see Table 5) of the chart is larger than the $ATS_1 = 40.62$ (see Table 4).

Table 5. The out-of-control profiles $AATS_1$ of the VSI and FSI upper-sided MOEWMA $\bar{X}$ charts when $ATS_0 = 200$.

								δ				
n	λ	Chart	UWL	UCL	0.1	0.3	0.5	1.0	1.5	2.0	2.5	3.0
3	0.05	FSI	-	0.1669	52.49	15.69	8.86	4.33	2.96	2.31	1.93	1.69
		VSI	0.0078	0.1669	39.59	7.63	3.81	1.56	0.88	0.57	0.40	0.28
	0.1	FSI	-	0.2797	58.63	15.90	8.29	3.80	2.57	2.00	1.67	1.47
		VSI	0.0218	0.2797	47.35	7.29	3.20	1.15	0.62	0.37	0.25	0.18
	0.15	FSI	-	0.3710	64.57	16.67	8.17	3.53	2.35	1.82	1.52	1.32
		VSI	0.0290	0.3710	53.09	7.51	2.88	0.93	0.47	0.28	0.18	0.14
	0.2	FSI	-	0.4511	69.70	17.77	8.30	3.37	2.20	1.70	1.42	1.22
		VSI	0.0388	0.4511	60.13	8.33	2.83	0.81	0.39	0.23	0.16	0.13
	0.25	FSI	-	0.5241	74.37	19.02	8.55	3.27	2.09	1.61	1.33	1.15
		VSI	0.0491	0.5241	66.74	9.48	2.90	0.74	0.34	0.20	0.14	0.12
5	0.05	FSI	-	0.1293	52.49	15.69	8.86	4.33	2.96	2.31	1.93	1.69
		VSI	0.0061	0.1293	27.28	5.39	2.76	1.10	0.60	0.37	0.25	0.18
	0.1	FSI	-	0.2169	58.63	15.90	8.29	3.80	2.57	2.00	1.67	1.47
		VSI	0.0169	0.2169	32.34	4.75	2.19	0.78	0.39	0.23	0.16	0.13
	0.15	FSI	-	0.2874	64.57	16.67	8.17	3.53	2.35	1.82	1.52	1.32
		VSI	0.0225	0.2874	36.99	4.57	1.89	0.61	0.29	0.18	0.13	0.11
	0.2	FSI	-	0.3494	69.70	17.77	8.30	3.37	2.20	1.70	1.42	1.22
		VSI	0.0300	0.3494	42.44	4.75	1.74	0.51	0.24	0.15	0.12	0.10
	0.25	FSI	-	0.4058	74.37	19.02	8.55	3.27	2.09	1.61	1.33	1.15
		VSI	0.0380	0.4058	47.82	5.16	1.70	0.45	0.21	0.13	0.11	0.10

5. A Real Data Application

To show the application of the REWMA, SEWMA, IEWMA, and the proposed MOEWMA $\bar{X}$ charts, in what follows, a real dataset of semiconductor manufacturing in Montgomery [9] is used to illustrate the charts' implementation. The photolithography process is important in semiconductor manufacturing. It transfers a geometric pattern from a mask to the surface of a silicon wafer using light-sensitive photoresist materials. This process is complex as it involves many engineering steps, for instance, chemical cleaning of the wafers, formation of barrier layer using silicon dioxide, and hard-baking process to increase photoresist adherence to the wafer surface. During the hard-baking process, the flow width of the photoresist is an important quality characteristic that needs to be monitored, as a minor variation (10 nm) in the thickness of photoresist will change the interference color and discolor the photoresist film.

Suppose that flow width can be controlled at a mean $\mu_0 = 1.5$ microns and the standard deviation $\sigma_0 = 0.15$ microns of a normally distributed process and the quality practitioner anticipates an upward shift size $\delta = 0.3$ in the process when the process is out-of-control. Then the upper-sided MOEWMA $\bar{X}$ chart is implemented for the process monitoring at each sampling point. For the FSI (VSI) chart, the desired ARL_0 (ATS_0) is maintained as 200, and $(h_S, h_L) = (0.1, 1.6)$ are selected.

In Table 6, 20 samples, each with size $n = 5$, are generated from an out-of-control normal distribution of the flow width with the mean $\mu_1 = \mu_0 + \delta \times \sigma_0 = 1.5 + 0.3 \times 0.15 = 1.545$ and the standard deviation σ_0. All sample mean values $\{\bar{X}_1, \bar{X}_2, \ldots, \bar{X}_{20}\}$ and the corresponding values of the different EWMA charting statistics are listed in the table. As a comparison, the upper-sided SEWMA, REWMA, and IEWMA $\bar{X}$ charts together with the MOEWMA $\bar{X}$ chart are plotted in Figure 1. It can be noted from Figure 1 that all control charts give an out-of-control signal at the 8th sample point, except for the upper-sided REWMA $\bar{X}$ chart, where the chart gives an out-of-control signal at the 9th sample point (see the bolded values in Table 6). This example shows that these FSI EWMA charts take about 8 or 9 time units to detect the assignable cause while, on average, we can note from Table 1 that the MOEWMA chart detect the shift $\delta = 0.3$ more quick than the SEWMA, REWMA, and IEWMA $\bar{X}$ charts.

Moreover, for the VSI-MOEWMA chart, the charting statistics Z_2^+ and Z_3^+ fall in the central region $[0, UWL]$, which leads to a large sampling interval $h_L = 1.6$ to find the subsequent samples. For the charting statistic at other sampling time point, the corresponding sampling interval is $h_S = 0.1$. This leads to a $ATS_1 = 3.8$ time unit of the VSI-MOEWMA $\bar{X}$ chart to detect the assignable cause. Thus, it is better to adopt the VSI-MOEWMA $\bar{X}$ chart to monitor the process.

Table 6. Dataset from the hard-baking process and the corresponding values of the charting statistics.

No.	$X_{t,1}$	$X_{t,2}$	$X_{t,3}$	$X_{t,4}$	$X_{t,5}$	$\bar{X}_t$	$\frac{\bar{X}_t - \mu_0}{\sigma_0}$	SEWMA Z_t	IEWMA Z_t^+	REWMA Z_t^+	MOEWMA Z_t^+
1	1.4843	1.5121	1.4521	1.6615	1.5718	1.5364	0.2424	0.0121	0.0123	0.0121	0.0121
2	1.6242	1.4130	1.4370	1.2060	1.6841	1.4729	−0.1809	0.0025	−0.0225	0.0025	0.0025
3	1.3940	1.4969	1.5511	1.4603	1.5285	1.4862	−0.0923	−0.0023	−0.0556	0.0000	0.0000
4	1.7084	1.4273	1.4462	1.6802	1.7809	1.6086	0.7239	0.0340	0.0517	0.0362	0.0340
5	1.8127	1.4903	1.4504	1.6042	1.6291	1.5973	0.6489	0.0648	0.1392	0.0668	0.0648
6	1.4994	1.5626	1.6364	1.5457	1.4819	1.5452	0.3015	0.0766	0.1558	0.0786	0.0766
7	1.5437	1.5712	1.6624	1.6105	1.5219	1.5819	0.5462	0.1001	0.2185	0.1019	0.1001
8	1.6210	1.5127	1.9105	1.7145	1.5037	1.6525	1.0165	**0.1459**	**0.3680**	0.1477	**0.1459**
9	1.7255	1.5221	1.5904	1.5681	1.5812	1.5974	0.6496	0.1711	0.4399	**0.1728**	0.1711
10	1.6233	1.5501	1.5537	1.4312	1.6582	1.5633	0.4220	0.1836	0.4645	0.1852	0.1836
11	1.6046	1.6137	1.4589	1.5180	1.5012	1.5393	0.2618	0.1876	0.4573	0.1891	0.1876
12	1.4726	1.7372	1.5157	1.5138	1.6138	1.5706	0.4709	0.2017	0.4904	0.2032	0.2017
13	1.5103	1.6380	1.5374	1.6795	1.8083	1.6347	0.8980	0.2365	0.6037	0.2379	0.2365
14	1.6370	1.5020	1.2816	1.6068	1.6847	1.5424	0.2829	0.2389	0.5935	0.2401	0.2389
15	1.7974	1.6347	1.5064	1.6271	1.6688	1.6469	0.9793	0.2759	0.7172	0.2771	0.2759
16	1.6303	1.5082	1.6574	1.5672	1.4228	1.5572	0.3811	0.2811	0.7202	0.2823	0.2811
17	1.3641	1.2779	1.4594	1.4907	1.4649	1.4114	−0.5908	0.2375	0.6500	0.2386	0.2375
18	1.6100	1.1929	1.6191	1.5542	1.5814	1.5115	0.0767	0.2295	0.5980	0.2306	0.2295
19	1.5312	1.2880	1.6937	1.5775	1.5299	1.5241	0.1604	0.2260	0.5647	0.2270	0.2260
20	1.5084	1.5094	1.7066	1.3353	1.3012	1.4722	−0.1854	0.2055	0.5023	0.2064	0.2055

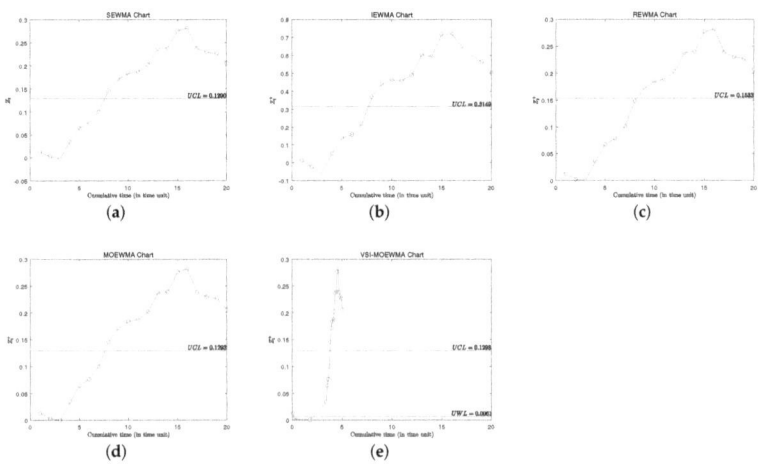

Figure 1. One-sided EWMA type charts applied to the dataset in Table 6. (**a**) SEWMA Chart (**b**) IEWMA Chart (**c**) REWMA Chart (**d**) MOEWMA Chart (**e**) VSI-MOEWMA Chart.

6. Conclusions and Recommendations

In this paper, we study the performance of one-sided MOEWMA $\bar{X}$ chart without- and with VSI features. Both the zero-state and steady-state performances of the FSI and VSI MOEWMA $\bar{X}$ chart are investigated by using extensive Monte-Carlo simulations. Through a comprehensive comparison with the SEWMA, REWMA, and IEWMA $\bar{X}$ charts, it is found that the MOEWMA $\bar{X}$ chart is shown to perform better than the REWMA $\bar{X}$ chart, especially for small shifts and it performs better than the IEWMA $\bar{X}$ chart for small shifts and worse for moderate to large shifts. Moreover, the MOEWMA $\bar{X}$ chart is always a little better than the SEWMA $\bar{X}$ chart. In addition, by investigating the optimal performance of the MOEWMA $\bar{X}$ chart, it can be concluded that the optimal MOEWMA $\bar{X}$ chart has a good performance over a wide range of shifts rather than a scheme to optimize the control charts at a specified shift. Finally, by adding the VSI feature to the MOEWMA $\bar{X}$ chart, it is shown that the VSI MOEWMA $\bar{X}$ chart is uniformly better than its counterpart with FSI, especially for small shifts.

As the current research works are based on the assumption of known process parameters, the manner in which the control chart performs with estimated process parameters remains an issue. Future works could be extended to this aspect. Moreover, this research is focused on the monitoring of the process mean. The methodology can also be extended to monitor the process variance, the ratio of two distributions, and so on.

Author Contributions: Conceptualization, X.H. and S.Z.; methodology, X.H.; software, S.Z.; validation, X.H., S.Z. and G.S.; formal analysis, G.S.; investigation, J.Z.; resources, S.W.; data curation, S.W.; writing—original draft preparation, S.Z. and G.S.; writing—review and editing, X.H. and J.Z.; visualization, S.W.; supervision, X.H.; project administration, X.H.; funding acquisition, X.H. All authors have read and agreed to the published version of the manuscript.

Funding: This research was funded by National Natural Science Foundation of China grant number 71802110, 71801049, 11701437 and Key Research Base of Philosophy and Social Sciences in Jiangsu-Information Industry Integration Innovation and Emergency Management Research Center and the Excellent Innovation Teams of Philosophy and Social Science in Jiangsu Province grant number 2017ZSTD022 and Postgraduate Research and Practice Innovation Program of Jiangsu Province grant number KYCX21_0840.

Institutional Review Board Statement: Not applicable.

Informed Consent Statement: Not applicable.

Data Availability Statement: All relevant data are within the manuscript.

Acknowledgments: The authors would like to express appreciation to Fupeng Xie from Nanjing University of Science and Technology for his works on Software.

Conflicts of Interest: The authors declare no conflict of interest.

Abbreviations

The following abbreviations are used in this manuscript:

EWMA	Exponentially Weighted Moving Average
CUSUM	Cumulative Sum
MOEWMA	Modified One-sided EWMA
SEWMA	The simple one-sided EWMA chart
REWMA	EWMA chart with resetting the charting statistic to the target
IEWMA	EWMA chart with truncating the sample mean to the target
RL	Run Length
ARL	Average Run Length
ARL_0	In-control ARL
ARL_1	Out-of-control ARL

SDRL	Standard Deviation of Run Length
$SDRL_0$	In-control SDRL
$SDRL_1$	Out-of-control SDRL
ATS	Average Time to Signal
ATS_0	In-control ATS
ATS_1	Out-of-control ATS
AATS	Average Adjusted Time to Signal
$AATS_0$	In-control AATS
$AATS_1$	Out-of-control AATS
VSI	Variable Sampling Interval
FSI	Fixed Sampling Interval
UCL	Upper Control Limit
LCL	Lower Control Limit
UWL	Upper Warning Limit
LWL	Lower Warning Limit
ZS	Zero-State
SS	Steady-State

References

1. Brook, D.; Evans, D. An Approach to the Probability Distribution of CUSUM Run Length. *Biometrika* **1972**, *59*, 539–549. [CrossRef]
2. Nelson, L. The Shewhart Control Chart–Tests for Special Causes. *J. Qual. Technol.* **1984**, *16*, 237–239. [CrossRef]
3. Lucas, J.; Saccucci, M. Exponentially weighted moving average control schemes: Properties and enhancements. *J. Qual. Technol.* **1990**, *32*, 1–12.
4. Hawkins, D.; Olwell, D. *Cumulative Sum Charts and Charting for Quality Improvement*; Springer: New York, NY, USA, 1999.
5. Li, Z.; Zou, C.; Gong, Z.; Wang, Z. The computation of average run length and average time to signal: An overview. *J. Stat. Comput. Simul.* **2014**, *84*, 1779–1802. [CrossRef]
6. Mukherjee, A.; Rakitzis, A.C. Some simultaneous progressive monitoring schemes for the two parameters of a zero-inflated Poisson process under unknown shifts. *J. Qual. Technol.* **2019**, *51*, 257–283. [CrossRef]
7. Zwetsloot, I.M.; Mahmood, T.; Woodall, W.H. Multivariate Time-Between-Events Monitoring–An overview and some (overlooked) underlying complexities. *Qual. Eng.* **2020**, *33*, 13–25. [CrossRef]
8. Perry, M.B. An EWMA control chart for categorical processes with applications to social network monitoring. *J. Qual. Technol.* **2020**, *52*, 182–197. [CrossRef]
9. Montgomery, D.C. *Introduction to Ststistical Quality Control*, 7th ed.; Wiley: Hoboken, NJ, USA, 2009.
10. Crowder, S.V. A Simple Method for Studying Run-Length Distributions of Exponentially Weighted Moving Average Charts. *Technometrics* **1987**, *29*, 401–407.
11. Domangue, R.; Patch, S.C. Some Omnibus Exponentially Weighted Moving Average Statistical Process Monitoring Schemes. *Technometrics* **1991**, *33*, 299–313. [CrossRef]
12. Borror, C.M.; Montgomery, D.C.; Runger, G.C. Robustness of the EWMA Control Chart to Non-Normality. *J. Qual. Technol.* **1999**, *31*, 309–316. [CrossRef]
13. Lu, C.W.; Reynolds, M.R., Jr. EWMA Control Charts for Monitoring the Mean of Autocorrelated Processes. *J. Qual. Technol.* **1999**, *31*, 166–188. [CrossRef]
14. Jones, L.A.; Champ, C.W.; Rigdon, S.E. The Performance of Exponentially Weighted Moving Average Charts With Estimated Parameters. *Technometrics* **2001**, *43*, 156–167. [CrossRef]
15. Celano, G.; Castagliola, P.; Trovato, E.; Fichera, S. Shewhart and EWMA *t* control charts for short production runs. *Qual. Reliab. Eng. Int.* **2011**, *27*, 313–326. [CrossRef]
16. Calzada, M.E.; Scariano, S.M. The Synthetic *t* and Synthetic EWMA *t* Charts. *Qual. Technol. Quant. Manag.* **2013**, *10*, 37–56. [CrossRef]
17. Haq, A.; Abidin, Z.U.; Khoo, M.B.C. An enhanced EWMA-*t* control chart for monitoring the process mean. *Commun. -Stat.-Theory Methods* **2019**, *48*, 1333–1350. [CrossRef]
18. Castagliola, P.; Celano, G.; Psarakis, S. Monitoring the Coefficient of Variation Using EWMA Charts. *J. Qual. Technol.* **2011**, *43*, 249–265. [CrossRef]
19. Tran, K.P.; Castagliola, P.; Celano, G. Monitoring the Ratio of Two Normal Variables Using EWMA Type Control Charts. *Qual. Reliab. Eng. Int.* **2016**, *32*, 1853–1869. [CrossRef]
20. Tran, K.P.; Knoth, S. Steady-state ARL analysis of ARL-unbiased EWMA-RZ control chart monitoring the ratio of two normal variables. *Qual. Reliab. Eng. Int.* **2018**, *34*, 377–390. [CrossRef]
21. Zhang, J.; Li, Z.; Chen, B.; Wang, Z. A new exponentially weighted moving average control chart for monitoring the coefficient of variation. *Comput. Ind. Eng.* **2014**, *78*, 205–212. [CrossRef]
22. Muhammad, A.N.B.; Yeong, W.C.; Chong, Z.L.; Lim, S.L.; Khoo, M.B.C. Monitoring the coefficient of variation using a variable sample size EWMA chart. *Comput. Ind. Eng.* **2018**, *126*, 378–398. [CrossRef]

23. Nguyen, H.D.; Tran, K.P.; Heuchenne, H.L. CUSUM control charts with variable sampling interval for monitoring the ratio of two normal variables. *Qual. Reliab. Eng. Int.* **2020**, *36*, 474–497. [CrossRef]
24. Haq, A. Weighted adaptive multivariate CUSUM charts with variable sampling intervals. *J. Stat. Comput. Simul.* **2018**, *89*, 478–491. [CrossRef]
25. Coelho, M.; Graham, M.; Chakraborti, S. Nonparametric signed-rank control charts with variable sampling intervals. *Qual. Reliab. Eng. Int.* **2017**, *33*, 2181–2192. [CrossRef]
26. Yue, J.; Liu, L. Multivariate nonparametric control chart with variable sampling interval. *Appl. Math. Model.* **2017**, *52*, 603–612. [CrossRef]
27. Yeong, W.C.; Khoo, M.B.C.; Tham, L.K.; Teoh, W.L.; Rahim, M.A. Monitoring the Coefficient of Variation Using a Variable Sampling Interval EWMA Chart. *J. Qual. Technol.* **2017**, *49*, 380–401. [CrossRef]
28. Amdouni, A.; Castagliola, P.; Taleb, H.; Celano, G. A variable sampling interval Shewhart control chart for monitoring the coefficient of variation in short production runs. *Int. J. Prod. Res.* **2017**, *55*, 5521–5536. [CrossRef]
29. Matrix, C.; Reynolds, M.R., Jr.; Cho, G.Y. Multivariate Control Charts for Monitoring the Mean Vector and Covariance Matrix with Variable Sampling Intervals. *Seq. Anal.* **2011**, *30*, 230–253.
30. Lee, M.H.; Khoo, M.B.C. Multivariate Synthetic $|S|$ Control Chart with Variable Sampling Interval. *Commun. Stat. Simul. Comput.* **2015**, *44*, 924–942. [CrossRef]
31. Chew, X.; Khoo, M.B.; Teh, S.; Castagliola, P. The variable sampling interval run sum $\bar{X}$ control chart. *Comput. Ind. Eng.* **2015**, *90*, 25–38. [CrossRef]
32. Robinson, P.B.; Ho, T.Y. Average Run Lengths of Geometric Moving Average Charts by Numerical Methods. *Technometrics* **1978**, *20*, 85–93. [CrossRef]
33. Hamilton, M.D.; Crowder, S.V. Average Run Lengths of EWMA Control Charts for Monitoring a Process Standard Deviation. *J. Qual. Technol.* **1992**, *24*, 44–50. [CrossRef]
34. Gan, F. Designs of one- and two-sided exponential EWMA charts. *J. Qual. Technol.* **1998**, *30*, 55–69. [CrossRef]
35. Shu, L.; Jiang, W. A New EWMA Chart for Monitoring Process Dispersion. *J. Qual. Technol.* **2008**, *40*, 319–331. [CrossRef]
36. Shu, L.; Jiang, W.; Wu, S. A One-Sided EWMA Control Chart for Monitoring Process Means. *Commun.-Stat.-Simul. Comput.* **2007**, *36*, 901–920. [CrossRef]
37. Haq, A. One-sided and two one-sided MEWMA charts for monitoring process mean. *J. Stat. Comput. Simul.* **2020**, *90*, 699–718. [CrossRef]
38. Dickinson, R.; Roberts, D.; Driscoll, A.; Woodall, W.; Vining, G. CUSUM Charts for Monitoring the Characteristic Life of Censored Weibull Lifetimes. *J. Qual. Technol.* **2014**, *46*, 340–358. [CrossRef]
39. Sparks, R.S. CUSUM Charts for Signalling Varying Location Shifts. *J. Qual. Technol.* **2000**, *32*, 157–171. [CrossRef]
40. Xu, S.; Jeske, D.R. Weighted EWMA charts for monitoring type I censored Weibull lifetimes. *J. Qual. Technol.* **2018**, *50*, 220–230. [CrossRef]
41. Reynolds, M.R.; Amin, R.W.; Arnold, J.C.; Nachlas, J.A. $\bar{X}$ Charts With Variable Sampling Intervals. *Technometrics* **1988**, *30*, 181–192. [CrossRef]
42. Reynolds, M.R.; Amin, R.W.; Arnold, J.C. CUSUM Charts with Variable Sampling Intervals. *Technometrics* **1990**, *32*, 371–384. [CrossRef]

Article

Copula-Based Estimation Methods for a Common Mean Vector for Bivariate Meta-Analyses

Jia-Han Shih [1], Yoshihiko Konno [2], Yuan-Tsung Chang [3] and Takeshi Emura [4],*

[1] Institute of Statistical Science, Academia Sinica, Taipei 11529, Taiwan; jhshih@stat.sinica.edu.tw
[2] Department of Mathematical and Physical Sciences, Japan Women's University, Tokyo 112-8681, Japan; konno@fc.jwu.ac.jp
[3] Department of Social Information, Mejiro University, Tokyo 161-8539, Japan; chogenso@gmail.com
[4] Biostatistics Center, Kurume University, Kurume, Fukuoka 830-0011, Japan
* Correspondence: takeshiemura@gmail.com

Abstract: Traditional bivariate meta-analyses adopt the bivariate normal model. As the bivariate normal distribution produces symmetric dependence, it is not flexible enough to describe the true dependence structure of real meta-analyses. As an alternative to the bivariate normal model, recent papers have adopted "copula" models for bivariate meta-analyses. Copulas consist of both symmetric copulas (e.g., the normal copula) and asymmetric copulas (e.g., the Clayton copula). While copula models are promising, there are only a few studies on copula-based bivariate meta-analysis. Therefore, the goal of this article is to fully develop the methodologies and theories of the copula-based bivariate meta-analysis, specifically for estimating the common mean vector. This work is regarded as a generalization of our previous methodological/theoretical studies under the FGM copula to a broad class of copulas. In addition, we develop a new R package, "*CommonMean.Copula*", to implement the proposed methods. Simulations are performed to check the proposed methods. Two real dataset are analyzed for illustration, demonstrating the insufficiency of the bivariate normal model.

Keywords: bivariate distribution; copula; correlation; FGM copula; maximum likelihood estimator; meta-analysis; normal distribution

1. Introduction

Bivariate outcomes often arise in meta-analyses on scientific studies, such as education and medicine. Educational researchers may analyze bivariate exam scores on verbal and mathematics [1,2], or on mathematics and statistics [3]. Medical experts may analyze bivariate risk scores on myocardial infection and cardiovascular death for diabetes patients [4,5]. Bivariate meta-analyses are statistical methods designed for these meta-analytical studies [6]. Dependence between two outcomes should be considered while performing bivariate meta-analyses. If one simply considers univariate (marginal) analysis for each outcome separately, any possible dependence between the outcomes is ignored. Riley [2] and Copas et al. [7] showed that ignoring the dependence between two outcomes increases the error for estimating parameters due to the loss of information. In medical research, dependence itself can be of clinical importance, e.g., dependence between two survival outcomes in meta-analysis [8–11].

In the traditional bivariate meta-analyses, the parameters of interest are the means of a bivariate normal model [6]. However, the bivariate normal model is not flexible enough to describe the true dependence structure of real meta-analyses. It will be shown that the bivariate normal mode fits poorly to the dependence structure of real bivariate meta-analyses (Section 8). This has motivated researchers to consider alternative models.

As an alternative to the bivariate normal model, recent papers have adopted "copula" models for bivariate meta-analyses [3,5,12–15]. Copula models are flexible as they allow a variety of dependence structures. Copulas consist of both symmetric copulas (e.g., the normal copula) and asymmetric copulas (e.g., the Clayton copula). Copula models have become very popular in all areas of science by replacing the traditional multivariate normal models. In astronomy, Takeuchi [16] constructed the bivariate luminosity density functions using the FGM copula; see reference [17] for the application of the FGM copula to engineering. In ecology, Ghosh et al. [18] applied copulas to model the dependence structure in environmental and biological variables. In environmental science, Alidoost et al. [19] used bivariate copulas in the analysis of temperature. See the survey of [20] for applications to energy, forestry, and environmental sciences. The books of [21,22] are devoted to the applications of copulas in survival analysis; see also references [11,23–25].

While bivariate copula models for meta-analyses are promising, there are only a few methodologically and theoretically solid studies on copula-based bivariate meta-analysis. For instance, the detailed theoretical studies of [3] are limited to the FGM copula. Other copula-based meta-analyses published in biostatistical journals, such as [5,12–15], are proposed without theoretical details. Furthermore, copula-based bivariate meta-analyses have not been implemented in a free software environment.

Therefore, the goal of this article is to fully develop the methodologies and theories of the copula-based bivariate meta-analysis for estimating the common mean vector. This work is regarded as a large generalization of our previous methodological/theoretical studies under the FGM copula model [3] to a broad class of copula models. In this article, we obtain theoretical results, including the formula of the information matrix and large sample theories. Our theoretical results guarantee the applications of many copulas, such as the Clayton, Gumbel, Frank, and normal copulas, in addition to the FGM copula. In addition, we developed a new R package, "CommonMean.Copula" [26], to implement the proposed methods under the five copulas. Therefore, the aim of the article is to make a solid development of the methodologies, theories, and practical implementations of copula-based bivariate meta-analysis for the common mean, which are not yet available in the literature.

The article is organized as follows. Section 2 reviews the background of this research. Section 3 introduces the proposed model and estimator. Section 4 provides the asymptotic theory and Section 5 gives confidence sets. Section 6 introduces our new R package. Section 7 conducts simulations to check the accuracy of the proposed methods. Section 8 analyzes two real datasets for illustration. Section 9 extends the proposed methods to non-normal data. Finally, Section 10 concludes with a discussion.

2. Background

This section reviews the literature on bivariate meta-analyses and the concept of copulas.

2.1. Bivariate Meta-Analysis

We review the bivariate meta-analysis method for bivariate continuous outcomes [6,27]. For each study i, let the bivariate outcomes, Y_{i1} and Y_{i2}, follow a bivariate normal distribution

$$Y_i = \begin{bmatrix} Y_{i1} \\ Y_{i2} \end{bmatrix} \sim N\left(\mu = \begin{bmatrix} \mu_1 \\ \mu_2 \end{bmatrix}, \Omega_i = \begin{bmatrix} \sigma_{i1}^2 & \rho_i \sigma_{i1} \sigma_{i2} \\ \rho_i \sigma_{i1} \sigma_{i2} & \sigma_{i2}^2 \end{bmatrix} \right), \quad i = 1, 2, \ldots, n, \quad (1)$$

where $\rho_i \in (-1, 1)$ is the within-study correlation for each i. In Equation (1), all the responses (Y_is) share the common mean vector (μ). The covariance matrix Ω_i is assumed to be known (from the i-th study) in usual bivariate meta-analyses. We do not consider a setting where the covariance is unknown [28,29].

Then, the MLE of the common mean vector is quite easily computed as

$$\hat{\mu}_n^{\text{Normal}} = \begin{bmatrix} \hat{\mu}_{n,1}^{\text{Normal}} \\ \hat{\mu}_{n,2}^{\text{Normal}} \end{bmatrix} = \left(\sum_{i=1}^n \Omega_i^{-1} \right)^{-1} \sum_{i=1}^n \Omega_i^{-1} Y_i.$$

One could use the R package *mvmeta* [30], although the above computation is easy.

The bivariate normal model (1) does not allow for a different dependence structure between the two outcomes. In practice, the bivariate normal model (1) can be too restrictive, as there are various dependence patterns between two outcomes. For example, to model the luminosity function of galaxies, Takeuchi [16] pointed out that the FGM copula model offers a more ideal shape than the normal copula model from a physical point of view. Such a limitation motivates us to construct a *general* copula model that can describe various dependence structures.

2.2. Copulas

This subsection prepares the basic terms on copulas that will subsequently be used.

A copula is a bivariate distribution function whose margins are uniformly distributed on the unit interval [31,32]. Copulas are indispensable tools when modelling a dependence structure between two random variables. We specifically consider the following *parametric* copulas.

The normal copula: The copula function is

$$C_\rho^{\text{Normal}}(u,v) = \Phi_\rho\{\Phi^{-1}(u), \Phi^{-1}(v)\}, \quad -1 < \rho < 1, \quad 0 < u,v < 1,$$

where $\Phi_\rho(\cdot,\cdot)$ is the cumulative distribution function (CDF) of the bivariate standard normal distribution with correlation ρ and Φ^{-1} is the inverse of the standard normal CDF Φ. While this copula is easy to understand, it has a complex form involving two implicit functions Φ_ρ and Φ^{-1}. The following two copulas provide simpler forms than the normal copula.

The Farlie–Gumbel–Morgenstern (FGM) copula [33]: The copula function is

$$C_\theta^{\text{FGM}}(u,v) = uv\{1 + \theta(1-u)(1-v)\}, \quad -1 \leq \theta \leq 1, 0 < u,v < 1.$$

The FGM copula has a very simple form, and is a fundamental copula, which has been extended to a variety of copulas, called the generalized FGM copulas [34–38].

The Clayton copula [39]: The copula function is

$$C_\alpha^{\text{Clayton}}(u,v) = (u^{-\alpha} + v^{-\alpha} - 1)^{-1/\alpha}, \quad \alpha > 0, 0 < u,v < 1.$$

The Clayton copula is one of the simplest and most frequently used copulas in applications. The Clayton copula is derived from the gamma frailty model, leading to its remarkable popularity in survival data analysis [22,40]. It has a lower tail dependence [31], but is not tractable for modeling negative dependence.

The Gumbel copula [41]: The copula function is

$$C_\beta^{\text{Gumbel}}(u,v) = \exp[-\{(-\log u)^\beta + (-\log v)^\beta\}^{1/\beta}], \quad \beta \geq 1, 0 < u,v < 1.$$

The Gumbel copula is a popular copula with upper tail dependence [31]. The Gumbel copula does not offer a negative dependence, as in the Clayton copula.

The Frank copula [42]: The copula function is

$$C_\gamma^{\text{Frank}}(u,v) = -\frac{1}{\gamma} \log\left\{1 + \frac{(e^{-\gamma u} - 1)(e^{-\gamma v} - 1)}{e^{-\gamma} - 1}\right\}, \quad \gamma \neq 0, 0 < u,v < 1.$$

The Frank copula does not have tail dependence [31]. Unlike the Clayton and Gumbel copulas, it can model both positive and negative dependences as the normal copula.

Under the null parameter (e.g., $\theta = 0$), all the above copulas reduce to the independence copula $\Pi(u,v) = uv$. As the parameter departs from the null, the dependence gets stronger.

We define the notations for partial derivatives (if they exist) as

$$C^{[j,k]}(u,v) = \frac{\partial^{j+k}}{\partial u^j \partial v^k} C(u,v); \quad j,k \in \{0,1,2,\ldots\}.$$

For instance,

$$C^{[1,0]}(u,v) = \frac{\partial}{\partial u}C(u,v), \quad C^{[0,1]}(u,v) = \frac{\partial}{\partial v}C(u,v), \quad C^{[1,1]}(u,v) = \frac{\partial^2}{\partial u \partial v}C(u,v),$$

where $C^{[1,1]}$ is called the copula density.

The copula is symmetric if $C^{[1,1]}(u,v) = C^{[1,1]}(1-u, 1-v)$. This means that the normal and FGM copulas are symmetric while the Clayton and Gumbel copulas are asymmetric. This symmetry should not be confused with the exchangeability $C(u,v) = C(v,u)$. All the aforementioned parametric copulas are exchangeable.

3. Proposed Methods

This section proposes a general copula-based approach for estimating a bivariate common mean vector. We first define the bivariate copula model and provide sufficient conditions for the copula parameter to be identifiable. We then develop a maximum likelihood estimator (MLE) for the common mean vector. In addition, we derive the expression for the information matrix.

3.1. General Copula Model for the Common Mean

This subsection proposes a new model for estimating the common mean in bivariate meta-analyses.

For $i = 1, 2, \ldots, n$, let $Y_i = (Y_{i1}, Y_{i2})$ be a random vector satisfying

$$Y_{i1} \sim N\left(\mu_1, \sigma_{i1}^2\right), Y_{i2} \sim N\left(\mu_2, \sigma_{i2}^2\right), \mu \equiv E(Y_i) = \begin{bmatrix} E(Y_{i1}) \\ E(Y_{i2}) \end{bmatrix} = \begin{bmatrix} \mu_1 \\ \mu_2 \end{bmatrix},$$

$$\Omega_i \equiv Cov(Y_i) = \begin{bmatrix} Var(Y_{i1}) & Cov(Y_{i1}, Y_{i2}) \\ Cov(Y_{i1}, Y_{i2}) & Var(Y_{i2}) \end{bmatrix} = \begin{bmatrix} \sigma_{i1}^2 & \rho_i \sigma_{i1} \sigma_{i2} \\ \rho_i \sigma_{i1} \sigma_{i2} & \sigma_{i2}^2 \end{bmatrix}.$$

Here, we call $\mu = (\mu_1, \mu_2)$ the 'common mean vector' since it is common across $i = 1, 2, \ldots, n$. Our target is the estimation of μ when Ω_i, $i = 1, 2, \ldots, n$ are known. In general, $\Omega_i \neq \Omega_j$ for some $i \neq j$, and, therefore, the random vectors Y_i, $i = 1, 2, \ldots, n$ are independent but not identically distributed (i.n.i.d.). While the marginal normality is specified, the bivariate normality is unspecified. We only specify the equation $Corr(Y_{i1}, Y_{i2}) = \rho_i$, where ρ_i is known.

We now specify a bivariate distribution for Y_i. According to Sklar's Theorem [43], for copulas C_{θ_i}, $i = 1, 2, \ldots, n$, we define the bivariate CDFs

$$Pr(Y_{i1} \leq y_1, Y_{i2} \leq y_2) = C_{\theta_i}\left\{\Phi\left(\frac{y_1 - \mu_1}{\sigma_{i1}}\right), \Phi\left(\frac{y_2 - \mu_2}{\sigma_{i2}}\right)\right\}, i = 1, 2, \ldots, n.$$

However, since ρ_i is known, the copula can be restricted. To see the problem clearly, we define the *correlation function* $\rho_C : \Theta \mapsto R_C$ as

$$\rho_C(\theta) = E\left\{\left(\frac{Y_{i1} - \mu_1}{\sigma_{i1}}\right)\left(\frac{Y_{i2} - \mu_2}{\sigma_{i2}}\right)\right\} = \int_{-\infty}^{\infty}\int_{-\infty}^{\infty} z_1 z_2 dC_\theta\{\Phi(z_1), \Phi(z_2)\},$$

where $R_C \equiv \{\rho_C(\theta) : \theta \in \Theta\}$ denotes the range of ρ_C that depends on the choice of C_θ. The correlation function ρ_C does not depend on μ. For the copula to be useful in real meta-analyses, θ_i has to be identifiable from ρ_i. This means that one has to be able to solve the equation $\rho_C(\theta) = \rho$. Now, we define our general copula model for a bivariate common mean vector.

Definition 1. (Copula-based common mean model): The copula-based common mean model is

$$Pr(Y_{i1} \leq y_1, Y_{i2} \leq y_2) = C_{\theta_i}\left\{\Phi\left(\frac{y_1-\mu_1}{\sigma_{i1}}\right), \Phi\left(\frac{y_2-\mu_2}{\sigma_{i2}}\right)\right\}, \quad i=1,2,\ldots,n, \quad (2)$$

where the copula parameter θ_i is identified by $\rho_C(\theta_i) = \rho_i$ for $i = 1, 2, \ldots, n$.

To explain the flexibility and generality of our model, we give examples for C_{θ_i}.

Example 1. (the normal copula): Under the normal copula, the model in Equation (2) becomes

$$Pr(Y_{i1} \leq y_1, Y_{i2} \leq y_2) = C_{\rho_i}^{\text{Normal}}\left\{\Phi\left(\frac{y_1-\mu_1}{\sigma_{i1}}\right), \Phi\left(\frac{y_2-\mu_2}{\sigma_{i2}}\right)\right\} = \Phi_{\rho_i}\left(\frac{y_1-\mu_1}{\sigma_{i1}}, \frac{y_2-\mu_2}{\sigma_{i2}}\right).$$

Under this model, the correlation function is the identity function $\rho_{C^{\text{Normal}}}(\rho) = \rho$. In addition, one has the copula parameter space $\Theta_{C^{\text{Normal}}} = (-1,1)$, and the range of correlations $R_{C^{\text{Normal}}} = (-1,1)$. Without doubt, for any $\rho_i \in (-1,1)$, the copula parameter can be identified.

Example 2. (the FGM copula): Under the FGM copula, the model in Equation (2) becomes

$$Pr(Y_{i1} \leq y_1, Y_{i2} \leq y_2) = \Phi\left(\frac{y_1-\mu_1}{\sigma_{i1}}\right)\Phi\left(\frac{y_2-\mu_2}{\sigma_{i2}}\right)\left[1+\theta_i\left\{1-\Phi\left(\frac{y_1-\mu_1}{\sigma_{i1}}\right)\right\}\left\{1-\Phi\left(\frac{y_2-\mu_2}{\sigma_{i2}}\right)\right\}\right].$$

Under this model, the correlation function is $\rho_{C^{\text{FGM}}}(\theta) = \theta/\pi$ for $-1 \leq \theta \leq 1$ [44]. Thus, the copula parameter is identified by $\theta_i = \pi\rho_i$, as long as $\rho_i \in [-1/\pi, 1/\pi] \approx [-0.32, 0.32]$. If $\rho_i \notin [-1/\pi, 1/\pi]$, we suggest $\theta_i = -1$ or $\theta_i = 1$, using $\theta_i \equiv \pi\rho_i^*$, where $\rho_i^* = \min[-1/\pi, \max\{\rho_i, 1/\pi\}]$. Hence, θ_i can still be identified by ρ_i. This boundary enforcement is illustrated in Figure 1.

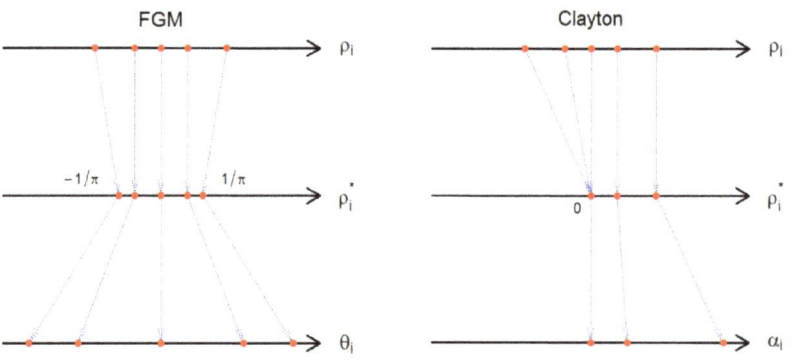

Figure 1. The boundary correction for the correlation coefficient under the bivariate FGM and Clayton models. The first step forces the correlation ρ_i to fall in a range that can be modeled by the chosen copula. The second step transforms the corrected correlation ρ_i^* to the corresponding copula parameter.

Example 3. (The Clayton copula): Under the Clayton copula, the model in Equation (2) becomes

$$Pr(Y_{i1} \leq y_1, Y_{i2} \leq y_2) = \left\{\Phi\left(\frac{y_1-\mu_1}{\sigma_{i1}}\right)^{-\alpha_i} + \Phi\left(\frac{y_2-\mu_2}{\sigma_{i2}}\right)^{-\alpha_i} - 1\right\}^{-1/\alpha_i}.$$

for $\alpha_i > 0$. The correlation function does not have a closed-form, and is written as

$$\rho_{C\text{Clayton}}(\alpha) = (\alpha+1) \int_{-\infty}^{\infty} \int_{-\infty}^{\infty} \frac{z_1 z_2 \varphi(z_1) \varphi(z_2)}{\Phi(z_1)^{\alpha+1} \Phi(z_2)^{\alpha+1} \left\{ \Phi(z_1)^{-\alpha} + \Phi(z_2)^{-\alpha} - 1 \right\}^{1/\alpha+2}} dz_1 dz_2.$$

It is known that $\lim_{\alpha \to 0} \rho_{C\text{Clayton}}(\alpha) = 0$ and $\lim_{\alpha \to \infty} \rho_{C\text{Clayton}}(\alpha) = 1$. In addition, if $\alpha_2 \geq \alpha_1$ then $C_{\alpha_2}^{\text{Clayton}}(u,v) \geq C_{\alpha_1}^{\text{Clayton}}(u,v)$ for all $u,v \in (0,1)$ [45]. Then, we conclude that the range of the correlation is $R_{C\text{Clayton}} = (0,1)$. Thus, one can identify by solving $\rho_{C\text{Clayton}}(\alpha_i) = \rho_i$ numerically if $\rho_i > 0$. If $\rho_i \leq 0$, we suggest the independence model (Figure 1)

$$Pr(Y_{i1} \leq y_1, Y_{i2} \leq y_2) = \Phi\left(\frac{y_1 - \mu_1}{\sigma_{i1}}\right) \Phi\left(\frac{y_2 - \mu_2}{\sigma_{i2}}\right).$$

Example 4. (The Gumbel copula): Under the Gumbel copula, the model in Equation (2) becomes

$$Pr(Y_{i1} \leq y_1, Y_{i2} \leq y_2) = \exp\left(-\left[\left\{-\log \Phi\left(\frac{y_1 - \mu_1}{\sigma_{i1}}\right)\right\}^{\beta_i} + \left\{-\log \Phi\left(\frac{y_2 - \mu_2}{\sigma_{i2}}\right)\right\}^{\beta_i}\right]^{1/\beta_i}\right)$$

for $\beta_i \geq 1$. Similar to the Clayton copula, the correlation function does not have a closed-form, and is not displayed here. It is known that $\rho_{C\text{Gumbel}}(1) = 0$ and $\lim_{\beta \to \infty} \rho_{C\text{Gumbel}}(\beta) = 1$. If $\rho_i < 0$, we suggest the independence model as in the Clayton copula.

Example 5. (The Frank copula): Under the Frank copula, the model in Equation (2) becomes

$$Pr(Y_{i1} \leq y_1, Y_{i2} \leq y_2) = -\frac{1}{\gamma_i} \log\left(1 + \frac{\left[\exp\left\{-\gamma_i \Phi\left(\frac{y_1-\mu_1}{\sigma_{i1}}\right)\right\} - 1\right]\left[\exp\left\{-\gamma_i \Phi\left(\frac{y_2-\mu_2}{\sigma_{i2}}\right)\right\} - 1\right]}{e^{-\gamma_i} - 1}\right)$$

for $\gamma_i \neq 0$. Again, the correlation function does not have a closed-form, and is not displayed here. It is known that $\lim_{\gamma \to -\infty} \rho_{C\text{Frank}}(\gamma) = -1$ and $\lim_{\gamma \to \infty} \rho_{C\text{Frank}}(\gamma) = 1$. Thus, the Frank copula parameter does not require boundary correction.

3.2. Statistical Inference Methods

This subsection develops statistical inference methods under the proposed model. We propose the MLE for μ under the general copula model (Definition 1) in Equation (2). Suppose that the copula density $C_\theta^{[1,1]}$ exists. Then, the joint density of Y_i is

$$f_{i,\mu}(y) = \frac{\partial^2}{\partial y_1 \partial y_2} Pr(Y_{i1} \leq y_1, Y_{i2} \leq y_2) = \frac{1}{\sigma_{i1}\sigma_{i2}} \varphi\left(\frac{y_1-\mu_1}{\sigma_{i1}}\right) \varphi\left(\frac{y_2-\mu_2}{\sigma_{i2}}\right) C_{\theta_i}^{[1,1]}\left\{\Phi\left(\frac{Y_1-\mu_1}{\sigma_{i1}}\right), \Phi\left(\frac{Y_2-\mu_2}{\sigma_{i2}}\right)\right\}.$$

where $y = (y_1, y_2)$ and $\varphi(\cdot)$ is the density of $N(0,1)$. Given the samples, the log-likelihood function is

$$\ell_n(\mu) = \text{constant} + \sum_{i=1}^{n} \log\left[C_{\theta_i}^{[1,1]}\left\{\Phi\left(\frac{Y_{i1}-\mu_1}{\sigma_{i1}}\right), \Phi\left(\frac{Y_{i2}-\mu_2}{\sigma_{i2}}\right)\right\}\right] - \frac{1}{2}\sum_{j=1}^{2}\sum_{i=1}^{n}\left(\frac{Y_{ij}-\mu_j}{\sigma_{ij}}\right)^2.$$

The MLE of the common mean vector is defined as

$$\hat{\mu}_n = \begin{bmatrix} \hat{\mu}_{n,1} \\ \hat{\mu}_{n,2} \end{bmatrix} = \underset{\mu \in R^2}{\operatorname{argmax}} \ell_n(\mu),$$

where $R = (-\infty, \infty)$ is a real line. The MLE does not have a closed-form expression except for the normal copula. Thus, the MLE can also be obtained by the Newton–Raphson algorithm or some software functions (e.g., the R functions *optim* or *nlm*). One may also apply our R package *CommonMean.Copula* [26], which will be explained in Section 6.

3.3. Information Matrix

For the MLE to be well-behaved, it is necessary to show that the (Fisher) information matrix exists and is non-singular. In other words, the MLE, without verifying these conditions, may have some problems, e.g., the non-existence, inconsistency, or inefficiency of the MLE. Furthermore, the information matrix describes how a copula influences the MLE.

We define the 2×2 information matrix $I_i(\mu)$ for $i = 1, 2, \ldots, n$ as

$$I_{i,jk}(\mu) = E\left\{\frac{\partial \log f_{i,\mu}(Y_i)}{\partial \mu_j} \frac{\partial \log f_{i,\mu}(Y_i)}{\partial \mu_k}\right\}, \quad j, k = 1, 2.$$

The following theorem gives the formula of the information matrix.

Lemma 1. *If $C_\theta^{[3,1]}$, $C_\theta^{[1,3]}$, and $C_\theta^{[2,2]}$ exist in $(0,1)^2$, for each i, the following equalities hold*

$$E\left\{\frac{\partial \log f_{i,\mu}(Y_i)}{\partial \mu_j} \frac{\partial \log f_{i,\mu}(Y_i)}{\partial \mu_k}\right\} = E\left\{-\frac{\partial^2 \log f_{i,\mu}(Y_i)}{\partial \mu_j \partial \mu_k}\right\}; \quad j, k = 1, 2.$$

The proof of Lemma 1 is given in Appendix A.1.

Many copulas have $C_\theta^{[3,1]}$, $C_\theta^{[1,3]}$, and $C_\theta^{[2,2]}$ in $(0,1)^2$, such as the normal, FGM, and Clayton copulas (Appendix A.2.). The following theorem gives the formula of the information matrix.

Theorem 1. *Under the copula-based model (Definition 1), the information matrix does not depend on μ. Furthermore, if $C_\theta^{[3,1]}$, $C_\theta^{[1,3]}$, and $C_\theta^{[2,2]}$ exist in $(0,1)^2$, it can be decomposed into the sum of the information matrix for the independent model and the additional information by the copula,*

$$I_i = \begin{bmatrix} \frac{1}{\sigma_{i1}^2} & 0 \\ 0 & \frac{1}{\sigma_{i2}^2} \end{bmatrix} + \begin{bmatrix} \frac{1}{\sigma_{i1}^2} E_C^{11}(\theta_i) & \frac{1}{\sigma_{i1}\sigma_{i2}}\{E_C^{12}(\theta_i) - \rho_C(\theta_i)\} \\ \frac{1}{\sigma_{i1}\sigma_{i2}}\{E_C^{12}(\theta_i) - \rho_C(\theta_i)\} & \frac{1}{\sigma_{i2}^2} E_C^{22}(\theta_i) \end{bmatrix}, \quad (3)$$

where

$$E_C^{11}(\theta_i) = E\left\{\frac{\varphi(Z_{i1})C_{\theta_i}^{[2,1]}\{\Phi(Z_{i1}), \Phi(Z_{i2})\}}{C_{\theta_i}^{[1,1]}\{\Phi(Z_{i1}), \Phi(Z_{i2})\}}\right\}^2,$$

$$E_C^{22}(\theta_i) = E\left\{\frac{\varphi(Z_{i2})C_{\theta_i}^{[1,2]}\{\Phi(Z_{i1}), \Phi(Z_{i2})\}}{C_{\theta_i}^{[1,1]}\{\Phi(Z_{i1}), \Phi(Z_{i2})\}}\right\}^2,$$

$$E_C^{12}(\theta_i) = E\left[\frac{\varphi(Z_{i1})\varphi(Z_{i2})C_{\theta_i}^{[2,1]}\{\Phi(Z_{i1}), \Phi(Z_{i2})\}C_{\theta_i}^{[1,2]}\{\Phi(Z_{i1}), \Phi(Z_{i2})\}}{C_{\theta_i}^{[1,1]}\{\Phi(Z_{i1}), \Phi(Z_{i2})\}^2}\right].$$

Theorem 1 can be proved by straightforward calculations as Lemma 1 (Appendix A.1.). Theorem 1 helps us interpret the role of the copula C_{θ_i} on the information matrix.

Theorem 2. *The determinant of I_i can be expressed as*

$$\det(I_i) = \frac{1}{\sigma_{i1}^2\sigma_{i2}^2}\left\{E_C^{11}(\theta_i)E_C^{22}(\theta_i) - E_C^{12}(\theta_i)^2\right\}$$

$$+ \frac{1}{\sigma_{i1}^2\sigma_{i2}^2}\left\{E_C^{11}(\theta_i) + E_C^{22}(\theta_i) + 2\rho_C(\theta_i)E_C^{12}(\theta_i)\right\} + \frac{1}{\sigma_{i1}^2\sigma_{i2}^2}\left\{1 - \rho_C(\theta_i)^2\right\}.$$

In addition, $\det(I_i) > 0$ and I_i is positive definite.

Proof of Theorem 2. The expression of $\det(I_i)$ is obtained by straightforward calculations. Clearly, we have $|\rho_C(\theta_i)| < 1$. Then, by the Cauchy-Schwarz inequality,

$$E_C^{11}(\theta_i) E_C^{22}(\theta_i) \geq E_C^{12}(\theta_i)^2.$$

Furthermore, by the arithmetic-geometric mean inequality, we have

$$E_C^{11}(\theta_i) + E_C^{22}(\theta_i) \geq 2\left\{E_C^{11}(\theta_i) E_C^{22}(\theta_i)\right\}^{1/2} \geq 2\left|E_C^{12}(\theta_i)\right| > 2\left|\rho_C(\theta_i) E_C^{12}(\theta_i)\right|.$$

Then we obtain $\det(I_i) > 0$. Since $E_C^{11}(\theta_i)/\sigma_{i1}^2 + 1/\sigma_{i1}^2 > 0$, both the upper left 1×1 and 2×2 determinants of I_i are positive. Thus, I_i is positive definite. □

Based on Theorem 1, one can derive the information matrix $I_i(\mu)$ for parametric copulas. Below, we show examples of the normal, FGM, and Clayton copulas.

Example 6. *(The normal copula):* Under the normal copula

$$E_{C\text{Normal}}^{11}(\rho_i) = E_{C\text{Normal}}^{22}(\rho_i) = \frac{\rho_i^2}{1-\rho_i^2}, \quad E_{C\text{Normal}}^{12}(\rho_i) = -\frac{\rho_i^3}{1-\rho_i^2}.$$

Then, by Theorem 1, the information matrix in Equation (3) becomes

$$I_i = \begin{bmatrix} \frac{1}{\sigma_{i1}^2} & 0 \\ 0 & \frac{1}{\sigma_{i2}^2} \end{bmatrix} + \begin{bmatrix} \frac{1}{\sigma_{i1}^2}\frac{\rho_i^2}{1-\rho_i^2} & \frac{1}{\sigma_{i1}\sigma_{i2}}\left(-\frac{\rho_i^3}{1-\rho_i^2}-\rho_i\right) \\ \frac{1}{\sigma_{i1}\sigma_{i2}}\left(-\frac{\rho_i^3}{1-\rho_i^2}-\rho_i\right) & \frac{1}{\sigma_{i2}^2}\frac{\rho_i^2}{1-\rho_i^2} \end{bmatrix}$$

$$= \frac{1}{1-\rho_i^2}\begin{bmatrix} \frac{1}{\sigma_{i1}^2} & -\frac{\rho_i}{\sigma_{i1}\sigma_{i2}} \\ -\frac{\rho_i}{\sigma_{i1}\sigma_{i2}} & \frac{1}{\sigma_{i2}^2} \end{bmatrix} = \Omega_i^{-1}.$$

and its determinant is $\det(I_i^{\text{Normal}}) = 1/(\sigma_{i1}^2\sigma_{i2}^2)$. Clearly, I_i^{Normal} is positive definite.

Example 7. *(The FGM copula):* Under the FGM copula

$$E_{C\text{FGM}}^{11}(\theta_i) = E_{C\text{FGM}}^{22}(\theta_i) = 4\theta_i^2 \int_{-\infty}^{\infty}\int_{-\infty}^{\infty} \frac{\varphi(z_1)^3\{1-2\Phi(z_2)\}^2\varphi(z_2)}{1+\theta_i\{1-2\Phi(z_1)\}\{1-2\Phi(z_2)\}} dz_1 dz_2,$$

$$E_{C\text{FGM}}^{12}(\theta_i) = 4\theta_i^2 \int_{-\infty}^{\infty}\int_{-\infty}^{\infty} \frac{\varphi(z_1)^2\{1-2\Phi(z_1)\}\varphi(z_2)^2\{1-2\Phi(z_2)\}}{1+\theta_i\{1-2\Phi(z_1)\}\{1-2\Phi(z_2)\}} dz_1 dz_2, \quad \rho_{C\text{FGM}}(\theta) = \frac{\theta}{\pi}.$$

Then, by Theorem 1, the information matrix in Equation (3) becomes

$$I_i^{\text{FGM}} = \begin{bmatrix} \frac{1}{\sigma_{i1}^2} & 0 \\ 0 & \frac{1}{\sigma_{i2}^2} \end{bmatrix} + \begin{bmatrix} \frac{1}{\sigma_{i1}^2}E_{C\text{FGM}}^{11}(\theta_i) & \frac{1}{\sigma_{i1}\sigma_{i2}}E_{C\text{FGM}}^{12}(\theta_i) - \frac{\theta_i}{\pi\sigma_{i1}\sigma_{i2}} \\ \frac{1}{\sigma_{i1}\sigma_{i2}}E_{C\text{FGM}}^{12}(\theta_i) - \frac{\theta_i}{\pi\sigma_{i1}\sigma_{i2}} & \frac{1}{\sigma_{i2}^2}E_{C\text{FGM}}^{22}(\theta_i) \end{bmatrix}.$$

By Theorem 2, its determinant is

$$\det(I_i) = \frac{1}{\sigma_{i1}^2\sigma_{i2}^2}\left\{E_{C\text{FGM}}^{11}(\theta_i)^2 - E_{C\text{FGM}}^{12}(\theta_i)^2\right\}$$
$$+ \frac{2}{\sigma_{i1}^2\sigma_{i2}^2}\left\{E_{C\text{FGM}}^{11}(\theta_i) + \frac{\theta_i}{\pi}E_{C\text{FGM}}^{12}(\theta_i)\right\} + \frac{1}{\sigma_{i1}^2\sigma_{i2}^2}\left(1-\frac{\theta_i^2}{\pi^2}\right).$$

This result agrees with [3] who considered the FGM model.

Example 8. *(The Clayton copula):* Under the Clayton copula

$$E^{11}_{C\text{Clayton}}(\alpha_i) = E^{22}_{C\text{Clayton}}(\alpha_i) = (\alpha_i+1)\int_{-\infty}^{\infty}\int_{-\infty}^{\infty}\frac{\varphi(z_1)^3\varphi(z_2)\{\alpha_i\Phi(z_1)^{-\alpha_i}-(\alpha_i+1)\Phi(z_2)^{-\alpha_i}+(\alpha_i+1)\}^2}{\Phi(z_1)^{\alpha_i+3}\Phi(z_2)^{\alpha_i+1}\{\Phi(z_1)^{-\alpha_i}+\Phi(z_2)^{-\alpha_i}-1\}^{1/\alpha_i+4}}dz_1 dz_2,$$

$$E^{12}_{C\text{Clayton}}(\alpha_i) = \int_{-\infty}^{\infty}\int_{-\infty}^{\infty}\frac{\varphi(z_1)^2\{\alpha_i\Phi(z_1)^{-\alpha_i}-(\alpha_i+1)\Phi(z_2)^{-\alpha_i}+(\alpha_i+1)\}}{\Phi(z_1)^{\alpha_i+2}\{\Phi(z_1)^{-\alpha_i}+\Phi(z_2)^{-\alpha_i}-1\}^{1/2\alpha_i+2}}$$

$$\times \frac{\varphi(z_2)^2\{\alpha_i\Phi(z_2)^{-\alpha_i}-(\alpha_i+1)\Phi(z_1)^{-\alpha_i}+(\alpha_i+1)\}}{\Phi(z_2)^{\alpha_i+2}\{\Phi(z_1)^{-\alpha_i}+\Phi(z_2)^{-\alpha_i}-1\}^{1/2\alpha_i+2}}dz_1 dz_2,$$

$$\rho_{C\text{Clayton}}(\alpha_i) = (\alpha_i+1)\int_{-\infty}^{\infty}\int_{-\infty}^{\infty}\frac{z_1 z_2 \varphi(z_1)\varphi(z_2)}{\Phi(z_1)^{\alpha_i+1}\Phi(z_2)^{\alpha_i+1}\{\Phi(z_1)^{-\alpha_i}+\Phi(z_2)^{-\alpha_i}-1\}^{1/\alpha_i+2}}dz_1 dz_2.$$

Then, by Theorems 1 and 2, we obtain I_i^{Clayton} and $\det(I_i^{\text{Clayton}})$ accordingly.

4. Asymptotic Theory

To assess the sampling variability of $\hat{\mu}_n$, its asymptotic distribution is presented in this section.

A technical burden comes from the fact that our samples Y_i, $i = 1, 2, \ldots, n$ are independent and *non-identically* distributed (i.n.i.d.) owing to heterogeneous variances ($\Omega_i \neq \Omega_j, i \neq j$). The existence of the asymptotic distribution requires the stabilization of the information matrix [3,46,47] in large samples. For the asymptotic variance of $\hat{\mu}_n$, to be defined, we assume the existence of a 2×2 positive definite matrix $I \equiv \lim_{n\to\infty}\sum_{i=1}^{n} I_i/n$. We further assume that the copula's derivatives $C_\theta^{[4,1]}$, $C_\theta^{[3,2]}$, $C_\theta^{[2,3]}$, and $C_\theta^{[1,4]}$ exist in $(0,1)^2$. With these conditions and many other technical conditions given in [48], we establish the consistency and asymptotic normality of $\hat{\mu}_n$:

Theorem 3. *Under the copula model (Definition 1), if some regularity conditions hold, then*

(a) *Existence and consistency: With probability tending to one, there exists the MLE $\hat{\mu}_n = (\hat{\mu}_{n,1}, \hat{\mu}_{n,2})$ such that $\hat{\mu}_n \to_p \mu$, as $n \to \infty$;*

(b) *Asymptotic normality: $n^{1/2}(\hat{\mu}_n - \mu) \to_d N(0, I^{-1})$, as $n \to \infty$.*

The proof of Theorem 3 and the required regularity conditions are given in the Ph.D dissertation of [48]. The proof approximates $n^{1/2}(\hat{\mu}_n - \mu)$ by the sum of independent random variables, and then applies the weak law of large numbers for i.n.i.d. random variables from Theorem 1.14 in [49] and the Lindeberg–Feller multivariate central limit theorem from Proposition 2.27 in [50]. The proof is fairly technical, but similar to those of Theorem 6.5.1 in [51], Theorem 1 in [47], and Theorem 5.1 in [3].

5. SE and Confidence Sets

As Section 4 has established the asymptotic theory to evaluate the variability of the proposed MLE, we can derive the SE, confidence interval (CI), and confidence ellipse (CE). Let $g: R^2 \mapsto R$ be a differentiable function, and $g(\mu)$ be the parameter of interest. For instance, $g(\mu) = \mu_1$ and $g(\mu) = \mu_2 - \mu_1$ can be considered. The SE of $g(\hat{\mu}_n)$ is

$$\text{SE}\{g(\hat{\mu}_n)\} = \left[\left\{\frac{\partial g(\mu)}{\partial \mu}\right\}^T \left\{-\frac{\partial^2 \ell_n(\mu)}{\partial \mu \partial \mu^T}\right\}^{-1}\left\{\frac{\partial g(\mu)}{\partial \mu}\right\}\bigg|_{\mu=\hat{\mu}_n}\right]^{1/2}.$$

This formula is based on the delta method and the large sample approximation

$$I \approx \frac{1}{n}\sum_{i=1}^{n} I_i \approx -\frac{1}{n}\frac{\partial^2 \ell_n(\mu)}{\partial \mu \partial \mu^T}\bigg|_{\mu=\hat{\mu}_n}.$$

The 95% CI for $g(\mu)$ is $g(\hat{\mu}_n) \pm 1.96 \times \text{SE}\{g(\hat{\mu}_n)\}$.
Moreover, based on Theorem 3, we construct a 95% CE for μ:

$$\text{CE} = \left\{\mu : (\hat{\mu}_n - \mu)^T \left(-\frac{\partial^2 \ell_n(\mu)}{\partial \mu \partial \mu^T}\bigg|_{\mu=\hat{\mu}_n}\right)(\hat{\mu}_n - \mu) \leq \chi^2_{df=2, 0.95}\right\},$$

where $\chi^2_{df=2,0.95}$ is be the 95% point of the χ^2-distribution with two degrees of freedom.

6. R Package

We implement the proposed methods in an R package *CommonMean.Copula* [26]. R users can easily compute the MLE with its SE and 95% CI under the FGM, Clayton, Gumbel, Frank, and normal copulas. In this package, the log-likelihood is maximized by the R *optim* function, where the initial values are set as the univariate estimators

$$\mu_j^{(0)} = \left(\sum_{i=1}^{n}\frac{1}{\sigma_{ij}^2}\right)^{-1}\sum_{i=1}^{n}\frac{Y_{ij}}{\sigma_{ij}^2}, \quad j=1,2.$$

For illustration, we fitted the Clayton copula by the following R codes:

```
> library(CommonMean.Copula)
> Y1 = c(35,25,30,50,60) # outcome 1
> Y2 = c(30,30,50,65,40) # outcome 2
> Sigma1 = c(1.3,1.4,1.5,2.0,1.8) # SE of outcome 1
> Sigma2 = c(1.7,1.9,2.5,2.2,1.8) # SE of outcome 2
> rho = c(0.4,0.7,0.6,0.7,0.6) # correlation between two outcomes
> CommonMean.Copula(Y1,Y2,Sigma1,Sigma2,rho,copula = "Clayton") # input
```

- some outputs are omitted for brevity –

```
$`CommonMean 1`
 estimate        SE       Lower      Upper
33.9505331 0.4393516 33.0894198 34.8116463

$`CommonMean 2`
 estimate        SE       Lower      Upper
41.9926717 0.6039963 40.8088607 43.1764827

$V
          [,1]      [,2]
[1,] 0.1930298 0.2507297
[2,] 0.2507297 0.3648115

$`Log-likelihood values`
         1         2         3         4          5      total
  -46.30760 -21.14432 -18.78560 -89.05592 -110.36095 -285.65438
```

Here, $CommonMean1 shows $\hat{\mu}_{n,1}^{Clayton} = 33.95$, $SE(\hat{\mu}_{n,1}^{Clayton}) = 0.439$, and the 95% CI (33.089, 34.812); $CommonMean2 is similar. $V shows the covariance matrix $Cov(\hat{\mu}_n^{Clayton})$. $'Log-likelihood values' shows $\ell_n^{Clayton}(\hat{\mu}_n^{Clayton}) = -285.65$. One can fit other copulas by changing "Clayton" to "FGM", "Gumbel", "Frank", or "normal".

7. Simulation Studies

We conducted Monte Carlo simulations to examine the accuracy of the proposed methods. We report the results for the Clayton copula; more results are available from [48].

We generated Y_i, $i = 1, 2, \ldots, n$, under the Clayton copula with $\alpha_i \sim Gamma(64, 1/8)$, $Gamma(4, 1/2)$, or $Gamma(1, 1)$, leading to $E[\alpha_i] = 8$, $E[\alpha_i] = 2$, or $E[\alpha_i] = 1$, respectively. In all three cases, we have $Var[\alpha_i] = 1$. Without loss of generality, we set $\mu = (0, 0)$. To set σ_{i1}^2 and σ_{i2}^2, we followed the simulation setting of [52]. That is, $\sigma_{i1}^2, \sigma_{i2}^2 \sim \chi_{df=1}^2/4$, restricted in the interval $[0.009, 0.6]$. This setting leads to $E[\sigma_{i1}^2] = E[\sigma_{i2}^2] = 0.173$. Based on the generated data, we computed $\hat{\mu}_{n,1}^{Clayton}$, $\hat{\mu}_{n,2}^{Clayton} - \hat{\mu}_{n,1}^{Clayton}$, and $\hat{\mu}_n^{Clayton}$, and their SEs and 95% CIs (CEs) by using the R function *CommonMean.Copula* (Section 6). We then evaluated the coverage probability (CP) of the 95% CI (CE) to see how the confidence set can cover the true value. We consider a small sample size $n \in \{5, 10, 15\}$ and a large sample size $n \in \{50, 100, 300\}$. Our simulations are based on 1000 repetitions.

Table 1 summarizes the results. For $\hat{\mu}_{n,1}^{Clayton}$ and $\hat{\mu}_{n,2}^{Clayton} - \hat{\mu}_{n,1}^{Clayton}$, the SDs of the estimates decrease when n increases from $n = 5$ to $n = 300$. We report the boxplots summarizing the 1000 repetitions for $\hat{\mu}_{n,1}^{Clayton}$ in Figure 2. This clearly visualizes how the variability of the estimates vanishes as the sample sizes increase. Table 1 also shows that the SDs are close to the average SEs, except for $n = 5$ (due to the very small samples). Consequently, the CPs are close enough to the nominal level of 0.95, especially when sample sizes are large, which is consistent with our asymptotic theories. For $\hat{\mu}_n^{Clayton}$, the CPs of the 95% CEs are also reasonably close to the nominal level. In summary, the proposed estimators and the asymptotic theory work fairly well in finite samples.

Table 1. Simulation results based on 1000 repetitions.

Parameters	n	$\hat{\mu}_{n,1}^{Clayton}$			$\hat{\mu}_{n,2}^{Clayton} - \hat{\mu}_{n,1}^{Clayton}$			$\hat{\mu}_n^{Clayton}$
		SD	SE	CP	SD	SE	CP	CP
$E[\alpha_i] = 8$	5	0.064	0.046	0.888	0.042	0.033	0.885	0.859
	10	0.033	0.026	0.913	0.023	0.019	0.931	0.894
	15	0.021	0.019	0.933	0.015	0.014	0.936	0.919
	50	0.010	0.009	0.952	0.007	0.007	0.954	0.950
	100	0.007	0.006	0.955	0.005	0.005	0.943	0.944
	300	0.004	0.004	0.948	0.003	0.003	0.942	0.948
$E[\alpha_i] = 2$	5	0.105	0.092	0.938	0.100	0.086	0.920	0.909
	10	0.061	0.057	0.937	0.060	0.055	0.929	0.919
	15	0.049	0.045	0.938	0.045	0.042	0.943	0.930
	50	0.023	0.023	0.959	0.022	0.021	0.944	0.943
	100	0.016	0.016	0.942	0.015	0.015	0.957	0.950
	300	0.009	0.009	0.946	0.008	0.008	0.946	0.949
$E[\alpha_i] = 1$	5	0.115	0.105	0.932	0.128	0.120	0.935	0.922
	10	0.069	0.068	0.950	0.079	0.075	0.937	0.937
	15	0.058	0.053	0.941	0.062	0.058	0.947	0.937
	50	0.028	0.027	0.942	0.029	0.030	0.955	0.943
	100	0.019	0.019	0.942	0.021	0.020	0.936	0.945
	300	0.010	0.011	0.958	0.011	0.012	0.960	0.959

SD = standard deviation, SE = standard error, CP = coverage probability of the 95% CI (CE).

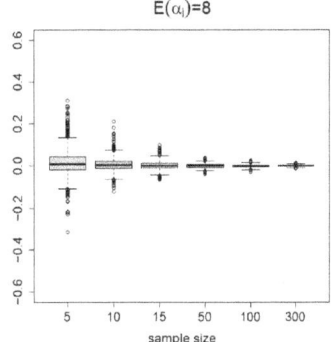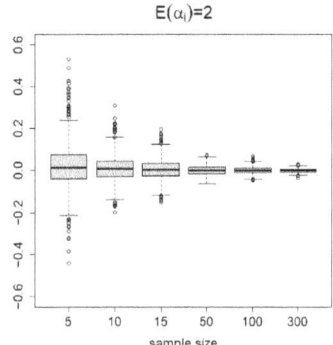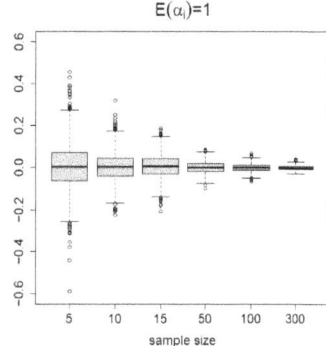

Figure 2. The boxplots summarizing the 1000 repetitions for $\hat{\mu}_{n,1}^{Clayton}$ with true parameter $\mu_1 = 0$ under the copula parameters $E[\alpha_i] = 8$, $E[\alpha_i] = 2$, or $E[\alpha_i] = 1$. The sample size varies from $n = 5$ to $n = 300$.

8. Data Analysis

We analyze two real datasets to illustrate the usefulness of the proposed methods.

8.1. The Entrance Exam Data

The first dataset we analyzed was the entrance exam scores on mathematics and statistics, which was introduced by [3]. The data come from undergrad students who took written exams from 2013 to 2017 to enter the Graduate Institute of Statistics, National Central University, Taiwan. The possible score range is from 0 to 100 for both subjects. Let $i = 1, 2, \ldots, 5$ be indices for years 2013, 2014, ..., 2017. Table 2 provides the data, including the values of mathematics (Y_{i1} = mean math score) and statistics (Y_{i2} = mean stat score), and their covariance matrix (Ω_i).

Table 2. The entrance exam data from [3].

i	Year	Mean Math Score (Y_{i1})	Mean Stat Score (Y_{i2})	Covariance Matrix (Ω_i)	Copula Parameter			
					ρ_i	θ_i	α_i	β_i	γ_i
1	2013	35.17	30.41	$\begin{bmatrix} 1.77 & 0.89 \\ 0.89 & 2.99 \end{bmatrix}$	0.38	1.00	0.67	1.34	2.68
2	2014	23.43	31.63	$\begin{bmatrix} 1.89 & 1.76 \\ 1.76 & 3.61 \end{bmatrix}$	0.67	1.00	1.92	1.90	6.00
3	2015	30.74	48.11	$\begin{bmatrix} 2.15 & 2.12 \\ 2.12 & 6.13 \end{bmatrix}$	0.58	1.00	1.37	1.65	4.67
4	2016	50.91	65.22	$\begin{bmatrix} 3.87 & 2.91 \\ 2.91 & 5.02 \end{bmatrix}$	0.66	1.00	1.82	1.85	5.76
5	2017	61.62	40.22	$\begin{bmatrix} 3.17 & 2.10 \\ 2.10 & 3.29 \end{bmatrix}$	0.65	1.00	1.75	1.83	5.60

ρ_i = the Pearson correlation; θ_i = the FGM copula parameter; α_i = the Clayton copula parameter; β_i = the Gumbel copula parameter; γ_i = the Frank copula parameter.

We fitted the data to the proposed model using the R function *CommonMean.Copula(.)* in our R package (Section 6). Table 3 summarizes the fitted results for the FGM, Clayton, Gumbel, Frank, and normal copulas. According to the values of the log-likelihood, the Gumbel copula produces the best fit, the Frank copula the second best, and the bivariate normal model the worst fit. The FGM copula failed to capture the dependence and fitted at the boundary $\theta_i = 1$ for all i (Table 2).

Table 3. Estimation results for the entrance exam data.

Copula	Math: Estimate (95% CI)	Stat: Estimate (95% CI)	Log-likelihood	CV
FGM	37.16 (35.85, 38.47)	41.17 (39.65, 42.70)	−291.80	2723.91
Clayton	32.56 (31.71, 33.40)	43.80 (42.55, 45.05)	−322.84	2644.03
Gumbel	37.67 (36.30, 39.03)	42.56 (40.79, 44.33)	−279.28	2860.21
Frank	37.23 (35.97, 38.49)	39.76 (38.13, 41.40)	−287.63	2738.09
Normal	35.83 (34.51, 37.16)	38.64 (36.94, 40.34)	−342.65	2773.41

Since the number of unknown parameters across different copulas is the same, model selection by the Akaike information criterion (AIC) is equivalent to model selection by the log-likelihood value. An alternative way of selecting a copula is based on a leave-one-out cross validation (CV), defined as

$$CV = \sum_{i=1}^{n}\{\left(Y_{i1} - \hat{\mu}_{n,1}^{(-i)}\right)^2 + \left(Y_{i2} - \hat{\mu}_{n,2}^{(-i)}\right)^2\},$$

where $\hat{\mu}_{n,1}^{(-i)}$ and $\hat{\mu}_{n,2}^{(-i)}$ are the MLE obtained without the ith sample. Here, CV measures how a sample is predicted by the others under a copula model. A smaller CV corresponds to a better performance of the model.

Table 3 reports the values of CV for each copula. It shows that the Clayton copula has the best performance while the Gumbel copula has the worst. The normal copula has the second worst performance. Overall, our analysis clearly shows the insufficiency of the bivariate normal model.

Figure 3 shows the 95% CEs for the mean vector μ. This visualizes how the resultant estimates vary from the choice of copulas. Interestingly, the CE under the Clayton copula is far away from the other four, although it has a larger log-likelihood value than the normal copula. The normal and Clayton copulas produce the rotated oval shape of the CEs, representing a positive dependence between math and stat scores. The FGM and Gumbel copulas produce similar shapes for their CE. We adopt the 95% CE given by the Gumbel copula because it has the largest log-likelihood value.

Figure 4 gives the 3D plot of the log-likelihood surface under the Gumbel copula model. The plot shows that the estimate of the common mean $\hat{\mu}_n^{\text{Gumbel}} = (37.67, 42.56)$ attains the global maximum of the log-likelihood function.

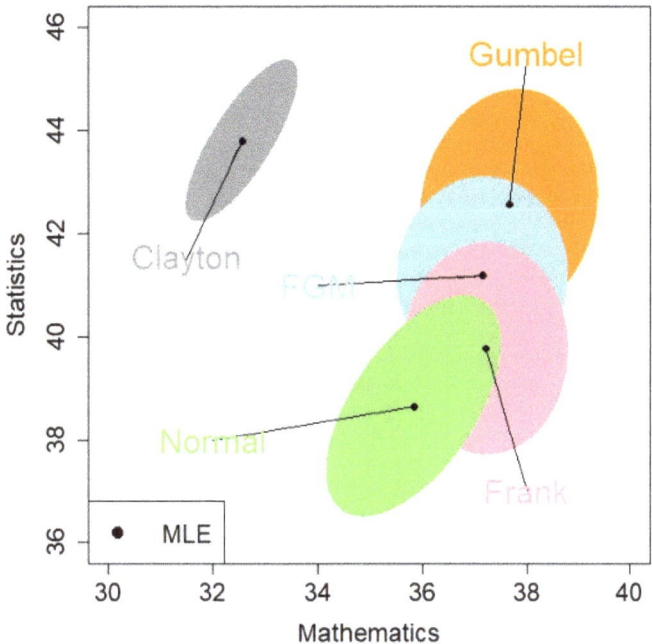

Figure 3. The MLE and the 95% CE (colored region) for the common means based on the exam score data. The copulas are signified by colors: blue = FGM; gray = Clayton; orange = Gumbel; pink = Frank; green = normal.

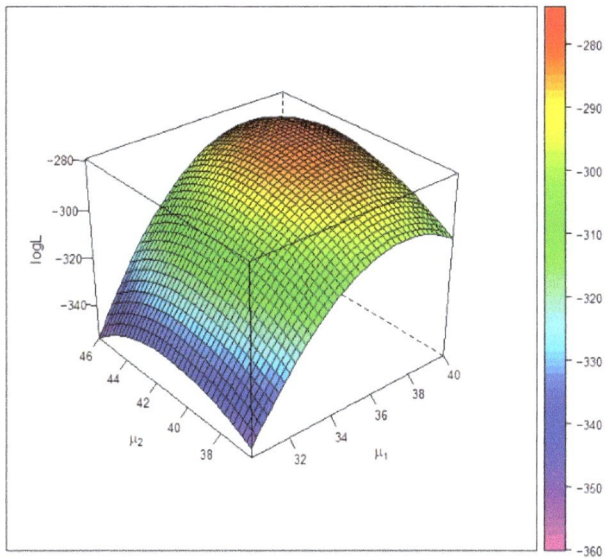

Figure 4. The 3D plot of the log-likelihood value under the Gumbel copula based on the entrance exam data. The maximum occurs at $\hat{\mu}_n^{\text{Gumbel}} = (37.67, 42.56)$.

8.2. The Blood Pressure Data

The second dataset we used contains 10 studies that examined the effectiveness of hypertension treatment for lowering blood pressure. Each study provides complete data on two treatment effects, the difference in systolic blood pressure (SBP) and diastolic blood pressure (DBP) between the treatment and the control groups, where these differences are adjusted for the participants' baseline blood pressures. The within-study correlations of the two outcomes range from $\rho_i = 0.45$ to $\rho_i = 0.78$, exhibiting positive dependence. This dataset is available in R package *mvmeta* [30] and was previously analyzed by [53].

We fitted the data to the proposed copula models using the R function *CommonMean.Copula(.)* in our R package (Section 6). Table 4 summarizes the fitted results for all the copulas. Based on the log-likelihood values, the Frank copula produces the best fit, the Gumbel copula the second best, and the Clayton copula produces the worst fit. The FGM copula failed to capture the dependence and fitted at the boundary $\theta_i = 1$ for all i. Again, our analysis reveals the insufficiency of the bivariate normal model; the Frank copula best captured the correlations in the blood pressure data. We also compared *CV* across all the copulas (Table 4). The results show that the Clayton copula has the best performance while the normal copula has the worst. Again, our analysis shows the insufficiency of the normal model.

Table 4. Estimation results for the blood pressure data.

Copula	SBP: Estimate (95% CI)	DBP: Estimate (95% CI)	Log-likelihood	CV
FGM	−9.18 (−9.32, −9.04)	−3.94 (−4.00, −3.89)	−530.29	177.23
Clayton	−9.53 (−9.70, −9.36)	−4.34 (−4.38, −4.29)	−787.02	163.04
Gumbel	−8.99 (−9.16, −8.83)	−3.94 (−4.00, −3.89)	−514.67	184.67
Frank	−9.20 (−9.40, −9.00)	−3.94 (−3.99, −3.88)	−513.34	179.81
Normal	−8.43 (−8.60, −8.25)	−3.95 (−4.01, −3.90)	−771.82	206.49

SBP = the difference in systolic blood pressure; DBP = the difference in diastolic blood pressure.

Figure 5 shows the 95% CEs for the mean vector μ. The CE under the Clayton and normal copula are far away from the other three. The CE under the FGM copula was almost fully covered by the CE under the Frank copula. We adopt the 95% CE given by the Frank copula, since it has the largest log-likelihood value (Table 4).

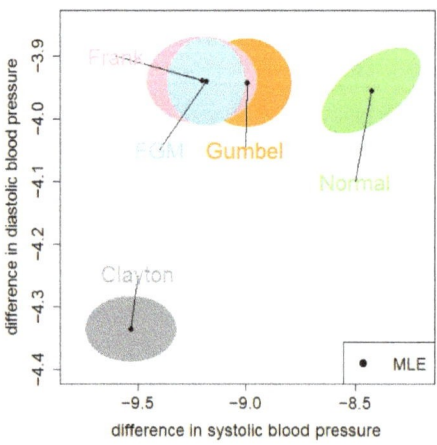

Figure 5. The MLE and the 95% CE (colored region) for the common means based on the blood pressure data. The correspondence copulas of the colored regions are: blue = FGM; gray = Clayton; orange = Gumbel; pink = Frank; green = normal.

Figure 6 depicts the 3D plot of the log-likelihood surface under the Frank copula model. The plot shows that the estimate of the common mean $\hat{\mu}_n^{\text{Frank}} = (-9.20, -3.94)$ attains the global maximum of the log-likelihood function.

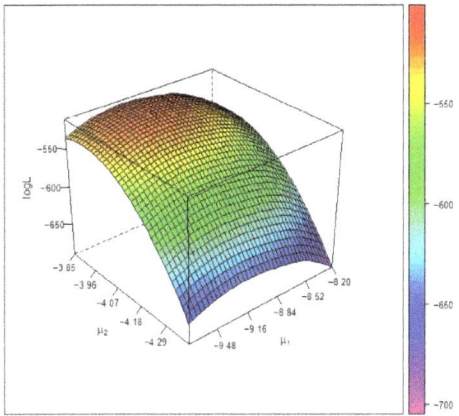

Figure 6. The 3D plot of the log-likelihood value under the Frank copula based on the blood pressure data. The maximum occurs at $\hat{\mu}_n^{\text{Frank}} = (-9.20, -3.94)$.

9. Extension to Non-Normal Models

So far, we have considered a common mean model under the marginal normality. This section explains how the proposed methods can be extended to non-normal models. For this reason, we specifically consider a common mean model under the marginal exponential distributions.

$$\bar{F}_j(y) \equiv Pr(Y_{ij} > y) = \exp(-\lambda_j y), \quad y > 0, \quad \lambda_j > 0, \quad j = 1, 2.$$

Thus, the common mean vector is $\mu = (1/\lambda_1, 1/\lambda_2)$.

We consider the Clayton copula to specify the bivariate distribution because it has simple derivatives with respect to the copula parameter [54]. Therefore, we propose a bivariate common mean Clayton copula model with exponential margins as follows:

$$Pr(Y_{i1} > y_1, Y_{i2} > y_2) = C_{\alpha_i}^{\text{Clayton}}\{\bar{F}_1(y_1), \bar{F}_2(y_2)\} = \{\exp(\alpha_i \lambda_1 y_1) + \exp(\alpha_i \lambda_2 y_2) - 1\}^{-1/\alpha_i}, \quad (4)$$

where α_i is known for $i = 1, 2, \ldots, n$. Note that copula $C_{\alpha_i}^{\text{Clayton}}$ is a survival copula for (Y_{i1}, Y_{i2}) as the usual way to model a survival function [22]. Using similar arguments to [55], the information matrix with respect to $\lambda = (\lambda_1, \lambda_2)$ can be decomposed as

$$I_i(\lambda) = \begin{bmatrix} \frac{1}{\lambda_1^2} & 0 \\ 0 & \frac{1}{\lambda_2^2} \end{bmatrix} + \begin{bmatrix} \frac{2\alpha_i^2(\alpha_i+1)}{\lambda_1^2(3\alpha_i+1)} & -\frac{\alpha_i(2\alpha_i+1)}{\lambda_1\lambda_2}\phi(\alpha_i) \\ -\frac{\alpha_i(2\alpha_i+1)}{\lambda_1\lambda_2}\phi(\alpha_i) & \frac{2\alpha_i^2(\alpha_i+1)}{\lambda_2^2(3\alpha_i+1)} \end{bmatrix}, \quad (5)$$

where

$$\phi(\alpha) = \frac{1}{3\alpha+1} + \frac{1}{2(3\alpha+1)(2\alpha+1)}\left\{\Psi\left(\frac{1}{2\alpha}\right) - \Psi\left(\frac{\alpha+1}{2\alpha}\right)\right\}, \quad \Psi(\alpha) = \frac{d^2 \log \Gamma(\alpha)}{d\alpha^2}.$$

See Appendix A.3. for detailed derivations. The expression of $I_i(\lambda)$ is an extension of Theorem 3 to the exponential model. With the information matrix, the properties of the MLE and the asymptotic theory are similar to the normal models.

We conducted Monte Carlo simulations to examine the correctness of Equation (5) by comparing it with their empirical version. We set $\lambda_1 = \lambda_2 = 1$ and $\alpha_i = 1$ for all i. We generated data (Y_{i1}, Y_{i2}), $i = 1, \ldots, n$ from the model in Equation (4) and computed the empirical versions of $I_{i,11}(\lambda)$ and $I_{i,12}(\lambda)$ as

$$\frac{1}{n}\sum_{i=1}^{n}\frac{\partial^2 \log f_{i,\lambda}^{\text{Clayton}}(Y_{i1}, Y_{i2})}{\partial \lambda_1^2}, \quad \frac{1}{n}\sum_{i=1}^{n}\frac{\partial^2 \log f_{i,\lambda}^{\text{Clayton}}(Y_{i1}, Y_{i2})}{\partial \lambda_1 \partial \lambda_2}.$$

The formulas for the derivatives of the log-density are found in Equations (A1) and (A2) in Appendix A.3. Our simulations were based on 1000 repetitions with $n \in \{100, 200, 300, 400, 500\}$.

Figure 7 depicts the simulation results based on 1000 repetitions. It clearly shows that the empirical versions are scattered around the theoretical values of $I_{i,11}(\lambda) = 2$ and $I_{i,12}(\lambda) = -1.16$. The variability of the empirical versions vanishes as n increases. The simulation results assert the correctness of Equation (5).

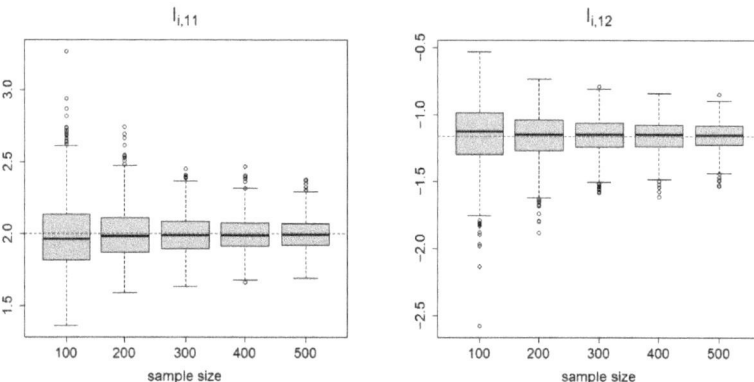

Figure 7. The boxplots summarizing the 1000 repetitions for the empirical versions of $I_{i,11}(\lambda) = 2$ and $I_{i,12}(\lambda) = -1.16$ (dashed lines) under the Clayton copula model in Equation (4) with parameter = 1. The sample size varies from $n = 100$ to $n = 300$.

10. Conclusions

At present, copula models are very popular in all areas of science. Bivariate meta-analyses are among those research areas that require sophisticated copula-based methods and theories. Nonetheless, there are only a few studies on copula-based bivariate meta-analysis from a methodological/theoretical perspective. This article fully develops the methodologies and theories of the copula-based bivariate meta-analysis, specifically for estimating the common mean vector. These developments will provide solid methodological/theoretical bases that are not available to date.

In this article, we emphasize the flexibility of the proposed copula models that allow for a variety of dependence structures. In the two real data examples, we employed the log-likelihood value as a criterion for model selection (Section 8). Even if the best copula is selected, it still raises the issue of goodness-of-fit, which is difficult to assess under the meta-analysis setting. The classical methods, such as Kolmogorov–Smirnov or Cramér–von Mises type statistics, cannot be directly applied to the non-identically distributed samples for which the empirical distribution function is difficult to interpret. Therefore, the development of goodness-of-fit tests is a possible research direction.

The fundamental assumption made in the proposed model is the common mean model, with known within-study correlations. The common mean assumption, although convenient for summarizing the data for a small number of studies [56], may not always hold in real meta-analyses [6]. Therefore, the extension of the proposed estimator to random means (random-effects models) or ordered means [57,58] is an important direction for future research. To model the random effects, we need another bivariate copula. The estimation problem for these hierarchical copula-based models is beyond the scope of the paper. Nonetheless, the results presented in this paper serve as fundamental knowledge before the exploration of more advanced models.

Author Contributions: Conceptualization, J.-H.S. and T.E.; methodology, J.-H.S. and T.E.; data curation, J.-H.S. and T.E.; writing, J.-H.S., Y.K., Y.-T.C. and T.E.; supervision, J.-H.S., Y.K., Y.-T.C. and T.E.; funding acquisition, Y.K. and Y.-T.C. All authors have read and agreed to the published version of the manuscript.

Funding: Konno Y. is financially supported by JSPS KAKENHI Grant Number 19K11867. Chang Y.-T. is supported by JSPS KAKENHI Grant Numbers JP26330047 and JP18K11196.

Institutional Review Board Statement: Not applicable.

Informed Consent Statement: Not applicable.

Data Availability Statement: Not applicable.

Acknowledgments: The authors thank five reviewers for their helpful comments that improved the manuscript. The authors kindly thank the Special Issue editors for their invitation to submit our work to *Symmetry*.

Conflicts of Interest: The authors declare no conflict of interest.

Appendix A

Appendix A.1. Proof of Lemma 1

We first prepare a lemma:

Lemma A1. *Under the general copula model (Definition 1), if $C_\theta^{[2,2]}$ exists in $(0,1)^2$, the correlation function has alternative expressions*

$$\rho_C(\theta_i) = E\left[\frac{Z_{i2}\varphi(Z_{i1})C_{\theta_i}^{[2,1]}\{\Phi(Z_{i1}),\Phi(Z_{i2})\}}{C_{\theta_i}^{[1,1]}\{\Phi(Z_{i1}),\Phi(Z_{i2})\}}\right]$$

$$= E\left[\frac{Z_{i1}\varphi(Z_{i2})C_{\theta_i}^{[1,2]}\{\Phi(Z_{i1}),\Phi(Z_{i2})\}}{C_{\theta_i}^{[1,1]}\{\Phi(Z_{i1}),\Phi(Z_{i2})\}}\right]$$

$$= E\left[\frac{\varphi(Z_{i1})\varphi(Z_{i2})C_{\theta_i}^{[2,2]}\{\Phi(Z_{i1}),\Phi(Z_{i2})\}}{C_{\theta_i}^{[1,1]}\{\Phi(Z_{i1}),\Phi(Z_{i2})\}}\right],$$

where Z_{i1} and Z_{i2} have the joint density

$$f_i(z_1, z_2) = \varphi(z_1)\varphi(z_2)C_{\theta_i}^{[1,1]}\{\Phi(z_1), \Phi(z_2)\}.$$

Proof of Lemma A1. We only prove the first identity for illustration. If $C_\theta^{[2,2]}$ exists, then

$$\rho_C(\theta_i) = \int_{-\infty}^{\infty} z_2\varphi(z_2) \int_{-\infty}^{\infty} z_1\varphi(z_1)C_{\theta_i}^{[1,1]}\{\Phi(z_1),\Phi(z_2)\}dz_1 dz_2$$
$$= \int_{-\infty}^{\infty} z_2\varphi(z_2) \int_{-\infty}^{\infty} \varphi(z_1)^2 C_{\theta_i}^{[2,1]}\{\Phi(z_1),\Phi(z_2)\}dz_1 dz_2,$$

where the last equality follows from Stein's identity. Thus, we obtain

$$\rho_C(\theta_i) = \int_{-\infty}^{\infty}\int_{-\infty}^{\infty} z_2 \varphi(z_2)\varphi(z_1)^2 C_{\theta_i}^{[2,1]}\{\Phi(z_1),\Phi(z_2)\}dz_1 dz_2$$

$$= \int_{-\infty}^{\infty}\int_{-\infty}^{\infty} z_2 \varphi(z_1) \frac{C_{\theta_i}^{[2,1]}\{\Phi(z_1),\Phi(z_2)\}}{C_{\theta_i}^{[1,1]}\{\Phi(z_1),\Phi(z_2)\}} f_i(z_1,z_2)dz_1 dz_2$$

$$= E\left[\frac{Z_{i2}\varphi(Z_{i1})C_{\theta_i}^{[2,1]}\{\Phi(Z_{i1}),\Phi(Z_{i2})\}}{C_{\theta_i}^{[1,1]}\{\Phi(Z_{i1}),\Phi(Z_{i2})\}}\right].$$

The proof completes. □

Lemma A1 is a generalization of Lemma 3.2 in [3].

Now, we prove Lemma 1 for $j = 1$ and $k = 2$. If $C_{\theta}^{[2,2]}$ exists, by straightforward calculations,

$$E\left\{\frac{\partial \log f_{i,\mu}(Y_i)}{\partial \mu_j}\frac{\partial \log f_{i,\mu}(Y_i)}{\partial \mu_k}\right\}$$

$$= \frac{1}{\sigma_{i1}\sigma_{i2}}\left(E(Z_{i1}Z_{i2}) - E\left[\frac{Z_{i2}\varphi(Z_{i1})C_{\theta_i}^{[2,1]}\{\Phi(Z_{i1}),\Phi(Z_{i2})\}}{C_{\theta_i}^{[1,1]}\{\Phi(Z_{i1}),\Phi(Z_{i2})\}}\right]\right.$$

$$-E\left[\frac{Z_{i1}\varphi(Z_{i2})C_{\theta_i}^{[1,2]}\{\Phi(Z_{i1}),\Phi(Z_{i2})\}}{C_{\theta_i}^{[1,1]}\{\Phi(Z_{i1}),\Phi(Z_{i2})\}}\right]$$

$$\left.+E\left[\frac{\varphi(Z_{i1})\varphi(Z_{i2})C_{\theta_i}^{[2,1]}\{\Phi(Z_{i1}),\Phi(Z_{i2})\}C_{\theta_i}^{[1,2]}\{\Phi(Z_{i1}),\Phi(Z_{i2})\}}{C_{\theta_i}^{[1,1]}\{\Phi(Z_{i1}),\Phi(Z_{i2})\}^2}\right]\right).$$

On the other hand,

$$E\left\{-\frac{\partial^2 \log f_{i,\mu}(Y_i)}{\partial \mu_j \partial \mu_k}\right\}$$

$$= \frac{1}{\sigma_{i1}\sigma_{i2}}\left(E\left[\frac{\varphi(Z_{i1})\varphi(Z_{i2})C_{\theta_i}^{[2,1]}\{\Phi(Z_{i1}),\Phi(Z_{i2})\}C_{\theta_i}^{[1,2]}\{\Phi(Z_{i1}),\Phi(Z_{i2})\}}{C_{\theta_i}^{[1,1]}\{\Phi(Z_{i1}),\Phi(Z_{i2})\}^2}\right]\right.$$

$$\left.-E\left[\frac{\varphi(Z_{i1})\varphi(Z_{i2})C_{\theta_i}^{[2,2]}\{\Phi(Z_{i1}),\Phi(Z_{i2})\}}{C_{\theta_i}^{[1,1]}\{\Phi(Z_{i1}),\Phi(Z_{i2})\}}\right]\right).$$

Based on the above results, it suffices to show

$$E(Z_{i1}Z_{i2}) - E\left[\frac{Z_{i2}\varphi(Z_{i1})C_{\theta_i}^{[2,1]}\{\Phi(Z_{i1}),\Phi(Z_{i2})\}}{C_{\theta_i}^{[1,1]}\{\Phi(Z_{i1}),\Phi(Z_{i2})\}}\right]$$

$$-E\left[\frac{Z_{i1}\varphi(Z_{i2})C_{\theta_i}^{[1,2]}\{\Phi(Z_{i1}),\Phi(Z_{i2})\}}{C_{\theta_i}^{[1,1]}\{\Phi(Z_{i1}),\Phi(Z_{i2})\}}\right]$$

$$+E\left[\frac{\varphi(Z_{i1})\varphi(Z_{i2})C_{\theta_i}^{[2,2]}\{\Phi(Z_{i1}),\Phi(Z_{i2})\}}{C_{\theta_i}^{[1,1]}\{\Phi(Z_{i1}),\Phi(Z_{i2})\}}\right] = 0$$

which is asserted by Lemma A1. Hence, the proof is completed. □

Appendix A.2. Derivatives for Copulas

The normal copula:

$$C_\rho^{\text{Normal }[1,1]}(u,v) = \frac{1}{\sqrt{1-\rho^2}}\exp\left\{-\frac{\rho^2 \Phi^{-1}(u)^2}{2(1-\rho^2)} - \frac{\rho^2 \Phi^{-1}(v)^2}{2(1-\rho^2)} + \frac{\rho \Phi^{-1}(u)\Phi^{-1}(v)}{1-\rho^2}\right\},$$

$$C_\rho^{\text{Normal }[2,1]}(u,v) = \frac{\sqrt{2\pi}}{\sqrt{1-\rho^2}} \exp\left\{\frac{(1-2\rho^2)\Phi^{-1}(u)^2}{2(1-\rho^2)} - \frac{\rho^2\Phi^{-1}(v)^2}{2(1-\rho^2)} + \frac{\rho\Phi^{-1}(u)\Phi^{-1}(v)}{1-\rho^2}\right\}$$
$$\times \left\{\frac{\rho\Phi^{-1}(v)}{1-\rho^2} - \frac{\rho^2\Phi^{-1}(u)}{1-\rho^2}\right\},$$

$$C_\rho^{\text{Normal }[2,2]}(u,v) = \frac{2\pi}{\sqrt{1-\rho^2}} \exp\left\{\frac{(1-2\rho^2)\Phi^{-1}(u)^2}{2(1-\rho^2)} - \frac{(1-2\rho^2)\Phi^{-1}(v)^2}{2(1-\rho^2)} + \frac{\rho\Phi^{-1}(u)\Phi^{-1}(v)}{1-\rho^2}\right\}$$
$$\times \left[\left\{\frac{\rho\Phi^{-1}(u)}{1-\rho^2} - \frac{\rho^2\Phi^{-1}(v)}{1-\rho^2}\right\}\left\{\frac{\rho\Phi^{-1}(v)}{1-\rho^2} - \frac{\rho^2\Phi^{-1}(u)}{1-\rho^2}\right\} + \frac{\rho}{1-\rho^2}\right],$$

$$C_\rho^{\text{Normal }[3,1]}(u,v) = \frac{2\pi}{\sqrt{1-\rho^2}} \exp\left\{\frac{(2-3\rho^2)\Phi^{-1}(u)^2}{2(1-\rho^2)} - \frac{\rho^2\Phi^{-1}(v)^2}{2(1-\rho^2)} + \frac{\rho\Phi^{-1}(u)\Phi^{-1}(v)}{1-\rho^2}\right\}$$
$$\times \left[\left\{\frac{(1-2\rho^2)\Phi^{-1}(u)}{1-\rho^2} + \frac{\rho\Phi^{-1}(v)}{1-\rho^2}\right\}\left\{\frac{\rho\Phi^{-1}(v)}{1-\rho^2} - \frac{\rho^2\Phi^{-1}(u)}{1-\rho^2}\right\} - \frac{\rho^2}{1-\rho^2}\right],$$

$$C_\rho^{\text{Normal }[3,2]}(u,v) = \frac{(2\pi)^{3/2}}{\sqrt{1-\rho^2}} \exp\left\{\frac{(2-3\rho^2)\Phi^{-1}(u)^2}{2(1-\rho^2)} - \frac{(1-2\rho^2)\Phi^{-1}(v)^2}{2(1-\rho^2)} + \frac{\rho\Phi^{-1}(u)\Phi^{-1}(v)}{1-\rho^2}\right\}$$
$$\times \left[\left\{\frac{(1-2\rho^2)\Phi^{-1}(u)}{1-\rho^2} + \frac{\rho\Phi^{-1}(v)}{1-\rho^2}\right\}\left\{\frac{\rho\Phi^{-1}(v)}{1-\rho^2} - \frac{\rho^2\Phi^{-1}(u)}{1-\rho^2}\right\} - \frac{\rho^2}{1-\rho^2}\right.$$
$$\left. + \frac{\rho}{1-\rho^2}\left\{\frac{\rho\Phi^{-1}(v)}{1-\rho^2} + \frac{\rho^2\Phi^{-1}(u)}{1-\rho^2}\right\} + \frac{\rho}{1-\rho^2}\left\{\frac{(1-2\rho^2)\Phi^{-1}(u)}{1-\rho^2} + \frac{\rho\Phi^{-1}(v)}{1-\rho^2}\right\}\right],$$

$$C_\rho^{\text{Normal }[4,1]}(u,v) = \frac{(2\pi)^{3/2}}{\sqrt{1-\rho^2}} \exp\left\{\frac{(3-4\rho^2)\Phi^{-1}(u)^2}{2(1-\rho^2)} - \frac{\rho^2\Phi^{-1}(v)^2}{2(1-\rho^2)} + \frac{\rho\Phi^{-1}(u)\Phi^{-1}(v)}{1-\rho^2}\right\}$$
$$\times \left[\left\{\frac{(1-2\rho^2)\Phi^{-1}(u)}{1-\rho^2} + \frac{\rho\Phi^{-1}(v)}{1-\rho^2}\right\}\left\{\frac{\rho\Phi^{-1}(v)}{1-\rho^2} - \frac{\rho^2\Phi^{-1}(u)}{1-\rho^2}\right\} - \frac{\rho^2}{1-\rho^2}\right.$$
$$\left. + \frac{1-2\rho^2}{1-\rho^2}\left\{\frac{\rho\Phi^{-1}(v)}{1-\rho^2} + \frac{\rho^2\Phi^{-1}(u)}{1-\rho^2}\right\} - \frac{\rho^2}{1-\rho^2}\left\{\frac{(1-2\rho^2)\Phi^{-1}(u)}{1-\rho^2} + \frac{\rho\Phi^{-1}(v)}{1-\rho^2}\right\}\right].$$

The FGM copula:

$$C_\theta^{\text{FGM }[1,1]}(u,v) = 1 + \theta(1-2u)(1-2v), \quad C_\theta^{\text{FGM }[2,1]}(u,v) = -2\theta(1-2v),$$

$$C_\theta^{\text{FGM }[2,2]}(u,v) = 4\theta, \quad C_\theta^{\text{FGM }[3,1]}(u,v) = C_\theta^{\text{FGM }[3,2]}(u,v) = C_\theta^{\text{FGM }[4,1]}(u,v) = 0.$$

The Clayton copula:

$$C_\alpha^{\text{Clayton }[j,k]}(u,v) = (\alpha+1)u^{-\alpha-j}v^{-\alpha-k}\left(u^{-\alpha}+v^{-\alpha}-1\right)^{-1/\alpha-(j+k)}\omega_{j,k}(u,v),$$

where $(j,k) \in \{(1,1),(2,1),(2,2),(3,1),(3,2),(4,1)\}$,

$$\omega_{1,1}(u,v) = 1, \quad \omega_{2,1}(u,v) = \alpha u^{-\alpha} + (\alpha+1)\left(1-v^{-\alpha}\right),$$

$$\omega_{2,2}(u,v) = -\alpha(\alpha+1)u^{-2\alpha} - (\alpha+1)u^{-\alpha} + \left(4\alpha^2+3\alpha+1\right)u^{-\alpha}v^{-\alpha} - \alpha(\alpha+1)v^{-2\alpha} - (\alpha+1)v^{-\alpha} + (\alpha+1)^2.$$

$$\omega_{3,1}(u,v) = \alpha(\alpha-1)u^{-2\alpha} + (4\alpha-1)(\alpha+1)\left(1-v^{-\alpha}\right)u^{-\alpha} + (\alpha+1)(\alpha+2)\left(1-v^{-\alpha}\right)^2,$$

$$\omega_{3,2}(u,v) = -\alpha(\alpha-1)(\alpha+1)u^{-3\alpha} - (\alpha+1)\left(3\alpha^2+4\alpha-1\right)u^{-2\alpha} + 3(\alpha-1)(\alpha+1)^2 u^{-\alpha}$$

$$+ \alpha(\alpha+1)(\alpha+2)v^{-3\alpha} - (\alpha-1)(\alpha+1)(\alpha+2)v^{-2\alpha} - (\alpha+1)(\alpha+2)^2 v^{-\alpha}$$

$$+ \left(11\alpha^3 + 7\alpha^2 + \alpha - 1\right) u^{-2\alpha} v^{-\alpha} - (\alpha+1)\left(11\alpha^2 + 5\alpha + 2\right) u^{-\alpha} v^{-2\alpha}$$

$$+ (\alpha+1)\left(8\alpha^2 + 5\alpha + 5\right) u^{-\alpha} v^{-\alpha} + (\alpha+1)^2(\alpha+2).$$

$$\omega_{4,1}(u,v) = \alpha(\alpha-1)(\alpha-2)u^{-3\alpha} + (\alpha-1)(\alpha+1)(11\alpha-2)(1-v^{-\alpha})u^{-2\alpha}$$

$$+ (\alpha+1)\left(11\alpha^2 + 14\alpha - 7\right)(1-v^{-\alpha})^2 u^{-\alpha} + (\alpha+1)(\alpha+2)(\alpha+3)(1-v^{-\alpha})^3.$$

Appendix A.3. The Information Matrix under the Clayton Copula with Exponential Margins

The Clayton copula model with exponential margins is given as

$$Pr(Y_{i1} > y_1, Y_{i2} > y_2) = C_{\alpha_i}^{\text{Clayton}}\{\bar{F}_1(y_1), \bar{F}_2(y_2)\} = \{\exp(\alpha_i \lambda_1 y_1) + \exp(\alpha_i \lambda_2 y_2) - 1\}^{-1/\alpha_i}.$$

Then, the joint density is

$$f_{i,\lambda}^{\text{Clayton}}(y_1, y_2) = \frac{\partial^2}{\partial y_1 \partial y_2} Pr(Y_{i1} > y_1, Y_{i2} > y_2) = \frac{(\alpha_i + 1)\lambda_1 \lambda_2 e^{\alpha_i \lambda_1 y_1 + \alpha_i \lambda_2 y_2}}{(e^{\alpha_i \lambda_1 y_1} + e^{\alpha_i \lambda_2 y_2} - 1)^{1/\alpha_i + 2}},$$

where $\lambda = (\lambda_1, \lambda_2)$. The log-density is

$$\log f_{i,\lambda}^{\text{Clayton}}(y_1, y_2) = \log(\alpha_i + 1) + \log \lambda_1 + \log \lambda_2 + \alpha_i \lambda_1 y_1 + \alpha_i \lambda_2 y_2 - \left(\frac{1}{\alpha_i} + 2\right)\log\left(e^{\alpha_i \lambda_1 y_1} + e^{\alpha_i \lambda_2 y_2} - 1\right).$$

The first-order partial derivative of $\log f_{i,\lambda}^{\text{Clayton}}(y_1, y_2)$ with respect to λ_j is

$$\frac{\partial \log f_{i,\lambda}^{\text{Clayton}}(y_1, y_2)}{\partial \lambda_j} = \frac{1}{\lambda_j} + \alpha_i y_j - (2\alpha_i + 1)\frac{y_j e^{\alpha_i \lambda_j y_j}}{e^{\alpha_i \lambda_1 y_1} + e^{\alpha_i \lambda_2 y_2} - 1}, \quad j = 1, 2.$$

The second-order partial derivatives of $\log f_{\alpha_i}^{\text{Clayton}}(y_1, y_2)$ are

$$\frac{\partial^2 \log f_{i,\lambda}^{\text{Clayton}}(y_1, y_2)}{\partial \lambda_j^2} = -\frac{1}{\lambda_j^2} - \alpha_i(2\alpha_i + 1)\left\{\frac{y_j^2 e^{\alpha_i \lambda_j y_j}}{e^{\alpha_i \lambda_1 y_1} + e^{\alpha_i \lambda_2 y_2} - 1} - \frac{y_j^2 e^{2\alpha_i \lambda_j y_j}}{(e^{\alpha_i \lambda_1 y_1} + e^{\alpha_i \lambda_2 y_2} - 1)^2}\right\}, \quad j = 1, 2, \quad \text{(A1)}$$

$$\frac{\partial^2 \log f_{i,\lambda}^{\text{Clayton}}(y_1, y_2)}{\partial \lambda_1 \partial \lambda_2} = \alpha_i(2\alpha_i + 1)\frac{y_1 y_2 e^{\alpha_i \lambda_1 y_1 + \alpha_i \lambda_2 y_2}}{(e^{\alpha_i \lambda_1 y_1} + e^{\alpha_i \lambda_2 y_2} - 1)^2}. \quad \text{(A2)}$$

Then, the Fisher information matrix is

$$I_{i,jk}^{\text{Clayton}}(\lambda) = E\left\{-\frac{\partial^2 \log f_{i,\lambda}^{\text{Clayton}}(Y_i)}{\partial \lambda_j \partial \lambda_k}\right\}, \quad j, k = 1, 2.$$

For $j = k = 1$, we have

$$I_{i,11}^{\text{Clayton}}(\lambda) = E\left\{-\frac{\partial^2 \log f_{i,\lambda}^{\text{Clayton}}(Y_i)}{\partial \lambda_1^2}\right\}$$

$$= \frac{1}{\lambda_1^2} + \frac{\alpha_i(2\alpha_i+1)}{\lambda_1^2}\left[E\left(\frac{\lambda_1^2 Y_{i1}^2 e^{\alpha_i \lambda_1 Y_{i1}}}{e^{\alpha_i \lambda_1 Y_{i1}} + e^{\alpha_i \lambda_2 Y_{i2}} - 1}\right) - E\left\{\frac{\lambda_1^2 Y_{i1}^2 e^{2\alpha_i \lambda_1 Y_{i1}}}{(e^{\alpha_i \lambda_1 Y_{i1}} + e^{\alpha_i \lambda_2 Y_{i2}} - 1)^2}\right\}\right].$$

To compute the first expectation, we consider the change in variable $\lambda_j y_j = x_j$, $j = 1, 2$. Then,

$$E\left(\frac{\lambda_1^2 Y_{i1}^2 e^{\alpha_i \lambda_1 Y_{i1}}}{e^{\alpha_i \lambda_1 Y_{i1}} + e^{\alpha_i \lambda_2 Y_{i2}} - 1}\right) = (\alpha_i + 1) \int_0^\infty \int_0^\infty \frac{\lambda_1^3 y_1^2 \lambda_2 e^{2\alpha_i \lambda_1 y_1 + \alpha_i \lambda_2 y_2}}{(e^{\alpha_i y_1} + e^{\alpha_i y_2} - 1)^{1/\alpha_i + 3}} dy_1 dy_2$$

$$= (\alpha_i + 1) \int_0^\infty \int_0^\infty \frac{x_1^2 e^{2\alpha_i x_1 + \alpha_i x_2}}{(e^{\alpha_i x_1} + e^{\alpha_i x_2} - 1)^{1/\alpha_i + 3}} dx_1 dx_2$$

$$= (\alpha_i + 1) \int_0^\infty x_1^2 e^{2\alpha_i x_1} \int_0^\infty \frac{e^{\alpha_i x_2}}{(e^{\alpha_i x_1} + e^{\alpha_i x_2} - 1)^{1/\alpha_i + 3}} dx_1 dx_2.$$

For the inner integral,

$$\int_0^\infty \frac{e^{\alpha_i x_2}}{(e^{\alpha_i x_1} + e^{\alpha_i x_2} - 1)^{1/\alpha_i + 3}} dx_2 = -\frac{1}{2\alpha_i + 1}\left\{\frac{1}{(e^{\alpha_i x_1} + e^{\alpha_i x_2} - 1)^{1/\alpha_i + 2}}\Big|_0^\infty\right\} = \frac{1}{2\alpha_i + 1} e^{-(2\alpha_i + 1)x_1}.$$

It follows that

$$\int_0^\infty x_1^2 e^{2\alpha_i x_1} \left\{\frac{1}{2\alpha_i + 1} e^{-(2\alpha_i + 1)x_1}\right\} dx_1 = \frac{1}{2\alpha_i + 1} \int_0^\infty x_1^2 e^{-x_1} dx_1 = \frac{2}{2\alpha_i + 1}.$$

Thus, we obtain

$$E\left(\frac{\lambda_1^2 Y_{i1}^2 e^{\alpha_i \lambda_1 Y_{i1}}}{e^{\alpha_i \lambda_1 Y_{i1}} + e^{\alpha_i \lambda_2 Y_{i2}} - 1}\right) = \frac{2(\alpha_i + 1)}{2\alpha_i + 1}.$$

The second expectation is computed as

$$E\left\{\frac{\lambda_1^2 Y_{i1}^2 e^{2\alpha_i \lambda_1 Y_{i1}}}{(e^{\alpha_i \lambda_1 Y_{i1}} + e^{\alpha_i \lambda_2 Y_{i2}} - 1)^2}\right\} = (\alpha_i + 1) \int_0^\infty \int_0^\infty \frac{\lambda_1^3 y_1^2 \lambda_2 e^{3\alpha_i \lambda_1 y_1 + \alpha_i \lambda_2 y_2}}{(e^{\alpha_i y_1} + e^{\alpha_i y_2} - 1)^{1/\alpha_i + 4}} dy_1 dy_2$$

$$= (\alpha_i + 1) \int_0^\infty \int_0^\infty \frac{x_1^2 e^{3\alpha_i x_1 + \alpha_i x_2}}{(e^{\alpha_i x_1} + e^{\alpha_i x_2} - 1)^{1/\alpha_i + 4}} dx_1 dx_2$$

$$= (\alpha_i + 1) \int_0^\infty x_1^2 e^{3\alpha_i x_1} \int_0^\infty \frac{e^{\alpha_i x_2}}{(e^{\alpha_i x_1} + e^{\alpha_i x_2} - 1)^{1/\alpha_i + 4}} dx_1 dx_2.$$

For the inner integral,

$$\int_0^\infty \frac{e^{\alpha_i x_2}}{(e^{\alpha_i x_1} + e^{\alpha_i x_2} - 1)^{1/\alpha_i + 4}} dx_2 = -\frac{1}{3\alpha_i + 1}\left\{\frac{1}{(e^{\alpha_i x_1} + e^{\alpha_i x_2} - 1)^{1/\alpha_i + 3}}\Big|_0^\infty\right\} = \frac{1}{3\alpha_i + 1} e^{-(3\alpha_i + 1)x_1}.$$

It follows that

$$\int_0^\infty x_1^2 e^{3\alpha_i x_1} \left\{\frac{1}{3\alpha_i + 1} e^{-(3\alpha_i + 1)x_1}\right\} dx_1 = \frac{1}{3\alpha_i + 1} \int_0^\infty x_1^2 e^{-x_1} dx_1 = \frac{2}{3\alpha_i + 1}.$$

Thus, we obtain

$$E\left\{\frac{\lambda_1^2 Y_{i1}^2 e^{2\alpha_i \lambda_1 Y_{i1}}}{(e^{\alpha_i \lambda_1 Y_{i1}} + e^{\alpha_i \lambda_2 Y_{i2}} - 1)^2}\right\} = \frac{2(\alpha_i + 1)}{3\alpha_i + 1}.$$

Combining the above results, we have

$$I_{i,11}^{\text{Clayton}}(\lambda) = \frac{1}{\lambda_1^2} + \frac{1}{\lambda_1^2}\frac{2\alpha_i^2(\alpha_i+1)}{3\alpha_i+1}.$$

In a similar fashion, for $j = k = 2$, we also have

$$I_{i,22}^{\text{Clayton}}(\lambda) = \frac{1}{\lambda_2^2} + \frac{1}{\lambda_2^2}\frac{2\alpha_i^2(\alpha_i+1)}{3\alpha_i+1}.$$

For $j = 1, k = 2$, we have

$$I_{i,12}^{\text{Clayton}}(\lambda) = E\left\{-\frac{\partial^2 \log f_{i,\lambda}^{\text{Clayton}}(Y_i)}{\partial \lambda_1 \partial \lambda_2}\right\} = -\left(\frac{1}{\alpha_i}+2\right)E\left\{\frac{\lambda_1 \lambda_2 Y_{i1} Y_{i2} e^{\alpha_i \lambda_1 Y_{i1} + \alpha_i \lambda_2 Y_{i2}}}{(e^{\alpha_i \lambda_1 Y_{i1}} + e^{\alpha_i \lambda_2 Y_{i2}} - 1)^2}\right\}$$

$$= -\frac{\alpha_i(2\alpha_i+1)}{\lambda_1 \lambda_2} E\left\{\frac{\lambda_1 \lambda_2 Y_{i1} Y_{i2} e^{\alpha_i \lambda_1 Y_{i1} + \alpha_i \lambda_2 Y_{i2}}}{(e^{\alpha_i \lambda_1 Y_{i1}} + e^{\alpha_i \lambda_2 Y_{i2}} - 1)^2}\right\}.$$

We consider

$$E\left\{\frac{\lambda_1 \lambda_2 Y_{i1} Y_{i2} e^{\alpha_i \lambda_1 Y_{i1} + \alpha_i \lambda_2 Y_{i2}}}{(e^{\alpha_i \lambda_1 Y_{i1}} + e^{\alpha_i \lambda_2 Y_{i2}} - 1)^2}\right\} = (\alpha_i+1)\int_0^\infty \int_0^\infty \frac{\lambda_1^2 \lambda_2^2 y_1 y_2 e^{2\alpha_i \lambda_1 y_1 + 2\alpha_i \lambda_2 y_2}}{(e^{\alpha_i y_1} + e^{\alpha_i y_2} - 1)^{1/\alpha_i+4}} dy_1 dy_2$$

$$= (\alpha_i+1)\int_0^\infty \int_0^\infty \frac{x_1 x_2 e^{2\alpha_i x_1 + 2\alpha_i x_2}}{(e^{\alpha_i x_1} + e^{\alpha_i x_2} - 1)^{1/\alpha_i+4}} dx_1 dx_2$$

$$= (\alpha_i+1)\int_0^\infty x_1 e^{2\alpha_i x_1} \int_0^\infty \frac{x_2 e^{2\alpha_i x_2}}{(e^{\alpha_i x_1} + e^{\alpha_i x_2} - 1)^{1/\alpha_i+4}} dx_1 dx_2.$$

For the inner integral,

$$\int_0^\infty \frac{x_2 e^{2\alpha_i x_2}}{(e^{\alpha_i x_1} + e^{\alpha_i x_2} - 1)^{1/\alpha_i+4}} dx_1$$

$$= -\frac{1}{3\alpha_i+1}\int_0^\infty x_2 e^{\alpha_i x_2} d\left\{\frac{1}{(e^{\alpha_i x_1} + e^{\alpha_i x_2} - 1)^{1/\alpha_i+3}}\right\}$$

$$= -\frac{1}{3\alpha_i+1}\left\{\frac{x_2 e^{\alpha_i x_2}}{(e^{\alpha_i x_1} + e^{\alpha_i x_2} - 1)^{1/\alpha_i+3}}\bigg|_0^\infty - \int_0^\infty \frac{1}{(e^{\alpha_i x_1} + e^{\alpha_i x_2} - 1)^{1/\alpha_i+3}} d(x_2 e^{\alpha_i x_2})\right\}$$

$$= \frac{1}{3\alpha_i+1}\int_0^\infty \frac{e^{\alpha_i x_2} + \alpha_i x_2 e^{\alpha_i x_2}}{(e^{\alpha_i x_1} + e^{\alpha_i x_2} - 1)^{1/\alpha_i+3}} dx_2$$

$$= \frac{1}{3\alpha_i+1}\int_0^\infty \frac{e^{\alpha_i x_2}}{(e^{\alpha_i x_1} + e^{\alpha_i x_2} - 1)^{1/\alpha_i+3}} dx_2 + \frac{\alpha_i}{3\alpha_i+1}\int_0^\infty \frac{x_2 e^{\alpha_i x_2}}{(e^{\alpha_i x_1} + e^{\alpha_i x_2} - 1)^{1/\alpha_i+3}} dx_2,$$

where the second equality follows from integration by parts. For the first integral,

$$\frac{1}{3\alpha_i+1}\int_0^\infty \frac{e^{\alpha_i x_2}}{(e^{\alpha_i x_1} + e^{\alpha_i x_2} - 1)^{1/\alpha_i+3}} dx_2$$

$$= -\frac{1}{(3\alpha_i+1)(2\alpha_i+1)}\left(\frac{1}{(e^{\alpha_i x_1} + e^{\alpha_i x_2} - 1)^{1/\alpha_i+2}}\bigg|_0^\infty\right)$$

$$= \frac{1}{(3\alpha_i+1)(2\alpha_i+1)} e^{-2(\alpha_i+1)x_1}.$$

The second integral is

$$\frac{\alpha_i}{3\alpha_i+1}\int_0^\infty \frac{x_2 e^{\alpha_i x_2}}{(e^{\alpha_i x_1}+e^{\alpha_i x_2}-1)^{1/\alpha_i+3}}dx_2$$

$$=-\frac{\alpha_i}{(3\alpha_i+1)(2\alpha_i+1)}\int_0^\infty x_2 d\left(\frac{1}{(e^{\alpha_i x_1}+e^{\alpha_i x_2}-1)^{1/\alpha_i+2}}\right)$$

$$=-\frac{\alpha_i}{(3\alpha_i+1)(2\alpha_i+1)}\left\{\frac{x_2}{(e^{\alpha_i x_1}+e^{\alpha_i x_2}-1)^{1/\alpha_i+2}}\bigg|_0^\infty - \int_0^\infty \frac{1}{(e^{\alpha_i x_1}+e^{\alpha_i x_2}-1)^{1/\alpha_i+2}}dx_2\right\}$$

$$=\frac{\alpha_i}{(3\alpha_i+1)(2\alpha_i+1)}\int_0^\infty \frac{1}{(e^{\alpha_i x_1}+e^{\alpha_i x_2}-1)^{1/\alpha_i+2}}dx_2,$$

where the second equality follows from integration by parts. Now, the expectation becomes

$$E\left\{\frac{\lambda_1\lambda_2 Y_{i1} Y_{i2} e^{\alpha_i\lambda_1 Y_{i1}+\alpha_i\lambda_2 Y_{i2}}}{(e^{\alpha_i\lambda_1 Y_{i1}}+e^{\alpha_i\lambda_2 Y_{i2}}-1)^2}\right\}$$

$$=\frac{\alpha_i+1}{(3\alpha_i+1)(2\alpha_i+1)}\int_0^\infty x_1 e^{-x_1}dx_1 + \frac{\alpha_i(\alpha_i+1)}{(3\alpha_i+1)(2\alpha_i+1)}\int_0^\infty\int_0^\infty \frac{x_1 e^{2\alpha_i x_2}}{(e^{\alpha_i x_1}+e^{\alpha_i x_2}-1)^{1/\alpha_i+2}}dx_1 dx_2,$$

$$=\frac{\alpha_i+1}{(3\alpha_i+1)(2\alpha_i+1)} + \frac{\alpha_i(\alpha_i+1)}{(3\alpha_i+1)(2\alpha_i+1)}\int_0^\infty\int_0^\infty \frac{x_1 e^{2\alpha_i x_2}}{(e^{\alpha_i x_1}+e^{\alpha_i x_2}-1)^{1/\alpha_i+2}}dx_1 dx_2.$$

For the integral in the above expression, we consider its inner integral,

$$\int_0^\infty \frac{x_1 e^{2\alpha_i x_2}}{(e^{\alpha_i x_1}+e^{\alpha_i x_2}-1)^{1/\alpha_i+2}}dx_1$$

$$=-\frac{1}{\alpha_i+1}\int_0^\infty x_1 e^{\alpha_i x_1} d\left\{\frac{1}{(e^{\alpha_i x_1}+e^{\alpha_i x_2}-1)^{1/\alpha_i+1}}\right\}$$

$$=-\frac{1}{\alpha_i+1}\left\{\frac{x_1 e^{\alpha_i x_1}}{(e^{\alpha_i x_1}+e^{\alpha_i x_2}-1)^{1/\alpha_i+1}}\bigg|_0^\infty - \int_0^\infty \frac{1}{(e^{\alpha_i x_1}+e^{\alpha_i x_2}-1)^{1/\alpha_i+1}}d(x_1 e^{\alpha_i x_1})\right\}$$

$$=\frac{1}{\alpha_i+1}\int_0^\infty \frac{e^{\alpha_i x_2}+\alpha_i x_1 e^{\alpha_i x_1}}{(e^{\alpha_i x_1}+e^{\alpha_i x_2}-1)^{1/\alpha_i+1}}dx_1$$

$$=\frac{1}{\alpha_i+1}\int_0^\infty \frac{e^{\alpha_i x_2}}{(e^{\alpha_i x_1}+e^{\alpha_i x_2}-1)^{1/\alpha_i+1}}dx_1 + \frac{\alpha_i}{\alpha_i+1}\int_0^\infty \frac{x_1 e^{\alpha_i x_1}}{(e^{\alpha_i x_1}+e^{\alpha_i x_2}-1)^{1/\alpha_i+1}}dx_1,$$

where the second last equality follows from integration by parts. We compute the above two integrals separately. We have

$$\frac{1}{\alpha_i+1}\int_0^\infty \frac{e^{\alpha_i x_2}}{(e^{\alpha_i x_1}+e^{\alpha_i x_2}-1)^{1/\alpha_i+1}}dx_1 = -\frac{1}{\alpha_i+1}\left\{\frac{1}{(e^{\alpha_i x_1}+e^{\alpha_i x_2}-1)^{1/\alpha_i}}\bigg|_0^\infty\right\} = \frac{1}{\alpha_i+1}e^{-x_2}.$$

On the other hand, we have

$$\frac{\alpha_i}{\alpha_i+1}\int_0^\infty \frac{x_1 e^{\alpha_i x_1}}{(e^{\alpha_i x_1}+e^{\alpha_i x_2}-1)^{1/\alpha_i+1}}dx_1$$

$$=-\frac{\alpha_i}{\alpha_i+1}\int_0^\infty x_1 d\left\{\frac{1}{(e^{\alpha_i x_1}+e^{\alpha_i x_2}-1)^{1/\alpha_i}}\right\}$$

$$= -\frac{\alpha_i}{\alpha_i+1}\left\{\frac{x_1}{(e^{\alpha_i x_1}+e^{\alpha_i x_2}-1)^{1/\alpha_i}}\bigg|_0^\infty - \int_0^\infty \frac{1}{(e^{\alpha_i x_1}+e^{\alpha_i x_2}-1)^{1/\alpha_i}}dx_1\right\}$$

$$= \frac{\alpha_i}{\alpha_i+1}\int_0^\infty \frac{1}{(e^{\alpha_i x_1}+e^{\alpha_i x_2}-1)^{1/\alpha_i}}dx_1.$$

Then,

$$\int_0^\infty\left\{\frac{1}{\alpha_i+1}e^{-x_2}+\frac{\alpha_i}{\alpha_i+1}\int_0^\infty\frac{1}{(e^{\alpha_i x_1}+e^{\alpha_i x_2}-1)^{1/\alpha_i}}dx_1\right\}dx_2 = \frac{1}{\alpha_i+1}+\frac{\alpha_i}{\alpha_i+1}\int_0^\infty\int_0^\infty\frac{1}{(e^{\alpha_i x_1}+e^{\alpha_i x_2}-1)^{1/\alpha_i}}dx_1 dx_2.$$

Combine all the results, one has

$$E\left\{\frac{\lambda_1\lambda_2 Y_{i1}Y_{i2}e^{\alpha_i\lambda_1 Y_{i1}+\alpha_i\lambda_2 Y_{i2}}}{(e^{\alpha_i\lambda_1 Y_{i1}}+e^{\alpha_i\lambda_2 Y_{i2}}-1)^2}\right\}$$

$$= \frac{\alpha_i+1}{(3\alpha_i+1)(2\alpha_i+1)}+\frac{\alpha_i}{(3\alpha_i+1)(2\alpha_i+1)}+\frac{\alpha_i^2}{(3\alpha_i+1)(2\alpha_i+1)}\int_0^\infty\int_0^\infty\frac{1}{(e^{\alpha_i x_1}+e^{\alpha_i x_2}-1)^{1/\alpha_i}}dx_1 dx_2$$

$$= \frac{1}{3\alpha_i+1}+\frac{\alpha_i^2}{(3\alpha_i+1)(2\alpha_i+1)}\int_0^\infty\int_0^\infty\frac{1}{(e^{\alpha_i x_1}+e^{\alpha_i x_2}-1)^{1/\alpha_i}}dx_1 dx_2.$$

Let $\alpha_i x_1 = s$ and $\alpha_i x_2 = t$, according to [52], we have

$$\int_0^\infty\int_0^\infty\frac{\alpha_i^2}{(e^{\alpha_i x_1}+e^{\alpha_i x_2}-1)^{1/\alpha_i}}dx_1 dx_2 = \int_0^\infty\int_0^\infty\frac{1}{(e^s+e^t-1)^{1/\alpha_i}}ds dt = \frac{1}{2}\left\{\Psi\left(\frac{1}{2\alpha_i}\right)-\Psi\left(\frac{\alpha_i+1}{2\alpha_i}\right)\right\}.$$

Hence, we obtain

$$E\left\{\frac{\lambda_1\lambda_2 Y_{i1}Y_{i2}e^{\alpha_i\lambda_1 Y_{i1}+\alpha_i\lambda_2 Y_{i2}}}{(e^{\alpha_i\lambda_1 Y_{i1}}+e^{\alpha_i\lambda_2 Y_{i2}}-1)^2}\right\} = \frac{1}{3\alpha_i+1}+\frac{1}{2(3\alpha_i+1)(2\alpha_i+1)}\left\{\Psi\left(\frac{1}{2\alpha_i}\right)-\Psi\left(\frac{\alpha_i+1}{2\alpha_i}\right)\right\}.$$

Finally, combining the above results, we have

$$I_{i,12}^{\text{Clayton}}(\lambda) = -\frac{\alpha_i(2\alpha_i+1)}{\lambda_1\lambda_2}\phi(\alpha_i),$$

where

$$\phi(\alpha) = \frac{1}{3\alpha_i+1}+\frac{1}{2(3\alpha+1)(2\alpha+1)}\left\{\Psi\left(\frac{1}{2\alpha}\right)-\Psi\left(\frac{\alpha+1}{2\alpha}\right)\right\}.$$

References

1. Gleser, L.J.; Olkin, L. Stochastically dependent effect sizes. In *The Handbook of Research Synthesis*; Russel Sage Foundation: New York, NY, USA, 1994.
2. Riley, R.D. Multivariate meta-analysis: The effect of ignoring within-study correlation. *J. R. Stat. Soc. Ser. A Stat. Soc.* 2009, 172, 789–811. [CrossRef]
3. Shih, J.-H.; Konno, Y.; Chang, Y.-T.; Emura, T. Estimation of a common mean vector in bivariate meta-analysis under the FGM copula. *Statistics* 2019, 53, 673–695. [CrossRef]
4. Nissen, S.E.; Wolski, K. Effect of Rosiglitazone on the Risk of Myocardial Infarction and Death from Cardiovascular Causes. *N. Engl. J. Med.* 2007, 356, 2457–2471. [CrossRef] [PubMed]
5. Yamaguchi, Y.; Maruo, K. Bivariate beta-binomial model using Gaussian copula for bivariate meta-analysis of two binary outcomes with low incidence. *Jpn. J. Stat. Data Sci.* 2019, 2, 347–373. [CrossRef]
6. Mavridis, D.; Salanti, G. A practical introduction to multivariate meta-analysis. *Stat. Methods Med. Res.* 2011, 22, 133–158. [CrossRef]
7. Copas, J.B.; Jackson, D.; White, I.; Riley, R.D. The role of secondary outcomes in multivariate meta-analysis. *J. R. Stat. Soc. Ser. C Appl. Stat.* 2018, 67, 1177–1205. [CrossRef]

8. Burzykowski, T.; Molenberghs, G.; Buyse, M.; Geys, H.; Renard, D. Validation of surrogate end points in multiple randomized clinical trials with failure time end points. *J. R. Stat. Soc. Ser. C Appl. Stat.* **2001**, *50*, 405–422. [CrossRef]
9. Rotolo, F.; Paoletti, X.; Michiels, S. surrosurv: An R package for the evaluation of failure time surrogate endpoints in individual patient data meta-analysis of randomized clinical trials. *Comput. Methods Programs Biomed.* **2018**, *155*, 189–198. [CrossRef]
10. Rotolo, F.; Paoletti, X.; Burzykowski, T.; Buyse, M.; Michiels, S. A Poisson approach to the validation of failure time surrogate endpoints in individual patient data meta-analyses. *Stat. Methods Med. Res.* **2019**, *28*, 170–183. [CrossRef]
11. Emura, T.; Sofeu, C.L.; Rondeau, V. Conditional copula models for correlated survival endpoints: Individual patient data meta-analysis of randomized controlled trials. *Stat. Methods Med. Res.* **2021**, *30*, 2634–2650. [CrossRef]
12. Kuss, O.; Hoyer, A.; Solms, A. Meta-analysis for diagnostic accuracy studies: A new statistical model using beta-binomial dis-tributions and bivariate copulas. *Stat. Med.* **2014**, *33*, 17–30. [CrossRef]
13. Nikoloulopoulos, A.K. A vine copula mixed effect model for trivariate meta-analysis of diagnostic test accuracy studies ac-counting for disease prevalence. *Stat. Methods Med. Res.* **2017**, *26*, 2270–2286. [CrossRef]
14. Nikoloulopoulos, A.K. A D-vine copula mixed model for joint meta-analysis and comparison of diagnostic tests. *Stat. Methods Med. Res.* **2018**, *28*, 3286–3300. [CrossRef]
15. Nikoloulopoulos, A.K. A multinomial quadrivariate D-vine copula mixed model for meta-analysis of diagnostic studies in the presence of non-evaluable subjects. *Stat. Methods Med. Res.* **2020**, *29*, 2988–3005. [CrossRef]
16. Takeuchi, T.T. Constructing a bivariate distribution function with given marginals and correlation: Application to the galaxy luminosity function. *Mon. Not. R. Astron. Soc.* **2010**, *406*, 1830–1840. [CrossRef]
17. Ota, S.; Kimura, M. Effective estimation algorithm for parameters of multivariate Farlie–Gumbel–Morgenstern copula. *Jpn. J. Stat. Data Sci.* **2021**, *4*, 1049–1078. [CrossRef]
18. Ghosh, S.; Sheppard, L.W.; Holder, M.T.; Loecke, T.D.; Reid, P.C.; Bever, J.D.; Reuman, D.C. Copulas and their potential for ecology. *Adv. Ecol. Res.* **2020**, *62*, 409–468. [CrossRef]
19. Alidoost, F.; Stein, A.; Su, Z. The use of bivariate copulas for bias correction of reanalysis air temperature data. *PLoS ONE* **2019**, *14*, e0216059. [CrossRef]
20. Bhatti, M.I.; Do, H.Q. Recent development in copula and its applications to the energy, forestry and environmental sciences. *Int. J. Hydrog. Energy* **2019**, *44*, 19453–19473. [CrossRef]
21. Emura, T.; Chen, Y.H. *Analysis of Survival Data with Dependent Censoring: Copula-Based Approaches*; JSS Research Series in Statistics; Springer: Singapore, 2018.
22. Emura, T.; Matsui, S.; Rondeau, V. *Survival Analysis with Correlated Endpoints, Joint Frailty-Copula Models*; JSS Research Series in Statistics; Springer: Singapore, 2019.
23. Emura, T.; Shih, J.-H.; Ha, I.D.; Wilke, R.A. Comparison of the marginal hazard model and the sub-distribution hazard model for competing risks under an assumed copula. *Stat. Methods Med. Res.* **2020**, *29*, 2307–2327. [CrossRef]
24. Peng, M.; Xiang, L.; Wang, S. Semiparametric regression analysis of clustered survival data with semi-competing risks. *Comput. Stat. Data Anal.* **2018**, *124*, 53–70. [CrossRef]
25. Huang, X.-W.; Wang, W.; Emura, T. A copula-based Markov chain model for serially dependent event times with a dependent terminal event. *Jpn. J. Stat. Data Sci.* **2020**, *4*, 917–951. [CrossRef]
26. Shih, J.H. Common Mean. Copula: Bivariate Common Mean Vector under Copula Models; CRAN. 2022. Available online: https://CRAN.R-project.org/package=CommonMean.Copula (accessed on 8 January 2022).
27. Berkey, C.S.; Hoaglin, D.C.; Antczak-bouckoms, A.; Mosteller, F.; Colditz, G.A. Meta-analysis of multiple outcomes by regression with random effect. *Stat. Med.* **1998**, *17*, 2537–2550. [CrossRef]
28. Shinozaki, N. A note on estimating the common mean of k normal distributions and the stein problem. *Commun. Stat.-Theory Methods* **1978**, *7*, 1421–1432. [CrossRef]
29. Malekzadeh, A.; Kharrati-Kopaei, M. Inferences on the common mean of several normal populations under hetero-scedasticity. *Comput. Stat.* **2018**, *33*, 1367–1384. [CrossRef]
30. Gasparrini, A. Mvmeta: Multivariate and Univariate Meta-Analysis and Meta-Regression; CRAN. 2019. Available online: https://CRAN.R-project.org/package=mvmeta (accessed on 8 January 2022).
31. Nelsen, R. An Introduction to Copulas. *Technometrics. Lett.* **2000**, *42*, 317. [CrossRef]
32. Durante, F.; Sempi, C. *Principles of Copula Theory*; CRC/Chapman & Hall: Boca Raton, FL, USA, 2016.
33. Morgenstern, D. Einfache Beispiele zweidimensionaler Verteilungen. *Mitt. Für Math. Stat.* **1956**, *8*, 34–235.
34. Bairamov, I.G.; Kotz, S.; Bekci, M. New generalized Farlie-Gumbel-Morgenstern distributions and concomitants of order statistics. *J. Appl. Stat.* **2001**, *28*, 521–536. [CrossRef]
35. Bairamov, I.; Kotz, S. Dependence structure and symmetry of Hunag-Kotz FGM distributions and their extensions. *Metrika* **2002**, *56*, 55–72. [CrossRef]
36. Amini, M.; Jabbari, H.; Borzadaran, G.R.M. Aspects of Dependence in Generalized Farlie-Gumbel-Morgenstern Distributions. *Commun. Stat.-Simul. Comput.* **2011**, *40*, 1192–1205. [CrossRef]
37. Domma, F.; Giordano, S. A copula-based approach to account for dependence in stress-strength models. *Stat. Pap.* **2012**, *54*, 807–826. [CrossRef]
38. Chesneau, C. A new two-dimensional relation copula inspiring generalized version of the Farlie-Gumbel-Morgenstern copula. *Res. Commun. Math. Math. Sci.* **2021**, *13*, 99–128.

39. Clayton, D.G. A model for association in bivariate life tables and its application in epidemiological studies of familial tendency in chronic disease incidence. *Biometrika* **1978**, *65*, 141–151. [CrossRef]
40. Duchateau, L.; Janssen, P. *The Frailty Model*; Springer: New York, NY, USA, 2007.
41. Gumbel, E.J. Distributions de valeurs extrêmes en plusieurs dimensions. *Publ. Inst. Statist. Univ. Paris* **1960**, *9*, 171–173.
42. Frank, M.J. On the simultaneous associativity of F(x, y) and x+y−F(x, y). *Aequ. Math.* **1979**, *19*, 194–226. [CrossRef]
43. Sklar, A. Fonctions de répartition à n dimensions et leurs marges. *Publ. Inst. Statist. Univ. Paris* **1959**, *8*, 229–231.
44. Schucany, W.R.; Parr, W.C.; Boyer, J.E. Correlation structure in Farlie-Gumbel-Morgenstern distributions. *Biometrika* **1978**, *65*, 650–653. [CrossRef]
45. Nelsen, R.B. Dependence and Order in Families of Archimedean Copulas. *J. Multivar. Anal.* **1997**, *60*, 111–122. [CrossRef]
46. Bradley, R.A.; Gart, J.J. The asymptotic properties of ML estimators when sampling from associated populations. *Biometrika* **1962**, *49*, 205–214. [CrossRef]
47. Emura, T.; Hu, Y.H.; Konno, Y. Asymptotic inference for maximum likelihood estimators under the special exponential family with double-truncation. *Stat. Pap.* **2017**, *58*, 877–909. [CrossRef]
48. Shih, J.H. Copula-Based Statistical Inferences for a Common Mean Vector and Correlation Ratios Using Bivariate Data. Ph.D. Thesis, National Central University Library, Taoyuan, Taiwan, 2020. Available online: https://etd.lib.nctu.edu.tw/cgi-bin/gs32/ncugsweb.cgi/ccd=GLZeNP/record?r1=2&h1=2 (accessed on 3 October 2020).
49. Shao, J. *Mathematical Statistics*; Springer: New York, NY, USA, 2003.
50. Van der Vaart, A.W. *Asymptotic Statistics*; Cambridge University Press: Cambridge, UK, 1998.
51. Lehmann, E.L.; Casella, G. *Theory of Point Estimation*, 2nd ed.; Springer: New York, NY, USA, 1998.
52. Kontopantelis, E.; Reeves, D. Performance of statistical methods for meta-analysis when true study effects are non-normally distributed: A simulation study. *Stat. Methods Med Res.* **2010**, *21*, 409–426. [CrossRef]
53. Jackson, D.; White, I.R.; Riley, R.D. A matrix-based method of moments for fitting the multivariate random effects model for meta-analysis and meta-regression. *Biom. J.* **2013**, *55*, 231–245. [CrossRef]
54. Schepsmeier, U.; Stöber, J. Derivatives and Fisher information of bivariate copulas. *Stat. Pap.* **2013**, *55*, 525–542. [CrossRef]
55. Oakes, D. A Model for Association in Bivariate Survival Data. *J. R. Stat. Soc. Ser. B Stat. Methodol.* **1982**, *44*, 414–422. [CrossRef]
56. Nakatochi, M.; Kanai, M.; Nakayama, A.; Hishida, A.; Kawamura, Y.; Ichihara, S.; Matsuo, H. Genome-wide me-ta-analysis identifies multiple novel loci associated with serum uric acid levels in Japanese individuals. *Commun. Biol.* **2019**, *2*, 1–10. [CrossRef]
57. Taketomi, N.; Konno, Y.; Chang, Y.-T.; Emura, T. A Meta-Analysis for Simultaneously Estimating Individual Means with Shrinkage, Isotonic Regression and Pretests. *Axioms* **2021**, *10*, 267. [CrossRef]
58. Taketomi, N.; Michimáe, H.; Chang, Y.-T.; Emura, T. meta.shrinkage: An R package for meta-analyses for simultaneously estimating individual means. *Algorithms*, 2022; accepted.

Article

Type II Half-Logistic Odd Fréchet Class of Distributions: Statistical Theory and Applications

Salem A. Alyami [1], Moolath Girish Babu [2,†], Ibrahim Elbatal [1,†], Naif Alotaibi [1,†] and Mohammed Elgarhy [3,*,†]

[1] Department of Mathematics and Statistics, College of Science Imam Mohammad Ibn Saud Islamic University (IMSIU), Riyadh 11432, Saudi Arabia; saalyami@imamu.edu.sa (S.A.A.); iielbatal@imamu.edu.sa (I.E.); nmaalotaibi@imamu.edu.sa (N.A.)

[2] Department of Statistics, CHMKM Government Arts and Science College, Kozhikode 673 572, India; giristat@gmail.com

[3] The Higher Institute of Commercial Sciences, Al Mahalla Al Kubra 31951, Algharbia, Egypt

* Correspondence: m_elgarhy85@sva.edu.eg

† These authors contributed equally to this work.

Abstract: A new class of statistical distributions called the Type II half-Logistic odd Fréchet-G class is proposed. The new class is a continuation of the unusual Fréchet class. This class is analytically feasible and could be used to evaluate real-world data effectively. The new suggested class of distributions has many new symmetrical and asymmetrical sub-models. We propose new four sub-models from the new class of distributions which are called Type II half-Logistic odd Fréchet exponential distribution, Type II half-Logistic odd Fréchet Rayleigh distribution, Type II half-Logistic odd Fréchet Weibull distribution, and Type II half-Logistic odd Fréchet Lindley distribution. Some statistical features of Type II half-Logistic odd Fréchet-G class such as ordinary moments (ORMs), incomplete moments (INMs), moment generating function (MGEF), residual life (REL), and reversed residual life (RREL) functions, and Rényi entropy (RéE) are derived. Six methods of estimation such as maximum likelihood, least-square, a maximum product of spacing, weighted least square, Cramér-von Mises, and Anderson–Darling are produced to estimate the parameters. To test the six estimation methods' performance, a simulation study is conducted. Four real-world data sets are utilized to highlight the importance and applicability of the proposed method.

Keywords: half-logistic class; odd Fréchet class; entropy; simulation; estimation method

1. Introduction

Today, there is a need for mathematical models required to retrieve all of the information from data and the ability to engage with it and make it usable in engineering, biological study, economics, and environmental sciences, to name a few examples. A lot of generations of academics have so far concentrated their efforts to build larger classes of distributions. The classic strategy consists of adding (parameters) to a scale or shape to the baseline model, also through the use of special functions (beta, gamma, excessive geometry, etc.), which makes the resulting distribution more adaptable, which is useful for understanding the behavior of density shapes and hazard rate shapes, for checking the goodness of fit of proposed distributions, or the flexibility on some important modeling aspects such as mean $E(X)$, variance $V(X)$, distribution tails, skewness (SK), kurtosis (KU), etc. Consequently, new different classes of continuous distributions have been offered, including those produced in the statistical literature listed below. Some well-known classes are the Fréchet class defined in [1], Marshall–Olkin class given in [2], beta-class given in [3], the generalized log-logistic class given in [4], the odd exponentiated half logistic (HL) class given in [5], the generalized odd log-logistic class given in [6], the Type I HL class given in [7], the logistic-X class given in [8], generalized odd log-logistic class given in [9], Kumaraswamy Type I HL class given in [10], the transmuted odd Fréchet (OF)-class given in [11], extended OF-G class given in [12], transmuted geometric-G [13], odd Perks-G class [14], odd Lindley-G in [15], truncated Cauchy power Weibull-G [16], generalized transmuted-G [17], truncated Cauchy power-G in [18], Burr X-G (BX-G) class [19], odd inverse power generalized Weibull-G [20], Type II exponentiated half-Logistic-G in [21], Topp Leone -G in [22], exponentiated M-G by [23], odd Nadarajah–Haghighi-G in [24], exponentiated truncated inverse Weibull-G in [25], T-X generator proposed in [26], among others.

Several Fréchet classes have been judged successful in a variety of statistical applications in the last years as [27] proposed a four-parameter model named the exponential transmuted Fréchet distribution, which extends the Fréchet distribution. Ref [1] proposed the $OF - G$ class of distributions with distribution function (cdf) and density function (pdf), respectively, are follows, for $x > 0$

$$G_{OF_r}(x;\theta) = e^{-\left(\frac{\overline{G}(x,\varphi)}{G(x,\varphi)}\right)^{\theta}}, \tag{1}$$

and

$$g_{OF_r}(x;\theta) = \frac{\theta g(x,\varphi)(1 - G(x,\varphi))^{\theta-1}}{G(x,\varphi)^{\theta+1}} e^{-\left(\frac{\overline{G}(x,\varphi)}{G(x,\varphi)}\right)^{\theta}}, \tag{2}$$

where $\theta > 0$ is a shape parameter, $G(x,\varphi)$ and $g(x,\varphi)$ are the pdf and cdf of a baseline continuous distribution with φ as parameter vector, respectively.

The $OF - G$ class was successfully considered in various statistical applications over the last few years. This reputation can be explained by its simple and versatile exponential-odd form, with the use of just one additional parameter, very different from the other current families. Ref [28] represented a new class of continuous distributions with an extra scale parameter $\alpha > 0$ called the Type II HL-G ($TIIHL - G$) class. The cdf and pdf of the $TIIHL - G$ class of distributions, respectively, are provided by

$$F(x) = \frac{2[G(x)]^{\alpha}}{1 + [G(x)]^{\alpha}}, \tag{3}$$

and

$$f(x) = 2\alpha g(x)[G(x)]^{\alpha-1}[1 + [G(x)]^{\alpha}]^{-2}. \tag{4}$$

The failure (hazard) rate function (hrf) is defined by

$$\tau(x) = \frac{2\alpha g(x)[G(x)]^{\alpha-1}}{1 - [G(x)]^{2\alpha}}. \tag{5}$$

In this paper, we discuss a new extension of the odd Fréchet-G class for a given baseline distribution with cdf $G(x,\varphi)$ using the Type II HL generator and this class is called the Type II HL odd Fréchet-G ($TIIHLOF - G$) class of distributions. This new suggested class of distributions is very flexible and has many new symmetrical and asymmetrical sub-models. The cdf of ($TIIHLOF - G$) class is obtained by inserting Equation (1) in Equation (3), we get

$$F(x,\alpha,\theta,\varphi) = \frac{2e^{-\alpha\left(\frac{\overline{G}(x,\varphi)}{G(x,\varphi)}\right)^{\theta}}}{1 + e^{-\alpha\left(\frac{\overline{G}(x,\varphi)}{G(x,\varphi)}\right)^{\theta}}}, x > 0. \tag{6}$$

For each baseline G, the $TIIHLOF - G$ cdf is given by Equation (6). The corresponding pdf is

$$f(x;\alpha,\theta,\varphi) = \frac{2\alpha\theta g(x,\varphi)\overline{G}(x,\varphi)^{\theta-1}}{G(x,\varphi)^{\theta+1}} e^{-\alpha\left(\frac{\overline{G}(x,\varphi)}{G(x,\varphi)}\right)^{\theta}}\left[1 + e^{-\alpha\left(\frac{\overline{G}(x,\varphi)}{G(x,\varphi)}\right)^{\theta}}\right]^{-2}. \tag{7}$$

The hrf of $TIIHLOF-G$ class is provided by

$$\chi(x) = \frac{2\alpha\theta g(x,\varphi)\overline{G}(x,\varphi)^{\theta-1}e^{-\alpha\left(\frac{\overline{G}(x,\varphi)}{G(x,\varphi)}\right)^{\theta}}}{G(x,\varphi)^{\theta+1}\left[1-e^{-2\alpha\left(\frac{\overline{G}(x,\varphi)}{G(x,\varphi)}\right)^{\theta}}\right]}.$$

The $TIIHLOF-G$ quantile function (qf) is given below

$$F^{-1}(u) = Q_G(u) = G^{-1}\left[\frac{1}{1+\left\{\frac{-1}{\alpha}\log(\frac{u}{2-u})\right\}^{\frac{1}{\theta}}}\right]. \quad (8)$$

The fundamental goal of the article under consideration is to introduce a new class of statistical distributions called the Type II half-Logistic odd Fréchet-G class (TIIHLOF-G for short) as well as to investigate its statistical characteristics. The following points provide sufficient incentive to study the proposed class of distributions. We specify it as follows: (i) the new class of distributions are very flexible and have many new symmetrical and asymmetrical sub-models; (ii) it is remarkable to observe the flexibility of the proposed family with the diverse graphical shapes of probability density functions (pdf) and hazard rate functions (hrf). So, the form analysis of the corresponding pdf and hrf has shown new characteristics, revealing the unseen fitting potential of the TIIHLOF-G; (iii) the new suggested class has a closed form of the quantile function; (iv) six methods of estimation are proposed to assess the behavior of the parameters; (v) the TIIHLOF-G is very flexible and applicable. This ability of the new class is explored using four real-life data sets proving the practical utility of the model being featured.

The substance of the article is arranged as follows: Section 2 presents a linear representation of the $TIIHLOF-G$ class density. Four new sub-models are provided in Section 3. Section 4 contains a number of statistical features such as ORMs, INMs, MGEF, REL, and RREL functions, and RéE. In Section 5, different estimation methods of the model parameters are determined. Section 6 shows simulation results. Section 7 investigates three real-world data sets to demonstrate the flexibility and potential of the $TIIHLOF-G$ class using the $TIIHLOFExp$ and $TIIHLOFW$ distributions. Finally, in Section 8, the conclusions are offered.

2. Useful Expansion

Assuming $|z|<1$ and $b>0$ be a real non-integer, then the next binomial expansions occur.

$$(1+z)^{-b} = \sum_{k=0}^{\infty}(-1)^k \frac{\Gamma(b+k)}{k!\Gamma(b)}z^k. \quad (9)$$

Applying Equation (9) to the last term in Equation (7), then

$$f_{TIIHLOF-G}(x) = \frac{2\alpha\theta g(x,\varphi)\overline{G}(x,\varphi)^{\theta-1}}{G(x,\varphi)^{\theta+1}}\sum_{i=0}^{\infty}(i+1)e^{-\alpha(i+1)\left(\frac{\overline{G}(x,\varphi)}{G(x,\varphi)}\right)^{\theta}}. \quad (10)$$

The exponential function's power series now yields

$$e^{-\alpha(i+1)\left(\frac{\overline{G}(x,\varphi)}{G(x,\varphi)}\right)^{\theta}} = \sum_{j=0}^{\infty}\frac{(-1)^j\alpha^j(i+1)^j}{j!}\frac{\overline{G}(x,\varphi)^{\theta j}}{G(x,\varphi)^{\theta j}}. \quad (11)$$

Inserting Equation (11) in Equation (10), then

$$f_{TIIHLOF-G}(x) = g(x,\varphi) \sum_{i,j=0}^{\infty} \frac{2\theta(-1)^j \alpha^{j+1}(i+1)^{j+1}}{j!} \frac{\overline{G}(x,\varphi)^{\theta(j+1)-1}}{G(x,\varphi)^{\theta(j+1)+1}}, \quad (12)$$

using the generalized binomial expansion to $(1 - G(x;\varphi))^{-[\theta(j+1)+1]}$,

$$(1 - G(x;\varphi))^{-[\theta(j+1)+1]} = \sum_{k=0}^{\infty} \frac{\Gamma(\theta(j+1)+k+1)}{k!\Gamma(\theta(j+1)+1)} G(x;\varphi)^k, \quad (13)$$

and

$$(1 - G(x;\varphi))^{[\theta(j+1)+k+1]} = \sum_{d=0}^{\infty} (-1)^d \binom{\theta(j+1)+k+1}{d} G(x;\varphi)^d. \quad (14)$$

The TIIHLOF pdf is an endless combination of exp-G pdfs

$$f_{TIIHLOF-G}(x) = \sum_{d=0}^{\infty} \varpi_d h_{(d+1)}(x), \quad (15)$$

where

$$\varpi_d = \sum_{i,j,k=0}^{\infty} \frac{2\theta(-1)^{j+d}\alpha^{j+1}(i+1)^{j+1}\Gamma(\theta(j+1)+k+1)}{j!k!\Gamma(\theta(j+1)+1)(d+1)} \binom{\theta(j+1)+k+1}{d},$$

and $h_{(d+1)}(x) = (d+1)g(x)G^d(x)$.

3. Submodels of the TIIHLOF-G Class

We exhibit four sub-models of the $TIIHLOF - G$ distribution class.

3.1. Type II Half-Logistic Odd Fréchet Exponential (TIIHLOFExp) Distribution

Let $G(x)$ and $g(x)$ in Equations (6) and (7) be the cdf and pdf of Exp distribution where $G(x;\varphi) = 1 - e^{-\lambda x}$ and $g(x;\varphi) = \lambda e^{-\lambda x}$. The cdf and pdf of Type II half-Logistic odd Fréchet Exp (TIIHLOFExp) are given below

$$F(x) = \frac{2e^{-\alpha\left(\frac{e^{-\lambda x}}{1-e^{-\lambda x}}\right)^\theta}}{1+e^{-\alpha\left(\frac{e^{-\lambda x}}{1-e^{-\lambda x}}\right)^\theta}}, x > 0,$$

and

$$f(x) = \frac{2\alpha\theta\lambda e^{-\lambda x}(e^{-\lambda x})^{\theta-1}}{(1-e^{-\lambda x})^{\theta+1}} e^{-\alpha\left(\frac{e^{-\lambda x}}{1-e^{-\lambda x}}\right)^\theta} \left[1+e^{-\alpha\left(\frac{e^{-\lambda x}}{1-e^{-\lambda x}}\right)^\theta}\right]^{-2}.$$

Figure 1 describes the different forms of the pdf of TIIHLOFExp distribution.

3.2. Type II Half-Logistic Odd Fréchet Rayleigh (TIIHLOFR) Distribution

Here we take $G(x) = 1 - e^{-\frac{1}{2}x^2}$ and $g(x;\varphi) = \lambda x e^{-\frac{1}{2}x^2}$ be the Rayleigh distribution. The cdf and pdf of $TIIHLOFR$ model, are given below

$$F(x) = \frac{2e^{-\alpha\left(\frac{e^{-\frac{1}{2}x^2}}{1-e^{-\frac{1}{2}x^2}}\right)^\theta}}{1+e^{-\alpha\left(\frac{e^{-\frac{1}{2}x^2}}{1-e^{-\frac{1}{2}x^2}}\right)^\theta}}, x > 0,$$

and

$$f(x) = \frac{2\alpha\theta\lambda x e^{-\frac{\lambda}{2}x^2}(e^{-\frac{\lambda}{2}x^2})^{\theta-1}}{(1-e^{-\frac{\lambda}{2}x^2})^{\theta+1}} e^{-\alpha\left(\frac{e^{-\frac{\lambda}{2}x^2}}{1-e^{-\frac{\lambda}{2}x^2}}\right)^{\theta}} \left[1+e^{-\alpha\left(\frac{e^{-\frac{\lambda}{2}x^2}}{1-e^{-\frac{\lambda}{2}x^2}}\right)^{\theta}}\right]^{-2}.$$

Figure 2 describes the different forms of the pdf of $TIIHLOFR$ distribution.

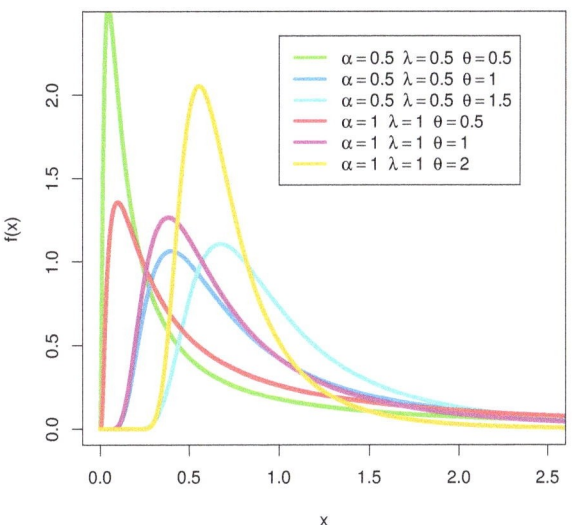

Figure 1. Shapes of the pdf of TIIHLOFExp $(\alpha, \lambda, \theta)$ for various values of parameter.

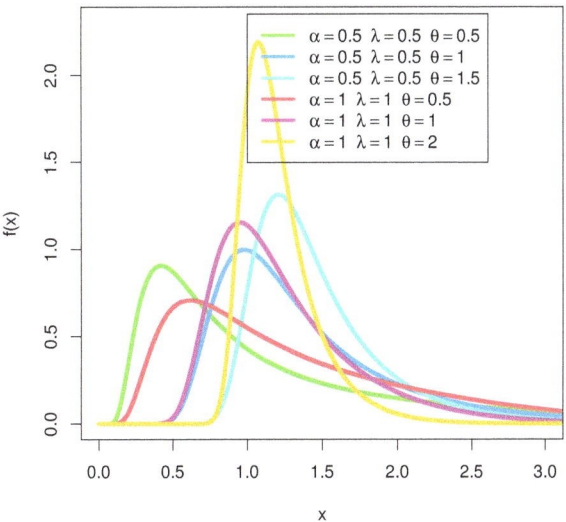

Figure 2. Shapes of the pdf of TIIHLOFR (α, β, θ) for various values of parameter.

3.3. Type II Half-Logistic Odd Fréchet Weibull (TIIHLOFW) Distribution

Let $G(x)$ and $g(x)$ in Equations (6) and (7) be the cdf and pdf of Weibull distribution, where $G(x;\varphi) = 1 - e^{-(\lambda x)^\mu}$ and $g(x;\varphi) = \mu\lambda^\mu x^{\mu-1} e^{-(\lambda x)^\mu}$. The cdf and pdf of (TIIHLOFW) distribution are given below

$$F(x) = \frac{2e^{-\alpha\left(\frac{e^{-(\lambda x)^\mu}}{1-e^{-(\lambda x)^\mu}}\right)^\theta}}{1+e^{-\alpha\left(\frac{e^{-(\lambda x)^\mu}}{1-e^{-(\lambda x)^\mu}}\right)^\theta}}, x > 0,$$

and

$$f(x) = \frac{2\alpha\theta\mu\lambda^\mu x^{\mu-1} e^{-\theta(\lambda x)^\mu}}{(1-e^{-(\lambda x)^\mu})^{\theta+1}} e^{-\alpha\left(\frac{e^{-(\lambda x)^\mu}}{1-e^{-(\lambda x)^\mu}}\right)^\theta} \left[1+e^{-\alpha\left(\frac{e^{-(\lambda x)^\mu}}{1-e^{-(\lambda x)^\mu}}\right)^\theta}\right]^{-2}.$$

Figure 3 describes the different forms of the pdf of TIIHLOFW distribution.

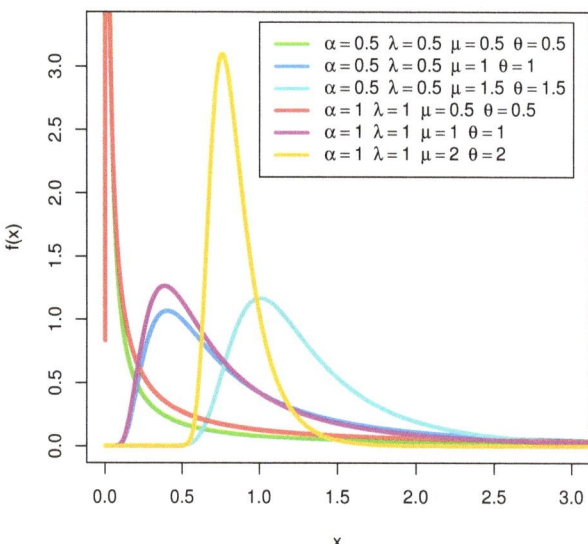

Figure 3. Shapes of the pdf of TIIHLOFW $(\alpha, \lambda, \mu, \theta)$ for various values of parameter.

3.4. Type II Half-Logistic Odd Fréchet Lindely (TIIHLOFL) Distribution

Let Lindely be the baseline distribution having cdf and pdf $G(x;\varphi) = 1 - (1 + \frac{\lambda}{\lambda+1}x)e^{-\lambda x}$ and $g(x;\varphi) = \frac{\lambda^2}{\lambda+1}(x+1)e^{-\lambda x}$. The cdf and pdf of TIIHLOFL model are provided below

$$F(x) = \frac{2e^{-\alpha\left(\frac{(1+\frac{\lambda}{\lambda+1}x)e^{-\lambda x}}{1-(1+\frac{\lambda}{\lambda+1}x)e^{-\lambda x}}\right)^\theta}}{1+e^{-\alpha\left(\frac{(1+\frac{\lambda}{\lambda+1}x)e^{-\lambda x}}{1-(1+\frac{\lambda}{\lambda+1}x)e^{-\lambda x}}\right)^\theta}}, x > 0,$$

and

$$f(x) = \frac{2\alpha\theta\lambda^2(x+1)e^{-\lambda x}((1+\frac{\lambda}{\lambda+1}x)e^{-\lambda x})^{\theta-1}e^{-\alpha\left(\frac{(1+\frac{\lambda}{\lambda+1}x)e^{-\lambda x}}{1-(1+\frac{\lambda}{\lambda+1}x)e^{-\lambda x}}\right)^{\theta}}}{(\lambda+1)(1-(1+\frac{\lambda}{\lambda+1}x)e^{-\lambda x})^{\theta+1}\left[1+e^{-\alpha\left(\frac{(1+\frac{\lambda}{\lambda+1}x)e^{-\lambda x}}{1-(1+\frac{\lambda}{\lambda+1}x)e^{-\lambda x}}\right)^{\theta}}\right]^2}.$$

Figure 4 describes the different forms of the pdf of TIIHLOFL distribution.

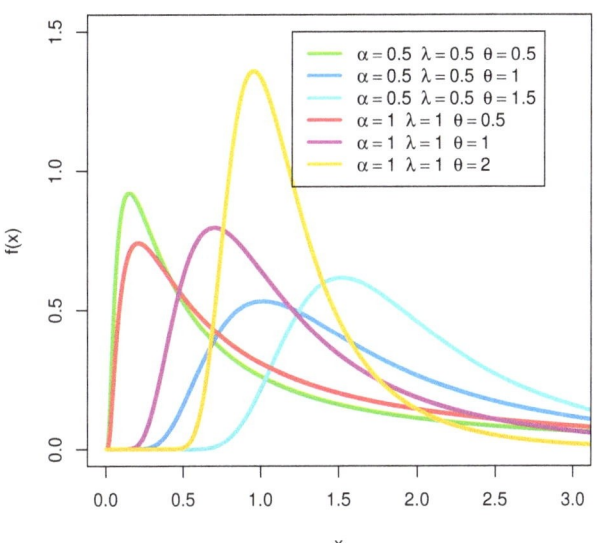

Figure 4. Shapes of the pdf of TIIHLOFL $(\alpha, \lambda, \theta)$ for various values of parameter.

4. Statistical Properties

In this section, we derive some statistical features for the $TIIHLOF - G$ class including ORMs, INMs, MGEF, REL, and RREL functions, and RéE.

4.1. Different Types of Moments

The rth ORM of the $TIIHLOF - G$ is

$$\mu'_r = E(X^r) = \sum_{d=0}^{\infty} \varpi_d E(Z^r_{(d+1)}). \tag{16}$$

Tables 1–3 show the numerical values of $E(X)$, $E(X^2)$, $E(X^3)$, $E(X^4)$, Var(X), SK, KU, and coefficient of variation (CV) of the $TIIHLOFExp$ and $TIIHLOFR$ distributions.

The sth INMs of the $TIIHLOF - G$ noted by $\zeta_s(t)$ for any real $s > 0$, is

$$\zeta_s(t) = \int_{-\infty}^{t} x^s f(x)dx = \sum_{d=0}^{\infty} \varpi_d \int_{-\infty}^{t} x^s h_{(d+1)}(x)dx. \tag{17}$$

The MGEF of the $TIIHLOF - G$ is

$$M_X(t) = E(e^{tX}) = \sum_{d=0}^{\infty} \varpi_d M_{(d+1)}(t),$$

53

where $M_{(d+1)}(t)$ is the MGEF of $Z_{(d+1)}$.

Table 1. Numerical values of $E(X)$, $E(X^2)$, $E(X^3)$, $E(X^4)$, Var(X), SK, KU, and CV of the TIIHLOFExp distribution.

α	λ	θ	$E(X)$	$E(X^2)$	$E(X^3)$	$E(X^4)$	Var(X)	SK	KU	CV
		0.5	1.386	8.647	98.110	1546.203	6.726	3.868	3.868	1.871
	0.5	0.9	1.183	3.394	18.738	154.587	1.994	3.552	3.552	1.193
		1.5	1.177	2.068	5.795	24.788	0.684	3.099	3.099	0.703
		0.5	0.770	2.669	16.823	147.291	2.076	3.868	3.868	1.871
0.5	0.9	0.9	0.657	1.048	3.213	14.726	0.616	3.552	3.552	1.193
		1.5	0.654	0.638	0.994	2.361	0.211	3.099	3.099	0.703
		0.5	0.462	0.961	3.634	19.089	0.747	3.868	3.868	1.871
	1.5	0.9	0.394	0.377	0.694	1.908	0.222	3.552	3.552	1.193
		1.5	0.392	0.230	0.215	0.306	0.076	3.100	3.100	0.703
		0.5	2.286	15.368	176.118	2781.125	10.144	2.929	2.929	1.393
	0.5	0.9	1.736	5.827	33.439	277.737	2.813	2.872	2.872	0.966
		1.5	1.531	3.239	9.975	44.119	0.894	2.693	2.693	0.617
		0.5	1.270	4.743	30.199	264.930	3.131	2.929	2.929	1.393
0.9	0.9	0.9	0.964	1.798	5.730	26.457	0.868	2.868	2.868	0.966
		1.5	0.851	1.000	1.710	4.203	0.276	2.693	2.693	0.617
		0.5	0.762	1.708	6.523	34.335	1.127	2.929	2.929	1.393
	1.5	0.9	0.579	0.647	1.238	3.429	0.313	2.868	2.868	0.966
		1.5	0.510	0.360	0.369	0.545	0.099	2.693	2.693	0.617
		0.5	3.395	24.984	291.692	4626.890	13.460	2.339	2.339	1.081
	0.5	0.9	2.351	9.119	54.810	461.069	3.590	2.424	2.424	0.806
		1.5	1.895	4.683	15.753	72.331	1.091	2.408	2.408	0.551
		0.5	1.886	7.711	50.016	440.757	4.154	2.339	2.339	1.081
1.5	0.9	0.9	1.306	2.814	9.398	43.921	1.108	2.424	2.424	0.806
		1.5	1.053	1.445	2.701	6.890	0.337	2.408	2.408	0.551
		0.5	1.132	2.776	10.803	57.122	1.496	2.339	2.339	1.081
	1.5	0.9	0.784	1.013	2.030	5.692	0.399	2.424	2.424	0.806
		1.5	0.632	0.520	0.583	0.893	0.121	2.408	2.408	0.551

The rth-order moment of the REL of the $TIIHLOF - G$ is

$$\psi_r(t) = \frac{1}{\overline{F}(t)} \int_t^\infty (x-t)^r f(x) dx, r \geq 1$$

$$= \frac{1}{\overline{F}(t)} \sum_{d=0}^\infty \varpi_d^* \int_t^\infty x^r h_{(d+1)}(x) dx, \quad (18)$$

where $\varpi_d^* = \sum_{d=0}^\infty \varpi_d \sum_{m=0}^r \binom{r}{m} (-t)^{r-m}$. The rth-order moment of the RREL of the $TIIHLOF - G$ is

$$m_r(t) = \frac{1}{F(t)} \int_0^t (t-x)^r f(x) dx, r \geq 1$$

$$= \frac{1}{F(t)} \sum_{d=0}^{\infty} \omega_d^* \int_0^t x^r h_{(d+1)}(x) dx, \qquad (19)$$

Table 2. Numerical values of $E(X)$, $E(X^2)$, $E(X^3)$, $E(X^4)$, Var(X), SK, KU, and CV of the $TIIHLOFR$ distribution.

α	λ	θ	$E(X)$	$E(X^2)$	$E(X^3)$	$E(X^4)$	Var(X)	SK	KU	CV
		0.5	1.260	2.772	8.786	34.588	1.184	1.793	1.793	0.863
	0.5	0.9	1.374	2.367	5.122	13.578	0.478	1.684	1.684	0.503
		1.5	1.469	2.353	4.170	8.274	0.195	1.629	1.629	0.300
		0.5	0.939	1.540	3.638	10.675	0.658	1.793	1.793	0.863
0.5	0.9	0.9	1.024	1.315	2.121	4.191	0.266	1.684	1.684	0.503
		1.5	1.095	1.307	1.727	2.554	0.108	1.629	1.629	0.300
		0.5	0.728	0.924	1.691	3.843	0.395	1.793	1.793	0.863
	1.5	0.9	0.793	0.789	0.986	1.509	0.159	1.684	1.684	0.503
		1.5	0.848	0.784	0.803	0.919	0.065	1.629	1.629	0.300
		0.5	1.777	4.571	15.319	61.470	1.412	1.295	1.295	0.669
	0.5	0.9	1.714	3.472	8.322	23.309	0.534	1.384	1.384	0.426
		1.5	1.689	3.063	6.023	12.957	0.210	1.463	1.463	0.271
		0.5	1.325	2.540	6.343	18.972	0.785	1.295	1.295	0.669
0.9	0.9	0.9	1.278	1.929	3.446	7.194	0.297	1.384	1.384	0.426
		1.5	1.259	1.702	2.494	3.999	0.117	1.463	1.463	0.271
		0.5	1.026	1.524	2.948	6.830	0.471	1.295	1.295	0.669
	1.5	0.9	0.990	1.157	1.602	2.590	0.178	1.384	1.384	0.426
		1.5	0.975	1.021	1.159	1.440	0.070	1.463	1.463	0.271
		0.5	2.304	6.789	24.223	99.935	1.483	0.970	0.970	0.529
	0.5	0.9	2.036	4.702	12.327	36.474	0.555	1.180	1.180	0.366
		1.5	1.890	3.790	8.124	18.731	0.218	1.343	1.343	0.247
		0.5	1.717	3.772	10.030	30.844	0.824	0.970	0.970	0.529
1.5	0.9	0.9	1.518	2.612	5.104	11.257	0.309	1.180	1.180	0.366
		1.5	1.409	2.106	3.364	5.781	0.121	1.343	1.343	0.247
		0.5	1.330	2.263	4.662	11.104	0.494	0.970	0.970	0.529
	1.5	0.9	1.176	1.567	2.372	4.053	0.185	1.180	1.180	0.366
		1.5	1.091	1.263	1.563	2.081	0.073	1.343	1.343	0.247

4.2. Rényi Entropy

The RéE of the $TIIHLOF - G$ is given below

$$I_R(\rho) = \frac{1}{1-\rho} \log \left[\int_{-\infty}^{\infty} f^\rho(x) dx \right], \rho > 0, \rho \neq 1. \qquad (20)$$

Employing Equation (9) and the same manner of the beneficial expansion of Equation (15), we obtain, after a little simplification,

$$f^{\rho}(x) = \sum_{d=0}^{\infty} \eta_d g(x)^{\rho} G(x)^d,$$

where

$$\eta_d = \sum_{i,k,m=0}^{\infty} \frac{(-1)^{k+m+d}(\alpha i + \rho)^k}{k!} \binom{-2\rho}{i}\binom{-\theta(\rho+k)-\rho}{m}\binom{\theta(\rho+k)+m-\rho}{d}.$$

Table 3. Numerical values of $E(X)$, $E(X^2)$, $E(X^3)$, $E(X^4)$, Var(X), SK, KU, and CV of the TIIHLOFL distribution.

α	λ	θ	E(X)	E(X²)	E(X³)	E(X⁴)	Var(X)	SK	KU	CV
		0.5	2.260	16.846	217.906	3836.068	11.740	3.152	3.152	1.516
	0.5	0.9	2.167	8.636	57.738	554.210	3.940	2.806	2.806	0.916
		1.5	2.256	6.553	25.753	138.065	1.463	2.469	2.469	0.536
		0.5	1.146	4.735	33.986	331.428	3.422	3.273	3.273	1.614
0.5	0.9	0.9	1.068	2.276	8.404	44.729	1.135	2.935	2.935	0.997
		1.5	1.102	1.634	3.424	10.065	0.419	2.579	2.579	0.587
		0.5	0.633	1.550	6.632	38.591	1.150	3.405	3.405	1.695
	1.5	0.9	0.574	0.703	1.536	4.867	0.373	3.086	3.086	1.065
		1.5	0.586	0.479	0.576	0.997	0.136	2.719	2.719	0.630
		0.5	3.595	29.612	390.003	6893.547	16.687	2.399	2.399	1.136
	0.5	0.9	3.022	14.300	101.607	991.829	5.165	2.314	2.314	0.752
		1.5	2.810	9.681	42.469	240.672	1.785	2.195	2.195	0.475
		0.5	1.849	8.356	60.885	595.744	4.938	2.476	2.476	1.202
0.9	0.9	0.9	1.518	3.820	14.865	80.168	1.514	2.397	2.397	0.810
		1.5	1.395	2.466	5.738	17.692	0.519	2.272	2.272	0.516
		0.5	1.030	2.742	11.889	69.381	1.682	2.568	2.568	1.260
	1.5	0.9	0.826	1.190	2.726	8.731	0.507	2.502	2.502	0.862
		1.5	0.750	0.734	0.976	1.761	0.172	2.373	2.373	0.552
		0.5	5.147	47.337	642.109	11444.724	20.848	1.932	1.932	0.887
	0.5	0.9	3.920	21.553	163.639	1635.462	6.187	1.991	1.991	0.635
		1.5	3.353	13.303	64.309	385.166	2.058	2.000	2.000	0.428
		0.5	2.680	13.430	100.417	989.623	6.248	1.981	1.981	0.933
1.5	0.9	0.9	1.998	5.830	24.091	132.505	1.837	2.047	2.047	0.678
		1.5	1.685	3.446	8.815	28.564	0.605	2.057	2.057	0.462
		0.5	1.506	4.425	19.635	115.307	2.156	2.045	2.045	0.975
	1.5	0.9	1.100	1.834	4.438	14.455	0.624	2.123	2.123	0.718
		1.5	0.915	1.040	1.516	2.862	0.203	2.135	2.135	0.492

Thus the RéE of $TIIHLOF - G$ class is given below

$$I_R(\rho) = \frac{1}{1-\rho} \log\left\{\sum_{d=0}^{\infty} \eta_d \int_{-\infty}^{\infty} g(x)^{\rho} G(x)^d dx\right\}. \tag{21}$$

5. Estimation Methods

To evaluate the estimation problem of the $TIIHLOF - G$ family parameters, this part uses six estimate methods: maximum likelihood, least-square, a maximum product of spacing, weighted least square, Cramér-von Mises, and Anderson–Darling. For more examples see [29–33].

5.1. Method of Maximum Likelihood Estimation

Suppose $x_1,\ldots,x_n$ represent a random sample of size n from the $TIIHLOF - G$ class having parameters α, θ and φ. Consider $\Psi = (\alpha, \theta, \varphi)^T$ be a $p \times 1$ parameter vector. The log-likelihood (LL) function is defined as follows:

$$\begin{aligned} L_n &= n\log(2\alpha) + n\log(\theta) + \sum_{i=1}^{n} \log g(x_i; \varphi) + (\theta-1)\sum_{i=1}^{n} \log \overline{G}(x_i; \varphi) \\ &\quad -(\theta+1)\sum_{i=1}^{n} \log(G(x_i; \varphi)) - \alpha \sum_{i=1}^{n} d_i^{\theta} \\ &\quad -2\sum_{i=1}^{n} \log\left\{1 + e^{-\alpha d_i^{\theta}}\right\}, \end{aligned} \qquad (22)$$

where $d_i = \frac{\overline{G}(x_i;\varphi)}{G(x_i;\varphi)}$. The components of score vector $U_n(\Psi) = \frac{\partial L_n}{\partial \Psi} = \left(\frac{\partial L_n}{\partial \alpha}, \frac{\partial L_n}{\partial \theta}, \frac{\partial L_n}{\partial \varphi_k}\right)$ are given below

$$U_\alpha = \frac{\partial L_n}{\partial \alpha} = \frac{n}{\alpha} - \sum_{i=1}^{n} d_i^{\theta} + 2\sum_{i=1}^{n} \frac{d_i^{\theta} e^{-\alpha d_i^{\theta}}}{1 + e^{-\alpha d_i^{\theta}}}, \qquad (23)$$

$$\begin{aligned} U_\theta &= \frac{\partial L_n}{\partial \theta} = \frac{n}{\theta} + \sum_{i=1}^{n} \log \overline{G}(x_i;\varphi) - \sum_{i=1}^{n} \log(G(x_i;\varphi)) \\ &\quad - \alpha \sum_{i=1}^{n} d_i^{\theta} \log(d_i) + 2\sum_{i=1}^{n} \frac{\alpha d_i^{\theta} \log(d_i) e^{-\alpha d_i^{\theta}}}{1 + e^{-\alpha d_i^{theta}}}, \end{aligned} \qquad (24)$$

and

$$\begin{aligned} U_{\varphi_k} &= \frac{\partial L_n}{\partial \varphi_k} = \sum_{i=1}^{n} \frac{g'(x_i;\varphi)}{g(x_i;\varphi)} + (\theta-1)\sum_{i=1}^{n} \frac{G'(x_i;\varphi)}{G(x_i;\varphi)} - (\theta+1)\sum_{i=1}^{n} \frac{\overline{G}'(x_i;\varphi)}{\overline{G}(x_i;\varphi)} \\ &\quad -\alpha\theta \sum_{i=1}^{n} d_i^{\theta-1} \partial d_i \partial \varphi_k - 2\sum_{i=1}^{n} \frac{\alpha\theta d_i^{\theta-1} e^{-\alpha d_i^{\theta}}}{1 + e^{-\alpha d_i^{\theta}}} \partial d_i \partial \varphi_k, \end{aligned} \qquad (25)$$

where $g'(x_i;\varphi) = \frac{\partial g(x_i;\varphi)}{\partial \varphi_k}$, $G'(x_i;\varphi) = \frac{\partial G(x_i;\varphi)}{\partial \varphi_k}$, $\overline{G}'(x_i;\varphi) = \frac{\partial \overline{G}(x_i;\varphi)}{\partial \varphi_k}$.

5.2. Ordinary Least Squares and Weighted Least Squares Methods

The methods of ordinary least squares (OLS) and weighted least squares (WLS) are used to estimate the parameters of diverse distributions. Let $x_{(1)} < \cdots < x_{(n)}$ be a random sample with the $\Psi = (\alpha, \theta, \varphi)^T$ parameters from the $TIIHLOF - G$ class having parameters. OLS estimators (OLSE) and WLS estimators (WLSE) of the $\Psi = (\alpha, \theta, \varphi)^T$ distribution parameters of $TIIHLOF - G$ can be obtained by minimizing the following:

$$V(\Psi) = \sum_{i=1}^{n} v_i \left[\frac{2e^{-\alpha\left(\frac{\overline{G}(x_{(i)},\varphi)}{G(x_{(i)},\varphi)}\right)^{\theta}}}{1 + e^{-\alpha\left(\frac{\overline{G}(x_{(i)},\varphi)}{G(x_{(i)},\varphi)}\right)^{\theta}}} \right]^2 \qquad (26)$$

$v_i = 1$ for OLSE and $v_i = \frac{(n+1)^2(n+2)}{[i(n-I+1)]}$ for WLSE with respect to α, θ, and φ. Furthermore, by resolving the nonlinear equations, the OLSE and WLSE with respect to α, θ, and φ.

5.3. Maximum Product of Spacings Method

If $x_{(1)} < \cdots < x_{(n)}$ is a random sample of the size n, you can describe the uniform spacing of the $TIIHLOF - G$ family as:

$$D_i(\Psi) = F(x_{(i)}, \Psi) - F(x_{(i-1)}, \Psi); \ i = 1, \ldots, n+1 \tag{27}$$

where $D_i(\Psi)$ denotes to the uniform spacings, $F(x_{(0)}, \Psi) = 0$, $F(x_{(n+1)}, \Psi) = 1$ and $\sum_{i=1}^{n+1} D_i(\Psi) = 1$. The maximum product of spacing (MPS) estimators (MPSE) of the $TIIHLOF - G$ family parameters can be obtained by maximizing

$$G(\Psi) = \frac{1}{n+1} \sum_{i=1}^{n+1} \ln \left\{ \left[\frac{2e^{-\alpha\left(\frac{\bar{G}(x_{(i)},\varphi)}{G(x_{(i)},\varphi)}\right)^\theta}}{1+e^{-\alpha\left(\frac{\bar{G}(x_{(i)},\varphi)}{G(x_{(i)},\varphi)}\right)^\theta}} \right]^2 - \left[\frac{2e^{-\alpha\left(\frac{\bar{G}(x_{(i-1)},\varphi)}{G(x_{(i-1)},\varphi)}\right)^\theta}}{1+e^{-\alpha\left(\frac{\bar{G}(x_{(i-1)},\varphi)}{G(x_{(i-1)},\varphi)}\right)^\theta}} \right]^2 \right\} \tag{28}$$

with respect to α, θ, and φ. Further, the MPSE of the $TIIHLOF - G$ family can also be obtained by solving nonlinear equation of derivatives of $G(\Psi)$ with respect to α, θ, and φ.

5.4. Cramér-von-Mises Method

In Cramér–von-Mises (CVM), we obtain the $TIIHLOF - G$ family by minimizing the following function with respect to α, θ, and φ; the CVM estimators (CVME) of the $TIIHLOF - G$ family parameters α, θ, and φ are obtained.

$$C(\Psi) = \frac{1}{12} + \sum_{i=1}^{n} \left(\left[\frac{2e^{-\alpha\left(\frac{\bar{G}(x_{(i)},\varphi)}{G(x_{(i)},\varphi)}\right)^\theta}}{1+e^{-\alpha\left(\frac{\bar{G}(x_{(i)},\varphi)}{G(x_{(i)},\varphi)}\right)^\theta}} \right]^2 - \frac{2i-1}{2n} \right)^2 \tag{29}$$

In addition, we resolve the nonlinear equations of derivatives of $C(\Psi)$ with respect to α, θ, and φ.

5.5. Anderson-Darling Method

In Anderson–Darling (AD), other forms of minimum distance estimators are the AD estimators (ADE). The ADE of the parameters of the $TIIHLOF - G$ family is acquired by minimizing

$$A(\Psi) = -n - \frac{1}{n} \sum_{i=1}^{n} (2i-1) \left(\ln \left(\left[\frac{2e^{-\alpha\left(\frac{\bar{G}(x_{(i)},\varphi)}{G(x_{(i)},\varphi)}\right)^\theta}}{1+e^{-\alpha\left(\frac{\bar{G}(x_{(i)},\varphi)}{G(x_{(i)},\varphi)}\right)^\theta}} \right]^2 \right) - \ln \left(1 - \left[\frac{2e^{-\alpha\left(\frac{\bar{G}(x_{(n+1-i)},\varphi)}{G(x_{(n+1-i)},\varphi)}\right)^\theta}}{1+e^{-\alpha\left(\frac{\bar{G}(x_{(n+1-i)},\varphi)}{G(x_{(n+1-i)},\varphi)}\right)^\theta}} \right]^2 \right) \right) \tag{30}$$

for α, θ, and φ, respectively. It is also possible to obtain the ADE by resolving the nonlinear equations of derivatives of $A(\Psi)$ with respect to α, θ, and φ.

6. Numerical Outcomes

In this section, Monte Carlo simulations are run to evaluate the correctness and consistency of the new class's six estimation methods. For the sake of example, the simulations are run with the estimators of the $TIIHLOFW$ distribution's parameters. The simulation replication is taken as $N = 1000$ and samples of sizes $n = 50, 100$ and 150 are generated by using the inverse transformation,

$$x_i = \frac{1}{\lambda}\left[-\log\left(1 - \frac{1}{1+[-\frac{1}{\alpha}\log(\frac{u}{2-u})]^{\frac{1}{\theta}}}\right)\right]^{\frac{1}{\mu}}, i = 1, 2, \ldots, n, \tag{31}$$

where U is a uniform distribution on $(0,1)$. The numerical outcomes are evaluated depending on the estimated relative biases (RB) and mean square errors (MSE). Table 4, shows the estimated RB and the MSE for the estimators of the parameters. Set four arbitrarily true values of $(\alpha, \theta, \lambda$ and $\mu)$ such as Case I: $(\alpha = 0.5; \theta = 0.5; \lambda = 0.5; \mu = 0.5)$, Case II: $(\alpha = 1.5; \theta = 1.5; \lambda = 0.5; \mu = 2)$, Case III: $(\alpha = 3; \theta = 1.5; \lambda = 3; \mu = 2)$, and Case IV: $(\alpha = 3; \theta = 1.5; \lambda = 3; \mu = 0.5)$.

Extensive computations were carried out using the R statistical programming language software, with the most useful statistical package being the "stats" package, which used the conjugate-gradient maximization algorithm.

From Table 4, we are able to make the following observations. The performances of the proposed estimates of α, θ, λ, and μ in terms of their RB and MSE become better as n increases, as expected, where the results revealed that as the sample size increases, RB and MSE decrease. These findings clearly demonstrate the estimation methods estimators' accuracy and consistency. As a result, the six estimation methods approach performs well in estimating the parameters of the $TIIHLOFW$ distribution. By the results of Table 4 and Figure 5, we show the OLS method and CVM method of estimation are better than other methods.

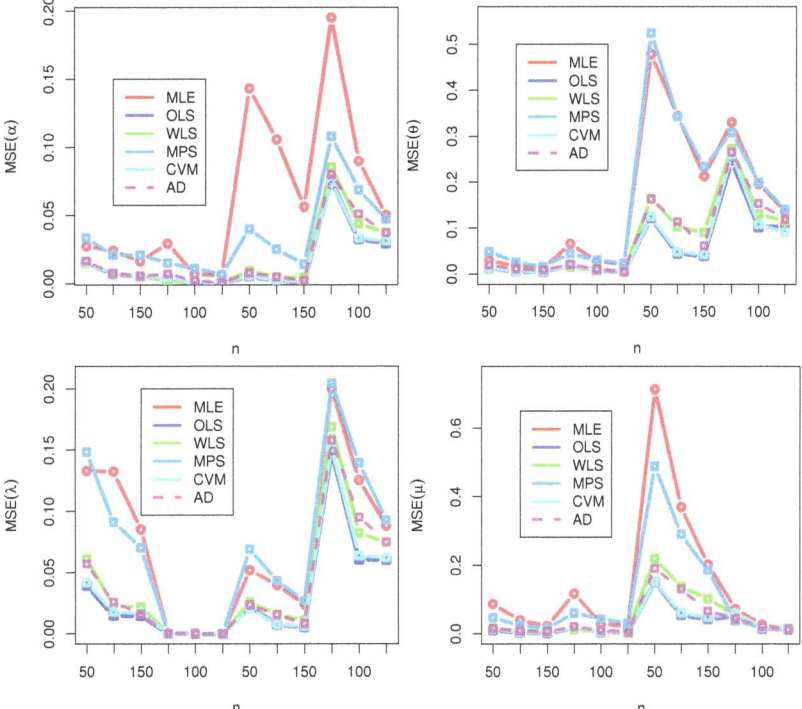

Figure 5. MSE with different sample sizes.

Table 4. The MLE, OLS, WLS, MPS, CVM, and AD estimated RB and MSE of the TIIHLOFW distribution.

Case	n		MLE RB	MLE MSE	OLS RB	OLS MSE	WLS RB	WLS MSE	MPS RB	MPS MSE	CVM RB	CVM MSE	AD RB	AD MSE
	50	α	0.0900	0.0274	0.0289	0.0154	0.0296	0.0150	0.0897	0.0335	0.0039	0.0153	0.0280	0.0167
		θ	0.0823	0.0296	0.0120	0.0142	0.0355	0.0188	0.0826	0.0494	−0.0043	0.0142	0.0364	0.0201
		λ	0.1366	0.1331	0.0488	0.0395	0.0545	0.0615	0.1357	0.1484	0.0801	0.0418	0.0875	0.0574
		μ	0.0280	0.0870	0.0247	0.0115	0.0209	0.0169	0.0278	0.0480	0.0777	0.0139	0.0279	0.0155
I	100	α	0.0686	0.0241	0.0104	0.0074	0.0062	0.0076	0.0687	0.0211	−0.0024	0.0078	0.0118	0.0078
		θ	0.0648	0.0183	0.0077	0.0066	0.0263	0.0105	0.0651	0.0262	0.0015	0.0066	0.0301	0.0115
		λ	0.1086	0.1325	0.0091	0.0151	0.0038	0.0224	0.1084	0.0913	0.0240	0.0177	0.0340	0.0260
		μ	−0.0169	0.0395	0.0067	0.0046	0.0065	0.0091	−0.0171	0.0247	0.0302	0.0051	0.0066	0.0090
	150	α	0.0496	0.0164	0.0059	0.0053	−0.0007	0.0051	0.0620	0.0210	0.0002	0.0054	0.0047	0.0056
		θ	0.0425	0.0126	0.0058	0.0057	0.0174	0.0099	0.0429	0.0165	−0.0014	0.0056	0.0218	0.0088
		λ	0.0915	0.0855	0.0091	0.0149	0.0037	0.0221	0.0915	0.0705	0.0237	0.0169	0.0138	0.0162
		μ	−0.0153	0.0225	0.0060	0.0039	0.0052	0.0081	−0.0163	0.0165	0.0301	0.0045	0.0062	0.0063
	50	α	0.0030	0.0293	0.0028	0.0037	0.0025	0.0021	0.0029	0.0153	0.0075	0.0045	0.0078	0.0072
		θ	−0.0122	0.0660	−0.0082	0.0194	−0.0011	0.0158	−0.0123	0.0452	0.0075	0.0199	0.0009	0.0212
		λ	−0.0066	0.0008	−0.0022	0.0003	−0.0021	0.0003	−0.0067	0.0006	−0.0004	0.0003	−0.0008	0.0003
		μ	−0.0178	0.1174	0.0009	0.0168	0.0027	0.0129	−0.0180	0.0614	0.0143	0.0191	0.0078	0.0214
II	100	α	−0.0024	0.0065	−0.0014	0.0007	0.0004	0.0010	−0.0025	0.0113	0.0014	0.0008	0.0015	0.0023
		θ	0.0041	0.0277	−0.0062	0.0083	−0.0011	0.0071	0.0041	0.0307	0.0004	0.0077	−0.0008	0.0099
		λ	−0.0055	0.0003	−0.0002	0.0002	0.0005	0.0002	−0.0055	0.0004	0.0009	0.0002	0.0005	0.0002
		μ	−0.0172	0.0301	−0.0004	0.0057	−0.0001	0.0057	−0.0172	0.0439	0.0032	0.0056	0.0006	0.0100
	150	α	−0.0024	0.0064	−0.0012	0.0006	−0.0004	0.0009	−0.0024	0.0068	0.0004	0.0007	−0.0004	0.0006
		θ	0.0040	0.0217	−0.0003	0.0062	0.0011	0.0070	0.0040	0.0241	0.0003	0.0057	0.0007	0.0049
		λ	−0.0053	0.0002	−0.0001	0.0001	−0.0003	0.0001	−0.0054	0.0003	0.0007	0.0001	0.0002	0.0001
		μ	−0.0129	0.0211	−0.0004	0.0051	−0.0001	0.0057	−0.0149	0.0314	0.0013	0.0046	−0.0006	0.0040
	50	α	0.0201	0.1430	0.0056	0.0055	0.0078	0.0095	0.0200	0.0401	0.0082	0.0059	0.0087	0.0077
		θ	0.1100	0.4787	−0.0042	0.1231	0.0105	0.1636	0.1107	0.5244	−0.0011	0.1252	0.0167	0.1633
		λ	−0.0090	0.0519	0.0037	0.0217	0.0014	0.0260	−0.0092	0.0692	0.0028	0.0205	−0.0002	0.0234
		μ	−0.0111	0.7129	0.0298	0.1515	0.0330	0.2199	−0.0119	0.4888	0.0568	0.1518	0.0356	0.1916
III	100	α	0.0148	0.1057	0.0012	0.0021	0.0037	0.0049	0.0147	0.0253	0.0019	0.0022	0.0039	0.0048
		θ	0.0977	0.3444	−0.0042	0.0452	0.0041	0.1036	0.0978	0.3428	0.0010	0.0485	0.0137	0.1142
		λ	−0.0081	0.0397	0.0033	0.0076	0.0013	0.0157	−0.0081	0.0433	0.0017	0.0077	0.0002	0.0153
		μ	−0.0103	0.3699	0.0070	0.0559	0.0205	0.1377	−0.0113	0.2907	0.0159	0.0610	0.0175	0.1306
	150	α	0.0107	0.0562	0.0002	0.0015	0.0033	0.0045	0.0108	0.0142	0.0010	0.0017	0.0014	0.0022
		θ	0.0848	0.2128	0.0031	0.0400	0.0040	0.0902	0.0862	0.2343	0.0010	0.0428	0.0120	0.0615
		λ	−0.0080	0.0240	0.0001	0.0057	−0.0009	0.0113	−0.0081	0.0269	−0.0005	0.0063	−0.0002	0.0083
		μ	−0.0106	0.2019	−0.0014	0.0433	0.0038	0.1024	−0.0106	0.1858	0.0072	0.0486	0.0012	0.0668
	50	α	0.0062	0.1951	−0.0112	0.0759	−0.0106	0.0852	0.0064	0.1080	−0.0140	0.0745	−0.0064	0.0797
		θ	0.0272	0.3304	−0.0230	0.2467	−0.0230	0.2735	0.0274	0.3084	−0.0362	0.2605	−0.0200	0.2659
		λ	−0.0129	0.2002	0.0064	0.1492	0.0059	0.1692	−0.0131	0.2047	0.0091	0.1519	0.0050	0.1579
		μ	0.0509	0.0720	0.1289	0.0521	0.1382	0.0543	0.0502	0.0384	0.1805	0.0601	0.1350	0.0447
IV	100	α	0.0062	0.0898	−0.0044	0.0327	−0.0073	0.0439	0.0057	0.0688	−0.0077	0.0334	−0.0059	0.0510
		θ	0.0261	0.1960	0.0069	0.1027	−0.0064	0.1301	0.0237	0.1994	−0.0118	0.1083	−0.0132	0.1535
		λ	−0.0101	0.1254	0.0018	0.0608	0.0035	0.0824	−0.0102	0.1395	0.0057	0.0639	0.0047	0.0952
		μ	0.0080	0.0266	0.0330	0.0159	0.0558	0.0202	0.0077	0.0199	0.0635	0.0191	0.0735	0.0223
	150	α	0.0060	0.0501	−0.0027	0.0296	−0.0020	0.0373	0.0046	0.0471	−0.0032	0.0313	0.0007	0.0374
		θ	0.0251	0.1355	0.0058	0.1032	0.0059	0.1154	0.0161	0.1409	0.0059	0.0911	0.0127	0.1197
		λ	−0.0093	0.0882	−0.0006	0.0607	−0.0017	0.0748	−0.0101	0.0928	−0.0006	0.0625	−0.0045	0.0752
		μ	−0.0073	0.0126	0.0309	0.0138	0.0350	0.0136	−0.0069	0.0107	0.0440	0.0139	0.0300	0.0130

7. Applications

Here, we provide three applications to demonstrate the adaptability of the new recommended family. Some measures of goodness of fit are used to illustrate the flexibility of the TIIHLOF-G: the values of negative LL function (−LL), KAINC (Akaike Information Criterion (INC)), KCAINC (Akaike INC with correction), KBINC (Bayesian INC), and KHQINC (Hannon–Quinn INC) are computed for all competitive models in order to verify which distribution fits the data more closely. The best distribution has the lowest numerical values of −LL, KAINC, KCAINC, KBINC, and KHQINC.

7.1. The Biomedical Data Set

The set of data just on relief times of 20 patients who received an analgesic (Gross and Clark, 1975) is 1.50, 1.20, 2.30, 1.80, 2.20, 1.70, 1.10, 4.10, 1.80, 1.60, 1.40, 1.40, 3.00, 1.70, 1.30, 1.60, 1.70, 1.90, 2.70, 2.00.

Throughout this subsection, we apply the TIIHLOFExp model to a real-world data set to assess its adaptability. To compare the TIIHLOFExp model to the other ten fitted distributions, one, two, three, four, and five parameters are employed. We compare the TIIHLOFExp distribution with the beta transmuted Weibull (BTW), Type I half-Logistic inverse power Ailamujia (TIHLIPA), McDonald log-logistic (McLL), Marshall–Olkin exponential (M-OExp), McDonald Weibull (McW), Burr X-Ex (BrXExp), transmuted exponentiated Chen (TEC), Kumaraswamy Ex (KwExp), generalized Marshall–Olkin Ex (GM-OExp), transmuted complementary Weibull-geometric (TCWG), beta Ex (BExp), Kumaraswamy Marshall–Olkin Ex (KwM-OExp), transmuted Chen (TC), Ailamujia (A), inverse Ailamujia (IA), Exp, beta Lomax (BL), gamma-Chen (GaC), Chen (C), Weibull Lomax (WL), Kumaraswamy Chen (KwC), odd log-logistic Weibull (OLL-W), beta Weibull (BW), beta-Chen (BC), Weibull (W), and Marshall–Olkin Chen (M-OC) models. All of these competitive models are mentioned in Al-Moisheer and Alotaibi (2022).

The parameter estimates and the numerical value of negative LL are presented in Table 5. Additionally, the numerical values of KAINC, KCAINC, KBINC, and KHQINC statistics for the biomedical data are presented in Table 6.

Table 5. The parameter estimates and the numerical values of $-LL$ of the biomedical data.

Model	ML Estimates	$-LL$
TIIHLOFExp	$\hat{\alpha} = 0.052, \hat{\lambda} = 0.179, \hat{\theta} = 2.973$	15.392
BTW	$\hat{\alpha} = 5.619, \hat{\beta} = 0.531, \hat{a} = 53.344, \hat{b} = 3.568, \hat{\lambda} = -0.772$	16.831
TIHLIPA	$\hat{\alpha} = 0.246, \hat{\beta} = 4.713, \hat{\gamma} = -6.781$	16.095
McLL	$\hat{\alpha} = 0.881, \hat{\beta} = 2.070, \hat{a} = 19.225, \hat{b} = 32.033, \hat{c} = 1.926$	16.526
M-OExp	$\hat{\alpha} = 54.474, \hat{\beta} = 2.316$	19.755
McW	$\hat{\alpha} = 2.774, \hat{\beta} = 0.380, \hat{a} = 79.108, \hat{b} = 17.898, \hat{c} = 3.006$	16.927
BrXExp	$\hat{\alpha} = 1.164, \hat{\beta} = 0.321$	22.050
TEC	$\hat{\alpha} = 300.010, \hat{\beta} = 0.500, \hat{a} = 2.430, \hat{b} = 0.340$	15.780
KwExp	$\hat{a} = 83.756, \hat{b} = 0.568, \hat{\beta} = 3.333$	17.890
GM-OExp	$\hat{\lambda} = 0.519, \hat{\alpha} = 89.462, \hat{\beta} = 3.169$	18.375
TCWG	$\hat{\alpha} = 43.663, \hat{\beta} = 5.127, \hat{\gamma} = 0.282, \hat{\lambda} = -0.271$	16.587
BExp	$\hat{a} = 81.633, \hat{b} = 0.542, \hat{\beta} = 3.514$	18.740
KwM-OExp	$\hat{\alpha} = 8.868, \hat{\beta} = 4.899, \hat{a} = 34.826, \hat{b} = 0.299$	17.400
TC	$\hat{\alpha} = 0.750, \hat{a} = 0.070, \hat{b} = 1.020$	23.815
A	$\hat{\beta} = 0.950$	26.160
IA	$\hat{\beta} = 3.449$	25.827
Exp	$\hat{\beta} = 0.526$	32.835
BL	$\hat{a} = 41.070, \hat{b} = 1.929, \hat{\theta} = 5.774, \hat{\lambda} = 0.429$	16.110
GaC	$\hat{\alpha} = 7.590, \hat{\beta} = 1.990, \hat{a} = 5.000, \hat{b} = 0.530$	23.175
C	$\hat{a} = 0.140, \hat{b} = 0.950$	24.570
WL	$\hat{a} = 14.739, \hat{b} = 5.585, \hat{\theta} = 0.263, \hat{\lambda} = 0.219$	19.631
KwC	$\hat{\alpha} = 160.070, \hat{\beta} = 0.490, \hat{a} = 2.210, \hat{b} = 0.520$	16.010
OLL-W	$\hat{\alpha} = 31.414, \hat{\lambda} = 0.134, \hat{\theta} = 26.771$	16.551
BW	$\hat{\alpha} = 0.831, \hat{\beta} = 0.613, \hat{a} = 29.947, \hat{b} = 11.632$	16.804
BC	$\hat{\alpha} = 85.870, \hat{\beta} = 0.480, \hat{a} = 2.010, \hat{b} = 0.55$	16.255
W	$\hat{\lambda} = 0.002, \hat{\theta} = 1.435$	20.586
M-OC	$\hat{\alpha} = 400.010, \hat{a} = 2.320, \hat{b} = 0.430$	19.440

From Tables 5 and 6, the values of −LL, KAINC, KCAINC, KBINC, and KHQINC are minimum for the $TIIHLOFExp$ distribution. Thus the $TIIHLOFExp$ distribution is a better model for the biomedical data as compared with the other twenty-six models.

Table 6. The numerical values of KAINC, KCAINC, KBINC, and KHQINC statistics for the biomedical data.

Models	KAINC	KCAINC	KBINC	KHQINC
TIIHLOFExp	36.784	38.284	34.688	37.368
BTW	43.662	50.124	39.468	44.828
TIHLIPA	38.189	39.112	36.092	38.772
McLL	43.051	47.337	39.556	44.023
M-OExp	43.51	45.51	44.22	43.9
McW	43.854	48.14	40.359	44.826
BrXExp	48.1	50.1	48.8	48.5
TEC	39.56	42.227	36.764	40.338
KwExp	41.78	44.75	43.28	42.32
GM-OExp	42.75	45.74	44.25	43.34
TCWG	51.173	55.459	47.678	52.145
BExp	43.48	46.45	44.98	44.02
KwM-OExp	42.8	46.84	45.55	43.6
TC	53.63	55.13	51.533	54.213
A	54.32	55.31	54.54	54.5
IA	53.653	53.888	52.954	53.847
Exp	67.67	68.67	67.89	67.87
BL	40.219	42.886	37.423	40.997
GaC	46.35	49.017	43.554	47.128
C	53.14	53.846	51.742	53.529
WL	47.261	49.928	44.465	48.039
KwC	40.02	42.687	37.224	40.798
OLL-W	39.101	40.601	37.004	39.684
BW	41.607	44.274	38.811	42.385
BC	40.51	43.177	37.714	41.288
W	45.1728	45.8786	45.5615	47.1642
M-OC	44.88	46.38	42.783	45.463

7.2. Engineering Data Set

The second data have been obtained from [34], it is for the time between failures (thousands of hours) of secondary reactor pumps. The data are as follows:
1.9210, 4.0820, 0.1990, 2.1600, 0.7460, 6.5600, 4.9920, 0.3470, 0.1500, 0.3580, 0.1010, 1.3590, 3.4650, 1.0600, 0.6140, 0.6050, 0.4020, 0.9540, 0.4910, 0.2730, 0.0700, 0.0620, 5.320.

We compare the fit of the $TIIHLOFW$ distribution with the following continuous lifetime distributions:

(i) Extended OF Weibull (EOFW) distribution of [12] has pdf given by

$$f(x;\lambda,\alpha,\mu,\theta) = \frac{\alpha\theta\mu\lambda^\mu x^{\mu-1} e^{-(\lambda x)^\mu}[1-(1-e^{-(\lambda x)^\mu})^\alpha]^{\theta-1}}{[1-e^{-(\lambda x)^\mu}]^{\alpha\theta+1}}, x > 0.$$

(ii) Type II HL Weibull (TIIHLW) distribution of [28] has pdf given by

$$f(x;\lambda,\alpha,\mu,\theta) = \frac{2\theta\mu\lambda^\mu x^{\mu-1} e^{-(\lambda x)^\mu}(1-e^{-(\lambda x)^\mu})^{\theta-1}}{[1+(1-e^{-(\lambda x)^\mu})^\theta]^2}, x > 0.$$

(iii) OF Weibull (OFW) distribution of [1] has pdf given by

$$f(x;\lambda,\mu,\theta) = \frac{\theta\mu\lambda^\mu x^{\mu-1} e^{-(\lambda x)^\mu}(e^{-(\lambda x)^\mu})^{\theta-1} e^{-\left(\frac{e^{-(\lambda x)^\mu}}{1-e^{-(\lambda x)^\mu}}\right)^\theta}}{(1-e^{-(\lambda x)^\mu})^{\theta+1}}, x > 0.$$

The parameter estimates and the numerical value of negative LL are presented in Table 7. Additionally, the numerical values of KAINC, KCAINC, KBINC, and KHQINC statistics for the engineering data are presented in Table 8.

Table 7. The parameter estimates and the numerical values of −LL of the engineering data.

Model	ML Estimates	−LL
TIIHLOFW	$\hat{\lambda} = 0.3901, \hat{\alpha} = 0.5884, \hat{\mu} = 1.4299, \hat{\theta} = 0.3758$	30.759
EOFW	$\hat{\lambda} = 0.5436, \hat{\alpha} = 0.9057, \hat{\mu} = 0.3694, \hat{\theta} = 0.1980$	45.418
TIIHLW	$\hat{\lambda} = 0.3474, \hat{\mu} = 0.8837, \hat{\theta} = 0.9501$	32.574
OFW	$\hat{\lambda} = 0.0464, \hat{\mu} = 0.0575, \hat{\theta} = 0.7175$	60.544

Table 8. The numerical values of KAINC, KCAINC, KBINC, and KHQINC statistics for the engineering data.

Models	KAINC	KCAINC	KBINC	KHQINC
TIIHLOFW	69.519	71.741	74.061	70.661
EOFW	98.836	101.058	103.378	99.978
TIIHLW	71.147	72.410	74.554	72.004
OFW	127.087	128.350	130.494	127.944

From Tables 7 and 8, the values of −LL, KAINC, KCAINC, KBINC, and KHQINC are minimum for the $TIIHLOFW$ distribution. Thus the $TIIHLOFW$ distribution is a better model for the engineering data as compared with the other three models. Figure 6 displays the fitted pdf plots of the engineering data set.

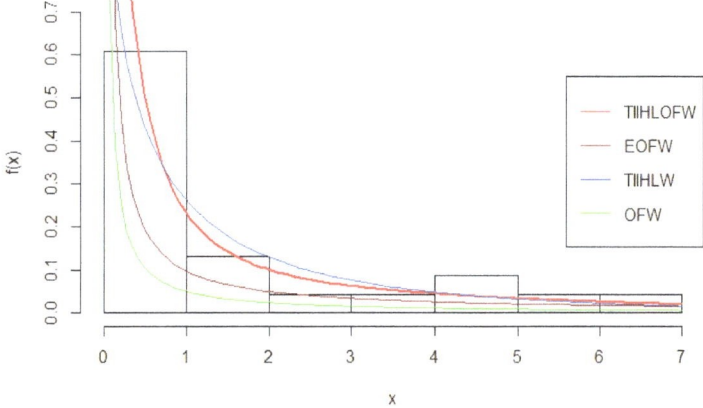

Figure 6. Fitted pdf for the engineering data set.

7.3. Environmental Data Set

The third data set is obtained from [35], it consists of thirty successive values of March precipitation (in inches) in Minneapolis/St Paul. The data are as follows:

1.180, 1.350, 4.750, 0.770, 1.950, 1.200, 0.470, 1.430, 3.370, 2.200, 3.000, 3.090, 1.510, 2.100, 0.520, 1.620, 1.310, 0.320, 0.590, 0.810, 2.810, 1.870, 2.480, 0.960, 1.890, 0.900, 1.740, 0.810, 1.200, 2.050.

We compare the fit of the $TIIHLOFW$ distribution with the following continuous lifetime distributions: EOFW, TIIHLW, and OFW models.

The parameter estimates and the numerical value of negative LL are presented in Table 9. Additionally, the numerical values of KAINC, KCAINC, KBINC, and KHQINC statistics for the environmental data are presented in Table 10.

From Tables 9 and 10, the values of −LL, KAINC, KCAINC, KBINC, and KHQINC are minimum for the $TIIHLOFW$ distribution. Thus the $TIIHLOFW$ distribution is a better model for the environmental data as compared with the other three models. Figure 7 displays the fitted pdf plots of the environmental data set.

Table 9. The parameter estimates and the numerical values of −LL of the environmental data.

Model	ML Estimates	−LL
TIIHLOFW	$\hat{\lambda} = 0.5477, \hat{\alpha} = 0.9205, \hat{\mu} = 1.8387, \hat{\theta} = 0.6241$	38.944
EOFW	$\hat{\lambda} = 0.2927, \hat{\alpha} = 0.8943, \hat{\mu} = 0.2182, \hat{\theta} = 1.0587$	55.876
TIIHLW	$\hat{\lambda} = 0.2675, \hat{\mu} = 0.9643, \hat{\theta} = 0.9297$	50.921
OFW	$\hat{\lambda} = 0.9615, \hat{\mu} = 1.5339, \hat{\theta} = 1.5469$	50.501

Table 10. The numerical values of KAINC, KCAINC, KBINC, and KHQINC statistics for the environmental data.

Models	KAINC	KCAINC	KBINC	KHQINC
TIIHLOFW	85.887	87.487	91.492	87.680
EOFW	119.752	121.352	125.357	121.545
TIIHLW	107.842	108.765	112.046	109.187
OFW	107.002	107.925	111.205	108.346

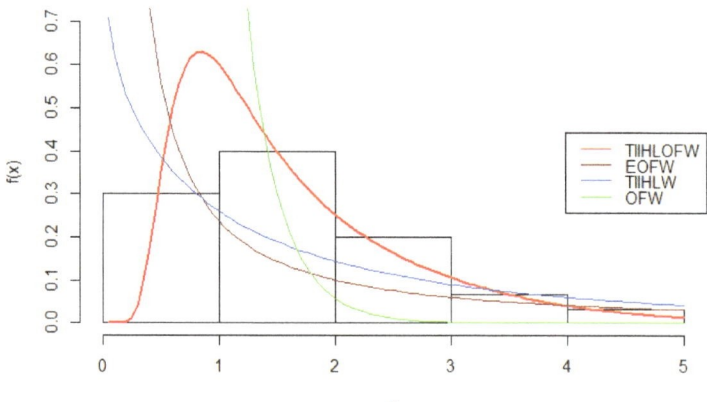

Figure 7. Fitted pdf for the environmental data.

7.4. Strength Data

The fourth data set is obtained from Ahmadini et al. [36], it consists of 56 values of strength data measured in GPA, the single carbon fibers, and 1000 impregnated carbon fiber tows. The data are as follows:

2.247, 2.64, 2.908, 3.099, 3.126, 3.245, 3.328, 3.355, 3.383, 3.572, 3.581, 3.681, 3.726, 3.727, 3.728, 3.783, 3.785, 3.786, 3.896, 3.912, 3.964, 4.05, 4.063, 4.082, 4.111, 4.118, 4.141, 4.246, 4.251, 4.262, 4.326, 4.402, 4.457, 4.466, 4.519, 4.542, 4.555, 4.614, 4.632, 4.634, 4.636, 4.678, 4.698, 4.738, 4.832, 4.924, 5.043, 5.099, 5.134, 5.359, 5.473, 5.571, 5.684, 5.721, 5.998, 6.06

We compare the fit of the $TIIHLOFW$ distribution with the following continuous lifetime distributions: Kumaraswamy Weibull (KW) by Cordeiro et al. [37], Marshall–Olkin alpha power Weibull (MOAPW) by Almetwally [38], Marshall–Olkin alpha power inverse Weibull (MOAPIW) by Basheer et al. [32], odd Perks Weibull (OPW) by Elbatal et al. [14], Marshall–Olkin alpha power Lomax (MOAPL) by Almongy et al. [33], and Odds exponential-Pareto IV (OWPIV) by Baharith et al. [39].

The parameter estimates and the numerical value of negative LL are presented in Table 11. Additionally, the numerical values of KAINC, KCAINC, KBINC, and KHQINC statistics for the environmental data are presented in Table 12.

From Tables 11 and 12, the values of −LL, KAINC, KCAINC, KBINC, and KHQINC are minimum for the $TIIHLOFW$ distribution. Thus the $TIIHLOFW$ distribution is a better model for the environmental data as compared with the other three models. Figure 8 displays the fitted pdf plots of the strength data set.

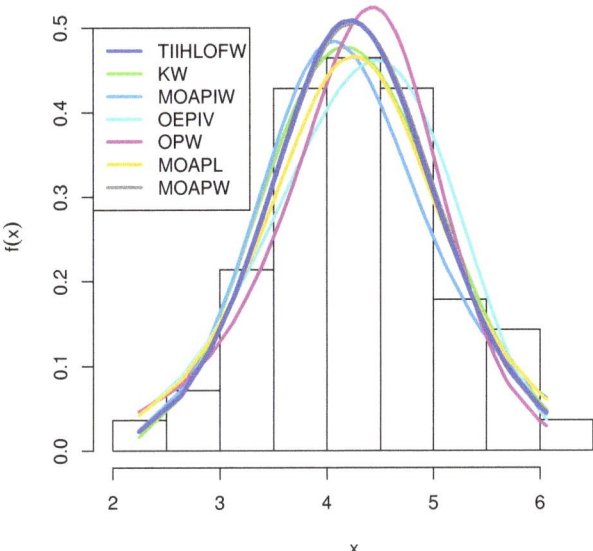

Figure 8. Fitted pdf for the strength data.

Table 11. The parameter estimates and the numerical values of −LL of the strength data.

Model	ML Estimates				−LL
TIIHLOFW	α = 5.2701,	0.3450	θ = 0.373,	μ = 3.2985,	67.7818
MOAPL	α = 281.8156,	β = 270.1004,	θ = 550.4996,	λ = 140.7209,	69.1317
MOAPW	α = 44.4414,	β = 7.5156,	θ = 0.0101,	λ = 5.7759,	67.9200
OPW	β = 0.0101,	θ = 0.1355,	λ = 0.3678,	δ = 0.5165,	70.2290
KW	α = 0.008,	β = 4.1936,	a = 2.8883,	b = 0.2909,	67.9350
MOAPIW	α = 10.5695,	β = 7.9752,	θ = 353.0412,	λ = 100.1504,	69.3700
OEPIV	α = 40.7601,	β = 0.1777,	θ = 54.1619,	λ = 18.1516,	69.0468

Table 12. The numerical values of KAINC, KCAINC, KBINC, and KHQINC statistics for the strength data.

Model	KAINC	KCAINC	KBINC	KHQINC
TIIHLOFW	143.5636	144.3479	151.6650	146.7045
MOAPL	146.2634	147.0477	154.3648	149.4043
MOAPW	143.8401	144.6244	151.9415	146.9810
OPW	148.4581	149.2424	156.5595	151.5990
KW	143.8700	144.6543	151.9714	147.0109
MOAPIW	146.7408	147.5251	154.8422	149.8817
OEPIV	146.0936	146.8779	154.1950	149.2345

8. Conclusions and Summary

We presented a new class of continuous distributions entitled the Type II half-Logistic odd Fréchet-G class in this work. The identifiability of the proposed model was proved and also studied its relationship with other families of distributions. Some statistical properties such as ORMs, INMs, MGEF, REL, RREL, and entropy are derived. The estimates of the parameters of the new model are estimated using the ML method. A simulation outcome was conducted to check the performance of the MLE method. Using four real-life data sets we illustrated the flexibility of the TIIHLOFExp and TIIHLOFW models. In our future works, the new suggested class of distributions will be used to generate more new statistical models, the statistical features of which will be explored. We also intend to study the statistical inferences of new models generated using the TIIHLOF-G class.

Author Contributions: Conceptualization, I.E.; methodology, I.E. and M.G.B.; software and M.E.; validation, N.A., S.A.A., M.E. and I.E.; formal analysis, M.G.B.; resources, I.E.; data curation, I.E., N.A. and S.A.A.; writing—original draft preparation, I.E. and M.E.; writing—review and editing, N.A., S.A.A. and M.E.; funding acquisition, I.E., N.A. and S.A.A. All authors have read and agreed to the published version of the manuscript.

Funding: The authors extend their appreciation to the Deanship of Scientific Research at Imam Mohammad Ibn Saud Islamic University for funding this work through Research Group no. RG-21-09-15.

Informed Consent Statement: Informed consent was obtained from all subjects involved in the study.

Data Availability Statement: Data sets are available in the application section.

Acknowledgments: The authors extend their appreciation to the Deanship of Scientific Research at Imam Mohammad Ibn Saud Islamic University for funding this work through Research Group no. RG-21-09-15.

Conflicts of Interest: The authors declare no conflict of interest.

References

1. Haq, A.; Elgarhy, M. The odd Fréchet-G class of probability distributions. *J. Stat. Appl. Probab.* **2018**, *7*, 189–203. [CrossRef]
2. Marshall, A.; Olkin, I. A new method for adding a parameter to a class of distributions with applications to the exponential and Weibull families. *Biometrika* **1997**, *84*, 641–652. [CrossRef]
3. Eugene, N.; Lee, C.; Famoye, F. Beta-normal distribution and its applications. *Commun. Stat. Theory Methods* **2002**, *31*, 497–512. [CrossRef]
4. Gleaton, J.U.; Lynch, J.D. Properties of generalized log-logistic families of lifetime distributions. *J. Probab. Stat. Sci.* **2006**, *4*, 51–64.
5. Afify, A.Z.; Altun, E.; Alizadeh, M.; Ozel, G.; Hamedani, G.G. The odd exponentiated half-logistic-G class: Properties, characterizations and applications. *Chil. J. Stat.* **2017**, *8*, 65–91.
6. Cordeiro, G.M.; Alizadeh, M.; Ozel, G.; Hosseini, B.; Ortega, E.M.M.; Altun, E. The generalized odd log-logistic class of distributions: Properties, regression models and applications. *J. Stat. Comput. Simul.* **2017**, *87*, 908–932. [CrossRef]
7. Cordeiro, G.M.; Alizadeh, M.; Diniz Marinho, P.R. The type I half-logistic class of distributions. *J. Stat. Comput. Simul.* **2015**, *86*, 707–728. [CrossRef]
8. Tahir, M.H.; Cordeiro, G.M.; Alzaatreh, A.; Mansoor, M.; Zubair, M. The Logistic-X class of distributions and its Applications. *Commun. Stat. Theory Method* **2016**, *45*, 7326–7349. [CrossRef]
9. Haghbin, H.; Ozel, G.; Alizadeh, M.; Hamedani, G.G. A new generalized odd log-logistic class of distributions. *Commun. Stat. Theory Methods* **2017**, *46*, 9897–9920. [CrossRef]

10. El-Sherpieny, E.; EL-Sehetry, M. Kumaraswamy Type I Half-logistic class of Distributions with Applications. *Gazi Univ. J. Sci.* **2019**, *32*, 333–349.
11. Badr, M.; Elbatal, I.; Jamal, F.; Chesneau, C.; Elgarhy, M. The Transmuted Odd Fréchet-G class of Distributions: Theory and Applications. *Mathematics* **2020**, *8*, 958. [CrossRef]
12. Nasiru, S. Extended Odd Fréchet-G class of Distributions. *J. Probab. Stat.* **2018**, *2018*, 2931326. [CrossRef]
13. Afify, A.Z.; Alizadeh, M.; Yousof, H.M.; Aryal, G.; Ahmad, M. The transmuted geometric-G family of distributions: Theory and applications. *Pak. J. Stat.* **2016**, *32*, 139–160.
14. Elbatal, I.; Alotaibi, N.; Almetwally, E.M.; Alyami, S.A.; Elgarhy, M. On Odd Perks-G Class of Distributions: Properties, Regression Model, Discretization, Bayesian and Non-Bayesian Estimation, and Applications. *Symmetry* **2022**, *14*, 883. [CrossRef]
15. Gomes, F.; Percontini, A.; de Brito, E.; Ramos, M.; Venancio, R.; Cordeiro, G. The odd Lindley-G family of distributions. *Austrian J. Stat.* **2017**, *1*, 57–79.
16. Alotaibi, N.; Elbatal, I.; Almetwally, E.M.; Alyami, S.A.; Al-Moisheer, A.S.; Elgarhy, M. Truncated Cauchy Power Weibull-G Class of Distributions: Bayesian and Non-Bayesian Inference Modelling for COVID-19 and Carbon Fiber Data. *Mathematics* **2022**, *10*, 1565. [CrossRef]
17. Nofal, Z.M.; Afify, A.Z.; Yousof, H.M.; Cordeiro, G.M. The generalized transmuted-G family of distributions. *Commun. Stat. Theory Methods* **2017**, *46*, 4119–4136. [CrossRef]
18. Aldahlan, M.A.; Jamal, F.; Chesneau, C.; Elgarhy, M.; Elbatal, I. The truncated Cauchy power family of distributions with inference and applications. *Entropy* **2020**, *22*, 346. [CrossRef]
19. Yousof, H.M.; Afify, A.Z.; Hamedani, G.G.; Aryal, G. The Burr X generator of distributions for lifetime data. *J. Stat. Theory Appl.* **2017**, *16*, 288–305. [CrossRef]
20. Al-Moisheer, A.S.; Elbatal, I.; Almutiry, W.; Elgarhy, M. Odd inverse power generalized Weibull generated family of distributions: Properties and applications. *Math. Probl. Eng.* **2021**, *2021*, 5082192. [CrossRef]
21. Al-Mofleh, H.; Elgarhy, M.; Afify, A.Z.; Zannon, M.S. Type II exponentiated half logistic generated family of distributions with applications. *Electron. J. Appl. Stat. Anal.* **2020**, *13*, 36–561.
22. Al-Shomrani, A.; Arif, O.; Shawky, A.; Hanif, S.; Shahbaz, M.Q. Topp–Leone family of distributions: Some properties and application. *Pak. J. Stat. Oper. Res.* **2016**, *12*, 443–451. [CrossRef]
23. Bantan, R.A.; Chesneau, C.; Jamal, F.; Elgarhy, M. On the analysis of new COVID-19 cases in Pakistan using an exponentiated version of the M family of distributions. *Mathematics* **2020**, *8*, 953. [CrossRef]
24. Nascimento, A.; Silva, K.F.; Cordeiro, M.; Alizadeh, M.; Yousof, H.; Hamedani, G. The odd Nadarajah–Haghighi family of distributions. *Prop. Appl. Stud. Sci. Math. Hung.* **2019**, *56*, 1–26.
25. Almarashi, A.M.; Jamal, F.; Chesneau, C.; Elgarhy, M. The Exponentiated truncated inverse Weibull-generated family of distributions with applications. *Symmetry* **2020**, *12*, 650. [CrossRef]
26. Alzaatreh, A.; Lee, C.; Famoye, F. A new method for generating families of continuous distributions. *Metron* **2013**, *71*, 63–79. [CrossRef]
27. Jayakumar, K.; Babu, M.G. A new generalization of the Fréchet distribution: Properties and application. *Statistica* **2019**, *79*, 267–289.
28. Hassan, A.S.; Elgarhy, M.; Shakil, M. Type II half-logistic class of distributions with applications. *Pak. J. Stat. Oper. Res.* **2017**, *13*, 245–264.
29. Ibrahim, G.M.; Hassan, A.S.; Almetwally, E.M.; Almongy, H.M. Parameter estimation of alpha power inverted Topp–Leone distribution with applications. *Intell. Autom. Soft Comput.* **2021**, *29*, 353–371. [CrossRef]
30. Almetwally, E.M. The odd Weibull inverse topp–leone distribution with applications to COVID-19 data. *Ann. Data Sci.* **2022**, *9*, 121–140. [CrossRef]
31. Almetwally, E.M.; Ahmad, H.H. A new generalization of the Pareto distribution and its applications. *Stat. Transit. New Ser.* **2020**, *21*, 61–84. [CrossRef]
32. Basheer, A.M.; Almetwally, E.M.; Okasha, H.M. Marshall-olkin alpha power inverse Weibull distribution: Non bayesian and bayesian estimations. *J. Stat. Appl. Probab.* **2021**, *10*, 327–345.
33. Almongy, H.M.; Almetwally, E.M.; Mubarak, A.E. Marshall–Olkin alpha power lomax distribution: Estimation methods, applications on physics and economics. *Pak. J. Stat. Oper. Res.* **2021**, *17*, 137–153. [CrossRef]
34. Salman, S.M.; Sangadji, P. Total time on test plot analysis for mechanical components of the RSG-GAS reactor. *Atom Indones* **1999**, *25*, 155–161.
35. Hinkley, D. On quick choice of power transformations. *J. R. Stat. Soc. Ser. Appl. Stat.* **1977**, *26*, 67–69. [CrossRef]
36. Ahmadini, A.A.H.; Hassan, A.S.; Mohamed, R.E.; Alshqaq, S.S.; Nagy, H.F. A New four-parameter moment exponential model with applications to lifetime data. *Intell. Autom. Soft Comput.* **2021**, *29*, 131–146. [CrossRef]
37. Cordeiro, G.M.; Ortega, E.M.; Nadarajah, S. The Kumaraswamy Weibull distribution with application to failure data. *J. Frankl. Inst.* **2010**, *347*, 1399–1429. [CrossRef]
38. Almetwally, E.M. Marshall olkin alpha power extended Weibull distribution: Different methods of estimation based on type i and type II censoring. *Gazi Univ. J. Sci.* **2022**, *35*, 293–312.
39. Baharith, L.A.; Al-Beladi, K.M.; Klakattawi, H.S. The Odds exponential-pareto IV distribution: Regression model and application. *Entropy* **2020**, *22*, 497. [CrossRef]

Article

Monitoring the Ratio of Two Normal Variables Based on Triple Exponentially Weighted Moving Average Control Charts with Fixed and Variable Sampling Intervals

Xuelong Hu [1], Guan Sun [1,*], Fupeng Xie [2] and Anan Tang [1]

Citation: Hu, X.; Sun, G.; Xie, F.; Tang, A. Monitoring the Ratio of Two Normal Variables Based on Triple Exponentially Weighted Moving Average Control Charts with Fixed and Variable Sampling Intervals. *Symmetry* 2022, 14, 1236. https://doi.org/10.3390/sym14061236

Academic Editors: Arne Johannssen, Nataliya Chukhrova, Quanxin Zhu, José Carlos R. Alcantud and Sergei D. Odintsov

Received: 22 April 2022
Accepted: 11 June 2022
Published: 14 June 2022

Publisher's Note: MDPI stays neutral with regard to jurisdictional claims in published maps and institutional affiliations.

Copyright: © 2022 by the authors. Licensee MDPI, Basel, Switzerland. This article is an open access article distributed under the terms and conditions of the Creative Commons Attribution (CC BY) license (https://creativecommons.org/licenses/by/4.0/).

[1] School of Management, Nanjing University of Posts and Telecommunications, Nanjing 210003, China; hxl0419@njupt.edu.cn (X.H.); tanganan2@sina.com (A.T.)
[2] School of Automation, Nanjing University of Science and Technology, Nanjing 210094, China; xfp@njust.edu.cn
* Correspondence: 1020112320@njupt.edu.cn; Tel.: +86-15950567942

Abstract: In statistical process control (SPC), the ratio of two normal random variables (RZ) is a valuable statistical indicator to be taken as the charting statistic. In this work, we propose a triple exponentially weighted moving average (TEWMA) chart for monitoring the RZ. Additionally, the variable sampling interval (VSI) strategy has been adopted to different control charts by researchers. With the application of this strategy, the VSI-TEWMA-RZ chart is then developed to further improve the performance of the proposed TEWMA-RZ chart. The run length (RL) properties of the proposed TEWMA-RZ and VSI-TEWMA-RZ charts are obtained by the widely used Monte-Carlo (MC) simulations. Through the comparisons with the VSI-EWMA-RZ and the VSI-DEWMA-RZ charts, the VSI-TEWMA-RZ chart is statistically more sensitive than the VSI-EWMA-RZ and the VSI-DEWMA-RZ charts in detecting small and moderate shifts. Moreover, it turned out that the VSI-TEWMA-RZ chart has better performance than the TEWMA-RZ chart on the whole. Furthermore, this paper illustrates the implementation of the proposed charts with an example from the food industry.

Keywords: SPC; RZ; EWMA chart; TEWMA chart; VSI-TEWMA chart

1. Introduction

The quality of products has become one of the most important factors in the company's market competition. For improving products' quality, Statistical Process Control (SPC) offers a lot of tools to supervise and control a process. Control chart, as one of the most critical tools in SPC, is often used to monitor the common or assignable causes. In the SPC literatures, control charts for monitoring the ratio of two normal random variables (RZ) have already been studied extensively. They have been used in various fields—for instance, the baking industry, the pharmaceutical industry, and the industrial production of materials, as seen in [1].

The research on the RZ control charts is mainly divided into three branches: the Shewhart type charts, the cumulative sum (CUSUM) charts and the exponentially weighted moving average (EWMA) charts. Among these three type control charts, the Shewhart control chart for monitoring the RZ was first discussed by Ref. [2], who investigated a quality control procedure for the insurance against unemployment. Ref. [3] pointed out that the distribution of the ratio was extremely complex and the statistical properties of the control chart can only be obtained by simulations. Ref. [4] put forward several guidelines to implement the Shewhart chart for supervising and controlling the ratio of glass oxide composition to its density in the glass industry. Ref. [1] discussed the Shewhart chart based on individual measurements, named as the Shewhart-RZ control chart. Following this work, Ref. [5] studied the RZ chart on the basis that subgroups consist of $n > 1$ units. Then, Ref. [6] stated that the synthetic control chart for supervising and controlling the RZ is statistically more sensitive than the Shewhart-RZ chart. As it is known to all, the Shewhart charts are ineffective in detecting small to moderate process shifts. Some researchers have suggested supplementing run rules for improving the Shewhart charts' statistical properties, see Refs. [7–9] and so on. To further improve the Shewhart-RZ chart's performance, Ref. [10] and Ref. [11] adopted the run rules to the Shewhart-RZ control charts, denoted as RR-RZ control charts for the purpose of increasing its sensitivity to small shifts.

To further overcome the shortcomings of the Shewhart-type charts in detecting a relatively small shift, some researchers have successively proposed EWMA and CUSUM charts. Both types of charts take full advantage use of the previous samples information, making charts faster in detecting relatively small shifts. For example, Refs. [12,13] proposed two one-sided EWMA-RZ charts, and it turned out that the EWMA-RZ chart is statistically more sensitive than the Shewhart -RZ chart on the whole. Additionality, Ref. [14] proposed and studied the statistical properties of two Phase II one-sided CUSUM-RZ control charts and the numerical results showed that the proposed CUSUM chart is more sensitive to small shifts than the Shewhart-RZ chart.

To further improve control charts' ability to adjust to small shifts, different methods for improving EWMA schemes have been shown in the SPC literature. These charts are considered an extension of EWMA charts. For example, Refs. [15,16] performed the exponential smoothing twice on the weighted coefficients of the EWMA charts, which was named a double exponential weighted moving average (DEWMA) chart. For more works on the DEWMA control charts, the reader may see Refs. [17,18]. Recently, Ref. [19] constructed the one-sided DEWMA chart for time between events (DEWMA-TBE) which has time-varying control limits based on the gamma distribution. It shows that the DEWMA-TBE chart is statistically more sensitive than competitors in detecting downward shifts. Moreover, Ref. [20] have improved the performance of the DEWMA-type control chart with additional run-rule schemes. Since then, Ref. [21] studied the nonparametric DEWMA chart on the basis of the Wilcoxon rank-sum test. Ref. [22] performed the exponential smoothing three times and proposed the triple exponentially weighted moving average (TEWMA) chart for monitoring a normally distributed process. Moreover, a TEWMA chart for monitoring time between events (TBE) was suggested by Ref. [23]. Recently, Ref. [24] proposed a new TEWMA chart for supervising and controlling the process dispersion, moreover the advantage of the chart is shown by comparing with some competitors in detecting small shifts. Later on, a new distribution-free TEWM chart on the basis of the Wilcoxon rank-sum statistic was proposed by Ref. [25]. The studies on the TEWMA chart have demonstrated its outstanding performance in the detection of small shifts.

In the related works of control charts, researchers have found that introducing the variable sampling interval (VSI) strategy to control charts can further improve the performance of traditional charts with a fixed sampling interval (FSI). The VSI strategy is the one that adjusts the next sampling interval based on the position of the current charting statistic on the control chart. For example, Ref. [26] proposed an EWMA-RZ chart by introducing the VSI strategy, denoted as the VSI-EWMA-RZ chart. As a result, the statistical performance of the VSI-EWMA-RZ chart is superior to the traditional EWMA-RZ charts. In addition, Ref. [27] further integrated the VSI into the CUSUM-RZ scheme, called the VSI-CUSUM-RZ chart, to enhance the CUSUM-RZ chart's performance.

Based on the above studies, it is found that the TEWMA chart has demonstrated its outstanding performance in the detection of small shifts in a normally distributed process. Motivated by this fact, this paper proposes a TEWMA chart for monitoring the RZ. Moreover, since the integration of the VSI strategy can improve the performance of the EWMA-RZ or CUSUM-RZ charts for small to moderate shifts, a VSI-TEWMA-RZ control chart is then proposed to further improve the performance of the proposed TEWMA-RZ chart.

The other parts of this paper are organized as follows: In Section 2, the distribution of the ratio Z between two normal random variables is briefly introduced. Then, the

TEWMA-RZ and VSI-TEWMA-RZ charts are introduced in next Section. Section 4 shows the design procedure of the proposed charts. The control limits and the ARL or the average time to signal (ATS) of the proposed charts are also shown in this section by using the widely used Monte-Carlo (MC) simulations. In Section 5, for different chart parameters, the performance of the VSI-TEWMA-RZ chart is compared with the TEWMA-RZ, the VSI-EWMA-RZ, and the VSI-DEWMA-RZ charts. Section 6 takes the food industry as an example and implement the proposed control chart in practice. At last, Section 7 gives several remarkable conclusions and proposals for future research works.

2. A Brief Review of the Distribution of the Ratio Z

In this section, the background of the distribution of the ratio Z is briefly outlined by considering two normally distributed random variables, X and Y—for example $\mathbf{W} = (X, Y)^T \sim N(\mu_W, \Sigma_W)$. Here, $\mathbf{W}$ is a bivariate normally distributed random vector with a mean vector and variance–covariance matrix, respectively, as below:

$$\mu_W = \begin{pmatrix} \mu_X \\ \mu_Y \end{pmatrix} \quad (1)$$

$$\Sigma_W = \begin{pmatrix} \sigma_X^2 & \rho\sigma_X\sigma_Y \\ \rho\sigma_X\sigma_Y & \sigma_Y^2 \end{pmatrix} \quad (2)$$

where ρ is the coefficient of correlation between X and Y. According to the definition, the coefficients of variation of the two random variables X and Y are defined as $\gamma_X = \frac{\sigma_X}{\mu_X}$ and $\gamma_Y = \frac{\sigma_Y}{\mu_Y}$, respectively, so the standard-deviation ratio is $\omega = \frac{\sigma_X}{\sigma_Y}$. Moreover, details of the interested ratio $Z = \frac{X}{Y}$ can refer to Refs. [28–30]. Although there is no closed-form expression for the distribution of the ratio Z, it can be approximated by applying a analogical method suggested by Refs. [5,31]. Thus, the approximated expression of the c.d.f. (cumulative distribution function) $F_Z(z \mid \gamma_X, \gamma_Y, \omega, \rho)$ of Z proposed by Ref. [5] can be obtained as follows:

$$F_Z(z \mid \gamma_X, \gamma_Y, \omega, \rho) \simeq \Phi\left(\frac{A}{B}\right), \quad (3)$$

where $\Phi(\cdot)$ is the c.d.f. of the standard normal distribution and $A = \frac{z}{\gamma_Y} - \frac{\omega}{\gamma_X}$ and $B = \sqrt{\omega^2 - 2\rho\omega z + z^2}$ are functions of z, γ_X, γ_Y, ω, and ρ. In addition, the p.d.f. (probability density function) $f_Z(z \mid \gamma_X, \gamma_Y, \omega, \rho)$ of Z can be given as follows:

$$f_Z(z \mid \gamma_X, \gamma_Y, \omega, \rho) \simeq \left(\frac{1}{B\gamma_Y} - \frac{(z - \rho\omega)A}{B^3}\right) \times \phi\left(\frac{A}{B}\right), \quad (4)$$

where $\phi(\cdot)$ is the p.d.f. of the standard normal distribution. The i.d.f. (inverse distribution function) $F_Z^{-1}(p \mid \gamma_X, \gamma_Y, \omega, \rho)$ of Z is,

$$F_Z^{-1}(p \mid \gamma_X, \gamma_Y, \omega, \rho) = \begin{cases} \frac{-C_2 - \sqrt{C_2^2 - 4C_1C_3}}{2C_1} & \text{if } p \in (0, 0.5], \\ \frac{-C_2 + \sqrt{C_2^2 - 4C_1C_3}}{2C_1} & \text{if } p \in [0.5, 1). \end{cases} \quad (5)$$

Here, $C_1 = \frac{1}{\gamma_Y^2} - \left(\Phi^{-1}(p)\right)^2$, $C_2 = 2\omega\left(\rho\left(\Phi^{-1}(p)\right)^2 - \frac{1}{\gamma_X\gamma_Y}\right)$ and $C_3 = \omega^2\left(\frac{1}{\gamma_X^2} - \left(\Phi^{-1}(p)\right)^2\right)$ are functions of γ_X, γ_Y, p, ω, and ρ. Moreover, $\Phi^{-1}(\cdot)$ is the i.d.f. of the standard normal distribution.

3. Construction of the TEWMA-RZ Control Charts

To implement the control chart for monitoring the ratio $Z = \frac{X}{Y}$, at each sampling point $i = 1, 2, \ldots$, we collect independent couples $\{\mathbf{W}_{i,1}, \mathbf{W}_{i,2}, \ldots, \mathbf{W}_{i,n}\}$ and each

$\mathbf{W}_{i,j} = (X_{i,j}, Y_{i,j})^T \sim N(\boldsymbol{\mu}_{w,i}, \boldsymbol{\Sigma}_{w,i}), j = 1, \ldots, n$, is a bivariate normal random vector with a mean vector and variance-covariance matrix, respectively, as follows:

$$\boldsymbol{\mu}_{w,i} = \begin{pmatrix} \mu_{X,i} \\ \mu_{Y,i} \end{pmatrix}, \tag{6}$$

$$\boldsymbol{\Sigma}_{w,i} = \begin{pmatrix} \sigma_{X,i}^2 & \rho_0 \sigma_{X,i} \sigma_{Y,i} \\ \rho_0 \sigma_{X,i} \sigma_{Y,i} & \sigma_{Y,i}^2 \end{pmatrix}. \tag{7}$$

where ρ_0 is the defined in-control correlation coefficient between two random variables X and Y. Following Ref. [5], several assumptions are made in this paper. First, the sample units are allowed to change among subgroups, which means $\boldsymbol{\mu}_{w,i} \neq \boldsymbol{\mu}_{w,k}$ and $\boldsymbol{\Sigma}_{w,i} \neq \boldsymbol{\Sigma}_{w,k}$ for $i \neq k$. Second, for variables X and Y, there is a linear relationship, $\sigma_{X,i} = \gamma_X \times \mu_{X,i}$ and $\sigma_{Y,i} = \gamma_Y \times \mu_{Y,i}$, where γ_X and γ_Y are the supposed known and constant coefficients of the variation of X and Y, respectively. Third, the known in-control value of the ratio is $z_0 = \frac{\mu_{X,i}}{\mu_{Y,i}}, i = 1, 2, \ldots$ for the in-control process.

3.1. A Brief Review of the VSI-EWMA-RZ Control Chart

To improve the performance of a Shewhart-RZ chart, Ref. [26] proposed a VSI-EWMA-RZ chart for monitoring the statistic $\hat{Z}_i$,

$$\hat{Z}_i = \frac{\hat{\mu}_{X,i}}{\hat{\mu}_{Y,i}} = \frac{\bar{X}_i}{\bar{Y}_i} = \frac{\sum_{j=1}^n X_{i,j}}{\sum_{j=1}^n Y_{i,j}}, i = 1, 2, \ldots \tag{8}$$

As it has been shown in Ref. [5], the c.d.f. $F_{\hat{Z}_i}(z \mid n, \gamma_X, \gamma_Y, z_0, \rho)$ and the i.d.f $F_{\hat{Z}_i}^{-1}(p \mid n, \gamma_X, \gamma_Y, z_0, \rho_0)$ of $\hat{Z}_i$ are equal to:

$$F_{\hat{Z}_i}(z \mid n, \gamma_X, \gamma_Y, z_0, \rho) = F_Z\left(z \mid \frac{\gamma_X}{\sqrt{n}}, \frac{\gamma_Y}{\sqrt{n}}, \frac{z_0 \gamma_X}{\gamma_Y}, \rho\right), \tag{9}$$

$$F_{\hat{Z}_i}^{-1}(p \mid n, \gamma_X, \gamma_Y, z_0, \rho_0) = F_Z^{-1}\left(p \mid \frac{\gamma_X}{\sqrt{n}}, \frac{\gamma_Y}{\sqrt{n}}, \frac{z_0 \gamma_X}{\gamma_Y}, \rho_0\right), \tag{10}$$

where $F_Z\left(z \mid \frac{\gamma_X}{\sqrt{n}}, \frac{\gamma_Y}{\sqrt{n}}, \frac{z_0 \gamma_X}{\gamma_Y}, \rho\right)$ is the c.d.f. of Z in Equation (3) and $F_Z^{-1}\left(p \mid \frac{\gamma_X}{\sqrt{n}}, \frac{\gamma_Y}{\sqrt{n}}, \frac{z_0 \gamma_X}{\gamma_Y}, \rho_0\right)$ is the i.d.f. of Z in Equation (5).

For detecting the upward shifts, the statistic Y_i^+ of the upper-sided VSI-EWMA-RZ (denoted as VSI-EWMA-RZ$^+$) chart is defined as:

$$Y_i^+ = \max\left(z_0, (1 - \lambda^+) Y_{i-1}^+ + \lambda^+ \hat{Z}_i\right), Y_0^+ = z_0, \tag{11}$$

With an upper control limit $UCL^+ = K^+ \times z_0$, where $\lambda^+ \in (0, 1]$ is the smoothing parameter and $K^+ > 1$ is chart parameter of the VSI-EWMA-RZ$^+$ chart. In addition, an upper warning limit $UWL^+ = W^+ \times z_0$ between $[z_0, UCL^+]$ is added to the chart, where $W^+ < K^+$ is the upper warning limit coefficient. A process is deemed to be out-of-control if the statistic $Y_i^+ > UCL^+$. Otherwise, the process is thought to be in-control if the statistic Y_i^+ falls within the warning region $(UWL^+, UCL^+]$, and a shorter sampling interval h_S is used to collect the next sampling point. The process is deemed to be in-control if the plotted statistic Y_i^+ falls within the safe region $[z_0, UWL^+]$, and a longer sampling interval h_L is used.

Similarly, for the detection of downward shifts, the statistic Y_i^- of the lower-sided VSI-EWMA-RZ (denoted as VSI-EWMA-RZ$^-$) chart is defined as:

$$Y_i^- = \min\left(z_0, (1 - \lambda^-) Y_{i-1}^- + \lambda^- \hat{Z}_i\right), Y_0^- = z_0, \tag{12}$$

With a lower control limit $LCL^- = K^- \times z_0$, where $\lambda^- \in (0, 1]$ is the smoothing parameter and $K^- < 1$ is the chart parameter of the VSI-EWMA-RZ$^-$ chart, respectively. In addition, a lower warning limit $LWL^- = W^- \times z_0$ between $[LCL^-, z_0]$ is added to the chart, where $W^- > K^-$ is the lower warning limit coefficient. A process is claimed to be out-of-control if the plotted statistic $Y_i^- < LCL^-$. Otherwise, the process is deemed to be in-control if the plotted statistic Y_i^- falls within the warning region $[LCL^- LWL^-)$ and a shorter sampling interval h_s is used. The process is deemed to be in-control if the plotted statistic Y_i^- falls within the safe region $[LWL^-, z_0]$ and a longer sampling interval h_L is used.

3.2. A Brief Review of the VSI-DEWMA-RZ Chart

According to Ref. [32], the one-sided VSI-DEWMA-RZ charts are constructed by making the smoothing twice and are defined as follows:

An upward VSI-DEWMA-RZ (denoted as VSI-DEWMA-RZ$^+$) chart is used to detect an increase in the process and the monitoring statistic U_i^- is:

$$Y_i^+ = \lambda^+ \hat{Z}_i + (1 - \lambda^+) Y_{i-1}^+, Y_0^+ = z_0, \tag{13}$$

$$U_i^+ = \lambda^+ Y_i^+ + (1 - \lambda^+) U_{i-1}^+, U_0^+ = z_0, \tag{14}$$

where $\lambda^+ \in (0, 1]$ is the smoothing parameter and $K^+ > 1$ is the chart parameter of the VSI-DEWMA-RZ$^+$ chart, respectively. The single control limit of the chart is $UCL^+ = K^+ \times z_0$. Also, an upper warning limit $UWL^+ = W^+ \times z_0$ between $[z_0, UCL^+]$ is added, where $W^+ < K^+$ is the upper warning limit coefficient. If the plotted statistic $U_i^+ > UCL^+$, the process is considered to be out-of-control. Otherwise, the process is claimed to be in-control if $UWL^+ < U_i^+ \leq UCL^+$ and a shorter sampling interval h_s is used to collect the next sampling point. The process is considered to be in-control if $z_0 \leq U_i^+ \leq UWL^+$ and a longer sampling interval h_L is used. The sampling interval h_i can be expressed as follows:

$$h_i = \begin{cases} h_s, & UWL^+ < U_i^+ \leq UCL^+ \\ h_L, & U_i^+ \leq UWL^+ \end{cases} \tag{15}$$

A downward VSI-DEWMA-RZ (denoted as VSI-DEWMA-RZ$^-$) chart is used to detect a decrease in the process and the statistic U_i^- can be similarly defined as:

$$Y_i^- = \lambda^- \hat{Z}_i + (1 - \lambda^-) Y_{i-1}^-, Y_0^- = z_0, \tag{16}$$

$$U_i^- = \lambda^- Y_i^- + (1 - \lambda^-) U_{i-1}^-, U_0^- = z_0, \tag{17}$$

where $\lambda^- \in (0, 1]$ and $K^- < 1$ are the smoothing and chart parameters of the FSI-DEWMA-RZ-chart, respectively. The single control limit of the chart is $LCL^- = K^- \times z_0$. A lower warning limit $LWL^- = W^- \times z_0$ between $[LCL^-, z_0]$ is added, where $W^- > K^-$ is the lower warning limit coefficient. If the plotted statistic $U_i^- < LCL^-$, the process is considered to be out-of-control. Otherwise, the process is claimed to be in-control if $LCL^- \leq U_i^- < LWL^-$ and a shorter sampling interval h_s is used. The process is considered to be in-control if $LWL^- \leq U_i^- \leq z_0$ and a longer sampling interval h_L is used. The sampling interval h_i can be expressed in a form similar to Equation (15).

3.3. The Proposed TEWMA-RZ Charts

To further enhance the advantage of the FSI- or VSI-EWMA-RZ charts, this paper performs the exponential smoothing three times on the weighted coefficients of the EWMA charts. As the distribution of Z is non-symmetric, two separate one-sided TEWMA-RZ charts are proposed for detecting increasing and decreasing shifts, respectively. Moreover, the VSI-TEWMA-RZ chart is further proposed to increase the sensitivity of the FSI-TEWMA-RZ chart.

3.3.1. The FSI-TEWMA-RZ Chart

An upward FSI-TEWMA-RZ (denoted as FSI-TEWMA-RZ$^+$) chart is used to detect an increase in the process, and the monitoring statistic V_i^+ is:

$$Y_i^+ = \lambda^+ \hat{Z}_i + (1-\lambda^+)Y_{i-1}^+, Y_0^+ = z_0, \tag{18}$$

$$U_i^+ = \lambda^+ Y_i^+ + (1-\lambda^+)U_{i-1}^+, U_0^+ = z_0, \tag{19}$$

$$V_i^+ = \lambda^+ U_i^+ + (1-\lambda^+)V_{i-1}^+, V_0^+ = z_0, \tag{20}$$

where $\lambda^+ \in (0,1]$ is the smoothing parameter and $K^+ > 1$ is the chart parameter of the FSI-TEWMA-RZ$^+$ chart, respectively. The single control limit of the chart is $UCL^+ = K^+ \times z_0$. A process is deemed to be out-of-control if the statistic V_i^+ falls above the UCL^+. Otherwise, the process is declared to be in-control.

A downward FSI-TEWMA-RZ (denoted as FSI-TEWMA-RZ$^-$) chart is used to detect downward process sifts and the statistic V_i^- can be similarly defined as:

$$Y_i^- = \lambda^- \hat{Z}_i + (1-\lambda^-)Y_{i-1}^-, Y_0^- = z_0, \tag{21}$$

$$U_i^- = \lambda^- Y_i^- + (1-\lambda^-)U_{i-1}^-, U_0^- = z_0, \tag{22}$$

$$V_i^- = \lambda^- U_i^- + (1-\lambda^-)V_{i-1}^-, V_0^- = z_0, \tag{23}$$

where $\lambda^- \in (0,1]$ is the smoothing parameter and $K^- < 1$ is the chart parameter of the TEWMA-RZ$^-$ chart, respectively. The single control limit of the chart is $LCL^- = K^- \times z_0$. A process is deemed to be out-of-control if the charting statistic V_i^- falls below the LCL^-. Otherwise, the process is declared to be in-control.

3.3.2. The VSI-TEWMA-RZ Chart

For further enhancing the sensitivity of the FSI-TEWMA-RZ chart for small or moderate shifts in the process, this paper introduces the VSI strategy into the FSI-TEWMA-RZ control chart in Section 3.3.1.

With respect to the proposed VSI-TEWMA-RZ chart, the control limit $UCL^+(LCL^-)$ is consistent with the FSI-TEWMA-RZ chart. For the upward VSI-TEWMA-RZ (denoted as VSI-TEWMA-RZ$^+$) control chart, an upper warning limit $UWL^+ = W^+ \times z_0$ between $[z_0, UCL^+]$ is added, where $W^+ < K^+$ is the upper warning limit coefficient. If the plotted statistic $V_i^+ > UCL^+$, the process is considered to be out-of-control. Otherwise, the process is claimed to be in-control if $UWL^+ < V_i^+ \leq UCL^+$ and a shorter sampling interval h_s is used to collect the next sampling point. The process is considered to be in-control if $z_0 \leq V_i^+ \leq UWL^+$ and a longer sampling interval h_L is used. The sampling interval h_i can be expressed as follows:

$$h_i = \begin{cases} h_s, UWL^+ < V_i^+ \leq UCL^+ \\ h_L, V_i^+ \leq UWL^+ \end{cases} \tag{24}$$

In terms of the downward VSI-TEWMA-RZ (denoted as VSI-TEWMA-RZ$^-$) control chart, a lower warning limit $LWL^- = W^- \times z_0$ between $[LCL^-, z_0]$ is added, where $W^- > K^-$ is the lower warning limit coefficient. If the plotted statistic $V_i^- < LCL^-$, the process is considered to be out-of-control. Otherwise, the process is claimed to be in-control if $LCL^- \leq V_i^- < LWL^-$ and a shorter sampling interval h_s is used. The process is considered to be in-control if $LWL^- \leq V_i^- \leq z_0$ and a longer sampling interval h_L is used. The sampling interval h_i can be expressed in a form similar to Equation (24).

4. Design of the Proposed TEWMA-RZ Charts

4.1. Design of the Proposed FSI-TEWMA-RZ Chart

Because of the complexity of the charting statistic of the FSI-TEWMA-RZ chart, the run length (RL) properties of the control chart are obtained by the MC simulation in this paper. Furthermore, to evaluate the performance of the FSI-TEWMA-RZ chart, the ARL measure, which indicates the average number of samples collected before going into out-of-control state, is selected. When the process is under control, the ARL is recorded as ARL_0. Otherwise, when the process gets out of control, the ARL is recorded as ARL_1. For illustration, the detailed procedure of the MC simulation of the FSI-TEWMA-RZ$^+$ chart is summarized as follows:

Step 1 Select the values of the sample size n, the in-control ratio z_0, the smoothing parameter λ^+, and the chart coefficient K^+. Compute the corresponding control limit $UCL^+ = K^+ \times z_0$.

Step 2 Generate a random sample from a multivariate normal distribution and compute the value of the charting statistic V_i^+ as in Equation (20).

Step 3 If the charting statistic V_i^+ falls below the UCL^+, the process is deemed to be in-control and returns to Step 2. Otherwise, the process is deemed to be out-of-control and then record the RL values.

Step 4 Repeat Steps 2 and 3 for . times, calculate the ARL values from the recorded RL values. The approximated expressions of the ARL can be written as:

$$ARL = \frac{\sum_{t=1}^{N} RL_t}{N}, t = 1, \ldots, N \qquad (25)$$

Without loss of generality, this paper assumes $ARL_0 = 200$ and further studies the ARL_1 performance of the proposed chart under different shifts. The performance of the FSI-TEWMA-RZ chart can be expressed as:

$$ARL_1 = ARL_1(n, \lambda, K, \gamma_X, \gamma_Y, z_0, \rho, \tau), \qquad (26)$$

Subject to the constraint:

$$ARL(n, \lambda, K, \gamma_X, \gamma_Y, z_0, \rho, \tau = 1) = ARL_0. \qquad (27)$$

When $\tau = 1$, the process is under control. Otherwise, when $\tau \neq 1$, the process is returns to be out-of-control. For the above model, considering different parameter combinations, this paper uses a bisection search algorithm to computer the value of K that satisfies the constraint of $ARL_0 = 200$, and then it is used to compute the ARL_1 values of the proposed chart.

4.2. Design of the Proposed VSI-TEWMA Charts

Since the sampling interval between the consecutive samples varies, it is not reasonable to assess the performance of the VSI-TEWMA-RZ chart by the ARL measure. Thus, the ATS is used to evaluate the performance of the VSI-TEWMA-RZ chart. The ATS represents the anticipant time before a control chart triggers an out-of-control signal. When the process is under control, it is recorded as ATS_0. Otherwise, when the process gets out-of-control, it is recorded as ATS_1.

For the FSI-TEWMA-RZ chart, the sampling interval h is fixed, which indicates that the $ATS^{FSI} = h \times ARL^{FSI}$. In general, the sampling interval of the FSI control chart is usually equal to one, that is, $h = 1$. Since the sampling interval h_i depends on the position of the currently monitoring statistic on the control chart, then the $ATS^{VSI} = E(h_i) \times ARL^{VSI}$, where $E(h_i)$ stands for the average sampling interval (ASI) of the VSI type chart. The detailed procedure of the MC simulation of the VSI-TEWMA-RZ$^+$ chart is summarized as below:

Step 1 Select the values of the sample size n, the in-control ratio z_0, the smoothing parameter λ^+, and the warning limit coefficient W^+ and K^+. Compute the corresponding warning limit $UWL^+ = W^+ \times z_0$ and the control limit $UCL^+ = K^+ \times z_0$.

Step 2 Generate a random sample from a multivariate normal distribution and compute the value of the charting statistic V_i^+ as in Equation (20).

Step 3 If $UWL^+ < V_i^+ \leq UCL^+$, a shorter sampling interval h_s is used to collect the next sampling point, and if $V_i^+ \leq UWL^+$, a longer sampling interval h_L is used to collect the next sampling point. Then, the process is declared to be in-control and returns to Step 2. The times t_S and t_L of the sampling intervals h_s and h_L are recorded, respectively. Otherwise, if the V_i^+ falls above the UCL^+, the process is declared to be out-of-control.

Step 4 Repeat Steps 2 and 3 for $N = 10^5$ times, calculate the ATS values from the recorded times of the sampling intervals h_s and h_L. The approximated expressions of the ATS can be written as:

$$ATS = h_S + h_S \times \frac{\sum_{t=1}^{N} t_S}{N} + h_L \times \frac{\sum_{t=1}^{N} t_L}{N}, t = 1, \ldots, N \tag{28}$$

Similarly, this paper assumes $ATS_0 = 200$ and further studies the ATS_1 performance of the proposed control charts under different process shifts.

The expressions of ATS^{FSI} and ATS^{VSI} are given as follows:

$$\begin{cases} ATS^{VSI} = ATS^{VSI}(n, h_S, h_L, \lambda, K, W, \gamma_0, \gamma_1, z_0, \rho, \tau) \\ ATS^{FSI} = h \times ARL_1^{FSI}(n, \lambda, K, \gamma_0, \gamma_1, z_0, \rho, \tau) \end{cases} \tag{29}$$

For the purpose of comparing the performance of the FSI-TEWMA-RZ and the VSI-TEWMA-RZ control charts, it is necessary to make sure that the control charts have the same controlled performance. The out-of-control performance of the VSI-TEWMA-RZ chart can be expressed as below:

$$ATS_1^{VSI} = ATS_1^{VSI}(n, h_S, h_L, \lambda, K, W, \gamma_0, \gamma_1, z_0, \rho, \tau)$$

Subject to the constraint:

$$ATS_0^{VSI} = ATS_0^{FSI} \tag{30}$$

$$ASI_0 = h = 1, \tag{31}$$

where ASI_0. is the controlled ASI of the VSI-TEWMA-RZ chart. Following the research work of Ref. [33], a general formula to determine the value of h_S and h_L are as follows:

$$\rho_S h_S + \rho_L h_L = h = 1 \text{ and } \rho_S + \rho_L = 1 \tag{32}$$

where ρ_S and ρ_L are the probabilities that the statistic V_i falls into the warning area and the safe area when the process is controlled, respectively. According to the research work of Ref. [34], this paper selects $(h_S, h_L) = (0.1, 1.9)$ and $\rho_S = \rho_L = 0.5$ for illustration.

In addition, a bisection search algorithm is used to calculate the control limit coefficient K and warning limit coefficient W by satisfying the constraint of $ATS_0 = 200$ and $ASI_0 = 1$. Then, these parameters are used to calculate the out-of-control ATS_1 values for the different process shift τ. According to the research of Ref. [26], we assume $z_0 = 1$ and select $\lambda \in \{0.2, 0.5\}$ and $n \in \{1, 5\}$ to discuss the performance of the VSI-TEWMA-RZ chart. For the selected combinations of (n, λ), Table 1 shows the values of K^+ and W^+ of the VSI-TEWMA-RZ control chart. Considering the space limitation, this article only gives the values of K^+ and W^+ under the condition that $\gamma_X = \gamma_Y$. It is noted that the value of K^+ of the VSI-TEWMA-RZ chart presented in Table 1, which is the same as the one from the corresponding FSI-TEWMA-RZ chart.

Table 1. K^+ and W^+ values of the VSI-TEWMA-RZ chart when $ATS_0 = 200$.

λ	($\gamma_X = 0.01, \gamma_Y = 0.01$)				($\gamma_X = 0.2, \gamma_Y = 0.2$)			
	$n = 1$		$n = 5$		$n = 1$		$n = 5$	
	K	W	K	W	K	W	K	W
				$\rho_0 = \rho_1 = -0.8$				
0.2	1.0067	0.9998	1.0030	0.9999	1.2480	1.0601	1.0762	1.0083
0.5	1.0161	1.0000	1.0071	0.9999	1.5315	1.0581	1.1699	1.0106
				$\rho_0 = \rho_1 = -0.4$				
0.2	1.0059	0.9998	1.0026	0.9999	1.2061	1.0467	1.0653	1.0061
0.5	1.0141	0.9999	1.0063	1.0000	1.4454	1.0452	1.1466	1.0069
				$\rho_0 = \rho_1 = 0$				
0.2	1.0050	0.9998	1.0022	0.9999	1.1618	1.0316	1.0534	1.0042
0.5	1.0119	0.9999	1.0053	1.0000	1.3544	1.0305	1.1210	1.0047
				$\rho_0 = \rho_1 = 0.4$				
0.2	1.0038	0.9998	1.0017	0.9999	1.1146	1.0179	1.0397	1.0019
0.5	1.0092	0.9999	1.0041	1.0000	1.2543	1.0179	1.0912	1.0028
				$\rho_0 = \rho_1 = 0.8$				
0.2	1.0022	0.9999	1.0010	1.0000	1.0574	1.0045	1.0216	1.0002
0.5	1.0053	1.0000	1.0024	1.0000	1.1316	1.0051	1.0504	1.0008

5. Numerical Results and Analysis

This section first compares the performance of the proposed VSI-TEWMA-RZ chart and the corresponding FSI-TEWMA-RZ control chart, and then compares the VSI-TEWMA-RZ chart's performance with the VSI-DEWMA-RZ chart in Ref. [32] and the VSI-EWMA-RZ chart proposed by Ref. [26]. Similar to the scenarios of Ref. [26], the parameter settings of the simulations are $\lambda \in \{0.2, 0.5\}$, $n \in \{1, 5\}$, $\gamma_X \in \{0.01, 0.2\}$, $\gamma_Y \in \{0.01, 0.2\}$ and $\rho_0 \in \{-0.8, -0.4, 0, 0.4, 0.8\}$, under different conditions $\{(\gamma_X = \gamma_Y, \rho_0 = \rho_1), (\gamma_X \neq \gamma_Y, \rho_0 = \rho_1), (\rho_0 \neq \rho_1, \gamma_X = \gamma_Y), (\rho_0 \neq \rho_1, \gamma_X \neq \gamma_Y)\}$. Since the proposed VSI-TEWMA-RZ control chart is mainly used to advance the sensitivity of the RZ chart for monitoring small shifts in a process and let us take the upward control chart for instance, we give priority to the performance of the RZ charts for the upward shifts $\tau \in \{1.001, 1.005, 1.01, 1.02, 1.05\}$.

5.1. Comparisons between the VSI-TEWMA-RZ and the FSI-TEWMA-RZ Charts

According to the above parameter settings and the values of K^+ and W^+ presented in Table 1, Figures 1–4 compare the performance of the upper-sided FSI-TEWMA-RZ and VSI-TEWMA-RZ charts when monitoring the upward shifts. The ARL_1 and ATS_1 represent the performances of the corresponding FSI and VSI control charts, respectively. It is pointed out that since the sampling interval of the FSI chart is $h = 1$, the FSI chart's ARL is equal to its ATS value. Then, the ARL_1 performance of the FSI chart can be directly compared with the ATS_1 performance of the VSI chart.

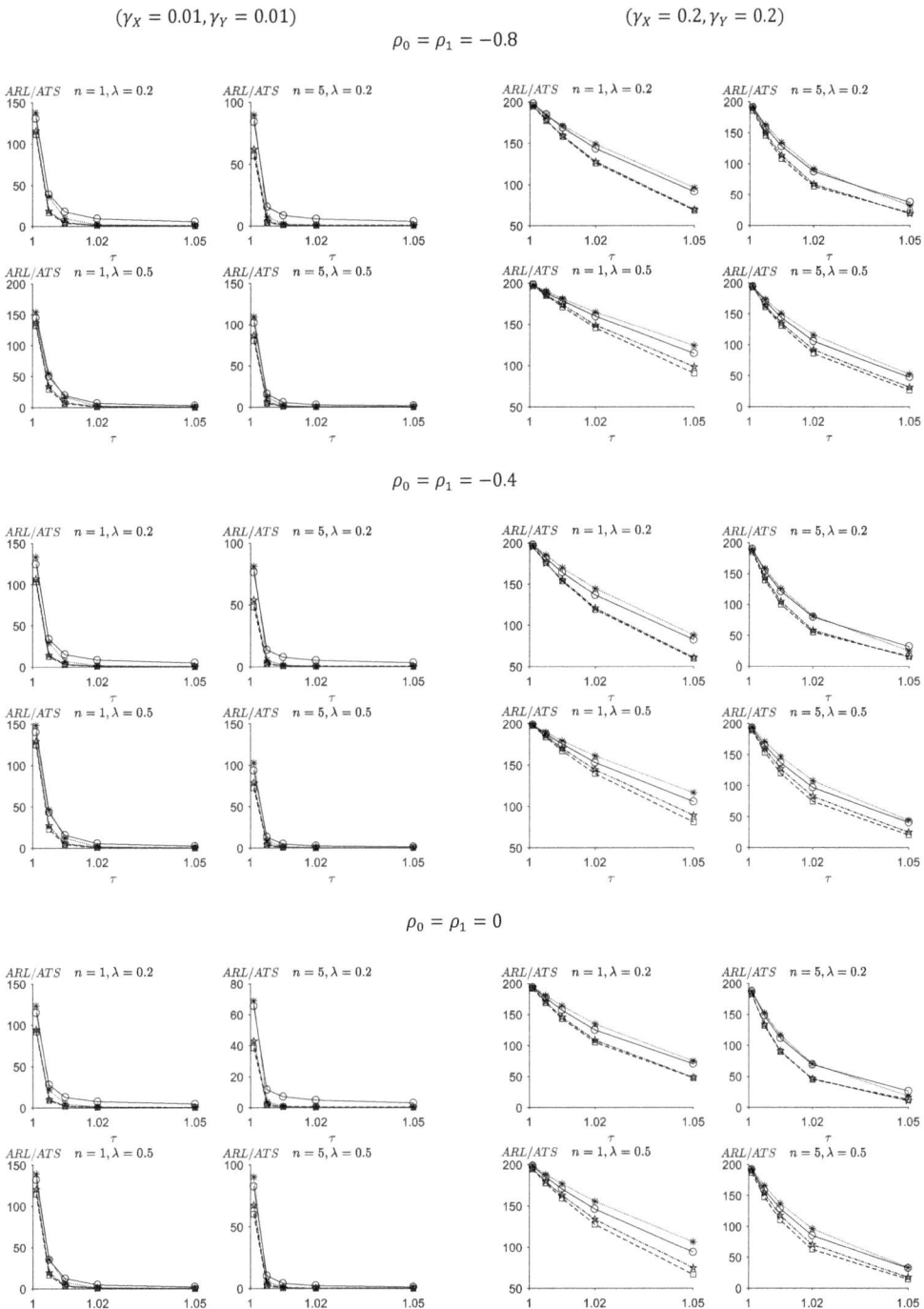

Figure 1. Cont.

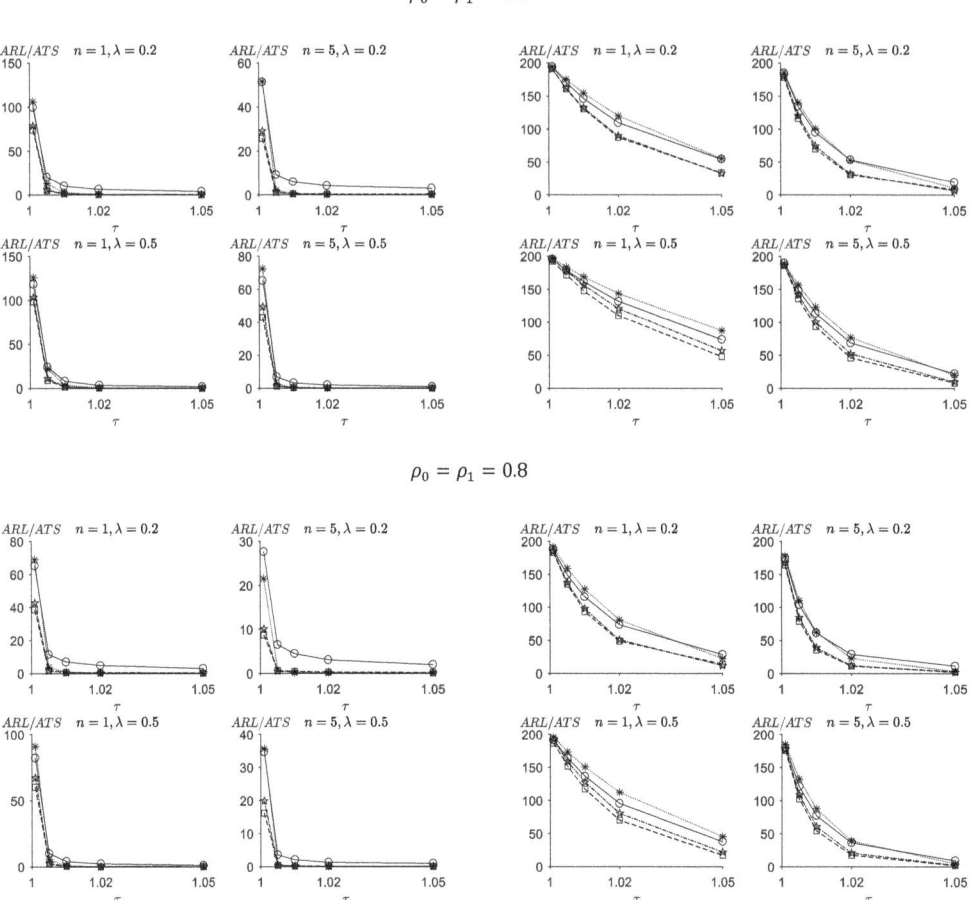

Figure 1. ARL values of the FSI-TEWMA-RZ (-○-) chart, ATS values of the VSI-DEWMA-RZ (-☆-), VSI-TEWMA-RZ (-□-), and VSI-EWMA-RZ (-✱-) charts for $\gamma_X \in \{0.01, 0.2\}$, $\gamma_Y \in \{0.01, 0.2\}$, $\gamma_X = \gamma_Y, \rho_0 \in \{-0.8, -0.4, 0, 0.4, 0.8\}$, $\rho_0 = \rho_1$, $\tau \in \{1.001, 1.005, 1.01, 1.02, 1.05\}$ and $n \in \{1, 5\}$.

Figures 1 and 2 show the out-of-control ARL_1 values of the FSI-TEWMA-RZ and the ATS_1 values of the proposed VSI-TEWMA-RZ chart under the conditions that $(\gamma_X = \gamma_Y, \rho_0 = \rho_1)$ and $(\gamma_X \neq \gamma_Y, \rho_0 = \rho_1)$, respectively. In Figures 1 and 2, when the process is in an out-of-control state, there is no shift in the correlation between X and Y, that is $\rho = \rho_0 = \rho_1$. From the results presented in Figures 1 and 2, some conclusions can be drawn as follows:

Generally, the proposed VSI-TEWMA-RZ chart reacts faster than the proposed FSI-TEWMA-RZ chart for detecting the process shifts. For instance, when $(\gamma_X, \gamma_Y) = (0.01, 0.01)$, $n = 1$, $\lambda = 0.2$, $\tau = 1.001$, and $\rho_0 = \rho_1 = -0.8$, we obtain $ATS_1 = 111.5$ for the VSI-TEWMA-RZ chart, which is much smaller than the $ARL_1 = 130.7$ for the FSI-TEWMA-RZ chart in Figure 1.

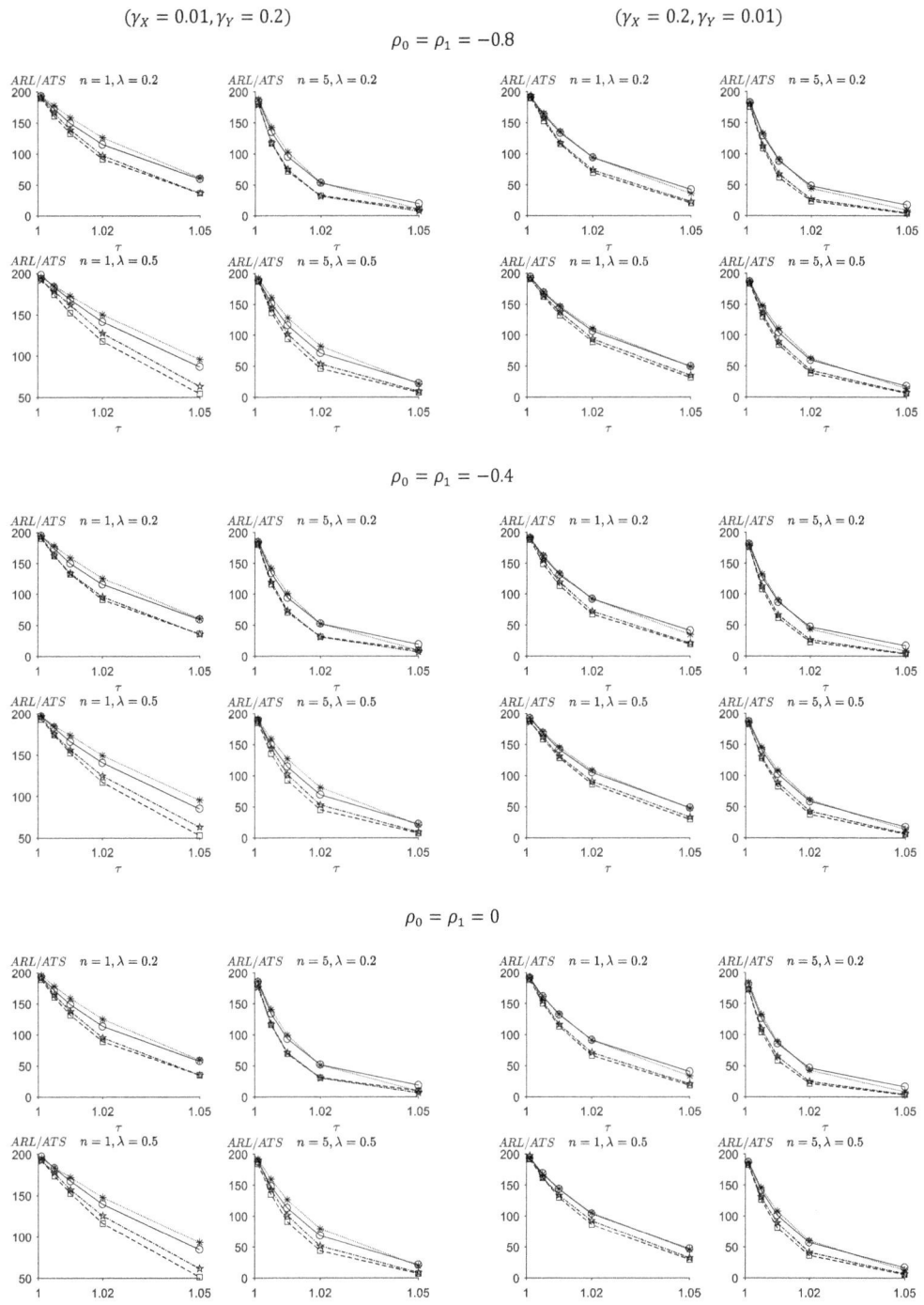

Figure 2. Cont.

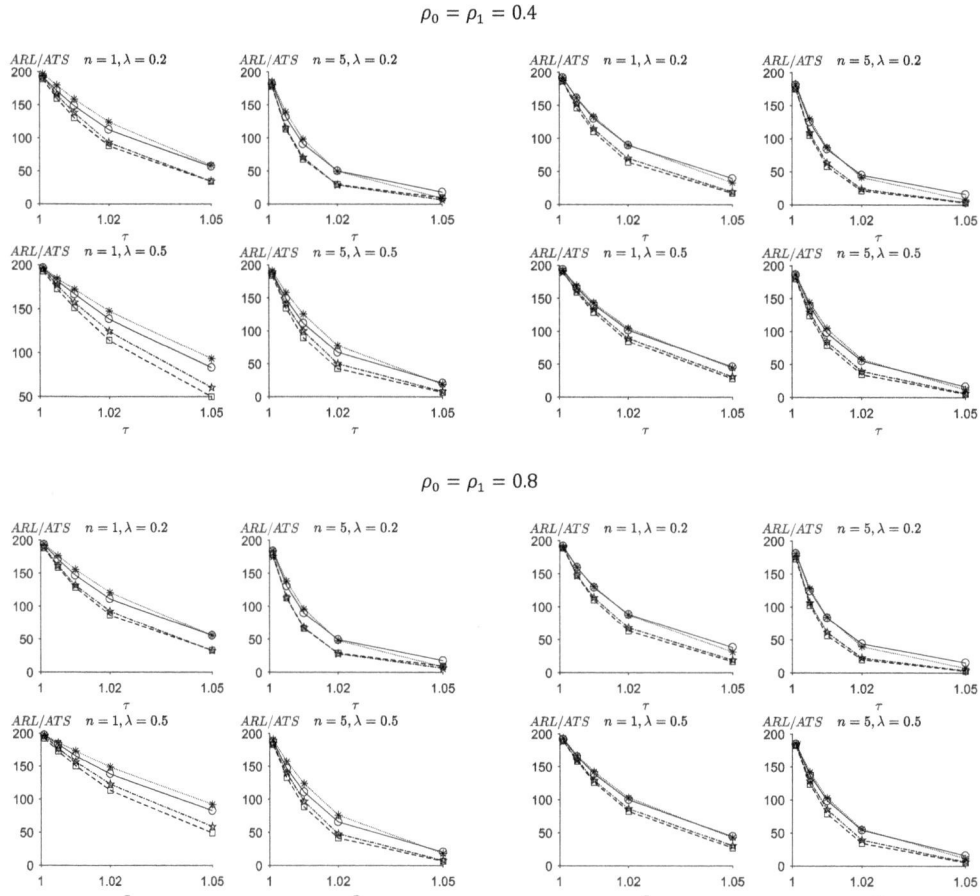

Figure 2. ARL values of the FSI-TEWMA-RZ (-○-) chart, ATS values of the VSI-DEWMA-RZ (-☆-), VSI-TEWMA-RZ (-□-), and VSI-EWMA-RZ (-✱-) charts for $\gamma_X \in \{0.01, 0.2\}$, $\gamma_Y \in \{0.01, 0.2\}$, $\gamma_X \neq \gamma_Y$, $\rho_0 \in \{-0.8, -0.4, 0, 0.4, 0.8\}$, $\rho_0 = \rho_1$, $\tau \in \{1.001, 1.005, 1.01, 1.02, 1.05\}$ and $n \in \{1, 5\}$.

The performances of the proposed FSI- and VSI-TEWMA-RZ charts are greatly affected by (γ_X, γ_Y). When $\gamma_X = \gamma_Y$, the smaller the coefficients of variation (γ_X, γ_Y), the better the performances of the proposed FSI- and VSI-TEWMA-RZ charts. For example, when $\rho_0 = \rho_1 = 0.4$, $n = 1$, $\lambda = 0.2$, and $\tau = 1.01$ in Figure 1, we have $ATS_1 = 10.2$ for the FSI-TEWMA-RZ chart and $ATS_1 = 1.3$ for the VSI-TEWMA-RZ chart when $(\gamma_X, \gamma_Y) = (0.01, 0.01)$. As a contrast, we have $ATS_1 = 146.0$ for the FSI-TEWMA-RZ chart and $ATS_1 = 130.6$ for the VSI-TEWMA-RZ chart when (γ_X, γ_Y) increases up to $(0.2, 0.2)$.

The performances of the proposed FSI- and VSI-TEWMA-RZ charts depend on ρ_0 and ρ_1. The performances of the proposed FSI- and VSI-TEWMA-RZ charts improve when ρ_0 increases. For example, when $(\gamma_X, \gamma_Y) = (0.01, 0.01)$, $n = 1$, $\lambda = 0.5$, $\tau = 1.001$, and $\rho_0 = \rho_1 = -0.8$, we have $ATS_1 = 144.9$ for the FSI-TEWMA-RZ chart and $ATS_1 = 132.3$ for the VSI-TEWMA-RZ chart in Figure 1. As a contrast, we obtain $ATS_1 = 82.1$ for the FSI-TEWMA-RZ chart and $ATS_1 = 60.2$ when ρ_0 and ρ_1 increase up to $(0.8, 0.8)$. The performances of the proposed FSI- and VSI-TEWMA-RZ charts are influenced by λ. The FSI- and VSI-TEWMA-RZ charts have a better performance in detecting small shifts when λ is generally small. As λ increases, their ability to detect small shifts gradually deteriorates. Instead, these charts are more sensitive to large shifts. For instance, when $(\gamma_X, \gamma_Y) = (0.2, 0.2)$, $\rho_0 = \rho_1 = 0.8$, $n = 5$, and $\tau = 1.001$, we obtain $ATS_1 = 174.6$ for the FSI-TEWMA-RZ chart and $ATS_1 = 164.4$ for the VSI-TEWMA-RZ chart when $\lambda = 0.2$ in Figure 1. If λ increases up to 0.5, we obtain $ATS_1 = 179.8$ for the FSI-TEWMA-RZ chart and $ATS_1 = 175.9$ for the VSI-TEWMA-RZ chart, which are larger than the ones of the $\lambda = 0.2$ case, respectively. Moreover, for a larger shift $\tau = 1.05$, we obtain $ATS_1 = 11$ for the FSI-TEWMA-RZ chart and $ATS_1 = 2.5$ for the VSI-TEWMA-RZ chart when $\lambda = 0.2$ in Figure 1. If λ increases up to 0.5, we obtain $ATS_1 = 9.1$ for the FSI-TEWMA-RZ chart and $ATS_1 = 2.0$ for the VSI-TEWMA-RZ chart, which are smaller than the ones of the $\lambda = 0.2$ case, respectively.

Figures 3 and 4 show the ARL_1 values of the FSI-TEWMA-RZ chart and the ATS_1 values of the proposed VSI-TEWMA-RZ chart under the conditions that $(\gamma_X = \gamma_Y, \rho_0 \neq \rho_1)$ and $(\gamma_X \neq \gamma_Y, \rho_0 \neq \rho_1)$, respectively. It is worth noting that the correlation coefficient between X and Y changes, that is $\rho_0 \neq \rho_1$. In order to facilitate the comparison and to be consistent with the research of Ref. [26], this paper chooses the in-control correlation coefficient $\rho_0 = \pm 0.4$ and the values of the studied shift in the correlation are 0.5 and 2, that is $\rho_1 = 0.5 \times \rho_0$ and $\rho_1 = 2 \times \rho_0$. From Figures 3 and 4, some conclusions can be summarized as follows:

With the increase in the level of the negative correlation coefficient, that is $\rho_0, \rho_1 < 0$, $|\rho_1| > |\rho_0|$, the performances of the proposed FSI- and VSI-TEWMA-RZ charts generally improve. For instance, when $(\gamma_X, \gamma_Y) = (0.2, 0.2)$, $\rho_0 = -0.4$, $\rho_1 = 2 \times \rho_0 = -0.8$, $n = 1$, $\lambda = 0.2$, and $\tau = 1.005$, we have $ATS_1 = 104$ for the FSI-TEWMA-RZ chart and $ATS_1 = 98.3$ for the VSI-TEWMA-RZ chart. While if $\rho_1 = \rho_0 = -0.4$, we obtain $ATS_1 = 181.6$ for the FSI-TEWMA-RZ chart and $ATS_1 = 176.3$ for the VSI-TEWMA-RZ chart. On the contrary, when the level of the negative correlation coefficient decreases, that is $|\rho_1| < |\rho_0|$ the performances of the proposed FSI- and VSI-TEWMA-RZ charts deteriorate. For example, when $\rho_1 = 0.5 \times \rho_0 = -0.2$, we obtain $ATS_1 = 273.6$ for the FSI-TEWMA-RZ chart and $ATS_1 = 272.2$ for the FSI-TEWMA-RZ chart. These ATS_1 values are all smaller than the ones of the $\rho_1 = \rho_0 = -0.4$ case, respectively.

$(\gamma_X = 0.01, \gamma_Y = 0.01)$ $(\gamma_X = 0.2, \gamma_Y = 0.2)$

$\rho_0 = -0.4, \rho_1 = -0.2$

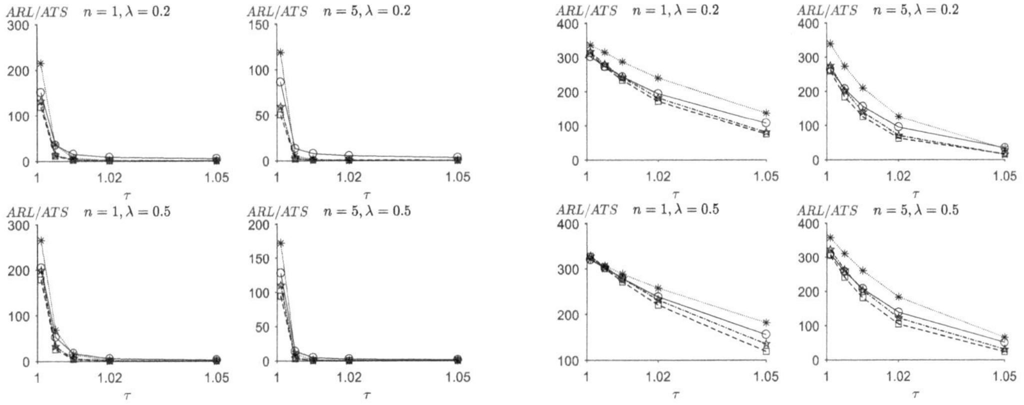

Figure 3. Cont.

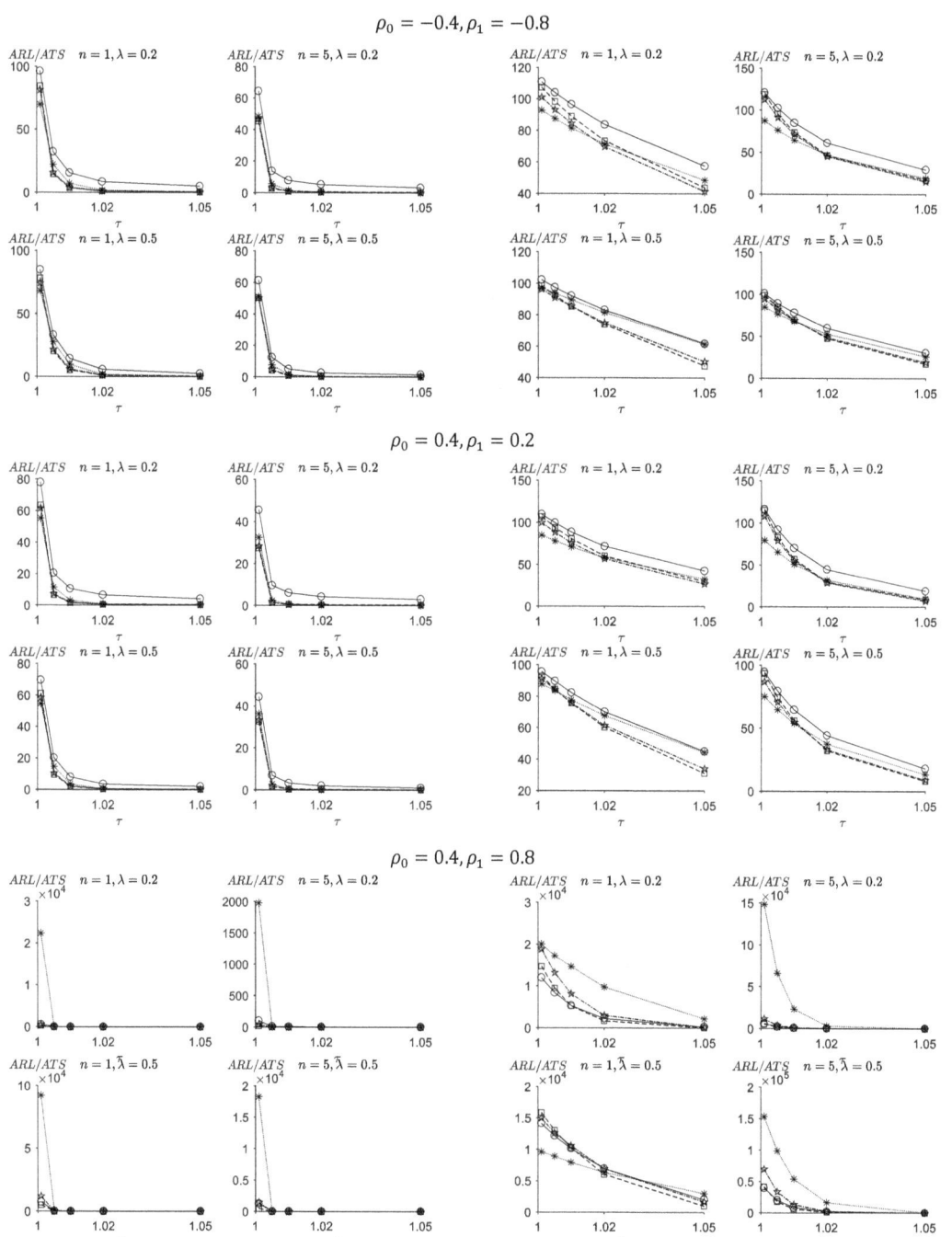

Figure 3. ARL values of the FSI-TEWMA-RZ (-○-) chart, ATS values of the VSI-DEWMA-RZ (-☆-), VSI-TEWMA-RZ (-□-), and VSI-EWMA-RZ (-✻-) charts for $\gamma_X \in \{0.01, 0.2\}$, $\gamma_Y \in \{0.01, 0.2\}$, $\gamma_X = \gamma_Y$, $\rho_0 \in \{-0.8, -0.4, 0, 0.4, 0.8\}$, $\rho_0 \neq \rho_1$, $\tau \in \{1.001, 1.005, 1.01, 1.02, 1.05\}$ and $n \in \{1, 5\}$.

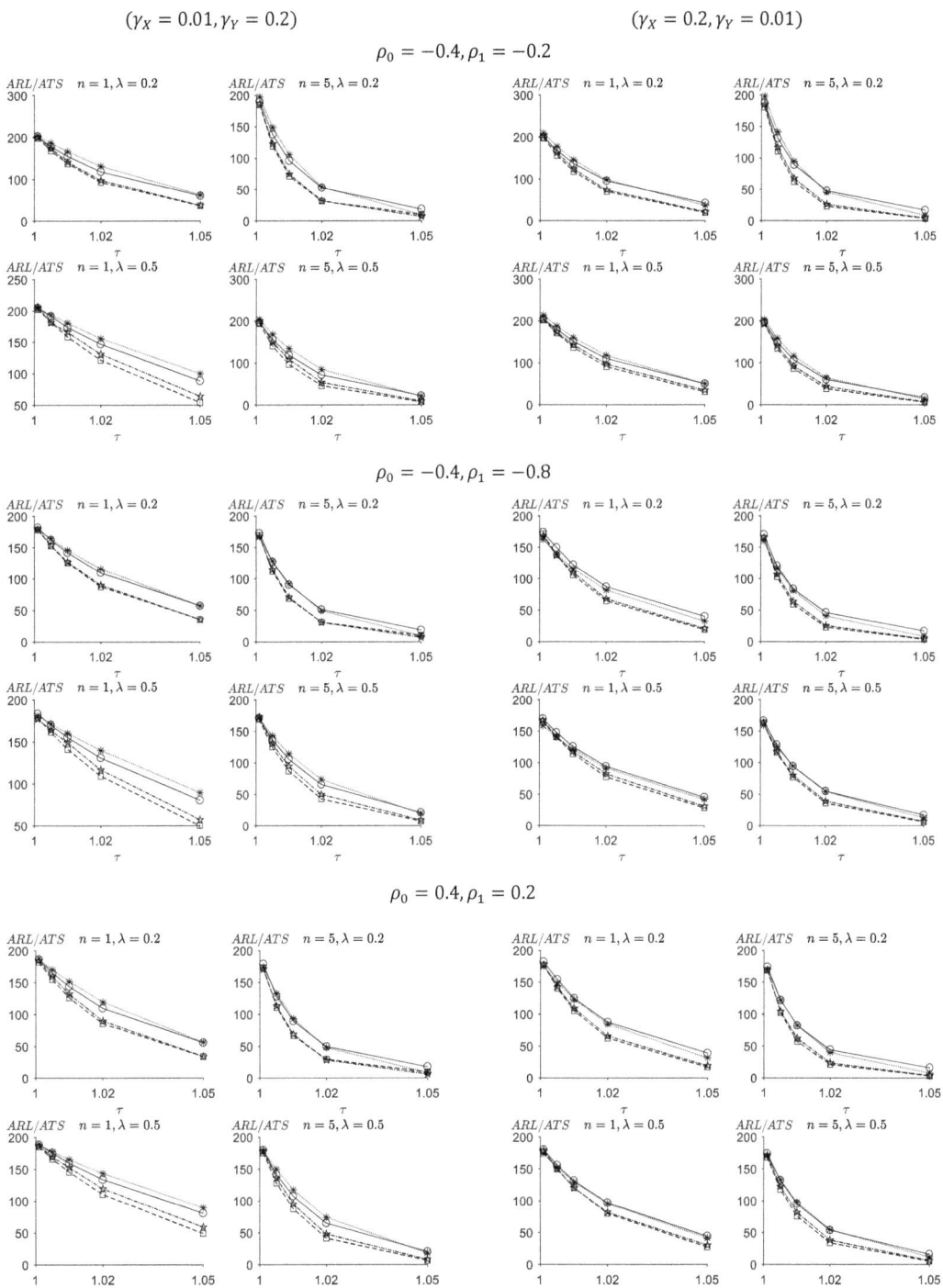

Figure 4. Cont.

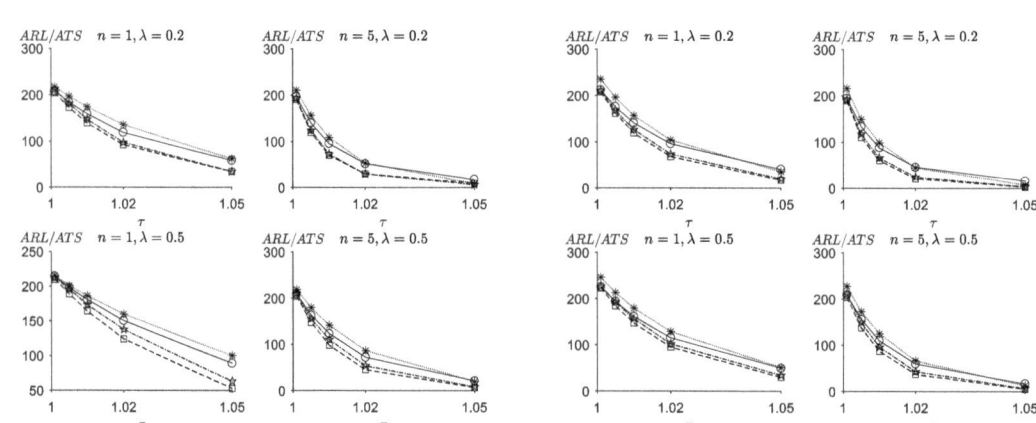

Figure 4. ARL values of the FSI-TEWMA-RZ (-○-) chart, ATS values of the VSI-DEWMA-RZ (-☆-), VSI-TEWMA-RZ (-□-) and VSI-EWMA-RZ (-✱-) charts for $\gamma_X \in \{0.01, 0.2\}$, $\gamma_Y \in \{0.01, 0.2\}$, $\gamma_X \neq \gamma_Y$, $\rho_0 \in \{-0.8, -0.4, 0, 0.4, 0.8\}$, $\rho_0 \neq \rho_1$, $\tau \in \{1.001, 1.005, 1.01, 1.02, 1.05\}$ and $n \in \{1, 5\}$.

With the increase in the level of the positive correlation coefficient, that is when $\rho_1 > \rho_0 > 0$, the performances of the proposed FSI- and VSI-TEWMA-RZ charts generally deteriorate. For instance, when $(\gamma_X, \gamma_Y) = (0.01, 0.01)$, $\rho_1 = 2 \times \rho_0 = 0.8$, $n = 1$, $\lambda = 0.2$, $\tau = 1.001$, we have $ATS_1 = 531.9$ for the FSI-TEWMA-RZ chart and $ATS_1 = 237.6$ for the VSI-TEWMA-RZ chart. While if $\rho_1 = \rho_0 = 0.4$, we obtain $ATS_1 = 99.6$ for the FSI-TEWMA-RZ chart and $ATS_1 = 73.9$ for the VSI-TEWMA-RZ chart. On the contrary, with the decrease in the level of the positive correlation coefficient, that is when $\rho_0 > \rho_1 > 0$, the performances of the proposed FSI- and VSI-TEWMA-RZ charts improve. For instance, when $\rho_1 = 0.5 \times \rho_0 = 0.2$, we have $ATS_1 = 77.9$ for the FSI-TEWMA-RZ chart and $ATS_1 = 63.5$ for the VSI-TEWMA-RZ chart. These ATS_1 values are all smaller than the ones of the $\rho_1 = \rho_0 = 0.4$ case, respectively.

5.2. Comparisons between the VSI-TEWMA-RZ Chart and the VSI-EWMA-RZ Chart

Similarly, based on the above parameter settings and the values of K^+ and W^+ presented in Table 1, Figures 1–4 also compare the performances of the VSI-TEWMA-RZ and VSI-EWMA-RZ control charts when monitoring the upward shifts. Figures 1 and 2 present the out-of-control ATS_1 values of the VSI-EWMA-RZ chart for the condition $\rho_0 = \rho_1$. While for the condition $\rho_0 \neq \rho_1$, the ATS_1 values of the VSI-EWMA-RZ chart are shown in Figures 3 and 4. Some conclusions can be drawn from Figures 1–4.

The proposed VSI-TEWMA-RZ control chart outperforms the VSI-EWMA-RZ control chart in the detection of the upward shifts for most cases, especially for small shifts. For instance, when $\rho_0 = \rho_1$ and $(\gamma_X, \gamma_Y) = (0.01, 0.01)$ in Figure 1, the VSI-TEWMA-RZ control chart has a better performance than the VSI-EWMA-RZ control chart for the shift $\tau \in [1.001, 1.005]$. On the contrary, the VSI-EWMA-RZ chart performs better than the VSI-TEWMA-RZ chart for the detection of a relatively large shift. For instance, when $n = 5$, $\lambda = 0.2$, $\rho_0 = -0.8$, $(\gamma_X, \gamma_Y) = (0.01, 0.01)$ and $\tau = 1.05$, we have $ATS_1 = 0.1$ for the VSI-EWMA-RZ chart, which is smaller than the $ATS_1 = 0.4$ for the VSI-TEWMA-RZ chart.

When the coefficient of variation γ_X or γ_Y increases, the advantage of the VSI-TEWMA-RZ chart over the VSI-EWMA-RZ chart increases. For example, when $(\gamma_X, \gamma_Y) = (0.01, 0.01)$, the VSI-TEWMA-RZ chart outperforms the VSI-EWMA-RZ chart only for the shift range $\tau \in [1.001, 1.005]$ in Figure 1. While if (γ_X, γ_Y) increase up to $(0.2, 0.2)$, the VSI-TEWMA-RZ chart outperforms the VSI-EWMA-RZ chart for all the upward shifts.

5.3. Comparisons between the VSI-TEWMA-RZ Chart and the VSI-DEWMA-RZ Chart

Furthermore, the proposed VSI-TEWMA-RZ is compared with the VSI-DEWMA-RZ chart when monitoring the upward shifts. It can be seen from Figures 1–4 that the proposed VSI-TEWMA-RZ chart is statistically more sensitive than the VSI-DEWMA-RZ chart for detecting the process shifts, especially for small shifts. For example, when $\rho_0 = \rho_1$ and $(\gamma_X, \gamma_Y) = (0.01, 0.01)$ in Figure 1, the VSI-TEWMA-RZ control chart has a better performance than the VSI-DEWMA-RZ chart for the shift $\tau \in [1.001, 1.005]$. On the contrary, the VSI-DEWMA-RZ chart is statistically more sensitive than the VSI-TEWMA-RZ chart for the detection of a relatively large shift. For instance, when $n = 5$, $\lambda = 0.2$, $\rho_0 = -0.4$, $(\gamma_X, \gamma_Y) = (0.01, 0.2)$, and $\tau = 1.1$ in Figure 2, we have $ATS_1 = 6.8$ for the VSI-DEWMA-RZ chart, which is smaller than the $ATS_1 = 10$ for the VSI-TEWMA-RZ chart.

It can be observed that when λ increases from 0.2 to 0.5, the advantage of the VSI-TEWMA-RZ chart over the VSI-DEWMA-RZ chart increases. For instance, when $n = 5$, $\lambda = 0.5$, $\rho_0 = \rho_1 = -0.4$, and $(\gamma_X, \gamma_Y) = (0.01, 0.2)$, the VSI-TEWMA-RZ chart is statistically more sensitive than the VSI-DEWMA-RZ chart for all the upward shifts in Figure 2. However, the VSI-TEWMA-RZ chart has a better performance than the VSI-DEWMA-RZ chart for the shift $\tau \in [1.001, 1.01]$ when $\lambda = 0.2$. In addition, when the coefficient of variation γ_X or γ_Y increases, the advantage of the VSI-TEWMA-RZ chart over the VSI-EWMA-RZ chart increases. For instance, when $n = 5$ and $(\gamma_X, \gamma_Y) = (0.01, 0.01)$, the VSI-TEWMA-RZ chart outperforms the VSI-DEWMA-RZ chart for the shift range $\tau \in [1.001, 1.005]$ in Figure 1. While if (γ_X, γ_Y) increase up to $(0.2, 0.2)$, the shift range that the VSI-TEWMA-RZ chart outperforms the VSI-DEWMA-RZ chart extends to $\tau \in [1.001, 1.02]$.

6. An Illustrative Example

This section discusses the implementation of the proposed FSI- and VSI-TEWMA-RZ control charts by adopting the dataset of a muesli brand recipe discussed in Ref. [6]. This recipe was composed of several ingredients, including sunflower oil, wildflower honey, seeds (pumpkin, flaxseeds, sesame, poppy), coconut milk powder, and rolled oats. To meet the nutritional requirements recommended by the brand and preserve the flavor of the mixture, the recipe has a requirement that the weights of 'pumpkin seeds' and 'flaxseeds' be equal. Their nominal proportions to the total weight of the box content are both fixed at $p_p = p_f = 0.1$. Moreover, the brand boxes produced by the company can be packaged in 250g or 500g. To check the deviation of the controlled ratio $z_0 = \frac{\mu_{p,i}}{\mu_{f,i}} = 1$, where $\mu_{p,i}$ and $\mu_{f,i}$ are the mean weights for 'pumpkin seeds' and 'flaxseeds', respectively, at time $i = 1, 2, \ldots$, the quality practitioners wanted to perform on-line SPC monitoring and collect a sample of $n = 5$ boxes at each sampling time. Since the box size varies from one sample to another, we can obtain $\mu_{p,i} \neq \mu_{p,k}$ and $\mu_{f,i} \neq \mu_{f,k}$, $\forall i \neq k$.

In the quality control program, the 'pumpkin seeds' and 'flaxseeds' are first separated from the muesli mixture and the sample average weights $\overline{W}_{p,i} = \frac{1}{n}\sum_{j=1}^{n} W_{p,i,j}$ and $\overline{W}_{f,i} = \frac{1}{n}\sum_{j=1}^{n} W_{f,i,j}$ are recorded. At last, the ratio $\hat{Z}_i = \frac{\overline{W}_{p,i}}{\overline{W}_{f,i}}$ is calculated and plotted in the FSI- and VSI-TEWMA-RZ charts. As it has been shown in Ref. [6], for $i = 1, 2, 3 \ldots$ and $j = 1, 2, 3, \ldots$, $W_{p,i,j}$ and $W_{f,i,j}$ can be well approximated as normal variables with constant coefficients of variation $\gamma_p = 0.02$ and $\gamma_f = 0.01$, which means $W_{p,i,j} \sim N(\mu_{p,i}, 0.02 \times \mu_{p,i})$ and $W_{f,i,j} \sim N(\mu_{f,i}, 0.01 \times \mu_{f,i})$. In addition, $\rho_0 = 0.8$ is considered as the in-control correlation coefficient between these two variables.

From an engineer's experience, a shift of 0.5% ($\tau = 1.005$) in the ratio should be interpreted as an assignable cause in the process monitoring. For this reason, we set the specified shift $\tau = 1.005$. Moreover, we chose the smoothing parameter $\lambda^+ = 0.5$ of the charts for the process monitoring. Given $n = 5$, $\lambda^+ = 0.5$, $\rho_0 = \rho_1 = 0.8$, and $(\gamma_X, \gamma_Y) = (0.02, 0.01)$, we obtained the control limit parameters $K^+ = 1.00497$ and $W^+ = 0.999899$ of the FSI-TEWMA-RZ$^+$ and VSI-TEWMA-RZ$^+ K^+ = 1.009089$ and

$W^+ = 1.000779$ of the VSI-EWMA-RZ$^+$ chart and $K^+ = 1.006163$ and $W^+ = 0.999942$ of the VSI-EWMA-RZ$^+$ chart and z_0 is set to be 1, then $UCL^+ = K^+$ and $UWL^+ = W^+$.

Table 2 presents the set of simulated sample data collected from the process. The process is deemed to be in-control up to sample #10 and from then on, an assignable cause occurs and shifts $Z_0 = 1$ to $Z_1 = 1.005$. When $(h_S, h_L) = (0.1, 1.9)$, Figure 5 presents the VSI-EWMA-RZ$^+$ chart, the VSI-DEWMA-RZ$^+$ chart, and the FSI- and VSI-TEWMA-RZ$^+$ control charts for the dataset in Table 2, where the index t in the axis is the cumulative time of the process monitoring. It can be seen from Figure 5 that the FSI- and VSI-TEWMA-RZ$^+$ chart triggers an out-of-control signal at sample #15 (in bold in Table 2), while the VSI-DEWMA-RZ$^+$ and VSI-EWMA-RZ$^+$ charts signal an out-of-control condition at sample #16 and #18 (in bold in Table 2), respectively. This example shows that the TEWMA-RZ charts outperform the VSI-DEWMA-RZ and the VSI-EWMA-RZ charts from the perspective of the number of samples.

Table 2. The food industry example data.

Sample Number	Box Size	$W_{p,i,j}$[gr] $W_{f,i,j}$[gr]					$\overline{W_{p,i}}$[gr] $\overline{W_{f,i}}$[gr]	$\hat{Z}_i = \frac{\overline{W_{p,i}}}{\overline{W_{f,i}}}$	VSI-EWMA		VSI-DEWMA		VSI-TEWMA	
									Y_i^+	t_i	U_i^+	t_i	V_i^+	t_i
1	250 gr	25.479 25.218	25.355 25.171	24.027 24.684	25.792 25.052	24.960 25.107	25.122 25.046	1.003	1.00150	0.1	1.00075	0.1	1.00038	0.1
2	250 gr	25.359 25.211	25.172 25.115	24.508 24.679	25.292 24.933	24.449 24.831	24.956 24.954	1.000	1.00075	0.2	1.00075	0.2	1.00056	0.2
3	250 gr	24.574 24.784	24.864 24.868	25.865 25.377	25.107 24.879	24.811 24.734	25.044 24.929	1.005	1.00288	2.1	1.00181	0.3	1.00119	0.3
4	250 gr	25.313 25.338	24.483 24.859	24.088 24.305	25.184 25.115	25.681 25.251	24.950 24.974	0.999	1.00094	2.2	1.00138	0.4	1.00128	0.4
5	250 gr	25.557 25.277	24.959 25.402	25.023 25.012	24.482 24.937	25.531 25.148	25.111 25.163	0.998	1.00000	2.3	1.00042	0.5	1.00085	0.5
6	250 gr	24.882 24.962	24.473 24.644	24.814 24.817	25.418 25.419	24.732 24.818	24.864 24.932	0.997	1.00000	4.2	0.99933	0.6	1.00009	0.6
7	500 gr	49.848 49.993	48.685 49.128	49.994 49.830	49.910 49.566	49.374 49.422	49.562 49.588	0.999	1.00000	6.1	0.99897	2.5	0.99953	0.7
8	500 gr	49.668 49.695	50.338 50.681	49.149 49.640	47.807 48.969	49.064 49.612	49.205 49.720	0.990	1.00000	8	0.99664	4.4	0.99809	2.6
9	500 gr	51.273 50.366	48.303 49.210	48.510 49.844	50.594 49.890	48.591 49.595	49.454 49.781	0.993	1.00000	9.9	0.99515	6.3	0.99662	4.5
10	500 gr	48.720 49.721	51.566 50.215	49.677 50.178	50.651 50.324	50.344 50.071	50.192 50.102	1.002	1.00100	11.8	0.99649	8.2	0.99655	6.4
11	500 gr	53.173 51.081	51.079 50.660	51.636 50.468	49.187 49.787	49.779 49.197	50.971 50.239	1.015	1.00800	11.9	1.00145	10.1	0.99900	8.3
12	500 gr	51.255 49.899	48.578 49.476	49.657 49.400	49.971 49.909	50.675 50.365	50.027 49.810	1.004	1.00600	12	1.00333	10.2	1.00116	10.2
13	500 gr	48.760 48.919	50.206 50.032	51.216 50.497	51.997 50.627	49.818 49.483	50.399 49.912	1.010	1.00800	12.1	1.00547	10.3	1.00332	10.3
14	500 gr	51.599 50.351	49.257 49.885	52.077 51.044	49.874 49.898	48.791 49.506	50.319 50.137	1.004	1.00600	12.2	1.00563	10.4	1.00447	10.4
15	500gr	49.178 49.104	51.188 50.348	50.602 50.621	50.221 50.018	50.433 50.085	50.325 50.035	1.006	1.00600	12.3	1.00577	10.5	**1.00512**	**10.5**
16	500gr	50.667 50.011	50.600 49.870	50.601 49.779	49.517 50.020	50.578 49.877	50.393 49.911	1.010	1.00800	12.4	**1.00686**	**10.6**	1.00599	10.6
17	500gr	50.925 50.579	49.036 49.735	50.971 50.196	51.888 50.740	50.741 49.959	50.712 50.242	1.009	1.00850	12.5	1.00767	10.7	1.00683	10.7
18	500gr	50.673 50.459	50.653 49.990	50.346 50.281	50.749 50.251	51.338 50.281	50.752 50.252	1.010	**1.00925**	**12.6**	1.00845	10.8	1.00764	10.8
19	250gr	25.390 25.158	25.554 25.278	25.799 25.073	23.869 24.349	25.041 25.085	25.131 24.989	1.006	1.00763	12.7	1.00804	10.9	1.00784	10.9
20	250gr	24.343 24.771	26.087 25.427	25.431 25.005	24.799 24.711	26.440 25.258	25.420 25.035	1.002	1.00481	12.8	1.00642	11.0	1.00713	11.0

In the VSI-TEWMA-RZ$^+$ chart, it is noted that the first six samples are in the warning region and a shorter sampling interval $h_s = 0.1$ is used to collect the next sampling point. The plotted sample point V_7^+ falls within the safe region $[z_0, UWL^+]$ and a longer sampling interval h_L is used. The VSI-TEWMA-RZ$^+$ chart needs 10.5-times the units to detect the assignable cause. As a comparison, the VSI-DEWMA-RZ$^+$ chart needs 10.6-times the units to trigger an out-of-control signal, while the VSI-EWMA-RZ$^+$ chart needs 12.6-times the units to trigger an out-of-control signal. This shows the advantage of the VSI-TEWMA-RZ$^+$ chart over the VSI-EWMA-RZ$^+$ chart and VSI-DEWMA-RZ$^+$ chart. Moreover, since the sampling interval of the FSI-TEWMA-RZ$^+$ control chart is 1, then it needs 15-times the units to trigger an out-of-control signal. If a control chart indicates an out-of-control signal, then the quality engineering should take corrective actions to search the potential assignable causes and make the process as controlled as possible.

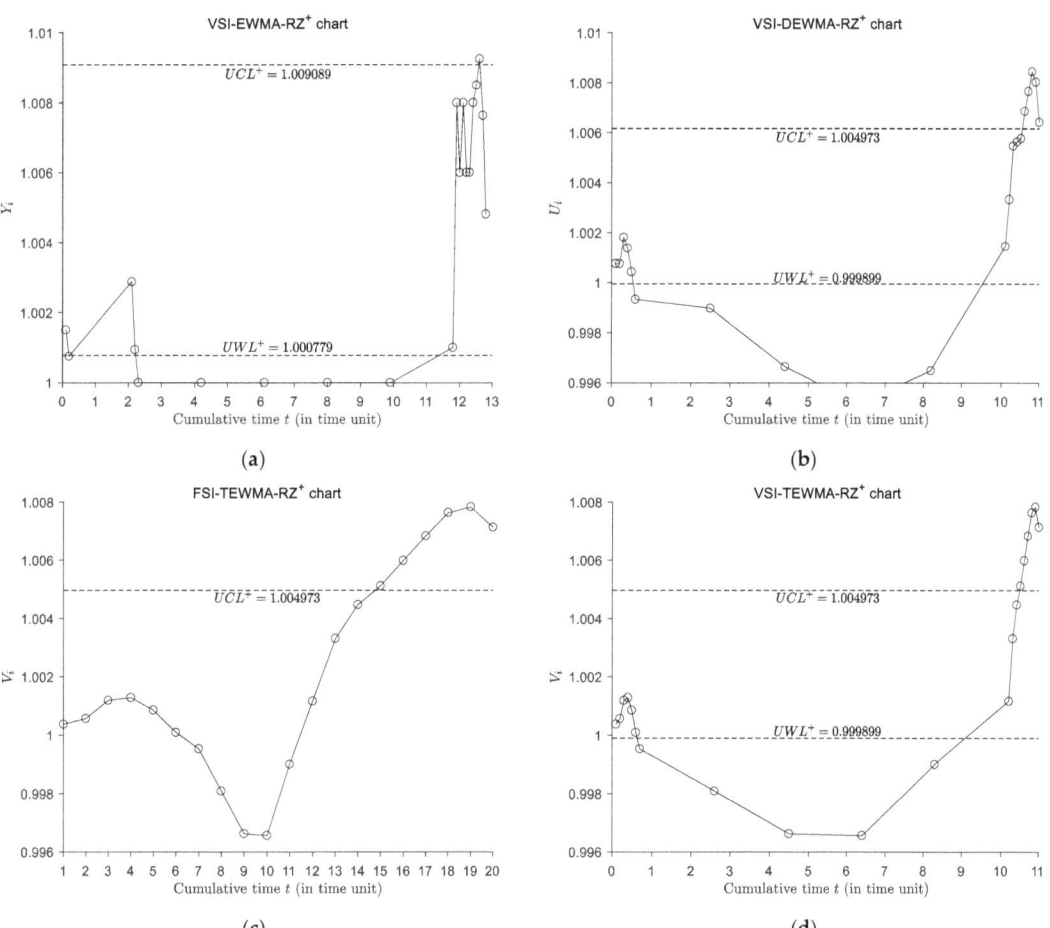

Figure 5. Different charts monitoring the food industry example. (**a**) The VSI-EWMA-RZ$^+$ chart, (**b**) the VSI-DEWMA-RZ$^+$ chart, (**c**) the proposed FSI-TEWMA-RZ$^+$ chart, and (**d**) the proposed VSI-TEWMA-RZ$^+$ charts.

7. Conclusions

In this paper, the major purpose is to propose the FSI- and VSI-TEWMA-RZ control charts by smoothing the coefficient of the EWMA-RZ chart three times. The RL properties of the proposed TEWMA-RZ charts are simulated using the MC method. Under different conditions, the performances of the VSI-TEWMA-RZ charts are presented and are compared with the FSI-TEWMA-RZ and the existing VSI-EWMA-RZ and the VSI-DEWMA-RZ charts in several figures. The results show that the performances of the proposed FSI- and VSI-TEWMA-RZ charts are greatly affected by (γ_X, γ_Y), ρ_0, and λ. Moreover, the comparison results show that the proposed VSI-TEWMA-RZ chart reacts faster than the FSI-TEWMA-RZ chart for all shifts, and the VSI-TEWMA-RZ chart also performs reacts faster than the VSI-EWMA-RZ and VSI-DEWMA-RZ charts in the detection of relatively small shifts.

Since this work is done on the assumption that both the two random variables X and Y are normally distributed, prospective research works can focus on other distributions of the two random variables to study the performance of charts for monitoring the RZ. Moreover, since some researchers have proposed distribution-free charts with the Wilcoxon rank-sum statistic, for instance Refs. [21,25,35] and so on, it would be possible to apply these distribution-free charts to monitor the RZ and study the distribution-free charts' robustness to the RZ distribution.

Author Contributions: Conceptualization, X.H. and G.S.; methodology, X.H.; software, G.S.; validation, F.X. and A.T.; formal analysis, G.S.; investigation, G.S.; resources, A.T.; data curation, X.H.; writing—original draft preparation, G.S.; writing—review and editing, X.H.; visualization, A.T.; supervision, X.H.; project administration, X.H.; funding acquisition, X.H. and A.T. All authors have read and agreed to the published version of the manuscript.

Funding: This work was supported by National Natural Science Foundation of China (Grant number: 71802110, 71671093, 72101123); China Scholarship Council (Grant number: 202006840086); The Excellent Innovation Teams of Philosophy and Social Science in Jiangsu Province (2017ZSTD022); Key Research Base of Philosophy and Social Sciences in Jiangsu Information Industry Integration Innovation and Emergency Management Research Center; Natural Science Foundation of JiangSu Province (BK20200750).

Institutional Review Board Statement: Not applicable.

Informed Consent Statement: Not applicable.

Data Availability Statement: Some or all data, models, or code generated or used during the study are available from the corresponding author by request.

Acknowledgments: This article would not have been possible without the valuable reference materials that I received from my supervisor, whose insightful guidance and enthusiastic encouragement in the course of my shaping this article definitely gain my deepest gratitude.

Conflicts of Interest: The authors declare no conflict of interest.

References

1. Celano, G.; Castagliola, P.; Faraz, A.; Fichera, S. Statistical performance of a control chart for individual observations monitoring the ratio of two normal variables. *Qual. Reliab. Eng. Int.* **2014**, *30*, 1361–1377. [CrossRef]
2. Spisak, A.W. A Control Chart for Ratios. *J. Qual. Technol.* **1990**, *22*, 34–37. [CrossRef]
3. Davis, R.B.; Woodall, W.H. Evaluation of control charts for ratios. In Proceedings of the 22nd Annual Pittsburgh Conference on Modeling and Simulation, Pittsburgh, PA, USA, 24–25 April 1975.
4. Öksoy, D.; Boulos, E.; Pye, L.D. Statistical process control by the quotient of two correlated normal variables. *Qual. Eng.* **1993**, *6*, 179–194. [CrossRef]
5. Celano, G.; Castagliola, P. Design of a phase II control chart for monitoring the ratio of two normal variables. *Qual. Reliab. Eng. Int.* **2016**, *32*, 291–308. [CrossRef]
6. Celano, G.; Castagliola, P. A synthetic control chart for monitoring the ratio of two normal variables. *Qual. Reliab. Eng. Int.* **2016**, *32*, 681–696. [CrossRef]
7. Antzoulakos, D.; Rakitzis, A. Runs rules schemes for monitoring process variability. *J. Appl. Stat.* **2010**, *37*, 1231–1247. [CrossRef]
8. Rakitzis, A.C. On the performance of modified runs rules charts with estimated parameters. *Commun. Stat. Simul. Comput.* **2017**, *46*, 1360–1380. [CrossRef]
9. Oh, J.; Wei, C.H. On the individuals chart with supplementary runs rules under serial dependence. *Methodol. Comput. Appl. Probab.* **2020**, *22*, 1257–1273. [CrossRef]
10. Tran, K.P. The efficiency of the 4-out-of-5 runs rules scheme for monitoring the ratio of population means of a bivariate normal distribution. *Int. J. Reliab. Qual. Saf. Eng.* **2016**, *23*, 1650020. [CrossRef]
11. Tran, K.P.; Castagliola, P.; Celano, G. Monitoring the ratio of two normal variables using Run Rules type control charts. *Int. J. Prod. Res.* **2015**, *54*, 1670–1688. [CrossRef]
12. Tran, K.P.; Castagliola, P.; Celano, G. Monitoring the ratio of two normal variables using EWMA type control charts. *Qual. Reliab. Eng. Int.* **2016**, *32*, 1853–1869. [CrossRef]
13. Tran, K.P.; Knoth, S. Steady-State ARL analysis of ARL-unbiased EWMA-RZ control chart monitoring the ratio of two normal variables. *Qual. Reliab. Eng. Int.* **2018**, *34*, 377–390. [CrossRef]
14. Tran, K.P.; Castagliola, P.; Celano, G. Monitoring the ratio of population means of a bivariate normal distribution using CUSUM type control charts. *Stat. Pap.* **2016**, *59*, 387–413. [CrossRef]

15. Shamma, S.E.; Amin, R.W.; Shamma, A.K. A double exponentially weigiited moving average control procedure with variable sampling intervals. *Commun. Stat.-Simul. Comput.* **1991**, *20*, 511–528. [CrossRef]
16. Shamma, S.E.; Shamma, A.K. Development and evaluation of control charts using double exponentially weighted moving averages. *Int. J. Qual. Reliab. Manag.* **1992**, *9*, 6. [CrossRef]
17. Zhang, L.; Chen, G. An extended EWMA mean chart. *Qual. Technol. Quant. Manag.* **2005**, *2*, 39–52. [CrossRef]
18. Mahmoud, M.A.; Woodall, W.H. An evaluation of the double exponentially weighted moving average control chart. *Commun. Stat. -Simul. Comput.* **2010**, *39*, 933–949. [CrossRef]
19. Alevizakos, V.; Koukouvinos, C. A double exponentially weighted moving average chart for time between events. *Commun. Stat. -Simul. Comput.* **2020**, *49*, 2765–2784. [CrossRef]
20. Adeoti, O.A.; Malela-Majika, J.-C. Double exponentially weighted moving average control chart with supplementary runs-rules. *Qual. Technol. Quant. Manag.* **2020**, *17*, 149–172. [CrossRef]
21. Malela-Majika, J.-C. New distribution-free memory-type control charts based on the Wilcoxon rank-sum statistic. *Qual. Technol. Quant. Manag.* **2021**, *18*, 135–155. [CrossRef]
22. Alevizakos, V.; Chatterjee, K.; Koukouvinos, C. The triple exponentially weighted moving average control chart. *Qual. Technol. Quant. Manag.* **2021**, *18*, 326–354. [CrossRef]
23. Alevizakos, V.; Chatterjee, K.; Koukouvinos, C. A triple exponentially weighted moving average control chart for monitoring time between events. *Qual. Reliab. Eng. Int.* **2021**, *37*, 1059–1079. [CrossRef]
24. Chatterjee, K.; Koukouvinos, C.; Lappa, A. A new S2-TEWMA control chart for monitoring process dispersion. *Qual. Reliab. Eng. Int.* **2021**, *37*, 1334–1354. [CrossRef]
25. Letshedi, T.I.; Malela-Majika, J.-C.; Castagliola, P.; Shongwe, S.C. Distribution-free triple EWMA control chart for monitoring the process location using the Wilcoxon rank-sum statistic with fast initial response feature. *Qual. Reliab. Eng. Int.* **2021**, *37*, 1996–2013. [CrossRef]
26. Nguyen, H.D.; Tran, K.P.; Heuchenne, C. Monitoring the ratio of two normal variables using variable sampling interval exponentially weighted moving average control charts. *Qual. Reliab. Eng. Int.* **2019**, *35*, 439–460. [CrossRef]
27. Nguyen, H.D.; Tran, K.P.; Heuchenne, H.L. CUSUM control charts with variable sampling interval for monitoring the ratio of two normal variables. *Qual. Reliab. Eng. Int.* **2019**, *36*, 474–497. [CrossRef]
28. Cedilnik, A.; Košmelj, K.; Blejec, A. The distribution of the ratio of jointly normal variables. *Metodoloski Zv.* **2004**, *1*, 99–108. [CrossRef]
29. Pham-Gia, T.; Turkkan, N.; Marchand, E. Density of the ratio of two normal random variables and applications. *Commun. Stat. Theory Methods* **2006**, *35*, 1569–1591. [CrossRef]
30. Oliveira, A.; Oliveira, T.; Macías, S.; Antonio. Distribution function for the ratio of two normal random variables. *AIP Conf. Proc.* **2015**, *1648*, 840005. [CrossRef]
31. Geary, R.C. The Frequency Distribution of the quotient of two normal variates. *J. R. Stat. Soc.* **1930**, *93*, 442–446. [CrossRef]
32. Sun, G.; Hu, X.; Xie, F.; Zhou, X.; Jiang, C. One-Sided double exponentially weighted moving average control charts for monitoring the ratio of two normal variables. *Sci. Iran.* **2022**. *under review*.
33. Reynolds, M.R.; Amin, R.W.; Arnold, J.C. CUSUM Charts with variable sampling intervals. *Technometrics* **1990**, *32*, 371–384.
34. Haq, A.; Akhtar, S. Auxiliary information based maximum EWMA and DEWMA charts with variable sampling intervals for process mean and variance. *Commun. Stat. -Theory Methods* **2020**, *51*, 3985–4005. [CrossRef]
35. Malela-Majika, J.-C.; Rapoo, E. Distribution-free cumulative sum and exponentially weighted moving average control charts based on the Wilcoxon rank-sum statistic using ranked set sampling for monitoring mean shifts. *J. Stat. Comput. Simul.* **2016**, *86*, 3715–3734. [CrossRef]

Article

Generating Optimal Discrete Analogue of the Generalized Pareto Distribution under Bayesian Inference with Applications

Hanan Haj Ahmad [1,*] and Ehab M. Almetwally [2,3]

[1] Department of Basic Science, Preparatory Year Deanship, King Faisal University, Hofuf 31982, Saudi Arabia
[2] Department of Statistical, Faculty of Business Administration, Delta University for Science and Technology, Gamasa 11152, Egypt; ehab.metwaly@deltauniv.edu.eg
[3] The Scientific Association for Studies and Applied Research, Al Manzalah 35646, Egypt; ehabxp_2009@hotmail.com
* Correspondence: hhajahmed@kfu.edu.sa

Abstract: This paper studies three discretization methods to formulate discrete analogues of the well-known continuous generalized Pareto distribution. The generalized Pareto distribution provides a wide variety of probability spaces, which support threshold exceedances, and hence, it is suitable for modeling many failure time issues. Bayesian inference is applied to estimate the discrete models with different symmetric and asymmetric loss functions. The symmetric loss function being used is the squared error loss function, while the two asymmetric loss functions are the linear exponential and general entropy loss functions. A detailed simulation analysis was performed to compare the performance of the Bayesian estimation using the proposed loss functions. In addition, the applicability of the optimal discrete generalized Pareto distribution was compared with other discrete distributions. The comparison was based on different goodness-of-fit criteria. The results of the study reveal that the discretized generalized Pareto distribution is quite an attractive alternative to other discrete competitive distributions.

Keywords: discretization methods; Bayesian estimation; symmetric and asymmetric loss functions; prior distribution; simulation analysis; Monte Carlo Markov chain; goodness-of-fit measures

MSC: 65C20; 60E05; 62P30; 62L15

Citation: Haj Ahmad, H.; Almetwally, E.M. Generating Optimal Discrete Analogue of the Generalized Pareto Distribution under Bayesian Inference with Applications. *Symmetry* **2022**, *14*, 1457. https://doi.org/10.3390/sym14071457

Academic Editors: Arne Johannssen, Nataliya Chukhrova and Quanxin Zhu

Received: 20 June 2022
Accepted: 14 July 2022
Published: 16 July 2022

Publisher's Note: MDPI stays neutral with regard to jurisdictional claims in published maps and institutional affiliations.

Copyright: © 2022 by the authors. Licensee MDPI, Basel, Switzerland. This article is an open access article distributed under the terms and conditions of the Creative Commons Attribution (CC BY) license (https://creativecommons.org/licenses/by/4.0/).

1. Introduction

The amount of data available in nature has become larger, demanding new statistical distributions to modify the description of each phenomenon or experiment under study. Most lifetime data are continuous, while they are discrete in observation, which leads to a need for appropriate methods to discretize the continuous distribution to better fit these data. Almost always, the observed values are in fact discrete because they are restrained to only a finite number of decimal places and cannot really create all points in a continuum. In some other cases, because of the accuracy of the measuring apparatus or the need to save space, continuous variables are measured by the frequencies of separate class intervals, whose union creates the whole range of random variables, and multinomial law is used to model this situation. Therefore, considering them as discrete values is more appropriate. Even for a continuous life experiment, records in an interval of time result in a discrete model, which seems more suitable than a continuous model.

Recently, many discrete distributions have been identified, particularly in reliability and survival analyses. For a special description and the role of discrete distributions, one may refer to [1–8], among others. Hence, many authors have conducted much work to originate and develop discrete reliability theory from various points of view.

The characterization of continuous random variables can be performed either by their probability density function (pdf), cumulative distribution function (CDF), moments, hazard rate functions, or others. Usually, creating a discrete analogue from a continuous distribution is based on the principle of preserving one or more characteristic properties of the continuous one. Consequently, different ways to discretize a continuous distribution appear in the literature, depending on the property the researcher aims to preserve (see, for example, [9,10]). In [11], the author provided an extensive survey of different discretization methods that preserve different functions.

There are many useful tips for creating discrete random variables from continuous ones: through discretization, data can actually be summarized and simplified; in addition, they can also become easier to understand, use, and explain for researchers (see [12]). Other tests appearing in the literature are suitable for both discrete and continuous distributions (see, for example, [13,14]).

Therefore, it is desirable to study a suitable discrete distribution created from the underlying continuous models.

In the present paper, we discretize the continuous generalized Pareto distribution (GPD) using three different discretization methods. Almost all authors have used one discretization method, which depends on the survival function. In [6,7], discrete normal and discrete Rayleigh distributions were introduced, respectively, and the author used the survival discretization approach. Using the same approach, discrete Burr type II was studied in [15]. Additionally, [16] introduced the discrete additive Weibull distribution (see also [17–23]). However, there remains a need to improve discrete models and generate new ones for the sake of describing and fitting the huge amount of data that appear and spread evenly throughout humans' daily lives. Further, [24] discussed the discrete odd Perks-G class of distributions. Reference [25] introduced a new novel discrete distribution with an application to COVID-19, and [26] obtained a discrete Weibull Marshall–Olkin family of distributions.

We aim to discretize the GPD since it has extensive applications and can model many real-life distributions. Recently, many authors have studied the continuous GPD; for example, one may refer to [27], in which the authors discussed baseline methods for parameter estimation. The authors of [28] performed statistical inference of the dynamic conditional GPD with weather and air quality factors, and [29] discussed outlier-robust truncated maximum likelihood parameter estimators of the GPD. Reference [30] introduced risk analysis using the GPD.

The originality of this work stems from the fact that no earlier research has been conducted in this area using the suggested discretization method and compared it with other methods from a Bayesian point of view. Symmetric and asymmetric loss functions are performed in the Bayesian estimation method using different parameter values. Therefore, the main objective of this paper is to illustrate the efficiency and performance of discrete generalized Pareto distributions (DGPDs) for modeling different COVID-19 daily death cases.

The rest of this paper is organized as follows: Section 2 contains the model description and the discretization methods. Section 3 presents Bayesian inference for unknown parameters, and both point and interval estimations are performed for the three DGPDs. In Section 4, the simulation study is described. Real data examples are provided in Section 5. Finally, conclusions are provided in Section 6.

2. Model Description and Discretization Methods

The generalized Pareto distribution is a continuous distribution with two parameters. However, its continuous distributional form is limited in characterizing data of discrete forms. Discretizing the GPD, therefore, produces a consequent distribution that accommodates count data while preserving the vital tail-modeling feature of the GPD. In this paper, we perform three discrete versions of the two-parameter GPD and use these counterparts to model real-life data.

The probability density function (pdf) of the continuous GPD is given as

$$f(x;\theta,\lambda) = \begin{cases} \frac{1}{\lambda}\left(1+\frac{\theta}{\lambda}x\right)^{-(1+\frac{1}{\theta})} & \theta \neq 0 \\ \frac{1}{\lambda}e^{-x/\lambda} & \theta = 0 \end{cases}, \quad (1)$$

and the cumulative distribution function (CDF) is given by

$$F(x;\theta,\lambda) = \begin{cases} 1-\left(1+\frac{\theta}{\lambda}x\right)^{-\frac{1}{\theta}} & \theta \neq 0 \\ 1-e^{-x/\lambda} & \theta = 0 \end{cases}, \quad (2)$$

where $\lambda > 0$ is the scale parameter, and θ is the shape parameter, $-\infty < \theta < \infty$. The domain of the random variable x depends on the value of θ, particularly whether it is positive or negative; hence, we have two cases: first, when $\theta > 0$, $x > 0$, and when $\theta < 0$, the support of x will be bounded, i.e., $0 < x < -\frac{\lambda}{\theta}$. For $\theta > 0$, the GPD is the well-known Pareto distribution. When $\theta \to 0$, the GPD reduces to the exponential distribution, as shown in Equation (1).

The GPD has a mean of $(\lambda/(1-\theta))$ and a variance $\frac{\lambda^2}{(1-\theta)^2(1-2\theta)}$, provided $\theta < 0.5$. The survival function $S(x;\theta,\lambda)$ and the hazard rate function HR are given, respectively, as follows:

$$S(x;\theta,\lambda) = \left(1+\frac{\theta x}{\lambda}\right)^{-\frac{1}{\theta}}, \quad (3)$$

and

$$h(x;\theta,\lambda) = \frac{1}{\lambda}\left(1+\frac{\theta}{\lambda}x\right)^{-1}. \quad (4)$$

The three discretization methods are presented in the next subsections. The first method aims to preserve the survival function, while the second method preserves the pdf, and the third method preserves the hazard rate.

2.1. Survival Discretization Method

The probability mass function (*pmf*) of a discrete distribution is defined by [6,7] as follows:

$$P(X=k) = S(k) - S(k+1), k = 0,1,2,\ldots \quad (5)$$

where $S(x)$ is the survival function given by Equation (3). Hence, the *pmf* of the first discrete generalized Pareto distribution (DGPD1) is

$$P(X=k) = \left(1+\frac{\theta k}{\lambda}\right)^{-\frac{1}{\theta}} - \left(1+\frac{\theta(k+1)}{\lambda}\right)^{-\frac{1}{\theta}} \quad (6)$$

The CDF of the DGPD1 distribution in the survival discretization method can be written as:

$$P(X<k) = F(k+1) = 1 - \left(1+\frac{\theta(k+1)}{\lambda}\right)^{-\frac{1}{\theta}} \quad (7)$$

2.2. Methodology II

In this method, the *pmf* of the discrete random variable is derived as an analogue of the continuous random variable with pdf $f(x)$ as

$$P(X=k) = \frac{f(k)}{\sum_{j=0}^{\infty}f(j)}, \quad k=0,1,2,\ldots \quad (8)$$

For more details and examples of this method, one can refer to [11]. When applying this method to the continuous GPD, we perceive a second discrete distribution, namely, DGPD2. Accordingly, the *pmf* can be written as:

$$P(X = k) = \frac{\left(1 + \frac{\theta k}{\lambda}\right)^{-(\frac{1}{\theta}+1)}}{\left(\frac{\theta}{\lambda}\right)^{-(\frac{1}{\theta}+1)} \zeta\left(1 + \frac{1}{\theta}, \frac{\lambda}{\theta}\right)}, \quad k = 0, 1, 2, \ldots. \quad (9)$$

The corresponding CDF is derived as

$$P(X < k) = \frac{1}{\left(\frac{\theta}{\lambda}\right)^{-(\frac{1}{\theta}+1)} \zeta\left(1 + \frac{1}{\theta}, \frac{\lambda}{\theta}\right)} \sum_{x=0}^{k} \left(1 + \frac{\theta x}{\lambda}\right)^{-(\frac{1}{\theta}+1)}, \quad (10)$$

where $\zeta(s, a) = \sum_{i=0}^{\infty}(\iota + a)^{-s}$ represents the Hurwitz zeta function.

2.3. Methodology III (Hazard Rate)

This methodology preserves the hazard rate function. It is performed as a two-stage method. In the first stage, the continuous random variable X with CDF F(x) defined on [0, +∞) is used to construct a new continuous random variable X_1 with the hazard rate function $h_{X_1}(x) = e^{-F(x)}$, (x ≥ 0). For more details about this methodology, a good reference is [11]. The survival function of the discrete analogue Y is given by

$$P(Y \geq k) = \left(1 - h_{X_1}(1)\right)\left(1 - h_{X_1}(2)\right) \ldots \left(1 - h_{X_1}(k-1)\right), \quad k = 1, 2, \ldots, m. \quad (11)$$

The corresponding *pmf* is then given by

$$P(Y = k) = \begin{cases} h_{X_1}(0), & k = 0, \\ \left(1 - h_{X_1}(1)\right)\left(1 - h_{X_1}(2)\right) \ldots \left(1 - h_{X_1}(k-1)\right) h_{X_1}(k), & k = 1, 2, \ldots, m \\ 0, & \text{otherwise} \end{cases} \quad (12)$$

Note that the range of Y is the value of m (m need not be finite) and is determined so that it satisfies the condition $0 \leq h(y) \leq 1$.

For the GPD model, the hazard rate function of X_1 will be $h_{X_1}(y) = e^{-1+\left(1+\frac{\theta y}{\lambda}\right)^{-\frac{1}{\theta}}}$; hence, the above condition holds. The survival function in Equation (11) for the third version of the discrete GP distribution (DGPD3) is

$$P(Y \geq k) = \prod_{i=1}^{k-1}\left(1 - e^{-1+\left(1+\frac{\theta * i}{\lambda}\right)^{-\frac{1}{\theta}}}\right),$$

Therefore, the CDF is

$$P(Y < k) = 1 - \prod_{i=1}^{k-1}\left(1 - e^{-1+\left(1+\frac{\theta * i}{\lambda}\right)^{-\frac{1}{\theta}}}\right).$$

The corresponding *pmf* is then given by

$$P(Y = k) = \begin{cases} 1, & k = 0 \\ e^{-1+\left(1+\frac{\theta k}{\lambda}\right)^{-\frac{1}{\theta}}} \prod_{i=1}^{k-1}\left(1 - e^{-1+\left(1+\frac{\theta * i}{\lambda}\right)^{-\frac{1}{\theta}}}\right), & k = 1, 2, \ldots, m \end{cases} \quad (13)$$

In Figures 1–3, the *pmfs* of DGPD1, DGPD2, and DGPD3 are plotted, respectively, for different parameter values. They possess a decreasing trend with different selected parameter values.

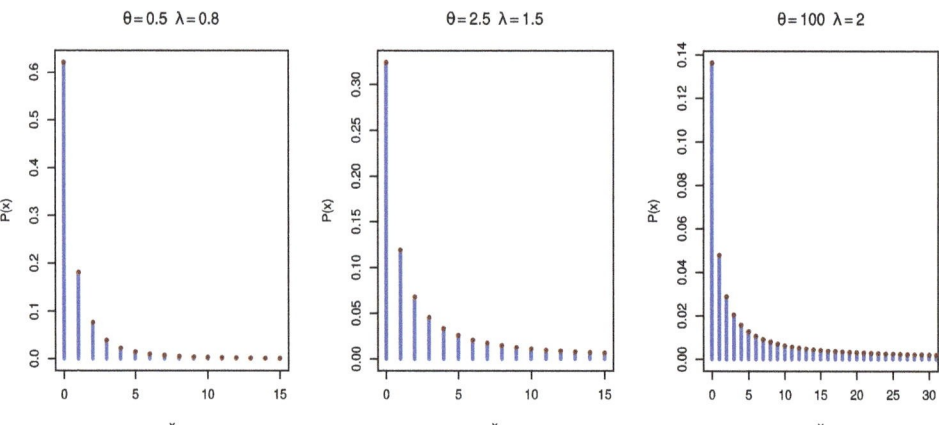

Figure 1. Plots of *pmf* of the DGPD1 distribution with different values of the parameters λ and θ.

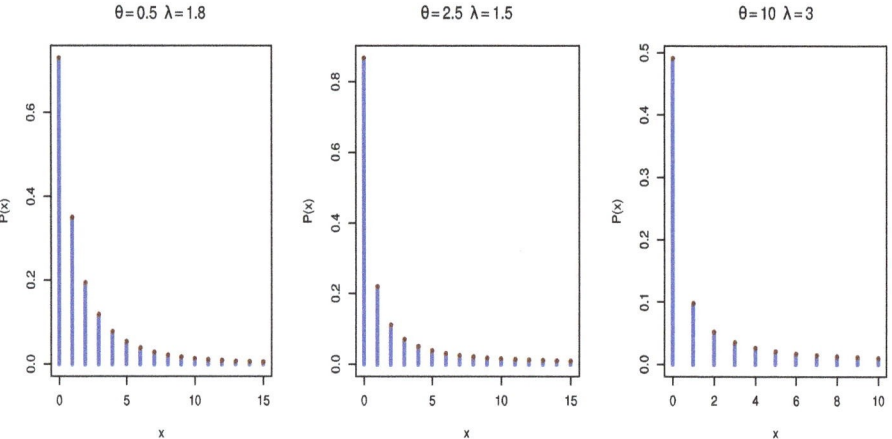

Figure 2. Plots of *pmf* of the DGPD2 distribution with different values of the parameters λ and θ.

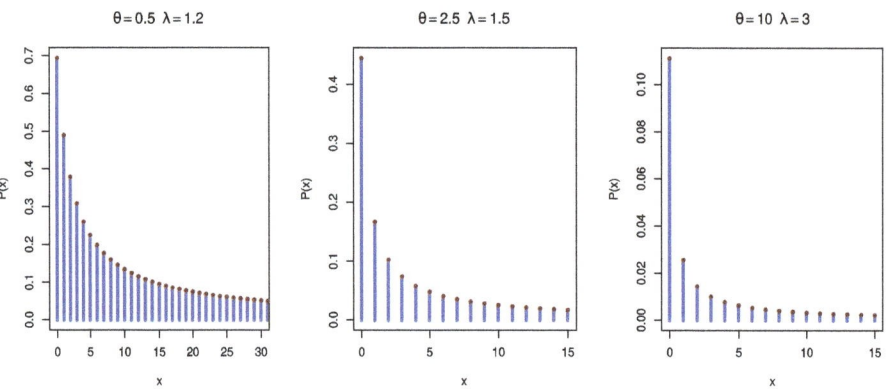

Figure 3. Plots of the *pmf* of the DGPD3 distribution with different values of the parameters λ and θ.

3. Parameter Estimation

In this section, we estimate the unknown parameters of the three versions of the DGPD distribution using the Bayesian estimation method. Numerical techniques are utilized for Bayesian calculations, such as the Monte Carlo Markov Chain (MCMC) technique.

In the Bayesian method, the parameters of the model are assumed to be random variables with a certain distribution called the prior distribution. Usually, the prior information is not available; hence, we need to specify a suitable choice of the prior. In this work, we decided to use a natural joint conjugate prior distribution for the parameters λ and θ, which is known as the modified Lwin Prior; it is defined by assuming a gamma distribution for λ and the Pareto (I) distribution for θ. Hence,

$$\lambda \sim Gamma(a_1, b_1),$$

and

$$\theta|\lambda \sim Pareto(I)(\lambda a_2, b_2),$$

where a_1, a_2, b_1 and b_2 are nonnegative hyperparameters of the assumed distributions. The authors of [31] mentioned that it is more meaningful to express θ conditional on λ rather than vice versa. Moreover, they strongly believed that it is more appropriate to consider that the prior distributions for λ and θ are independent of each other.

Therefore, the prior distributions for λ and θ can be written as

$$\pi_1(\lambda) = \frac{b_1^{a_1}}{\Gamma(a_1)} \lambda^{a_1-1} e^{-b_1 \lambda},$$

$$\pi_2(\theta|\lambda) = \frac{\lambda a_2}{b_2} \left(\frac{\theta}{b_2}\right)^{-a_2 \lambda}.$$

Hence, the joint prior for λ and θ is

$$\pi(\lambda, \theta) \propto \lambda^{a_1} e^{-b_1 \lambda} \left(\frac{\theta}{b_2}\right)^{-a_2 \lambda}. \tag{14}$$

The joint posterior of λ and θ given the data is defined as

$$p(\lambda, \theta / \underline{x}) = \frac{1}{K} L(\underline{x}/\lambda, \theta) \pi(\lambda, \theta),$$

where $L(\underline{x}/\lambda, \theta)$ is the likelihood function of the DGPD, $\pi(\lambda, \theta)$ is the joint prior given by Equation (14), and $K = \iint L(\underline{x}/\lambda, \theta) \pi(\lambda, \theta) d\lambda d\theta$.

The estimation for the parameters of the DGPD can be performed using different loss functions, such as (i) squared error (SE), (ii) LINEX, and (iii) general entropy (GE) loss functions. The performance of the estimators using the said loss functions was investigated using a simulation study. The bias, the mean square error (MSE), and the length of the credible interval were used as criteria for determining the superiority of the respective estimates.

3.1. Loss Functions

The following loss functions are used for posterior estimation.

3.1.1. Squared Error (SE) Loss Function

Assuming the SE loss function, Bayesian estimation for the parameters λ and θ is defined as the mean or expected value with respect to the joint posterior:

$$\hat{\lambda}_{SE} = \frac{1}{k} \iint \lambda L(\underline{x}/\lambda, \theta) \pi(\lambda, \theta) d\lambda d\theta, \tag{15}$$

and
$$\hat{\theta}_{SE} = \frac{1}{k} \iint \theta L(\underline{x}/\lambda,\theta) \pi(\lambda,\theta) d\lambda d\theta. \qquad (16)$$

3.1.2. LINEX Loss Function

With the LINEX loss function, Bayesian estimation for the parameters λ and θ are formulated as

$$\begin{aligned}\hat{\lambda}_{LIN} &= -\frac{1}{h} \ln[\frac{1}{K} \iint e^{-h\lambda} L(\underline{x}/\lambda,\theta) \pi(\lambda,\theta) d\lambda d\theta] \\ \hat{\theta}_{LIN} &= -\frac{1}{h} \ln[\frac{1}{K} \iint e^{-h\theta} L(\underline{x}/\lambda,\theta) \pi(\lambda,\theta) d\lambda d\theta].\end{aligned} \qquad (17)$$

3.1.3. General Entropy (GE) Loss Functions

Using the GE loss function, Bayesian estimation for the parameters λ and θ is given by

$$\begin{aligned}\hat{\lambda}_{GE} &= \left(\frac{1}{k} \iint \lambda^{-q} L(\underline{x}/\lambda,\theta) \pi(\lambda,\theta) d\lambda d\theta\right)^{-1/q}, \\ \hat{\theta}_{GE} &= \left(\frac{1}{k} \iint \theta^{-q} L(\underline{x}/\lambda,\theta) \pi(\lambda,\theta) d\lambda d\theta\right)^{-1/q}.\end{aligned} \qquad (18)$$

3.2. Bayesian Estimation

For evaluating the above-expected values and double integration, numerical methods are essential. We opted to use the Markov Chain Monte Carlo (MCMC) technique by using the Gibbs sampling method and by formulating the suitable R code. For more details, one may refer to [32]. Many authors have used Bayesian estimation for different lifetime models with many real data applications (see, for example, [33–35]).

Since we implement three different discretization methods on the GP distribution, we have to deal with three cases of Bayesian inference based on the different *pmfs* of DGPDs that are written in Equations (6), (9), and (13).

3.2.1. Case 1

When applying the survival discretization method, we obtain DGPD1 with the *pmf* given by Equation 6. The joint posterior density is

$$p_1(\lambda,\theta/\underline{x}) = \frac{1}{K} \prod_{i=1}^{n} \left[\left(1+\frac{\theta x_i}{\lambda}\right)^{-\frac{1}{\theta}} - \left(1+\frac{\theta x_i+1}{\lambda}\right)^{-\frac{1}{\theta}}\right] \lambda^{a_1} e^{-b_1\lambda} \left(\frac{\theta}{b_2}\right)^{-a_2\lambda} \qquad (19)$$

$$= G_\lambda(a_1+1, b_1) Q(\lambda,\theta),$$

where $Q(\lambda,\theta) = \frac{1}{K} \prod_{i=1}^{n} \left[\left(1+\frac{\theta x_i}{\lambda}\right)^{-\frac{1}{\theta}} - \left(1+\frac{\theta x_i+1}{\lambda}\right)^{-\frac{1}{\theta}}\right] \left(\frac{\theta}{b_2}\right)^{-a_2\lambda}$, and $G(.,.)$ represents the gamma distribution.

Bayesian estimation for the parameters λ and θ using the SE loss function is performed using Equations (15) and (16) with the posterior density Equation (19), respectively:

$$\hat{\lambda}_{SE} = \frac{1}{k} \iint \prod_{i=1}^{n} \left[\left(1+\frac{\theta x_i}{\lambda}\right)^{-\frac{1}{\theta}} - \left(1+\frac{\theta x_i+1}{\lambda}\right)^{-\frac{1}{\theta}}\right] \lambda^{a_1+1} e^{-b_1\lambda} \left(\frac{\theta}{b_2}\right)^{-a_2\lambda} d\lambda d\theta,$$

$$\hat{\theta}_{SE} = \frac{1}{k} \iint \prod_{i=1}^{n} \left[\left(1+\frac{\theta x_i}{\lambda}\right)^{-\frac{1}{\theta}} - \left(1+\frac{\theta x_i+1}{\lambda}\right)^{-\frac{1}{\theta}}\right] \theta^{-a_2\lambda+1} \lambda^{a_1} e^{-b_1\lambda} (b_2)^{a_2\lambda} d\lambda d\theta.$$

For the LINEX loss function, Bayesian estimation is obtained by using Equation (17) and the posterior density Equation (18):

$$\hat{\lambda}_{LIN} = -\frac{1}{h} \ln[\frac{1}{K} \iint \prod_{i=1}^{n} \left[\left(1+\frac{\theta x_i}{\lambda}\right)^{-\frac{1}{\theta}} - \left(1+\frac{\theta x_i+1}{\lambda}\right)^{-\frac{1}{\theta}}\right] \lambda^{a_1} e^{-(b_1+h)\lambda} \left(\frac{\theta}{b_2}\right)^{-a_2\lambda} d\lambda d\theta]$$

$$\hat{\theta}_{LIN} = -\frac{1}{h}\ln[\frac{1}{K}\iint \prod_{i=1}^{n}\left[\left(1+\frac{\theta x_i}{\lambda}\right)^{-\frac{1}{\theta}} - \left(1+\frac{\theta x_i+1}{\lambda}\right)^{-\frac{1}{\theta}}\right]\lambda^{a_1}e^{-b_1\lambda-h\theta}\left(\frac{\theta}{b_2}\right)^{-a_2\lambda}d\lambda d\theta]$$

Bayesian estimation for the parameters λ and λ using the GE loss function is obtained using Equations (18) and (19) and is given by

$$\hat{\lambda}_{GE} = \left(\frac{1}{k}\iint \prod_{i=1}^{n}\left[\left(1+\frac{\theta x_i}{\lambda}\right)^{-\frac{1}{\theta}} - \left(1+\frac{\theta x_i+1}{\lambda}\right)^{-\frac{1}{\theta}}\right]\lambda^{a_1-q}e^{-b_1\lambda}\left(\frac{\theta}{b_2}\right)^{-a_2\lambda}d\lambda d\theta\right)^{-1/q}$$

3.2.2. Case 2

For the second form of discrete GPD, namely, DGPD2, with the *pmf* given by Equation (9), the joint posterior density is given by

$$p_2(\lambda,\theta/\underline{x}) = \frac{1}{K}\prod_{i=1}^{n}\left[\frac{\left(1+\frac{\theta x_i}{\lambda}\right)^{-(\frac{1}{\theta}+1)}\theta^{-a_2\lambda+(\frac{1}{\theta}+1)}}{b_2^{-a_2\lambda}\varsigma\left(1+\frac{1}{\theta},\frac{\lambda}{\theta}\right)}\right]\lambda^{a_1-(\frac{1}{\theta}+1)}e^{-b_1\lambda} \quad (20)$$

$$= G_\lambda\left(a_1-\frac{1}{\theta},b_1\right)R(\lambda,\theta),$$

where $R(\lambda,\theta)= \frac{1}{K}\prod_{i=1}^{n}\left[\frac{\left(1+\frac{\theta x_i}{\lambda}\right)^{-(\frac{1}{\theta}+1)}\theta^{-a_2\lambda+(\frac{1}{\theta}+1)}}{b_2^{-a_2\lambda}\varsigma\left(1+\frac{1}{\theta},\frac{\lambda}{\theta}\right)}\right]$.

Bayesian estimation for the parameters λ and θ using the SE loss function is given as

$$\hat{\lambda}_{SE} = \frac{1}{k}\iint \prod_{i=1}^{n}\left[\frac{\left(1+\frac{\theta x_i}{\lambda}\right)^{-(\frac{1}{\theta}+1)}\theta^{-a_2\lambda+(\frac{1}{\theta}+1)}}{b_2^{-a_2\lambda}\varsigma\left(1+\frac{1}{\theta},\frac{\lambda}{\theta}\right)}\right]\lambda^{a_1-\frac{1}{\theta}}e^{-b_1\lambda}d\lambda d\theta,$$

$$\hat{\theta}_{SE} = \frac{1}{k}\iint \prod_{i=1}^{n}\left[\frac{\left(1+\frac{\theta x_i}{\lambda}\right)^{-(\frac{1}{\theta}+1)}\theta^{-a_2\lambda+(\frac{1}{\theta}+2)}}{b_2^{-a_2\lambda}\varsigma\left(1+\frac{1}{\theta},\frac{\lambda}{\theta}\right)}\right]\lambda^{a_1-(\frac{1}{\theta}+1)}e^{-b_1\lambda}d\lambda d\theta.$$

For the LINEX loss function, Bayesian estimation is found by the following integrations:

$$\hat{\lambda}_{LIN} = -\frac{1}{h}\ln[\frac{1}{K}\iint \prod_{i=1}^{n}\left[\frac{\left(1+\frac{\theta x_i}{\lambda}\right)^{-(\frac{1}{\theta}+1)}\theta^{-a_2\lambda+(\frac{1}{\theta}+1)}}{b_2^{-a_2\lambda}\varsigma\left(1+\frac{1}{\theta},\frac{\lambda}{\theta}\right)}\right]\lambda^{a_1-(\frac{1}{\theta}+1)}e^{-(b_1+h)\lambda}d\lambda d\theta],$$

$$\hat{\theta}_{LIN} = -\frac{1}{h}\ln[\frac{1}{K}\iint \prod_{i=1}^{n}\left[\frac{\left(1+\frac{\theta x_i}{\lambda}\right)^{-(\frac{1}{\theta}+1)}\theta^{-a_2\lambda+(\frac{1}{\theta}+1)}}{b_2^{-a_2\lambda}\varsigma\left(1+\frac{1}{\theta},\frac{\lambda}{\theta}\right)}\right]\lambda^{a_1-(\frac{1}{\theta}+1)}e^{-b_1\lambda-h\theta}d\lambda d\theta]$$

For the GE loss function, Bayesian estimation for parameters λ and θ is given by

$$\hat{\lambda}_{GE} = \left(\frac{1}{k}\iint \prod_{i=1}^{n}\left[\frac{\left(1+\frac{\theta x_i}{\lambda}\right)^{-(\frac{1}{\theta}+1)}\theta^{-a_2\lambda+(\frac{1}{\theta}+1)}}{b_2^{-a_2\lambda}\varsigma\left(1+\frac{1}{\theta},\frac{\lambda}{\theta}\right)}\right]\lambda^{a_1-(\frac{1}{\theta}+1)-q}e^{-b_1\lambda}d\lambda d\theta\right)^{-1/q}$$

$$\hat{\theta}_{GE} = \left(\frac{1}{k}\iint\prod_{i=1}^{n}\left[\frac{\left(1+\frac{\theta x_i}{\lambda}\right)^{-(\frac{1}{\theta}+1)}e^{-a_2\lambda+(\frac{1}{\theta}+1)-q}}{b_2^{-a_2}\zeta\left(1+\frac{1}{\theta},\frac{\lambda}{\theta}\right)}\right]\lambda^{a_1-(\frac{1}{\theta}+1)}e^{-b_1\lambda}d\lambda d\theta\right)^{-1/q}$$

3.2.3. Case 3

The third discretization method of GP yields DGPD3 with the *pmf* described by Equation (13), and the joint posterior density is

$$p_3(\lambda,\theta/\underline{x}) = \frac{1}{k}\prod_{j=1}^{n}e^{-1+(1+\frac{\theta x_j}{\lambda})^{-\frac{1}{\theta}}}\left[\prod_{i=1}^{x_j-1}(1-e^{-1+(1+\frac{\theta*i}{\lambda})^{-\frac{1}{\theta}}})\right]\lambda^{a_1}e^{-b_1\lambda}\left(\frac{\theta}{b_2}\right)^{-a_2\lambda}$$

$$= \frac{1}{k}G_\lambda(a_1+1,b_1)S(\lambda,\theta),$$

where $S(\lambda,\theta) = \prod_{j=1}^{n}e^{-1+(1+\frac{\theta x_j}{\lambda})^{-\frac{1}{\theta}}}\left[\prod_{i=1}^{x_j-1}(1-e^{-1+(1+\frac{\theta*i}{\lambda})^{-\frac{1}{\theta}}})\right]\left(\frac{\theta}{b_2}\right)^{-a_2\lambda}.$

Bayesian estimation for the parameters λ and θ using the SE loss function is given as

$$\hat{\lambda}_{SE} = \frac{1}{k}\iint\prod_{j=1}^{n}e^{-1+(1+\frac{\theta x_j}{\lambda})^{-\frac{1}{\theta}}}\left[\prod_{i=1}^{x_j-1}(1-e^{-1+(1+\frac{\theta*i}{\lambda})^{-\frac{1}{\theta}}})\right]\lambda^{a_1+1}e^{-b_1\lambda}\left(\frac{\theta}{b_2}\right)^{-a_2\lambda}d\lambda d\theta, \quad (21)$$

$$\hat{\theta}_{SE} = \frac{1}{k}\iint\prod_{j=1}^{n}e^{-1+(1+\frac{\theta x_j}{\lambda})^{-\frac{1}{\theta}}}\left[\prod_{i=1}^{x_j-1}(1-e^{-1+(1+\frac{\theta*i}{\lambda})^{-\frac{1}{\theta}}})\right]b_2\lambda^{a_1}e^{-b_1\lambda}\left(\frac{\theta}{b_2}\right)^{-a_2\lambda+1}d\lambda d\theta.$$

For the LINEX loss function, Bayesian estimation is found by the following integrations:

$$\hat{\lambda}_{LIN} = -\frac{1}{h}\ln[\frac{1}{K}\iint\prod_{j=1}^{n}e^{-1+(1+\frac{\theta x_j}{\lambda})^{-\frac{1}{\theta}}}\left[\prod_{i=1}^{x_j-1}(1-e^{-1+(1+\frac{\theta*i}{\lambda})^{-\frac{1}{\theta}}})\right]\lambda^{a_1}e^{-(b_1+h)\lambda}\left(\frac{\theta}{b_2}\right)^{-a_2\lambda}d\lambda d\theta],$$

$$\hat{\theta}_{LIN} = -\frac{1}{h}\ln[\frac{1}{K}\iint\prod_{j=1}^{n}e^{-1+(1+\frac{\theta x_j}{\lambda})^{-\frac{1}{\theta}}}\left[\prod_{i=1}^{x_j-1}(1-e^{-1+(1+\frac{\theta*i}{\lambda})^{-\frac{1}{\theta}}})\right]\lambda^{a_1}e^{-b_1\lambda-h\theta}\left(\frac{\theta}{b_2}\right)^{-a_2\lambda}d\lambda d\theta].$$

For the GE loss function, Bayesian estimation for parameters λ and θ is given by

$$\hat{\lambda}_{GE} = \left(\frac{1}{k}\iint\prod_{j=1}^{n}e^{-1+(1+\frac{\theta x_j}{\lambda})^{-\frac{1}{\theta}}}\left[\prod_{i=1}^{x_j-1}(1-e^{-1+(1+\frac{\theta*i}{\lambda})^{-\frac{1}{\theta}}})\right]\lambda^{a_1-q}e^{-b_1\lambda}\left(\frac{\theta}{b_2}\right)^{-a_2\lambda}d\lambda d\theta\right)^{-1/q},$$

$$\hat{\theta}_{GE} = \left(\frac{1}{k}\iint\prod_{j=1}^{n}e^{-1+(1+\frac{\theta x_j}{\lambda})^{-\frac{1}{\theta}}}\left[\prod_{i=1}^{x_j-1}(1-e^{-1+(1+\frac{\theta*i}{\lambda})^{-\frac{1}{\theta}}})\right]b_2^{-q}\lambda^{a_1}e^{-b_1\lambda}\left(\frac{\theta}{b_2}\right)^{-a_2\lambda-q}d\lambda d\theta\right)^{-1/q}.$$

4. Simulation Analysis

To evaluate the performance of the three discrete versions of the continuous GPD, we aim to compare the point estimation of the unknown parameters with respect to bias and MSE. Additionally, a comparison is conducted using the different loss functions described in Section 3. Some interesting conclusions and results are reported at the end of this section.

Random samples were generated with 10,000 iterations using the suitable R code; the different selected values of the parameters λ and θ were {0.5, 3}, and different sample sizes n = {20,50,100} were considered.

The simulation results of point and interval estimations for the three discrete versions of the GPD are reported in Tables 1–3. Figures 4–6 illustrate the MSE for the simulation results in Tables 1–3. The x-axis represents sample sizes, which take values of {20,50,100}.

For a fixed sample size, six different parameter values are presented. Therefore, lambda increases from 0.5 to 3 (the first six points) when theta is 0.5, and lambda increases from 0.5 to 3 (the last six points) when theta is 3.

Table 1. Bayesian inference for DGPD1 (bias, MSE, and length of CI) for different values of parameters.

θ	λ	n		SE			LINEX (−1.5)			LINEX (1.5)			GE (−1.5)			GE (1.5)		
				Bias	MSE	L.CCI	Bias	MSE	L.CCI	Bias	MSE	L.CCI	Bias	MSE	L.CCI	Bias	MSE	L.CCI
0.5	0.5	20	θ	0.0247	0.0887	0.5335	0.0601	0.0194	0.4371	−0.0066	0.0167	0.4630	0.0450	0.0820	0.6443	−0.0870	0.0245	0.4930
			λ	0.2946	0.1284	0.7412	0.3597	0.1870	0.8541	0.2368	0.0866	0.6692	0.3190	0.1458	0.7567	0.1631	0.0586	0.6918
		50	θ	−0.0130	0.0155	0.4394	0.0034	0.0167	0.4526	−0.0289	0.0150	0.4294	−0.0020	0.0155	0.4396	−0.0750	0.0215	0.4590
			λ	0.2666	0.0952	0.6031	0.2901	0.1120	0.6405	0.2429	0.0796	0.5616	0.2764	0.1014	0.6067	0.2132	0.0465	0.5528
		100	θ	−0.0084	0.0112	0.4062	−0.0025	0.0112	0.4070	−0.0144	0.0113	0.4062	−0.0041	0.0110	0.4023	−0.0316	0.0136	0.4360
			λ	0.1827	0.0424	0.3745	0.1923	0.0470	0.3914	0.1729	0.0381	0.3569	0.1872	0.0444	0.3781	0.1586	0.0326	0.3407
	3	20	θ	0.0353	0.0150	0.4610	0.0680	0.0162	0.4588	0.0064	0.0178	0.4533	0.0537	0.0126	0.4755	−0.0642	0.0159	0.4910
			λ	0.0704	0.0555	0.8743	0.1615	0.0852	0.9396	−0.0176	0.0469	0.8464	0.0803	0.0574	0.8773	0.0206	0.0500	0.8675
		50	θ	0.0009	0.0116	0.4267	0.0080	0.0120	0.4324	−0.0062	0.0114	0.4220	0.0057	0.0116	0.4274	−0.0248	0.0131	0.4528
			λ	0.0192	0.0276	0.6226	0.0301	0.0287	0.6274	0.0084	0.0269	0.6189	0.0204	0.0277	0.6217	0.0132	0.0274	0.6259
		100	θ	−0.0080	0.0079	0.3509	−0.0042	0.0079	0.3511	−0.0117	0.0079	0.3508	−0.0054	0.0078	0.3480	−0.0214	0.0087	0.3554
			λ	0.0230	0.0143	0.4554	0.0285	0.0148	0.4601	0.0175	0.0139	0.4513	0.0236	0.0143	0.4552	0.0200	0.0141	0.4526
3	0.5	20	θ	0.0121	0.0751	0.3389	0.0512	0.0107	0.3506	−0.0595	0.0779	0.3306	0.0164	0.0766	0.3387	−0.0935	0.0674	0.3351
			λ	0.2173	0.1645	0.8449	0.4302	0.1759	1.0064	0.2412	0.0961	0.7222	0.2527	0.1297	0.8780	0.2331	0.0514	0.7289
		50	θ	−0.0037	0.0098	0.3079	0.0348	0.0098	0.3335	−0.0405	0.0087	0.2944	0.0005	0.0076	0.3612	−0.0245	0.0080	0.2998
			λ	0.2719	0.1411	0.5948	0.3410	0.1623	0.6569	0.2115	0.0745	0.5119	0.2499	0.1272	0.6932	0.1251	0.0499	0.5576
		100	θ	−0.0321	0.0097	0.3052	0.0018	0.0092	0.3060	−0.0655	0.0061	0.2343	−0.0284	0.0069	0.3509	−0.0151	0.0061	0.2534
			λ	0.1317	0.1330	0.5668	0.3723	0.1380	0.6074	0.2068	0.0598	0.5096	0.2338	0.0148	0.6809	0.1021	0.0371	0.4620
	3	20	θ	0.0039	0.0705	0.3629	0.0430	0.0096	0.4776	−0.0339	0.0090	0.3625	0.0082	0.0071	0.3986	−0.0175	0.0724	0.4327
			λ	0.0440	0.0524	0.8789	0.1402	0.0791	0.9525	−0.0487	0.0489	0.8914	0.0545	0.0538	0.8868	−0.0091	0.0496	0.8982
		50	θ	0.0038	0.0575	0.3339	0.0421	0.0075	0.3526	−0.0333	0.0083	0.3348	0.0080	0.0070	0.3368	−0.0172	0.0167	0.3383
			λ	0.0443	0.0522	0.8095	0.1370	0.0773	0.8957	−0.0451	0.0409	0.8679	0.0544	0.0535	0.7960	−0.0069	0.0497	0.8517
		100	θ	−0.0152	0.0170	0.3049	−0.0080	0.0069	0.3489	−0.0224	0.0073	0.4917	−0.0144	0.0069	0.3049	−0.0192	0.0072	0.2491
			λ	0.0112	0.0233	0.5707	0.0197	0.0240	0.5772	0.0028	0.0228	0.5787	0.0122	0.0234	0.5702	0.0065	0.0231	0.5744

Table 2. Bayesian inference for DGPD2 (bias, MSE, and length of CI) for different values of parameters.

θ	λ	n		SE			LINEX (−1.5)			LINEX (1.5)			GE (−1.5)			GE (1.5)		
				Bias	MSE	L.CCI	Bias	MSE	L.CCI	Bias	MSE	L.CCI	Bias	MSE	L.CCI	Bias	MSE	L.CCI
0.5	0.5	20	θ	−0.1145	0.0668	0.7749	−0.1110	0.0652	0.7740	−0.1177	0.0681	0.7734	−0.1086	0.0630	0.7578	−0.1349	0.0793	0.7870
			λ	−0.4889	0.2491	0.0185	−0.4856	0.2459	0.0247	−0.4911	0.2412	0.0142	−0.4684	0.2296	0.0421	−0.4993	0.2493	0.0039
		50	θ	−0.0972	0.0525	0.7273	−0.0951	0.0518	0.7252	−0.0991	0.0531	0.7284	−0.0945	0.0511	0.7180	−0.1075	0.0574	0.7516
			λ	−0.4901	0.2402	0.0177	−0.4878	0.2380	0.0204	−0.4916	0.2417	0.0157	−0.4732	0.2240	0.0291	−0.4980	0.2480	0.0092
		100	θ	−0.0522	0.0186	0.4950	−0.0515	0.0184	0.4941	−0.0529	0.0187	0.4963	−0.0516	0.0184	0.4927	−0.0550	0.0192	0.4994
			λ	−0.4747	0.2254	0.0255	−0.4696	0.2206	0.0293	−0.4782	0.2288	0.0243	−0.4505	0.2031	0.0335	−0.4919	0.2420	0.0193
	3	20	θ	0.1424	0.0378	0.4501	0.1906	0.0604	0.5041	0.1000	0.0234	0.4023	0.1647	0.0459	0.4579	0.0206	0.0143	0.4190
			λ	−0.0366	0.0591	0.8932	0.0534	0.0699	0.9843	−0.1246	0.0681	0.8693	−0.0265	0.0588	0.9016	−0.0881	0.0641	0.8811
		50	θ	0.0248	0.0145	0.4295	0.0328	0.0154	0.4373	0.0167	0.0138	0.4241	0.0300	0.0147	0.4286	−0.0031	0.0137	0.4048
			λ	−0.0371	0.0312	0.6886	−0.0256	0.0300	0.6766	−0.0487	0.0327	0.6941	−0.0358	0.0310	0.6877	−0.0437	0.0323	0.6971
		100	θ	0.0068	0.0077	0.3405	0.0104	0.0078	0.3384	0.0032	0.0075	0.3367	0.0092	0.0077	0.3346	−0.0056	0.0079	0.3475
			λ	−0.0257	0.0113	0.4118	−0.0213	0.0109	0.4001	−0.0302	0.0117	0.4212	−0.0252	0.0113	0.4104	−0.0283	0.0116	0.4019

Table 2. Cont.

θ	λ	n			SE			LINEX (−1.5)			LINEX (1.5)			GE (−1.5)			GE (1.5)	
				Bias	MSE	L.CCI	Bias	MSE	L.CCI	Bias	MSE	L.CCI	Bias	MSE	L.CCI	Bias	MSE	L.CCI
3	0.5	20	θ	0.0315	0.0547	0.9001	0.0348	0.0549	0.9038	0.0282	0.0543	0.8926	0.0318	0.0547	0.9004	0.0297	0.0546	0.8976
			λ	−0.4798	0.2309	0.0569	−0.4715	0.2240	0.0845	−0.4850	0.2355	0.0409	−0.4503	0.2046	0.1119	−0.4998	0.2498	0.0006
		50	θ	0.0211	0.0169	0.4877	0.0234	0.0171	0.4883	0.0187	0.0166	0.4842	0.0214	0.0169	0.4879	0.0198	0.0168	0.4854
			λ	−0.3902	0.1568	0.2287	−0.3676	0.1406	0.2581	−0.4090	0.1710	0.1935	−0.3388	0.1195	0.2469	−0.4981	0.2490	0.0003
		100	θ	0.0183	0.0085	0.3602	0.0199	0.0086	0.3628	0.0166	0.0083	0.3570	0.0184	0.0085	0.3605	0.0173	0.0084	0.3587
			λ	−0.3494	0.1252	0.1901	−0.3246	0.1087	0.2058	−0.3715	0.1407	0.1709	−0.3002	0.0929	0.1893	−0.4992	0.2049	0.0002
	3	20	θ	0.0932	0.0255	0.6319	0.1333	0.0251	0.3280	0.0544	0.0195	0.5306	0.0975	0.0263	0.5319	0.0719	0.0219	0.5632
			λ	0.0225	0.0618	0.9381	0.1175	0.0857	1.0463	−0.0703	0.0608	0.8915	0.0330	0.0629	0.9506	−0.0309	0.0606	0.8925
		50	θ	0.0546	0.0203	0.5208	0.0640	0.0219	0.5218	0.0453	0.0189	0.5090	0.0556	0.0204	0.5209	0.0495	0.0196	0.5177
			λ	−0.0173	0.0281	0.6513	−0.0059	0.0272	0.6505	−0.0287	0.0293	0.6510	−0.0160	0.0279	0.6504	−0.0238	0.0290	0.6459
		100	θ	0.0451	0.0115	0.3816	0.0495	0.0123	0.3872	0.0406	0.0107	0.3728	0.0455	0.0116	0.3835	0.0426	0.0111	0.3791
			λ	−0.0042	0.0115	0.4137	0.0000	0.0115	0.4164	−0.0083	0.0117	0.4146	−0.0037	0.0115	0.4138	−0.0065	0.0116	0.4162

Table 3. Bayesian inference for DGPD3 (bias, MSE, and length of CI) for different values of parameters.

θ	λ	n			SE			LINEX (−1.5)			LINEX (1.5)			GE (−1.5)			GE (1.5)	
				Bias	MSE	L.CCI	Bias	MSE	L.CCI	Bias	MSE	L.CCI	Bias	MSE	L.CCI	Bias	MSE	L.CCI
0.5	0.5	20	θ	0.0231	0.0552	0.9405	0.0248	0.0552	0.9396	0.0214	0.0550	0.9399	0.0236	0.0552	0.9397	0.0208	0.0552	0.9422
			λ	−0.4908	0.2409	0.0134	−0.4879	0.2381	0.0189	−0.4927	0.2428	0.0097	−0.4710	0.2219	0.0349	−0.4998	0.2498	0.0005
		50	θ	0.0067	0.0134	0.4749	0.0075	0.0135	0.4757	0.0058	0.0133	0.4719	0.0069	0.0134	0.4750	0.0055	0.0133	0.4718
			λ	−0.4505	0.2032	0.0495	−0.4374	0.1916	0.0645	−0.4603	0.2120	0.0397	−0.4064	0.1655	0.0713	−0.4999	0.2499	0.0002
		100	θ	0.0291	0.0124	0.4307	0.0303	0.0134	0.4333	0.0028	0.0131	0.4255	0.0295	0.0130	0.4312	0.0274	0.0131	0.4246
			λ	−0.4204	0.1771	0.0642	−0.4030	0.1628	0.0796	−0.4342	0.1887	0.0521	−0.3742	0.1405	0.0841	−0.4946	0.2446	0.0097
	3	20	θ	0.0783	0.1698	1.3450	0.1181	0.2003	1.3980	0.0418	0.1425	1.2318	0.0989	0.1747	1.3478	−0.0302	0.1534	1.2360
			λ	−0.5967	0.4528	1.0853	−0.4890	0.3254	0.9966	−0.6941	0.5849	1.1111	−0.5818	0.4329	1.0580	−0.6704	0.5575	1.1327
		50	θ	−0.0389	0.0829	0.9246	−0.0219	0.0866	0.9413	−0.0558	0.0793	0.8868	−0.0247	0.0803	0.9205	−0.1120	0.1012	0.9059
			λ	−0.2242	0.0906	0.7755	−0.1974	0.0726	0.6992	−0.2507	0.1108	0.8376	−0.2207	0.0881	0.7653	−0.2414	0.1040	0.8219
		100	θ	−0.0457	0.0799	0.8656	−0.0290	0.0828	0.9041	−0.0622	0.0770	0.8300	−0.0314	0.0769	0.8707	−0.1192	0.0999	0.8511
			λ	−0.2203	0.0876	0.7755	−0.1938	0.0700	0.6992	−0.2466	0.1073	0.8376	−0.2169	0.0851	0.7653	−0.2373	0.1007	0.8219
3	0.5	20	θ	−0.0119	0.0524	0.8664	−0.0101	0.0523	0.8657	−0.0137	0.0524	0.8661	−0.0117	0.0524	0.8664	−0.0129	0.0525	0.8665
			λ	−0.4911	0.2411	0.0129	−0.4884	0.2385	0.0180	−0.4929	0.2429	0.0099	−0.4717	0.2226	0.0330	−0.4998	0.2498	0.0005
		50	θ	0.0029	0.0112	0.4081	0.0036	0.0112	0.4077	0.0022	0.0111	0.4081	0.0030	0.0112	0.4080	0.0025	0.0112	0.4082
			λ	−0.4495	0.2023	0.0525	−0.4360	0.1905	0.0672	−0.4596	0.2113	0.0404	−0.4048	0.1643	0.0736	−0.4999	0.2499	0.0002
		100	θ	0.0034	0.0049	0.2857	0.0040	0.0049	0.2853	0.0029	0.0049	0.2860	0.0035	0.0049	0.2857	0.0031	0.0049	0.2859
			λ	−0.4238	0.1799	0.0538	−0.4064	0.1654	0.0653	−0.4375	0.1916	0.0439	−0.3757	0.1415	0.0652	−0.4986	0.2486	0.0026
	3	20	θ	−0.0261	0.0370	0.6937	0.0126	0.0297	0.6419	−0.0640	0.0320	0.6453	−0.0218	0.0317	0.5972	−0.0478	0.0386	0.6255
			λ	−0.6123	0.4187	0.7591	−0.5002	0.3003	0.8630	−0.7168	0.5547	0.7219	−0.5969	0.4002	0.7670	−0.6900	0.5200	0.7443
		50	θ	−0.0277	0.0274	0.5896	−0.0182	0.0268	0.5730	−0.0372	0.0282	0.6052	−0.0267	0.0273	0.5874	−0.0331	0.0280	0.6017
			λ	−0.2226	0.0826	0.7089	−0.2005	0.0687	0.6596	−0.2449	0.0978	0.7456	−0.2198	0.0807	0.7030	−0.2368	0.0925	0.7363
		100	θ	−0.0252	0.0270	0.5209	−0.0159	0.0264	0.5730	−0.0345	0.0277	0.6052	−0.0242	0.0269	0.5874	−0.0305	0.0276	0.6017
			λ	−0.2207	0.0816	0.6709	−0.1990	0.0680	0.6596	−0.2423	0.0965	0.7456	−0.2179	0.0798	0.7030	−0.2344	0.0913	0.7363

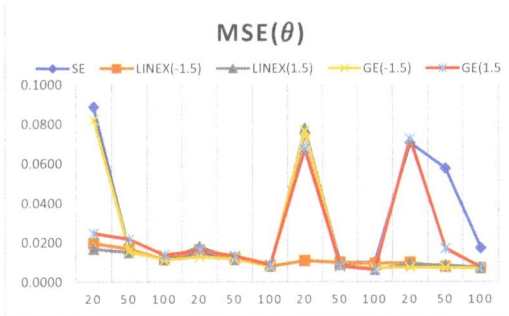
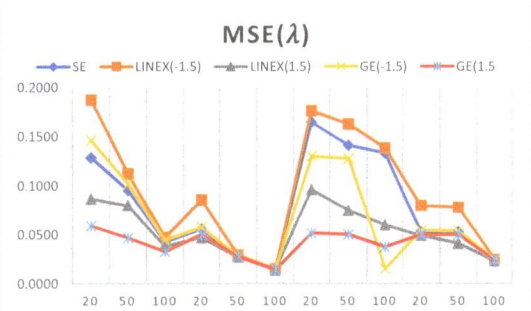

Figure 4. MSE of Bayesian inference for DGPD1.

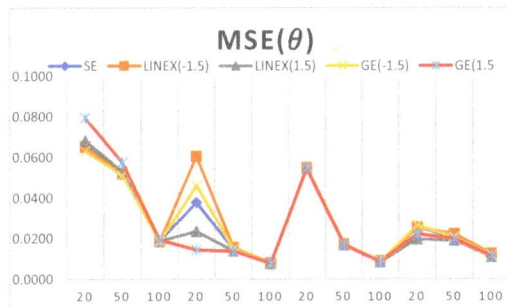
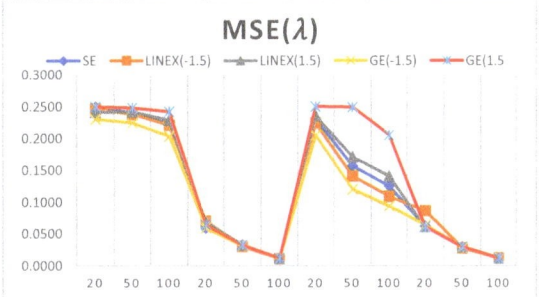

Figure 5. MSE of Bayesian inference for DGPD2.

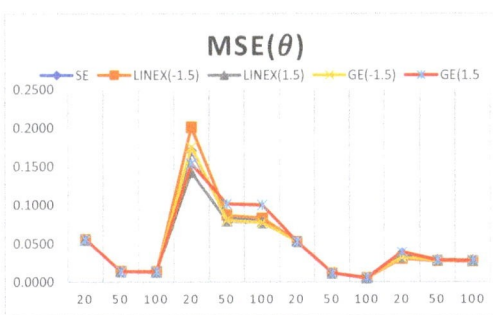
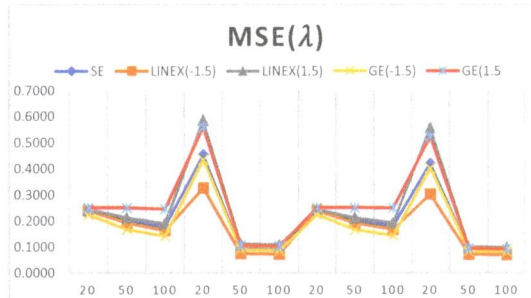

Figure 6. MSE of Bayesian inference for DGPD3.

The main simulation analysis points are as follows:

- It can be observed that the estimated values of the model parameters converge to their true values when increasing the sample size. This can be observed since the MSE and biases decrease as the sample size increases, which shows that the proposed estimators are consistent in nature.
- For a small sample size, the LINEX loss function provides the lowest values of MSE and bias when estimating θ, while the GE loss function provides the lowest values of MSE and bias when estimating λ.
- For a large sample size, the LINEX loss function provides the lowest values of MSE and bias when estimating both parameters λ and θ.

- In almost all cases, the LINEX and GE loss functions produce minimum bias and MSE values, and this is true for different sample sizes. Hence, LINEX and GE are recommended over SE in this study.
- For the credible CI, it is noted that the shortest interval length is obtained when using the LINEX loss function.
- The SE loss function has some advantages over other loss functions under some conditions; for example, when $\lambda = \theta = 3$ and for a small sample size (n = 20), the bias and MSE attain their minimum values when estimating θ.
- For a fixed value of λ, the bias decreases when the shape parameter θ increases. Similarly, for a fixed value of θ, the bias decreases when λ increases.
- The length of the credible interval decreases when the sample size increases, and this is true for all loss functions under study.

When comparing the performance of the three DGPD analogues, we observe the following:

- For almost all small-size cases, the first discrete analogue DGPD1 has the least bias and lowest MSE for different parameter values.
- For a large sample size, it is observed that the MSE attains its minimum values when using the second analogue, DGPD2.
- The advantage of using the third analogue, DGPD3, appears when finding the credible interval for the parameter θ using the GE loss function, where the interval length reaches its minimum value.

5. Real Data Examples

In this section, some real data are utilized for the purpose of proving the efficiency of the discrete analogues of the GP distribution.

Some goodness-of-fit measures are used, such as the chi-square test, Kolmogorov–Smirnov (KS), Akaike information criterion (AIC), Bayesian information criterion (BIC), corrected Akaike information criterion (CAIC), and Hannan–Quinn information criterion (HQIC). As a model selection criterion, the researcher should choose the model with the minimum value from the above-mentioned measures of fit.

Data set 1: The first set of data represents a 42-day COVID-19 data set from the United States Virgin Islands, recorded between 19 April 2021 and 30 May 2021. These data comprise daily new deaths. The data are as follows: 11, 2, 3, 10, 10, 4, 12, 0, 10, 3, 5, 12, 6, 9, 13, 4, 10, 26, 0, 32, 0, 0, 13, 10, 3, 20, 5, 6, 0, 3, 18, 2, 18, 14, 24, 7, 0, 30, 16, 26, 17, 23. The data are available on the Worldometer website at [36].

Table 4 summarizes the values of goodness-of-fit measures when comparing the DGPD with nine different discrete models, including those with one, two, and three parameters. The competitive models are discrete Marshal Olkin inverted Topp–Leone (DMOITL), which is introduced in [37], Discrete Burr (DB), which is introduced in [38], discrete Weibull (DW), which is introduced in [39], discrete inverse Weibull (DIW), which is obtained in [40], negative binomial NB in [41], Poisson, discrete generalized exponential (DGE), which is introduced in [42], discrete alpha power inverse Lomax (DAPIL) in [19], and discrete Lindley (DL) in [43].

Table 4 reveals the efficiency and suitability of DGPD1 for modeling COVID-19 cases with respect to other discrete candidate models, while Figure 7 shows PMF and CDF for the fitted DGPD1 of data set 1. The distribution that has smaller values of key statistics, such as AIC, BIC, CAIC, HQIC, KS-test statistics, and Chi2-test statistics, is generally the one that fits the data the best. These statistics show that among all fitted models, the DGPD1 has the lowest KS-statistical, Chi2-statistical, AIC, BIC, CAIC, and HQIC values. The P-value of KS-test statistics and Chi2-test statistics are compared at the 5% level of significance. For data set 1, Table 5 elucidates the performance of Bayesian estimation, which is marginally better than the well-known classical maximum likelihood estimation (MLE) with respect to minimizing SE.

Table 4. MLE estimates with goodness-of-fit test and different measures for different alternative models.

		Estimates	KS-Test	Chi2-Test	AIC	CAIC	BIC	HQIC
DGP	θ	−0.4052	0.1429	35.2645	284.7945	285.1021	288.2698	286.0683
	λ	15.6070	0.3581	0.3164				
DMOITL	θ	16.5627	0.1429	49.3821	297.3120	297.6197	300.7873	298.5859
	λ	1.8434	0.3581	0.0255				
DB	α	1.6460	0.3209	94.9821	325.9139	326.2216	329.3892	327.1877
	θ	0.7401	0.0004	0.0000				
DW	λ	0.9297	0.1429	38.7117	288.3261	288.6338	291.8014	289.6000
	β	1.0837	0.3581	0.1925				
DIW	λ	0.0642	0.2034	64.6983	315.3363	315.6439	318.8116	316.6101
	β	0.7797	0.0618	0.0005				
NB	P	0.8015	0.3072	28307.5450	431.9343	432.0343	433.6720	432.5712
			0.0007	0.0000				
Poisson	λ	10.4048	0.3277	677700.3282	482.2590	482.3590	483.9967	482.8960
			0.0002	0.0000				
DGE	α	0.9124	0.1595	38.3097	288.6633	288.9710	292.1386	289.9371
	θ	0.9986	0.2359	0.2049				
DAPL	α	48.5629	0.1804	44.5099	305.8090	306.4406	311.0221	307.7198
	θ	3.1137	0.1301	0.0697				
	λ	0.5752						
DL	θ	0.8437	0.1231	51.3964	289.7677	289.8677	291.5054	290.4046
			0.5479	0.0163				

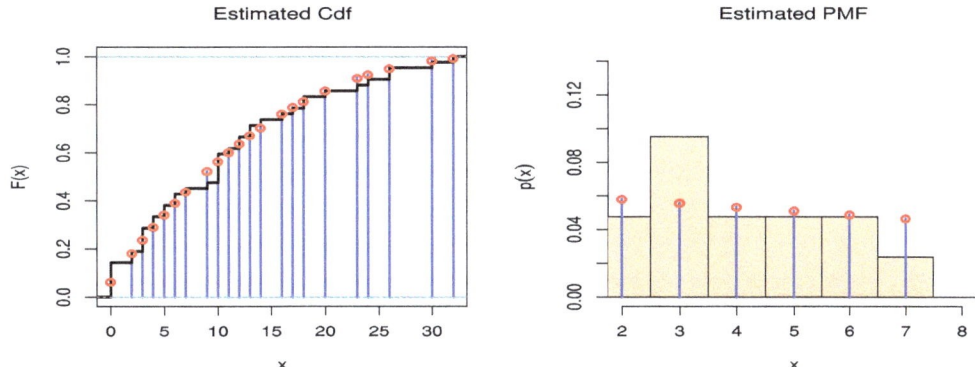

Figure 7. Plots of estimated pmf and CDF of DGPD1 for data set I.

Table 5. MLE and Bayesian estimates with SE for data set 1.

	MLE		Bayesian	
	Estimates	SE	Estimates	SE
θ	−0.4052	0.1651	−0.2337	0.1209
λ	15.6070	3.3902	15.5417	0.8679

To confirm this conclusion, we should check the convergence of the MCMC results. Figure 7 shows the trace and convergence plots of MCMC for parameter estimates of DGPD1. Figure 8 depicts the MCMC convergence of λ and θ. We confirm the results of MCMC that the parameters of DGPD1 have convergence by the MH algorithm. Figure 9 shows the posterior density plots of MCMC for parameter estimates of DGPD1 for data set 1, which has a normal curve, as per the proposed distribution of the MH algorithm.

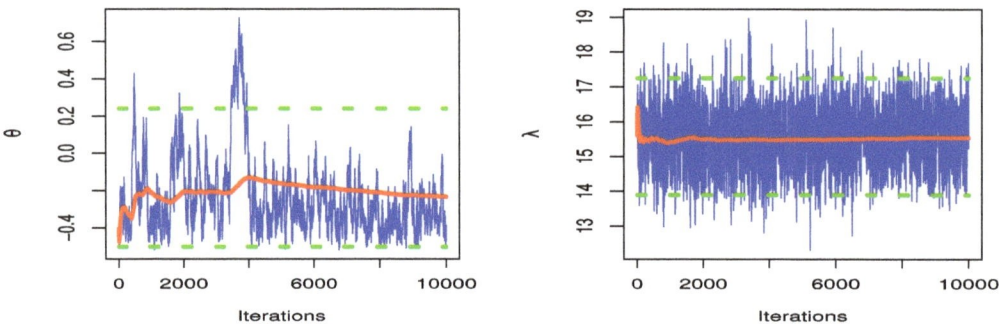

Figure 8. Trace and convergence plots of MCMC for parameter estimates of DGPD1 for data set I.

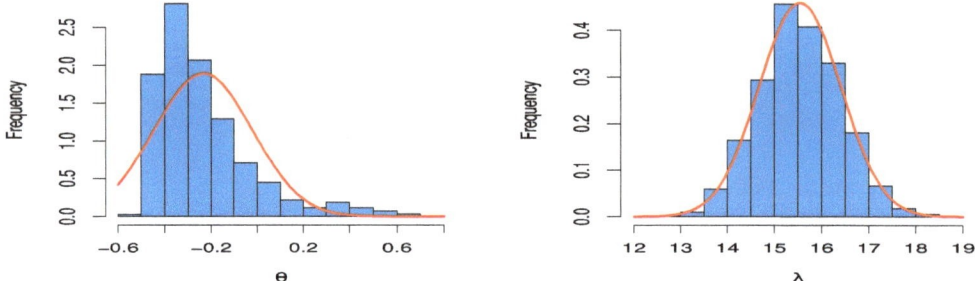

Figure 9. Posterior density plots of MCMC for parameter estimates of DGPD1 for data set I.

Data set 2: The second set of data represents a 53-day COVID-19 data set from Italy, recorded between 13 June 2021 and 4 August 2021. These data comprise daily new deaths. The data are as follows: 52, 26, 36, 63, 52, 37, 35, 28, 17, 21, 31, 30, 10, 56, 40, 14, 28, 42, 24, 21, 28, 22, 12, 31, 24, 14, 13, 25, 12, 7, 13, 20, 23, 9, 11, 13, 3, 7, 10, 21, 15, 17, 5, 7, 22, 24, 15, 19, 18, 16, 5, 20, 27. The data are available on the Worldometer website at [36].

Figure 10 shows PMF and CDF for the fitted DGP of data set 2. The SE values of the parameters of DGP are shown in Table 6 to compare between MLE and Bayesian estimation methods for data set 2. From the results of SE in Table 6, we note that Bayesian estimation is a superior estimation method for data set 2 compared to MLE. Figure 11 shows that the posterior density plots of MCMC for parameter estimates of DGPD1 for data set 2 have a normal curve, as per the proposed distribution of the MH algorithm. To confirm this conclusion, we should check the convergence of the MCMC results. Figure 12 shows the trace and convergence plots of MCMC for parameter estimates of DGPD1 for data set 2. In Figure 12, we confirm that the results of MCMC for the parameters of DGPD1 have convergence by the MH algorithm.

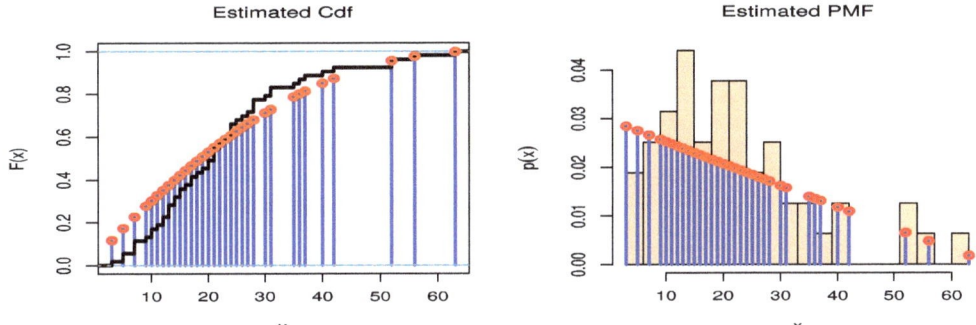

Figure 10. Plots of estimated pmf and CDF of DGPD1 for data set 2.

Table 6. MLE and Bayesian estimates with SE for data set 2.

	MLE		Bayesian	
	Estimates	SE	Estimates	SE
θ	−0.491911	0.103421	−0.41147	0.093889
λ	33.312755	5.266817	33.34727	0.886706

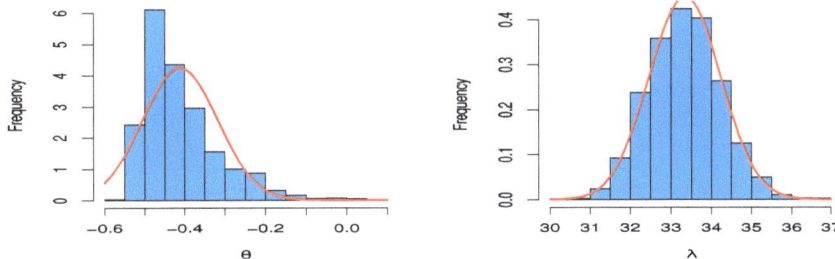

Figure 11. Posterior density plots of MCMC for parameter estimates of DGPD1 for data set 2.

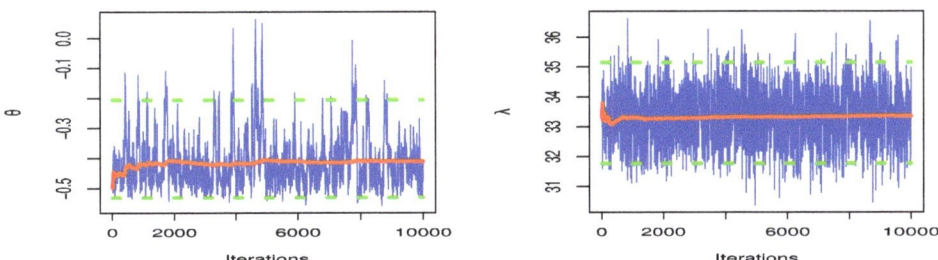

Figure 12. Trace and convergence plots of MCMC for parameter estimates of DGPD1 for data set 2.

6. Conclusions

In this study, we propose and study new discrete distributions that have a decreasing probability mass function for all choices of their parameters. The new distribution is called the discrete generalized Pareto distribution (DGPD). We used different discretization methods that introduced three discrete analogues of the DGPD. Point and interval estimations through the Bayesian method were obtained, and a simulation analysis was performed using R code to assess the efficiency of the three discrete models. Some loss functions were employed in this study, such as SE, LINEX, and GE loss functions. The tables presented in the simulation section show some good properties for each analogue. To check the validity of the DGPD, two real data examples were considered, which comprised COVID-19 death cases in two different regions. Our proposed DGPD1 was compared with other discrete candidates, and via goodness-of-fit tests, it was proved that DGPD1 fit the data very well. The tables and figures illustrate the efficiency of the new model as well. For further study, we suggest using other discretization methods and testing their performance and suitability using real-life data.

Author Contributions: Conceptualization, H.H.A. and E.M.A.; methodology, H.H.A.; software, E.M.A.; validation, H.H.A. and E.M.A.; formal analysis, H.H.A.; investigation, E.M.A.; resources, H.H.A. and E.M.A.; data curation, E.M.A.; writing—original draft preparation, H.H.A.; writing—review and editing, H.H.A. and E.M.A.; visualization, E.M.A.; supervision, H.H.A.; project administration, H.H.A.; funding acquisition, H.H.A. All authors have read and agreed to the published version of the manuscript.

Funding: This work was supported through the Annual Funding track by the Deanship of Scientific Research, Vice Presidency for Graduate Studies and Scientific Research, King Faisal University, Saudi Arabia [Project No. AN000537].

Institutional Review Board Statement: Not applicable.

Informed Consent Statement: Not applicable.

Data Availability Statement: The data is available in the text of this article.

Conflicts of Interest: The authors declare no conflict of interest.

References

1. Xekalaki, E. Hazard function and life distributions in discrete time. *Commun. Stat. Theory Methods* **1983**, *12*, 2503–2509. [CrossRef]
2. Hitha, N.; Nair, N.U. Characterization of some discrete models by properties of residual life function. *Calcutta Stat. Assoc. Bull.* **1989**, *38*, 219–223. [CrossRef]
3. Roy, D.; Gupta, R.P. Classifications of discrete lives. *Microelectron. Reliab.* **1992**, *32*, 459–1473. [CrossRef]
4. Roy, D.; Gupta, R.P. Stochastic modeling through reliability measures in the discrete case. *Stat. Probab. Lett.* **1999**, *43*, 197–206. [CrossRef]
5. Roy, D. On classifications of multivariate life distributions in the discrete set-up. *Microelectron. Reliab.* **1997**, *37*, 361–366. [CrossRef]
6. Roy, D. The discrete normal distribution. *Commun. Stat. Theory Methods* **2003**, *32*, 1871–1883. [CrossRef]
7. Roy, D. Discrete Rayleigh distribution. *IEEE. Trans. Reliab.* **2004**, *53*, 255–260. [CrossRef]
8. Roy, D.; Ghosh, T. A New Discretization Approach with Application in Reliability Estimation. *IEEE Trans. Reliab.* **2009**, *58*, 456–461. [CrossRef]
9. Bracquemond, C.; Gaudoin, O. A survey on discrete life time distributions. *Int. J. Reliab. Qual. Saf. Eng.* **2003**, *10*, 69–98. [CrossRef]
10. Lai, C.D. Issues concerning constructions of discrete lifetime models. *Qual. Technol. Quant. Manag.* **2013**, *10*, 251–262. [CrossRef]
11. Chakraborty, S. Generating discrete analogues of continuous probability distributions—A survey of methods and constructions. *J. Stat. Distrib. Appl.* **2015**, *2*, 6. [CrossRef]
12. Liu, H.; Hussain, F.; Tan, C.L.; Dash, M. Discretization: An Enabling Technique. *Data Min. Knowl. Discov.* **2002**, *6*, 393–423. [CrossRef]
13. Arnastauskaitė, J.; Ruzgas, T.; Bražėnas, M. An Exhaustive Power Comparison of Normality Tests. *Mathematics* **2021**, *9*, 788. [CrossRef]
14. Korkmaz, S.; Goksuluk, D.; Zararsiz, G. MVN: An R Package for Assessing Multivariate Normality. *R J.* **2014**, *6*, 151–162. [CrossRef]
15. Al-Huniti, A.A.; AL-Dayian, G.R. Discrete Burr type III distribution. *Am. J. Math. Stat.* **2012**, *2*, 145–152. [CrossRef]
16. Bebbington, M.; Lai, C.D.; Wellington, M.; Zitikis, R. The discrete additive Weibull distribution: A bathtub-shaped hazard for discontinuous failure data. *Reliab. Eng. Syst. Saf.* **2012**, *106*, 37–44. [CrossRef]
17. Sarhan, A.M. A two-parameter discrete distribution with a bathtub hazard shape. *Commun. Stat. Appl. Methods* **2017**, *24*, 15–27. [CrossRef]
18. Yari, G.; Tondpour, Z. Discrete Burr XII-Gamma Distributions: Properties and Parameter Estimations. *Iran. J. Sci. Technol. Trans. A Sci.* **2018**, *42*, 2237–2249. [CrossRef]
19. Almetwally, E.M.; Ibrahim, G.M. Discrete Alpha Power Inverse Lomax Distribution with Application of COVID-19 Data. *Int. J. Appl. Math.* **2020**, *9*, 11–22.

20. Eliwa, M.S.; Altun, E.; El-Dawoody, M.; El-Morshedy, M. A new three-parameter discrete distribution with associated INAR (1) process and applications. *IEEE Access* **2020**, *8*, 91150–91162. [CrossRef]
21. Almetwally, E.M.; Almongy, H.M.; Saleh, H.A. Managing risk of spreading "COVID-19" in Egypt: Modelling using a discrete Marshall-Olkin generalized exponential distribution. *Int. J. Probab. Stat.* **2020**, *9*, 33–41.
22. Al-Babtain, A.A.; Ahmed, A.H.N.; Afify, A.Z. A New Discrete Analog of the Continuous Lindley Distribution, with Reliability Applications. *Entropy* **2020**, *22*, 603. [CrossRef] [PubMed]
23. Eldeeb, A.S.; Ahsan-Ul-Haq, M.; Babar, A. A Discrete Analog of Inverted Topp-Leone Distribution: Properties, Estimation and Applications. *Int. J. Anal. Appl.* **2021**, *19*, 695–708.
24. Elbatal, I.; Alotaibi, N.; Almetwally, E.M.; Alyami, S.A.; Elgarhy, M. On Odd Perks-G Class of Distributions: Properties, Regression Model, Discretization, Bayesian and Non-Bayesian Estimation, and Applications. *Symmetry* **2022**, *14*, 883. [CrossRef]
25. Nagy, M.; Almetwally, E.M.; Gemeay, A.M.; Mohammed, H.S.; Jawa, T.M.; Sayed-Ahmed, N.; Muse, A.H. The new novel discrete distribution with application on covid-19 mortality numbers in Kingdom of Saudi Arabia and Latvia. *Complexity 2021*, **2021**, 7192833. [CrossRef]
26. Gillariose, J.; Balogun, O.S.; Almetwally, E.M.; Sherwani, R.A.K.; Jamal, F.; Joseph, J. On the Discrete Weibull Marshall–Olkin Family of Distributions: Properties, Characterizations, and Applications. *Axioms* **2021**, *10*, 287. [CrossRef]
27. Martín, J.; Parra, M.I.; Pizarro, M.M.; Sanjuán, E.L. Baseline Methods for the Parameter Estimation of the Generalized Pareto Distribution. *Entropy* **2022**, *24*, 178. [CrossRef]
28. Huang, C.; Zhao, X.; Cheng, W.; Ji, Q.; Duan, Q.; Han, Y. Statistical Inference of Dynamic Conditional Generalized Pareto Distribution with Weather and Air Quality Factors. *Mathematics* **2022**, *10*, 1433. [CrossRef]
29. Shui, P.-L.; Zou, P.-J.; Feng, T. Outlier-robust truncated maximum likelihood parameter estimators of generalized Pareto distributions. *Digit. Signal Process.* **2022**, *127*, 103527. [CrossRef]
30. He, Y.; Peng, L.; Zhang, D.; Zhao, Z. Risk Analysis via Generalized Pareto Distributions. *J. Bus. Econ. Stat.* **2021**, *40*, 852–867. [CrossRef]
31. Arnold, B.C.; Press, S.J. Compatible Conditional Distributions. *J. Am. Stat. Assoc.* **1989**, *84*, 152. [CrossRef]
32. Karandikar, R.L. On the Markov Chain Monte Carlo (MCMC) method. *Sadhana* **2006**, *31*, 81–104. [CrossRef]
33. Wang, Y.; Zhang, J.; Cai, C.; Lu, W.; Tang, Y. Semiparametric estimation for proportional hazards mixture cure model allowing non-curable competing risk. *J. Stat. Plan. Inference* **2020**, *211*, 171–189. [CrossRef]
34. Xu, A.; Zhou, S.; Tang, Y. A unified model for system reliability evaluation under dynamic operating conditions. *IEEE Trans. Reliab.* **2021**, *70*, 65–72. [CrossRef]
35. Luo, C.; Shen, L.; Xu, A. Modelling and estimation of system reliability under dynamic operating environments and lifetime ordering constraints. *Reliab. Eng. Syst. Saf.* **2022**, *218*, 108136. [CrossRef]
36. Worldometers. Available online: https://www.worldometers.info/coronavirus. (accessed on 1 June 2021).
37. Almetwally, E.M.; Abdo, D.A.; Hafez, E.H.; Jawa, T.M.; Sayed-Ahmed, N.; Almongy, H.M. The new discrete distribution with application to COVID-19 Data. *Results Phys.* **2021**, *32*, 104987. [CrossRef]
38. Krishna, H.; Pundir, P.S. Discrete Burr and discrete Pareto distributions. *Stat. Methodol.* **2009**, *6*, 177–188. [CrossRef]
39. Khan, M.A.; Khalique, A.; Abouammoh, A.M. On estimating parameters in a discrete Weibull distribution. *IEEE Trans. Reliab.* **1989**, *38*, 348–350. [CrossRef]
40. Jazi, M.A.; Lai, C.-D.; Alamatsaz, M.H. A discrete inverse Weibull distribution and estimation of its parameters. *Stat. Methodol.* **2010**, *7*, 121–132. [CrossRef]
41. Fisher, P. Negative Binomial Distribution. *Ann. Eugen.* **1941**, *11*, 182–787. [CrossRef]
42. Nekoukhou, V.; Alamatsaz, M.H.; Bidram, H. Discrete generalized exponential distribution of a second type. *Statistics* **2013**, *47*, 876–887. [CrossRef]
43. Gómez-Déniz, E.; Calderín-Ojeda, E. The discrete Lindley distribution: Properties and applications. *J. Stat. Comput. Simul.* **2011**, *81*, 1405–1416. [CrossRef]

Article

Estimation of Asymmetric Spatial Autoregressive Dependence on Irregular Lattices

Franz H. Harke [1,*,†], Miryam S. Merk [2,†] and Philipp Otto [1,†]

1. Faculty of Civil Engineering and Geodetic Science, Leibniz University Hannover, 30167 Hannover, Germany; philipp.otto@ikg.uni-hannover.de
2. Chairs of Statistics and Econometrics, University of Goettingen, Humboldtallee 3, 37073 Göttingen, Germany; miryamsarah.merk@uni-goettingen.de
* Correspondence: harke@ikg.uni-hannover.de
† These authors contributed equally to this work.

Abstract: In spatial econometrics, we usually assume that the spatial dependence structure is known and that all information about it is contained in a spatial weights matrix **W**. However, in practice, the structure of **W** is unknown a priori and difficult to obtain, especially for asymmetric dependence. In this paper, we propose a data-driven method to obtain **W**, whether it is symmetric or asymmetric. This is achieved by calculating the area overlap of the adjacent regions/districts with a given shape (a pizza-like shape, in our case). With **W** determined in this way, we estimate the potentially asymmetric spatial autoregressive dependence on irregular lattices. We verify our method using Monte Carlo simulations for finite samples and compare it with classical approaches such as Queen's contiguity matrices and inverse-distance weighting matrices. Finally, our method is applied to model the evolution of sales prices for building land in Brandenburg, Germany. We show that the price evolution and its spatial dependence are mainly driven by the orientation towards Berlin.

Keywords: spatial autoregressive model (SAR); weights matrix; model selection; Akaike information criterion (AIC); maximum likelihood estimation

1. Introduction

Geospatial analysis is based on Tobler's first law of geography, which points out that everything is connected to everything else, but that nearby objects dominate (Tobler [1]). Not every process can be described by applying this rule, and there is no precise and unique definition of "nearby". Therefore, it is often assumed that the dependence structure is known through underlying physical systems (e.g., river flows) or geographical information or network structures (e.g., public transport connections), or assumptions such as symmetry are made. Generally, to model spatial data, one needs to know the $n(n-1)$ potential interactions among the system's n objects. A major challenge is to obtain these interactions from the n data points in the sample.

There are various attempts to model such spatial dependence. For instance, the spatial covariance could directly be described by a parametric covariance function that has fewer parameters than all possible links. This approach is commonly known as the geostatistical approach (see, e.g., Cressie and Wikle [2]). Alternatively, spatial dependence could be modeled by explicitly including spatially lagged variables. These models are often referred to as spatial econometrics models. Processes in which the objects/regions influence each other can be modeled with spatial autoregressive (SAR) models (LeSage [3], LeSage and Pace [4]). SAR models describe processes in which the observed value of one region influences the observed value in other regions and vice versa. An exemplary question that such models attempt to answer is whether the average salary in one region influences the average salary in adjacent regions, and if so, to what extent. Such interplay among n regions is described by an $n \times n$ spatial weights matrix **W**.

These autoregressive-type approaches involving the specification of a weights matrix have been widely used in different areas. For instance, in environmental statistics, the effects of weather conditions on fertilizer application were modelled (Billé and Rogna [5]) and environmental expenditure interactions among OECD countries were investigated. In addition, the impact of COVID on financial returns was investigated (Billé and Caporin [6]), and studies of the labour market have employed spatial weight matrices (Billé [7]). Furthermore, in health economics, Donegan et al. [8] used spatial econometrics approaches for modelling community health.

There are different methods for obtaining a suitable $\mathbf{W}$. One is to assume that all regions sharing a common border influence each other. This method is also called the Queen's contiguity matrix, alluding to the chessboard (LeSage and Pace [4]). If region A and region B share a common border, the Queen's contiguity matrix is then constructed with $W_{AB} = W_{BA} = 1$. Other methods involve geographical distances such as those used in Lin Lawell [9] to model air pollution. They assume that the first-neighbour regions are the regions within 500 km of each other. Another method for constructing $\mathbf{W}$ is to assume that the regions' influences on each other declines as the distance between them increases. The so-called 'inverse-distance $\mathbf{W}$' was used by Boly et al. [10] to model real-estate valuation and by Zhao et al. [11] to describe air pollution in China. The inverse-distance matrix is constructed with $W_{AB} = W_{BA} = 1/distance(A,B)$. An advanced method also takes geographical or economical connections into account when constructing $\mathbf{W}$. Krisztin et al. [12] described the worldwide spread of the coronavirus by assuming that countries with a common border influence each other, as well as countries connected by an airline. Other suggested methods for constructing $\mathbf{W}$ include the parametric or semiparametric estimation method proposed by Pinkse et al. [13], the method of Stakhovych and Bijmolt [14], where $\mathbf{W}$ was selected from a set of possible candidates with a goodness-of-fit criterion, requiring that the true $\mathbf{W}$ is in the set of candidates, and that of Bhattacharjee and Jensen-Butler [15], where $\mathbf{W}$ was selected from an estimated spatial autocovariance matrix under the conditions of symmetry and a finite sample size of n.

Ahrens and Bhattacharjee [16] proposed to estimate $\mathbf{W}$ in two steps with a least absolute shrinkage and selection operator (lasso) approach. An alternative penalized estimation approach was proposed by Lam and Souza [17]. They selected $\mathbf{W}$ from a linear combination of different weights matrices by setting irrelevant components to zero. This linear combination could involve higher-order spatial lags (see, e.g., Cohen and Paul [18]). A method for selecting the best weights matrix from a set of candidates was also proposed by Debarsy and LeSage [19] or by Debarsy and Ertur [20]. Zhang and Yu [21] showed that the true weights matrix can consistently be selected from the set of candidates (if included) using Mallow's C_p criterion. If the true matrix is not in the set of candidates, the selection is still optimal, and they proposed a model averaging technique over different candidates. In addition, the method was illustrated by an analysis of historical rice prices in China.

Most of the studies have in common the fact that they apply symmetric weighting schemes (if A influences B, then B influences A, but with a potentially different magnitude). To the best of our knowledge, there are only a few references that deal with the construction of weights matrices accounting for asymmetry. Exceptions include, for instance, Zhou et al. [22], who constructed their asymmetric weights matrix by element-wise multiplication of a nearest-neighbour weights matrix (mostly symmetric) with a matrix that indicated whether the influence flowed from A to B or vice versa. The direction of the influence must be known in advance. A similar method for constructing an asymmetric weights matrix was proposed by Merk and Otto [23], to model $PM_{2.5}$ concentrations. In their approach, the directional component depended on the wind direction and wind speed, which strongly influenced the spatial dependence structure.

However, in practice, we often do not have prior knowledge about the asymmetrical or directional influences. Therefore, in this paper, we develop a data-driven method to estimate the interactions directly from the sample data and explicitly allow asymmetric dependence for irregular lattice data. We assume that the interactions are not dependent on the location of the region but are equal over the entire sample area. With this approach for irregular lattice data, we extend the work of Merk and Otto [24], who proposed a similar approach for obtaining the interactions for regular lattice data based on a lasso procedure. The proposed method respects the interactions from close neighbours, like the Queen's contiguity matrix or the inverse-distance matrix, but allows asymmetric interactions (if A influences B, B does not necessarily influence A). It is worth noting that the proposed method provides a method of obtaining a flexible weights matrix. This weights matrix can be an additional candidate for the selection of the weights matrix described above, for which good candidates must be available.

This paper is structured as follows. Section 2 describes the theoretical model. Section 3 covers a Monte Carlo simulation study. In Section 4, we apply our method to real-world data and analyse the evolution of land sale prices in Brandenburg, Germany, to show that the short-distance directional influences are coming from Berlin. We conclude by discussing new research directions in Section 5.

2. Theoretical Model

Let $\{Y(s) \in \mathbb{R} : s \in B\}$ be a univariate process in the spatial domain B. We explicitly consider B to be an irregular lattice, as would be the case for spatial polygon data. Shapes like this can be found in countries, states, and districts. An artificial example can be seen in Figure 1.

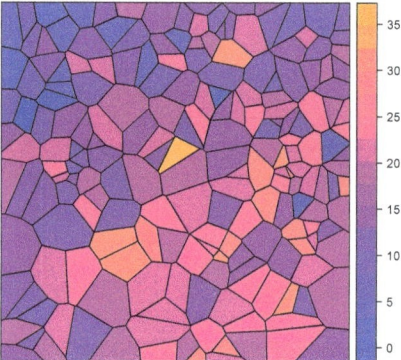

Figure 1. Example of simulated values for an $n = 200$ Voronoi map. The simulation is based on 8-setting-4 (see Figure 3).

Furthermore, suppose that the process is observed for a finite set of locations $B = \{s_1, \ldots, s_n\}$ and $Y = (Y(s_1), \ldots, Y(s_n))^t$. We consider that the process follows a spatial autoregressive model, i.e.,

$$Y = WY + X\beta + \epsilon, \tag{1}$$

where W is an unknown spatial weights matrix and β is a vector of p exogenous influences. Furthermore, X is a $(p+1) \times n$ matrix and ϵ is a random error vector, which is assumed to have zero mean with a diagonal, homoscedastic covariance matrix $\sigma_\epsilon^2 I$. The identity matrix is denoted by I. Since W consists of $n(n-1)$ unknown parameters, which must be estimated, and only n values of the response are observed, W is typically replaced by a multiple of a pre-specified matrix $\tilde{W}$, i.e., $W = \phi \tilde{W}$, where ϕ is an unknown scalar parameter to be estimated (Anselin [25]).

In the following, we aim to estimate the full spatial dependence structure W. To obtain a meaningful and easy-to-interpret representation, suppose that the spatial dependence can be separated into k directions and d distances (see Figure 2a). Furthermore, suppose that there is a unique weighting for each segment of the sectors such that **W** can be decomposed as

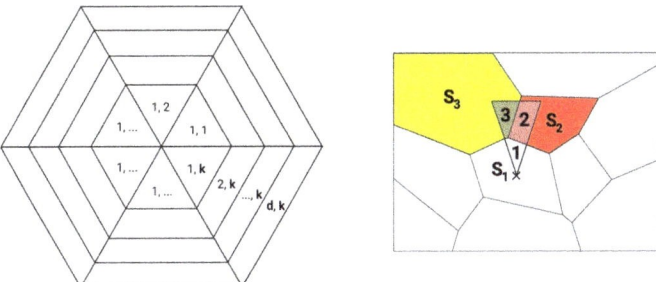

Figure 2. *Left*: schematic representation of dividing a spatial dependence structure into k directions and d distances. *Right*: evaluation of an arbitrary segment (ϕ_{ij}) of the spatial dependence structure referring to district S_1. Area **1** is not considered, since it is part of the region that is evaluated. The relative sizes of the overlaps **2** and **3** give the positive weights and are row-normalized to one. Here, we obtain approximations to the weights: $w_{ij,S_1 S_2} = 0.6$ and $w_{ij,S_1 S_3} = 0.4$.

$$\mathbf{W} = \sum_{i=1}^{k}\sum_{j=1}^{d} \phi_{ij} \tilde{\mathbf{W}}_{ij}, \tag{2}$$

where each matrix $\tilde{\mathbf{W}}_{ij}$ has positive weights for the (ij)th segment only (see Figure 2b). The weights are chosen to be proportional to the overlapping areas. That is,

$$\tilde{\mathbf{W}}_{ij} = \begin{pmatrix} 0 & w_{ij,12} & \cdots & w_{ij,1n} \\ w_{ij,21} & 0 & \cdots & w_{ij,2n} \\ \vdots & \vdots & \ddots & \vdots \\ w_{ij,n1} & w_{ij,n2} & \cdots & 0 \end{pmatrix} = (w_{ij,\iota\eta})_{\iota,\eta=1,\dots,n} \tag{3}$$

where $w_{ij,\iota\eta}$ is the relative area of the ηth location lying in the (ij)th segment with respect to region ι. For example, (see Figure 2b), one $w_{ij,\iota\eta}$ is the normalized area of **2**. Due to normalization, each $\tilde{\mathbf{W}}_{ij}$ is bounded by 1 in the row sums. Each of these matrices contains the relative overlapping areas of one segment with the n regions. Since a segment usually overlaps with a small fraction of the regions only, all $\tilde{\mathbf{W}}_{ij}$ are sparse.

Figure 2b depicts an artificial map of ten regions. An exemplary segment (ϕ_{ij}) determines the spatial dependence of the region S_1 towards the north by the relative sizes of its overlap with the neighbouring regions S_2 and S_3. As we exclude self-influences, the overlap with region S_1 is ignored, and the weights for the spatial dependence are normalized with respect to the two remaining intersections. Here, the weights are given by $w_{ij,12} = 0.6$ and $w_{ij,13} = 0.4$ for S_2 and S_3, respectively. With this construction, the matrix $(w_{ij,\iota\eta})$ is row-normalized, as $w_{ij,12}$ and $w_{ij,13}$ are the only non-zero entries in row $\iota = 1$.

This leads to the classical autoregressive model with higher-order spatial lags, given by

$$Y = \sum_{i=1}^{k}\sum_{j=1}^{d} \phi_{ij} \tilde{\mathbf{W}}_{ij} Y + \mathbf{X}\beta + \epsilon. \tag{4}$$

In the reduced form, we obtain with

$$\mathbf{S}\{\phi_{ij} : i = 1,\dots,k; j = 1,\dots,d\} = \mathbf{I} - \sum_{i=1}^{k}\sum_{j=1}^{d} \phi_{ij} \tilde{\mathbf{W}}_{ij} \tag{5}$$

that

$$Y = \left(I - \sum_{i=1}^{k}\sum_{j=1}^{d} \phi_{ij}\tilde{W}_{ij}\right)^{-1}(X\beta + \epsilon) = S\{\phi_{ij}\}^{-1}(X\beta + \epsilon). \quad (6)$$

In this paper, we consider that d and k are chosen to be large enough to obtain a flexible model reflecting the true underlying spatial dependence precisely, generally leading to a rich, parameterized description.

The inverse S^{-1} exists if the column-sum norm $\|W\|_1 < a$ or the row-sum norm $\|W\|_\infty < a$ is bounded by a finite number a. With the $\tilde{W}_{ij}$ row sums bounded by 1, this can be ensured under the assumption that

$$\sum_{i=1}^{k}\sum_{j=1}^{d}|\phi_{ij}| < 1. \quad (7)$$

A more general condition is discussed by Elhorst et al. [26]. Since we only want to describe the direction from which we see a stronger or weaker influence, we constrain ourselves to the first condition.

Implementing the model demands a proper choice of the parameters k and d, which determine the division of the direction and distance of the spatial dependence, respectively. Moreover, the actual length of each distance step can be optimally chosen. We perform a spatial partitioning analysis to obtain a robust choice of all three parameters.

Let l_q be the distance between the qth and $(q+1)$th distance steps. We suggest selecting $k \in K \subset \mathbb{N}$, $d \in D \subset \mathbb{N}$, and $l_q \in L \subset \mathbb{R}_{>0}$ using Akaike information criterion (AIC) selection (Akaike [27]). Therefore, we calculate all $\tilde{W}_{ij}(k, d, l_q)$ for different sets of $D \times K \times L$. Then, we estimate the unknown parameters β, ϕ_{ij} with maximum-likelihood methods and select the best-performing model based on its AIC. Having obtained the best-fitting $(\hat{k}, \hat{d}, \hat{l}_q)$, we estimate the final model in the next step.

We estimate the parameters $\{\beta, \phi_{ij}\}$ using the maximum-likelihood approach combined with parameter selection using minimal AIC. For both symmetric and asymmetric dependence, a large share of the ϕ_{ij} values can be expected to be zero, because k and d are large. For this reason, we repeat the estimation $d \times k$ times and, at every step, we drop the least significant ϕ_{ij} parameter (i.e., we set this particular ϕ_{ij} to zero). Finally, from these $d \times k$ estimations we choose the one with the lowest AIC.

In general, the unknown parameters $\{\beta, \phi_{ij}\}$ can be estimated. For that reason, the joint probability function, the log-likelihood function $f_Y(Y)$, is maximized with respect to parameters ϕ_{ij} and β. Assuming that $\epsilon \sim N(0, \sigma_\epsilon^2 I)$, the log-likelihood is given by

$$\mathcal{L}(Y|\beta, \phi_{ij}) = \frac{n}{2}\log(2\pi\sigma_\epsilon^2) - \frac{1}{2\sigma_\epsilon^2}\tilde{\epsilon}^t\tilde{\epsilon} + \log\det(S) \quad (8)$$

with

$$\tilde{\epsilon} = \left(I - \sum_{i=1}^{k}\sum_{j=1}^{d}\phi_{ij}\tilde{W}_{ij}\right)Y - X\beta = SY - X\beta. \quad (9)$$

The estimator is obtained by maximizing Equation (8) with respect to all parameters. For the consistency of the resulting estimators, we refer to Lee [28] and Gupta and Robinson [29].

3. Monte Carlo Simulations

For the simulation study, we simulate the irregular spatial lattice as Voronoi cells (Longley et al. [30], Sen [31]), where $n \in \{200, 500, 900\}$ centroids are sampled from a two-dimensional uniform distribution on the interval $[0, \sqrt{n}]^2$ (see Figure 1). Eventually, Y can be simulated as in Equation (6), with ϵ being uncorrelated realizations of a standard normal distribution. We choose $\beta = (3, 1, 2, 0, 5)^t$ and X has only ones in the first column. The remaining elements are standard normally distributed random values.

We consider four different specifications of the spatial dependence with $k = 8$ and $k = 16$, as shown in Figures 3 and 4. First, an isotropic process is considered where only the first lag has an influence, as in classical contiguity settings. Second, a directional process is considered with a clear north-to-south dependence. Third, we consider a nearest-neighbour dependence in the northwest direction only. Finally, the fourth setting is extended by adding another level of dependence strength, while retaining the mainly northwest directional dependence. Blue sections represent zero influence, orange sections represent the maximum influence, and purple sections represent 50% of the maximum influence. The maximum influence is obtained by setting $\sum_{i=1}^{k} \sum_{j=1}^{d} |\phi_{ij}| = 0.95$.

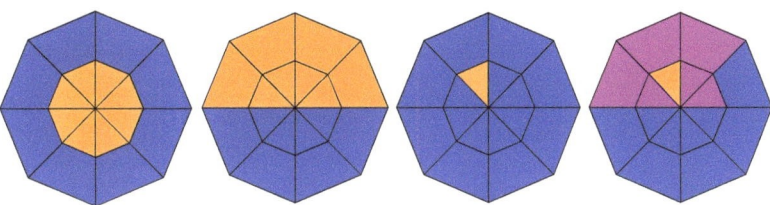

Figure 3. Four different spatial dependence structures implied by the parameters ϕ_{ij}. In the following, they will be denoted 8-setting-1 for the very left setting, to 8-setting-4 on the right. Blue: $\phi_{ij} = 0$, orange: $\phi_{ij} = $ max, and purple: $\phi_{ij} = \frac{max}{2}$. The value max comes from $\sum_{i=1}^{k} \sum_{j=1}^{d} |\phi_{ij}| = 0.95$.

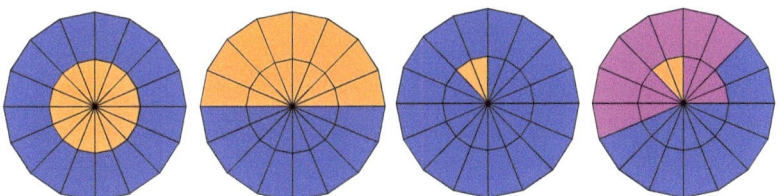

Figure 4. Four different spatial dependence structures implied by the parameters ϕ_{ij}. In the following, they will be denoted 16-setting-1 for the very left setting, to 16-setting-4 on the right. Blue: $\phi_{ij} = 0$, orange: $\phi_{ij} = $ max, and purple: $\phi_{ij} = \frac{max}{2}$. The value max comes from $\sum_{i=1}^{k} \sum_{j=1}^{d} |\phi_{ij}| = 0.95$.

We carried out two types of simulation. In the first type, we used $d = 2$, $k = 8$ and $l = 375$, employing the spatial dependence structures depicted in Figure 3. We first performed the spatial partitioning (results in Table 1 and Figure 5) to gain the best $\tilde{k}$ and $\tilde{l}$ for the estimation of $\hat{\phi}_{ij}$ (we use $\tilde{k}$ to denote the optimal parameter and $\hat{k}$ to denote an estimator). The procedure to determine $\tilde{k}$ and $\tilde{l}$ is described below, and was repeated 10^3 times. Then, using the optimal $(\tilde{k}, \tilde{l})$ from each of the 1000 estimations, we estimated $\hat{\phi}_{ij}$ and compared it to alternative estimations with the Queen's contiguity matrix, the inverse-distance neighbour matrix by AIC, and the sum of squared residuals (ϵ^2). The comparison can be found in Table 2, showing that our method works best.

In the second type of simulation, we show that we can re-estimate even higher-dimensional specifications of the spatial dependence, as depicted in Figure 4. We simulated Y with $d = 2$, $k = 16$ and $l_1 = l_2 = 375$ using this high-resolution spatial dependence and estimated $\hat{\phi}_{ij}$, conditionally upon selecting the true d, k and l as the best parameters. The results are summarized in Table 3. One can see that we can re-estimate these higher-dimensional settings with a true positive rate of at least 76%. The simulations were carried out in R using the packages *spdep* and *rgdal* (Bivand et al. [32], Bivand et al. [33]).

Table 1. Means and standard deviations of the best $\tilde{k}$ and $\tilde{l}$ for 10^3 estimations. For each setting, the best values are printed in bold. The greater the value of n, the closer we approach to the true values of $k = 8$ and $l = 375$.

n	8-Setting-1			8-Setting-2			8-Setting-3			8-Setting-4		
	200	500	900	200	500	900	200	500	900	200	500	900
mean($\tilde{k}$)	5.34	6.17	6.29	6.8	6.43	7.51	7.99	**8**	**8**	6.26	6.59	7.36
sd($\tilde{k}$)	1.31	1.39	1.35	1.37	1.44	1.07	0.16	**0**	**0**	1.31	1.47	1.22
mean($\tilde{l}$)	325	336	347	382	393	376	377	**375**	374	379	389	**375**
sd($\tilde{l}$)	86	65	66	58	37	30	18	7.1	**4.5**	69	36	37

The spatial partitioning algorithm to determine the optimal parameters $(\tilde{k}, \tilde{l})$ was implemented as follows. Initially, we select the distance $d = 2$ and split the spatial dependence into different lengths $l_q = l \in \{225, 250, \ldots, 525\}$ and various numbers of directions $k \in \{4, 5, 6, 7, 8, 9, 10\}$. For each spatial dependence structure, all $d \times k$ spatial weights matrices $\hat{W}_{ij}$ are calculated. We calculate 3×1000 sets of Y with $k = 8$ and $l = 375$ ($Y_{k=8, l=375}$) that differ by a random white noise element ϵ. Finally, we re-estimate $\hat{Y}_{kl}$ for all combinations of k and l and calculate their AIC values to select the best set of $(\tilde{k}, \tilde{l})$ for each of the 1000 $Y_{k=8, l=375}$. The results can be seen in Table 1 and Figure 5.

Figure 5 shows that for 8-setting-1, the symmetric setting, it is more difficult to estimate the correct k, because the models are observationally equivalent. The directional influence for this radially symmetric setting looks almost identical for $k = 4$ and $k = 8$. Since settings with fewer variables benefit from AIC selection, observation of this pattern is to be expected. The length of the slices (l; here the y-axis) can be identified.

However, 8-setting-2 is axially symmetric about the y-axis. Only the northern half of the sections can provide spatial influence. In this case, the spatial partitioning algorithm is less robust in determining the length parameter $\tilde{l}$. One plausible reason is the ambiguity between the length and the number of distance steps, which occurs particularly for this spatial dependence setting. For 8-setting-3, the true values of k and l are selected consistently. For 8-setting-4, estimation is more difficult, but the results show reasonable consistency for larger values of n. In general, $\tilde{k}$ was rarely selected to be too large, but the selection of $\tilde{l}$ was more difficult.

For each of the previous 10^3 estimations, we obtained the best values for $\tilde{k}$ and $\tilde{l}$. Now, using these $\tilde{k}$ and $\tilde{l}$ values, we estimate, 10^3 times, the values for the segments $\hat{\phi}_{ij}$, as described in Section 2. Finally, we compare the mean AIC values and the sum of squared residuals (ϵ^2) of those estimates to the commonly used Queen's contiguity matrices (Lin Lawell [9]) and inverse-distance weighting matrices (Boly et al. [10]).

The average AIC value and the sum of squared residuals are reported in Table 2. For all settings and all n, our method outperforms the common procedure, i.e., smaller values for AIC and ϵ^2 are obtained.

For the final estimation, the spatial dependence is split into $k = 16$ directions and $d = 2$ distances (see Figure 4), leading to $d \times k = 32$ spatial weight matrices $\bar{W}_{ij}$ with dimension $n \times n$. We assume knowledge of the true parameters of $(\tilde{k}, \tilde{d}, \tilde{l}_p)$, and we re-estimate the parameters of $\hat{\phi}_{ij}$. Table 3 shows the results of the simulation study for the different dependence structures (see Figure 4), with 500 estimations for each n and for each setting. Since we know the true values, we compare the BIAS and the RMSE of the estimations. For the BIAS and RMSE results, we distinguish two cases. Either the true values should be chosen to be zero ($\stackrel{!}{=} 0$), or the true values should be chosen to be greater than zero ($\stackrel{!}{>} 0$).

The true positive values represent the rate at which $\hat{\phi}_{ij}$ was correctly identified as positive. The false non-zero value represents the rate of falsely identifying zero values as positive. From Table 3, we can see that the results improve when a larger n is chosen. The minimal true positive rate was 76%, but, in most cases, the true positive rate exceeds

90%. Furthermore, we chose up to only 7% of the values as falsely non-zero. From the true positive and false non-zero values, one can see that, for a very simple dependence structure such as 16-setting-3, the sections $\hat{\phi}_{ij}$ are identified almost perfectly.

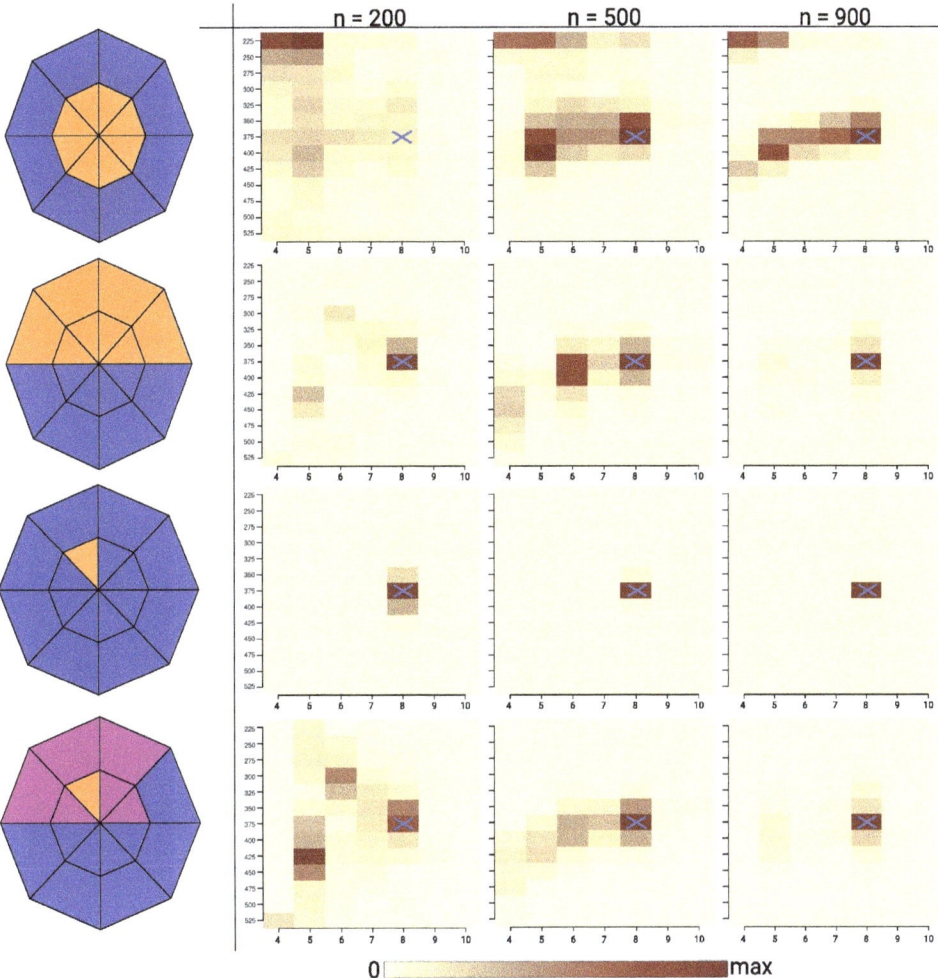

Figure 5. Results for spatial partitioning to choose the best $\tilde{k}$ and $\tilde{l}$ using the four spatial dependence structures from Figure 3. The 12 heatmaps show the best values for each estimation after 1000 realizations. Each heatmap depicts values of $k \in \{4, 5, 6, 7, 8, 9, 10\}$ on the x-axis and values of $l \in \{225, 250, \ldots, 525\}$ on the y-axis. The maximum of the colour scale is chosen for for each heatmap individually to achieve optimal visualization. Especially in 8-setting-3, the selections of $\tilde{k}$ and $\tilde{l}$ are very sharp. Therefore, every plot has its own scale, and we named the maximum value *max*. The blue crosses indicate the true parameters $k = 8$ and $l = 375$.

Table 2. One thousand estimations of $\hat{y}$ using this method. The results are compared, using the average AIC and ϵ^2, to estimations with Queen's contiguity matrices and inverse-distance weighting matrices. The values of $\bar{k}$ and $\bar{l}$ are chosen from spatial partitioning.

		8-Setting-1			8-Setting-2			8-Setting-3			8-Setting-4		
	n	200	500	900	200	500	900	200	500	900	200	500	900
AIC	Our Method	570	1431	2573	568	1426	2562	573	1439	2592	568	1425	2563
	Queen	671	1541	2846	654	1569	2965	785	2015	3438	644	1612	2901
	Inv. Dist.	652	1539	2859	652	1552	2868	775	2031	3445	636	1597	2815
ϵ^2	Our Method	0.954	0.987	1.000	0.947	0.984	0.995	1.016	1.035	1.040	0.957	0.986	0.996
	Queen	1.343	1.245	1.341	1.299	1.370	1.497	2.561	2.942	2.507	1.314	1.370	1.381
	Inv. Dist.	1.201	1.225	1.337	1.256	1.293	1.321	2.377	3.111	2.515	1.229	1.314	1.268

Table 3. Mean of 500 estimates for each of the 4 different settings with 3 different values of n. We compare the BIAS, RMSE, true positive selections, and false negative selections. The values for BIAS and RMSE are to the power of 10^{-3} and are separated between values that should be estimated as zero ($\stackrel{!}{=} 0$) and values that should be estimated as greater than zero ($\stackrel{!}{>} 0$).

		16-Setting-1			16-Setting-2			16-Setting-3			16-Setting-4		
	n	200	500	900	200	500	900	200	500	900	200	500	900
BIAS	$\stackrel{!}{=} 0$	1.835	0.892	0.595	1.920	1.103	0.729	0.668	0.323	0.243	2.113	1.107	0.757
(in 10^{-3})	$\stackrel{!}{>} 0$	−4.721	−3.934	−3.677	−4.961	−4.194	−3.824	−32.80	−28.74	−28.06	−5.091	−4.171	−3.855
RMSE	$\stackrel{!}{=} 0$	1.861	0.910	0.609	2.636	1.445	0.940	0.888	0.407	0.331	2.571	1.430	0.967
(in 10^{-3})	$\stackrel{!}{>} 0$	5.125	4.102	3.815	6.721	5.062	4.151	32.80	28.75	28.06	7.490	5.101	4.363
True positive		0.86	0.97	0.99	0.78	0.95	0.99	1.0	1.0	1.0	0.76	0.92	0.98
False non-zero		0.07	0.06	0.05	0.06	0.05	0.04	0.03	0.02	0.02	0.06	0.05	0.05

4. Real-World Application

In this section, we apply our approach to the evolution of land prices in Brandenburg, Germany. In general, spatial autoregressive or spatial lag models are widely applied to model housing prices or the evolution of house prices (e.g., Fingleton [34], Osland [35], Baltagi et al. [36,37], Jin and Lee [38]). Furthermore, Taşpınar et al. [39] showed that there are spatial interactions in the volatility of house-price returns. Below, we focus on the spatial dependence structure due to the specifics of the studied area. The state of Brandenburg, with 2370 districts, completely surrounds Berlin. Berlin does not belong to Brandenburg and is therefore not included in the dataset. It is to be expected that the distance to Berlin has a strong influence on the evolution of Brandenburg's sales prices. It is also to be expected that the influences the districts have on each other is stronger in the vicinity of Berlin.

We consider the sales prices of land that was sold as building land for the first time. The dataset contains the sales prices from 2005 to 2014 for the 2370 districts of Brandenburg. To model the evolution of the sales prices, we take the average prices per square metre for all regions between 2005 and 2009 and compute the difference from the average price for the regions from 2010 to 2014. For regions that do not have sufficient data, we replace the difference in selling price with zero, that is, we assume no price changes between these periods. The resulting map is plotted in Figure 6, on the right.

We wish to investigate whether the districts in the dataset exert a short-distance influence on each other, whether this influence is directional, and in which direction the influence flows. Therefore, we choose the setting such that our weights ϕ_{ij} are oriented towards Berlin (similarly to a compass pointing north, hence in Figure 6 the green pieces are pointing to Berlin). Furthermore, we include the following regressors: (1) the distance to Berlin for each district, (2) the squared distance to Berlin, (3) the inverse distance to

Berlin, and (4) an intercept of 1. To find the optimal number of directions k and the best length l, we calculate the $K \times L \, \tilde{\boldsymbol{W}}_{ij}$ for a subset of $n_0 = 58$ of the $n = 2370$ districts to lower the required computational effort (see Figure 6, left).

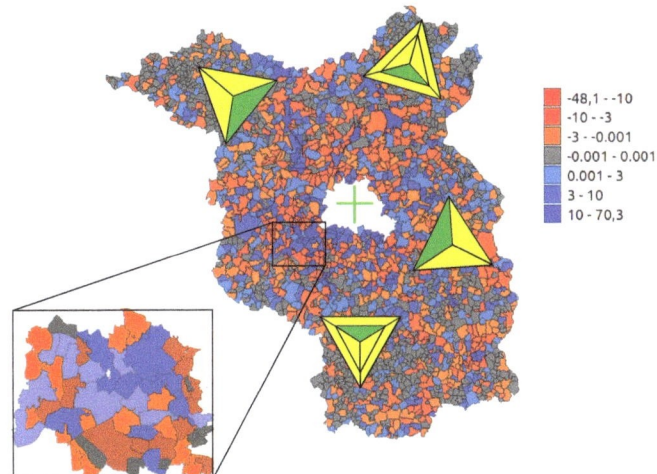

Figure 6. Brandenburg with its $n = 2370$ districts. Green cross: Berlin centre. Triangles: two example settings of the ϕ_{ij} with two different d and l. They are always chosen to be biased towards Berlin centre. The inset shows the sub-region of Brandenburg with $n_0 = 58$ districts which is used to determine the parameters $\{\tilde{d}, \tilde{k}, \tilde{l}\}$ by spatial partitioning.

The results of the spatial partitioning are plotted in Figure 7 for distances $d = 1$ and $d = 2$. In both cases, the best number of directions is $\tilde{k} = 3$. In the case where $d = 1$, the optimal length of the pieces is $\tilde{l} = 7000$ m, and in the case where $d = 2$, it is $\tilde{l} = 5250$ m. The global best choice, according to the AIC, is the latter setting. For the selection of the optimal length we use step sizes of $\delta l = 250$ m.

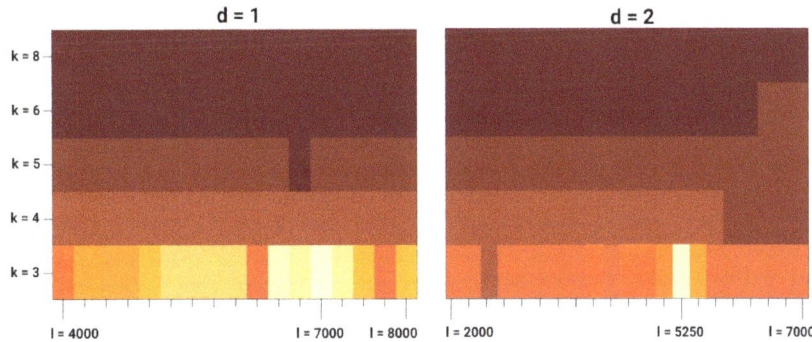

Figure 7. Heatmap of AIC values for different k, l, d. Lighter colours represent a smaller AIC value.

With the optimal settings, we estimated the parameters for $\hat{\beta}$ and $\hat{\phi}_{ij}$ as described in Section 2. We estimated the model $d \times k + p$ times and, after each step, removed the least significant parameter. Finally, we selected the best estimation according to the AIC. In both cases, the estimation with only one parameter was selected via the AIC. In both cases, the remaining parameter is the one pointing towards Berlin (see Figure 8). Furthermore, $\hat{\beta} = 0$ is selected by our method, which shows that the evolution of the sales prices is not dependent on the distance to Berlin. The result from the real-world study shows that the evolution of the sales prices can be described by a directional influence within the districts of Brandenburg, coming mainly from Berlin.

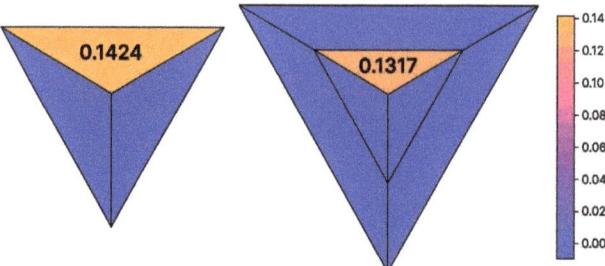

Figure 8. Results of the estimation for Brandenburg. The values represent the estimated values. There is only directional influence from Berlin. This plot visualizes the estimated directional influence between the districts in Brandenburg.

5. Discussion

Spatial weights matrices for SAR models are of interest in many areas, e.g., for the description of environmental processes such as air pollution or the description of the evolution of housing prices. Numerous methods have therefore been introduced to estimate the spatial weights matrix. However, methods applicable in asymmetric scenarios are lacking.

In this paper, we presented a method for calculating the $n \times n$ spatial weights matrix **W** for directional processes which can be symmetric as well as anti-symmetric. The directional influence is assumed to be the same in all regions of a map and is described by the value of the segments ϕ_{ij}. The proposed method can be used to estimate the directional influence in certain use-cases, such as in the modelling of $PM_{2.5}$ in a windy area (see Zhou et al. [22]). In other areas of application, spatial models are created in different environmental areas such as regions of ocean currents (mostly from the same direction). To date, the models have only allowed a symmetric influence or it was necessary to bias the directional influence by knowingly setting certain directions of influence to zero.

In Section 3, we presented Monte Carlo simulations to show that we can re-estimate the $\hat{\phi}_{ij}$ consistently. Additionally, we showed that weight matrices calculated with our method outperformed a Queen's contiguity matrix and an inverse-distance weighting matrix in the selection of four directional settings.

In Section 4, we applied our method to real-world data and showed that there is a short-distance influence in the evolution of land sales prices in Brandenburg, Germany. This directional influence flows from Berlin, at the centre of Brandenburg.

One limitation of the proposed method is that the effort required to calculate the overlapping areas of all pizza-like shapes for all regions is computationally demanding. For larger numbers of regions or larger d and k, the proposed method needs to be improved.

In future work, we intend to decrease the computational effort required to calculate the weights matrices W_{ij}, to allow a larger number of distances d for the segment shapes. With this in hand, one could investigate whether another means of selecting parameters—other than the AIC—could boost the results, since selection using the AIC always promotes fewer parameters. This could be achieved by predicting which area of which region overlap needs to be calculated. Another suggestion is to try different segment shapes. In this paper, we considered only a pizza-like slicing. It could also be worth investigating whether the estimation itself could be enhanced by using a lasso technique.

Author Contributions: F.H.H.: conceptualization, methodology, software, data curation, writing—original draft preparation, writing—review and editing, and visualization; M.S.M.: conceptualization, methodology, and writing—review and editing; P.O.: conceptualization, methodology, writing—original draft preparation, writing—review and editing, supervision, project administration, and funding acquisition. All authors have read and agreed to the published version of the manuscript.

Funding: This research received no external funding.

Institutional Review Board Statement: Not applicable.

Informed Consent Statement: Not applicable.

Data Availability Statement: All software code is open-source. The data are available upon request.

Acknowledgments: The results presented here were achieved by computations carried out on the cluster system at the Leibniz University Hannover, Germany.

Conflicts of Interest: The authors declare no conflict of interest.

References

1. Tobler, W.R. A computer movie simulating urban growth in the Detroit region. *Econ. Geogr.* **1970**, *46*, 234–240. [CrossRef]
2. Cressie, N.; Wikle, C.K. *Statistics for Spatio-Temporal Data*; John Wiley & Sons: Hoboken, NJ, USA, 2015.
3. LeSage, J.P. Bayesian estimation of spatial autoregressive models. *Int. Reg. Sci. Rev.* **1997**, *20*, 113–129. [CrossRef]
4. LeSage, J.; Pace, R.K. *Introduction to Spatial Econometrics*; Chapman and Hall/CRC: Boca Raton, FL, USA, 2009.
5. Billé, A.G.; Rogna, M. The effect of weather conditions on fertilizer applications: A spatial dynamic panel data analysis. *J. R. Stat. Soc. Ser. A (Stat. Soc.)* **2022**.
6. Billé, A.G.; Caporin, M. Impact of COVID-19 on Financial Returns: A Spatial Dynamic Panel Data Model with Random Effects. *Available SSRN 3990761* **2021**. Available online: https://papers.ssrn.com/sol3/papers.cfm?abstract_id=3990761 (accessed on 9 June 2022).
7. Billé, A.G. Spatial autoregressive nonlinear models in R with an empirical application in labour economics. In *Handbook of Research Methods and Applications in Empirical Microeconomics*; Edward Elgar Publishing: Cheltenham, UK, 2021; pp. 23–41.
8. Donegan, C.; Chun, Y.; Griffith, D.A. Modeling community health with areal data: Bayesian inference with survey standard errors and spatial structure. *Int. J. Environ. Res. Public Health* **2021**, *18*, 6856. [CrossRef]
9. Lin Lawell, C.Y.C. A Spatial Econometric Approach to Measuring air Pollution Externalities. *Available SSRN 675501* **2005**. Available online: https://papers.ssrn.com/sol3/papers.cfm?abstract_id=675501 (accessed on 9 June 2022).
10. Boly, A.; Coulibaly, S.; Kéré, E.N. Tax policy, foreign direct investment and spillover effects in Africa. *J. Afr. Econ.* **2020**, *29*, 306–331. [CrossRef]
11. Zhao, H.; Cao, X.; Ma, T. A spatial econometric empirical research on the impact of industrial agglomeration on haze pollution in China. *Air Qual. Atmos. Health* **2020**, *13*, 1305–1312. [CrossRef]
12. Krisztin, T.; Piribauer, P.; Wögerer, M. The spatial econometrics of the coronavirus pandemic. *Lett. Spat. Resour. Sci.* **2020**, *13*, 209–218. [CrossRef]
13. Pinkse, J.; Slade, M.E.; Brett, C. Spatial price competition: A semiparametric approach. *Econometrica* **2002**, *70*, 1111–1153. [CrossRef]
14. Stakhovych, S.; Bijmolt, T.H. Specification of spatial models: A simulation study on weights matrices. *Pap. Reg. Sci.* **2009**, *88*, 389–408. [CrossRef]
15. Bhattacharjee, A.; Jensen-Butler, C. Estimation of the spatial weights matrix under structural constraints. *Reg. Sci. Urban Econ.* **2013**, *43*, 617–634. [CrossRef]
16. Ahrens, A.; Bhattacharjee, A. Two-step lasso estimation of the spatial weights matrix. *Econometrics* **2015**, *3*, 128–155. [CrossRef]
17. Lam, C.; Souza, P.C. Estimation and selection of spatial weight matrix in a spatial lag model. *J. Bus. Econ. Stat.* **2020**, *38*, 693–710. [CrossRef]
18. Cohen, J.P.; Paul, C.M. The impacts of transportation infrastructure on property values: A higher-order spatial econometrics approach. *J. Reg. Sci.* **2007**, *47*, 457–478. [CrossRef]
19. Debarsy, N.; LeSage, J.P. Bayesian model averaging for spatial autoregressive models based on convex combinations of different types of connectivity matrices. *J. Bus. Econ. Stat.* **2022**, *40*, 547–558. [CrossRef]
20. Debarsy, N.; Ertur, C. Interaction matrix selection in spatial autoregressive models with an application to growth theory. *Reg. Sci. Urban Econ.* **2019**, *75*, 49–69. [CrossRef]
21. Zhang, X.; Yu, J. Spatial weights matrix selection and model averaging for spatial autoregressive models. *J. Econom.* **2018**, *203*, 1–18. [CrossRef]
22. Zhou, H.; Jiang, M.; Huang, Y.; Wang, Q. Directional spatial spillover effects and driving factors of haze pollution in North China Plain. *Resour. Conserv. Recycl.* **2021**, *169*, 105475. [CrossRef]
23. Merk, M.S.; Otto, P. Estimation of Anisotropic, Time-Varying Spatial Spillovers of Fine Particulate Matter Due to Wind Direction. *Geogr. Anal.* **2020**, *52*, 254–277. [CrossRef]

24. Merk, M.S.; Otto, P. Estimation of the spatial weighting matrix for regular lattice data—An adaptive lasso approach with cross-sectional resampling. *Environmetrics* **2022**, *31*, e2705. [CrossRef]
25. Anselin, L. *Spatial Econometrics: Methods and Models*; Springer Science & Business Media: Berlin/Heidelberg, Germany, 1988; Volume 4.
26. Elhorst, J.P.; Lacombe, D.J.; Piras, G. On model specification and parameter space definitions in higher order spatial econometric models. *Reg. Sci. Urban Econ.* **2012**, *42*, 211–220. [CrossRef]
27. Akaike, H. A new look at the statistical model identification. *IEEE Trans. Autom. Control.* **1974**, *19*, 716–723. [CrossRef]
28. Lee, L.F. Consistency and efficiency of least squares estimation for mixed regressive, spatial autoregressive models. *Econom. Theory* **2002**, *18*, 252–277. [CrossRef]
29. Gupta, A.; Robinson, P.M. Inference on higher-order spatial autoregressive models with increasingly many parameters. *J. Econom.* **2015**, *186*, 19–31. [CrossRef]
30. Longley, P.; Goodchild, M.; Maguire, D.; Rhind, D. *Geographic Information Systems and Science*; Wiley: Hoboken, NJ, USA, 2005.
31. Sen, Z. *Spatial Modeling Principles in Earth Sciences*; Springer International Publishing: Berlin/Heidelberg, Germany, 2016.
32. Keitt, T.; Bivand, R.; Pebesma, E.; Rowlingson, B. Package 'Rgdal'. Bindings for the Geospatial Data Abstraction Library. 2015. Available online: https://cran.r-project.org/web/packages/rgdal/index.html (accessed on 15 October 2017).
33. Bivand, R. Package 'Spdep'. *The Comprehensive R Archive Network*. 2015. Available online: https://www.yumpu.com/en/document/view/9283478/package-spdep-the-comprehensive-r-archive-network (accessed on 9 June 2022).
34. Fingleton, B. A generalized method of moments estimator for a spatial panel model with an endogenous spatial lag and spatial moving average errors. *Spat. Econ. Anal.* **2008**, *3*, 27–44. [CrossRef]
35. Osland, L. An application of spatial econometrics in relation to hedonic house price modeling. *J. Real Estate Res.* **2010**, *32*, 289–320. [CrossRef]
36. Baltagi, B.H.; Fingleton, B.; Pirotte, A. Spatial lag models with nested random effects: An instrumental variable procedure with an application to English house prices. *J. Urban Econ.* **2014**, *80*, 76–86. [CrossRef]
37. Baltagi, B.H.; Bresson, G.; Etienne, J.M. Hedonic housing prices in Paris: An unbalanced spatial lag pseudo-panel model with nested random effects. *J. Appl. Econom.* **2015**, *30*, 509–528. [CrossRef]
38. Jin, C.; Lee, G. Exploring spatiotemporal dynamics in a housing market using the spatial vector autoregressive Lasso: A case study of Seoul, Korea. *Trans. GIS* **2020**, *24*, 27–43. [CrossRef]
39. Taşpınar, S.; Doğan, O.; Chae, J.; Bera, A.K. Bayesian inference in spatial stochastic volatility models: An application to house price returns in Chicago. *Oxf. Bull. Econ. Stat.* **2021**, *83*, 1243–1272. [CrossRef]

Article

Reduction in Waiting Time in an M/M/1/N Encouraged Arrival Queue with Feedback, Balking and Maintaining of Reneged Customers

Ismailkhan Enayathulla Khan and Rajendran Paramasivam *

Department of Mathematics, School of Advanced Sciences, VIT University, Vellore 632014, Tamil Nadu, India
* Correspondence: prajendran@vit.ac.in

Abstract: In this research, we look at the work associated with the encouraged arrival line with feedback, balking and maintaining reneged clients. We analyse the quality control policy for the Markovian model using an iterative method to the nth customer in the system. We derive performance measures for the expected number of units in the system, as well as in the queue and the average number of occupied services and the expected waiting time in the system, as well as in the queue. To show the effectiveness, we provide numerical examples for the average default rate and average retention rate. The developed formula also satisfies Little's formula.

Keywords: encouraged arrival; quality control feedback; balking; maintaining; retention

1. Introduction

A queue in operations research signifies a certain number of clients waiting for service. In most cases, the consumer being served is not regarded as being in line. The queue's characteristics are described by queueing theory. In everyday life, everyone has to wait in a line or queue, whether it is at a food court, a clinic, or a bank cashier. It can be fascinating at times, but it is often frustrating for both the consumer and the service provider. Understanding queues or lines is one of the most critical aspects of operation research management.

Queuing theory as an area of research was introduced by A.K. Erlang. The customer enters a queue. Balking and reneging have been discussed [1,2], respectively. The mingled impact of the finite capacity queue of balking and reneging has been derived by [3,4].

An M/M/1/N queuing model with quality control policy and optimal policies are discussed [5]. Ref. [6] discussed an M/M/1/N with reneging and general balking distribution. Ref. [7] studied in quality control and an M/G/1 queue-like production system was discussed. Ref. [8] derived an optimal admission Markov queue under the quality of service constraints.

An M/M/1/N queuing system and Markovian feedback queue discussion about retention and reneged customers is found in [9]; a discussion around M/M/1/N queuing system and balking with the retention of reneged customers queuing model is found in [10], and a feedback queue with the retention of reneged customers has been discussed in [11]. An M/M/1/N queuing system and reverse balking is discussed in [12]; an M/M/1/N queuing system with encouraged arrival has been studied in [13]. An M/M/1/N quality control feedback with balking and retention of reneged customers has been discussed in [14]. Basic definitions of queuing theory be found in [15]. Impact of prioritization on the outpatient queuing system in the emergency department with limited medical resources has been studied [16]. A comparison between bivariate statistical models has been studied [17]. An MMAP/(PH.PH)/1 Queue with priority loss through feedback has been studied [18]

The goal of this study is to optimize various parameters in the quality control of a single server, including the encouraged arrivals in balking, retention, and reneging customers through a steady-state condition. This paper is arranged as follows: Notation and Mathematical model formulation is delivered in Section 2. A deal with performance measure and special cases in Section 3. We discuss about model Elaboration relation and solution of this model in Section 4. Section 5 deals with Main result and discussion, limitations. Conclusion is provided in Section 6.

2. Mathematical Model Formulation

The Following Were Assumed to Describe the Mathematical Model

1. Customers arrive one by one to a Poisson discipline process with rate $\lambda(1+\eta)$, where η represents past or observed data calculated by the customer. If a past organisation offered discounts and percentages, the number of customers observed values rise to $\eta = 0.5$ and $\eta = 1.2$, respectively.
2. Service time is exponential and identically distributed.
3. Customers follows the first in first out discipline.
4. After the completion of service, customers join at the end of the original queue as feedback with probability $(1-q)$.
5. The probability that a processing job is defective in the system with probability q.
6. For the feedback situation, g_n, could be a random event such that $g_n = 1$ reflects the event that there are N jobs in the system and $g_n = 0$ otherwise for $0 \leq n \leq N$. After joining a queue, for service to begin the probability is $(1-p)$.
7. If the service has not begun, the customer will leave the queue without getting service, as an impatient customer with probability $(n-1)pa$ for $2 \leq n \leq N$ for $n=1$, the value is zero.
8. An encouraged arrival will join the queue with probability β and will not join the queue with probability: $1-b$, when n units are ahead $0 \leq n \leq 1$. An encouraged arrival will join the queue with probability b and will not join the queue with probability: $1-b$, for $1 \leq n \leq N-1$ and $b=1$ otherwise.

We derive the following differential-difference equations:

$$\frac{d}{dt}p_0(t) = -\lambda(1+\eta)\,p_0(t) + \mu q g_1 p_1(t), \quad n=0 \tag{1}$$

$$\frac{d}{dt}p_1(t) = -(b\lambda(1+\eta) + \mu q g_1)p_1(t) + \lambda(1+\eta)p_0(t) + (\mu q g_2 + ap)p_2, \quad n=1 \tag{2}$$

$$\frac{d}{dt}p_n(t) = -(b\lambda(1+\eta) + \mu q g_n + (n-1)ap)p_n(t) + b\lambda(1+\eta)p_{n-1}(t) + (\mu q g_{n+1} + nap)p_{n+1}, \quad 1 \leq n < N \tag{3}$$

$$\frac{d}{dt}p_N(t) = -(\mu q g_N + (N-1)ap)p_N(t) + b\lambda(1+\eta)p_{N-1}(t), \quad n=N \tag{4}$$

Steady-State Solution:

$$-\lambda(1+\eta)p_0 + \mu q g_1 p_1 = 0, \quad n=0 \tag{5}$$

$$-(b\lambda(1+\eta) + \mu q g_1)p_1 + \lambda(1+\eta)p_0 + (\mu q g_2 + ap)p_2 = 0, \quad n=1 \tag{6}$$

$$-((b\lambda(1+\eta) + \mu q g_n + (n-1)ap)p_n + b\lambda(1+\eta)p_{n-1} + (\mu q g_{n+1} + nap)p_{n+1} = 0, \quad 1 < n < N \tag{7}$$

$$-(\mu q g_N + (N-1)ap)p_N + b\lambda(1+\eta)p_{N-1} = 0, \quad n=N \tag{8}$$

Solving the differential–difference Equations from (1) to (8) iteratively, we obtain,

$$(\mu q g_{n+1} + nap)p_{n+1} - b\lambda(1+\eta)p_n = (\mu q g_n + (n-1)ap)p_n - b\lambda(1+\eta) = \ldots (\mu q p_2 + ap)p_2 - b\lambda(1+\eta)p_1 = \ldots (\mu q g_1 p_1 - \lambda(1+\eta)p_0 = 0.$$

Now, the value of p_n is obtained as:

$$p_n = \frac{b\lambda(1+\eta)}{\mu q g_n + (n-1)ap} p_{n-1} \tag{9}$$

By using the recurrence formula given by Equation (9), the general formula is obtained as:

$$p_n = \frac{\lambda(1+\eta)(b\lambda(1+\eta))^n}{[\mu q g_n + (n-1)ap] * [\mu q g_{n-1} + (n-2)ap] * [\mu q g_2 + ap] * [\mu q g_1]} p_0$$

Now, the probability of 'n' units in the system is given by

$$p_n = \begin{cases} p_0 & n = 0 \\ \dfrac{\delta^n}{b \prod_{i=0}^{n-1}(\gamma g_{i+1} + i)} & 1 \leq n \leq N \end{cases}$$

where $\delta = \dfrac{b\lambda(1+\eta)}{ap}$ and $\gamma = \dfrac{\mu q}{ap}$.

Now to find the probability that there is no unit in the service, which is denoted by p_0, we use the boundary condition $1 = \sum_{n=0}^{N} p_n$.

That is, $1 = p_0 + \sum_{n=1}^{N} \dfrac{\delta^n}{b \prod_{i=0}^{n-1}(\gamma g_{i+1} + i)}$,

$$p_0^{-1} = 1 + \frac{1}{b} \sum_{n=1}^{N} \frac{\delta^n}{\prod_{i=0}^{n-1}(\gamma g_{i+1} + i)} \tag{10}$$

3. Performance Measures

Now we obtain the formula for various measures as given below:
The expected number of units in the system is given by:

$$L = \frac{p_0}{b} \sum_{n=1}^{N} \frac{n\delta^n}{\prod_{i=0}^{n-1}(\gamma g_{i+1} + i)} \tag{11}$$

The expected number of units in the queue is given by:

$$L_q = L - (1 - p_0) \tag{12}$$

The average number of occupied services is given by:

$$L_s = L - L_q \tag{13}$$

The expected waiting time in the system is given by:

$$W = \frac{L}{\lambda(1+\eta)} \tag{14}$$

and

The expected waiting time in the queue is given by:

$$w_q = \frac{L_q}{\lambda(1+\eta)} \tag{15}$$

The Equations (14) and (15) are called Little's formula.
The expected service time is given by:

$$W_s = W - W_q = \frac{L - L_q}{\lambda(1+\eta)} \tag{16}$$

The average reneging rate is given by:

$$R_E = \sum_{n=1}^{N}(n-1)app_n \tag{17}$$

The average maintaining rate is given by:

$$R_e = \sum_{n=1}^{N}(n-1)app_n \tag{18}$$

Particular Cases

Case 1: when we put $a = 0$, $b = 1$, $p = 1$, $q = 1$, $g_n = 1$, this is the quality control queue: M/M/1/N with feedback, balking and retention of reneged customers.

Case 2: when we put $q = 1$, $g_n = 1$, and $a = 0$, we get the model M/M/1/N, which is the same as Gross and Harris [15].

4. Model Elaboration

The values of the parameters of this M/M/1/N queuing model are given.

λ	η	λ (1+η)	N	P	q	q	g_i
4	0.5	6	4	0.1	0.9	0.25, 0.50, 1	0 or 1

The following Tables 1–4 of values is obtained for L-expected number of units in the system by using the relation [11] for b = 0.25, 0.50, 1.

Table 1. The values of L for different values of b = 0.25, 0.50, 1.

a	L at b = 0.25	L at b = 0.50	L at b = 1
0.05	3.995225	3.996138	3.998365
0.06	3.996334	3.816372	3.999065
0.07	3.991855	3.978771	3.988408
0.08	3.898826	3.998237	3.988041
0.09	3.992406	3.969705	3.998728
0.10	3.972794	3.996458	3.997931
0.11	3.991761	3.994401	3.979199
0.12	3.990751	3.995094	3.921691
0.13	3.989561	3.989560	3.981316
0.14	3.988700	3.999407	3.977291
0.15	3.988784	3.994852	3.975339

Table 2. Comparison of L-Expected number of units in the system between poisson and encouraged arrival.

a	Poisson Arrival L at b = 0.50	Encouraged Arrival L at b = 0.50
0.06	3.967179	3.816372

Table 3. Comparison of L-Expected number of units in the system between poisson and encouraged arrival.

a	Poisson Arrival L at b = 1	Encouraged Arrival L at b = 1
0.08	3.985963	3.988041
0.11	3.980742	3.979199
0.12	3.979004	3.921691

Solution of the system is determined by scheming L against "a" for some values of b, as given in Figure 1.

Remark 1. *From the Figure 1, it is evident that, the value of L-Expected number of units in the system is less at a = 0.06, 0.08, 0.12 comparing the poisson arrival.*

The value of the parameters of this M/M/1/N queuing models are given.

λ	η	λ (1+η)	N	P	q	q	g_i
4	0.6	6.4	4	0.1	0.9	0.25, 0.50, 1	0 or 1

The following Tables 5–8 of values is obtained for L-expected number of units in the system by using the relation [11] for b = 0.25, 0.50, 1.

Table 4. Verification of Little's law.

S.No	b	a	L	W	L/W	λ
1	0.25	0.05	3.995225	0.66587083	5.999998498	6
2	0.5	0.05	3.996334	0.66605567	5.999996997	6
3	1	0.05	3.998365	0.66639417	6.000001501	6
4	0.25	0.06	3.996334	0.66605567	5.999996997	6
5	0.5	0.06	3.816372	0.63606200	6	6
6	1	0.06	3.999065	0.66651083	5.9999985	6
7	0.25	0.07	3.991855	0.66531417	5.999956412	6
8	0.5	0.07	3.978771	0.66312850	5.999995476	6
9	1	0.07	3.988408	0.66473467	5.999996991	6
10	0.25	0.08	3.898826	0.64980433	6.000003078	6
11	0.5	0.08	3.998237	0.66637283	5.999998499	6
12	1	0.08	3.988041	0.66467350	5.999995487	6
13	0.25	0.09	3.992406	0.6654010	6	6
14	0.5	0.09	3.969705	0.6616175	5.999995466	6
15	1	0.09	3.998728	0.6664546	5.999996999	6
16	0.25	0.1	3.972794	0.6621323	6.000003021	6
17	0.5	0.1	3.996458	0.6660763	6.000003003	6
18	1	0.1	3.997931	0.6663218	5.999998499	6
19	0.25	0.11	3.991761	0.6652935	5.999995491	6
20	0.5	0.11	3.994401	0.6657335	5.999995494	6
21	1	0.11	3.979199	0.6631998	5.999998492	6
22	0.25	0.12	3.990751	0.6651251	6.000001503	6
23	0.5	0.12	3.995094	0.6658490	6	6
24	1	0.12	3.921691	0.6536151	6.00000153	6
25	0.25	0.13	3.989561	0.6649268	5.999998496	6
26	0.5	0.13	3.989560	0.6649266	5.999996992	6
27	1	0.13	3.981316	0.6635526	5.999996986	6
28	0.25	0.14	3.988700	0.6647833	6.000003009	6
29	0.5	0.14	3.999407	0.6665678	5.9999985	6
30	1	0.14	3.977291	0.6628818	5.999998491	6
31	0.25	0.15	3.988784	0.6647973	6.000030085	6
32	0.5	0.15	3.994852	0.6658086	5.999996996	6
33	1	0.15	3.975339	0.6625560	5.999995472	6

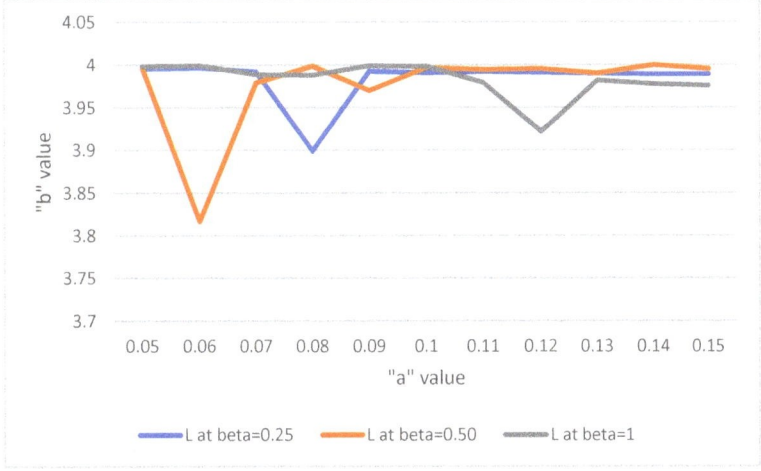

Figure 1. The relationship between L and "a" when "b" = 0.25, 0.50.

Table 5. The values of L for different values of b = 0.25, 0.50, 1.

a	L at b = 0.25	L at b = 0.50	L at b = 1
0.05	3.984371	3.994342	3.670805
0.06	3.989045	3.994022	3.991227
0.07	3.994445	3.978169	3.990492
0.08	3.991879	3.997466	3.816650
0.09	3.991760	3.997145	3.993229
0.10	3.992748	3.995779	3.964409
0.11	3.990344	3.972103	3.998272
0.12	3.992591	3.995301	3.997578
0.13	3.992015	3.991104	3.962625
0.14	3.968499	3.906548	3.901016
0.15	3.988080	3.992987	3.985997

Table 6. Comparison of L-Expected number of units in the system between poisson and encouraged arrival.

a	Poisson Arrival L at b = 0.50	Encouraged Arrival L at b = 0.50
0.14	3.924853	3.906548

Table 7. Comparison of L-Expected number of units in the system between poisson and encouraged arrival.

a	Poisson Arrival L at b = 1	Encouraged Arrival L at b = 1
0.05	3.991214	3.670805
0.08	3.985968	3.816650
0.10	3.982482	3.964409
0.13	3.977268	3.962625
0.14	3.975535	3.901016

Solution of the system is determined by scheming L against "a" for some values of b, as given in Figure 2.

Remark 2. *From the Figure 2, it is evident that, the value of L-Expected number of units in the system is less at a = 0.05, 0.08, 0.14 comparing the poisson arrival.*

The value of the parameters of this M/M/1/N queuing models are given.

λ	η	$\lambda(1+\eta)$	N	P	q	q	g_i
4	0.7	6.8	4	0.1	0.9	0.25, 0.50, 1	0 or 1

The following Tables 9–12 of values is obtained for L-expected number of units in the system by using the relation [11] for b = 0.25, 0.50, 1.

Table 8. Verification of Little's law.

S.No	b	a	L	W	L/W	λ
1	0.25	0.05	3.984371	0.62255797	6.399999679	6.4
2	0.5	0.05	3.994342	0.62411594	6.399999359	6.4
3	1	0.05	3.670805	0.57356328	6.400003138	6.4
4	0.25	0.06	3.989045	0.62328828	6.400002888	6.4
5	0.5	0.06	3.994022	0.62406594	6.399999359	6.4
6	1	0.06	3.990492	0.62351438	6.400003849	6.4
7	0.25	0.07	3.994445	0.62413203	6.400008332	6.4

Table 8. Cont.

S.No	b	a	L	W	L/W	λ
8	0.5	0.07	3.978169	0.62158891	6.399999035	6.4
9	1	0.07	3.990492	0.62351438	6.400003849	6.4
10	0.25	0.08	3.991879	0.62373109	6.400000962	6.4
11	0.5	0.08	3.997466	0.62460406	6.40000064	6.4
12	1	0.08	3.816650	0.59635156	6.399995305	6.4
13	0.25	0.09	3.991760	0.62371250	6.399994869	6.4
14	0.5	0.09	3.997145	0.62455391	6.399999039	6.4
15	1	0.09	3.993229	0.62394203	6.400000321	6.4
16	0.25	0.1	3.992748	0.62386688	6.399998718	6.4
17	0.5	0.1	3.995779	0.62434047	6.400004805	6.4
18	1	0.1	3.964409	0.61943891	6.399999031	6.4
19	0.25	0.11	3.990344	0.62349125	6.400002566	6.4
20	0.5	0.11	3.972103	0.62064109	6.400000967	6.4
21	1	0.11	3.998272	0.62473000	6.4	6.4
22	0.25	0.12	3.992591	0.62384234	6.400003527	6.4
23	0.5	0.12	3.995301	0.62426578	6.399997757	6.4
24	1	0.12	3.997578	0.62466844	6.399524227	6.4
25	0.25	0.13	3.992015	0.62375234	6.400003527	6.4
26	0.5	0.13	3.991104	0.62361000	6.4	6.4
27	1	0.13	3.962625	0.61916016	6.400001615	6.4
28	0.25	0.14	3.968499	0.62007797	6.399999677	6.4
29	0.5	0.14	3.906548	0.61039813	6.400001311	6.4
30	1	0.14	3.901016	0.60953375	6.399997375	6.4
31	0.25	0.15	3.988080	0.6231375	6.399994865	6.4
32	0.5	0.15	3.992987	0.62390422	6.400002244	6.4
33	1	0.15	3.985997	0.62281203	6.400000321	6.4

Figure 2. The relationship between L and "a" when "b" = 0.25, 0.50, 1.

Table 9. The values of L for different values of b = 0.25, 0.50, 1.

a	L at b = 0.25	L at b = 0.50	L at b = 1
0.05	3.691028	3.998519	3.999239
0.06	3.996364	3.998222	3.999115
0.07	3.995741	3.997918	3.998966
0.08	3.995176	3.997620	3.998820

Table 9. Cont.

a	L at b = 0.25	L at b = 0.50	L at b = 1
0.09	3.994538	3.997342	3.998671
0.10	3.993821	3.997006	3.998423
0.11	3.993171	3.996615	3.998422
0.12	3.992940	3.873728	3.998231
0.13	3.991847	3.996127	3.998082
0.14	3.991183	3.995767	3.997902
0.15	3.990506	3.995525	3.997780

Table 10. Comparison of L-Expected number of units in the system between poisson and encouraged arrival.

a	Poisson Arrival L at b = 0.50	Encouraged Arrival L at b = 0.50
0.05	3.908215	3.691028

Table 11. Comparison of L-Expected number of units in the system between poisson and encouraged arrival.

a	Poisson Arrival L at b = 1	Encouraged Arrival L at b = 1
0.12	3.935285	3.873728

Solution of the system is determined by scheming L against "a" for some values of b, as given in Figure 3.

Remark 3. *From the Figure 3, it is evident that, the value of L-Expected number of units in the system is less at a = 0.05, 0.12 comparing the poisson arrival.*

The value of the parameters of this M/M/1/N queuing models are given.

λ	η	$\lambda(1+\eta)$	N	P	q	q	g_i
4	0.8	7.2	4	0.1	0.9	0.25, 0.50, 1	0 or 1

The following Tables 13–16 of values is obtained for L-expected number of units in the system by using the relation [11] for $b = 0.25, 0.50, 1$.

Table 12. Verification of Little's law.

S.No	B	a	L	W	L/W	λ
1	0.25	0.05	3.691028	0.54279824	6.800002948	6.8
2	0.5	0.05	3.998519	0.58801750	6.799994218	6.8
3	1	0.05	3.999239	0.58812338	6.800004421	6.8
4	0.25	0.06	3.996364	0.58770059	6.799995236	6.8
5	0.5	0.06	3.998222	0.58797382	6.799997959	6.8
6	1	0.06	3.999115	0.58810515	6.8000017	6.8
7	0.25	0.07	3.995741	0.58760897	6.79999966	6.8
8	0.5	0.07	3.997918	0.58792912	6.800001361	6.8
9	1	0.07	3.998966	0.58808324	6.800002721	6.8
10	0.25	0.08	3.995176	0.58752588	6.799998638	6.8
11	0.5	0.08	3.997620	0.58788529	6.800003402	6.8
12	1	0.08	3.998820	0.58806176	6.799997279	6.8
13	0.25	0.09	3.994538	0.58743206	6.800000681	6.8
14	0.5	0.09	3.997342	0.58784441	6.800004763	6.8
15	1	0.09	3.998671	0.58803985	6.799998299	6.8

Table 12. Cont.

S.No	B	a	L	W	L/W	λ
16	0.25	0.1	3.993821	0.58732662	6.799995573	6.8
17	0.5	0.1	3.997006	0.58779500	6.8	6.8
18	1	0.1	3.998423	0.58800338	6.800004422	6.8
19	0.25	0.11	3.993171	0.58723103	6.800000341	6.8
20	0.5	0.11	3.996615	0.58773750	6.799994215	6.8
21	1	0.11	3.998422	0.58800324	6.800002721	6.8
22	0.25	0.12	3.992940	0.58719706	6.800000681	6.8
23	0.5	0.12	3.873728	0.56966588	6.799998596	6.8
24	1	0.12	3.998231	0.58797515	6.800001701	6.8
25	0.25	0.13	3.991847	0.58703632	6.800003748	6.8
26	0.5	0.13	3.996127	0.58766574	6.799996937	6.8
27	1	0.13	3.998082	0.58795324	6.800002721	6.8
28	0.25	0.14	3.991183	0.58693868	6.799996252	6.8
29	0.5	0.14	3.995767	0.58761279	6.799997617	6.8
30	1	0.14	3.997902	0.58792676	6.799997279	6.8
31	0.25	0.15	3.990506	0.58683912	6.800001363	6.8
32	0.5	0.15	3.995525	0.58757721	6.800002383	6.8
33	1	0.15	3.997780	0.58790882	6.799997959	6.8

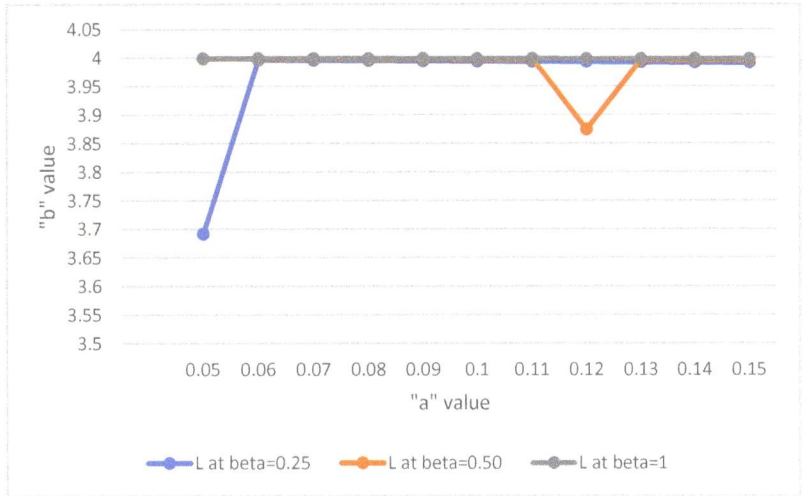

Figure 3. The relationship between L and "a" when "b" = 0.25, 0.50, 1.

Table 13. The values of L for different values of b = 0.25, 0.50, 1.

a	L at b = 0.25	L at b = 0.50	L at b = 1
0.05	3.984716	3.995301	3.998185
0.06	3.994041	3.991779	3.944412
0.07	3.964199	3.997761	3.994704
0.08	3.949832	3.967141	3.973384
0.09	3.970734	3.963279	3.982187
0.10	3.992297	3.972509	3.956158
0.11	3.984562	3.988086	3.993573
0.12	3.992639	3.985290	3.997242
0.13	3.959906	3.989724	3.980712
0.14	3.989582	3.909560	3.997553
0.15	3.996673	3.982409	3.981590

Table 14. Comparison of L-Expected number of units in the system between poisson and encouraged arrival.

a	Poisson Arrival L at $b = 0.50$	Encouraged Arrival L at $b = 0.50$
0.14	3.924853	3.909560

Table 15. Comparison of L-Expected number of units in the system between poisson and encouraged arrival.

a	Poisson Arrival L at $b = 1$	Encouraged Arrival L at $b = 1$
0.06	3.989463	3.944412
0.08	3.985968	3.973384
0.09	3.984224	3.982187
0.10	3.982482	3.956158

The solution of the system is determined by scheming L against "a" for some values of b, as given in Figure 4.

Remark 4. *From the Figure 4, it is evident that, the value of L-Expected number of units in the system is less at $a = 0.06, 0.08, 0.09, 0.10, 0.12, 0.13, 0.14$ comparing the poisson arrival.*

The value of the parameters of this M/M/1/N queuing models are given.

λ	η	$\lambda(1+\eta)$	N	P	q	q	g_i
4	0.9	7.6	4	0.1	0.9	0.25, 0.50, 1	0 or 1

The following Tables 17–21 of values is obtained for L-expected number of units in the system by using the relation [11] for $b = 0.25, 0.50, 1$.

Table 16. Verification of Little's law.

S.No	b	a	L	W	L/W	λ
1	0.25	0.05	3.984716	0.55343278	7.199997109	7.2
2	0.5	0.05	3.995301	0.55490292	7.199998919	7.2
3	1	0.05	3.998185	0.55530347	7.200006123	7.2
4	0.25	0.06	3.994041	0.55472792	7.199998918	7.2
5	0.5	0.06	3.991779	0.55441375	7.199996753	7.2
6	1	0.06	3.944412	0.54783500	7.2	7.2
7	0.25	0.07	3.964199	0.55058319	7.200002543	7.2
8	0.5	0.07	3.997761	0.55524458	7.199994597	7.2
9	1	0.07	3.994704	0.55482000	7.2	7.2
10	0.25	0.08	3.949832	0.54858778	7.199997083	7.2
11	0.5	0.08	3.967141	0.55099181	7.199997459	7.2
12	1	0.08	3.973384	0.55185889	7.19999855	7.2
13	0.25	0.09	3.970734	0.55149083	7.199997824	7.2
14	0.5	0.09	3.963279	0.55045542	7.20000545	7.2
15	1	0.09	3.982187	0.55308153	7.199993853	7.2
16	0.25	0.1	3.992297	0.55448569	7.199996032	7.2
17	0.5	0.1	3.972509	0.55173736	7.200004712	7.2
18	1	0.1	3.956158	0.54946639	7.200005096	7.2
19	0.25	0.11	3.984562	0.55341139	7.20000506	7.2
20	0.5	0.11	3.988086	0.55390083	7.199997834	7.2
21	1	0.11	3.993573	0.55466292	7.199998918	7.2
22	0.25	0.12	3.992639	0.55453319	7.200002525	7.2
23	0.5	0.12	3.985290	0.55351250	7.199993496	7.2
24	1	0.12	3.997242	0.55517250	7.199993516	7.2
25	0.25	0.13	3.959906	0.54998694	7.199999273	7.2

Table 16. Cont.

S.No	b	a	L	W	L/W	λ
26	0.5	0.13	3.989724	0.55412833	7.200004331	7.2
27	1	0.13	3.980712	0.55287667	7.199995659	7.2
28	0.25	0.14	3.989582	0.55410861	7.199994947	7.2
29	0.5	0.14	3.909560	0.54299444	7.200005893	7.2
30	1	0.14	3.997553	0.55521569	7.199996038	7.2
31	0.25	0.15	3.996673	0.55509347	7.200006125	7.2
32	0.5	0.15	3.982409	0.55311236	7.200004701	7.2
33	1	0.15	3.981590	0.55299861	7.199994937	7.2

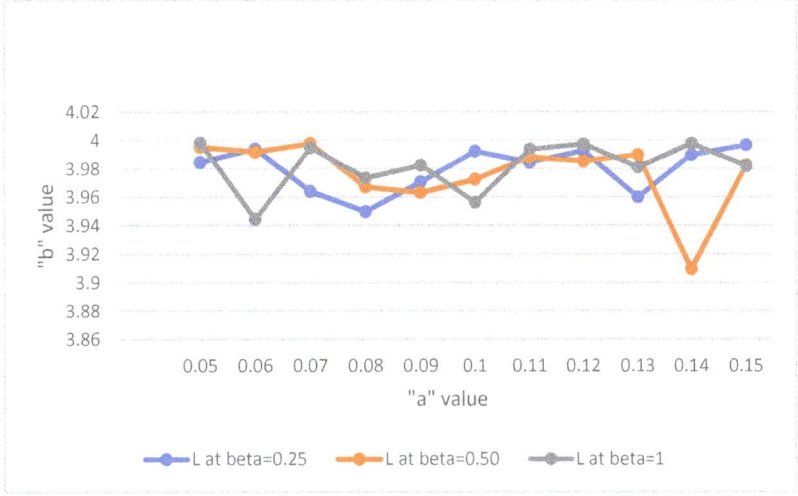

Figure 4. The relationship between L and "a" when "b" = 0.25, 0.50, 1.

Table 17. The values of L for different values of b = 0.25, 0.50, 1.

a	L at b = 0.25	L at b = 0.50	L at b = 1
0.05	3.80713	3.95550	3.89270
0.06	3.96457	3.80124	3.37690
0.07	3.88220	3.87680	3.71920
0.08	3.71410	3.97520	3.98390
0.09	3.98960	3.93560	3.96960
0.10	3.80066	3.94490	3.63780
0.11	3.83620	3.75970	3.95590
0.12	3.98890	3.94710	3.99470
0.13	3.98770	3.99320	3.97470
0.14	3.98853	3.97796	3.98021
0.15	3.96290	3.69889	3.97548

Table 18. Comparison of L-Expected number of units in the system between poisson and encouraged arrival.

a	Poisson Arrival L at b = 0.25	Encouraged Arrival L at b = 0.25
0.05	3.908215	3.80713
0.08	3.856900	3.71410
0.10	3.824116	3.80066

Table 19. Comparison of L-Expected number of units in the system between poisson and encouraged arrival.

a	Poisson Arrival L at b = 0.50	Encouraged Arrival L at b = 0.50
0.05	3.972583	3.95550
0.06	3.967179	3.80124
0.07	3.961800	3.87680
0.09	3.951119	3.93560
0.10	3.945816	3.94490
0.11	3.940538	3.75970
0.15	3.919673	3.69889

Table 20. Comparison of L-Expected number of units in the system between poisson and encouraged arrival.

a	Poisson Arrival L at b = 1	Encouraged Arrival L at b = 1
0.05	3.9912	3.8927
0.06	3.9894	3.3769
0.07	3.9877	3.7192
0.08	3.9859	3.9839
0.09	3.9842	3.9696
0.10	3.9824	3.6378
0.11	3.9807	3.9559
0.13	3.9772	3.9747

Table 21. Verification of Little's law.

S.No	b	a	L	W	L/W	λ
1	0.25	0.05	3.80713	0.50093816	7.600002396	7.6
2	0.5	0.05	3.95550	0.52046053	7.599993083	7.6
3	1	0.05	3.89270	0.51219737	7.600109334	7.6
4	0.25	0.06	3.96457	0.52165395	7.599999233	7.6
5	0.5	0.06	3.80124	0.50016316	7.600002399	7.6
6	1	0.06	3.37690	0.44432895	7.599999100	7.6
7	0.25	0.07	3.88220	0.51081579	7.599996868	7.6
8	0.5	0.07	3.87680	0.51010526	7.600003921	7.6
9	1	0.07	3.71920	0.48936842	7.600006539	7.6
10	0.25	0.08	3.71410	0.48869737	7.600005730	7.6
11	0.5	0.08	3.97520	0.52305263	7.599994647	7.6
12	1	0.08	3.98390	0.52419737	7.600005342	7.6
13	0.25	0.09	3.98960	0.52494737	7.600005334	7.6
14	0.5	0.09	3.93560	0.51784211	7.600001545	7.6
15	1	0.09	3.96960	0.52231579	7.599996937	7.6
16	0.25	0.1	3.80066	0.50008684	7.599997600	7.6
17	0.5	0.1	3.94490	0.51906579	7.599996918	7.6
18	1	0.1	3.63780	0.47865789	7.599998329	7.6
19	0.25	0.11	3.83620	0.50476316	7.600002377	7.6
20	0.5	0.11	3.75970	0.49469737	7.60000566	7.6
21	1	0.11	3.95590	0.52051316	7.600002305	7.6
22	0.25	0.12	3.98890	0.52485526	7.600003811	7.6
23	0.5	0.12	3.94710	0.51935526	7.600003851	7.6
24	1	0.12	3.99470	0.52561842	7.600006088	7.6
25	0.25	0.13	3.98770	0.52469737	7.600005336	7.6
26	0.5	0.13	3.99320	0.52542105	7.600000761	7.6
27	1	0.13	3.97470	0.52298684	7.599997705	7.6
28	0.25	0.14	3.98853	0.52480658	7.599993903	7.6
29	0.5	0.14	3.97796	0.52341579	7.599996943	7.6

Table 21. Cont.

S.No	b	a	L	W	L/W	λ
30	1	0.14	3.98021	0.52371184	7.599997709	7.6
31	0.25	0.15	3.96290	0.52143526	7.600003836	7.6
32	0.5	0.15	3.69889	0.48669605	7.600000822	7.6
33	1	0.15	3.97548	0.52308947	7.600006882	7.6

The solution of the system is determined by scheming L against a for some values of b, as given in Figure 5.

Figure 5. The relationship between L and "a" when "b" = 0.25, 0.50, 1.

Remark 5. *From the Figure 5, it is evident that, the value of L-Expected number of units in the system is less at a = 0.06, 0.08, 0.09, 0.10, 0.11, 0.12, 0.14, 0.15 comparing the poisson arrival.*

The value of the parameters of this M/M/1/N queuing models are given below.

λ	η	λ (1+η)	N	P	q	q	g_i
4	0.11	4.44	4	0.1	0.9	0.25, 0.50, 1	0 or 1

The following Tables 22–26 of values is obtained for L-expected number of units in the system by using the relation [11] for b = 0.25, 0.50, 1.

Table 22. The values of L for different values of b = 0.25, 0.50, 1.

a	L at b = 0.25	L at b = 0.50	L at b = 1
0.05	3.995100	3.546800	3.998800
0.06	3.854856	3.939360	3.994395
0.07	3.996000	3.621280	3.993300
0.08	3.991044	3.999263	3.980034
0.09	3.990490	3.934637	3.927608
0.10	3.884795	3.982260	3.957856
0.11	3.987600	3.655474	3.969599
0.12	3.941250	3.991380	3.922006
0.13	3.983723	3.995832	3.757424
0.14	3.983723	3.987378	3.996665
0.15	3.983001	3.992066	3.978019

Table 23. Comparison of L-Expected number of units in the system between poisson and encouraged arrival.

a	Poisson Arrival L at b = 0.25	Encouraged Arrival L at b = 0.25
0.06	3.890814	3.854856

Table 24. Comparison of L-Expected number of units in the system between poisson and encouraged arrival.

a	Poisson Arrival L at b = 0.50	Encouraged Arrival L at b = 0.50
0.05	3.97258	3.54680
0.06	3.96717	3.93936
0.07	3.96180	3.62128
0.09	3.95111	3.93463
0.11	3.94053	3.65547

Table 25. Comparison of L-Expected number of units in the system between poisson and encouraged arrival.

a	Poisson Arrival L at b = 1	Encouraged Arrival L at b = 1
0.08	3.98596	3.980034
0.09	3.98422	3.927608
0.10	3.98248	3.957856
0.11	3.98074	3.969599
0.13	3.97726	3.757424

Table 26. Verification of Little's law.

S.No	b	a	L	W	L/W	λ
1	0.25	0.05	3.9951	0.8997973	4.440001467	4.44
2	0.5	0.05	3.5468	0.79882883	4.439999049	4.44
3	1	0.05	3.9988	0.90063063	4.439998179	4.44
4	0.25	0.06	3.854856	0.86821081	4.439999032	4.44
5	0.5	0.06	3.93936	0.88724324	4.440001217	4.44
6	1	0.06	3.9943953	0.89963858	4.439997933	4.44
7	0.25	0.07	3.996	0.9	4.44	4.44
8	0.5	0.07	3.62128	0.8156036	4.439997842	4.44
9	1	0.07	3.9933	0.89939189	4.439999466	4.44
10	0.25	0.08	3.991044	0.89888378	4.439998932	4.44
11	0.5	0.08	3.999263	0.90073491	4.439999556	4.44
12	1	0.08	3.980034	0.89640405	4.440000268	4.44
13	0.25	0.09	3.99049	0.89875901	4.440000045	4.44
14	0.5	0.09	3.934637	0.8861795	4.439997517	4.44
15	1	0.09	3.927608	0.8845964	4.44000199	4.44
16	0.25	0.1	3.884795	0.87495383	4.439999131	4.44
17	0.5	0.1	3.98226	0.89690541	4.440002007	4.44
18	1	0.1	3.957856	0.89140901	4.440000045	4.44
19	0.25	0.11	3.9876	0.89810811	4.440000534	4.44
20	0.5	0.11	3.655474	0.82330495	4.439999757	4.44
21	1	0.11	3.969599	0.89405383	4.43999915	4.44
22	0.25	0.12	3.94125	0.88766892	4.439999594	4.44
23	0.5	0.12	3.99138	0.89895946	4.440002269	4.44
24	1	0.12	3.922006	0.88333468	4.439998415	4.44
25	0.25	0.13	3.983723	0.89723491	4.439999554	4.44
26	0.5	0.13	3.995832	0.89996216	4.4400008	4.44
27	1	0.13	3.757424	0.84626667	4.439998251	4.44
28	0.25	0.14	3.983723	0.89723491	4.439999554	4.44
29	0.5	0.14	3.987378	0.89805811	4.440000534	4.44
30	1	0.14	3.996665	0.90014977	4.439998889	4.44

Table 26. *Cont.*

S.No	b	a	L	W	L/W	λ
31	0.25	0.15	3.9830014	0.89707239	4.440001917	4.44
32	0.5	0.15	3.992066	0.89911396	4.439999822	4.44
33	1	0.15	3.978019	0.89595023	4.440001116	4.44

The solution of the system is determined by scheming L against a for some values of b, as given in Figure 6.

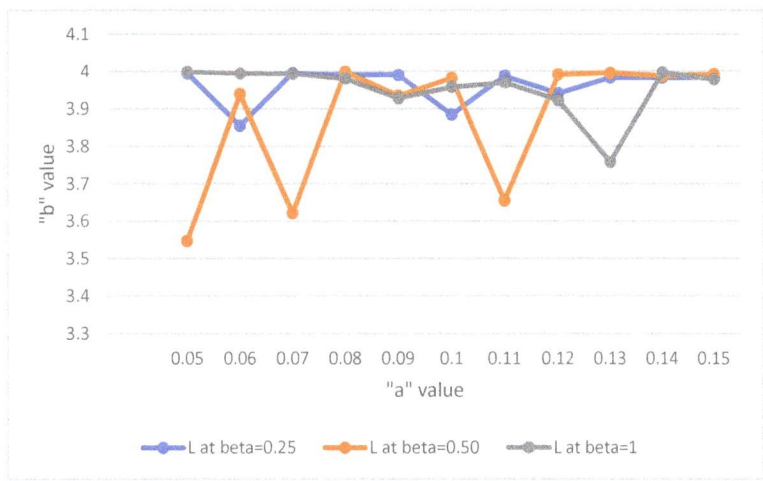

Figure 6. The relationship between L and "a" when "b" = 0.25, 0.50, 1.

Remark 6. *From the Figure 6, it is evident that, the value of L-Expected number of units in the system is less at a = 0.05, 0.06, 0.07, 0.11, 0.13, comparing the poisson arrival.*

The value of the parameters of this M/M/1/N queuing models are given.

λ	η	λ (1+η)	N	P	q	q	g_i
4	0.12	4.48	4	0.1	0.9	0.25, 0.50, 1	0 or 1

The following Tables 27–29 of values is obtained for L-expected number of units in the system by using the relation [11] for b = 0.25, 0.50, 1.

Table 27. The values of L for different values of b = 0.25, 0.50, 1.

a	L at b = 0.25	L at b = 0.50	L at b = 1
0.05	3.995172	3.997721	3.998884
0.06	3.994119	3.997247	3.998651
0.07	3.993030	3.996783	3.995359
0.08	3.991918	3.996305	3.998160
0.09	3.990777	3.995824	3.997972
0.10	3.980430	3.990005	3.955846
0.11	3.988407	3.978139	3.993533
0.12	3.987155	3.977938	3.973857
0.13	3.985937	3.984462	3.981141
0.14	3.984280	3.993300	3.990031
0.15	3.981860	3.991190	3.993370

Table 28. Comparison of L-Expected number of units in the system between poisson and encouraged arrival.

a	Poisson Arrival L at b = 1	Encouraged Arrival L at b = 1
0.10	3.98248	3.955846

Table 29. Verification of Little's law.

S.No	b	a	L	W	L/W	λ
1	0.25	0.05	3.995172	0.89177946	4.480002332	4.48
2	0.5	0.05	3.997721	0.89234844	4.480002196	4.48
3	1	0.05	3.998884	0.89260804	4.480000179	4.48
4	0.25	0.06	3.994119	0.89154442	4.480002109	4.48
5	0.5	0.06	3.997247	0.89224263	4.479998162	4.48
6	1	0.06	3.998651	0.89255603	4.480000134	4.48
7	0.25	0.07	3.99303	0.89130134	4.480001705	4.48
8	0.5	0.07	3.996783	0.89213906	4.480000314	4.48
9	1	0.07	3.995359	0.89182121	4.480001032	4.48
10	0.25	0.08	3.991918	0.89105313	4.480000628	4.48
11	0.5	0.08	3.996305	0.89203237	4.480001838	4.48
12	1	0.08	3.99816	0.89244643	4.480002151	4.48
13	0.25	0.09	3.990777	0.89079844	4.4800022	4.48
14	0.5	0.09	3.995824	0.8919317	4.47996484	4.48
15	1	0.09	3.997972	0.89240446	4.480002331	4.48
16	0.25	0.1	3.98043	0.88848884	4.47999919	4.48
17	0.5	0.1	3.990005	0.89062612	4.480000584	4.48
18	1	0.1	3.955846	0.88300134	4.480001721	4.48
19	0.25	0.11	3.988407	0.89026942	4.480002112	4.48
20	0.5	0.11	3.978139	0.88797746	4.480002297	4.48
21	1	0.11	3.993533	0.89141362	4.47999807	4.48
22	0.25	0.12	3.987155	0.88998996	4.479999775	4.48
23	0.5	0.12	3.977938	0.88793259	4.479997928	4.48
24	1	0.12	3.973857	0.88702165	4.479998241	4.48
25	0.25	0.13	3.985937	0.88971808	4.480000405	4.48
26	0.5	0.13	3.9844625	0.88938895	4.479999753	4.48
27	1	0.13	3.981141	0.88864754	4.479997704	4.48
28	0.25	0.14	3.98428	0.88934821	4.480001079	4.48
29	0.5	0.14	3.9933	0.89136161	4.479998025	4.48
30	1	0.14	3.990031	0.89063192	4.479999596	4.48
31	0.25	0.15	3.98186	0.88880804	4.48000018	4.48
32	0.5	0.15	3.99119	0.89089063	4.479998114	4.48
33	1	0.15	3.99337	0.89137723	4.480001167	4.48

The solution of the system is determined by scheming L against "a" for some values of b, as given in Figure 7.

Remark 7. *From the Figure 5, it is evident that, the value of L-Expected number of units in the system is less at a = 0.10, 0.11, 0.12 comparing the poisson arrival.*

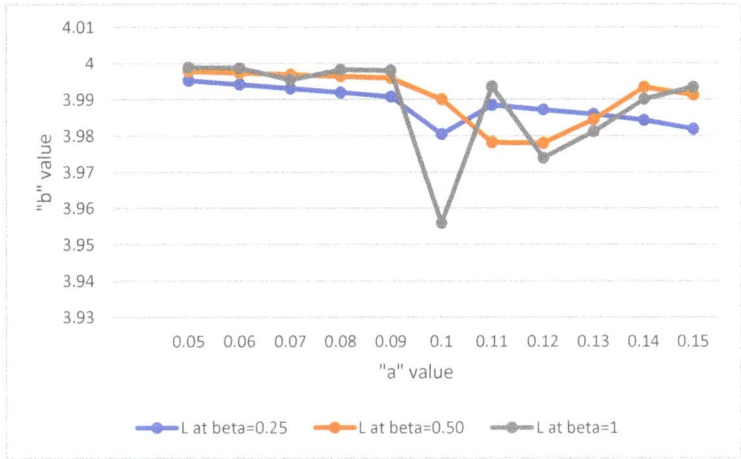

Figure 7. The relationship between L and "a" when "b" = 0.25, 0.50, 1.

5. Main Result and Discussion

When compared to Poisson arrival, encouraged arrival is more effective in handling service without delays. The (Tables 1–16 and 22–29) shows that L-Expected number of units in the system is lower for the model prescribed here on comparing with the Poisson arrival model. It is also found that the Tables 17–20 shows that adopting encouraged arrivals as well as increasing discounts in place of the model with Poisson arrival, greatly reduces W—the expected waiting time in the system.

Limitations

- This concept only suitable for M/M/1/N and M/M/1/K Queuing model;
- This concept will reduce the waiting time of customers for M/M/1/N Queuing model;
- This concept is valid for all real life applications with single service mechanism;
- The real life applications are always with finite capacity.

6. Conclusions

The encouraged arrival is quite valuable for many different businesses in terms of managing operations, deliberating, outlining, implementation, service development, and so on for consumers. In this study, we explored feedback, balking, retaining reneged clients and the quality control technique impact the encouraged arrival queuing model. The steady state scenario and iterative technique approach were utilized to create an analytical solution for the feedback M/M/1/N model's quality control. From to (Tables 1–16 and 22–29), the system's waiting time is much decreased by adopting the encouraged arrivals and increasing discounts supplied instead of Poisson arrivals. Tables 17–20 also shows that the waiting time is minimized to the greatest degree possible.

Author Contributions: R.P., contributes methodology, supervision, validation, formal analysis, review and editing. I.E.K., contributes MS EXCEL for conceptional, methodology and typing draft. All authors have read and agreed to the published version of the manuscript.

Funding: The research work is supported by Vellore Institute of Technology, Vellore-632014.

Institutional Review Board Statement: Not applicable.

Informed Consent Statement: Not applicable.

Data Availability Statement: Not applicable.

Acknowledgments: The author thank the management of Vellore Institute of Technology—632014 and School of Advanced Sciences authorities, for their continuous support and encouragement to bring out this research paper.

Conflicts of Interest: The authors declare no conflict of interest.

References

1. Haight, F.A. Queuing with balking, I. *Biometrika* **1960**, *47*, 285–296. [CrossRef]
2. Haight, F.A. Queueing with Reneging. *Metrika* **1959**, *2*, 186–197. [CrossRef]
3. Ancker, C.J., Jr.; Gafarian, A.V. Some queuing problems with balking and reneging I. *Oper. Res.* **1963**, *11*, 88–100. [CrossRef]
4. Ancker, C.J., Jr.; Gafarian, A.V. Some queuing problems with balking and reneging II. *Oper. Res.* **1963**, *11*, 928–937. [CrossRef]
5. Hsu, L.; Tapiero, C.S. An economic model for determining the optimal quality and process control policy in a queue-like production system. *Int. J. Prod. Res.* **1990**, *28*, 1447–1457. [CrossRef]
6. Abou-El-Ata, M.O. The State-Dependent Queue: M/M/1/N with Reneging and General Balk Functions. *Microelectron. Reliab.* **1991**, *31*, 1001–1007. [CrossRef]
7. Hsu, L.; Tapiero, C.S. Integration of process monitoring, quality control and maintenance in an M/G/1 queue-like production system. *Int. J. Prod. Res.* **1992**, *30*, 2363–2379. [CrossRef]
8. Fan-Orzechowski, X.; Feinberg, E.A. Optimal Admission Control for a Markovian Queue under the Quality of Service Constraint. In Proceedings of the 44th IEEE Conference on Decision and Control and the European Control Conference, Seville, Spain, 12–15 December 2005; pp. 1729–1734.
9. Kumar, R.; Sharma, S.K. M/M/1/N Queuing System with Retention of Reneged Customers. *Pak. J. Stat. Oper. Res.* **2012**, *8*, 859–866. [CrossRef]
10. Kumar, R.; Sharma, S.K. An M/M/1/N Queuing Model with Retention of reneged customers and Balking. *Am. J. Oper. Res.* **2012**, *2*, 1–5.
11. Sharma, S.K.; Kumar, R. A Markovian Feedback Queue with Retention of Reneged Customers. *Adv. Model. Optim.* **2012**, *14*, 681–688.
12. Jain, N.K.; Kumar, R.; Som, B.K. An M/M/1/N Queuing system with reverse balking. *Am. J. Oper. Res.* **2014**, *4*, 17–20.
13. Som, B.K.; Seth, S. An M/M/1/N queuing system with encouraged arrivals. *Glob. J. Pure Appl. Math.* **2017**, *17*, 3443–3453.
14. Kotb, K.A.M.; El-Ashkar, H.A. Quality Control for Feedback M/M/1/N Queue with Balking and Retention of Reneged Customers. *Filomat* **2020**, *34*, 167–174. [CrossRef]
15. Gross, D.; Harris, C. *Fundamentals of Queueing Theory*, 4th ed.; John Wiley and Sons: Hoboken, NJ, USA, 2018.
16. Zhang, A.; Zhu, X.; Lu, Q.; Zhang, R. Impact of Prioritization on the Outpatient Queuing System in the Emergency Department with Limited Medical Resources. *Symmetry* **2019**, *11*, 796. [CrossRef]
17. Li, R.; Wang, N. Landslide Susceptibility Mapping for the Muchuan County (China): A Comparison between Bivariate Statistical Models (WoE, EBF, and IoE) and Their Ensembles with Logistic Regression. *Symmetry* **2019**, *11*, 762. [CrossRef]
18. Nair, D.V.; Krishnamoorthy, A.; Melikov, A.; Alieyeva, S. MMAP/(PH.PH)/1 Queue with priority loss through feedback. *Mathematics* **2021**, *9*, 1797. [CrossRef]

Article

Statistical Analysis of Alpha Power Inverse Weibull Distribution under Hybrid Censored Scheme with Applications to Ball Bearings Technology and Biomedical Data

Hanan Haj Ahmad [1,*,†], Ehab M. Almetwally [2,3,†], Ahmed Rabaiah [4,†] and Dina A. Ramadan [5,†]

1. Department of Basic Science, Preparatory Year Deanship, King Faisal University, Hofuf 31982, Al Ahsa, Saudi Arabia
2. Department of Statistics, Faculty of Business Administration, Delta University for Science and Technology, Gamasa 11152, Egypt
3. The Scientific Association for Studies and Applied Research, Al Manzalah 35642, Egypt
4. Department of Electrical Engineering, College of Engineering, King Faisal University, Hofuf 31982, Al Ahsa, Saudi Arabia
5. Department of Mathematics, Faculty of Science, Mansoura University, Mansoura 35516, Egypt
* Correspondence: hhajahmed@kfu.edu.sa
† All authors contributed equally to this work.

Abstract: Applications in medical technology have a massive contribution to the treatment of patients. One of the attractive tools is ball bearings. These balls support the load of the application as well as minimize friction between the surfaces. If a heavy load is applied to a ball bearing, there is the risk that the balls may be damaged and cause the bearing to fail earlier. Hence, we aim to study the model of the failure times of ball bearings. A hybrid Type-II censoring scheme is recommended to minimize the experimental time and cost where the components are following alpha power inverse Weibull distribution. A ball bearing is one example; the other is the resistance of guinea pigs exposed to dosages of virulent tubercle bacilli. We use different estimation methods to obtain point and interval estimates of the unknown parameters of the distribution; consequently, estimating statistical functions such as the hazard rate and the survival functions are observed. The maximum likelihood method and the maximum product spacing methods are used, in addition to the Bayesian estimation method, in which symmetric and asymmetric loss functions are utilized. Interval estimators are obtained for the unknown parameters using three different criteria: approximate, credible, and bootstrap confidence intervals. The performance of the parameters' estimation is accomplished via simulation analysis and numerical methods such as Newton–Raphson and Monte Carlo Markov chains. Finally, results and conclusions support the suitability of alpha power inverse Weibull distribution under a hybrid Type-II censoring scheme for modeling real biomedical data.

Keywords: alpha power inverse Weibull distribution; hybrid Type-II censoring; ball bearing; maximum likelihood estimator; Bayes estimator; symmetric and asymmetric loss functions; Monte Carlo Markov chain; maximum product spacing

1. Introduction

Many bearing types and styles provide an extensive range of solutions that are useful for applications across various industries, including mechanical, medical, global aerospace, and others. In biomaterials, ball bearing technology is used for "Hip Joint Replacement", where it is necessary for a patient's life suffering from arthritis; for more details, refer to [1]. When ball bearings are operating, they can be inclined to spoil for different reasons; it can be due to lack of lubrication, changeable load, vibration, or pollutants. All can cause a fast failure time of the bearings. Accordingly, modeling components' lifetimes have considerable attention in many applied sciences.

Another important application in the biomedical area is studying the resistance of living organs to a certain kind of bacteria. Tuberculosis is still considered one of the main health problems, taking millions of lives annually. The World Health Organization reported that 30% of the world's population had been infected with the tubercle bacillus, and the risk of infection is still increasing; see [2]. We considered a sample of guinea pigs that were exposed to dosages of virulent tubercle bacilli (VTB), and their resistance was recorded with respect to their living times. Modeling the lifetimes of guinea pigs is our second purpose in this work.

Dealing with samples in real-life experiments may confront obstacles such as missing or eliminating components during the experiment and/or lack of money and time; therefore, statisticians are spending considerable effort in investigating components' breakdown times (failures) as the main structure of the performing systems in industry and mechanics. The researchers usually analyze the observation of operating unit failure, the recorded lifetimes of those units, and their application of statistical analysis methods from data obtained to data collected for the whole system. However, certain experimental units are costly and highly efficient, requiring to decrease in the number of tested components and their lifetimes. A measurement system that can save time and resources for all outputs is the main requirement. It will subsequently be taken into consideration because the composite data show the exact times of failure of such damaged components. Failure data should be fitted to an appropriate parametric statistical distribution to estimate its unknown parameters and furthermore to estimate its reliability and hazard functions. Estimating the reliability and hazard functions helps statisticians predict and make the right decision about the survival factor or hazard factor of these models in probabilistic meaning with a high level of confidence that may reach 95%.

In this paper, some statistical inference approaches are handled, such as the maximum likelihood, the maximum product spacing, and the Bayesian methods.

A system of censoring schemes that can balance (i) the total experimental time spent, (ii) the number of test components, and (iii) the efficiency of the experimental statistical inference is of great concern and is highly evaluated. A hybrid censoring scheme (HCS) is a consolidation between the two types of censoring schemes (Type-I and Type-II), which may be explained by using similar elements. The analysis is decided with the failure of r units, or reaching a specified time T in the experiment. If the i-th ordered failure time is symbolized by $X_{i:n}$, the test may be ended at $T_1 = \min\{X_{r:n}, T\}$ or at $T_2 = \max\{X_{r:n}, T\}$. Time T_1 means the end of the experiment for hybrid Type-I censoring ($HT1CS$) test units. T_2 is the end time for hybrid Type-II censored ($HT2CS$) test units. Epstein [3] suggested the $HT1CS$ and studied a lifetime experiment that assumes the life cycle of every component to be exponentially distributed.

Many researchers have worked on $HT1CS$, such as Ebrahimi [4]. One of the disadvantages of $HT1CS$ is that a small number of failures may occur until after a fixed period T under $HT1CS$. Childs et al. [5] developed $HT2CS$, which assures a minimum of r failures. If r failures actually occurred before T, the experiment would remain until the r-th failure occurred, and we would see r failures of the data exactly at this point. The applications of the $HT2CS$ have been discussed by several authors, and the reader can refer to Mansour and Ramadan [6], Salah et al. [7], Yousef et al. [8], Yadav et al. [9], Mahmoud et al. [10], Aldahlan et al. [11], Mohamed et al. [12], Ramadan et al. [13] and Nassr et al. [14].

In this article, alpha power inverse Weibull (APIW) distribution is used to model the ball-bearing lifetimes and the resistance of VTB. APIW distribution was first proposed by [15]. Let X be a random variable with an APIW distribution; then, the cumulative distribution function (CDF) and the probability density function (pdf) are determined as

$$F_{APIW}(x; \alpha, \beta, \lambda) = \frac{\alpha^{e^{-\lambda x^{-\beta}}} - 1}{\alpha - 1} \quad ; \alpha \neq 1, x, \alpha, \lambda, \beta > 0 \qquad (1)$$

and

$$f_{APIW}(x;\alpha,\beta,\lambda) = \frac{\log \alpha}{\alpha-1}\lambda\,\beta\,x^{-(\beta+1)}e^{-\lambda x^{-\beta}}\alpha^{e^{-\lambda x^{-\beta}}}\quad;\alpha\neq 1, x, \alpha, \lambda, \beta > 0, \quad (2)$$

respectively. The survival and the hazard functions of APIW distribution are

$$S(x) = \frac{\alpha - \alpha^{e^{-\lambda x^{-\beta}}}}{\alpha - 1}; \alpha \neq 1, x, \alpha, \lambda, \beta > 0 \quad (3)$$

and

$$h(x) = \frac{\log(\alpha)\,\lambda\,\beta\,x^{-(\beta+1)}\,e^{-\lambda x^{-\beta}}\alpha^{e^{-\lambda x^{-\beta}}}}{\alpha - \alpha^{e^{-\lambda x^{-\beta}}}};\ \alpha \neq 1, x, \alpha, \lambda, \beta > 0, \quad (4)$$

respectively. The APIW statistical characteristics were discussed recently by [15]. It was shown that the pdf of APIW is unimodal; it can be either symmetric or skewed to the right depending on the parameter values. In addition, the hazard rate function can be an increasing or decreasing curve. Hence, this model is a good candidate for describing several real data which can be symmetric or asymmetric (positively skewed).

Point and interval estimation of the unknown parameters were explored on the basis of a complete sample. Not much work handled the hybrid Type-II censoring for the alpha power family of distribution and used it for modeling biological issues; hence, we aim to study the APIW lifetimes under $HT2CS$ using classical estimation methods in addition to the Bayesian method based on informative priors with symmetric and asymmetric loss functions. A simulation analysis using R software is performed to compare the different methods of estimation and test the quality of the new model under $HT2CS$ sampling when fitting it to some real-life data. The Newton–Raphson method of maximization is used in the "maxLik" software to compute the MLE and MPS. Additionally, the 'CODA' package, which analyzes Markov chain Monte Carlo (MCMC) outputs and diagnoses lack of convergence, is used to compute the Bayesian estimation.

The rest of this article is prepared accordingly: In Section 2, the maximum likelihood estimators are obtained for the APIW parameters, and hence, estimations of the hazard rate and reliability functions are obtained. In Section 3, estimates are observed using the MPS method. Bayesian estimation is derived in Section 4 under various loss functions, including the squared error loss function (SEL) and the linear exponential loss function ($LINEX$). Confidence intervals are evaluated in Section 5. In Section 6, the actual data set is tested and analyzed. Simulation analysis is observed in Section 7 to study and evaluate the quality of the various estimators studied in this research. Conclusions and related results are reported in Section 8.

2. The Maximum Likelihood Estimator

The classical well-known maximum likelihood estimation (MLE) method is used in this section. Point estimations of the parameters are performed assuming the censoring $HT2CS$. Hence, let n be identical components that are placed in an experiment and assume their lifetimes follow the APIW distribution with pdf as in Equation (2). The experiment is stopped at the pre-fixed time (T) and at a pre-specified number of failures ($r \leq n$) whichever comes later; therefore, the experiment is stopped at the $\max(x_{r:n}, T)$, in which $x_{r:n}$ denotes the r-th failure. Under $HT2CS$, the random failures are achieved according to the cases:

Case 1: $\{x_{1:n} < \ldots < x_{r:n}\}$ if $T < x_{r:n}$;
Case 2: $\{x_{1:n} < \ldots < x_{r+1:n} < \ldots < x_{m:n} < T\}$ if $T > x_{r:n}$;
m: The number of units that fail before time T and $r \leq m \leq n$.

The likelihood function for case 1 is

$$L_1(\alpha, \beta, \lambda | data) = \frac{n!}{(n-r)!} \left(\frac{(\log \alpha)^r \lambda^r \beta^r}{(\alpha-1)^r} \prod_{i=1}^{r} x_{i:n}^{-(\beta+1)} e^{-\lambda \sum_{i=1}^{r} x_{i:n}^{-\beta}} \sum_{\alpha^{i=1}}^{r} e^{-\lambda x_{i:n}^{-\beta}} \right)$$

$$\left(\frac{(\alpha-1) - \alpha^{-1+e^{-\lambda x_{r:n}^{-\beta}}}}{\alpha-1} \right)^{n-r}.$$

For case 2, the likelihood function is

$$L_2(\alpha, \beta, \lambda | data) = \frac{n!}{(n-m)!} \left(\frac{(\log \alpha)^m \lambda^m \beta^m}{(\alpha-1)^N} \prod_{i=1}^{m} x_{i:n}^{-(\beta+1)} e^{-\lambda \sum_{i=1}^{m} x_{i:n}^{-\beta}} \sum_{\alpha^{i=1}}^{m} e^{-\lambda x_{i:n}^{-\beta}} \right)$$

$$\left(\frac{\alpha - 1 - \alpha^{-1+e^{-\lambda x_{m:n}^{-\beta}}}}{\alpha-1} \right)^{n-m}.$$

The combined likelihood function can be represented as

$$L(\alpha, \beta, \lambda | data) = C \left(\frac{(\log \alpha)^H \lambda^H \beta^H}{(\alpha-1)^H} \prod_{i=1}^{H} x_{i:n}^{-(\beta+1)} e^{-\lambda \sum_{i=1}^{H} x_{i:n}^{-\beta}} \sum_{\alpha^{i=1}}^{H} e^{-\lambda x_{i:n}^{-\beta}} \right)$$

$$\left(\frac{\alpha - 1 - \alpha^{-1+e^{-\lambda u^{-\beta}}}}{\alpha-1} \right)^{n-H}, \quad (5)$$

where $C = \frac{n!}{(n-H)!}$, H indicates the number of failures, $u = x_{r:n}$ if $H = r$ and $u = x_{m:n}$ if $H = m$.

By taking the logarithm of Equation (5), we obtain Equation (6)

$$\log L(\alpha, \beta, \lambda | data) = \log(C) + H \log(\log(\alpha)) + H \log(\lambda) + H \log(\beta) - (n-H) \log(\alpha-1)$$

$$-(\beta+1) \sum_{i=1}^{H} \log(x_{i:n}) - \lambda \sum_{i=1}^{H} x_{i:n}^{-\beta} + \log(\alpha) \sum_{i=1}^{H} e^{-\lambda x_{i:n}^{-\beta}} \quad (6)$$

$$+ (n-H) \log(\alpha - 1 - \alpha^{-1+e^{-\lambda u^{-\beta}}}).$$

The MLEs of the parameters denoted by $\hat{\alpha}, \hat{\beta}$ and $\hat{\lambda}$ can be attained by solving the simultaneous nonlinear log-likelihood equations as follows, respectively:

$$\frac{H}{\alpha \log(\alpha)} - \frac{n-H}{\alpha-1} + \alpha^{-1} \sum_{i=1}^{H} e^{-\lambda x_{i:n}^{-\beta}} + \frac{(n-H) \left[1 - \alpha^{-2+e^{-\lambda u^{-\beta}}} (-1 + e^{-\lambda u^{-\beta}}) \right]}{\left(\alpha - 1 - \alpha^{-1+e^{-\lambda u^{-\beta}}} \right)} = 0, \quad (7)$$

$$\frac{H}{\beta} - \sum_{i=1}^{H} \log(x_{i:n}) + \lambda \sum_{i=1}^{H} x_{i:n}^{-\beta} \log(x_{i:n}) + \lambda \log(\alpha) \left[\sum_{i=1}^{H} x_i^{-\beta} \log(x_{i:n}) e^{-\lambda x_{i:n}^{-\beta}} \right]$$

$$- \frac{(n-H)\lambda u^{-\beta} \log(u) \log(\alpha) e^{-\lambda u^{-\beta}} \alpha^{-1+e^{-\lambda u^{-\beta}}}}{\left(\alpha - 1 - \alpha^{-1+e^{-\lambda u^{-\beta}}} \right)} = 0 \quad (8)$$

and

$$\frac{H}{\lambda} - \sum_{i=1}^{H} x_{i:n}^{-\beta} - \log(\alpha) \left[\sum_{i=1}^{H} x_{i:n}^{-\beta} e^{-\lambda x_{i:n}^{-\beta}} \right]$$

$$+\frac{(n-H)\,u^{-\beta}\log(\alpha)\,e^{-\lambda u^{-\beta}}\,\alpha^{-1+e^{-\lambda u^{-\beta}}}}{\left(\alpha-1-\alpha^{-1+e^{-\lambda u^{-\beta}}}\right)}=0. \qquad (9)$$

An implicit solution is not an easy task for solving the above system. Hence, some numerical techniques will be helpful to find a numerical approximate solution. The Newton–Raphson technique is used to find a numerical solution. The Newton–Raphson algorithm is described in detail in EL-Sagheer [16].

Furthermore, using the invariant property of the MLEs, we can find the MLEs of $S(x)$ and $h(x)$, after replacing α, β and λ by $\hat{\alpha}, \hat{\beta}$ and $\hat{\lambda}$ in Equations (3) and (4); hence, we obtain

$$\hat{S}(x) = \frac{\hat{\alpha} - \hat{\alpha}^{e^{-\hat{\lambda} x^{-\hat{\beta}}}}}{\hat{\alpha} - 1}; \alpha \neq 1, x, \alpha, \lambda, \beta > 0 \qquad (10)$$

and

$$\hat{h}(x) = \frac{\log(\hat{\alpha})\,\hat{\lambda}\,\hat{\beta}\,x^{-(\hat{\beta}+1)}e^{-\hat{\lambda} x^{-\hat{\beta}}}\hat{\alpha}^{e^{-\hat{\lambda} x^{-\hat{\beta}}}}}{\hat{\alpha} - \hat{\alpha}^{e^{-\hat{\lambda} x^{-\hat{\beta}}}}}; \alpha \neq 1, x, \alpha, \lambda, \beta > 0. \qquad (11)$$

3. Maximum Product Spacing

The maximum product spacing method (MPS) is an alternative efficient estimation method that demonstrates improvements compared with other point estimation methods; one may refer to Cheng and Amin [17] for more details. The MPS is performed to estimate the unknown parameters of APIW distribution. Once again, it is necessary to deal with a system of nonlinear equations; these equations are emanated from the partial derivatives of the logarithm of the product spacing function $\Phi(\alpha, \lambda, \beta)$, which is written as:

$$\Phi(\alpha, \lambda, \beta) = \left(\prod_{i=1}^{n+1} D_i\right)^{\frac{1}{n+1}}, \qquad (12)$$

where Φ is the geometric mean of the product spacing function D_i that is defined as

$$\begin{aligned} D_1 &= F(x_1) \\ D_i &= F(x_i) - F(x_{i-1}); i = 2, \ldots, n \\ D_{n+1} &= 1 - F(x_n). \end{aligned} \qquad (13)$$

The MPS function under HT2CS is written as:

$$\Phi(x_i; \alpha, \lambda, \beta) = CF(x_1)(1 - F(u))^{n-H}\prod_{i=2}^{H}(F(x_i) - F(x_{i-1})) \qquad (14)$$

where u is defined similarly as in Section 2. Using the CDF in Equation (1) and substituting in Equation (14), we obtain the MPS function as:

$$\Phi(x_i; \alpha, \lambda, \beta) = C\frac{1}{(\alpha-1)^n}(\alpha^{e^{-\lambda x_1^{-\beta}}} - 1)(\alpha - \alpha^{e^{-\lambda u^{-\beta}}})^{n-H}\prod_{i=2}^{H}\left[\alpha^{e^{-\lambda x_i^{-\beta}}} - \alpha^{e^{-\lambda x_{i-1}^{-\beta}}}\right] \qquad (15)$$

consequently,

$$\log \Phi(x_i; \alpha, \lambda, \beta) = \log c - n\log(\alpha - 1) + \log(\alpha^{e^{-\lambda x_1^{-\beta}}} - 1) + \\ (n-H)\log(\alpha - \alpha^{e^{-\lambda u^{-\beta}}}) + \sum_{i=2}^{H}\log[\alpha^{e^{-\lambda x_i^{-\beta}}} - \alpha^{e^{-\lambda x_{i-1}^{-\beta}}}] \qquad (16)$$

The estimators under the MPS method are attained by taking the partial derivatives of Equation (16) and then solving the system of nonlinear equations numerically; this can be executed by using the Newton–Raphson method. The numerical results are later exposed in Section 7.

4. Bayes Estimation

A Bayesian approach, which is highly effective in reliability analysis, is created by the capacity to combine prior information within the test, as the restricted availability of data is a significant difficulty in relation with reliability analysis. The unknown α, β, and λ parameters versus the functions of loss for SEL and $LINEX$ are estimates of Bayesian. Suppose that the unknown parameters α, β and λ have Gamma prior distributions independently.

$$\begin{aligned} \pi_1(\alpha) &\propto \alpha^{a_1-1} e^{-b_1 \alpha}, & \alpha &> 0, a_1 > 0, b_1 > 0, \\ \pi_2(\beta) &\propto \beta^{a_2-1} e^{-b_2 \beta}, & \beta &> 0, a_2 > 0, b_2 > 0, \\ \pi_3(\lambda) &\propto \lambda^{a_3-1} e^{-b_3 \lambda}, & \lambda &> 0, a_3 > 0, b_3 > 0. \end{aligned} \quad (17)$$

where the hyper-parameters a_i and b_i, $i = 1, 2, 3$ are the hyper-parameters that contain the prior information. Many authors, such as Kundu and Howlader [18], Dey and Dey [19], Dey et al. [20] and Dey et al. [21] developed Bayesian estimation for their parameter models using informative gamma priors. The posterior distribution of α, β and λ is defined by $\pi^*(\alpha, \beta, \lambda | data)$ and can be procured by combining the likelihood function Equation (5) with the prior Equation (17) and can be written as

$$\pi^*(\alpha, \beta, \lambda \mid data) = \frac{L(\alpha, \beta, \lambda \mid data) \, \pi_1(\alpha) \, \pi_2(\beta) \, \pi_3(\lambda)}{\int_0^\infty \int_0^\infty \int_0^\infty L(\alpha, \beta, \lambda \mid data) \, \pi_1(\alpha) \, \pi_2(\beta) \, \pi_3(\lambda) \, d\alpha \, d\beta \, d\lambda}. \quad (18)$$

A square error loss (SEL) function, which is a commonly used function, is a symmetric loss function, which is defined as

$$L(\phi, \hat{\phi}) = (\hat{\phi} - \phi), \quad (19)$$

here, $\hat{\phi}$ is an estimate of ϕ.

The Bayes estimate of any function of α, β and λ, say $g(\alpha, \beta, \lambda)$ under the SEL function can be determined as

$$\hat{g}_{BS}(\alpha, \beta, \lambda | x) = E_{\alpha, \beta, \lambda | x}(g(\alpha, \beta, \lambda)), \quad (20)$$

where

$$E_{\alpha, \beta, \lambda | data}(g(\alpha, \beta, \lambda)) = \frac{\int_0^\infty \int_0^\infty \int_0^\infty g(\alpha, \beta, \lambda) \, \pi_1(\alpha) \, \pi_2(\beta) \, \pi_3(\lambda) \, L(\alpha, \beta, \lambda \mid data) \, d\alpha \, d\beta \, d\lambda}{\int_0^\infty \int_0^\infty \int_0^\infty \pi_1(\alpha) \, \pi_2(\beta) \, \pi_3(\lambda) \, L(\alpha, \beta, \lambda \mid data) \, d\alpha \, d\beta \, d\lambda}. \quad (21)$$

The $LINEX$ function is the most universally used asymmetric loss function. The asymmetric loss function is considered more comprehensive in many respects; see Varian [22]. It is

$$L(\Delta) = \left(e^{\varepsilon \Delta} - \varepsilon \Delta - 1 \right), \, \varepsilon \neq 0, \, \Delta = \hat{\phi} - \phi, \quad (22)$$

where ε is a loss function scale parameter. The LINEX loss function is nearly the same as the SEL function for the option of positive or negative values of ε (close to zero).

The Bayes estimate of any function of α, β and λ, say $g(\alpha, \beta, \lambda)$ under the LINEX function can be determined as

$$\hat{g}_{BL}(\alpha, \beta, \lambda \mid data) = -\frac{1}{\varepsilon} \log \left[E \left(e^{-\varepsilon g(\alpha, \beta, \lambda)} \mid data \right) \right], \, \varepsilon \neq 0, \quad (23)$$

$$E\left(e^{-\varepsilon g(\alpha,\beta,\lambda)} \mid \text{data}\right) = \frac{\int_0^\infty \int_0^\infty \int_0^\infty e^{-\varepsilon g(\alpha,\beta,\lambda)} \pi_1(\alpha) \pi_2(\beta) \pi_3(\lambda) L(\alpha,\beta,\lambda \mid \text{data}) d\alpha d\beta d\lambda}{\int_0^\infty \int_0^\infty \int_0^\infty \pi_1(\alpha) \pi_2(\beta) \pi_3(\lambda) L(\alpha,\beta,\lambda \mid \text{data}) d\alpha d\beta d\lambda}. \quad (24)$$

It is noticed that the ratio of multiple integrals in Equations (21) and (24) cannot be obtained in an explicit form.

MCMC is developed to create samples of the joint posterior function in Equation (18). The MCMC mechanism is primarily concerned with calculating an estimated integral value. We consider the Gibbs in the Metropolis–Hasting sampler approach in order to implement the MCMC technique. From Equations (5) and (17), the joint posterior distribution can be written as

$$\pi^*(\alpha,\beta,\lambda \mid x) \propto \alpha^{a_1-1} \beta^{H+a_2-1} \lambda^{H+a_3-1} e^{-\alpha b_1 - \beta b_2 - \lambda b_3} \frac{n!}{(n-H)!} \frac{(\log \alpha)^H}{(\alpha-1)^H}$$
$$\left[\prod_{i=1}^H x_{i:n}^{-(\beta+1)} \sum_{i=1}^H e^{-\lambda x_{i:n}^{-\beta}} \sum_{i=1}^H e^{-\lambda x_{i:n}^{-\beta}} \alpha^{i=1}\right] \left[\frac{(\alpha-1) - \alpha^{-1+e^{-\lambda u^{-\beta}}}}{\alpha-1}\right]^{n-H}. \quad (25)$$

We rewrite conditionals for α, β and λ as follows:

$$\pi_1^*(\alpha \mid \beta,\lambda,x) \propto \frac{n!}{(n-H)!} \frac{\alpha^{a_1-1}(\log \alpha)^H}{(\alpha-1)^H} e^{-\alpha b_1} \alpha^{\sum_{i=1}^H e^{-\lambda x_{i:n}^{-\beta}}} \left[\frac{(\alpha-1) - \alpha^{-1+e^{-\lambda u^{-\beta}}}}{\alpha-1}\right]^{n-H}, \quad (26)$$

$$\pi_2^*(\beta \mid \alpha,\lambda,x) \propto \frac{n!}{(n-H)!} \beta^{a_2-H-1} e^{-\beta b_2} \sum_{i=1}^H e^{-\lambda x_{i:n}^{-\beta}} \sum_{i=1}^H e^{-\lambda x_{i:n}^{-\beta}} \alpha^{i=1} \left(\prod_{i=1}^H x_{i:n}^{-(\beta+1)}\right)$$
$$\left[\frac{(\alpha-1) - \alpha^{-1+e^{-\lambda u^{-\beta}}}}{\alpha-1}\right]^{n-H} \quad (27)$$

and

$$\pi_3^*(\lambda \mid \alpha,\beta,x) \propto \frac{n!}{(n-H)!} \lambda^{a_3-H-1} e^{-\lambda b_3} \sum_{i=1}^H e^{-\lambda x_{i:n}^{-\beta}} \sum_{i=1}^H e^{-\lambda x_{i:n}^{-\beta}} \alpha^{i=1}$$
$$\left[\frac{(\alpha-1) - \alpha^{-1+e^{-\lambda u^{-\beta}}}}{\alpha-1}\right]^{n-H}. \quad (28)$$

The conditional posteriors of α, β and λ in Equations (26)–(28) thus do not have normal forms. As a result, the MCMC method will be used to compute the Bayesian estimates of α, β and λ in addition to the Bayesian estimates of the survival function and hazard function as well as the related credible intervals. See Robert [23,24] for a detailed description of the MCMC method.

5. Confidence Intervals

In this section, we study three types of confidence intervals. A numerical analysis is performed to compare the efficacy of these intervals with respect to interval length and coverage probability.

5.1. Approximate Confidence Intervals

This subsection will present the observed Fisher's information matrix, which is frequently used to construct asymptotic confidence intervals (ACIs). The principle of missing information is as follows:

Observed information = Complete information − Missing information.

The MLEs $(\hat{\alpha}, \hat{\beta}, \hat{\lambda})$ are approximately bivariate normal with a mean $(\hat{\alpha}, \hat{\beta}, \hat{\lambda})$ and variance matrix $I^{-1}(\hat{\alpha}, \hat{\beta}, \hat{\lambda})$. Here, $\hat{I}(\alpha, \beta, \lambda)$ is the observed Fisher information matrix, and it is defined as

$$\hat{I}(\alpha, \beta, \lambda) = \begin{pmatrix} -\frac{\partial^2 \ell}{\partial \alpha^2} & -\frac{\partial^2 \ell}{\partial \alpha \partial \beta} & -\frac{\partial^2 \ell}{\partial \alpha \partial \lambda} \\ -\frac{\partial^2 \ell}{\partial \beta \partial \alpha} & -\frac{\partial^2 \ell}{\partial \beta^2} & -\frac{\partial^2 \ell}{\partial \beta \partial \lambda} \\ -\frac{\partial^2 \ell}{\partial \lambda \partial \alpha} & -\frac{\partial^2 \ell}{\partial \lambda \partial \beta} & -\frac{\partial^2 \ell}{\partial \lambda^2} \end{pmatrix}_{(\alpha,\beta,\lambda)=(\hat{\alpha},\hat{\beta},\hat{\lambda})}, \quad (29)$$

where

$$\frac{\partial^2 \ell}{\partial \alpha^2} = \frac{-H}{(\alpha \log(\alpha))^2} + \frac{n-H}{(\alpha-1)^2} + \alpha^{-2} \sum_{i=1}^{H} e^{-\lambda x_{i:n}^{-\beta}}$$

$$+ (n-H)\left(\alpha - 1 - \alpha^{-1+e^{-\lambda u^{-\beta}}}\right)^{-2}$$

$$\times \left[\left(1 - \alpha^{-2+e^{-\lambda u^{-\beta}}}(-1 + e^{-\lambda u^{-\beta}})\right)^2 - \left(\alpha - 1 - \alpha^{-1+e^{-\lambda u^{-\beta}}}\right)\left(-2 + e^{-\lambda u^{-\beta}}\right)(-1 + e^{-\lambda u^{-\beta}})\alpha^{-3+e^{-\lambda u^{-\beta}}} \right],$$

$$\frac{\partial^2 \ell}{\partial \alpha \partial \beta} = \frac{\lambda}{\alpha} \sum_{i=1}^{H} x_{i:n}^{-\beta} \log(x_{i:n}) e^{-\lambda x_{i:n}^{-\beta}}$$

$$+ (n-H)\lambda u^{-\beta} e^{-2\lambda u^{-\beta}} \log(u) \alpha^{-1+e^{-\lambda u^{-\beta}}}\left(\alpha - \alpha^2 + \alpha e^{e^{-\lambda u^{-\beta}}}\right)^{-2}$$

$$\times \left[e^{-\lambda u^{-\beta}}\left(\alpha - \alpha^2 + \alpha e^{e^{-\lambda u^{-\beta}}}\right) + \alpha \log(\alpha)(1 - \alpha + (2\alpha - 1)e^{-\lambda u^{-\beta}}) \right],$$

$$\frac{\partial^2 \ell}{\partial \alpha \partial \lambda} = \frac{-1}{\alpha} \sum_{i=1}^{H} x_{i:n}^{-\beta} e^{-\lambda x_{i:n}^{-\beta}} + (n-H) u^{-\beta} e^{-2\lambda u^{-\beta}} \alpha^{-1+e^{-\lambda u^{-\beta}}}\left(\alpha - \alpha^2 + \alpha e^{e^{-\lambda u^{-\beta}}}\right)^{-2}$$

$$\times \left[-e^{\lambda u^{-\beta}}\left(\alpha - \alpha^2 + \alpha e^{e^{-\lambda u^{-\beta}}}\right) - \alpha \log(\alpha)(1 - \alpha + e^{\lambda u^{-\beta}}) \right],$$

$$\frac{\partial^2 \ell}{\partial \beta^2} = \frac{-H}{\beta^2} - \lambda \sum_{i=1}^{H} x_{i:n}^{-\beta} (\log(x_{i:n}))^2$$

$$+ \lambda \log(\alpha) \sum_{i=1}^{H} (x_{i:n}^{-\beta} \log(x_{i:n}))^2 e^{-\lambda x_{i:n}^{-\beta}} [\lambda - 1]$$

$$- (n-H)\lambda u^{-2\beta}(\log(u))^2 \log(\alpha) e^{-2\lambda u^{-\beta}} \alpha^{e^{-\lambda u^{-\beta}}}\left(\alpha - \alpha^2 + \alpha e^{e^{-\lambda u^{-\beta}}}\right)^{-2}$$

$$\times \left[(\lambda - u^\beta) e^{\lambda u^{-\beta}}\left(\alpha - \alpha^2 + \alpha e^{e^{-\lambda u^{-\beta}}}\right) - (\alpha - 1)\alpha \lambda \log(\alpha) \right],$$

$$\frac{\partial^2 \ell}{\partial \beta \partial \lambda} = \sum_{i=1}^{H} x_{i:n}^{-\beta} \log(x_{i:n}) - \log(\alpha) \sum_{i=1}^{H} x_i^{-\beta} \log(x_{i:n}) \, e^{-\lambda x_{i:n}^{-\beta}} \left[1 - \lambda x_{i:n}^{-\beta}\right]$$

$$+ (n-H)\, u^{-2\beta} \log(u) \log(\alpha)\, e^{-2\lambda u^{-\beta}} \alpha e^{-\lambda u^{-\beta}} \left(\alpha - \alpha^2 + \alpha e^{-\lambda u^{-\beta}}\right)^{-2}$$

$$\times \left[(u^{\beta} - \lambda) e^{\lambda u^{-\beta}} \left(\alpha - \alpha^2 + \alpha e^{-\lambda u^{-\beta}}\right) + (\alpha - 1)\alpha\lambda \log(\alpha) \right]$$

and

$$\frac{\partial^2 \ell}{\partial \lambda^2} = \frac{-H}{\lambda^2} - \sum_{i=1}^{H} x_{i:n}^{-\beta} - \log(\alpha) \sum_{i=1}^{H} \left(x_{i:n}^{-\beta}\right)^2 e^{-\lambda x_{i:n}^{-\beta}}$$

$$+ (n-H)\, u^{-2\beta} \log(\alpha)\, e^{-2\lambda u^{-\beta}} \alpha e^{-\lambda u^{-\beta}} \left(\alpha - \alpha^2 + \alpha e^{-\lambda u^{-\beta}}\right)^{-2}$$

$$\times \left[e^{\lambda u^{-\beta}} \left(\alpha - \alpha^2 + \alpha e^{-\lambda u^{-\beta}}\right) + (\alpha - 1)\alpha \log(\alpha) \right].$$

As a result, the approximate (or observed) asymptotic variance-covariance matrix $[\hat{V}]$, for MLEs is derived by inverting the observed information matrix $\hat{I}(\alpha, \beta, \lambda)$ or equivalent

$$[\hat{V}] = \hat{I}^{-1}(\alpha, \beta, \lambda) = \begin{pmatrix} \widehat{Var}(\hat{\alpha}) & \widehat{cov}(\hat{\alpha}, \hat{\beta}) & \widehat{cov}(\hat{\alpha}, \hat{\lambda}) \\ \widehat{cov}(\hat{\alpha}, \hat{\beta}) & \widehat{Var}(\hat{\beta}) & \widehat{cov}(\hat{\beta}, \hat{\lambda}) \\ \widehat{cov}(\hat{\alpha}, \hat{\lambda}) & \widehat{cov}(\hat{\beta}, \hat{\lambda}) & \widehat{Var}(\hat{\lambda}) \end{pmatrix}. \quad (30)$$

It is well known that $(\hat{\alpha}, \hat{\beta}, \hat{\lambda})$ is approximately distributed as multivariate normal with mean (α, β, λ) and covariance matrix $I^{-1}(\alpha, \beta, \lambda)$ under some regularity conditions, see Lawless [25]. The $100(1-\gamma)\%$ two-sided confidence intervals can be given by

$$\hat{\alpha} \pm Z_{\frac{\gamma}{2}} \sqrt{\widehat{Var}(\hat{\alpha})},\, \hat{\beta} \pm Z_{\frac{\gamma}{2}} \sqrt{\widehat{Var}(\hat{\beta})} \text{ and } \hat{\lambda} \pm Z_{\frac{\gamma}{2}} \sqrt{\widehat{Var}(\hat{\lambda})}. \quad (31)$$

where $Z_{\frac{\gamma}{2}}$ is the percentile of the standard normal distribution with right-tail probability $\frac{\gamma}{2}$.

The delta method is used to obtain approximate estimates of the variances of $\hat{S}(t)$ and $\hat{h}(t)$. Greene [26] explained a general approach to computing CIs for functions of MLEs. The variance of $\hat{S}(t)$ and $\hat{h}(t)$ can be estimated using this method, respectively.

$$\hat{\sigma}^2_{\hat{S}(t)} = \left[\nabla \hat{S}(t)\right]^T [\hat{V}] \left[\nabla \hat{S}(t)\right] \text{ and } \hat{\sigma}^2_{\hat{h}(t)} = \left[\nabla \hat{h}(t)\right]^T [\hat{V}] \left[\nabla \hat{h}(t)\right],$$

where $\nabla \hat{S}(t)$ and $\nabla \hat{h}(t)$ are, respectively, the gradient of $\hat{S}(t)$ and $\hat{h}(t)$ with respect to α, β and λ as follows:

$$\nabla \hat{S}(t) = \begin{pmatrix} \frac{\partial S(t)}{\partial \alpha} \\ \frac{\partial S(t)}{\partial \beta} \\ \frac{\partial S(t)}{\partial \lambda} \end{pmatrix}$$

and

$$\nabla \hat{h}(t) = \begin{pmatrix} \frac{\partial h(t)}{\partial \alpha} \\ \frac{\partial h(t)}{\partial \beta} \\ \frac{\partial h(t)}{\partial \lambda} \end{pmatrix}$$

where

$$\frac{\partial S(t)}{\partial \alpha} = \frac{e^{-\lambda t^{-\beta}}\left((1-\alpha)\alpha^{e^{-\lambda t^{-\beta}}} + \alpha e^{\lambda t^{-\beta}}\left(-1 + \alpha^{e^{-\lambda t^{-\beta}}}\right)\right)}{\alpha(\alpha-1)^2},$$

$$\frac{\partial S(t)}{\partial \beta} = \frac{-\lambda t^{-\beta} e^{-\lambda t^{-\beta}} \alpha^{e^{-\lambda t^{-\beta}}} \log(\alpha) \log(t)}{\alpha - 1},$$

$$\frac{\partial S(t)}{\partial \lambda} = \frac{t^{-\beta} e^{-\lambda t^{-\beta}} \alpha^{e^{-\lambda t^{-\beta}}} \log(\alpha)}{\alpha - 1},$$

$$\frac{\partial h(t)}{\partial \alpha} = \frac{-\lambda \beta t^{-(\beta+1)} e^{-2\lambda t^{-\beta}} \alpha^{e^{-\lambda t^{-\beta}}-1}}{(\alpha - \alpha^{e^{-\lambda t^{-\beta}}})^2} \left[e^{\lambda t^{-\beta}}(-\alpha + \alpha^{e^{-\lambda t^{-\beta}}}) + \alpha \log(\alpha)(e^{\lambda t^{-\beta}} - 1) \right],$$

$$\frac{\partial h(t)}{\partial \beta} = \frac{\lambda \log(\alpha) t^{-(2\beta+1)} e^{-2\lambda t^{-\beta}} \alpha^{e^{-\lambda t^{-\beta}}}}{(\alpha - \alpha^{e^{-\lambda t^{-\beta}}})^2} \left[\begin{array}{c} t^\beta e^{\lambda t^{-\beta}}(\alpha - \alpha^{e^{-\lambda t^{-\beta}}}) \\ + \beta \log(t)\left(e^{\lambda t^{-\beta}}(t^\beta - \lambda)(-\alpha + \alpha^{e^{-\lambda t^{-\beta}}}) + \alpha\lambda\log(\alpha)\right) \end{array} \right]$$

and

$$\frac{\partial h(t)}{\partial \lambda} = \frac{-\beta \log(\alpha) t^{-(2\beta+1)} e^{-2\lambda t^{-\beta}} \alpha^{e^{-\lambda t^{-\beta}}}}{(\alpha - \alpha^{e^{-\lambda t^{-\beta}}})^2} \left[e^{\lambda t^{-\beta}}(t^\beta - \lambda)(-\alpha + \alpha^{e^{-\lambda t^{-\beta}}}) + \alpha\lambda\log(\alpha) \right].$$

Then, the $100(1-\gamma)\%$ two-sided confidence intervals of $S(t)$ and $h(t)$ can be given, respectively, by

$$\hat{S}(t) \pm Z_{\frac{\gamma}{2}} \sqrt{\hat{\sigma}^2_{\hat{S}(t)}} \text{ and } \hat{h}(t) \pm Z_{\frac{\gamma}{2}} \sqrt{\hat{\sigma}^2_{\hat{h}(t)}}. \quad (32)$$

A disadvantage of an approximate $100(1-\gamma)\%$ confidence interval is that it can produce a negative lower bound even if the parameter only accepts positive values. The negative value is modified by zero in this case. Optionally, Meeker and Escobar [27] proposed using a log transformation to obtain approximate confidence intervals for parameters with positive values. Thus, the approximate two-sided $100(1-\gamma)\%$ confidence interval derived in this manner for $\varphi = (\alpha, \beta, \lambda, S(t), h(t))$ is provided by

$$\left\{ \hat{\varphi} \exp\left[-\frac{Z_{\frac{\gamma}{2}}\widehat{Var}(\hat{\varphi})}{\varphi}\right], \hat{\varphi} \exp\left[\frac{Z_{\frac{\gamma}{2}}\widehat{Var}(\hat{\varphi})}{\varphi}\right] \right\}, \quad (33)$$

where $\hat{\varphi} = \left(\hat{\alpha}, \hat{\beta}, \hat{\lambda}, \hat{S}(t), \hat{h}(t)\right)$.

5.2. Credible CI

The credible confidence interval (CCI) is obtained by using the algorithm of Metropolis-Hastings within the Gibbs sampling technique. We summarized these algorithm steps as follows:

(1) Start with initial guess $\left(\alpha^{(0)}, \beta^{(0)}, \lambda^{(0)}\right)$.
(2) Set $j = 1$.
(3) From the normal proposal distributions $N\left(\alpha^{(j-1)}, var(\alpha)\right)$, $N\left(\beta^{(j-1)}, var(\beta)\right)$ and $N\left(\lambda^{(j-1)}, var(\lambda)\right)$, generate $\alpha^{(j)}, \beta^{(j)}$ and $\lambda^{(j)}$ from $\pi_1^*\left(\alpha^{(j-1)} | \beta^{(j-1)}, \lambda^{(j-1)}, data\right)$, $\pi_2^*\left(\beta^{(j-1)} | \alpha^{(j)}, \lambda^{(j-1)}, data\right)$ and $\pi_3^*\left(\lambda^{(j-1)} | \alpha^{(j)}, \beta^{(j)}, data\right)$ and from the main crossways in inverse Fisher information matrix can be obtained $var(\alpha), var(\beta)$ and $var(\lambda)$.

(4) From $N\left(\alpha^{(j-1)}, var(\alpha)\right)$, $N\left(\beta^{(j-1)}, var(\beta)\right)$ and $N\left(\lambda^{(j-1)}, var(\lambda)\right)$, generate proposals α^*, β^* and λ^*.

(i) Evaluate the acceptance probabilities

$$\eta_\alpha = \min\left[1, \frac{\pi_1^*\left(\alpha^* \mid \beta^{(j-1)}, \lambda^{(j-1)}, data\right)}{\pi_1^*\left(\alpha^{(j-1)} \mid \beta^{(j-1)}, \lambda^{(j-1)}, data\right)}\right],$$

$$\eta_\beta = \min\left[1, \frac{\pi_2^*\left(\beta^* \mid \alpha^{(j)}, \lambda^{(j-1)}, data\right)}{\pi_2^*\left(\beta^{(j-1)} \mid \alpha^{(j)}, \lambda^{(j-1)}, data\right)}\right],$$

$$\eta_\lambda = \min\left[1, \frac{\pi_3^*\left(\lambda^* \mid \alpha^{(j)}, \beta^{(j)}, data\right)}{\pi_3^*\left(\lambda^{(j-1)} \mid \alpha^{(j)}, \beta^{(j)}, data\right)}\right].$$

(ii) From a uniform $(0,1)$ distribution, generate u_1, u_2 and u_3.
(iii) If $u_1 < \eta_\alpha$, accept and set $\alpha^{(j)} = \alpha^*$; else, set $\alpha^{(j)} = \alpha^{(j-1)}$.
(iv) If $u_2 < \eta_\beta$, accept and set $\beta^{(j)} = \beta^*$; else, set $\beta^{(j)} = \beta^{(j-1)}$.
(v) If $u_3 < \eta_\lambda$, accept and set $\lambda^{(j)} = \lambda^*$; else, set $\lambda^{(j)} = \lambda^{(j-1)}$.

(5) Set $j = j + 1$.
(6) Repeat Steps (3)–(5) N times and obtain $\alpha^{(i)}, \beta^{(i)}$ and $\lambda^{(i)}, i = 1, 2, \ldots N$.
(7) To compute the CRs of $\psi_k^{(i)}, k = 1, 2, 3, (\psi_1, \psi_2, \psi_3) = (\alpha, \beta, \lambda)$
as $\psi_k^{(1)} < \psi_k^{(2)} \ldots < \psi_k^{(N)}$; then, the $100(1-\gamma)\%$ CRIs of ψ_k is

$$\left(\psi_{k(N\gamma/2)}, \psi_{k(N(1-\gamma/2))}\right).$$

The first simulated M variations will be eliminated in order to promote convergence and devote attention to the selection of initial values. The samples have chosen $\psi_k^{(j)}$, $j = M+1, \ldots N$, an approximate posterior sample generated for sufficiently large N, which may be required to develop the inferences of Bayes.

The approximate Bayes estimates of ψ_k based on the SEL function are obtained by

$$\hat{\psi}_k = \frac{1}{N-M} \sum_{j=M+1}^{N} \psi_k^{(j)}, \tag{34}$$

The approximate Bayes estimates for ψ_k based on the $LINEX$ loss function are obtained by

$$\hat{\psi}_k = \frac{-1}{c} \ln\left[\frac{1}{N-M} \sum_{j=M+1}^{N} e^{-c\,\psi_k^{(j)}}\right], k = 1, 2, 3. \tag{35}$$

5.3. Bootstrap CI

When the sample size is small, the percentile bootstrap (Boot-p) and the bootstrap-t (Boot-t) confidence interval presented by [28–31] allows for the computation of the confidence interval for the parameters of interest. Two parametric bootstrap algorithms are offered to calculate the bootstrap confidence intervals of $\alpha, \beta, \lambda, S(t)$ and $h(t)$. Bootstrap-t was created using a studentized 'pivot' and requires an estimator of the variance of the MLE of $\alpha, \beta, \lambda, S(t)$ and $h(t)$.

5.3.1. Parametric Boot-p

(1) Based on $x = x_{1:m:n}, x_{2:m:n}, \ldots, x_{m:m:n}$, obtain $\hat{\alpha}, \hat{\beta}$ and $\hat{\lambda}$ by maximizing Equations (7)–(9).
(2) Generate $x^* = x_{1:m:n}^*, x_{2:m:n}^*, \ldots, x_{m:m:n}^*$ from the APIW distribution with parameters $\hat{\alpha}, \hat{\beta}$ and $\hat{\lambda}$ based on hybrid Type-II censoring, using the algorithm described in [32].

(3) Obtain the bootstrap estimate $\hat{\psi}_i^* = \left(\hat{\alpha}_i^*, \hat{\beta}_i^*, \hat{\lambda}_i^*, \hat{S}_i^*(t), \hat{h}_i^*(t)\right), i = 1, 2, 3, \ldots, N$ boot by the MLEs under the bootstrap sample.

(4) Repeat Steps (2) and (3) N boot times, and obtain $\hat{\psi}_1^*, \hat{\psi}_2^*, \ldots, \hat{\psi}_{N\,boot'}^*$ where $\hat{\psi}_i^* = \left(\hat{\alpha}_i^*, \hat{\beta}_i^*, \hat{\lambda}_i^*, \hat{S}_i^*(t), \hat{h}_i^*(t)\right), i = 1, 2, 3, \ldots, N$ boot.

(5) Obtain $\hat{\psi}_{(1)}^*, \hat{\psi}_{(2)}^*, \ldots, \hat{\psi}_{(N\,boot)}^*$ by arrange $\hat{\psi}_i^*, i = 1, 2, 3, \ldots, N$ boot in ascending orders.

Define $\hat{\psi}_{boot-p} = G_1^{-1}(z)$ for given z, where $G_1(z) = P(\hat{\psi}^* \leq z)$ is the cumulative distribution function of $\hat{\psi}^*$. The approximate bootstrap-p $100(1-\gamma)\%$ CI of $\hat{\psi}$ is given by

$$\left[\hat{\psi}_{boot-p}\left(\frac{\gamma}{2}\right), \hat{\psi}_{boot-p}\left(1 - \frac{\gamma}{2}\right)\right]. \tag{36}$$

5.3.2. Parametric Boot-t

(1) Repeat the steps of the parametric Boot-p from (1) to (3).

(2) The variance–covariance matrix $I^{-1*}\left(\frac{\partial \ell}{\partial \alpha}, \frac{\partial \ell}{\partial \beta}, \frac{\partial \ell}{\partial \lambda}\right)$ and the approximate estimates of the variance $S(t)$ and $h(t)$ based on the asymptotic variance–covariance matrix and delta method are computed.

(3) The $T^{*\psi}$ statistic is defined as

$$T^{*\psi} = \frac{(\hat{\psi}^* - \hat{\psi})}{\sqrt{\widehat{var(\hat{\psi}^*)}}}$$

(4) Obtain $T_1^{*\psi}, T_2^{*\psi}, \ldots, T_{N\,boot}^{*\psi}$ from repeating steps 2–5, NBoot times

(5) Obtain the ordered sequences $T_{(1)}^{*\psi}, T_{(2)}^{*\psi}, \ldots, T_{(N\,boot)}^{*\psi}$ by arranging $\hat{\psi}_i^*, i = 1, 2, 3, \ldots, N$ boot in $T_1^{*\psi}, T_2^{*\psi}, \ldots, T_{N\,boot}^{*\psi}$ in ascending order.

Define $\hat{\psi}_{boot-t} = \hat{\psi} + G_2^{-1}(z)\sqrt{\widehat{var(\hat{\psi}^*)}}$, where $G_2(z) = P(T^* \leq z)$ is the cumulative distribution function of T^* for a given z.

Then, the approximate bootstrap-t $100(1-\gamma)\%$ CI of $\hat{\psi}$ is obtained by

$$\left[\hat{\psi}_{boot-t}\left(\frac{\gamma}{2}\right), \hat{\psi}_{boot-t}\left(1 - \frac{\gamma}{2}\right)\right]. \tag{37}$$

6. Application to Real-Life Data

Two real data examples are discussed in this section. We aim to model the failure times of a sample of ball bearings using APIW distribution, and the resistances in a sample of guinea pigs are modeled using APIW distribution. A goodness of fit measure is utilized for that purpose. Point and interval estimations are performed via numerical methods using suitable R-codes.

6.1. Data Set I

Leiblein et al. [33] employ the suggested approaches in this section to determine how many millions of spins a large sample of 23 ball bearings can withstand before failing. The data are shown in Table 1. The difference between the empirical Kolmogorov–Smirnov (KSD) distribution and the CDF for the APIW distribution is 0.0937, and the p-value (PVKS) is 0.9876, which indicates the goodness of fit using the APIW model. Therefore, the APIW distribution is consistent with the information supplied.

Table 1. Failure times for a group of 23 ball bearings in a life endurance test.

17.88	28.92	33.00	41.52	42.12	45.60
48.48	51.84	51.96	54.12	55.56	67.80
68.64	68.64	68.88	84.12	93.12	98.64
105.12	105.84	127.92	128.04	173.40	

Table 2 details the MLE, the MPS, and the Bayesian estimates of the parameters with the standard errors (SE) and describes the Kolmogorov–Smirnov goodness of fit test for data set I. While analyzing data set I, it was discovered that the Bayesian estimates have lower SE values for estimating α, while the MPS has less SE when estimating β and λ. The best goodness of fit with respect to KSD is attained for its minimum value, and this is achieved under Bayesian estimation; similarly, the highest PVKS is obtained under Bayesian estimation. Therefore, according to Bayesian estimations, the APIW distribution offers a better fit. Figure 1 illustrates the APIW distribution's theoretical and empirical pdf, CDF, and P-P plot using data set I, and it can be seen that the APIW is fitting data set I very well.

Table 2. MLE, MPS, and Bayesian estimates with SE values and KS test.

		Estimates	SE	KSD	PVKS
MLE	α	64.1705	154.1028	0.0937	0.9876
	β	2.3255	0.3061		
	λ	2556.7180	3050.7065		
MPS	α	74.6228	49.1516	0.1136	0.9281
	β	2.0332	0.0634		
	λ	745.7198	16.0139		
Bayesian	α	64.1103	15.4170	0.0924	0.9894
	β	2.3246	0.3057		
	λ	2558.2005	305.4596		

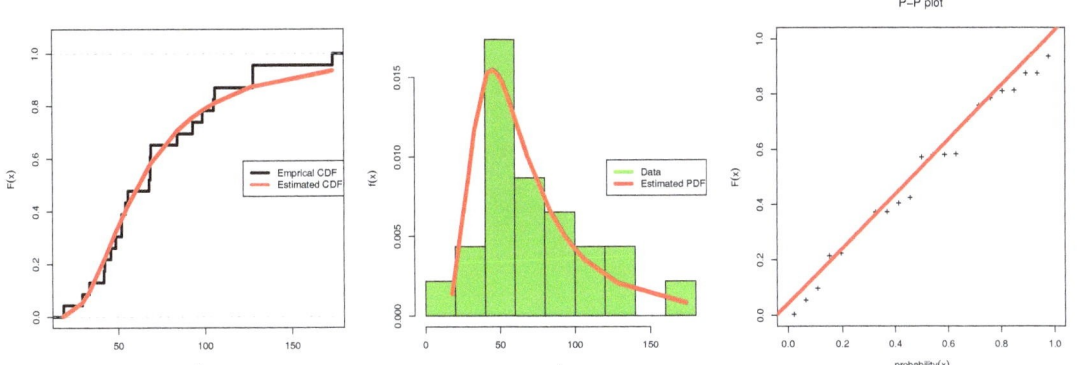

Figure 1. Estimated CDF, pdf, and pp-plot: data set I.

To check the performance of the MLE, we plot the profile likelihood function, where the x-label is one parameter with different values and the y-label is the log-likelihood value keeping the other parameters to be fixed. The profile likelihood of data set I is sketched in Figure 2, where the blue line is a log-likelihood values with different value of parameter and dot is the MLE estimator of parameter with max log-likelihood value, and it confirms that the MLE estimates have maximum values for data set I, which is consistent with the values of MLE observed in Table 2, and it is also clear that data set I behave very well as the three roots of the parameter are global maxima.

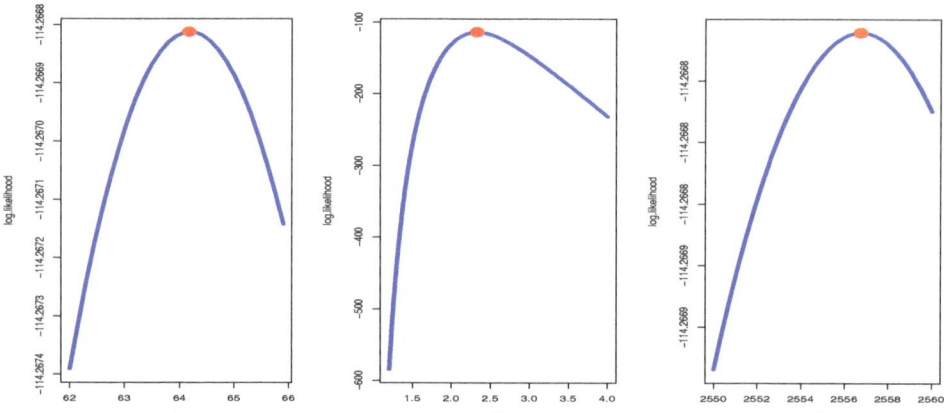

Figure 2. The Profile likelihood curve with maximum point for data set I.

The plots of the MCMC trace, the auto-correlation (ACF) tests, the posterior sample histogram, and the convergence of MCMC are all performed to diagnose the issues related to MCMC samples. An essential tool for evaluating a chain's mixing is a trace plot. The auto-correlation plot, also known as the ACF plot, shows the serial correlation in time-varying data. Therefore, we plot MCMC trace, ACF plot, and a histogram of posterior density of MCMC results, and the convergence of the MCMC results for data set I are presented in Figures 3–6, respectively.

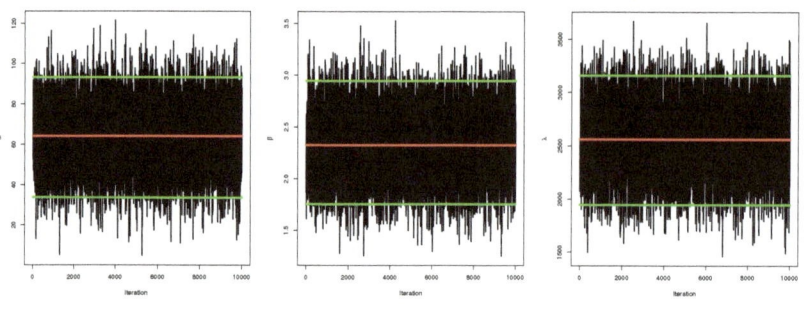

Figure 3. MCMC trace: data set I.

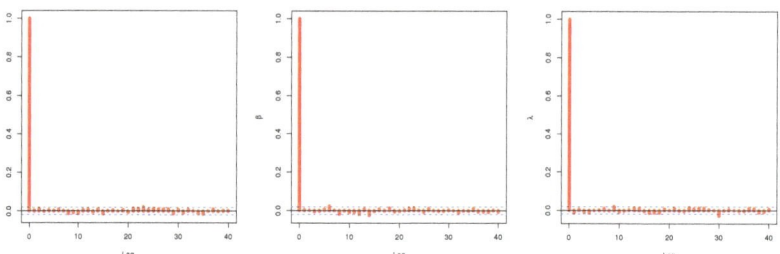

Figure 4. Auto-correlation test: data set I.

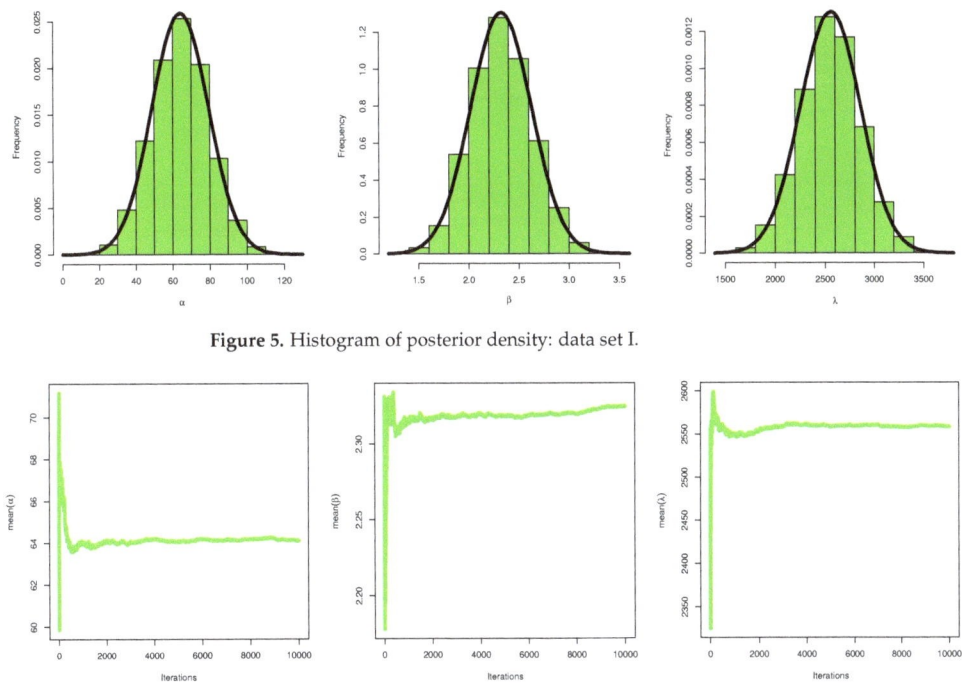

Figure 5. Histogram of posterior density: data set I.

Figure 6. Convergence of MCMC results: data set I.

Figures 3, 5, and 6 confirm that the MCMC trace has normal results and convergence measures for data set I. Furthermore, this shows the histograms for the marginal posterior density estimates of the parameters based on 5000 chain values and the Gaussian kernel. The estimation in Figure 5 clearly indicates that all generated posteriors are symmetric with respect to the theoretical posterior density function. Figure 4 explores the auto-correlation test which revealed that the auto-correlation test for the MCMC is the correlation between an iteration series with a decreased version of itself. The auto-correlation function started to slow down at zero, which represents the correlation of the iteration series with itself, and then, it resulted in a correlation of one.

Table 3 provides the MLE, the MPS, and the Bayesian estimates for parameters of APIW distribution based on hybrid censored samples for data set I. Table 4 presents the survival and hazard of APIW distribution based on hybrid censored samples with data set I.

It is observed from the numerical results in Table 3 that the Bayesian estimators act better than alternative methods for estimating the parameter α, while the MPS is the best choice for estimating the parameters β and λ. Table 4 demonstrates the efficiency of the MPS estimation method since the survival estimation is maximized and the hazard rate estimation is minimized under the MPS estimation method.

Table 3. MLE, MPS, and Bayesian estimates based on hybrid censored samples: data set I.

T	r		MLE		MPS		Bayesian	
			Estimates	SE	Estimates	SE	Estimates	SE
68	12	α	46.3400	163.7701	83.8863	351.3109	46.3076	3.9134
		β	1.9705	0.4337	1.6145	0.4176	1.9692	0.4331
		λ	747.1634	1407.1232	156.5471	329.6032	747.8127	156.7151
	16	α	46.0169	162.8815	74.4494	322.0154	45.9893	3.2896
		β	1.9650	0.4308	2.0330	0.2510	1.9637	0.4302
		λ	733.8110	1375.322	745.4669	10.3476	734.6510	131.6786
110	16	α	55.8774	166.4168	79.4264	16.2216	55.8488	3.2118
		β	2.1265	0.3848	1.8119	0.0638	2.1254	0.3742
		λ	1246.7484	2026.3962	320.7453	8.6051	1247.550	169.1073
	20	α	60.7348	157.5242	75.2723	10.3590	60.7075	3.0404
		β	2.2491	0.3624	1.9606	0.0645	2.2480	0.3319
		λ	1935.9909	1875.5629	565.5794	10.3615	1937.155	139.9357

Table 4. Survival and hazard based on hybrid censored samples: data set I.

T	r		MLE	MPS	Bayesian
68	12	survival	0.4857	0.5113	0.4877
		hazard	0.0188	0.0150	0.0188
	16	survival	0.4850	0.5107	0.4869
		hazard	0.0188	0.0150	0.0187
110	16	survival	0.3253	0.3563	0.3268
		hazard	0.0197	0.0163	0.0197
	20	survival	0.1978	0.2277	0.1988
		hazard	0.0185	0.0158	0.0185

6.2. Data Set II

A real data set II from Okash et al. [34] is considered. To demonstrate the reliability of the APIW distribution to fit these data, 72 observations of resistance in guinea pigs were exposed to various dosages of virulent tubercle bacilli. The observed data set II has been shown in Table 5.

Table 5. Survival times (in days) of resistance in guinea pigs exposed to various dosages of virulent tubercle bacilli.

12	15	22	24	24	32	32	33
38	38	43	44	48	52	53	54
55	56	57	58	58	59	60	60
60	61	62	63	65	65	67	68
70	72	73	75	76	76	81	83
85	87	91	95	96	98	99	109
121	127	129	131	143	146	146	175
211	233	258	258	263	297	341	341

Table 6 details MLE, MPS, and Bayesian estimates with SE and DKS goodness of fit test for data set II. While analyzing data set II, it is realized that the MPS estimates have lower SE values for the estimated APIW parameters. For modeling purposes, the Bayesian estimation has the minimum KSD (0.1091) and highest PVKS (0.3581); hence, the APIW distribution offers a better fit under Bayesian estimation. Figure 7 illustrates the APIW distribution's theoretical and empirical pdf, CDF, and P-P plot using data set II, and it can be seen that the APIW is suitable and reliable for fitting data set II.

Table 6. MLE, MPS, and Bayesian estimates with SE values and KS test: data set II.

		Estimates	SE	Lower	Upper	KSD	PVKS
MLE	α	99.0793	46.2628	8.4043	189.7544	0.1096	0.3524
	β	1.7889	0.1558	1.4835	2.0944		
	λ	344.2289	143.1508	63.6533	624.8045		
MPS	α	122.7002	4.7472	113.3957	132.0046	0.1186	0.2637
	β	1.6840	0.0358	1.6139	1.7542		
	λ	210.6960	2.5855	205.6284	215.7635		
Bayesian	α	98.9326	15.7863	68.4324	129.4730	0.1091	0.3581
	β	1.7885	0.1556	1.4991	2.1047		
	λ	344.2667	24.3636	295.4979	392.3949		

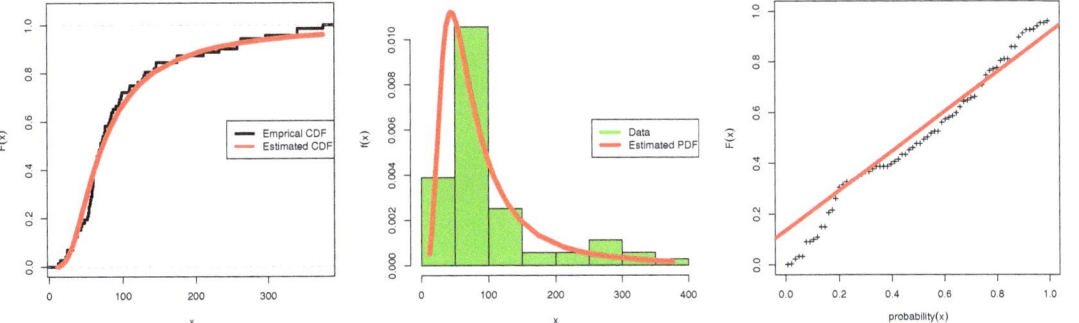

Figure 7. Estimated CDF, pdf and pp-plot: data set II.

Figure 8 confirms that the MLE estimates have the maximum likelihood values for data set II for the estimated parameter values that coincide with the MLE estimates in Table 6. Figure 9, describing the trace of the MCMC and its convergence. Figure 10 states that there is no auto-correlation for the MCMC series; the values started with zero and end up with one. In Figure 11, it is emphasized that the MCMC results have a normal curve with symmetric histograms of the posterior density, while Figure 12 shows that the MCMC trace has convergence results. Table 7 summarizes the MLE, the MPS, and the Bayesian estimates for parameters of APIW distribution based on hybrid censored samples for data set II with different values of T and r. The Bayesian estimators are better for estimating the parameter α, while the MPS is the best choice for estimating the parameters β and λ. Table 8 shows the estimated values of the survival and the hazard of APIW distribution based on the hybrid censored samples with data set II with different values of T and r. It is clear that the maximum survival is attained under MPS estimation and also the minimum hazard rate is obtained under MPS estimation, which supports the selection of the MPS method for efficient failure data analysis.

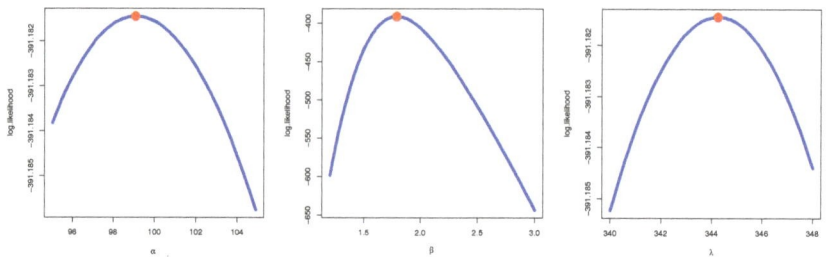

Figure 8. The Profile likelihood curve with the maximum point for data set II.

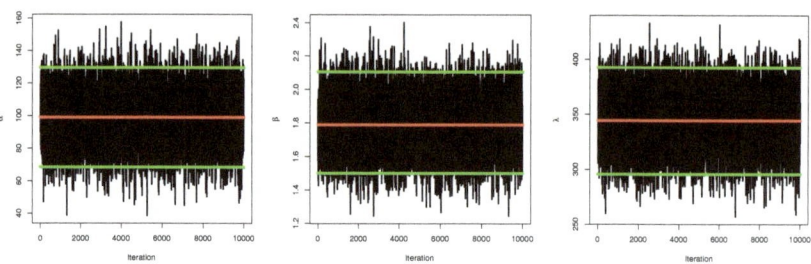

Figure 9. MCMC trace: data set II.

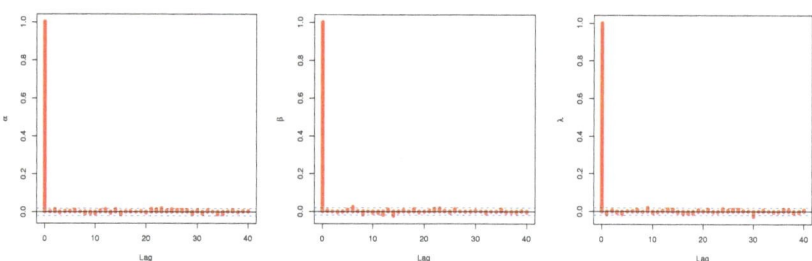

Figure 10. Auto-correlation test: data set II.

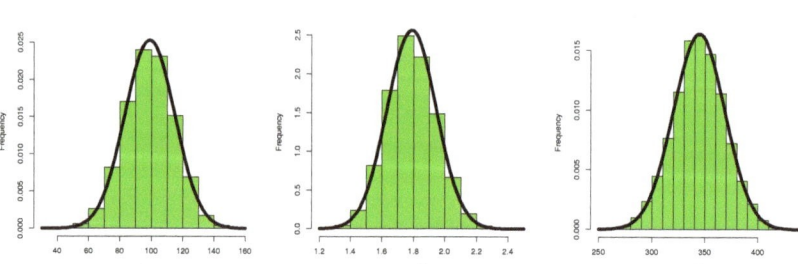

Figure 11. Histogram of posterior density: data set II.

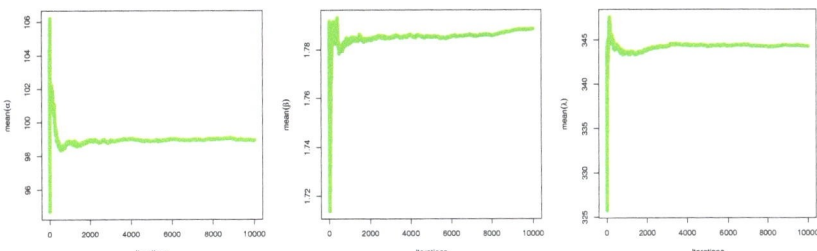

Figure 12. Convergence of MCMC results: data set II.

Table 7. MLE, MPS, and Bayesian estimates based on hybrid censored samples: data set II.

T	r		MLE		MPS		Bayesian	
			Estimates	SE	Estimates	SE	Estimates	SE
100	50	α	101.0733	164.6184	125.1150	67.7176	101.0304	3.9380
		β	1.7786	0.1811	1.6609	0.0656	1.7781	0.1809
		λ	327.2383	259.4398	191.2807	22.0057	327.2877	28.8832
	60	α	103.0959	164.5881	126.4073	9.2812	103.0530	3.9373
		β	1.7976	0.1786	1.6819	0.0363	1.7970	0.1783
		λ	349.4182	271.6575	206.2780	5.2838	349.4698	30.2434
110	50	α	101.0733	164.6184	125.1150	67.7176	101.0304	3.9380
		β	1.7786	0.1811	1.6609	0.0656	1.7781	0.1809
		λ	327.2383	259.4398	191.2807	22.0057	327.2877	28.8832
	60	α	101.2719	164.0169	125.7735	16.0496	101.2291	3.9237
		β	1.7814	0.1748	1.6686	0.0365	1.7808	0.1745
		λ	330.4588	255.2788	196.5964	4.9556	330.5050	28.4200

Table 8. Survival and hazard based on hybrid censored samples: data set II.

T	r		MLE	MPS	Bayesian
100	50	survival	0.3523	0.3647	0.3530
		hazard	0.0141	0.0130	0.0141
	60	survival	0.3286	0.3412	0.3293
		hazard	0.0140	0.0130	0.0140
110	50	survival	0.3523	0.3647	0.3530
		hazard	0.0141	0.0130	0.0141
	60	survival	0.2906	0.3040	0.2912
		hazard	0.0131	0.0121	0.0131

7. A Simulation Study

A simulation analysis was carried out using 5000 iterations for hybrid Type-II censored samples. For the generated simulated sample from APIW distribution, descriptive statistics are computed to evaluate the consistency of this simulated data, Table 9 summarizes some measures in addition to skewness and kurtosis measures. Each simulation compares the APIW distribution parameter estimators by likelihood, product spacing, and Bayesian. Censored APIW samples are with the initial values:

In Table 10: $\alpha = 0.6, \beta = 0.6, \lambda = 0.7$ and $\alpha = 1.3, \beta = 0.6, \lambda = 0.7$.

In Table 11: $\alpha = 0.6, \beta = 0.6, \lambda = 2$ and $\alpha = 2, \beta = 0.6, \lambda = 2$.
In Table 12: $\alpha = 0.8, \beta = 2, \lambda = 2$ and $\alpha = 2, \beta = 2, \lambda = 2$.

For the development of a hybrid censored sample, we selected different sample sizes as n = 50 and 100 and different censored sample sizes as r = 30, 40, and 50 for n = 50, r = 70, 90, and 100 for n = 100.

The relative bias (RB), mean square error (MSE), length of asymptotic confidence intervals (LACI), length of bootstrap-p (LBP), and length of bootstrap-t (LBT) are calculated, and a comparison was considered between the different approaches of the resulting estimators with respect to the RB of α, β, and λ. In addition, the MSE was utilized for the same purpose such that $MSE(\psi_k) = \frac{1}{M} \sum_{i=1}^{M} \left(\hat{\psi}_k^{(i)} - \psi_k \right)^2$, where $M = 5000$ is the number of simulated samples, and $(\psi_1 = \alpha, \psi_2 = \beta, \psi_3 = \lambda)$. Overall, 95% of the CIs are obtained from asymptotic distributions from MLEs and CRIs and are also compared with a further criterion. The comparison is between the average confidence interval length (ACL). In order to assess the type of prior, estimates of the parameters in the Bayes technique are computed from informative priors. The hyperparameters in the case of informative priors are chosen by elective hyperparameters using MLE information to show the results of estimated parameters.

Table 9. Summary of simulated data from APIW distribution.

α	β	λ	Minimum	Q1	Q2	Mean	Q3	Maximum	SD	SK	KT
0.6	0.6	0.2	0.0019	0.0375	0.0968	9.3625	0.3837	2525.81	117.8092	17.2574	320.5176
		0.7	0.0341	0.2744	0.781	28.6615	3.2646	3533.482	188.5746	12.4815	188.0099
		1.2	0.0504	0.564	1.6943	554.9259	6.8621	373,379.5	12,016.08	30.0298	929.0447
		1.7	0.1445	1.1408	3.2773	112.0147	12.4232	25308.46	988.7543	18.8949	440.0531
		2.2	0.1183	1.7701	4.6629	758.7959	18.144	254,110.1	9603.757	21.2078	516.2217
		2.7	0.136	2.4891	7.0995	12,403.68	29.2255	621,3521	244,427.2	22.5586	527.7023
	1.5	0.2	0.0817	0.2689	0.3929	0.7271	0.6817	22.9594	1.492	9.6082	119.4912
		0.7	0.2587	0.5961	0.9059	1.6512	1.6052	26.2592	2.4575	4.8751	34.0851
		1.2	0.3026	0.7953	1.2348	2.449	2.1606	169.3792	7.1983	15.4838	314.6141
		1.7	0.4613	1.0541	1.6077	2.8005	2.7396	57.7173	4.1289	6.1401	56.8222
		2.2	0.4258	1.2566	1.8512	3.8492	3.1878	145.2141	8.8066	9.0808	110.2727
		2.7	0.4502	1.4402	2.1902	5.3273	3.8574	521.597	24.5777	16.9134	322.1059
	3	0.2	0.2859	0.5186	0.6269	0.7411	0.8256	4.7916	0.4218	4.1298	29.9656
		0.7	0.5087	0.7721	0.9518	1.1322	1.267	5.1244	0.608	2.6053	11.9396
		1.2	0.5501	0.8918	1.1112	1.3201	1.4699	13.0146	0.8409	5.8075	58.3727
		1.7	0.6792	1.0267	1.268	1.4908	1.6552	7.5972	0.7606	2.7864	14.7529
		2.2	0.6526	1.121	1.3606	1.662	1.7854	12.0505	1.0431	4.2566	29.2693
		2.7	0.671	1.2001	1.4799	1.8111	1.964	22.8385	1.4315	8.0332	97.9213

Table 9. Cont.

α	β	λ	Minimum	Q1	Q2	Mean	Q3	Maximum	SD	SK	KT
1.5	0.6	0.2	0.0021	0.0576	0.1675	20.1354	0.7441	5453.285	254.3222	17.2608	320.6308
		0.7	0.0395	0.4161	1.3517	61.1988	6.3512	7620.369	406.3593	12.502	188.5294
		1.2	0.0561	0.8339	2.8926	1196.982	13.2257	806,474.1	25,953.44	30.0314	929.1182
		1.7	0.167	1.7169	5.6449	239.0572	23.9633	54,604.49	2132.057	18.9211	441.0744
		2.2	0.1306	2.6675	7.9627	1633.918	34.8865	548,731.3	20,735.8	21.2142	516.483
		2.7	0.1484	3.7507	12.2307	26,786.65	56.6635	13,422,188	527,997	22.5588	527.7134
	1.5	0.2	0.0989	0.343	0.5117	0.9127	0.8951	25.1911	1.6971	8.8703	105.0283
		0.7	0.2976	0.7198	1.1197	1.9816	2.0002	28.5589	2.7859	4.5374	30.0123
		1.2	0.3396	0.9341	1.4893	2.8184	2.6335	164.0482	7.2539	14.1928	271.0224
		1.7	0.5111	1.2247	1.9137	3.2503	3.291	59.7669	4.4974	5.6013	48.348
		2.2	0.4661	1.4447	2.1772	4.3322	3.7888	141.9907	8.9929	8.4079	96.0569
		2.7	0.4889	1.6417	2.5574	5.7369	4.5445	470.9055	22.6724	16.1496	299.0034
	3	0.2	0.2912	0.5651	0.6995	0.8348	0.9426	5.589	0.502	4.0018	28.582
		0.7	0.5239	0.8392	1.0621	1.2755	1.4473	5.9758	0.7261	2.5326	11.4722
		1.2	0.5622	0.9643	1.2367	1.4842	1.676	15.1816	0.9981	5.6295	55.6979
		1.7	0.6991	1.1142	1.4136	1.6778	1.8876	8.8602	0.9095	2.6968	14.0562
		2.2	0.6655	1.2168	1.5143	1.8717	2.0348	14.0563	1.2387	4.1458	28.1226
		2.7	0.6828	1.3026	1.65	2.0412	2.2421	26.6419	1.6898	7.8521	94.6963
3	0.6	0.2	0.0023	0.0837	0.2587	33.3614	1.1989	9044.133	421.7753	17.2616	320.6565
		0.7	0.0453	0.5991	2.0877	101.2154	10.2436	12,634.96	673.6439	12.5066	188.6474
		1.2	0.062	1.1807	4.4402	1984.686	21.2686	1,337,645	43,047.07	30.0318	929.1349
		1.7	0.191	2.4597	8.6994	395.314	38.5459	90,546.07	3534.951	18.9271	441.3064
		2.2	0.1428	3.825	12.2242	2708.01	56.0588	910,095.2	34,390.2	21.2156	516.5424
		2.7	0.1605	5.3781	18.8508	44,427.34	91.2935	22,263,025	875,773	22.5589	527.7159
	1.5	0.2	0.102	0.3945	0.6023	1.0877	1.0704	30.4535	2.0548	8.8479	104.636
		0.7	0.3133	0.8252	1.3179	2.3613	2.3929	34.5215	3.3769	4.5215	29.8511
		1.2	0.3524	1.0643	1.7489	3.3579	3.147	198.3252	8.7774	14.1699	270.3686
		1.7	0.5375	1.4015	2.2507	3.869	3.9332	72.248	5.4519	5.5778	48.0366
		2.2	0.4819	1.6538	2.5569	5.1663	4.5263	171.6554	10.8861	8.3911	95.7611
		2.7	0.5035	1.8793	3.0078	6.855	5.4345	569.3038	27.4201	16.1402	298.7514
	3	0.2	0.296	0.6089	0.7631	0.9119	1.037	6.1841	0.5605	3.9338	27.9076
		0.7	0.5385	0.9026	1.1586	1.3933	1.5925	6.6117	0.8119	2.4899	11.2289
		1.2	0.5734	1.0338	1.3473	1.6196	1.8431	16.7984	1.1133	5.5364	54.3872
		1.7	0.7182	1.1972	1.5413	1.8319	2.0758	9.8033	1.0177	2.6452	13.7014
		2.2	0.6775	1.3078	1.6498	2.0443	2.2373	15.5531	1.3815	4.0881	27.5711
		2.7	0.6935	1.4	1.7991	2.2299	2.4665	29.4793	1.8797	7.7641	93.1916

Table 10. Bayesian and non-Bayesian estimation for parameters of APIW distribution based on hybrid censored samples where $\beta = 0.6$, $\theta = 0.7$.

$\beta = 0.6, \theta = 0.7$					MLE					MPS					Bayesian		
α	n	T	r		RB	MSE	LACI	LBP	LBT	RB	MSE	LACI	LBP	LBT	RB	MSE	LCCI
1.3	50	1.4	30	α	0.0012	0.0791	1.1039	0.0476	0.0483	−0.0249	0.0679	1.0143	0.0437	0.0464	0.0748	0.0256	0.5025
				β	0.0365	0.0108	0.3989	0.0199	0.0199	−0.0496	0.0100	0.3743	0.0167	0.0167	−0.2786	0.0091	0.4369
				λ	0.0200	0.0255	0.6239	0.0298	0.0298	0.0520	0.0264	0.6212	0.0302	0.0318	−0.2234	0.0240	0.4759
			40	α	0.0010	0.0619	1.0723	0.0479	0.0479	−0.0024	0.0176	1.0065	0.0372	0.0371	0.0627	0.0178	0.4171
		7		β	0.0267	0.0070	0.3228	0.0146	0.0148	−0.0412	0.0066	0.3030	0.0139	0.0135	−0.2631	0.0061	0.3763
				λ	0.0182	0.0219	0.5790	0.0244	0.0239	0.0309	0.0235	0.5961	0.0249	0.0248	−0.2190	0.0140	0.3908
		999	50	α	−0.0014	0.0507	0.9554	0.0386	0.0468	−0.0019	0.0125	0.9899	0.0287	0.0288	0.0313	0.0073	0.2778
				β	0.0102	0.0053	0.2839	0.0119	0.0120	−0.0416	0.0058	0.2590	0.0107	0.0108	−0.2344	0.0046	0.2703
				λ	0.0162	0.0204	0.4719	0.0233	0.0233	0.0291	0.0214	0.5761	0.0237	0.0237	−0.2109	0.0128	0.2981
	100	1.4	70	α	0.0360	0.2776	2.0930	0.1478	0.1481	−0.0577	0.1186	1.3516	0.0622	0.0625	0.1368	0.0470	0.4726
				β	0.0195	0.0043	0.2520	0.0119	0.0119	−0.0311	0.0045	0.2529	0.0116	0.0115	−0.3606	0.0016	0.3682
				λ	0.0083	0.0211	0.4019	0.0273	0.0172	0.0316	0.0143	0.4616	0.0211	0.0212	−0.3061	0.0155	0.3704
		7	90	α	0.0308	0.2697	1.9132	0.1309	0.0908	0.0405	0.1041	1.2503	0.0611	0.0611	0.1163	0.0344	0.4199
				β	0.0101	0.0039	0.2443	0.0101	0.0101	−0.0304	0.0042	0.2455	0.0111	0.0109	−0.4388	0.0015	0.3200
				λ	0.0318	0.0197	0.3944	0.0234	0.0162	0.0314	0.0123	0.3602	0.0202	0.0209	−0.4305	0.0150	0.3220
		999	100	α	0.0428	0.2500	1.7648	0.1216	0.0812	−0.0401	0.0985	1.2854	0.0513	0.0513	0.0623	0.0114	0.2600
				β	−0.0045	0.0038	0.2419	0.0091	0.0100	−0.0316	0.0042	0.2354	0.0107	0.0106	−0.3557	0.0009	0.2399
				λ	0.0263	0.0137	0.3735	0.0213	0.0133	0.0291	0.0106	0.3488	0.0200	0.0237	−0.3547	0.0114	0.2948

Table 10. Cont.

$\beta = 0.6, \theta = 0.7$				MLE						MPS			Bayesian		
α	n	T	r		RB	MSE	LACI	LBP	LBT	RB	MSE	LACI	LBP	LBT	RB	MSE	LCCI
0.6	50	0.5	30	α	0.0616	0.0412	0.7829	0.0350	0.0348	−0.0301	0.0370	0.7512	0.0352	0.0355	0.1988	0.0290	0.4688
				β	0.0596	0.0126	0.4182	0.0194	0.0195	−0.0571	0.0106	0.3818	0.0166	0.0166	−0.1291	0.0106	0.3893
				λ	−0.0187	0.0261	0.6321	0.0271	0.0272	0.0902	0.0374	0.7172	0.0312	0.0308	−0.1567	0.0128	0.5101
		5	40	α	0.0577	0.0417	0.7004	0.0344	0.0315	−0.0301	0.0353	0.6903	0.0341	0.0341	0.1239	0.0283	0.3812
				β	0.0320	0.0079	0.3413	0.0157	0.0159	−0.0493	0.0072	0.3116	0.0143	0.0143	−0.1234	0.0079	0.3346
				λ	0.0106	0.0257	0.6404	0.0260	0.0270	0.0752	0.0330	0.6827	0.0279	0.0277	−0.1271	0.0125	0.3717
		99,999	50	α	0.1308	0.0125	0.6835	0.0316	0.0259	−0.0280	0.0311	0.5259	0.0354	0.0255	0.1137	0.0121	0.2803
				β	0.0335	0.0068	0.3139	0.0141	0.0144	−0.0467	0.0070	0.2986	0.0141	0.0137	−0.1197	0.0069	0.2393
				λ	0.0064	0.0231	0.6191	0.0213	0.0231	0.0612	0.0349	0.6180	0.0238	0.0238	−0.1090	0.0102	0.3190
	100	0.5	70	α	0.1568	0.1709	1.5798	0.0743	0.0745	−0.0893	0.1224	1.3568	0.0605	0.0605	0.3783	0.0640	0.4302
				β	0.0221	0.0086	0.3598	0.0154	0.0154	−0.0714	0.0096	0.3456	0.0164	0.0161	−0.1407	0.0091	0.3560
				λ	0.0357	0.0532	0.8997	0.0411	0.0408	0.1771	0.0779	0.9813	0.0448	0.0448	−0.2168	0.0351	0.4293
		5	90	α	0.2180	0.1523	1.2823	0.0750	0.0682	0.0120	0.1182	1.3675	0.0607	0.0602	0.3728	0.0618	0.3257
				β	0.0170	0.0044	0.2584	0.0110	0.0111	−0.0487	0.0054	0.2634	0.0123	0.0126	−0.1287	0.0036	0.2954
				λ	0.0075	0.0344	0.7277	0.0330	0.0329	0.1039	0.0532	0.8592	0.0391	0.0398	−0.2042	0.0294	0.3247
		99,999	100	α	0.1976	0.1224	1.2799	0.0677	0.0658	−0.0169	0.1022	1.2844	0.0585	0.0588	0.2379	0.0244	0.2489
				β	0.0124	0.0042	0.2468	0.0102	0.0102	−0.0371	0.0047	0.2484	0.0123	0.0123	−0.1264	0.0035	0.2385
				λ	0.0226	0.0315	0.7310	0.0318	0.0319	0.1007	0.0471	0.7933	0.0342	0.0342	−0.1321	0.0156	0.3095

Table 11. Bayesian and non-Bayesian estimation for parameters of APIW distribution based on hybrid censored samples where $\beta = 0.6, \theta = 2$.

						MLE							MPS				Bayesian		
α	β = 0.6, θ = 2	n	T	r		RB	MSE	LACI	LBP	LBT	RB	MSE	LACI	LBP	LBT	RB	MSE	LCCI
0.6		50	1.4	30	α	0.5022	0.6443	2.9192	0.1332	0.1314	0.1281	0.5495	2.8997	0.1347	0.1377	0.1649	0.0247	0.4886
					β	0.0198	0.0100	0.3889	0.0179	0.0198	−0.1065	0.0135	0.3808	0.0179	0.0177	−0.3502	0.0095	0.3791
					λ	0.0087	0.2139	1.8136	0.0792	0.0792	0.0566	0.2394	1.8677	0.0874	0.0867	−0.0478	0.0295	0.5636
				40	α	0.5263	0.6337	2.8674	0.1257	0.1282	0.1210	0.4745	2.6878	0.1160	0.1163	0.1672	0.0216	0.4103
					β	0.0547	0.0091	0.3410	0.0169	0.0185	−0.0678	0.0128	0.3414	0.0178	0.0181	−0.3339	0.0085	0.2883
					λ	−0.0097	0.1465	1.4999	0.0718	0.0725	0.0304	0.1519	1.5104	0.0703	0.0700	−0.0326	0.0241	0.4540
			7	50	α	0.1792	0.1318	1.3605	0.0603	0.0607	−0.1141	0.1057	1.2317	0.0537	0.0545	0.1095	0.0096	0.2808
					β	0.0535	0.0081	0.3249	0.0159	0.0172	−0.0579	0.0126	0.3246	0.0168	0.0172	−0.2406	0.0062	0.2289
					λ	0.0389	0.1410	1.4413	0.0648	0.0651	0.0302	0.1495	1.4070	0.0613	0.0598	−0.0301	0.0098	0.2934
			999		α	0.1216	0.1193	1.3246	0.0623	0.0652	−0.1856	0.0907	1.0981	0.0497	0.0497	0.2768	0.0400	0.4275
				70	β	0.0154	0.0074	0.3355	0.0153	0.0153	−0.0829	0.0088	0.3113	0.0124	0.0125	−0.5069	0.0070	0.2629
					λ	0.0214	0.0974	1.2132	0.0568	0.0604	0.0675	0.1189	1.2450	0.0545	0.0545	−0.0894	0.0496	0.5074
		100	1.4		α	0.1407	0.1028	1.2361	0.0614	0.0620	−0.0333	0.0787	1.0978	0.0451	0.0496	0.2681	0.0384	0.3780
				90	β	0.0190	0.0050	0.2728	0.0119	0.0120	−0.0413	0.0051	0.2624	0.0116	0.0121	−0.4668	0.0048	0.2168
					λ	0.0001	0.0430	1.1381	0.0361	0.0368	0.0078	0.0413	0.7955	0.0355	0.0355	−0.0891	0.0145	0.4277
			7		α	0.0442	0.0941	1.1989	0.0546	0.0550	−0.0220	0.0611	1.0021	0.0436	0.0456	0.1824	0.0168	0.2568
				100	β	0.0031	0.0042	0.2554	0.0106	0.0107	−0.0181	0.0048	0.2488	0.0103	0.0112	−0.3617	0.0025	0.1912
			999		λ	0.0275	0.0372	1.0306	0.0346	0.0346	0.0072	0.0412	0.6226	0.0305	0.0315	−0.0541	0.0138	0.3084

Table 11. Cont.

α	$\beta=0.6, \theta=2$				MLE						MPS			Bayesian		
	n	T	r		RB	MSE	LACI	LBP	LBT	RB	MSE	LACI	LBP	LBT	RB	MSE	LCCI
2	50	4	30	α	−0.0049	0.8570	3.6322	0.1661	0.1670	−0.0257	0.8294	3.5679	0.1661	0.1658	0.0166	0.0233	0.5513
				β	0.0138	0.0083	0.2758	0.0131	0.0127	−0.0575	0.0054	0.2558	0.0112	0.0152	−0.2798	0.0078	0.3962
				λ	0.0657	0.1980	1.6680	0.0756	0.0754	−0.0072	0.1540	1.5390	0.0704	0.0701	−0.0401	0.0252	0.5318
		22	40	α	0.0194	0.4354	2.5847	0.1154	0.1161	0.0256	0.5350	2.8432	0.1193	0.1216	0.0159	0.0131	0.4276
				β	0.0253	0.0068	0.2319	0.0125	0.0121	−0.0430	0.0046	0.2305	0.0110	0.0142	−0.2492	0.0064	0.2740
				λ	0.0454	0.1786	1.6195	0.0749	0.0716	−0.0092	0.1392	1.4333	0.0655	0.0653	−0.0470	0.0232	0.4449
		99,999	50	α	0.0068	0.0965	1.2178	0.0534	0.0535	−0.0116	0.1648	1.5901	0.0698	0.0694	0.0132	0.0064	0.2937
				β	0.0597	0.0062	0.2137	0.0116	0.0110	−0.0357	0.0030	0.2155	0.0195	0.0135	−0.2189	0.0052	0.2133
				λ	0.0522	0.1581	0.8506	0.0709	0.0691	−0.0062	0.1013	1.2392	0.0558	0.0551	−0.0328	0.0106	0.3105
	100	4	70	α	0.0254	0.4205	2.5368	0.1136	0.1155	−0.0166	0.2736	2.0482	0.0951	0.0953	0.0236	0.0187	0.4739
				β	0.0297	0.0084	0.3525	0.0157	0.0158	−0.0443	0.0079	0.3325	0.0151	0.0152	−0.4132	0.0068	0.3206
				λ	0.0263	0.0757	1.0599	0.0477	0.0474	−0.0081	0.0649	0.9977	0.0460	0.0472	−0.0764	0.0431	0.5429
		22	90	α	−0.0065	0.0729	1.0584	0.0463	0.0453	−0.0135	0.0375	0.7523	0.0323	0.0322	0.0210	0.0157	0.4303
				β	0.0131	0.0032	0.2204	0.0099	0.0100	−0.0286	0.0033	0.2136	0.0096	0.0095	−0.4079	0.0016	0.2093
				λ	0.0255	0.0650	0.9804	0.0449	0.0450	−0.0081	0.0540	0.9009	0.0405	0.0405	−0.0696	0.0410	0.4314
		99,999	100	α	0.0028	0.0629	1.0104	0.0390	0.0389	0.0124	0.0246	0.5092	0.0319	0.0239	0.0213	0.0082	0.2936
				β	0.0066	0.0027	0.2032	0.0097	0.0095	−0.0236	0.0033	0.2080	0.0092	0.0092	−0.3042	0.0011	0.1713
				λ	0.0163	0.0579	0.9094	0.0436	0.0426	−0.0072	0.0485	0.8127	0.0353	0.0395	−0.0621	0.0215	0.3091

Table 12. Bayesian and non-Bayesian estimation for parameters of APIW distribution based on hybrid censored samples where $\beta = 2, \theta = 2$.

$\beta = 2, \theta = 2$					MLE					MPS				Bayesian		
α	n	T	r		RB	MSE	LACI	LBP	LBT	RB	MSE	LACI	LBP	LBT	RB	MSE	LCCI
0.8	50	1.5	30	α	0.3767	0.7387	3.1630	0.2334	0.2282	−0.1050	0.4568	2.6352	0.1943	0.1950	0.1140	0.0253	0.5532
				β	0.0402	0.2281	1.8497	0.1278	0.1290	−0.1186	0.2520	1.7381	0.1227	0.1230	−0.0496	0.0303	0.5508
				λ	0.0631	0.3817	2.3764	0.1554	0.1548	0.1214	0.3962	2.2821	0.1698	0.1678	−0.0505	0.0310	0.6040
		3	40	α	0.3105	0.6978	3.0153	0.2033	0.2013	0.1029	0.4169	2.6153	0.1820	0.2934	0.1240	0.0211	0.4089
				β	0.0495	0.1812	1.6247	0.0694	0.0687	−0.0569	0.1871	1.6375	0.0732	0.0738	−0.0484	0.0214	0.4397
				λ	−0.0143	0.2779	2.0654	0.0892	0.0886	0.0860	0.3350	2.2711	0.1008	0.1019	−0.0502	0.0249	0.4433
		99	50	α	0.2901	0.6495	2.6126	0.1931	0.1873	0.1026	0.4053	2.5852	0.1830	0.1830	0.0791	0.0094	0.2958
				β	0.0211	0.1413	1.4660	0.0672	0.0667	−0.0512	0.1822	1.5636	0.0726	0.0777	−0.0279	0.0089	0.2905
				λ	0.0131	0.2533	2.0125	0.0820	0.0830	0.0092	0.2464	2.0574	0.0711	0.0710	−0.0305	0.0104	0.3250
	100	1.5	70	α	0.3635	0.6536	2.9600	0.1373	0.1360	−0.0689	0.5129	2.8018	0.1278	0.1259	0.1916	0.0383	0.4662
				β	0.0276	0.1214	1.3497	0.0604	0.0585	−0.0964	0.1572	1.3598	0.0586	0.0589	−0.0749	0.0426	0.5332
				λ	0.0189	0.2072	1.7800	0.0849	0.0864	0.1073	0.2985	1.9715	0.0853	0.0872	−0.0803	0.0451	0.5308
		3	90	α	0.3467	0.6173	2.3847	0.1241	0.1129	0.0598	0.4938	2.7555	0.1218	0.1128	0.1924	0.0453	0.3753
				β	0.0129	0.0916	1.1830	0.0551	0.0553	−0.0558	0.1249	1.3158	0.0585	0.0589	−0.0718	0.0393	0.3852
				λ	0.0248	0.2013	1.6856	0.0823	0.0825	0.0462	0.3020	1.9125	0.0799	0.0878	−0.0791	0.0462	0.4199
		99	100	α	0.2929	0.5981	2.1152	0.1127	0.1113	0.0463	0.4866	2.3417	0.1206	0.1027	0.1378	0.0171	0.2769
				β	0.0152	0.0916	1.1818	0.0523	0.0523	−0.0479	0.1140	1.3319	0.0580	0.0561	−0.0549	0.0179	0.2981
				λ	−0.0062	0.1928	1.6020	0.0819	0.0810	0.0458	0.3008	1.8910	0.0798	0.0799	−0.0534	0.0177	0.3142

Table 12. Cont.

$\beta=2, \theta=2$				MLE						MPS			Bayesian		
α	n	T	r		RB	MSE	LACI	LBP	LBT	RB	MSE	LACI	LBP	LBT	RB	MSE	LCCI
2	50	2	30	α	0.1108	2.1771	5.7241	0.2747	0.2759	0.1555	3.6273	7.3730	0.3179	0.3503	0.0246	0.0212	0.5163
				β	0.0198	0.1346	1.4314	0.0680	0.0668	−0.0698	0.1504	1.4197	0.0647	0.0647	−0.0524	0.0317	0.5489
				λ	0.0679	0.2229	1.7742	0.0785	0.0785	0.0013	0.1940	1.7283	0.0803	0.0774	−0.0535	0.0339	0.5863
			40	α	0.1034	1.0666	4.2958	0.2410	0.2312	0.1426	3.4818	6.6843	0.3142	0.3227	0.0236	0.0151	0.4241
				β	0.0055	0.1049	1.2701	0.0589	0.0590	−0.0623	0.1218	1.2788	0.0587	0.0600	−0.0497	0.0220	0.4423
				λ	0.0881	0.2039	1.3575	0.0711	0.0781	0.0013	0.1837	1.6395	0.0801	0.0691	−0.0524	0.0253	0.4364
			50	α	0.0924	0.9740	4.0544	0.2419	0.2147	0.1448	3.0179	5.8231	0.2763	0.3081	0.0151	0.0075	0.3239
				β	−0.0106	0.1007	1.2482	0.0577	0.0575	−0.0610	0.1161	1.1344	0.0575	0.0572	−0.0312	0.0104	0.3003
		99		λ	0.1231	0.1504	1.1614	0.0612	0.0612	0.0019	0.1853	1.4771	0.0361	0.0611	−0.0289	0.0099	0.3013
	100	2	70	α	0.0622	1.2694	4.3940	0.1994	0.1961	0.0554	1.4031	4.6277	0.1925	0.1922	0.0492	0.0269	0.5138
				β	−0.0048	0.0576	0.9413	0.0446	0.0447	−0.0582	0.0725	0.9522	0.0446	0.0443	−0.0921	0.0513	0.5276
				λ	0.0432	0.1285	1.3653	0.0648	0.0645	0.0080	0.1371	1.4517	0.0694	0.0689	−0.0955	0.0556	0.5253
			90	α	0.0522	0.9516	2.2214	0.1909	0.1900	0.0512	0.9671	2.0285	0.1832	0.1823	0.0483	0.0211	0.4262
				β	−0.0227	0.0583	0.9304	0.0407	0.0400	−0.0600	0.0772	0.9828	0.0462	0.0462	−0.0868	0.0407	0.4078
				λ	0.0907	0.1267	1.0897	0.0618	0.0584	0.0074	0.1285	0.1064	0.0592	0.0590	−0.1036	0.0554	0.4244
			100	α	0.0413	0.9290	1.6319	0.1897	0.1880	0.0501	0.9155	2.0033	0.1733	0.1633	0.0277	0.0095	0.3026
				β	−0.0144	0.0582	0.9397	0.0394	0.0395	−0.0617	0.0695	0.9060	0.0451	0.0451	−0.0534	0.0175	0.2841
		99		λ	0.0831	0.1133	0.9915	0.0619	0.0493	0.0041	0.1141	0.1005	0.0411	0.0401	−0.0552	0.0184	0.3156

165

From the simulation analysis, we point out the following results:

1. The RB and the MSE decrease for estimated parameters of MLE and MPS as the sample size increases and the Bayes estimates for α, β and λ attain the minimum MSE. See Tables 10–12.
2. In almost all cases, the Bayes estimates perform better than the MLEs with respect to RB, MSE, LACI, LBP, and LBT.
3. In most cases, the MPS estimates are better than the MLE with respect to MSE.
4. The performance increases when the censored sample size r increases, such that the sample size n and the time of the hybrid censored sample are kept fixed.
5. The performance increases when the time of a hybrid censored sample increases when keeping sample size n and censored sample size r as fixed values.
6. When the number of failures r is fixed and sample size n increases, the MSEs and width of the LACI, LBP, and LBT of the MLEs, MPS, and Bayes estimations are decreased. However, the MPS process performs well in terms of estimating the parameters of APIW. See Tables 10–12.
7. The MSEs and the widths of the confidence intervals of the ACI, BP, and BT of the MLEs, MPS, and Bayes estimations decrease as the number of failures r increases for a fixed sample size n.
8. As the sample size n increases, the average length of all intervals decreases. On average, the credible CI estimates are better than the ACI.
9. As the sample size n increases, the bootstrap CI estimates are better than the traditional CI.

8. Conclusions

Modeling some biomedical data was performed in this study, the new APIW continuous distribution was utilized and the hybrid Type-II censoring scheme was recommended. Three estimation methods were performed to estimate the unknown parameters of the APIW distribution and hence estimate the survival and hazard functions. In real data analysis, the classical alternative (MPS) for the well-known MLE method confirmed the power fullness of the MPS over the MLE for estimating parameters, survival, and hazard function. In simulation analysis, the Bayesian approach for the inference of APIW parameters was relatively acting much better compared to the classical methods. A comparison was conducted with respect to the mean squared error and relative bias, and all results were summarized in tables and plotted in figures. The MCMC approach was employed as estimates from Bayesian are not directly obtainable. The model was applied to two real-life data sets, including failure statistical data for certain ball-bearing components and the resistance in guinea pigs exposed to various dosages of virulent tubercle bacilli.

Author Contributions: Conceptualization, D.A.R. and H.H.A.; methodology, D.A.R. and E.M.A.; software, E.M.A.; validation, D.A.R., H.H.A. and A.R.; formal analysis, E.M.A.; investigation, D.A.R.; resources, H.H.A.; data curation, A.R.; writing—original draft preparation, D.A.R. and E.M.A.; writing—review and editing, D.A.R., H.H.A. and E.M.A. All authors have read and agreed to the published version of the manuscript.

Funding: This work was supported by the Deanship of Scientific Research, Vice Presidency for Graduate Studies and Scientific Research, King Faisal University, Saudi Arabia [Grant No. 2245].

Data Availability Statement: Data are available in this paper.

Conflicts of Interest: The authors declare no conflict of interest.

References

1. Ghalme, S.G.; Mankar, A.; Bhalerao, Y. Biomaterials in Hip Joint Replacement. *Int. J. Mater. Sci. Eng.* **2016**, *4*, 113–125. . [CrossRef]
2. Kochi, A. The global tuberculosis situation and the new control strategy of the World Health Organization. *Tubercle* **1991**, *72*, 1–6. [CrossRef]
3. Epstein, B. Truncated life tests in the exponential case. *Ann. Socite Pol. Math.* **1954**, *25*, 555–564. [CrossRef]

4. Ebrahimi, N. Estimating the parameters of an exponential distribution from hybrid life test. *J. Stat. Plan. Inference* **1986**, *14*, 255–261. [CrossRef]
5. Childs, A.; Chand Rasekhar, B.; Balakrishnan, N.; Kundu, D.E. Likelihood inference based on type-I and type-II hybrid censored samples from the exponential distribution. *Ann. Inst. Stat. Math.* **2003**, *55*, 319–330. [CrossRef]
6. Mansour, M.M.M.; Ramadan, D.A. Statistical inference of the parameters of the modified extended exponential distribution under the type-II hybrid censoring scheme. *J. Appl. Probab. Stat.* **2020**, *15*, 19–44.
7. Salah, M.M.; Ahmed, E.A.; Alhussain, Z.A.; Ahmed, H.H.; El-Morshedy, M.; Eliwa, M.S. Statistical inferences for type-II hybrid censoring data from the alpha power exponential distribution. *PLoS ONE* **2021**, *16*, e0244316. [CrossRef] [PubMed]
8. Yousef, M.M.; Almetwally, E.M. Bayesian Inference for the Parameters of Exponential Chen Distribution Based on Hybrid Censoring. *Pak. J. Stat.* **2022**, *38*, 145–164.
9. Yadav, A.S.; Singh, S.K.; Singh, U. On hybrid censored inverse Lomax distribution: Application to the survival data. *Statistica* **2016**, *76*, 185–203.
10. Mahmoud, M.A.W.; Ramadan, D.A.; Mansour, M.M.M. Estimation of lifetime parameters of the modified extended exponential distribution with application to a mechanical model. *Commun. Stat. Simul. Comput.* **2020**, *51*, 7005–7018. [CrossRef]
11. Aldahlan, M.A.; Bakoban, R.A.; Alzahrani, L.S. On Estimating the Parameters of the Beta Inverted Exponential Distribution under Type-II Censored Samples. *Mathematics* **2022**, *10*, 506. [CrossRef]
12. Mohammed, H.S.; Nassar, M.; Alotaibi, R.; Elshahhat, A. Analysis of Adaptive Progressive Type-II Hybrid Censored Dagum Data with Applications. *Symmetry* **2022**, *14*, 2146. [CrossRef]
13. Ramadan, D.A.; Aboshady, M.S.; Mansour, M.M.M. Inference for modified extended exponential distribution based on progressively Type-I hybrid censored data with application to some mechanical models. *J. Appl. Probab. Stat.* **2022**, *17*, 69–88.
14. Nassr, S.G.; Almetwally, E.M.; El Azm, W.S.A. Statistical inference for the extended weibull distribution based on adaptive type-II progressive hybrid censored competing risks data. *Thail. Stat.* **2021**, *19*, 547–564.
15. Ramadan, D.A.; Magdy, W.A. On the alpha-power inverse Weibull. *Int. J. Comput. Appl.* **2018**, *181*, 975–8887.
16. El-Sagheer, R.M. Estimation of parameters of Weibull-Gamma distribution based on progressively censored data. *Stat. Pap.* **2018**, *59*, 725–757. [CrossRef]
17. Cheng, R.C.H.; Amin, N.A.K. Estimating parameters in continuous univariate distributions with a shifted origin. *J. R. Stat. Soc. Ser. B Methodol.* **1983**, *45*, 394–403. [CrossRef]
18. Kundu, D.; Howlader, H. Bayesian inference and prediction of the inverse Weibull distribution for Type-II censored data. *Comput. Stat. Data Anal.* **2010**, *54*, 1547–1558. [CrossRef]
19. Dey, S.; Dey, T. On progressively censored generalized inverted exponential distribution. *J. Appl. Stat.* **2014**, *41*, 2557–2576. [CrossRef]
20. Dey, S.; Ali, S.; Park, C. Weighted exponential distribution: Properties and different methods of estimation. *J. Stat. Comput. Simul.* **2015**, *85*, 3641–3661. [CrossRef]
21. Dey, S.; Singh, S.; Tripathi, Y.M.; Asgharzadeh, A. Estimation and prediction for a progressively censored generalized inverted exponential distribution. *Stat. Methodol.* **2016**, *32*, 185–202. [CrossRef]
22. Varian, H.R. Bayesian approach to real estate assessment. In *Studies in Bayesian Econometrics and Statistics in Honor of L.J. Savage*; Feinderg, S.E., Zellner, A., Eds.; North-Holland: Amsterdam, The Netherlands, 1975; pp. 195–208.
23. Robert, C.P. *Monte Carlo Statistical Methods*; Springer: New York, NY, USA, 2004.
24. Tolba, A. Bayesian and Non-Bayesian Estimation Methods for Simulating the Parameter of the Akshaya Distribution. *Comput. J. Math. Stat. Sci.* **2022**, *1*, 13–25. [CrossRef]
25. Lawless, J.F. *Statistical Models and Methods for Lifetime Data*; John Wiley and Sons: New York, NY, USA, 1982.
26. Greene, W.H. *Econometric Analysis*, 4th ed.; Prentice-Hall: New York, NY, USA, 2000.
27. Meeker, W.Q.; Escobar, L.A. *Statistical Methods for Reliability Data*; Wiley: New York, NY, USA, 1998.
28. Efron, B. The bootstrap and other resampling plans. In *CBMS-NSF Regional Conference Series in Applied Mathematics*; SIAM: Philadelphia, PA, USA, 1982.
29. Hall, P. Theoretical Comparison of Bootstrap Confidence Intervals. *Ann. Stat.* **1988**, *16*, 927–953. [CrossRef]
30. Almongy, H.M.; Almetwally, E.M.; Alharbi, R.; Alnagar, D.; Hafez, E.H.; Mohie El-Din, M.M. The Weibull generalized exponential distribution with censored sample: Estimation and application on real data. *Complexity* **2021**, *2021*, 6653534. [CrossRef]
31. Muhammed, H.Z.; Almetwally, E.M. Bayesian and non-Bayesian estimation for the bivariate inverse weibull distribution under progressive type-II censoring. *Ann. Data Sci.* **2020**, 1–32. [CrossRef]
32. Balakrishnan, N.; Sandhu, R.A. Best linear unbiased and maximum likelihood estimation for exponential distributions under general progressive Type-II censored samples. *Indian J. Stat. Ser. B* **1996**, *58*, 1–9.
33. Leiblein, J.; Zelen, M. Statistical investigation of fatigue life of deep groove ball bearings. *Res. Natl. Bur. Stand.* **1956**, *57*, 273–316. [CrossRef]
34. Okasha, H.M.; El-Baz, A.H.; Tarabia, A.M.K.; Basheer, A.M. Extended inverse weibull distribution with reliability application. *J. Egypt. Math. Soc.* **2017**, *25*, 343–349. [CrossRef]

Disclaimer/Publisher's Note: The statements, opinions and data contained in all publications are solely those of the individual author(s) and contributor(s) and not of MDPI and/or the editor(s). MDPI and/or the editor(s) disclaim responsibility for any injury to people or property resulting from any ideas, methods, instructions or products referred to in the content.

Article

Computational Analysis for Fréchet Parameters of Life from Generalized Type-II Progressive Hybrid Censored Data with Applications in Physics and Engineering

Refah Alotaibi [1], Hoda Rezk [2] and Ahmed Elshahhat [3,*]

[1] Department of Mathematical Sciences, College of Science, Princess Nourah bint Abdulrahman University, P.O. Box 84428, Riyadh 11671, Saudi Arabia
[2] Department of Statistics, Al-Azhar University, Cairo 11884, Egypt
[3] Faculty of Technology and Development, Zagazig University, Zagazig 44519, Egypt
* Correspondence: aelshahhat@ftd.zu.edu.eg

Abstract: Generalized progressive hybrid censored procedures are created to reduce test time and expenses. This paper investigates the issue of estimating the model parameters, reliability, and hazard rate functions of the Fréchet (Fr) distribution under generalized Type-II progressive hybrid censoring by making use of the Bayesian estimation and maximum likelihood methods. The appropriate estimated confidence intervals of unknown quantities are likewise built using the frequentist estimators' normal approximations. The Bayesian estimators are created using independent gamma conjugate priors under the symmetrical squared-error loss. The Bayesian estimators and the associated greatest posterior density intervals cannot be computed analytically since the joint likelihood function is obtained in complex form, but they may be assessed using Monte Carlo Markov chain (MCMC) techniques. Via extensive Monte Carlo simulations, the actual behavior of the proposed estimation methodologies is evaluated. Four optimality criteria are used to choose the best censoring scheme out of all the options. To demonstrate how the suggested approaches may be utilized in real scenarios, two real applications reflecting the thirty successive values of precipitation in Minneapolis–Saint Paul for the month of March as well as the number of vehicle fatalities for thirty-nine counties in South Carolina during 2012 are examined.

Keywords: Fréchet model; symmetric Bayes inference; MCMC techniques; maximum likelihood; reliability analysis; generalized Type-II progressive hybrid censoring

Citation: Alotaibi, R.; Rezk, H.; Elshahhat, A. Computational Analysis for Fréchet Parameters of Life from Generalized Type-II Progressive Hybrid Censored Data with Applications in Physics and Engineering. *Symmetry* **2023**, *15*, 348. https://doi.org/10.3390/sym15020348

Academic Editors: Arne Johannssen, Nataliya Chukhrova and Quanxin Zhu

Received: 16 January 2023
Revised: 22 January 2023
Accepted: 24 January 2023
Published: 27 January 2023

Copyright: © 2023 by the authors. Licensee MDPI, Basel, Switzerland. This article is an open access article distributed under the terms and conditions of the Creative Commons Attribution (CC BY) license (https://creativecommons.org/licenses/by/4.0/).

1. Introduction

Reliability technology, as a measure of a system's capacity to properly perform its intended function under predetermined conditions for a specific period of time, is currently increasingly significant. In this regard, many research studies have been conducted, see for example, Chen et al. [1] and Luo et al. [2]. In the literature, progressive Type-II censoring (PC-T2) has received a lot of attention because it allows surviving subjects to be removed during an experiment at various stages other than the termination point, see Balakrishnan and Cramer [3]. To conduct this censoring, a researcher must first put n independent units into a test at time zero and determine the number of failures m and the progressive censoring $\underline{R} = (R_1, R_2, \ldots, R_m)$, where $n = \sum_{i=1}^{m} R_i + m$. At the moment of the first recorded failure (say $X_{1:m:n}$), the surviving units R_1 out of $n-1$ units are randomly chosen and removed from the test. Similarly, R_2 of $n - R_1 - 2$ are selected at random and removed from the test at the time of the second failure (say $X_{2:m:n}$) observed, and so on. All remaining survival units, $R_m = n - m - \sum_{j=1}^{m-1} R_j$, are withdrawn from the test at the moment of the mth failure (say $X_{m:m:n}$) observed, see Panahi [4]. The main disadvantage of this censoring is that it may take a longer time to complete the test when the experimental units are extremely trustworthy. To overcome this problem, the progressive Type-I hybrid censoring

(PHC-T1), which combines PC-T2 and traditional Type-I censoring, was presented by Kundu and Joarder [5]. However, PHC-T1 had the disadvantage that there are relatively few failures that may occur before time T, meaning that maximum likelihood estimators (MLEs) could not always be derived. To address this issue, Childs et al. [6] proposed the progressive Type-II hybrid censoring (PHC-T2) in which the experiment terminates at $T^* = \max\{X_{m:m:n}, T\}$, for details see Panahi [7]. On the other hand, to improve the efficiency of statistical inference, Ng et al. [8] proposed the adaptive progressively Type-II hybrid censoring, for further details see Panahi and Moradi [9].

Although the PHS-T2 guarantees an efficient number of observable failures, it may take a long time to collect the desired failures. Therefore, the generalized progressive Type-II hybrid censoring (GPHC-T2) was introduced by Lee et al. [10]. Assume that the two thresholds T_i, $i = 1, 2$ and the number m are preassigned such that $1 < m \leq n$ and $0 < T_1 < T_2$. The total number of failures up to periods T_1 and T_2 are shown as d_1 and d_2, respectively. Next, R_1 of $n - 1$ are arbitrarily removed from the test at $X_{1:m:n}$; R_2 of $n - R_1 - 2$ are then removed at $X_{2:m:n}$, and so on. At $T^* = \max\{T_1, \min\{X_{m:m:n}, T_2\}\}$, the experiment is terminated and all remaining units are removed. If $X_{m:n} < T_1$, we continue to observe failures without any additional withdrawals up to time T_1 (Case-I); if $T_1 < X_{m:m:n} < T_2$, we end the test at $X_{m:m:n}$ (Case-II); otherwise, we end the test at time T_2 (Case-III). It is important to remember that the GPHC-T2 alters the PHC-T2 by ensuring that the test is finished at the designated time T_2. Thus, T_2 shows the maximum amount of time that the researcher is prepared to permit the experiment to run. As a result, the experimenter will see one of the following three data formats:

$$\{\underline{X}, \underline{R}\} = \begin{cases} \{(X_{1:m:n}, R_1), \ldots, (X_{m-1:m:n}, R_{m-1}), (X_{m:m:n}, 0), \ldots, (X_{d_1:n}, 0)\}; & \text{Case-I,} \\ \{(X_{1:m:n}, R_1), \ldots, (X_{d_1:n}, R_{d_1}), \ldots, (X_{m-1:m:n}, R_{m-1}), (X_{m:m:n}, R_m)\}; & \text{Case-II,} \\ \{(X_{1:m:n}, R_1), \ldots, (X_{d_1:n}, R_{d_1}), \ldots, (X_{d_2-1:n}, R_{d_2-1}), (X_{d_2:n}, R_{d_2})\}; & \text{Case-III.} \end{cases}$$

Assume that the variables $\underline{X}, \underline{R}$ stand for the respective lives in a distribution with cumulative distribution function (CDF) $F(\cdot)$ and probability density function (PDF) $f(\cdot)$. This leads to the following expression for the GPHC-T2 likelihood function as follows:

$$L_\rho(\theta|\underline{X}) = C_\rho \mathcal{R}_\rho(T_\tau; \theta) \prod_{j=1}^{D_\rho} f(x_{j:m:n}; \theta) [1 - F(x_{j:m:n}; \theta)]^{R_j}, \quad (1)$$

where Case-I, Case-II, and Case-III denoted by $\rho = 1, 2, 3$, correspondingly, $\tau = 1, 2$, and $\mathcal{R}_\rho(\cdot)$ is a composite form of reliability functions. From (1), the GPHC-T2 notations are listed in Table 1. Moreover, from (1), different censoring plans can be obtained as special cases, namely:

- PHC-T1 if $T_1 \to 0$.
- PHC-T2 if $T_2 \to \infty$.
- Hybrid-T1 if $T_1 \to 0$, $R_j = 0$, $j = 1, 2, \ldots, m - 1$, $R_m = n - m$.
- Hybrid-T2 if $T_2 \to \infty$, $R_j = 0$, $j = 1, 2, \ldots, m - 1$, $R_m = n - m$.
- Type-I censoring if $T_1 = 0$, $m = 1$, $R_j = 0$, $j = 1, 2, \ldots, m - 1$, $R_m = n - m$.
- Type-II censoring if $T_1 = 0$, $T_2 \to \infty$, $R_j = 0$, $j = 1, 2, \ldots, m - 1$, $R_m = n - m$.

Table 1. The GPHC-T2 notations.

ρ	C_ρ	D_ρ	$\mathcal{R}_\rho(T_\tau; \theta)$	$R^*_{d_\tau+1}$
1	$\prod_{j=1}^{d_1} \sum_{i=j}^{m} (R_i + 1)$	d_1	$[1 - F(T_1)]^{R^*_{d_1+1}}$	$n - d_1 - \sum_{i=1}^{m-1} R_i$
2	$\prod_{j=1}^{m} \sum_{i=j}^{m} (R_i + 1)$	m	1	0
3	$\prod_{j=1}^{d_2} \sum_{i=j}^{m} (R_i + 1)$	d_2	$[1 - F(T_2)]^{R^*_{d_2+1}}$	$n - d_2 - \sum_{i=1}^{d_2} R_i$

On the basis of GPHC-T2, other research has also been carried out. For instance, the maximum likelihood and Bayes estimators of the Weibull parameters were produced by Ashour and Elshahhat [11]. The prediction problem of failure times from the Burr-XII distribution was studied by Ateya and Mohammed [12]. Seo [13] developed an objective Bayesian analysis with limited information about the Weibull distribution. The competing risks from exponential data were addressed by Cho and Lee [14], and more recently, Nagy et al. [15] looked at both the point and interval estimates of the Burr-XII parameters, and Wang et al. [16] addressed the estimation problem of the Kumaraswamy parameters using classical and Bayesian procedures.

The inverse Weibull (or Gumbel Type-II) distribution, commonly known as the two-parameter Fréchet (Fr) distribution, is well suited for data modeling with decreasing and upside-down bathtub hazard rates. To illustrate many environmental phenomena, including earthquakes, floods, wind speeds, rainfall, breakdown of insulating fluid, sea waves, etc., it has been widely employed. This model was originally proposed by Fréchet [17], and Kotz and Nadarajah [18] later discussed it. Suppose that X is a lifetime random variable that follows the Fr distribution, which is represented by the notation $Fr(\delta, \theta)$, where $\delta > 0$ is the scale parameter and $\theta > 0$ is the shape parameter. Its PDF, CDF, and hazard rate function (HRF), denoted by $f(\cdot)$, $F(\cdot)$, and $h(\cdot)$, are provided by

$$f(x; \delta, \theta) = \delta\theta x^{-(\theta+1)} e^{-\delta x^{-\theta}}, \ x > 0; \tag{2}$$

$$F(x; \delta, \theta) = e^{-\delta x^{-\theta}}, \ x > 0; \tag{3}$$

and

$$h(t; \delta, \theta) = \frac{\delta\theta t^{-(\theta+1)}}{e^{\delta t^{-\theta}} - 1}, \ t > 0, \tag{4}$$

respectively, and its reliability function (RF), $R(\cdot)$, is given by $R(\cdot) = 1 - F(\cdot)$.

To our knowledge, no work has been done that estimates the Fr model parameters or survival characteristics in the presence of data from the generalized Type-II progressive hybrid censoring. Our goals in this study were the following in order to close this gap. The likelihood inference for the unknown Fr parameters and/or any function of them, such as $R(t)$, or $h(t)$, was first derived. The second goal was to create Bayes estimates for the same unknown parameters using independent gamma priors from the squared-error loss (SEL). Additionally, using the suggested estimating techniques, for all unknown parameters, the asymptotic confidence intervals (ACIs) and highest posterior density (HPD) interval estimators were obtained. The R programming language's "maxLik" and "coda" packages were used to calculate the acquired estimates because the theoretical results of δ and θ obtained by the proposed estimation methods cannot be expressed in closed form. These packages were proposed by Henningsen and Toomet [19] and Plummer et al. [20]. The final goal was to come up with the most effective progressive censoring scheme using four optimality criteria. A Monte Carlo simulation was used to examine the efficacy of the different estimators using various combinations of the total sample size, effective sample size, threshold times, and progressive censoring. All acquired estimators were compared using their simulated root-mean-square errors, mean relative absolute biases, average confidence lengths, and coverage percentages. To determine how well the suggested approaches worked in practice and choose the best censoring strategy, two different data sets the from physical and engineering domains were analyzed. The rest of the study is structured as follows: In Sections 2 and 3, the maximum likelihoods and Bayes inferences of the unknown parameters and reliability characteristics are obtained, respectively. In Section 4, the asymptotic and credible intervals are derived. The outcomes of the Monte Carlo simulation are detailed in Section 5. Section 6 investigates the methodology for determining the best progressive censoring strategy. In Section 7, two real applications are examined. Finally, in Section 8, some concluding remarks of the study are provided.

2. Likelihood Inference

Suppose $\underline{X} = \{(X_{1:m:n}, R_1), .., (X_{d_1:n}, R_{d_1}), .., (X_{d_2:n}, R_{d_2})\}$ is a GPHC-T2 sample of size d_2 obtained from $Fr(\delta, \theta)$. Thus, by inserting (2) and (3) into (1), where x_j is used in place of $x_{j:m:n}$, the likelihood function of GPHC-T2 may be expressed as

$$L_\rho(\delta, \theta | \underline{x}) \propto \prod_{j=1}^{D_\rho} \delta \theta x_j^{-(\theta+1)} e^{-\delta x_j^{-\theta}} \left(1 - e^{-\delta x_j^{-\theta}}\right)^{R_j} \mathcal{R}_\rho(T_\tau; \delta, \theta), \qquad (5)$$

where $\mathcal{R}_2(T_\tau; \delta, \theta) = 1$
$\mathcal{R}_1(T_1; \delta, \theta) = \left(1 - e^{-\delta T_1^{-\theta}}\right)^{R_{d_1}^*+1}$ and $\mathcal{R}_3(T_2; \delta, \theta) = \left(1 - e^{-\delta T_2^{-\theta}}\right)^{R_{d_2}^*+1}$.

The log-likelihood function $\ell_\rho \propto L_\rho$ of (5) becomes

$$\ell_\rho(\delta, \theta | \underline{x}) \propto D_\rho \ln(\delta \theta) - (\theta + 1) \sum_{j=1}^{D_\rho} \ln(x_j) - \delta \sum_{j=1}^{D_\rho} x_j^{-\theta} + \sum_{j=1}^{D_\rho} R_j \ln\left(1 - e^{-\delta x_j^{-\theta}}\right) + Y_\rho(T_\tau; \delta, \theta), \qquad (6)$$

where $Y_2(T_\tau; \delta, \theta) = 0$
$Y_1(T_1; \delta, \theta) = R_{d_1+1}^* \ln\left(1 - e^{-\delta T_1^{-\theta}}\right)$, and $Y_3(T_2; \delta, \theta) = R_{d_2+1}^* \ln\left(1 - e^{-\delta T_2^{-\theta}}\right)$.

The following two results are obtained by partly differentiating (6) with regard to δ and θ. To produce the MLEs $\hat{\delta}$ and $\hat{\theta}$, the following likelihood equations must be solved concurrently after being equated to zero as

$$\frac{\partial \ell_\rho}{\partial \delta} = \frac{D_\rho}{\delta} - \sum_{j=1}^{D_\rho} x_j^{-\theta} + \sum_{j=1}^{D_\rho} \frac{R_j x_j^{-\theta} e^{-\delta x_j^{-\theta}}}{\left(1 - e^{-\delta x_j^{-\theta}}\right)} + \frac{\partial Y_\rho(T_\tau; \delta, \theta)}{\partial \delta}, \qquad (7)$$

and

$$\frac{\partial \ell_\rho}{\partial \theta} = \frac{D_\rho}{\theta} - \sum_{j=1}^{D_\rho} \ln(x_j) + \delta \sum_{j=1}^{D_\rho} x_j^{-\theta} \ln(x_j) - \sum_{j=1}^{D_\rho} \frac{R_j \delta x_j^{-\theta} \ln(x_j) e^{-\delta x_j^{-\theta}}}{\left(1 - e^{-\delta x_j^{-\theta}}\right)} - \frac{\partial Y_\rho(T_\tau; \delta, \theta)}{\partial \theta}, \qquad (8)$$

where for $\rho = 1, 3$ and $\tau = 1, 2$, we have
$\frac{\partial Y_\rho(T_\tau; \delta, \theta)}{\partial \delta} = \frac{R_{d_\tau+1}^* T_\tau^{-\theta} e^{-\delta T_\tau^{-\theta}}}{\left(1 - e^{-\delta T_\tau^{-\theta}}\right)}$, $\frac{\partial Y_\rho(T_\tau; \delta, \theta)}{\partial \theta} = \frac{R_{d_\tau+1}^* \delta T_\tau^{-\theta} \ln(T_\tau) e^{-\delta T_\tau^{-\theta}}}{\left(1 - e^{-\delta T_\tau^{-\theta}}\right)}$.

As shown in (7) and (8), the MLEs of δ and θ must be obtained by solving a system of two nonlinear equations. Therefore, there is no closed-form analytical solution for $\hat{\delta}$ or $\hat{\theta}$. As a result, it may be calculated for every given GPHC-T2 data set using numerical methods such the Newton–Raphson iterative approach. The MLEs $\hat{R}(t)$ and $\hat{h}(t)$ can also be obtained by replacing δ and θ with $\hat{\delta}$ and $\hat{\theta}$, respectively.

3. Bayes Inference

The Bayes estimators of $\delta, \theta, R(t)$ and $h(t)$ and their corresponding HPD intervals are created in this section based on the SEL function. In order to do this, the Fr parameters δ and θ are taken to have independent gamma ($G(\cdot)$) priors with the form $G(\nu_1, \vartheta_1)$ and $G(\nu_2, \vartheta_2)$, respectively. Gamma priors should be taken into account for a number of reasons, including the fact that they (i) offer different shapes depending on parameter values, (ii) are adaptable, and (iii) are quite simple, brief, and might not produce a result with a difficult estimate problem. The joint prior density of δ and θ becomes

$$\pi(\delta, \theta) \propto \delta^{\nu_1 - 1} \theta^{\nu_2 - 1} e^{-(\delta \vartheta_1 + \theta \vartheta_2)}, \qquad (9)$$

where $v_i > 0$ and $\vartheta_i > 0$ for $i = 1, 2$, are known. From (5) and (9), the joint posterior PDF of δ and θ is

$$\pi_\rho(\delta, \theta | \underline{x}) \propto \delta^{D_\rho + v_1 - 1} \theta^{D_\rho + v_2 - 1} e^{-(\delta \vartheta_1 + \theta \vartheta_2)} \prod_{j=1}^{D_\rho} e^{-\delta x_j^{-\theta}} x_j^{-\theta} \left(1 - e^{-\delta x_j^{-\theta}}\right)^{R_j} \mathcal{R}_\rho(T_\tau; \delta, \theta). \quad (10)$$

There are many reasons to consider the SEL in a Bayesian analysis: (i) it is the commonly used symmetric loss; (ii) it is simple, clear, concise, and fairly easy; (iii) it assumes that the overestimation and underestimation are treated equally; and (iv) it develops the Bayes estimator directly by taking the posterior mean. However, under the SEL function, the posterior expectation of (10) yields the Bayes estimate of δ and θ (say $\tilde{\varphi}(\cdot)$) as

$$\tilde{\varphi}(\delta, \theta) = \int_0^\infty \int_0^\infty \varphi(\delta, \theta) \pi_\rho(\delta, \theta | \underline{x}) d\delta d\theta.$$

It is obvious from (10), that the explicit expression of the marginal PDFs of δ and θ is not possible. Thus, to compute the acquired Bayes estimates and create their HPD intervals, we suggest generating samples from (10) using Bayesian MCMC techniques. Therefore, from (10), the conditional PDFs of δ and θ are provided, respectively, as

$$\pi_\rho^\delta(\delta | \theta, \underline{x}) \propto \delta^{D_\rho + v_1 - 1} e^{-\delta \vartheta_1} \prod_{j=1}^{D_\rho} e^{-\delta x_j^{-\theta}} \left(1 - e^{-\delta x_j^{-\theta}}\right)^{R_j} \mathcal{R}_\rho(T_\tau; \delta, \theta), \quad (11)$$

and

$$\pi_\rho^\theta(\theta | \delta, \underline{x}) \propto \theta^{D_\rho + v_2 - 1} e^{-\theta \left(\vartheta_2 + \sum_{j=1}^{D_\rho} \ln(x_j)\right)} \prod_{j=1}^{D_\rho} e^{-\delta x_j^{-\theta}} \left(1 - e^{-\delta x_j^{-\theta}}\right)^{R_j} \mathcal{R}_\rho(T_\tau; \delta, \theta). \quad (12)$$

It is clear, from (11) and (12), that there is no analytical way to reduce the posterior PDFs of δ and θ, respectively, to any known distribution. Thus, the Metropolis–Hastings (M-H) method is seen to be the best option for solving this issue; for detail see Gelman et al. [21] and Lynch [22]. The M-H algorithm's sampling procedure based on the normal proposal distribution is carried out as follows:

Step-1: Set the starting values $\delta^{(0)} = \hat{\delta}$ and $\theta^{(0)} = \hat{\theta}$.

Step-2: Set $s = 1$.

Step-3: Create δ^* and θ^* from $N(\hat{\delta}, \hat{\sigma}_\delta^2)$ and $N(\hat{\theta}, \hat{\sigma}_\theta^2)$, respectively.

Step-4: Find $\xi_\delta = \min\left\{1, \frac{\pi_\rho^\delta(\delta^* | \theta^{(s-1)}; \underline{x})}{\pi_\rho^\delta(\delta^{(s-1)} | \theta^{(s-1)}; \underline{x})}\right\}$ and $\xi_\theta = \min\left\{1, \frac{\pi_\rho^\theta(\theta^* | \delta^{(s)}; \underline{x})}{\pi_\rho^\theta(\theta^{(s-1)} | \delta^{(s)}; \underline{x})}\right\}$.

Step-5: Create samples u_1 and u_2 using the uniform $U(0, 1)$ distribution.

Step-6: If both u_1 and u_2 are less than ξ_δ and ξ_θ, respectively, then set $\delta^{(s)} = \delta^*$ and $\theta^{(s)} = \theta^*$, respectively. Otherwise, set $\delta^{(s)} = \delta^{(s-1)}$ and $\theta^{(s)} = \theta^{(s-1)}$, respectively.

Step-7: Set $s = s + 1$.

Step-8: Redo steps 3–7 $\mathcal{H}$ times to get $\delta^{(s)}$ and $\theta^{(s)}$ for $s = 1, 2, \ldots, \mathcal{H}$.

Step-9: Use $\delta^{(s)}$ and $\theta^{(s)}$, for $t > 0$, to compute the reliability $R(t)$ and hazard rate $h(t)$ parameters, respectively, as

$$R^{(s)}(t) = 1 - e^{-\delta^{(s)} t^{-\theta^{(s)}}} \quad \text{and} \quad h^{(s)}(t) = \frac{\delta^{(s)} \theta^{(s)} t^{-\theta^{(s)} - 1}}{e^{\delta^{(s)} t^{-\theta^{(s)}}} - 1}.$$

In order to ensure the MCMC sampler's convergence and to eliminate the impact of initial guesses $\delta^{(0)}$ and $\theta^{(0)}$, the first simulated samples (say $\mathcal{H}_0$) are eliminated as burn-in.

The Bayesian estimates using the SEL function are therefore calculated using the remaining $\tilde{\mathcal{H}} = \mathcal{H} - \mathcal{H}_0$ samples of δ, θ, $R(t)$, and $h(t)$, (say $\tilde{\varphi}(\cdot)$) as

$$\tilde{\varphi}(\delta,\theta) = \frac{1}{\tilde{\mathcal{H}}} \sum_{s=\mathcal{H}_0+1}^{\mathcal{H}} \varphi^{(s)}(\delta,\theta).$$

Since the choice of symmetric (or asymmetric) loss is one of the main issues in the Bayes analysis, one may incorporated any other type of loss function instead of the SEL easily.

4. Interval Inference

In this section, the ACIs (based on observed Fisher information) and HPD intervals (based on MCMC simulated variates) of δ, θ, $R(t)$, and $h(t)$ are created.

4.1. Asymptotic Intervals

The asymptotic variance–covariance (AVC) matrix, which is created by inverting the Fisher information matrix, must first be computed in order to create the ACIs for δ and θ. The MLEs $(\hat{\delta}, \hat{\theta})$ under some regularity criteria are normally distributed with mean (δ, θ) and variance $\mathbf{I}^{-1}(\delta, \theta)$. Following Lawless [23], we estimate $\mathbf{I}^{-1}(\delta, \theta)$ by $\mathbf{I}^{-1}(\hat{\delta}, \hat{\theta})$ by substituting $\hat{\delta}$ and $\hat{\theta}$ in place of δ and θ as

$$\mathbf{I}^{-1}(\hat{\delta}, \hat{\theta}) \cong \begin{bmatrix} -\mathcal{L}_{11} & -\mathcal{L}_{12} \\ -\mathcal{L}_{21} & -\mathcal{L}_{22} \end{bmatrix}^{-1}_{(\hat{\delta},\hat{\theta})} = \begin{bmatrix} \hat{\sigma}_\delta^2 & \hat{\sigma}_{\delta\theta} \\ \hat{\sigma}_{\theta\delta} & \hat{\sigma}_\theta^2 \end{bmatrix}, \tag{13}$$

where $\mathcal{L}_{ij}$ for $i,j = 1,2$ are

$$\mathcal{L}_{11} = -\frac{D_\rho}{\delta^2} - \sum_{j=1}^{D_\rho} \frac{R_j x_j^{-2\theta} e^{-\delta x_j^{-\theta}}}{\left(1 - e^{-\delta x_j^{-\theta}}\right)^2} + \frac{\partial^2 Y_\rho(T_\tau; \delta, \theta)}{\partial \delta^2},$$

$$\mathcal{L}_{22} = -\frac{D_\rho}{\theta^2} - \delta \sum_{j=1}^{D_\rho} x_j^{-\theta} \ln^2(x_j) - \delta \sum_{j=1}^{D_\rho} \frac{R_j x_j^{-\theta} \ln^2(x_j) e^{-\delta x_j^{-\theta}} \left(e^{-\delta x_j^{-\theta}} + \delta x_j^{-\theta} - 1\right)}{\left(1 - e^{-\delta x_j^{-\theta}}\right)^2} - \frac{\partial^2 Y_\rho(T_\tau; \delta, \theta)}{\partial \theta^2},$$

and

$$\mathcal{L}_{12} = \sum_{j=1}^{D_\rho} x_j^{-\theta} \ln(x_j) - \sum_{j=1}^{D_\rho} \frac{R_j x_j^{-\theta} \ln(x_j) e^{-\delta x_j^{-\theta}} \left(1 - 2e^{-\delta x_j^{-\theta}}\right)}{\left(1 - e^{-\delta x_j^{-\theta}}\right)^2} - \frac{\partial^2 Y_\rho(T_\tau; \delta, \theta)}{\partial \theta \partial \delta},$$

$$\frac{\partial^2 Y_\rho(T_\tau; \delta, \theta)}{\partial \delta^2} = -\frac{R^*_{d_\tau+1} T_\tau^{-2\theta} e^{-\delta T_\tau^{-\theta}}}{\left(1 - e^{-\delta T_\tau^{-\theta}}\right)^2},$$

$$\frac{\partial^2 Y_\rho(T_\tau; \delta, \theta)}{\partial \theta^2} = \frac{R^*_{d_\tau+1} \delta \ln^2(T_\tau) T_\tau^{-\theta} e^{-\delta T_\tau^{-\theta}} \left(e^{-\delta T_\tau^{-\theta}} + \delta T_\tau^{-\theta} - 1\right)}{\left(1 - e^{-\delta T_\tau^{-\theta}}\right)^2},$$

and

$$\frac{\partial^2 Y_\rho(T_\tau; \delta, \theta)}{\partial \theta \partial \delta} = \frac{R^*_{d_\tau+1} T_\tau^{-\theta} \ln(T_\tau) e^{-\delta T_\tau^{-\theta}} \left(1 - \delta T_\tau^{-\theta} - e^{-\delta T_\tau^{-\theta}}\right)}{\left(1 - e^{-\delta T_\tau^{-\theta}}\right)^2}.$$

Thus, for δ and θ, respectively, the two-sided $100(1-\gamma)\%$ ACIs are provided by

$$\hat{\delta} \pm Z_{\frac{\gamma}{2}}\sqrt{\hat{\sigma}_{\hat{\delta}}^2} \quad \text{and} \quad \hat{\theta} \pm Z_{\frac{\gamma}{2}}\sqrt{\hat{\sigma}_{\hat{\theta}}^2},$$

where $Z_{\frac{\gamma}{2}}$ denotes the top $\frac{\gamma}{2}$ percentage points of the standard normal distribution.

Additionally, we use the delta approach to first determine the estimated variance of $\hat{R}(t)$ and $\hat{h}(t)$ (see Greene [24]) before building the ACIs of $R(t)$ and $h(t)$ as

$$\hat{\sigma}_{\hat{R}(t)}^2 = \nabla_{\hat{R}}^T I^{-1}(\hat{\delta},\hat{\theta})\nabla_{\hat{R}} \quad \text{and} \quad \hat{\sigma}_{\hat{h}(t)}^2 = \nabla_{\hat{h}}^T I^{-1}(\hat{\delta},\hat{\theta})\nabla_{\hat{h}},$$

where $\nabla_{\hat{R}}^T = \left[\frac{\partial R(t)}{\partial \delta} \frac{\partial R(t)}{\partial \theta}\right]_{(\hat{\delta},\hat{\theta})}$ and $\nabla_{\hat{h}}^T = \left[\frac{\partial h(t)}{\partial \delta} \frac{\partial h(t)}{\partial \theta}\right]_{(\hat{\delta},\hat{\theta})}$.

Following that, the two-sided $100(1-\gamma)\%$ ACIs of $R(t)$ and $h(t)$ are provided, respectively, by

$$\hat{R}(t) \pm Z_{\frac{\gamma}{2}}\sqrt{\hat{\sigma}_{\hat{R}(t)}^2} \quad \text{and} \quad \hat{h}(t) \pm Z_{\frac{\gamma}{2}}\sqrt{\hat{\sigma}_{\hat{h}(t)}^2}.$$

4.2. HPD Intervals

Using the approach proposed by Chen and Shao [25], the $100(1-\gamma)\%$ HPD interval estimations of δ, θ, $R(t)$, or $h(t)$ are constructed. First, we rank the MCMC samples of $\varphi^{(s)}$ for $s = \mathcal{H}_0 + 1, \mathcal{H}_0 + 2, \ldots, \mathcal{H}$ as $\varphi_{(\mathcal{H}_0+1)}, \varphi_{(\mathcal{H}_0+2)}, \ldots, \varphi_{(\mathcal{H})}$. Hence, the $100(1-\gamma)\%$ two-sided HPD interval of φ is provided by

$$\varphi_{(j^*)}, \varphi_{(j^*+(1-\gamma)\mathcal{H})},$$

where $j^* = \mathcal{H}_0 + 1, \mathcal{H}_0 + 2, \ldots, \mathcal{H}$ is selected so that

$$\varphi_{(j^*+[(1-\gamma)(\mathcal{H})])} - \varphi_{(j^*)} = \min_{1 \leq j \leq \gamma \mathcal{H}}\left[\varphi_{(j+[(1-\gamma)\mathcal{H}])} - \varphi_{(j)}\right].$$

5. Monte Carlo Simulation

To evaluate the true performance of the acquired point/interval estimators of δ, θ, $R(t)$, and $h(t)$, Monte Carlo simulations were conducted based on various combinations of $T_i, i = 1, 2$ (threshold points), n (size of experimental items), m (size of effective sample), and $\underline{R}$ (removal pattern). To establish this goal, for $Fr(0.5, 1.5)$, we replicated the GPHC-T2 mechanism 1000 times. At $t = 0.3$, the true values of $R(t)$ and $h(t)$ were 0.9523 and 0.7620, respectively. Taking $(T_1, T_2) = (0.4, 0.8)$ and $(0.8, 1.2)$, two different choices of n and m were used as $n(=40, 80)$ and the choices of m were taken as failure percentages (FPs) of each n such as $\frac{m}{n}(=50, 80)\%$. Additionally, for each (n, m), three progressive censoring plans $\underline{R}$ were used, namely,

Scheme-1: $\underline{R} = (n - m, 0^*(m - 1))$,

Scheme-2: $\underline{R} = \left(0^*\left(\frac{m}{2} - 1\right), n - m, 0^*\left(\frac{m}{2}\right)\right)$,

Scheme-3: $\underline{R} = (0^*(m - 1), n - m)$,

where $\underline{R} = (3, 0, 0, 4)$ was used as $\underline{R} = (3, 0^*2, 4)$

Once 1000 GPHC-T2 samples had been collected, via R 4.2.2 programming software by installing the "maxLik" package (by Henningsen and Toomet [19]), the MLEs and 95% ACI estimates of δ, θ, $R(t)$, and $h(t)$ were evaluated. Via the "coda" package (by Plummer et al. [20]) in R 4.2.2 programming software, to obtain the Bayes point estimates along with their HPD interval estimates of the same unknown parameters, we simulated 12,000 MCMC samples and ignored the first 2000 iterations as burn-in. According to the prior mean and prior variance criteria, two sets called Prior-I and -II of the hyperparameters (a_1, a_2, b_1, b_2) were considered as $(2.5, 7.5, 5, 5)$ and $(5, 15, 10, 10)$, respectively.

Specifically, the average point estimates (APEs) of δ, θ, $R(t)$, or $h(t)$ (say Ω) were given by

$$\overline{\check{\Omega}_\tau} = \frac{1}{\mathcal{B}} \sum_{i=1}^{\mathcal{B}} \check{\Omega}_\tau^{(i)}, \ \tau = 1, 2, 3, 4,$$

where $\mathcal{B}$ is the number of replications, $\check{\Omega}^{(i)}$ is the estimate of Ω at the ith sample, $\Omega_1 = \delta$, $\Omega_2 = \theta$, $\Omega_3 = R(t)$, and $\Omega_4 = h(t)$.

A comparison between point estimates of Ω was made based on their root-mean-square errors (RMSEs) and mean relative absolute biases (MRABs), respectively, as

$$\text{RMSE}(\check{\Omega}_\tau) = \sqrt{\frac{1}{\mathcal{B}} \sum_{i=1}^{\mathcal{B}} \left(\check{\Omega}_\tau^{(i)} - \Omega_\tau \right)^2}, \ \tau = 1, 2, 3, 4,$$

and

$$\text{MRAB}(\check{\Omega}_\tau) = \frac{1}{\mathcal{B}} \sum_{i=1}^{\mathcal{B}} \frac{1}{\Omega_\tau} \left| \check{\Omega}_\tau^{(i)} - \Omega_\tau \right|, \ \tau = 1, 2, 3, 4.$$

On the other hand, the comparison between the interval estimates of Ω was made based on their average confidence lengths (ACLs) and coverage percentages (CPs) as

$$\text{ACL}_{(1-\gamma)\%}(\Omega_\tau) = \frac{1}{\mathcal{B}} \sum_{i=1}^{\mathcal{B}} \left(\mathcal{U}_{\check{\Omega}_\tau^{(i)}} - \mathcal{L}_{\check{\Omega}_\tau^{(i)}} \right), \ \tau = 1, 2, 3, 4,$$

and

$$\text{CP}_{(1-\gamma)\%}(\Omega_\tau) = \frac{1}{\mathcal{B}} \sum_{i=1}^{\mathcal{B}} \mathbf{1}_{\left(\mathcal{L}_{\check{\Omega}_\tau^{(i)}}, \mathcal{U}_{\check{\Omega}_\tau^{(i)}} \right)}(\Omega_\tau), \ \tau = 1, 2, 3, 4,$$

respectively, where $\mathbf{1}(\cdot)$ is the indicator function, $(\mathcal{L}(\cdot), \mathcal{U}(\cdot))$ denote the (lower, upper) bounds of $(1-\gamma)\%$ ACI (or HPD) interval of Ω_τ.

Via a heatmap data visualization in R version 4.2.2 programming software (available in https://cran.r-project.org/bin/windows/base (accessed on 23 January 2023), the simulated RMSEs, MRABs, ACLs, and CPs of δ, θ, $R(t)$, or $h(t)$ are shown in Figures 1–4, respectively, while their numerical tables are available as Supplementary Materials. For specialization, some notations of the proposed methods have been defined on the "x-axis" line in Figures 1–3 such that (for Prior-I (say P1) as an example) the Bayes estimates is referred to as "BE-P1" and the HPD interval estimates is denoted as "HPD-P1".

From Figures 1–4, in terms of the lowest RMSE, MRAB, and ACL values as well as the highest CP values, useful observations were found and can be easily reported as:

- The main general point is that the proposed estimates of δ, θ, $R(t)$, or $h(t)$ provided good performance.
- As n (or m) increased, all estimates of μ, $R(t)$, and $h(t)$ performed satisfactory. A similar result was obtained when $\sum_{i=1}^{m} R_i$ decreased.
- As (T_1, T_2) increased, in most situations, the RMSEs, MRABs, and ACLs of all unknown parameters decreased while their CPs increased.
- The Bayes estimates of δ, θ, $R(t)$, or $h(t)$, due to the gamma information, behaved better compared to the other estimates as expected. A similar comment could also be made in the case of HPD credible intervals.
- Since the variance of Prior-II was smaller than the variance of Prior-I, the MCMC calculations under Prior-II provided more accurate estimates than others for all unknown parameters.
- Comparing the proposed schemes 1, 2, and 3, in most cases, it was noted that the proposed estimates of δ, θ, $R(t)$, and $h(t)$ behaved better using scheme 3 than the others.

- As a result, the Bayes M-H algorithm sampler is recommended to estimate the Fr parameters or its reliability characteristics in the presence of data obtained from generalized Type-II progressive hybrid censoring.

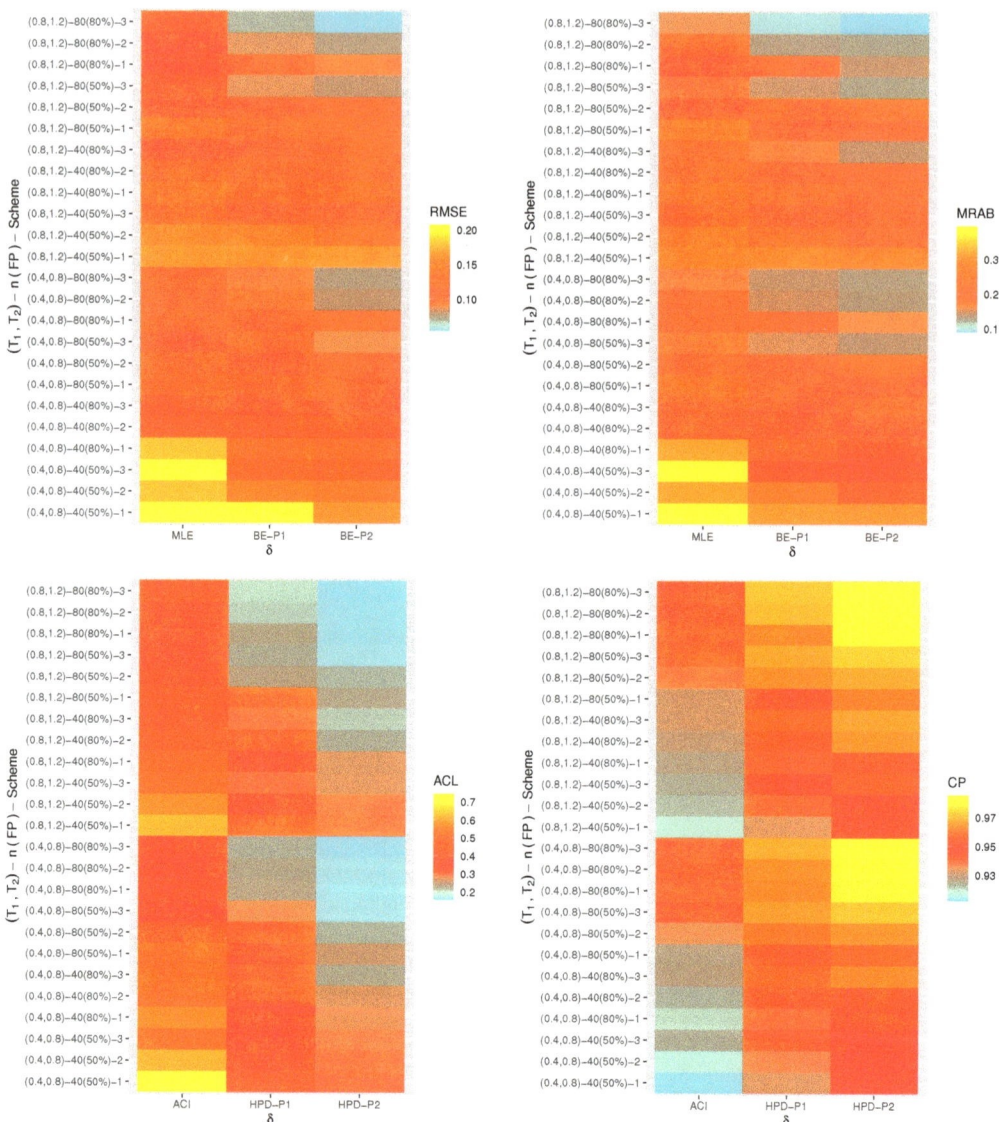

Figure 1. Heatmap plots for the simulation outputs of δ.

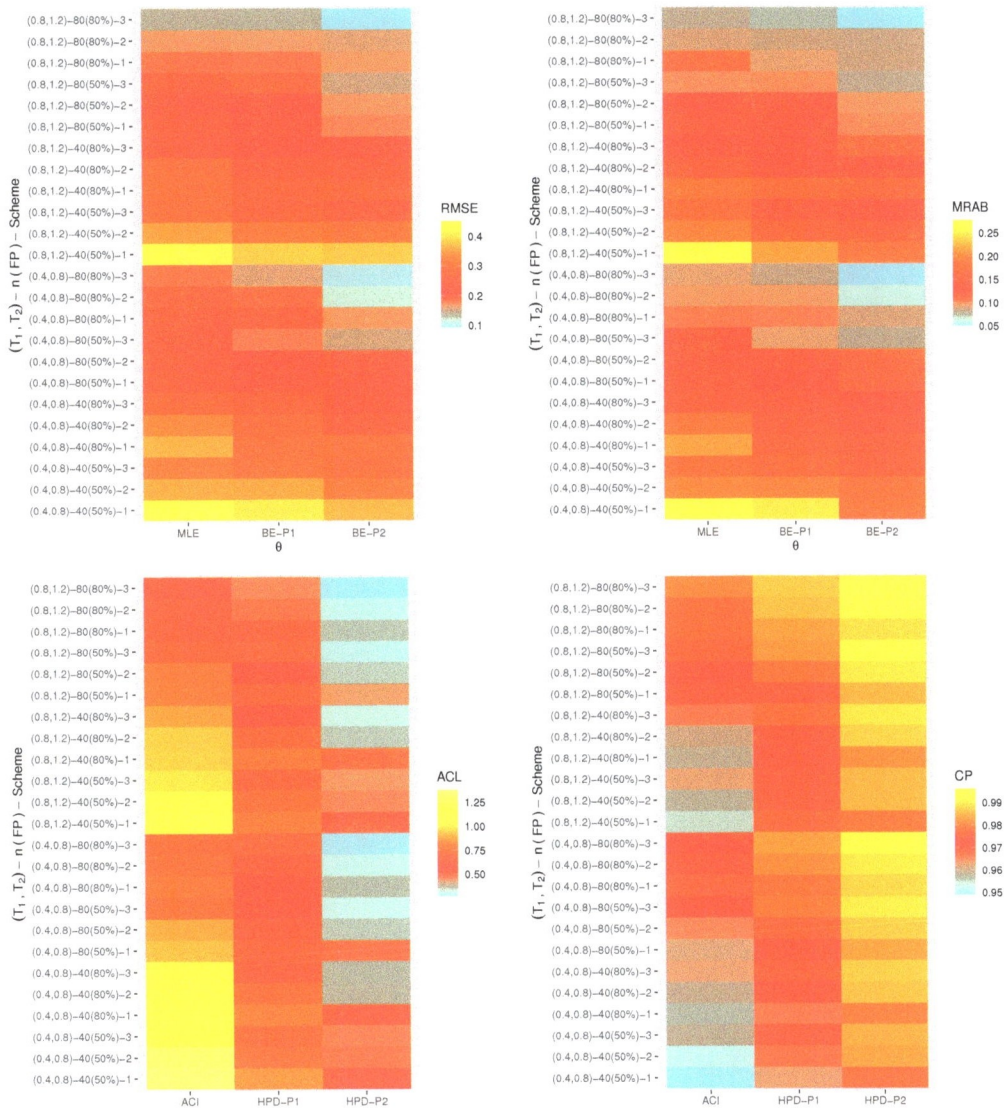

Figure 2. Heatmap plots for the simulation outputs of θ.

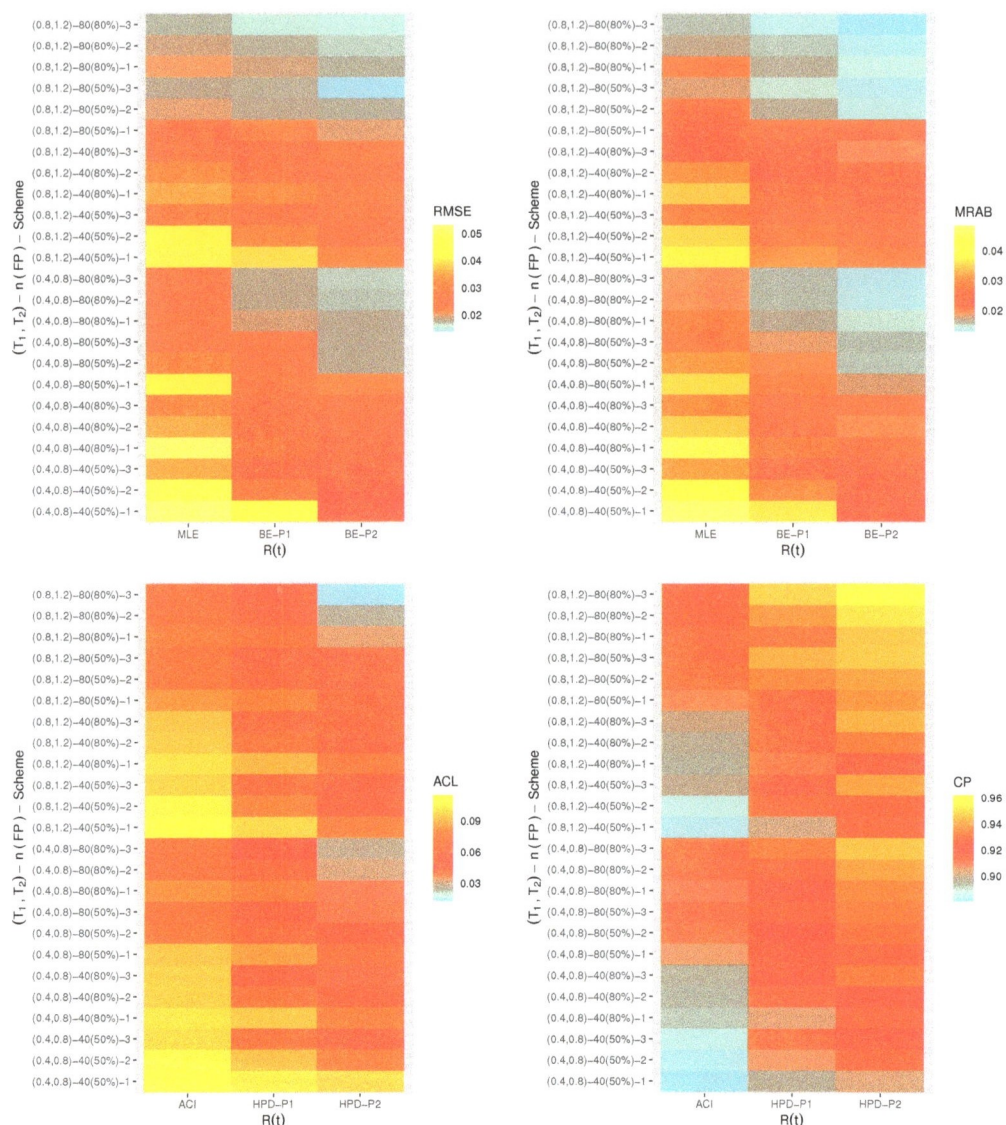

Figure 3. Heatmap plots for the simulation outputs of $R(t)$.

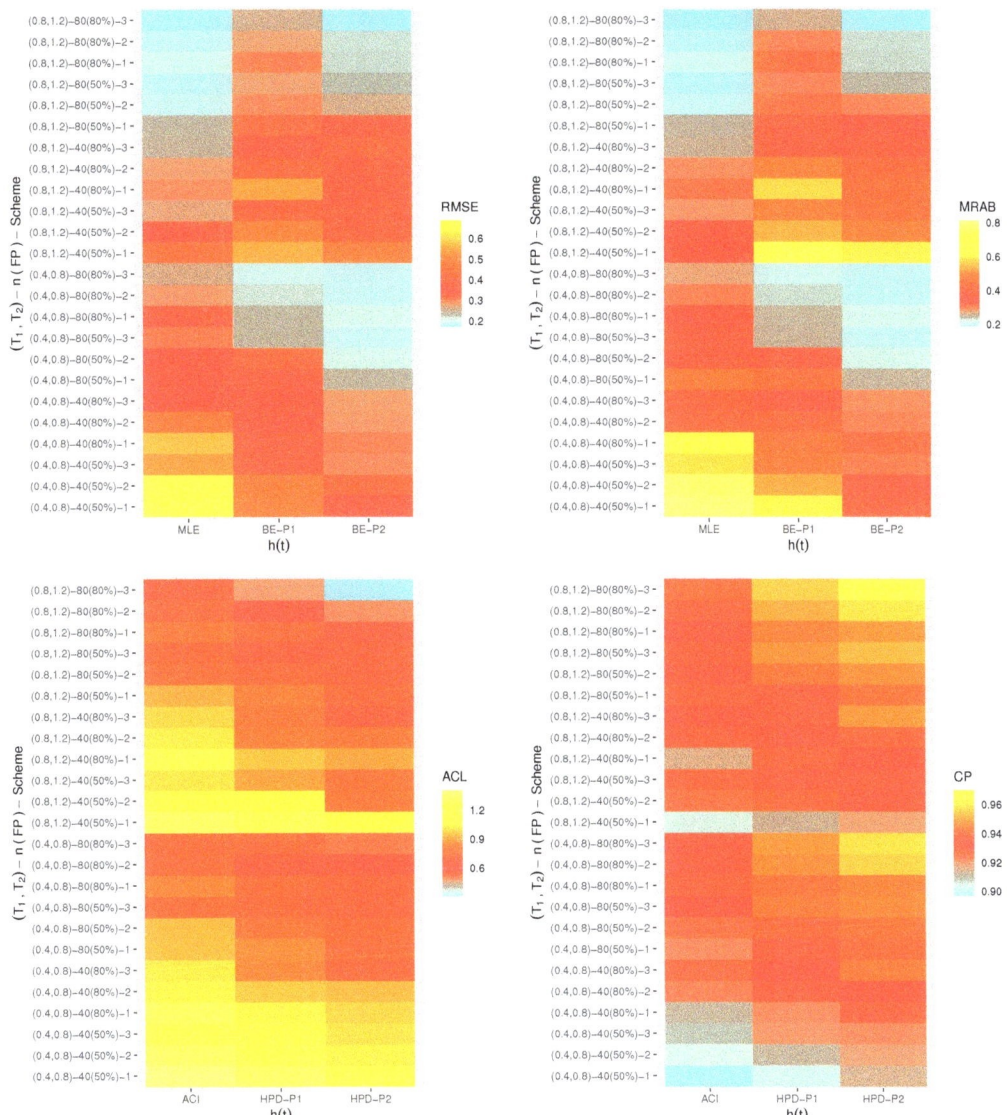

Figure 4. Heatmap plots for the simulation outputs of $h(t)$.

6. Optimal PC-T2 Designs

The experimenter may want to choose the "best" censoring scheme from a collection of all accessible censoring schemes in order to offer the most information about the unknown parameters under research, especially in the context of dependability. First, Balakrishnan and Aggarwala [26] looked at the issue of selecting the best censoring approach in various situations. However, several optimality criteria have been put forth, and many conclusions on the best censoring schemes have been examined. The ideal censoring design $\underline{R} = (R_1, R_2, \ldots, R_m)$ such that $n - m = \sum_{i=1}^{m} R_i$ can be proposed, and the precise values of n (size of test units), m (effective sample), and T_i, $i = 1, 2$ (ideal test thresholds) are chosen beforehand based on the availability of the units, experimental facilities, and cost considerations; for details, see Ng et al. [27].

The issue of contrasting two (or more) alternative censoring strategies has been addressed in a number of publications in the literature (for examples, see Sen et al. [28], Elshahhat and Abu El Azm [29], Elshahhat et al. [30], among others). In our situation, Table 2 provides a selection of frequently used metrics to assist us in selecting the ideal censoring approach, C_i.

Table 2. Useful criteria for the best PC-T2 plan.

Criterion	Target
C_1	Maximize trace$(I(\hat{\delta},\hat{\theta}))$
C_2	Minimize trace$(I^{-1}(\hat{\delta},\hat{\theta}))$
C_3	Minimize det$(I^{-1}(\hat{\delta},\hat{\theta}))$
C_4	Minimize $\widehat{var}(\log(\hat{\mathcal{T}}_\varrho))$

It is recommended to maximize the observed Fisher information, the $I^{-1}(\cdot)$ values for C_1. In addition, for criteria C_2 and C_3, we want to minimize the determinant and trace of $I^{-1}(\cdot)$. For multiparameter distributions, the ideal censoring approach may be chosen using scale-invariant criteria. While comparing the two Fisher information matrices is more difficult when dealing with unknown multiparameter distributions, scale-invariant criteria can be utilized to compare numerous criteria when dealing with single-parameter distributions C_4. Criterion C_4 tends to minimize the variance of the logarithmic MLE of the ϱth quantile, $\mathcal{T}_\varrho$. Thus, from (3), the logarithmic of the Fr distribution $\mathcal{T}_\varrho$ is given by

$$\log(\hat{\mathcal{T}}_\varrho) = \left[-\frac{\log(\varrho)}{\delta}\right]^{-\frac{1}{\theta}}_{(\hat{\delta},\hat{\theta})}, \quad 0 < \varrho < 1. \tag{14}$$

Applying the delta approach to (14), the approximation of the variance for the Fr distribution's $\log(\hat{\mathcal{T}}_\varrho)$ is obtained as

$$\widehat{var}(\log(\hat{\mathcal{T}}_\varrho)) = \Sigma^\mathsf{T}_{\log(\hat{\mathcal{T}}_\varrho)} I^{-1}(\hat{\delta},\hat{\theta}) \Sigma_{\log(\hat{\mathcal{T}}_\varrho)},$$

where

$$\Sigma^\mathsf{T}_{\log(\hat{\mathcal{T}}_\varrho)} = \left[\frac{\partial}{\partial \delta}\log(\hat{\mathcal{T}}_\varrho), \frac{\partial}{\partial \theta}\log(\hat{\mathcal{T}}_\varrho)\right]_{(\hat{\delta},\hat{\theta})}.$$

The highest value of the criteria C_1 and the minimum value of the criterion C_i for $i = 2, 3, 4$ correspond to the optimum censoring. Contrarily, the highest value of the criterion C_1 and the lowest value of other criteria correspond to the optimal censoring.

7. Real-Life Applications

To highlight the utility of the proposed estimation procedures and the applicability of the study objectives to actual situations, this section presents two different applications by analyzing two sets of useful real data taken from the physical and engineering fields. These applications show that the proposed inferential approaches work satisfactorily under real-life data using the proposed censoring plan.

7.1. March Precipitation

In this application, we considered a data set representing thirty successive values (in inches) of precipitation in Minneapolis–Saint Paul for the month of March, see Table 3. This data set was provided by Hinckley [31] and recently reanalyzed by Elshahhat et al. [32]. To examine whether March precipitation data fit the Fr distribution or not, the Kolmogorov–Smirnov (KS) statistic and its p-value were calculated. To establish this goal, from Table 3, the MLEs (with their standard errors (SEs)) of δ and θ were 1.0252 (0.1978) and 1.5496

(0.2027), respectively, meanwhile the KS (p-value) was 0.1524 (0.489). It means that the Fr lifetime model fit the March precipitation data well. Using a graphic visualization, based on the complete March precipitation data, Figure 5 displays (i) the estimated and empirical RFs and (ii) the contour of the log-likelihood function with respect to various choices of δ and θ. It supported the same findings as the KS test and showed that the MLEs $\hat{\delta} \cong 1.025$ and $\hat{\theta} \cong 1.550$ existed and were unique.

Table 3. Successive values of March precipitation.

0.77	1.74	0.81	1.20	1.95	1.20	0.47	1.43	3.37	2.20
3.00	3.09	1.51	2.10	0.52	1.62	1.31	0.32	0.59	0.81
2.81	1.87	1.18	1.35	4.75	2.48	0.96	1.89	0.90	2.05

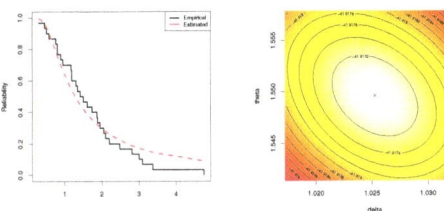

Figure 5. Empirical/fitted RFs (**left**); contour (**right**) plots from March precipitation data.

For the explanation of the proposed estimation methodologies, from the complete March precipitation data, three GPHC-T2 samples with $m = 10$ and various thresholds $T_i, i = 1, 2$ were generated and are reported in Table 4. Moreover, in Table 4, different censoring plans $\underline{R}$ were utilized, namely, $\mathcal{S}_1 : (2^*10)$, $\mathcal{S}_2 : (5^*2, 0^*6, 5^*2)$, $\mathcal{S}_3 : (6^*3, 0^*6, 2)$, and $\mathcal{S}_4 : (2, 0^*6, 6^*3)$. From Table 4, the maximum likelihood estimates (along with their SEs) as well as the ACI estimates (along with their widths) of δ, θ, $R(t)$, and $h(t)$ (at $t = 1$) were computed and are listed in Table 5. Since there was no prior information about the unknown Fr parameters δ and θ from the given data set, by repeating the MCMC sampler 50,000 times and ignoring the first 10,000 times as burn-in, the Bayes estimates (with their SEs) as well as the HPD interval estimates (with their widths) were evaluated using improper gamma priors and are provided in Table 5 as well. For the computational logic, the unknown hyperparameters were set to 0.001. It is clear, from Table 5, that the MCMC estimates of δ, θ, $R(t)$, and $h(t)$ behaved better than the others in terms of the smallest standard error and interval width values.

Table 4. GPHC-T2 samples from March precipitation data.

Scheme	Sample	$T_1(d_1)$	$T_2(d_2)$	Generated Data	R^*	T^*
$\mathcal{S}_1$	1	3.40(11)	5.00(11)	0.32, 0.59, 0.81, 1.18, 1.31, 1.51, 1.87, 2.05, 2.48, 3.09, 3.37	1	3.40
	2	2.00(7)	3.25(10)	0.32, 0.59, 0.81, 1.18, 1.31, 1.51, 1.87, 2.05, 2.48, 3.09	0	3.09
	3	2.00(7)	2.50(9)	0.32, 0.59, 0.81, 1.18, 1.31, 1.51, 1.87, 2.05, 2.48	3	2.50
$\mathcal{S}_2$	1	2.95(11)	3.05(11)	0.32, 0.81, 1.31, 1.35, 1.43, 1.51, 1.62, 1.74, 1.87, 2.48, 2.81	4	2.95
	2	2.25(9)	2.50(10)	0.32, 0.81, 1.31, 1.35, 1.43, 1.51, 1.62, 1.74, 1.87, 2.48	0	2.48
	3	1.50(5)	2.00(9)	0.32, 0.81, 1.31, 1.35, 1.43, 1.51, 1.62, 1.74, 1.87	6	2.00
$\mathcal{S}_3$	1	3.50(11)	4.80(11)	0.32, 0.90, 1.43, 2.05, 2.10, 2.20, 2.48, 2.81, 3.00, 3.09, 3.37	1	3.50
	2	2.75(7)	3.25(10)	0.32, 0.90, 1.43, 2.05, 2.10, 2.20, 2.48, 2.81, 3.00, 3.09	0	3.09
	3	2.25(6)	3.05(9)	0.32, 0.90, 1.43, 2.05, 2.10, 2.20, 2.48, 2.81, 3.00	3	3.05
$\mathcal{S}_4$	1	2.60(11)	4.80(11)	0.32, 0.59, 0.77, 0.81, 0.81, 0.90, 0.96, 1.18, 1.62, 2.20, 2.48	5	2.60
	2	1.10(7)	2.50(10)	0.32, 0.59, 0.77, 0.81, 0.90, 0.96, 1.18, 1.62, 2.20	0	2.20
	3	1.50(8)	2.10(9)	0.32, 0.59, 0.77, 0.81, 0.81, 0.90, 0.96, 1.18, 1.62	7	2.10

Table 5. Point and 95% interval estimates of δ, θ, $R(t)$, and $h(t)$ from March precipitation data.

Scheme	Sample	Par.	MLE		MCMC		ACI			HPD		
			Est.	SE	Est.	SE	Lower	Upper	Width	Lower	Upper	Width
S_1	1	δ	1.8514	0.3703	1.6588	0.2364	1.1256	2.5772	1.4517	1.3969	1.9224	0.5255
		θ	0.9547	0.1974	0.8078	0.1878	0.5677	1.3417	0.7739	0.5750	1.0277	0.4527
		$R(1)$	0.8430	0.0581	0.8079	0.0439	0.7290	0.9570	0.2279	0.7526	0.8538	0.1011
		$h(1)$	0.3292	0.1084	0.3162	0.0557	0.1168	0.5416	0.4248	0.2183	0.4275	0.2093
	2	δ	1.8803	0.3765	1.6879	0.2337	1.1424	2.6182	1.4758	1.4424	1.9576	0.5152
		θ	0.9039	0.1991	0.7523	0.1922	0.5136	1.2941	0.7804	0.5353	0.9912	0.4559
		$R(1)$	0.8475	0.0574	0.8135	0.0421	0.7349	0.9600	0.2251	0.7637	0.8588	0.0952
		$h(1)$	0.3059	0.1046	0.2889	0.0545	0.1010	0.5108	0.4098	0.1962	0.3969	0.2007
	3	δ	1.9040	0.3823	1.7049	0.2416	1.1547	2.6534	1.4988	1.4514	1.9965	0.5451
		θ	0.8633	0.2033	0.7049	0.1974	0.4648	1.2618	0.7970	0.4664	0.9247	0.4583
		$R(1)$	0.8510	0.0570	0.8165	0.0428	0.7394	0.9627	0.2233	0.7685	0.8662	0.0977
		$h(1)$	0.2877	0.1028	0.2679	0.0545	0.0862	0.4892	0.4030	0.1634	0.3608	0.1974
S_2	1	δ	2.3307	0.4210	2.1201	0.2523	1.5056	3.1559	1.6503	1.8228	2.3704	0.5476
		θ	0.8229	0.1722	0.6788	0.1806	0.4853	1.1605	0.6752	0.4675	0.8874	0.4199
		$R(1)$	0.9028	0.0409	0.8788	0.0294	0.8226	0.9830	0.1604	0.8466	0.9129	0.0662
		$h(1)$	0.2066	0.0680	0.1969	0.0374	0.0733	0.3398	0.2666	0.1295	0.2686	0.1391
	2	δ	1.8799	0.3918	1.6843	0.2392	1.1120	2.6479	1.5359	1.4255	1.9528	0.5273
		θ	1.0014	0.2118	0.8466	0.1956	0.5863	1.4164	0.8301	0.6217	1.0810	0.4594
		$R(1)$	0.8474	0.0598	0.8127	0.0432	0.7302	0.9646	0.2344	0.7596	0.8581	0.0985
		$h(1)$	0.3390	0.1155	0.3261	0.0565	0.1126	0.5654	0.4528	0.2244	0.4378	0.2134
	3	δ	1.8845	0.3952	1.6894	0.2366	1.1099	2.6591	1.5493	1.4467	1.9610	0.5144
		θ	0.9891	0.2206	0.8256	0.2046	0.5568	1.4214	0.8647	0.6076	1.0796	0.4720
		$R(1)$	0.8481	0.0600	0.8137	0.0425	0.7304	0.9658	0.2353	0.7646	0.8593	0.0946
		$h(1)$	0.3339	0.1184	0.3168	0.0570	0.1018	0.5660	0.4642	0.2180	0.4256	0.2075
S_3	1	δ	2.3735	0.4667	2.1580	0.2556	1.4589	3.2882	1.8294	1.8927	2.4194	0.5267
		θ	0.8882	0.1730	0.7458	0.1808	0.5490	1.2273	0.6783	0.5500	0.9770	0.4269
		$R(1)$	0.9069	0.0435	0.8834	0.0284	0.8216	0.9921	0.1704	0.8529	0.9141	0.0611
		$h(1)$	0.2165	0.0766	0.2109	0.0366	0.0664	0.3667	0.3002	0.1397	0.2787	0.1389
	2	δ	2.0295	0.4390	1.8276	0.2421	1.1691	2.8898	1.7207	1.5706	2.0924	0.5218
		θ	1.0130	0.2028	0.8574	0.1962	0.6155	1.4105	0.7950	0.6199	1.0857	0.4658
		$R(1)$	0.8686	0.0577	0.8378	0.0376	0.7555	0.9816	0.2261	0.7953	0.8787	0.0834
		$h(1)$	0.3110	0.1121	0.3012	0.0508	0.0914	0.5307	0.4393	0.2087	0.4009	0.1921
	3	δ	2.0708	0.4490	1.8624	0.2513	1.1908	2.9508	1.7600	1.5918	2.1203	0.5286
		θ	0.9542	0.2040	0.7971	0.1973	0.5545	1.3540	0.7996	0.5466	1.0094	0.4627
		$R(1)$	0.8739	0.0566	0.8432	0.0378	0.7630	0.9849	0.2219	0.7990	0.8817	0.0827
		$h(1)$	0.2851	0.1065	0.2737	0.0485	0.0764	0.4938	0.4173	0.1826	0.3615	0.1788
S_4	1	δ	1.7138	0.3237	1.5320	0.2232	1.0794	2.3482	1.2688	1.2781	1.7873	0.5092
		θ	0.8887	0.2006	0.7435	0.1850	0.4955	1.2820	0.7865	0.5247	0.9780	0.4532
		$R(1)$	0.8198	0.0583	0.7821	0.0471	0.7055	0.9341	0.2286	0.7277	0.8376	0.1099
		$h(1)$	0.3347	0.1087	0.3149	0.0590	0.1216	0.5478	0.4262	0.2034	0.4170	0.2136
	2	δ	1.6400	0.3231	1.4614	0.2202	1.0067	2.2733	1.2666	1.2305	1.7284	0.4979
		θ	0.9122	0.2171	0.7602	0.1941	0.4867	1.3377	0.8510	0.5090	0.9807	0.4717
		$R(1)$	0.8060	0.0627	0.7662	0.0500	0.6832	0.9289	0.2457	0.7115	0.8248	0.1133
		$h(1)$	0.3600	0.1228	0.3365	0.0655	0.1193	0.6007	0.4814	0.2122	0.4520	0.2398
	3	δ	1.6816	0.3330	1.4968	0.2297	1.0289	2.3343	1.3055	1.2307	1.7600	0.5293
		θ	0.8508	0.2181	0.6970	0.1939	0.4232	1.2783	0.8551	0.4756	0.9421	0.4665
		$R(1)$	0.8139	0.0620	0.7740	0.0506	0.6925	0.9354	0.2429	0.7130	0.8319	0.1189
		$h(1)$	0.3271	0.1185	0.3020	0.0639	0.0948	0.5594	0.4646	0.1882	0.4165	0.2283

Various properties, namely, the mean, mode, median, first/third quartiles, standard deviation (St.D), and skewness (Skew.) from 40,000 MCMC variates of δ, θ, $R(t)$, and $h(t)$ were obtained and are presented in Table 6. To highlight the convergence of the MCMC iterations, from each generated sample by S_1 (for example), Figure 6 displays both the density and trace plots of δ, θ, $R(t)$, and $h(t)$. For discrimination, the solid (—) line represents the Bayes estimate while the dashed (- - -) lines represent the HPD interval bounds. It is clear, from Figure 6, that the MCMC technique converged favorably, and the suggested size of the burn-in sample was sufficient to eliminate the influence of the suggested initial values. Moreover, for each sample, Figure 6 shows that the calculated estimates of δ, θ, and $h(t)$ were fairly symmetrical while those associated with $R(t)$ were negatively skewed.

Table 6. Summary of MCMC draws of δ, θ, $R(t)$, and $h(t)$ from March precipitation data.

Scheme	Sample	Par.	Mean	Mode	1st Quart.	Median	3rd Quart.	St.D	Skew.
S_1	1	δ	1.65884	1.44240	1.56456	1.66014	1.75286	0.13707	0.06177
		θ	0.80782	0.78396	0.72868	0.80569	0.88953	0.11712	0.03572
		$R(1)$	0.80785	0.76364	0.79082	0.80988	0.82672	0.02632	−0.30505
		$h(1)$	0.31615	0.34999	0.27967	0.31448	0.35220	0.05417	0.21963
	2	δ	1.68791	1.33249	1.59475	1.68677	1.77693	0.13267	0.04592
		θ	0.75233	0.75994	0.67512	0.74995	0.83252	0.11832	0.03766
		$R(1)$	0.81346	0.73618	0.79704	0.81488	0.83084	0.02478	−0.35833
		$h(1)$	0.28894	0.36288	0.25335	0.28748	0.32189	0.05183	0.24360
	3	δ	1.70488	1.39610	1.61328	1.70442	1.79652	0.13674	−0.00785
		θ	0.70490	0.56174	0.62146	0.70547	0.78358	0.11780	0.06035
		$R(1)$	0.81649	0.75244	0.80076	0.81812	0.83412	0.02523	−0.44389
		$h(1)$	0.26785	0.25802	0.23289	0.26549	0.30269	0.05073	0.26045
S_2	1	δ	2.12012	1.71551	2.02876	2.11993	2.21242	0.13895	−0.03581
		θ	0.67875	0.71366	0.60156	0.67956	0.75084	0.10878	0.07255
		$R(1)$	0.87881	0.82013	0.86851	0.87996	0.89056	0.01698	−0.48792
		$h(1)$	0.19689	0.26852	0.17194	0.19544	0.22075	0.03612	0.27805
	2	δ	1.68425	1.47094	1.58825	1.68506	1.77899	0.13749	0.07098
		θ	0.84661	0.83066	0.76259	0.84304	0.93005	0.11962	0.04259
		$R(1)$	0.81266	0.77029	0.79572	0.81457	0.83119	0.02572	−0.29661
		$h(1)$	0.32609	0.36437	0.28879	0.32443	0.36352	0.05503	0.21025
	3	δ	1.68935	1.47765	1.59572	1.68609	1.77855	0.13377	0.07314
		θ	0.82559	0.63312	0.74114	0.82271	0.90966	0.12298	0.07918
		$R(1)$	0.81371	0.77183	0.79724	0.81476	0.83112	0.02491	−0.32491
		$h(1)$	0.31675	0.27657	0.27736	0.31461	0.35079	0.05436	0.28526
S_3	1	δ	2.15798	1.86332	2.06271	2.15792	2.25137	0.13729	0.14454
		θ	0.74578	0.79158	0.67012	0.74546	0.82224	0.11142	0.11278
		$R(1)$	0.88336	0.84484	0.87289	0.88444	0.89475	0.01591	−0.22485
		$h(1)$	0.21087	0.27088	0.18488	0.20956	0.23429	0.03621	0.32873
	2	δ	1.82763	1.69518	1.73442	1.82638	1.91578	0.13367	0.12385
		θ	0.85736	0.76249	0.77643	0.85412	0.93867	0.11953	0.05221
		$R(1)$	0.83777	0.81643	0.82349	0.83901	0.85277	0.02159	−0.26012
		$h(1)$	0.30121	0.29062	0.26634	0.29833	0.33361	0.04988	0.29036
	3	δ	1.86243	1.63762	1.76459	1.86529	1.95677	0.14061	0.12317
		θ	0.79707	0.61631	0.72013	0.80131	0.87467	0.11919	0.03519
		$R(1)$	0.84317	0.80556	0.82874	0.84515	0.85869	0.02193	−0.23488
		$h(1)$	0.27368	0.24361	0.24158	0.27169	0.30419	0.04713	0.25244
S_4	1	δ	1.53202	1.32668	1.44701	1.53007	1.61764	0.12947	0.04637
		θ	0.74345	0.60097	0.66593	0.74052	0.82041	0.11459	0.07596
		$R(1)$	0.78209	0.73464	0.76473	0.78348	0.80163	0.02825	−0.34439
		$h(1)$	0.31494	0.28799	0.27636	0.31184	0.35151	0.05561	0.25228
	2	δ	1.46145	1.28186	1.37635	1.45918	1.54745	0.12887	0.04011
		θ	0.76024	0.68648	0.68097	0.75701	0.84119	0.12069	0.05982
		$R(1)$	0.76617	0.72248	0.74751	0.76757	0.78721	0.03021	−0.37683
		$h(1)$	0.33652	0.33802	0.29477	0.33514	0.37521	0.06116	0.26036
	3	δ	1.49676	1.11375	1.40627	1.49904	1.58976	0.13635	−0.05557
		θ	0.69695	0.63129	0.61659	0.69281	0.77564	0.11814	0.15571
		$R(1)$	0.77405	0.67168	0.75494	0.77666	0.79603	0.03108	0.47954
		$h(1)$	0.30203	0.34369	0.26199	0.29914	0.34097	0.05874	0.29132

According to the optimum criteria $\mathcal{C}_i$, $i = 1, 2, 3, 4$ presented in Section 6, utilizing the generated samples in Table 4, the best PC-T2 plan was also proposed; see Table 7. It is evident that

- Via criterion $\mathcal{C}_1$, the schemes $\mathcal{S}_2$ (in sample 1) and $\mathcal{S}_1$ (in samples 2 and 3) were the optimum plans.
- Via criteria $\mathcal{C}_i$, $i = 2, 3, 4$, the scheme $\mathcal{S}_4$ (in samples 1, 2, and 3) was the optimum plan.
- The ideal PC-T2 plans suggested here confirmed the findings listed in Section 5.

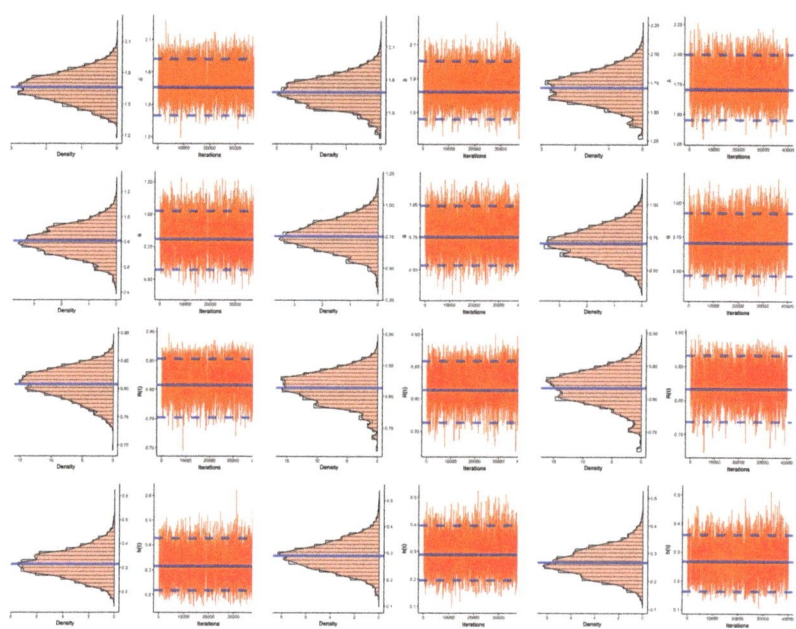

Figure 6. Density (**left**) and trace (**right**) plots of δ, θ, $R(t)$, and $h(t)$ from March precipitation data.

Table 7. Optimum PC-T2 plans from March precipitation data.

Sample $\varrho \rightarrow$	Scheme	$\mathcal{C}_1$	$\mathcal{C}_2$	$\mathcal{C}_3$	$\mathcal{C}_4$		
					0.3	0.6	0.9
1	$\mathcal{S}_1$	33.1788	0.17613	0.00531	0.13763	2.38870	311.913
	$\mathcal{S}_2$	40.1670	0.20691	0.00515	0.32813	6.92420	1148.77
	$\mathcal{S}_3$	38.4794	0.24774	0.00644	0.29390	4.63153	535.519
	$\mathcal{S}_4$	34.9765	0.14503	0.00415	0.12876	1.95256	182.945
2	$\mathcal{S}_1$	32.4967	0.18138	0.00558	0.17374	2.88478	333.724
	$\mathcal{S}_2$	28.9297	0.19837	0.00686	0.13316	2.11421	253.737
	$\mathcal{S}_3$	29.5870	0.23382	0.00790	0.16429	1.92208	137.821
	$\mathcal{S}_4$	31.9176	0.15153	0.00475	0.11751	1.70550	135.791
3	$\mathcal{S}_1$	31.2816	0.18753	0.00599	0.21677	4.17175	580.510
	$\mathcal{S}_2$	27.1783	0.20486	0.00754	0.16105	3.54841	556.485
	$\mathcal{S}_3$	29.0505	0.24319	0.00837	0.21440	2.93514	262.146
	$\mathcal{S}_4$	31.2035	0.15850	0.00508	0.14613	2.00214	168.034

7.2. Vehicle Fatalities

For this application, we analyzed a real data set representing the number of vehicle fatalities for thirty-nine counties in South Carolina during 2012. These data were obtained from the National Highway Traffic Safety Administration (www-fars.nhtsa.dot.gov/States) and reported first by Mann [33]; see Table 8. First, to check the fit status, the KS statistics (with its p-value) and MLEs (with their SEs) based on all of vehicle fatalities data were computed. From Table 8, the MLEs (SEs) of δ and θ were 7.8474 (1.8243) and 0.9719 (0.1068), respectively, meanwhile the KS (p-value) was 0.1648 (0.240). It showed that the Fr distribution was a suitable life model for the vehicle fatalities data. Additionally, Figure 7 corroborated the same goodness-of-fit results and suggested taking the estimates $\hat{\delta} \cong 7.8474$ and $\hat{\theta} \cong 0.9719$ (that is, $\hat{\theta}$ existed and was unique) as initial guesses to run any proposed numerical evaluations.

Table 8. Motor vehicle deaths in South Carolina for 2012.

22	26	17	4	48	9	9	31	27	20
12	6	5	14	9	16	3	33	9	20
68	13	51	13	2	4	17	16	6	52
50	48	23	12	13	10	15	8	1	

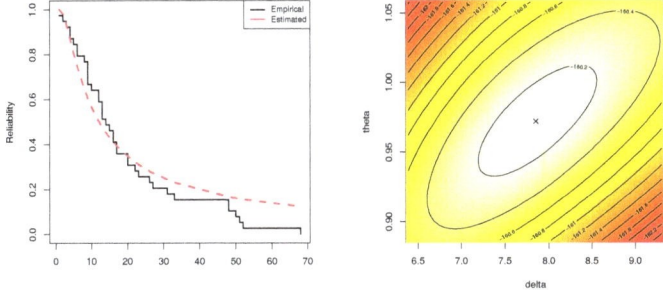

Figure 7. Empirical/fitted RFs (**left**); contour (**right**) plots from vehicle fatalities data.

To evaluate our acquired estimators, different artificial GPHC-T2 samples (when $m = 20$) based on different choices of $\underline{R}$ and T_i, $i = 1,2$ were obtained from the vehicle fatalities data and are presented in Table 9. The censoring mechanisms used here were designed as $\mathcal{S}_1 : (1^*19, 0)$, $\mathcal{S}_2 : (3^*3, 0^*13, 1, 3^*3)$, $\mathcal{S}_3 : (6^*3, 0^*16, 1)$, and $\mathcal{S}_4 : (1, 0^*16, 6^*3)$.

From Table 9, the point and interval estimates obtained via the maximum likelihood and Bayes estimation approaches of δ, θ, $R(t)$, and $h(t)$ (at $t = 5$) were determined and are provided in Table 10. The Bayesian results were carried out under the noninformative priors. As a result, from Table 10, the point estimates of the unknown parameters had the same behavior, as they appeared to be near each other. A similar behavior was also observed in the case of interval estimates. This was an expected result due to the lack of additional historical information that could be used, which in turn made no significant difference between the proposed frequentist and Bayesian estimates.

Table 9. GPHC-T2 samples from vehicle fatalities data.

Scheme	Sample	$T_1(d_1)$	$T_2(d_2)$	Generated Data	R^*	T^*
S_1	1	70(21)	75(21)	1, 2, 4, 5, 6, 9, 9, 10, 12, 13, 14, 16, 17, 20, 22, 26, 31, 48, 50, 52, 68	0	70
	2	35(17)	60(20)	1, 2, 4, 5, 6, 9, 9, 10, 12, 13, 14, 16, 17, 20, 22, 26, 31, 48, 50, 52	0	52
	3	25(15)	49(18)	1, 2, 4, 5, 6, 9, 9, 10, 12, 13, 14, 16, 17, 20, 22, 26, 31, 48	4	49
S_2	1	55(22)	70(22)	1, 4, 8, 9, 10, 12, 12, 13, 13, 13, 14, 15, 16, 16, 17, 17, 20, 22, 31, 50, 51, 52	1	55
	2	18(16)	60(20)	1, 4, 8, 9, 10, 12, 12, 13, 13, 13, 14, 15, 16, 16, 17, 17, 20, 22, 31, 50	0	50
	3	21(17)	40(19)	1, 4, 8, 9, 10, 12, 12, 13, 13, 13, 14, 15, 16, 16, 17, 17, 20, 22, 31	4	40
S_3	1	70(21)	75(21)	1, 6, 12, 16, 16, 17, 17, 20, 20, 22, 23, 26, 27, 31, 33, 48, 48, 50, 51, 52, 68	0	70
	2	40(15)	70(20)	1, 6, 12, 16, 16, 17, 17, 20, 20, 22, 23, 26, 27, 31, 33, 48, 48, 50, 51, 52	0	52
	3	19(7)	49(17)	1, 6, 12, 16, 16, 17, 17, 20, 20, 22, 23, 26, 27, 31, 33, 48, 48	4	49
S_4	1	49(22)	70(22)	1, 3, 4, 4, 5, 6, 6, 8, 9, 9, 9, 9, 10, 12, 12, 13, 13, 13, 20, 33, 48, 48	4	49
	2	30(19)	50(20)	1, 3, 4, 4, 5, 6, 6, 8, 9, 9, 9, 9, 10, 12, 12, 13, 13, 13, 20, 33	0	33
	3	19(18)	32(19)	1, 3, 4, 4, 5, 6, 6, 8, 9, 9, 9, 9, 10, 12, 12, 13, 13, 13, 20	6	30

Table 10. Point and 95% interval estimates of δ, θ, $R(t)$, and $h(t)$ from vehicle fatalities data.

Scheme	Sample	Par.	MLE Est.	MLE SE	MCMC Est.	MCMC SE	ACI Lower	ACI Upper	ACI Width	HPD Lower	HPD Upper	HPD Width
∞_2	1	δ	6.4352	1.6264	6.2790	0.1963	3.2476	9.6229	6.3753	6.0529	6.5206	0.4677
		θ	0.6926	0.1043	0.6494	0.0729	0.4881	0.8971	0.4090	0.5393	0.7655	0.2262
		$R(5)$	0.8789	0.0430	0.8887	0.0252	0.7945	0.9632	0.1687	0.8425	0.9308	0.0883
		$h(5)$	0.0403	0.0106	0.0359	0.0093	0.0195	0.0611	0.0415	0.0215	0.0527	0.0313
	2	δ	6.2622	1.5457	6.0989	0.2048	3.2327	9.2917	6.0590	5.8370	6.3190	0.4820
		θ	0.6751	0.1031	0.6313	0.0734	0.4729	0.8772	0.4043	0.5138	0.7441	0.2303
		$R(5)$	0.8791	0.0424	0.8887	0.0252	0.7961	0.9621	0.1660	0.8417	0.9307	0.0889
		$h(5)$	0.0392	0.0104	0.0349	0.0092	0.0189	0.0596	0.0407	0.0201	0.0511	0.0310
	3	δ	5.8676	1.4876	5.6906	0.2217	2.9520	8.7833	5.8313	5.3873	5.9128	0.5255
		θ	0.6320	0.1048	0.5869	0.0731	0.4265	0.8375	0.4109	0.4742	0.6977	0.2236
		$R(5)$	0.8802	0.0426	0.8893	0.0243	0.7966	0.9638	0.1672	0.8429	0.9296	0.0866
		$h(5)$	0.0365	0.0099	0.0324	0.0086	0.0172	0.0558	0.0386	0.0188	0.0477	0.0288
S_2	1	δ	7.5035	2.0715	7.2561	0.2921	3.4434	11.564	8.1202	6.9272	7.5138	0.5866
		θ	0.6528	0.0995	0.6161	0.0627	0.4577	0.8479	0.3902	0.5127	0.7128	0.2001
		$R(5)$	0.9275	0.0326	0.9312	0.0155	0.8636	0.9914	0.1278	0.9007	0.9579	0.0572
		$h(5)$	0.0268	0.0078	0.0245	0.0062	0.0115	0.0421	0.0305	0.0141	0.0359	0.0218
	2	δ	7.7362	2.0966	7.4992	0.2785	3.6270	11.846	8.2186	7.2111	7.7641	0.5530
		θ	0.7523	0.1103	0.7077	0.0744	0.5362	0.9684	0.4323	0.5860	0.8211	0.2352
		$R(5)$	0.9003	0.0401	0.9079	0.0225	0.8216	0.9789	0.1573	0.8667	0.9483	0.0816
		$h(5)$	0.0384	0.0109	0.0344	0.0092	0.0170	0.0598	0.0428	0.0188	0.0507	0.0318
	3	δ	7.6067	2.0985	7.3867	0.2595	3.4937	11.720	8.2262	7.1073	7.6411	0.5337
		θ	0.7420	0.1124	0.6938	0.0783	0.5217	0.9623	0.4406	0.5712	0.8133	0.2421
		$R(5)$	0.9002	0.0404	0.9094	0.0236	0.8210	0.9794	0.1584	0.8676	0.9493	0.0817
		$h(5)$	0.0379	0.0108	0.0334	0.0095	0.0167	0.0592	0.0425	0.0178	0.0495	0.0317
S_3	1	δ	9.2039	2.7553	8.9694	0.2811	3.8036	14.604	10.801	8.6897	9.2987	0.6090
		θ	0.7815	0.1100	0.7387	0.0745	0.5658	0.9971	0.4313	0.6238	0.8582	0.2344
		$R(5)$	0.9270	0.0378	0.9333	0.0191	0.8529	0.9978	0.1449	0.8984	0.9652	0.0668
		$h(5)$	0.0322	0.0112	0.0287	0.0085	0.0102	0.0543	0.0441	0.0149	0.0440	0.0291
	2	δ	8.9795	2.6017	8.7588	0.2627	3.8802	14.079	10.199	8.5049	9.0478	0.5430
		θ	0.7661	0.1083	0.7230	0.0748	0.5539	0.9784	0.4246	0.5989	0.8415	0.2425
		$R(5)$	0.9270	0.0368	0.9336	0.0190	0.8548	0.9991	0.1444	0.8984	0.9662	0.0678
		$h(5)$	0.0316	0.0109	0.0280	0.0084	0.0102	0.0530	0.0427	0.0138	0.0428	0.0291
	3	δ	8.1794	2.3471	7.9443	0.2780	3.5792	12.780	9.2004	7.6748	8.2128	0.5381
		θ	0.7061	0.1083	0.6605	0.0774	0.4938	0.9184	0.4246	0.5440	0.7805	0.2366
		$R(5)$	0.9276	0.0361	0.9341	0.0194	0.8569	0.9983	0.1414	0.8988	0.9659	0.0671
		$h(5)$	0.0289	0.0100	0.0255	0.0081	0.0094	0.0485	0.0391	0.0124	0.0395	0.0271

Table 10. Cont.

Scheme	Sample	Par.	MLE		MCMC		ACI			HPD		
			Est.	SE	Est.	SE	Lower	Upper	Width	Lower	Upper	Width
S_4	1	δ	6.2440	1.5894	6.0212	0.2627	3.1289	9.3591	6.2302	5.7671	6.2754	0.5083
		θ	0.7337	0.1116	0.6827	0.0818	0.5149	0.9524	0.4375	0.5578	0.8022	0.2444
		$R(5)$	0.8530	0.0461	0.8641	0.0299	0.7625	0.9434	0.1809	0.8112	0.9156	0.1044
		$h(5)$	0.0485	0.0118	0.0431	0.0111	0.0254	0.0715	0.0461	0.0251	0.0616	0.0365
	2	δ	6.0989	1.6122	5.8599	0.2795	2.9389	9.2588	6.3199	5.6177	6.1841	0.5664
		θ	0.7190	0.1167	0.6667	0.0816	0.4902	0.9479	0.4577	0.5402	0.7844	0.2443
		$R(5)$	0.8530	0.0466	0.8637	0.0296	0.7615	0.9444	0.1829	0.8109	0.9164	0.1055
		$h(5)$	0.0475	0.0118	0.0422	0.0109	0.0245	0.0706	0.0461	0.0242	0.0600	0.0359
	3	δ	6.0137	1.5585	5.7737	0.2813	2.9591	9.0684	6.1093	5.4699	6.0277	0.5578
		θ	0.7203	0.1177	0.6635	0.0880	0.4896	0.9510	0.4614	0.5395	0.8025	0.2631
		$R(5)$	0.8484	0.0471	0.8609	0.0321	0.7561	0.9408	0.1847	0.7997	0.9141	0.1143
		$h(5)$	0.0486	0.0122	0.0426	0.0118	0.0247	0.0724	0.0478	0.0243	0.0630	0.0387

The vital statistics of δ, θ, $R(t)$, and $h(t)$, obtained based on 40,000 MCMC variates, namely, the mean, mode, median, first/third quartiles, St.D, and skewness were calculated and are listed in Table 11. Moreover, using the data sets generated by S_1 as an example, the density and trace plots of δ, θ, $R(t)$, and $h(t)$ were plotted and are displayed in Figure 8. They demonstrated that the MCMC method converged effectively. It is also clear that the MCMC iterations of δ and θ were fairly symmetrical while those associated with $R(t)$ and $h(t)$ were negatively and positively skewed, respectively.

Table 11. MCMC properties of δ, θ, $R(t)$, and $h(t)$ from vehicle fatalities data.

Scheme	Sample	Par.	Mean	Mode	1st Quart.	Median	3rd Quart.	St.D	Skew.
S_1	1	δ	6.27902	6.07238	6.19440	6.27871	6.35796	0.11885	0.12109
		θ	0.64937	0.60836	0.60836	0.64920	0.68829	0.05868	0.10751
		$R(5)$	0.88874	0.89782	0.87410	0.89025	0.90534	0.02314	−0.45401
		$h(5)$	0.03592	0.03158	0.02987	0.03539	0.04103	0.00819	0.47887
	2	δ	6.09886	5.83703	6.01562	6.10033	6.17950	0.12355	−0.00218
		θ	0.63130	0.59457	0.59062	0.63021	0.66983	0.05894	0.16323
		$R(5)$	0.88871	0.89373	0.87396	0.89032	0.90551	0.02330	−0.50969
		$h(5)$	0.03494	0.03169	0.02915	0.03425	0.03991	0.00811	0.54586
	3	δ	6.09886	5.83703	6.01562	6.10033	6.17950	0.12355	−0.00218
		θ	0.63130	0.59457	0.59062	0.63021	0.66983	0.05894	0.16323
		$R(5)$	0.88871	0.89373	0.87396	0.89032	0.90551	0.02330	−0.50969
		$h(5)$	0.03494	0.03169	0.02915	0.03425	0.03991	0.00811	0.54586
S_2	1	δ	7.25614	6.92722	7.14857	7.26059	7.36376	0.15535	−0.05403
		θ	0.61609	0.58145	0.58145	0.61666	0.65115	0.05087	0.09922
		$R(5)$	0.93118	0.93395	0.92209	0.93217	0.94205	0.01510	−0.47310
		$h(5)$	0.02451	0.02235	0.02046	0.02411	0.02811	0.00574	0.50290
	2	δ	7.49919	7.29232	7.39787	7.49533	7.59669	0.14611	0.14063
		θ	0.70769	0.71028	0.66841	0.70805	0.74481	0.05960	0.06435
		$R(5)$	0.90789	0.90220	0.89555	0.90828	0.92348	0.02120	−0.45521
		$h(5)$	0.03443	0.03580	0.02853	0.03409	0.03933	0.00825	0.47964
	3	δ	7.38668	7.10877	7.28818	7.38192	7.47749	0.13747	0.20688
		θ	0.69382	0.73684	0.65019	0.69430	0.73573	0.06176	0.08418
		$R(5)$	0.90938	0.88600	0.89566	0.91127	0.92470	0.02170	−0.53495
		$h(5)$	0.03341	0.04118	0.02753	0.03274	0.03856	0.00838	0.53320

Table 11. Cont.

Scheme	Sample	Par.	Mean	Mode	1st Quart.	Median	3rd Quart.	St.D	Skew.
$\mathcal{S}_3$	1	δ	8.96935	8.58414	8.87126	8.97489	9.07186	0.15489	−0.11977
		θ	0.73871	0.79551	0.69502	0.73939	0.78131	0.06101	0.07219
		$R(5)$	0.93335	0.90800	0.92240	0.93476	0.94659	0.01795	−0.57091
		$h(5)$	0.02873	0.03846	0.02306	0.02822	0.03361	0.00776	0.54583
	2	δ	8.75879	8.52297	8.65921	8.75582	8.85316	0.14244	0.13097
		θ	0.72303	0.66433	0.68138	0.72298	0.76373	0.06108	0.10960
		$R(5)$	0.93364	0.94638	0.92273	0.93515	0.94626	0.01782	−0.63479
		$h(5)$	0.02805	0.02203	0.02266	0.02752	0.03260	0.00762	0.61696
	3	δ	7.94430	7.67479	7.83967	7.94385	8.04518	0.14838	0.20050
		θ	0.66047	0.71265	0.61505	0.65708	0.70477	0.06251	0.13608
		$R(5)$	0.93411	0.91262	0.92193	0.93677	0.94782	0.01824	−0.63194
		$h(5)$	0.02554	0.03326	0.01996	0.02442	0.03041	0.00734	0.62253
$\mathcal{S}_4$	1	δ	6.02117	5.85999	5.91772	6.01872	6.11777	0.13903	0.23533
		θ	0.68273	0.61467	0.63882	0.68367	0.72573	0.06396	0.05950
		$R(5)$	0.86408	0.88685	0.84640	0.86541	0.88432	0.02776	−0.37107
		$h(5)$	0.04313	0.03418	0.03578	0.04260	0.04920	0.00973	0.39941
	2	δ	5.85988	5.53493	5.76293	5.85735	5.95667	0.14492	0.07564
		θ	0.66665	0.68793	0.62290	0.66654	0.70781	0.06254	0.07949
		$R(5)$	0.86374	0.83947	0.84488	0.86631	0.88260	0.02761	−0.37640
		$h(5)$	0.04218	0.04813	0.03531	0.04143	0.04813	0.00947	0.41417
	3	δ	5.77368	5.47975	5.67229	5.76992	5.87478	0.14664	0.09816
		θ	0.66351	0.63075	0.61691	0.66383	0.70766	0.06721	0.06895
		$R(5)$	0.86094	0.86270	0.84218	0.86270	0.88203	0.02955	−0.42338
		$h(5)$	0.04258	0.03986	0.03520	0.04198	0.04890	0.01013	0.45365

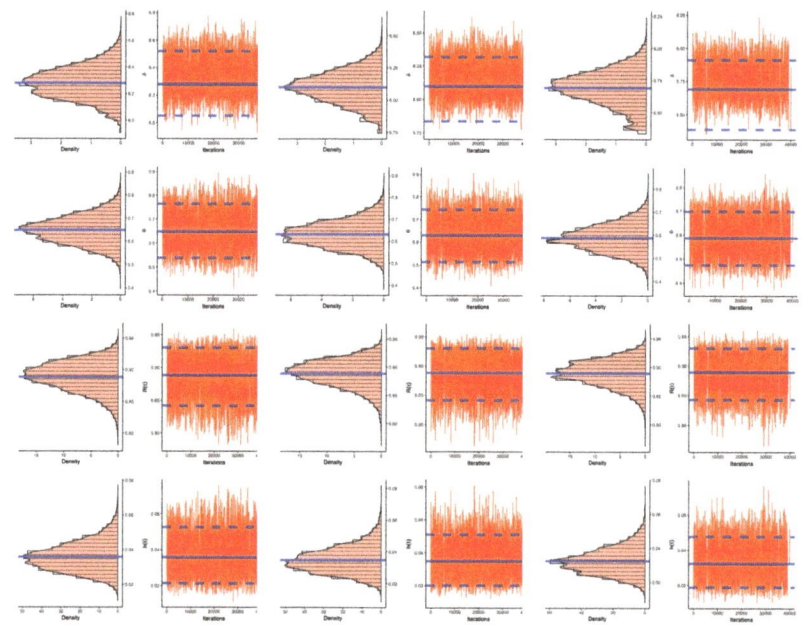

Figure 8. Density (**left**) and trace (**right**) plots of δ, θ, $R(t)$, and $h(t)$ from vehicle fatalities data.

Again, from Table 9, the problem of selecting an optimum PC-T2 plan is also illustrated based on vehicle fatalities data; see Table 12. It shows that:

- Via criterion $\mathcal{C}_1$, the schemes $\mathcal{S}_2$ (in samples 1 and 2) and $\mathcal{S}_3$ (in sample 3) were the optimum plans.
- Via criteria $\mathcal{C}_i$, $i = 2, 3$, the scheme $\mathcal{S}_1$ (in samples 1, 2, and 3) was the optimum plan.
- Via criterion $\mathcal{C}_4$; the scheme $\mathcal{S}_4$ (in samples 1, 2, and 3) was the optimum plan.
- The ideal PC-T2 plans provided here supported our findings from Section 5 as well.

Finally, based on both physical and engineering scenarios, we can draw the conclusion that the investigated approaches provided an adequate interpretation of the Fréchet lifetime model when a sample was generated from the generalized Type-II progressive hybrid censoring mechanism.

Table 12. Optimum PC-T2 plans from vehicle fatalities data.

Sample $\varrho \rightarrow$	Scheme	$\mathcal{C}_1$	$\mathcal{C}_2$	$\mathcal{C}_3$	$\mathcal{C}_4$		
					0.3	0.6	0.9
1	$\mathcal{S}_1$	224.0199	2.395783	0.010695	9.631151	256.7524	92,617.13
	$\mathcal{S}_2$	308.4324	4.30110	0.013945	17.72368	517.4279	227,824.3
	$\mathcal{S}_3$	205.2758	7.603747	0.037042	11.68548	179.4937	29,616.80
	$\mathcal{S}_4$	196.9198	2.538555	0.012891	4.878394	104.0239	26,231.06
2	$\mathcal{S}_1$	200.1599	2.492961	0.012455	8.04740	196.9935	60,769.58
	$\mathcal{S}_2$	206.0574	4.407945	0.021392	8.279247	157.4971	35,747.67
	$\mathcal{S}_3$	205.3611	6.780726	0.033019	12.5469	208.1168	37,439.37
	$\mathcal{S}_4$	190.6955	2.612971	0.01370	5.328222	125.0294	33,173.61
3	$\mathcal{S}_1$	201.6662	2.360953	0.011707	10.68031	328.4031	145,470.3
	$\mathcal{S}_2$	203.6842	4.416535	0.021683	8.808981	176.8395	40,252.86
	$\mathcal{S}_3$	207.2369	5.52049	0.026639	17.9720	393.9506	106,057.5
	$\mathcal{S}_4$	180.4068	2.442885	0.013541	5.187278	123.4222	34,735.87

8. Concluding Remarks

This work considered the generalized Type-II progressive hybrid censoring-based Fréchet model's reliability analysis of the unknown parameters, reliability and hazard rate functions. The Newton–Raphson iterative approach was used to calculate the frequentist estimates with their asymptotic confidence intervals for the unknown parameters and any function of them using the R programming language's "maxLik" package. The posterior density function was derived in nonlinear form since the likelihood function was generated in complex form. Therefore, using the Metropolis–Hastings method and taking into account the squared-error loss, the Bayesian estimates and the corresponding HPD intervals were constructed. Numerous simulation experiments based on various selections of total test units, observed failure data, threshold times, and progressive censoring plans were carried out to compare the behavior of the acquired estimates, and they demonstrated that the Bayes MCMC approach outperformed the frequentist approach quite satisfactorily. It is advised to use the Bayesian MCMC paradigm to estimate the Fréchet distribution's parameters, reliability, and hazard functions under generalized Type-II progressive hybrid censoring. To show how the suggested methods could be applied in practical situations, two applications representing the successive values (in inches) of precipitation in Minneapolis–Saint Paul and the number of vehicle fatalities in South Carolina were examined. We anticipate reliability practitioners will find the findings and methodology presented here useful and that they will be applied to further filtering strategies.

Supplementary Materials: The following supporting information can be downloaded at: https://www.mdpi.com/article/10.3390/sym15020348/s1, Table S1: The APEs (1st column), RMSEs (2nd column) and MRABs (3rd column) of δ; Table S2: The APEs (1st column), RMSEs (2nd column) and MRABs (3rd column) of θ; Table S3: The APEs (1st column), RMSEs (2nd column) and MRABs (3rd column) of $R(t)$; Table S4: The APEs (1st column), RMSEs (2nd column) and MRABs (3rd column) of $h(t)$; Table S5: The ACLs (1st column) and CPs (2nd column) of 95% ACI/HPD credible intervals of δ; Table S6: The ACLs (1st column) and CPs (2nd column) of 95% ACI/HPD credible intervals of θ;

Table S7: The ACLs (1st column) and CPs (2nd column) of 95% ACI/HPD credible intervals of $R(t)$;
Table S8: The ACLs (1st column) and CPs (2nd column) of 95% ACI/HPD credible intervals of $h(t)$.

Author Contributions: Methodology, A.E., R.A. and H.R.; funding acquisition, R.A.; software, A.E.; supervision A.E.; writing—original draft, R.A. and H.R.; writing—review and editing, H.R. All authors have read and agreed to the published version of the manuscript.

Funding: This research was funded by Princess Nourah bint Abdulrahman University Researchers Supporting Project number (PNURSP2023R50), Princess Nourah bint Abdulrahman University, Riyadh, Saudi Arabia.

Data Availability Statement: The authors confirm that the data supporting the findings of this study are available within the article.

Acknowledgments: Princess Nourah bint Abdulrahman University Researchers Supporting Project number (PNURSP2023R50), Princess Nourah bint Abdulrahman University, Riyadh, Saudi Arabia. The authors would also like to express their thanks to the editor and the anonymous referees for valuable comments and helpful observations.

Conflicts of Interest: The authors declare no conflict of interest.

References

1. Chen, P.; Xu, A.; Ye, Z.S. Generalized fiducial inference for accelerated life tests with Weibull distribution and progressively Type-II censoring. *IEEE Trans. Reliab.* **2016**, *65*, 1737–1744. [CrossRef]
2. Luo, C.; Shen, L.; Xu, A. Modelling and estimation of system reliability under dynamic operating environments and lifetime ordering constraints. *Reliab. Eng. Syst. Saf.* **2022**, *218*, 108136. [CrossRef]
3. Balakrishnan, N.; Cramer, E. *The Art of Progressive Censoring*; Springer: New York, NY, USA, 2014.
4. Panahi, H. Interval estimation of Kumaraswamy parameters based on progressively Type II censored sample and record values. *Miskolc Math. Notes* **2020**, *21*, 319–334. [CrossRef]
5. Kundu, D.; Joarder, A. Analysis of Type-II progressively hybrid censored data. *Comput. Stat. Data Anal.* **2006**, *50*, 2509–2528. [CrossRef]
6. Childs, A.; Chandrasekar, B.; Balakrishnan, N. Exact likelihood inference for an exponential parameter under progressive hybrid censoring schemes. In *Statistical Models and Methods for Biomedical and Technical Systems*; Vonta, F., Nikulin, M., Limnios, N., Huber-Carol, C., Eds.; Springer: Boston, MA, USA, 2008; pp. 319–330.
7. Panahi, H. Estimation methods for the generalized inverted exponential distribution under Type ii progressively hybrid censoring with application to spreading of micro-drops data. *Commun. Math. Stat.* **2017**, *5*, 159–174. [CrossRef]
8. Ng, H.K.T.; Kundu, D.; Chan, P.S. Statistical analysis of exponential lifetimes under an adaptive Type-II progressive censoring scheme. *Nav. Res. Logist.* **2009**, *56*, 687–698. [CrossRef]
9. Panahi, H.; Moradi, N. Estimation of the inverted exponentiated Rayleigh distribution based on adaptive Type II progressive hybrid censored sample. *J. Comput. Appl. Math.* **2020**, *364*, 112345. [CrossRef]
10. Lee, K.; Sun, H.; Cho, Y. Exact likelihood inference of the exponential parameter under generalized Type II progressive hybrid censoring. *J. Korean Stat. Soc.* **2016**, *45*, 123–136. [CrossRef]
11. Ashour, S.; Elshahhat, A. Bayesian and non-Bayesian estimation for Weibull parameters based on generalized Type-II progressive hybrid censoring scheme. *Pak. J. Stat. Oper. Res.* **2016**, *12*, 213–226.
12. Ateya, S.; Mohammed, H. Prediction under Burr-XII distribution based on generalized Type-II progressive hybrid censoring scheme. *J. Egypt. Math. Soc.* **2018**, *26*, 491–508.
13. Seo, J.I. Objective Bayesian analysis for the Weibull distribution with partial information under the generalized Type-II progressive hybrid censoring scheme. *Commun.-Stat.-Simul. Comput.* **2020**, *51*, 5157–5173. [CrossRef]
14. Cho, S.; Lee, K. Exact Likelihood Inference for a Competing Risks Model with Generalized Type II Progressive Hybrid Censored Exponential Data. *Symmetry* **2021**, *13*, 887. [CrossRef]
15. Nagy, M.; Bakr, M.E.; Alrasheedi, A.F. Analysis with applications of the generalized Type-II progressive hybrid censoring sample from Burr Type-XII model. *Math. Probl. Eng.* **2022**, *2022*, 1241303. [CrossRef]
16. Wang, L.; Zhou, Y.; Lio, Y.; Tripathi, Y.M. Inference for Kumaraswamy Distribution under Generalized Progressive Hybrid Censoring. *Symmetry* **2022**, *14*, 403. [CrossRef]
17. Fréchet, M. Sur la loi de probabilité de lécart maximum. *Ann. Soc. Pol. Math.* **1927**, *6*, 93–116.
18. Kotz, S.; Nadarajah, S. *Extreme Value Distributions: Theory and Applications*; Imperial College Press: London, UK, 2000.
19. Henningsen, A.; Toomet, O. maxLik: A package for maximum likelihood estimation in R. *Comput. Stat.* **2011**, *26*, 443–458. [CrossRef]
20. Plummer, M.; Best, N.; Cowles, K.; Vines, K. CODA: Convergence diagnosis and output analysis for MCMC. *R News* **2006**, *6*, 7–11.
21. Gelman, A.; Carlin, J.B.; Stern, H.S.; Rubin, D.B. *Bayesian Data Analysis*, 2nd ed.; Chapman and Hall/CRC: Boca Raton, FL, USA, 2004.

22. Lynch, S.M. *Introduction to Applied Bayesian Statistics and Estimation for Social Scientists*; Springer: New York, NY, USA, 2007.
23. Lawless, J.F. *Statistical Models and Methods for Lifetime Data*, 2nd ed.; John Wiley and Sons: Hoboken, NJ, USA, 2003.
24. Greene, W.H. *Econometric Analysis*, 4th ed.; Prentice-Hall: New York, NY, USA, 2000.
25. Chen, M.H.; Shao, Q.M. Monte Carlo estimation of Bayesian credible and HPD intervals. *J. Comput. Graph. Stat.* **1999**, *8*, 69–92.
26. Balakrishnan, N.L.; Aggarwala, R. *Progressive Censoring Theory, Methods and Applications*; Springer: Boston, MA, USA, 2000.
27. Ng, H.K.T.; Chan, P.S.; Balakrishnan, N. Optimal progressive censoring plans for the Weibull distribution. *Technometrics* **2004**, *46*, 470–481. [CrossRef]
28. Sen, T.; Tripathi, Y.M.; Bhattacharya, R. Statistical inference and optimum life testing plans under Type-II hybrid censoring scheme. *Ann. Data Sci.* **2018**, *5*, 679–708. [CrossRef]
29. Elshahhat, A.; Abu El Azm, W.S. Statistical reliability analysis of electronic devices using generalized progressively hybrid censoring plan. *Qual. Reliab. Eng. Int.* **2022**, *38*, 1112–1130. [CrossRef]
30. Elshahhat, A.; Mohammed, H.S.; Abo-Kasem, O.E. Reliability Inferences of the Inverted NH Parameters via Generalized Type-II Progressive Hybrid Censoring with Applications. *Symmetry* **2022**, *14*, 2379. [CrossRef]
31. Hinkley, D. On quick choice of power transformation. *J. R. Stat. Soc.* **1977**, *26*, 67–69. [CrossRef]
32. Elshahhat, A.; Bhattacharya, R.; Mohammed, H.S. Survival Analysis of Type-II Lehmann Fréchet Parameters via Progressive Type-II Censoring with Applications. *Axioms* **2022**, *11*, 700. [CrossRef]
33. Mann, S.P. *Introductoty Statistics*; John Wiley and Sons Inc.: New York, NY, USA, 2016.

Disclaimer/Publisher's Note: The statements, opinions and data contained in all publications are solely those of the individual author(s) and contributor(s) and not of MDPI and/or the editor(s). MDPI and/or the editor(s) disclaim responsibility for any injury to people or property resulting from any ideas, methods, instructions or products referred to in the content.

Article

An Improved Charting Scheme to Monitor the Process Mean Using Two Supplementary Variables

Muhammad Arslan [1], Sadia Anwar [2], Nevine M. Gunaime [3], Sana Shahab [4], Showkat Ahmad Lone [3,*] and Zahid Rasheed [5]

1. Department of Mathematics and Statistics, Institute of Southern Punjab, Multan 59300, Pakistan
2. Department of Mathematics, College of Arts and Science, Prince Sattam bin Abdul Aziz University, AL-Kharj 16242, Saudi Arabia
3. Department of Basic Science, College of Science and Theoretical Studies, Saudi Electronic University, Riyadh 11673, Saudi Arabia
4. Department of Business Administration, College of Business Administration, Princes Nourah bint Abdulrahman University, P.O. Box 84428, Riyadh 11671, Saudi Arabia
5. Department of Mathematics, Women University of Azad Jammu and Kashmir, Bagh AJ&K 12500, Pakistan
* Correspondence: s.lone@seu.edu.sa

Abstract: A control chart is the most well-known statistical monitoring tecnique to address unfavourable process parameter (s) changes. Quality practitioners always desire a charting device that promptly identifies the undesired changes in the process. This study intends to design a sensitive homogeneously weighted moving average chart using two supplementary variables (hereafter, TAHWMA). The two supplementary variables are correlated with the study variable in the form of a regression estimator, which is an efficient and unbiased estimator for the process mean. The suggested TAHWMA charting structure is checked out and compared in terms of appearance and non-appearance of multicollinearity amidst the two additional variables. Average run length-related measures are taken as performance measures. It is observed that the proposed TAHWMA scheme performs effectively when the two supplementary variables have no collinearity. A comprehensive comparison between the proposed TAHWMA and existing charts is also carried out, showing the proposed's supremacy over existing counterparts. For execution purposes, two illustrative examples, one belonging to carbon fibre manufacturing-related data and the other using a simulated dataset and where our simulated dataset belongs to symmetrical distribution, are also presented for the application of the recommended TAHWMA chart.

Keywords: average run length; control chart; multicollinearity; regression estimator; supplementary variable

Citation: Arslan, M.; Anwar, S.; Gunaime, N.M.; Shahab, S.; Lone, S.A.; Rasheed, Z. An Improved Charting Scheme to Monitor the Process Mean Using Two Supplementary Variables. *Symmetry* **2023**, *15*, 482. https://doi.org/10.3390/sym15020482

Academic Editors: Arne Johannssen, Nataliya Chukhrova and Quanxin Zhu

Received: 23 December 2022
Revised: 6 February 2023
Accepted: 6 February 2023
Published: 11 February 2023

Copyright: © 2023 by the authors. Licensee MDPI, Basel, Switzerland. This article is an open access article distributed under the terms and conditions of the Creative Commons Attribution (CC BY) license (https://creativecommons.org/licenses/by/4.0/).

1. Introduction

Quality control is an essential aspect of production management. Many management and engineering techniques are widely used to maintain the quality of goods and services that fulfil increasing customer demand. Companies can monitor their processes with the application of control charts for producing high-quality products. In an ongoing process, change/variation is an inevitable output factor. Statistical process control (SPC) is handy for controlling the variation of methods. Variations are divided into two significant categories: natural and unnatural variations, respectively. Suppose natural changes occur in any running process. In that case, the process is assumed to be statistically in-control (IC), while unusual changes lead the running process to an out-of-control (OOC) state (Montgomery [1]).

Control charts are customarily utilized when unnatural variations exist in the process. The charting mechanism based on the Shewhart [2] structure is a type of memoryless chart because it accepts only recent sample information. The cumulative sum (CUSUM)

charting scheme is an example of a memory-type charting mechanism that was originated by Page [3]. Another memory-type control chart, namely the exponentially weighted moving average (EWMA), was initiated by Roberts [4], and the homogenously weighted moving average proposed by Abbas [5] is also a memory-type chart. The above memory-type charts utilize the previous information along with recent sample information. In any manufacturing industry, SPC quality inspectors have adopted several supplementary techniques to improve the output of any continuing process.

To spot a shift in the process parameter (s) efficiently and enhance the control chart's sensitivity in SPC literature, utilising the supplementary information and different sampling schemes is considered the best option. Recently, the concept of supplementary information has been tested for enhancing the performance of the existing charting schemes by many researchers. The charting situation when the study characteristic is observed correlated with another supplementary feature; such a structure is called an AIB-based charting design (cf. Haq and Khoo [6]). The extraneous information at the estimation phase or information other than the sample is called supplementary or supplementary information.

The regression-based control charts were designed by Mandel [7] and Zhang [8] to screen the process. The utilization of supplementary information in the control chart was initiated by Riaz [9,10] for supervising the process dispersion and location parameters, respectively. Riaz et al. [11] suggested a new AIB-Shewhart control chart under normal and non-normal scenarios for monitoring the process. Furthermore, the (AIB-GWMCV) chart was proposed by Nuriman et al. [12]. Haq and Khoo [13] developed an AIB-synthetic charting scheme to improve the efficiency of the synthetic mean model. Recently, the monitoring of the coefficient of variation using supplementary information has been initiated by Abbasi [14]. In addition, Nuriman et al. [12] proposed a supplementary information-based control chart for efficiently monitoring the process CV. Muhammad Arslan et al. [15] studied a mixed EWMA Dual Crosier CUSUM chart with and without supplementary information. The interested readers are referred to Abbas et al. [16], Chen, J. H., & Lu, S. L. [17], Rasheed et al. [18], Aslam et al. [19], Anwar et al. [20], Rasheed et al. [21], and Zhang et al. [22] for more recent work on HWMA structure and supplementary information-based charting schemes.

Recently, Zichuan et al. [23] designed two AIB EWMA (name hereafter; TAEWMA) control charts to monitor small shifts in the process mean promptly. Taking inspiration from Zichuan et al. [23], this study proposes a new HWMA charting scheme based on two supplementary variables (TAHWMA) to monitor small changes in the process mean quickly. The proposed TAHWMA chart is also investigated under the appearance and non-appearance of the multicollinearity behaviour among the two supplementary variables. The performance of the proposed design has been evaluated using run-length (RL) characteristics, where run length is defined as the number of samples before a chart signal. The expected value of the run lengths is recognized as average run length (ARL). ARL_0 and ARL_1 known as IC ARL and OOC ARL values, respectively.

The rest of the article is organized as follows: The design structures of the existing control charts are briefly described in Section 2. The designed structure of the proposed TAHWMA chart and RL evaluation is presented in Section 3. The comparison of the proposed TAHWMA chart against the existing charts is presented in Section 4. Illustrative examples are conferred in Section 5, and the conclusions of this article are provided in Section 6.

2. Design Structures of Some Existing Control Charts

In this section of the article, existing counterparts are briefly described. The classical HWMA, AHWMA, classical EWMA, and AEWMA control charts are the competitors of the proposed TAHWMA control chart.

2.1. Design Structure of the HWMA Control Chart

Assume the quality characteristic $Y_{ij} \sim N(\mu, \sigma^2)$ to be monitored; when the process is IC, it is assumed that both process parameters μ and σ are known, i.e., $\mu = \mu_0$ and $\sigma = \sigma_y$, respectively. To monitor the process mean, the classical HWMA chart was recently designed by Abbas [5]. The plotting statistic of the HWMA chart is given as:

$$H_i = \lambda \overline{Y}_i + (1-\lambda)\overline{\overline{Y}}_{i-1}, \tag{1}$$

where λ is known as smoothing parameter that is parameter of the HWMA charting scheme; its value lies between 0 and 1. The HWMA chart is more efficient at small choices of the smoothing parameter λ. Abbas [5] showed that the Shewhart control chart becomes the particular case of the HWMA chart at $\lambda = 1$. Where $\overline{\overline{Y}}_{i-1} = \frac{\sum_{k=1}^{i-1} \overline{Y}_k}{i-1}$ is the mean of the remaining $(i-1)$ sample means, and The $\overline{Y}_i$ is the sample average of ith the sample. Control limits of the HWMA are given as:

$$LCL = \begin{cases} \mu_0 - L\sqrt{\frac{\lambda^2 \sigma_y^2}{n}}, & \text{if } i = 1 \\ \mu_0 - L\sqrt{\frac{\lambda^2 \sigma_y^2}{n} + (1-\lambda)^2 \frac{\sigma_y^2}{n(i-1)}}, & \text{if } i > 1 \end{cases}$$

$$CL = \mu_0, \tag{2}$$

$$UCL = \begin{cases} \mu_0 + L\sqrt{\frac{\lambda^2 \sigma_y^2}{n}}, & \text{if } i = 1 \\ \mu_0 + L\sqrt{\frac{\lambda^2 \sigma_y^2}{n} + (1-\lambda)^2 \frac{\sigma_y^2}{n(i-1)}}, & \text{if } i > 1 \end{cases}$$

where the width of the control chart is known as L. The HWMA chart produces an OOC signal if the H_i statistic presented in Equation (1) goes beyond the control limits described in Equation (2).

2.2. Design Structure of the AHWMA Control Chart

For monitoring the process location, the supplementary-based HWAM (AHWMA) chart was proposed by Adegoke et al. [20]. According to Adegoke et al. [24], the study variable Y_{ij} is correlated with the supplementary variable X_{ij} (Cochran [25]). The regression can be expressed as:

$$R_i = \overline{Y}_i + b_{YX}(\mu_X - \overline{X}_i) \tag{3}$$

where $b_{YX} = \rho_{YX}\left(\frac{\sigma_Y}{\sigma_X}\right)$ is expressed as the regression coefficient. The mean and the variance of the regression estimator are $\mu_R = \mu_Y$ and $\sigma_R^2 = \frac{\sigma_Y^2}{n}(1 - \rho_{YX}^2)$, respectively. The AHWMA charting scheme is given below,

$$D_i = \lambda R_i + (1-\lambda)\overline{R}_{i-1}. \tag{4}$$

In Equation (4) R_i is the regression estimate of the process variable while $\overline{R}_{i-1}$ is the average of all previous samples. The control limits of the AHWMA chart are expressed as:

$$LCL = \begin{cases} \mu_0 - L\sigma_Y\sqrt{\frac{\lambda^2}{n}(1 - \rho_{yx}^2)}, & \text{if } i = 1 \\ \mu_0 - L\sigma_Y\sqrt{(\frac{\lambda^2}{n} + \frac{(1-\lambda)^2}{n(i-1)})(1 - \rho_{yx}^2)}, & \text{if } i > 1 \end{cases}$$

$$CL = \mu_0, \tag{5}$$

$$UCL = \begin{cases} \mu_0 + L\sigma_Y\sqrt{\frac{\lambda^2}{n}(1 - \rho_{yx}^2)}, & \text{if } i = 1 \\ \mu_0 + L\sigma_Y\sqrt{(\frac{\lambda^2}{n} + \frac{(1-\lambda)^2}{n(i-1)})(1 - \rho_{yx}^2)}, & \text{if } i > 1 \end{cases}$$

where L is the width of control limits of the AHWMA control chart and λ is chosen to achieve a desired IC ARL for the chart. The AHWMA chart produces an OOC signal if the D_i statistic presented in Equation (4) goes outside the control limits given in Equation (5).

2.3. Design Structure of the Classical EWMA Control Chart

The classical EWMA charting scheme to examine the process location was suggested by Roberts [4]. The classical EWMA charting statistic is given below:

$$S_i = \lambda \overline{Y}_i + (1-\lambda) S_{i-1}, \tag{6}$$

where S_{i-1} is the information at $(i-1)$th time $E(S_i) = \mu_0$, and $Var(S_i) = \sigma_{\overline{Y}}^2 (\frac{\lambda}{2-\lambda}(1-(1-\lambda)^{2i}))$ are the mean and variance for the IC process. The control limits for the classical EWMA charts are:

$$\begin{aligned} LCL &= \left\{ \mu_0 - L\sigma_{\overline{Y}} \sqrt{\frac{\lambda}{2-\lambda}(1-(1-\lambda)^{2i})}, \right. \\ CL &= \mu_0, \\ UCL &= \left\{ \mu_0 + L\sigma_{\overline{Y}} \sqrt{\frac{\lambda}{2-\lambda}(1-(1-\lambda)^{2i})}. \right. \end{aligned} \tag{7}$$

It is interesting to note that the Shewhart chart is a special case of EWMA at $\lambda = 1$. The classical EWMA chart detects an OOC state if any plotting statistic S_i falls beyond the control limits described in Equation (7).

2.4. Design Structure of the AEWMA Control Chart

The supplementary variable-based EWMA chart for monitoring the process location was suggested by Abbas et al. [12]. Let us assume X_i known as a supplementary variable and is associated with the variable of interest Y_i. The term ρ_{YX} is known as the correlation between the two variables. The bivariate symmetrical distribution can be expressed as $(Y, X) \sim N_2(\mu_Y, \mu_X, \sigma_Y^2, \sigma_X^2, \rho_{YX})$. For monitoring the population mean μ_0, the regression estimator based on supplementary information is given as (Cochran [25]):

$$C_Y = \overline{Y} + b_{YX}(\mu_X - \overline{X}), \tag{8}$$

where $b_{YX} = \rho_{YX}\left(\frac{\sigma_Y}{\sigma_X}\right)$ is presenting change the measures Y due to a one-unit change in X, and in Equation (9) mean and variance of the regression estimator is given below

$$E(C_Y) = \mu_0, Var(C_Y) = \sigma_{\overline{Y}}^2 = \frac{\sigma_Y^2}{n}(1-\rho_{YX}^2) = \frac{\sigma_Y^2 - b_{YX}^2 \sigma_X^2}{n}, \tag{9}$$

C_Y is an unbiased estimator of μ_0 and $Var(C_Y) < Var(\overline{Y})$ for $\rho_{YX}^2 > 0$. The AEWMA statistic based on the regression estimator is defined as

$$E_i = \lambda C_Y + (1-\lambda) E_{i-1} \tag{10}$$

The value of EWMA statistics E_{i-1} presents past information and is taken from the initial to $(i-1)$ sample group. The value E_0 is commonly accepted as equal to the target mean μ_0. The variance $Var(C_Y) = \sigma_{\overline{Y}}^2 = \frac{\sigma_Y^2}{n}(1-\rho_{YX}^2) = \frac{\sigma_Y^2 - b_{YX}^2 \sigma_X^2}{n}$ and its means are the target value of the process. The control limits of the AHWMA control chart are given as;

$$\begin{aligned} LCL &= \left\{ \mu_0 - L\sigma_Y \sqrt{(1-\rho_{YX}^2)(\frac{\lambda}{2-\lambda}(1-(1-\lambda)^{2i}))}, \right. \\ CL &= \mu_0, \\ ULC &= \left\{ \mu_0 + L\sigma_Y \sqrt{(1-\rho_{YX}^2)(\frac{\lambda}{2-\lambda}(1-(1-\lambda)^{2i}))}. \right. \end{aligned} \tag{11}$$

The AEWMA charting scheme detects OOC if any plotting statistic falls beyond the control limits.

3. Proposed TAHWMA Control Chart

The design structure of the proposed TAHWMA control chart and performance metrics are discussed in this section. The proposed TAHWMA structure is designed under the presence and absence of multicollinearity.

3.1. Design Structure of the Proposed TAHWMA Control Chart

This section of the article provides the detailed design structure of the proposed TAHWMA charting scheme. Here three variables are selected from a trivariate symmetrical distribution such as Y, X, and Z. X and Z are the supplementary variables, and Y presents the study variable. The matrix form of the variables is organized below:

$$\begin{pmatrix} Y \\ X \\ Z \end{pmatrix} \sim N_3 \left(\begin{pmatrix} \mu_Y \\ \mu_X \\ \mu_Z \end{pmatrix}, \begin{pmatrix} \sigma_{yy} & \sigma_{yx} & \sigma_{yz} \\ \sigma_{xy} & \sigma_{xx} & \sigma_{xz} \\ \sigma_{zy} & \sigma_{zx} & \sigma_{zz} \end{pmatrix} \right)$$

The regression-based estimator initiated by Kadilar and Cingi [26] is given as,

$$G_i = \bar{y} + b_{yx}(\mu_x - \bar{x}) + b_{yz}(\mu_z - \bar{z}), \tag{12}$$

where $\left(b_{yx} = \frac{s_{yx}}{s_{xx}}\right)$ and $\left(b_{yz} = \frac{s_{yz}}{s_{zz}}\right)$ are the regression coefficient, s_{yx} and s_{yz} are sample covariances of Y, X and Y, Z. While s_{xx} and s_{zz} are the sample variances of X and Z, respectively. The mean and variance of Equation (12) are $E(G) = \mu_G = \mu_0$ $Var(G) = \sigma_G^2 = (1 - \rho_{yx}^2 - \rho_{yz}^2 + 2\rho_{yx}\rho_{yz}\rho_{xz})\frac{\sigma_Y^2}{n}$, respectively (cf. Kadilar and Cingi [27]). The proposed TAHWMA charting scheme based on the regression estimator (in Equation (12)) is given as,

$$H_i = \lambda G_i + (1 - \lambda)\overline{\overline{G}}_{i-1} \tag{13}$$

$$LCL = \begin{cases} \mu_0 - L\sqrt{\frac{\lambda^2 \sigma_G^2}{n}}, & \text{if } i = 1 \\ \mu_0 - L\sqrt{\frac{\lambda^2 \sigma_G^2}{n} + (1-\lambda)^2 \frac{\sigma_G^2}{n(i-1)}}, & \text{if } i > 1 \end{cases}$$

$$CL = \mu_0, \tag{14}$$

$$UCL = \begin{cases} \mu_0 + L\sqrt{\frac{\lambda^2 \sigma_G^2}{n}}, & \text{if } i = 1 \\ \mu_0 + L\sqrt{\frac{\lambda^2 \sigma_G^2}{n} + (1-\lambda)^2 \frac{\sigma_G^2}{n(i-1)}}, & \text{if } i > 1 \end{cases}$$

Control limits of the proposed TAHWMA control chart are presented in Equation (14), where L represents the width of the control limits. Simulation codes are established in R software for the performance evaluation of the proposed chart. The amount of shift in the process mean can be mathematically expressed as $\delta = \frac{|\mu_1 - \mu_0|}{\sigma_y/\sqrt{n}}$, where μ_1 denotes the shifted mean of the study variable and $n = 1$, has taken without loss generality. We use 50,000 iterations in simulation to find the desired average run length. The proposed TAHWMA control chart has two designed parameters λ, and L. λ is identified as the smoothing parameter, and the various values of the λ is $\lambda \in \{0.03, 0.05, 0.1, 0.25\}$ are considered in this study.

3.2. Performance Metrics

In this section, a detailed discussion of the run length properties of the proposed TAHWMA control chart is carried out using run-length (RL) characteristics. The run length (RL) is defined as the number of sample observations before a chart alarm describes as run-length (RL). Extra quadratic loss (EQL) is also taken as the performance measure of run-length properties, describing the charting schemes' overall effectiveness. EQL is mathematically defined as $EQL = \frac{1}{\delta_{max} - \delta_{min}} \int_{\delta_{min}}^{\delta_{max}} \sigma^2 ARL(\delta) d\delta$. Another performance measure is the relative mean index (RMI). Mathematically it is defined as $RMI = \frac{1}{N}\sum_{i=1}^{N}\frac{ARL(\delta)-ARL^*(\delta)}{ARL^*(\delta)}$. Where N represents the number of shifts to be considered. For the specific shift δ, $ARL(\delta)$ is the ARL_1 value of a control chart, while $ARL^*(\delta)$ represents the smallest value of the ARL_1. The percentage decrease in ARL is ARL_d, where $ARL_d = \left(\frac{ARL_0 - ARL_1}{ARL_0}\right) \times 100\%$. ARL_0 shows the ARL when the process is working in stable conditions and ARL_1 presents ARL values when the process is in an OOC situation. For each value of λ, the ARL_0 is fixed at 500 using the Monte Carlo simulation method. A comprehensive discussion on the RL distribution of the newly suggested TAHWMA charting scheme is examined under the appearance and non-appearance of the multicollinearity among the two supplementary characteristics.

3.2.1. Performance of the Proposed TAHWMA Control Chart under the Non-Appearance of Multicollinearity

In this section, we examined the performance of the suggested TAHWMA charting scheme under the appearance and non-appearance of multicollinearity among the two supplementary variables. If there is no relationship between the supplementary variable such as $\rho_{xz} = 0$, both supplementary variables have a partial effect on the study variable. Under the appearance of multicollinearity, the ARL values of the suggested TAHWMA charting scheme at several choices of the parameters are given in Table 1. For tracing the small shift in the process mean, it is obvious that small choices of smoothing parameter, high values of the ρ_{YX} and ρ_{YZ}, and the suggested TAHWMA charting scheme becomes more sensitive. The suggested TAHWMA charting scheme with designed parameters $\lambda = 0.03$, $L = 2.272$, $\rho_{YX} = 0.25$ and $\rho_{YZ} = 0.50$, provides $ARL_1 = 330.14$ and $ARL_d = 33.97\%$ at $\delta = 0.05$. At $\lambda = 0.03$, $L = 2.272$, $\rho_{YX} = 0.75$ and $\rho_{YZ} = 0.50$, at 3% increase in the process mean the suggested TAHWMA charting scheme yields $ARL_d = 65.05\%$ (see Table 1). The effect of the ρ_{YX} and ρ_{YZ} on the performance of the proposed TAHWMA model can be seen in Figures 1 and 2. From Figures 1 and 2, it can be observed that the values of ρ_{YX} and ρ_{YZ} increase, and the performance of the suggested TAHWMA charting scheme also becomes highly sensitive.

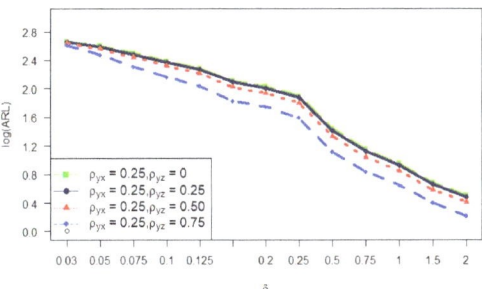

Figure 1. The performance of the proposed TAHWMA control chart at fixed ρ_{yx} and various choices of ρ_{yz}.

3.2.2. Performance of the Proposed TAHWMA Control Chart under the Appearance of Multicollinearity

If some linear relationship occurs between the two supplementary variables, this term is expressed as multicollinearity (cf. Hocking and Pendleton [26]). Unfortunately, multicollinearity happens due to mistakes or a lack of understanding of the model. It is vital to know about the effect of multicollinearity between two supplementary variables on the performance of the suggested TAHWMA charting scheme. The performance of the suggested TAHWMA charting scheme is reported at various choices of correlation between two supplementary characteristics, i.e., $\rho_{xz} \in 0.05, 0.15$, and 0.25 (cf. Table 2). In Table 2, it can be noticed that as the value ρ_{xz} increases, the performance of the suggested

TAEWMA charting structure decreases. For example, at $\lambda = 0.05$, $L = 2.633$ and $\rho_{xz} = 0.05$ at $\delta = 0.05$, the proposed scheme provides $ARL_1 = 349.49$ and at $\rho_{xz} = 0.25$, $\lambda = 0.05$ it gives $ARL_1 = 354.30$ respectively (cf. Table 2).

Table 1. ARL values of the proposed TAHWMA chart in absence of multicollinearity at various choices of design parameters.

	Small Shifts						Moderate Shifts						Large Shifts		
	$\lambda = 0.03, L = 2.272$			$\lambda = 0.05, L = 2.608$			$\lambda = 0.10, L = 2.938$			$\lambda = 0.25, L = 3.075$		
δ	$\rho_{yx}=0.25$	$\rho_{yx}=0.5$	$\rho_{yx}=0.75$	$\rho_{yx}=0.25$	$\rho_{yx}=0.5$	$\rho_{yx}=0.75$	$\rho_{yx}=0.25$	$\rho_{yx}=0.5$	$\rho_{yx}=0.75$	$\rho_{yx}=0.25$	$\rho_{yx}=0.5$	$\rho_{yx}=0.75$
	$\rho_{yz}=0.50, \rho_{xz}=0$			$\rho_{yz}=0.50, \rho_{xz}=0$			$\rho_{yz}=0.50, \rho_{xz}=0$			$\rho_{yz}=0.50, \rho_{xz}=0$		
0	499.92	500.59	500.50	500.87	500.48	500.00	499.70	499.68	500.22	500.96	499.81	500.92
0.03	422.12	393.17	291.19	432.70	408.11	315.37	439.43	421.68	335.05	466.80	455.76	398.38
0.05	330.14	288.40	174.72	345.68	310.76	194.21	362.74	330.82	218.70	419.96	392.24	290.20
0.075	226.50	193.27	104.73	254.06	217.28	120.66	272.73	237.35	136.16	346.73	310.04	189.49
0.1	165.07	136.69	69.23	186.99	157.06	81.87	208.11	173.65	91.86	274.62	239.11	127.87
0.125	125.40	100.83	48.69	144.15	118.10	59.37	160.82	132.53	66.29	223.38	184.65	89.11
0.175	79.36	62.04	28.51	92.93	74.41	35.17	103.92	83.45	39.74	145.17	114.72	50.07
0.2	64.22	50.32	22.92	76.32	60.70	28.69	85.96	68.58	32.40	117.87	92.28	39.13
0.25	45.82	35.69	15.80	55.40	43.76	19.81	62.29	48.84	22.81	82.98	63.02	26.01
0.5	14.74	11.35	5.34	18.53	14.13	6.48	21.19	16.43	7.44	24.20	18.19	7.52
0.75	7.69	6.09	3.08	9.40	7.33	3.61	11.02	8.57	4.08	11.53	8.76	3.95
1	5.01	4.02	2.11	6.00	4.75	2.46	6.88	5.44	2.71	7.09	5.44	2.61
1.5	2.89	2.36	1.21	3.40	2.76	1.35	3.81	3.08	1.50	3.68	2.93	1.45
2	1.97	1.58	1.02	2.31	1.84	1.03	2.58	2.07	1.06	2.44	1.95	1.06

Table 2. ARL values of proposed TAHWMA control chart under the presence of multicollinearity when $\rho_{yx} = 0.25$ and $\rho_{yz} = 0.50$.

| | $\rho_{xz} = 0.05$ | | | $\rho_{xz} = 0.15$ | | | $\rho_{xz} = 0.25$ | | |
| | $\lambda = 0.05, L = 2.633$ | | | $\lambda = 0.05, L = 2.679$ | | | $\lambda = 0.05, L = 2.719$ | | |
δ	ARL	SDRL	MDRL	ARL	SDRL	MDRL	ARL	SDRL	MDRL
0	501.18	372.02	438	499.75	372.26	437	495.53	368.77	436
0.03	434.94	329.12	376	434.31	331.05	373	429.45	329.72	367
0.05	349.49	274.23	291	353.02	278.69	295	354.30	279.99	294
0.075	253.89	200.40	210	261.87	204.59	216	262.13	205.74	218
0.1	190.50	147.65	160	192.57	150.72	161	196.71	154.48	164
0.125	145.68	110.16	123	150.41	114.68	127	151.95	116.03	127
0.175	94.24	69.61	81	96.52	71.67	82	98.10	73.09	83
0.2	78.06	56.57	67	79.25	57.85	68	81.47	59.95	69
0.25	56.42	40.24	49	57.62	41.41	50	58.68	41.95	51
0.5	18.59	12.44	16	19.24	12.93	17	19.58	13.27	17
0.75	9.53	5.95	8	9.87	6.20	9	10.08	6.33	9
1	6.17	3.49	6	6.23	3.51	6	6.41	3.67	6
1.5	3.44	1.74	3	3.52	1.77	3	3.60	1.85	3
2	2.34	1.26	3	2.40	1.28	3	2.44	1.31	3

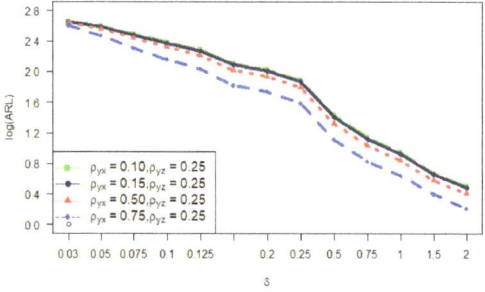

Figure 2. The performance of the proposed TAHWMA control chart at several choices of ρ_{yx} and fixed ρ_{yz}.

4. Comparative Study

In this section, a comparison of the proposed TAHWMA chart is provided against some existing control charts. The ARL is a comparative index for classical EWMA, AEWMA, HWMA, AHWMA, and proposed TAHWMA charts.

4.1. Proposed Versus EWMA and AEWMA Control Charts

The classical EWMA charting scheme is famous for examining the small shifts in the process; the classical EWMA chart was initiated by Roberts [4]. Abbas et al. [12] suggested a new charting scheme, AEWMA, for the efficient monitoring of the process mean. In Table 3, ARL values of both existing charting schemes such as classical EWMA and AEWMA are described. At $\lambda = 0.05$ and $\delta = 0.075$ classical EWMA yields $ARL_1 = 338.65$ and for AEWMA at $\lambda = 0.05$ and $\delta = 0.075$ $\rho_{yx} = 0.25$, $ARL_1 = 328.86$ respectively. The proposed TAHWMA chart at $\lambda = 0.05$, $\delta = 0.075$, $\rho_{yx} = 0.25$ and $\rho_{yz} = 0.50$ produces $ARL_1 = 254.06$, respectively (cf. Table 1). From Tables 1 and 3, we noticed that the suggested TAHWMA charting scheme performs more efficiently than AEWMA and classical EWMA charting schemes to detect small and moderate shifts in the process mean level.

Table 3. The ARL values of the EWMA and AEWMA control charts.

δ	EWMA				AEWMA ($\rho_{yx} = 0.25$)			
	$\lambda = 0.03$ $L = 2.483$	$\lambda = 0.05$ $L = 2.639$	$\lambda = 0.1$ $L = 2.824$	$\lambda = 0.25$ $L = 3.001$	$\lambda = 0.03$ $L = 2.483$	$\lambda = 0.05$ $L = 2.639$	$\lambda = 0.1$ $L = 2.824$	$\lambda = 0.25$ $L = 3.001$
0	500.64	499.68	500.94	499.79	500.33	500.36	500.39	500.78
0.03	456.41	462.91	480.81	488.19	453.72	466.58	475.58	484.32
0.05	388.18	412.31	438.70	466.30	382.72	408.43	438.29	462.55
0.075	304.78	338.65	376.08	435.67	301.97	328.86	372.44	427.63
0.1	232.24	266.78	318.91	390.56	229.75	262.54	314.47	384.82
0.125	181.85	211.65	264.66	346.91	177.55	202.55	251.93	336.03
0.175	113.49	135.20	177.02	262.29	110.97	130.36	168.29	254.75
0.2	93.56	111.53	148.70	224.77	90.34	106.50	139.50	219.07
0.25	67.29	76.75	102.97	169.33	63.26	73.58	97.39	161.22
0.5	21.19	23.74	29.12	47.85	20.25	22.26	26.81	44.31
0.75	10.77	11.93	13.58	19.27	10.14	11.18	12.78	18.02
1	6.60	7.40	8.25	10.38	6.34	6.92	7.71	9.76
1.5	3.42	3.77	4.17	4.79	3.29	3.59	3.98	4.49
2	2.25	2.41	2.65	2.93	2.15	2.31	2.52	2.80

4.2. Proposed Versus HWMA and AHWMA Control Charts

The HWMA scheme was recently developed by Abbas [5] to address small changes in the process mean. To increase the sensitivity of the HWMA model, Adegoke et al. [24] designed the AHWMA chart using a regression estimator that is based on the single supplementary variable. The values of ARL for both classical HWMA and AHWMA control charts are given in Table 4 at various combinations of designed parameters. For example, At $\lambda = 0.03$ the classical HWMA scheme yields $ARL_1 = 205.43$ at $\delta = 0.1$. For the AHWMA chart, at $\rho_{yx} = 0.25$, $\lambda = 0.3$ and $\delta = 0.1$, the value of $ARL_1 = 199.38$ (cf. Table 4). The suggested TAHWMA charting scheme at $\lambda = 0.03$, $\delta = 0.1$ and $\rho_{yx} = 0.25$ and $\rho_{yz} = 0.50$ yields $ARL_1 = 165.07$ (cf. Table 1). The supremacy of the suggested TAHWMA charting scheme is obvious over the classical HWMA and AHWMA schemes (cf. Tables 1 and 4).

In Table 5, the relative mean index (RMI) and extra quadratic loss (EQL) are also considered performance measures. For the proposed TAHWMA control chart $\lambda \in (0.03, 0.05, 0.1, 0.25)$ is used when $\rho_{yx} = 0.75$, $\rho_{yz} = 0.50$, and $\rho_{xz} = 0$. Other existing charting schemes such as HWMA, EWMA, AEWMA, and AHWMA are also considered when $\lambda = 0.03$. For the proposed TAHWMA chart, when $\lambda = 0.03$, RMI has a minimum value of zero and the proposed TAHWMA chart also has the minimum value of the EQL, which is 2.12. The minimum values of the RMI and EQL show the supremacy of the suggested TAHWMA charting scheme against its existing charting structure.

Table 4. The ARL values of the HWMA and AHWMA control charts.

δ	HWMA				AHWMA ($\rho_{yx}=0.25$)			
	$\lambda = 0.03$ $L = 2.272$	$\lambda = 0.05$ $L = 2.608$	$\lambda = 0.1$ $L = 2.938$	$\lambda = 0.25$ $L = 3.075$	$\lambda = 0.03$ $L = 2.272$	$\lambda = 0.05$ $L = 2.608$	$\lambda = 0.1$ $L = 2.938$	$\lambda = 0.25$ $L = 3.075$
0	500.70	499.35	499.48	499.69	499.98	500.18	500.96	500.34
0.03	440.12	449.24	456.35	473.57	442.47	448.12	453.61	473.88
0.05	359.03	382.47	397.11	441.31	359.39	380.54	393.94	445.27
0.075	274.16	298.00	313.35	382.72	266.64	286.42	310.21	377.80
0.1	205.43	229.66	250.83	329.77	199.38	222.00	242.77	317.69
0.125	158.89	179.95	201.22	270.99	151.54	174.35	191.82	265.10
0.175	101.43	119.55	133.63	187.62	97.86	115.19	127.79	179.99
0.2	84.52	99.66	111.81	158.76	80.32	96.17	106.49	148.73
0.25	61.19	73.06	81.59	113.01	58.59	69.15	78.16	106.86
0.5	20.08	25.26	28.57	33.96	19.09	23.76	27.27	31.84
0.75	10.36	12.80	14.89	16.12	9.82	12.25	14.07	15.24
1	6.64	7.99	9.37	9.74	6.28	7.63	8.81	9.14
1.5	3.72	4.41	4.97	4.92	3.56	4.22	4.75	4.66
2	2.55	3.00	3.33	3.18	2.44	2.85	3.18	3.05

Table 5. ARL comparisons of the proposed TAHWMA and the existing control chart.

Shift	TAHWMA				EWMA	AEWMA	HWMA	AHWMA
	$\lambda = 0.03$	$\lambda = 0.05$	$\lambda = 0.1$	$\lambda = 0.25$	$\lambda = 0.03$	$\lambda = 0.03$	$\lambda = 0.03$	$\lambda = 0.03$
0	500.5	500	500.22	500.92	500.64	500.33	500.7	499.98
0.03	291.19	315.37	335.05	398.38	456.41	453.72	440.12	442.47
0.05	174.72	194.21	218.7	290.2	388.18	382.72	359.03	359.39
0.075	104.73	120.66	136.16	189.49	304.78	301.97	274.16	266.64
0.1	69.23	81.87	91.86	127.87	232.24	229.75	205.43	199.38
0.125	48.69	59.37	66.29	89.11	181.85	177.55	158.89	151.54
0.175	28.51	35.17	39.74	50.07	113.49	110.97	101.43	97.86
0.2	22.92	28.69	32.4	39.13	93.56	90.34	84.52	80.32
0.25	15.8	19.81	22.81	26.01	67.29	63.26	61.19	58.59
0.5	5.34	6.48	7.44	7.52	21.19	20.25	20.08	19.09
0.75	3.08	3.61	4.08	3.95	10.77	10.14	10.36	9.82
1	2.11	2.46	2.71	2.61	6.6	6.34	6.64	6.28
1.5	1.21	1.35	1.5	1.45	3.42	3.29	3.72	3.56
2	1.02	1.03	1.06	1.06	2.25	2.15	2.55	2.44
EQL	2.12	2.37	2.61	2.60	6.28	6.01	6.48	6.18
RMI	0.00	0.17	0.30	0.52	2.21	2.10	2.03	1.91

In Figure 3, the supremacy of the proposed TAHWMA charting structure (in terms of smallest ARL$_1$) is evident compared to all the competitors at small, moderate and large shifts in the process mean. The performance of the AHWMA scheme is the second best.

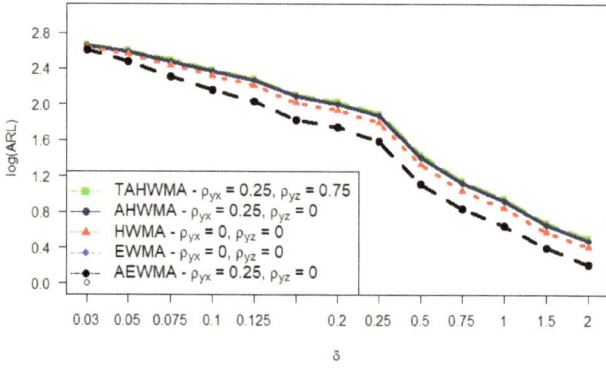

Figure 3. The OOC performance of the proposed TAHWMA and existing control charts.

5. Illustrative Example

Along with exploring the several properties of the suggested TAHWMA charting scheme hypothetically, it is necessary to offer an illustrative example of the developed design. Two examples are presented in this section to show the supremacy of the proposed TAHWMA chart; one consists of the real dataset and the second is based on simulated data. The first real dataset belongs to the carbon fibre tube (manufacturing data), and the second dataset is taken from the trivariate normal distribution.

5.1. Real-Life Application

In this section, a real dataset example related to manufacturing carbon fibre (graphite fibre) tubes is used to show the application of the proposed TAWHMA chart and its competitors. This carbon dataset is used from the R statistical package "MSQC" and is also used by Abbasi and Adegoke [28]. Carbon fibre tubes are frequently comprised of carbon atoms. It has numerous assets for illustration, high tensile strength, low weight, etc. (cf. Zhang et al. [29]). It is a polymer that is solid but lightweight. It is used to manufacture aircraft, cars, and many other machinery parts. Carbon fibre is produced from polyacrylonitrile (PAN) and a small quantity of petroleum pitch. Carbon fibre is much stronger than steel; it is a fibre having many characteristics, and the size of the fibre is nearly equal to 5 to 10 micrometres. It is low-density material but has high-temperature tolerance, high chemical resistance, high stiffness, and high tensile strength.

In this analysis, Y represents the inner diameter, X represents thickness, and Z represents length. These are the first and second supplementary variables, respectively. These variables belong to the manufacturing process of the fiber tubes. A dataset has 30 samples, where 10 samples are taken with 0.05 amount of shift in the process mean, and 20 samples are taken as the IC process. For the execution of the proposed TAHWMA plotting scheme and prevailing schemes, planned parameters are set at the desired value of ARL = 500 for all the charts included in this example. Some descriptive statistics of the carbon fibre data of the first 20 samples are; $\overline{X}$ is 1.022, and $\overline{Z}$ is 50.1005 and $\overline{Y}$ is 0.993. where $s_y^2 = 0.001706316$, $s_x^2 = 0.01139579$, $s_z^2 = 0.05572079$, $\rho_{yx} = 0.2778609$, $\rho_{yz} = 0.617334$, $\rho_{xz} = 0.1219354$. Figures 4 and 5 show that the HWMA and AHWMA charts are not detecting a 0.05 amount of shift at any sample, whereas the proposed TAHWMA charting structure drops this change at the 25th to 30th sample observations (cf. Figure 6).

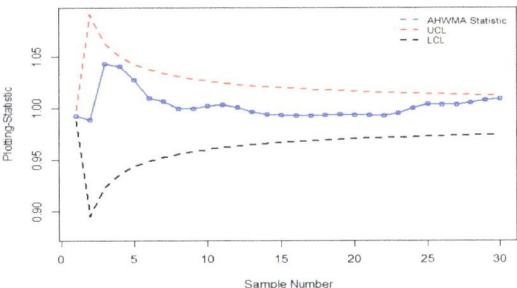

Figure 4. The real-life application of the AHWMA control chart when ($\rho_{YX} = 0.25$, $L = 2.608$).

In detecting the small changes in the process mean compared to its counterparts, the real-life application indicates that the suggested TAHWMA charting structure is the most powerful tool.

5.2. Simulation Study

This section describes the application using the hypothetical dataset to implement the planned design. In this simulated part of the study, the dataset consists of 50 samples. These 50 samples belong to trivariate symmetrical distribution; for the IC process, 25 samples are considered, and 25 samples are incorporated with a shift of 0.5 in the process mean for the

OOC process. The execution of the recommended charting structure is executed considering the appearance and non-appearance of multicollinearity among the two supplementary variables. Further details on the selection of designed parameters for the proposed and existing counterparts are given in Figures 7–10. From Figures 7–10, it can be observed that all the charts remain in the IC situation for the first 25 samples. In Figure 7, the application of the proposed TAHWMA chart is provided when there is no multicollinearity between the supplementary variables, and it traces a shift at the 39th samples. In Figure 8, the presentation of the proposed TAHWMA control chart is delivered when multicollinearity exists between the supplementary variables. The proposed TAHWMA chart traces the shift at the 41st samples in this case. In Figure 9, the existing chart, namely the HWMA chart, outlines the shift at the 49th samples. In Figure 10, the existing chart, namely the AHWMA chart, detects the shift at 49th samples. Based on the discussion, it is observed that the proposed TAHWMA charting scheme has performed efficiently against existing charting schemes, particularly in the non-appearance of multicollinearity among the two supplementary variables.

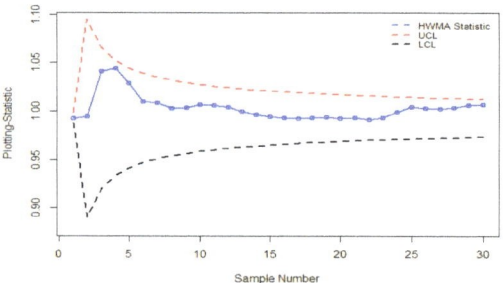

Figure 5. The real-life application of the HWMA control chart when ($L = 2.608$).

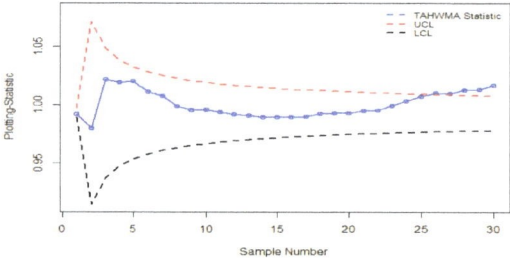

Figure 6. The real-life application of the proposed TAHWMA control chart when ($\lambda = 0.05$; $L = 2.608$).

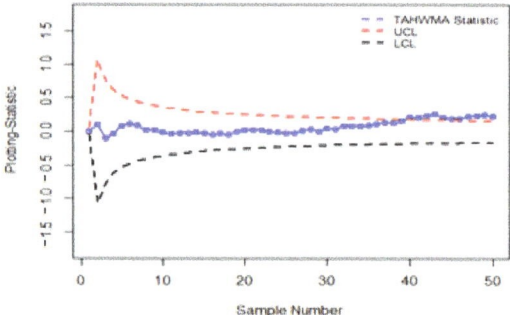

Figure 7. The real-life application of the proposed TAHWMA control chart without multicollinearity with design parameters $L = 2.608$, $\lambda = 0.05$, $\rho_{YX} = 0.25$, $\rho_{YZ} = 0.50$ and $\rho_{XZ} = 0$.

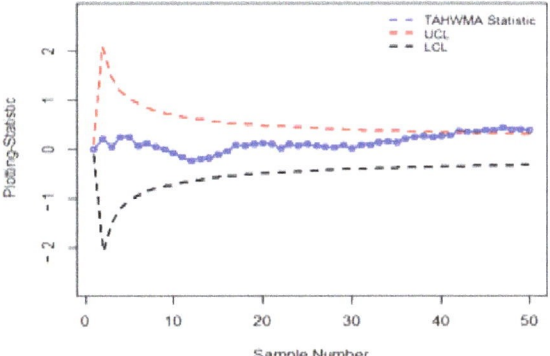

Figure 8. The real-life application of the proposed TAHWMA control chart with multicollinearity with designed parameters $L = 2.633$, $\lambda = 0.05$, $\rho_{YX} = 0.25$, $\rho_{YZ} = 0.50$ and $\rho_{XZ} = 0.05$.

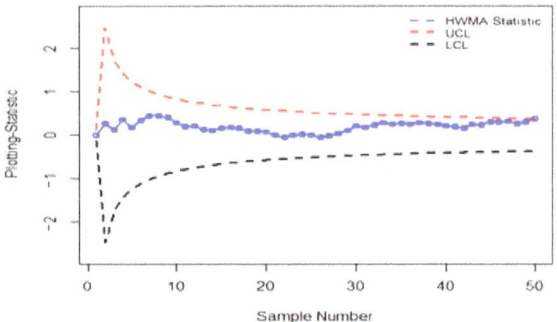

Figure 9. The real-life of the HWMA control chart design parameters ($L = 2.272$, $\lambda = 0.05$).

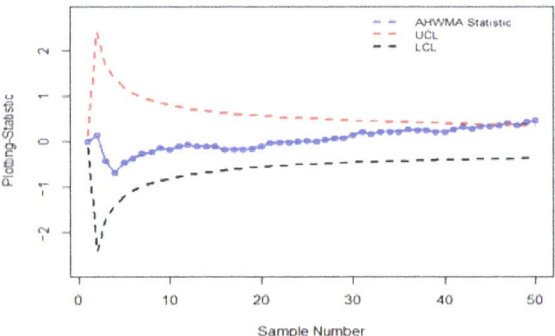

Figure 10. The real-life application of the AHWMA control chart with design parameters ($L = 2.272$, $\lambda = 0.05$, $\rho_{YX} = 0.25$).

6. Summary, Conclusions and Recommendations

The single supplementary information-based (AIB) homogeneously weighted moving (HWMA) chart is an innovative version of the HWMA charting scheme to monitor the process mean shift. This study aims to enhance the HWMA and AIB HWMA charts and propose an HWMA chart based on two supplementary variables, indicated as the TAHWMA charting scheme, to improve the process mean shift monitoring. The run-length characteristic of the proposed TAHWMA charting scheme has been discussed in the absence and presence of multicollinearity between the two supplementary variables. It has been observed that the proposed structure performs better for various correlation coefficient choices, particularly when both supplementary variables consume a fractional effect on the study variable.

To evaluate the performance of the proposed TAHWMA chart against other control existing charts, an algorithm is developed in R software using the Monte Carlo simulation technique to obtain numerical results. Based on numerical results, performance evaluation measures such as ARL, EQL, and RMI are calculated. The analysis based on performance evaluation measures and visual presentation reveals that the proposed charting scheme outperformed existing counterparts. Furthermore, two illustrative examples, one related to the hypothetical dataset and another with regard to a Carbon fibre tube (manufacturing process), are also provided to show the practical implementation of the proposed charting scheme. The proposed charting scheme can be extended for multivariate structures to monitor the process location, dispersion, or both parameters.

Author Contributions: Conceptualization, M.A., S.A.L. and S.A.; methodology, S.A.L. and S.S.; software, N.M.G. and M.A.; validation, S.A., N.M.G. and M.A.; formal analysis, S.A.L. and M.A.; investigation, S.A. and Z.R.; resources, M.A. and S.A.L.; data curation, S.S. and N.M.G.; writing—original draft preparation, M.A. and S.S.; writing—review and editing, Z.R. and S.A.L.; visualization, S.A.L. and Z.R.; supervision, S.A.L. and Z.R.; project administration, S.A.L. and Z.R.; funding acquisition, M.A. and S.A.L. All authors have read and agreed to the published version of the manuscript.

Funding: This research received no external funding.

Institutional Review Board Statement: Not applicable.

Informed Consent Statement: Not applicable.

Data Availability Statement: The data presented in this study are openly available, and a reference is provided.

Conflicts of Interest: The authors declare no conflict of interest.

References

1. Montgomery, D.C. *Introduction to Statistical Quality Control*, 7th ed.; John Wiley & Sons: New York, NY, USA, 2012.
2. Shewhart, W.A. Quality control charts. *Bell Syst. Tech. J.* **1926**, *5*, 593–603. [CrossRef]
3. Page, E.S. Continuous inspection schemes. *Biometrika* **1954**, *41*, 100–115. [CrossRef]
4. Roberts, S. Control chart tests based on geometric moving averages. *Technometrics* **1959**, *1*, 239–250. [CrossRef]
5. Abbas, N. Homogeneously weighted moving average control chart with an application in substrate manufacturing process. *Comput. Ind. Eng.* **2018**, *120*, 460–470. [CrossRef]
6. Haq, A.; Khoo, M.B.C. A new double sampling control chart for monitoring process mean using auxiliary information. *J. Stat. Comput. Simul.* **2017**, *88*, 869–899. [CrossRef]
7. Mandel, B. The regression control chart. *J. Qual. Technol.* **1969**, *1*, 1–9. [CrossRef]
8. Zhang, G. Cause-selecting control charts—A new type of quality control charts. *QR J.* **1985**, *12*, 221–225.
9. Riaz, M. Monitoring process mean level using auxiliary information. *Stat. Neerl.* **2008**, *62*, 458–481. [CrossRef]
10. Riaz, M. Monitoring process variability using auxiliary information. *Comput. Stat.* **2008**, *23*, 253–276. [CrossRef]
11. Riaz, M.; Mehmood, R.; Ahmad, S.; Abbasi, S.A. On the Performance of Auxiliary-based Control Charting under Normality and Nonnormality with Estimation Effects. *Qual. Reliab. Eng. Int.* **2013**, *29*, 1165–1179. [CrossRef]
12. Nuriman, M.A.; Mashuri, M.; Ahsan, M. Auxiliary information based generally weighted moving coefficient of variation (AIB-GWMCV) control chart. *IOP Conf. Ser. Mater. Sci. Eng.* **2021**, *1115*, 012033. [CrossRef]
13. Haq, A.; Khoo, M.B.C. A new synthetic control chart for monitoring process mean using auxiliary information. *J. Stat. Comput. Simul.* **2016**, *86*, 3068–3092. [CrossRef]
14. Abbasi, S.A. Efficient Control Charts for Monitoring Process CV Using Auxiliary Information. *IEEE Access* **2020**, *8*, 46176–46192. [CrossRef]
15. Arslan, M.; Ashraf, M.A.; Anwar, S.M.; Rasheed, Z.; Hu, X.; Abbasi, S.A. Novel Mixed EWMA Dual-Crosier CUSUM Mean Charts without and with Auxiliary Information. *Math. Probl. Eng.* **2022**, 1362193. [CrossRef]
16. Abbas, Z.; Nazir, H.Z.; Akhtar, N.; Riaz, M.; Abid, M. On designing a progressive mean chart for efficient monitoring of process location. *Qual. Reliab. Eng. Int.* **2020**, *36*, 1716–1730. [CrossRef]
17. Chen, J.H.; Lu, S.L. A New Sum of Squares Exponentially Weighted Moving Average Control Chart Using Auxiliary In-formation. *Symmetry* **2020**, *12*, 1888. [CrossRef]

18. Rasheed, Z.; Zhang, H.; Anwar, S.M.; Zaman, B. Homogeneously Mixed Memory Charts with Application in the Substrate Production Process. *Math. Probl. Eng.* **2021**, *2021*, 2582210. [CrossRef]
19. Aslam, M.; Anwar, S.M.; Khan, M.; Abiodun, N.L.; Rasheed, Z. Efficient Auxiliary Information–Based Control Charting Schemes for the Process Dispersion with Application of Glass Manufacturing Industry. *Math. Probl. Eng.* **2022**, 1265204. [CrossRef]
20. Anwar, S.M.; Aslam, M.; Zaman, B.; Riaz, M. Mixed memory control chart based on auxiliary information for simultaneously monitoring of process parameters: An application in glass field. *Comput. Ind. Eng.* **2021**, *156*, 107284. [CrossRef]
21. Rasheed, Z.; Khan, M.; Abiodun, N.L.; Anwar, S.M.; Khalaf, G.; Abbasi, S.A. Improved Nonparametric Control Chart Based on Ranked Set Sampling with Application of Chemical Data Modelling. *Math. Probl. Eng.* **2022**, 7350204. [CrossRef]
22. Zhang, H.; Rasheed, Z.; Khan, M.; Namangale, J.J.; Anwar, S.M.; Hamid, A. A Distribution-Free THWMA Control Chart under Ranked Set Sampling. *Math. Probl. Eng.* **2022**, *2022*, 3823013. [CrossRef]
23. Zichuan, M.; Arslana, M.; Abbasb, Z.; Abbasic, S.A.; Zafar, H. Improving the Performance of EWMA mean chart using Two Auxiliary Variables. *Rev. Argent. Clin. Psicol.* **2020**, *29*, 2016–2024.
24. Adegoke, N.A.; Smith, A.N.H.; Anderson, M.J.; Sanusi, R.A.; Pawley, M.D.M. Efficient Homogeneously Weighted Moving Average Chart for Monitoring Process Mean Using an Auxiliary Variable. *IEEE Access* **2019**, *7*, 94021–94032. [CrossRef]
25. Cochran, W.G. *Sampling Techniques*, 3rd ed.; Wiley: New York, NY, USA, 1977.
26. Abbas, N.; Ahmad, S.; Riaz, M. Reintegration of auxiliary information based control charts. *Comput. Ind. Eng.* **2022**, *171*, 108479. [CrossRef]
27. Kadilar, C.; Cingi, H. A new estimator using two auxiliary variables. *Appl. Math. Comput.* **2005**, *162*, 901–908. [CrossRef]
28. Abbasi, S.A.; Adegoke, N.A. Auxiliary—information—based efficient variability control charts for Phase I of SPC. *Qual. Reliabil. Eng. Int.* **2020**, *36*, 2322–2337. [CrossRef]
29. Zhang, G. A new type of control charts and a theory of diagnosis with control charts. In *World Quality Congress Transactions*; American Society for Quality Control: Milwaukee, WI, USA, 1984; pp. 175–185.

Disclaimer/Publisher's Note: The statements, opinions and data contained in all publications are solely those of the individual author(s) and contributor(s) and not of MDPI and/or the editor(s). MDPI and/or the editor(s) disclaim responsibility for any injury to people or property resulting from any ideas, methods, instructions or products referred to in the content.

Article

Estimation of the Modified Weibull Additive Hazards Regression Model under Competing Risks

Habbiburr Rehman [1], Navin Chandra [2,*], Takeshi Emura [3] and Manju Pandey [4]

1. Department of Medicine (Biomedical Genetics), Boston University Chobanian & Avedisian School of Medicine, Boston, MA 02118, USA
2. Department of Statistics, Ramanujan School of Mathematical Sciences, Pondicherry University, Puducherry 605014, India
3. Biostatistics Center, Kurume University, Kurume 8300011, Japan
4. Department of Zoology and DST Centre for Mathematical Sciences, Institute of Sciences, Banaras Hindu University, Varanasi 221005, India
* Correspondence: nc.stat@gmail.com

Abstract: The additive hazard regression model plays an important role when the excess risk is the quantity of interest compared to the relative risks, where the proportional hazard model is better. This paper discusses parametric regression analysis of survival data using the additive hazards model with competing risks in the presence of independent right censoring. In this paper, the baseline hazard function is parameterized using a modified Weibull distribution as a lifetime model. The model parameters are estimated using maximum likelihood and Bayesian estimation methods. We also derive the asymptotic confidence interval and the Bayes credible interval of the unknown parameters. The finite sample behaviour of the proposed estimators is investigated through a Monte Carlo simulation study. The proposed model is applied to liver transplant data.

Keywords: cause-specific hazard; regression model; additive hazard; modified Weibull distribution; Bayes estimate; MCMC

Citation: Estimation of the Modified Weibull Additive Hazards Regression Model under Competing Risks. *Symmetry* 2023, 15, 485. https://doi.org/10.3390/sym15020485

Academic Editors: Quanxin Zhu, Arne Johannssen and Nataliya Chukhrova

Received: 13 January 2023
Revised: 3 February 2023
Accepted: 5 February 2023
Published: 12 February 2023

Copyright: © 2023 by the authors. Licensee MDPI, Basel, Switzerland. This article is an open access article distributed under the terms and conditions of the Creative Commons Attribution (CC BY) license (https://creativecommons.org/licenses/by/4.0/).

1. Introduction

In time-to-event analysis, the survival time, $T > 0$, represents the duration until the occurrence of an event and is the variable of interest. The hazard function, $h(t)$, has received great attention among practitioners to model the risk of occurrence of an event in the particular interval $[t, t + \Delta t)$. Regression models are often used in survival analysis to investigate the causal relationship between survival outcome and covariates. In the statistical literature, the well-known proportional hazards (PH) approach [1] has gained popularity in modelling covariate effects on the survival of the individual. In the PH model, the effect of the covariates acts multiplicatively on some unknown baseline hazard rate function. However, there are occasions where a measure of the additive effect of covariates is preferred over a multiplicative effect [2,3]. Aalen [4] introduced an important alternative to the PH model that is the additive hazards (AH) regression model which was later studied by Lin and Ying [5,6]. In the AH model, the hazard with the associated covariates is defined as the sum of the baseline hazard rate and regression function of the covariates. In a two sample set-up, the PH model concerns the risks ratio, whereas the AH model addresses the risks difference.

In survival studies, it is often possible that an individual has a lifetime with $p \geq 2$ mutually exclusive types of events or competing risks [7,8]. In the competing risks setting, the occurrence of one type of event alters the chance of the occurrence of other types of events. For example, primary biliary cirrhosis (PBC) is a chronic liver disease in which an individual may receive a transplant and experience death in the waiting queue. In breast cancer clinical trials, investigators may be interested in observing events such as local relapse, auxiliary relapse, remote relapse, second malignancy of any kind, and death. Frequently used competing risks modelling methods depend on the observed value of the bivariate random vector (T, C), where T denotes the lifetime (possibly censored) and $C = j, j \in 1, 2, \ldots, p$ is the set of possible causes of failure. In this framework, the basic identifiable quantities are the cause-specific hazard (CSH) function and the cumulative incidence function (CIF). For a comprehensive review and recent developments in competing risks, one may refer to [7,9–13].

In the literature, there is a considerable amount of work on the parametric modelling of competing risks data in the presence of covariates. Jeong and Fine [14] considered the parametric regression analysis for competing risks using the Gompertz distribution as a baseline model. Anjana and Sankaran [15] proposed the reverse cause-specific PH model by assuming an inverse Weibull distribution under left censoring. Lee [16] provided the parametric quantile inference for the CSH function with adjustment of covariates. Lipowski et al. [17] suggested three parametric distributions for competing risks data. Rehman and Chandra [18] presented a survival analysis with competing risks using the parametric PH model under the middle censoring scheme.

Parametric regression modelling of competing risks survival data in the above-mentioned literature is mainly based on Cox's PH model [1]. However, researchers have commonly considered non-parametric and semi-parametric analysis of the AH model in the presence of competing risks. Shen and Cheng [19] proposed the confidence bands for CIF under the AH model. Sun et al. [20] considered the AH model for competing risks analysis of the case-cohort design. Zhang et al. [21] proposed a regression analysis of competing risks data via a semi-parametric AH model. Li et al. [22] analysed an additive sub-distribution hazard model for competing risks data.

Semi-parametric and non-parametric methods are distribution-free approaches, and they are useful in a situation where the distribution function of survival time T is unknown. If the model is adequately specified, however, parametric methods are more efficient than semi-parametric methods [9]. Parametric approaches have two major advantages: predicting future behaviour and the availability of straightforward estimation and inference methods based on the likelihood theory. In this article, we focus on the parametric approach for survival analysis based on the AH model instead of semi-parametric and non-parametric approaches. A parametric AH regression model may be developed by assuming some known distributional form for the baseline hazard function [23]. To the best of our knowledge, survival analysis with competing risks based on a parametric AH regression model has not received much attention, and this is the motivation behind the development of this article. Therefore, the main objective is to employ a parametric AH regression model for competing risks survival data. In this article, we study the modified Weibull distribution (MWD) with one scale and two shape parameters, which is capable of capturing various shapes of the hazard rate, such as bathtub failure rate, and it also accommodates many properties of exponential and Weibull distributions [24].

Another aim of this article is to consider both classical and Bayesian methods of estimation. In traditional statistical inference approaches, parameters are estimated based on the available data in which the maximum likelihood estimator (MLE) usually provides the solution. While dealing with lifetime data, it is obvious that some past information may be available in terms of the past record of the individuals. For example, in medical sciences, before examining a patient, the investigator may be interested in knowing the history of the disease. The MLE does not have the flexibility to incorporate prior information in data analysis. In this context, the Bayesian method of reasoning is well known for incorporating prior information. Furthermore, Bayesian methods provide more accurate estimation results than MLE when the sample size is small. In practice, researchers often consider the gamma prior as an informative prior even if it is not a conjugate prior [25]. However, other researchers consider Weibull, inverted gamma, and log-normal prior as an alternative choice of the gamma prior [26,27]. Therefore, in this article, we choose a class of baseline informative types of prior, namely gamma, Weibull, and log-normal priors for comparison purposes. For regression parameters, we assume uniform priors. The Bayes estimates are obtained based on two different loss functions, viz., squared error (symmetric) and LINEX (asymmetric) loss functions. Interval estimation is also obtained. Asymptotic and Bayes credible intervals of unknown parameters are derived in this setting with respect to classical and Bayesian approaches.

The rest of the paper is organised as follows: we propose a parametric cause-specific AH regression model in Section 2. In Section 3, we estimate the model parameters by using the MLE. In Section 4, the Bayesian estimation is considered under non-informative priors with two loss functions. In Section 5, interval estimation is considered. A Monte Carlo simulation study is carried out to examine the finite sample behaviour of the estimators in Section 6. In Section 7, the applicability of the proposed model is demonstrated with real data. Finally, the concluding remarks are given in Section 8.

2. The Proposed Model

In this study, to develop a regression model for competing risks survival data, we consider the AH regression model given in [5]. In this model, the effect of the covariates vector $x = (x_1, x_2, \ldots, x_m)^\top$ on the baseline hazard function is additive in nature. This model for the CSH rate turns out to be the following form:

$$h_j(t|x) = h_{0j}(t) + \beta_j^\top x, \quad j = 1, 2, \ldots, p, \tag{1}$$

where $h_j(t|x)$ represents the CSH rate for given covariates x, $h_{0j}(t)$ denotes the baseline CSH rate, and $\beta_j = (\beta_{j1}, \beta_{j2}, \ldots, \beta_{jm})^\top$ is the $m \times 1$ vector of cause-specific regression parameters. In the present work, we study the MWD with one scale parameter, a, and two shape parameters, α and λ, for lifetime variate T with the cumulative distribution function and the hazard function given as:

$$F(t) = 1 - \exp(-at^\alpha e^{\lambda t}), \quad t \geq 0, a > 0, \alpha \geq 0, \lambda > 0, \tag{2}$$

$$h(t) = a(\alpha + \lambda t)t^{\alpha-1}e^{\lambda t}, \quad t \geq 0, a > 0, \alpha \geq 0, \lambda > 0. \tag{3}$$

Lai et al. [24] developed the MWD and discussed some of its theoretical properties, for example, the bathtub behaviour of the hazard rate. Ng [28] estimated the parameters of the MWD for progressive type-II censored samples. Furthermore, some Bayesian estimations of MWD parameters were considered in [29,30]. The MWD is assumed here as a baseline model of the cause-specific AH analysis in (1), due to its flexibility to accommodate various shapes of the hazard function.

Accordingly, the CSH function, cumulative CSH function, and overall survival function are obtained as:

$$h_j(t; \Theta_j, x) = a_j(\alpha_j + \lambda_j t)t^{\alpha_j-1}e^{\lambda_j t} + \beta_j^\top x, \tag{4}$$

$$H_j(t; \Theta_j, x) = a_j t^{\alpha_j} e^{\lambda_j t} + \beta_j^\top xt, \tag{5}$$

and

$$S(t; \Theta, x) = \exp\left\{-\left(\sum_{j=1}^p a_j t^{\alpha_j} e^{\lambda_j t} + \beta_j^\top xt\right)\right\}, \tag{6}$$

where $\Theta = (\Theta_1, \Theta_2, \ldots, \Theta_p)$ and $\Theta_j = (a_j, \alpha_j, \lambda_j, \beta_j)$ are the vectors of cause-specific parameters. The main aim of this article is to develop estimation methods for the unknown parameters and cumulative CSH function as the quantity of interest.

3. Maximum Likelihood Estimation

Following the competing risks framework, let T be the observed lifetime which is defined by $T = \min(T^*, D)$, where T^* is the failure time and D is the censoring time. For the given covariate x, T^* and D are assumed to be independent. Furthermore, we assume that for each observed failure time, the associated cause of failure was also observed. Therefore, the censoring indicator is defined as $\delta_{ij} = I(T_i = T_i^*, C_i = j)$.

Let (t_i, δ_{ij}, x_i), $i = 1, 2, \ldots, n$ be the $n \in \mathbb{N}$ independently and identically distributed samples of (T, δ, x). Now, we can write the likelihood function for the observed data as:

$$L(\Theta) = \prod_{i=1}^{n} \left(\prod_{j=1}^{p} h_j(t_i; \Theta_j, x_i)^{\delta_{ij}} S(t_i; \Theta, x_i) \right). \tag{7}$$

The fully parameterized likelihood function based on (4) and (6) is given by:

$$L(\Theta) = \prod_{i=1}^{n} \left[\prod_{j=1}^{p} \left(a_j(\alpha_j + \lambda_j t_i) t_i^{\alpha_j - 1} e^{\lambda_j t_i} + \beta_j^\top x_i \right)^{\delta_{ij}} \right. \\ \left. \times \exp\left\{ -\left(\sum_{j=1}^{p} a_j t_i^{\alpha_j} e^{\lambda_j t_i} + \beta_j^\top x_i t_i \right) \right\} \right]. \tag{8}$$

The log likelihood function $\ell(\Theta) = \log L(\Theta)$ is given as:

$$\ell(\Theta) = \sum_{j=1}^{p} \sum_{i=1}^{n_j} \log\left(a_j(\alpha_j + \lambda_j t_i) t_i^{\alpha_j - 1} e^{\lambda_j t_i} + \beta_j^\top x_i \right) \\ - \sum_{i=1}^{n} \left(\sum_{j=1}^{p} a_j t_i^{\alpha_j} e^{\lambda_j t_i} + \beta_j^\top x_i t_i \right). \tag{9}$$

In Equation (9), n_j denotes the number of failures of type j. To obtain the estimates of the unknown parameters a_j, α_j, λ_j, and β_j, we maximize (9) by equating the partial derivatives of each parameter to zero. The score equations are obtained as:

$$\frac{\partial \ell(\Theta)}{\partial a_j} = \sum_{i=1}^{n_j} \frac{(\alpha_j + \lambda_j t_i) t_i^{\alpha_j - 1} e^{\lambda_j t_i}}{a_j(\alpha_j + \lambda_j t_i) t_i^{\alpha_j - 1} e^{\lambda_j t_i} + \beta_j^\top x_i} - \sum_{i=1}^{n} t_i^{\alpha_j} e^{\lambda_j t_i} = 0, \tag{10}$$

$$\frac{\partial \ell(\Theta)}{\partial \alpha_j} = \sum_{i=1}^{n_j} \frac{a_j t_i^{\alpha_j - 1} e^{\lambda_j t_i} + a_j \alpha_j t_i^{\alpha_j - 1} \log t_i e^{\lambda_j t_i} + a_j \lambda_j t_i^{\alpha_j} \log t_i e^{\lambda_j t_i}}{a_j(\alpha_j + \lambda_j t_i) t_i^{\alpha_j - 1} e^{\lambda_j t_i} + \beta_j^\top x_i} \\ - \sum_{i=1}^{n} a_j t_i^{\alpha_j} \log t_i e^{\lambda_j t_i} = 0, \tag{11}$$

$$\frac{\partial \ell(\Theta)}{\partial \lambda_j} = \sum_{i=1}^{n_j} \frac{a_j \alpha_j t_i^{\alpha_j} e^{\lambda_j t_i} + a_j t_i^{\alpha_j} e^{\lambda_j t_i} + a_j \lambda_j t_i^{\alpha_j + 1} e^{\lambda_j t_i}}{a_j(\alpha_j + \lambda_j t_i) t_i^{\alpha_j - 1} e^{\lambda_j t_i} + \beta_j^\top x_i} \\ - \sum_{i=1}^{n} a_j t_i^{\alpha_j + 1} e^{\lambda_j t_i} = 0, \tag{12}$$

$$\frac{\partial \ell(\Theta)}{\partial \beta_j} = \sum_{i=1}^{n_j} \frac{x_i}{a_j(\alpha_j + \lambda_j t_i) t_i^{\alpha_j - 1} e^{\lambda_j t_i} + \beta_j^\top x_i} - \sum_{i=1}^{n} x_i t_i = 0. \tag{13}$$

The score equations (10)–(13) are not in explicit form and cannot be solved analytically. Therefore, we use numerical methods to estimate the parameters.

Several methodologies are available for estimating parameters in the literature by solving score equations or directly maximizing the log-likelihood function. The Newton–Raphson method is the most frequently used approach for estimation because the derivatives of the scoring equations are simple to calculate. The initial values are critical in the numerical iterative procedure because of the logarithm function. We use the simplex method [31] to estimate the parameters through the optim function in R software. The simplex method is a straightforward method for estimating parameters by maximizing the likelihood function without having to optimize the function's derivatives. Once the parameter estimates are obtained, the function of the parameter estimates can be obtained using the invariance property of the MLE. Therefore, the MLE of the cumulative CSH $H_j(t; \Theta_j, x)$ is given by:

$$\hat{H}_j(t; \hat{\Theta}_j, x) = \hat{a}_j t^{\hat{\alpha}_j} e^{\hat{\lambda}_j t} + \hat{\beta}_j^\top x t.$$

4. Bayesian Estimation

In frequentist statistical techniques, prior information is not considered when analysing data. Bayesian inference is intriguing because it incorporates prior or previous information with observed data. As a result, this article explores the Bayesian analysis of a parametric cause-specific AH regression model. Prior assumptions are made based on previous experiences, mathematical convenience, and expert judgments, which can be informative, non-informative, or weakly informative. If the previous dataset is large enough, informative priors can be employed. A non-informative prior can be used when only limited or vague knowledge (a priori) about the parameters is available. This article considers informative types of priors for baseline parameters, such as the gamma, Weibull, and log-normal distributions. A uniform, non-informative prior is assumed for the regression parameters. Furthermore, it is assumed that all the chosen priors are independent.

4.1. Gamma Prior

We assume that the baseline model parameters a_j, α_j, and λ_j of the modified Weibull cause-specific AH model (4) are independent random variables with gamma informative types of priors. Furthermore, the regression parameters have the prior distributions as uniform distribution. Their respective marginal prior density functions are given as:

$$\begin{aligned}
\pi_{1j}(a_j) &\propto a_j^{q_{1j}-1} e^{-r_{1j} a_j}, & a_j > 0, q_{1j} > 0, r_{1j} > 0, \\
\pi_{1j}(\alpha_j) &\propto \alpha_j^{q_{2j}-1} e^{-r_{2j} \alpha_j}, & \alpha_j > 0, q_{2j} > 0, r_{2j} > 0, \\
\pi_{1j}(\lambda_j) &\propto \lambda_j^{q_{3j}-1} e^{-r_{3j} \lambda_j}, & \lambda_j > 0, q_{3j} > 0, r_{3j} > 0, \\
\pi_{1j}(\beta_j) &\propto \prod_{l=1}^{m} \frac{1}{(d_{jl} - c_{jl})}, & -\infty < c_{jl} < \beta_{jl} < d_{jl} < \infty,
\end{aligned} \quad (14)$$

where r_{1j}, r_{2j}, r_{3j} and q_{1j}, q_{2j}, q_{3j} are the rate and shape hyper-parameters of the baseline gamma priors of a_j, α_j, and λ_j, respectively. The joint prior density function based on the priors defined in (14) is given by:

$$\pi_1(\Theta) \propto \prod_{j=1}^{p} \frac{a_j^{q_{1j}-1} \alpha_j^{q_{2j}-1} \lambda_j^{q_{3j}-1}}{\prod_{l=1}^{m}(d_{jl} - c_{jl})} \exp\left\{-\left(r_{1j} a_j + r_{2j} \alpha_j + r_{3j} \lambda_j\right)\right\}. \quad (15)$$

The hyper-parameters are assumed to be known and chosen in such a way as to reflect the prior belief about the unknown parameters.

4.2. Weibull Prior

We assume that the baseline parameters a_j, α_j, and λ_j of the model (4) are independent random variables with the prior distributions as Weibull distributions. We also assume that the regression parameters have the prior distributions as uniform distributions. Thus, their respective prior density functions are given as:

$$
\begin{aligned}
\pi_{2j}(a_j) &\propto a_j^{k_{1j}-1} e^{-(\theta_{1j}a_j)^{k_{1j}}}, & a_j > 0, k_{1j} > 0, \theta_{1j} > 0, \\
\pi_{2j}(\alpha_j) &\propto \alpha_j^{k_{2j}-1} e^{-(\theta_{2j}\alpha_j)^{k_{2j}}}, & \alpha_j > 0, k_{2j} > 0, \theta_{2j} > 0, \\
\pi_{2j}(\lambda_j) &\propto \lambda_j^{k_{3j}-1} e^{-(\theta_{3j}\lambda_j)^{k_{3j}}}, & \lambda_j > 0, k_{3j} > 0, \theta_{3j} > 0, \\
\pi_{2j}(\beta_j) &\propto \prod_{l=1}^{m} \frac{1}{(d_{jl}-c_{jl})}, & -\infty < c_{jl} < \beta_{jl} < d_{jl} < \infty,
\end{aligned}
\qquad (16)
$$

where k_{1j}, k_{2j}, and k_{3j} are the shape hyper-parameters and θ_{1j}, θ_{2j}, and θ_{3j} are the rate hyper-parameters of the Weibull baseline priors. Therefore, the joint prior distribution of a_j, α_j, λ_j, and β_j, $j = 1, 2, \ldots, p$, based on their prior densities defined in (16), is given by:

$$
\pi_2(\Theta) \propto \frac{a_j^{k_{1j}-1} \alpha_j^{k_{2j}-1} \lambda_j^{k_{3j}-1}}{\prod_{l=1}^{m}(d_{jl}-c_{jl})} \exp\left\{ -\left((\theta_{1j}a_j)^{k_{1j}} + (\theta_{2j}\alpha_j)^{k_{2j}} + (\theta_{3j}\lambda_j)^{k_{3j}}\right) \right\}. \qquad (17)
$$

4.3. Log-Normal Prior

In this subsection, we assume the priors for the baseline parameters as the log-normal distributions. Regression parameters independently follow the uniform distributions. Their corresponding prior densities functions are given as:

$$
\begin{aligned}
\pi_{3j}(a_j) &\propto \frac{1}{a_j} e^{-\frac{1}{2}\left(\frac{\log a_j - \mu_{1j}}{\sigma_{1j}}\right)^2}, & a_j > 0, \sigma_{1j} > 0, -\infty < \mu_{1j} < \infty \\
\pi_{3j}(\alpha_j) &\propto \frac{1}{\alpha_j} e^{-\frac{1}{2}\left(\frac{\log \alpha_j - \mu_{2j}}{\sigma_{2j}}\right)^2}, & \alpha_j > 0, \sigma_{2j} > 0, -\infty < \mu_{2j} < \infty \\
\pi_{3j}(\lambda_j) &\propto \frac{1}{\lambda_j} e^{-\frac{1}{2}\left(\frac{\log \lambda_j - \mu_{3j}}{\sigma_{3j}}\right)^2}, & \lambda_j > 0, \sigma_{3j} > 0, -\infty < \mu_{3j} < \infty \\
\pi_{3j}(\beta_j) &\propto \prod_{l=1}^{m} \frac{1}{(d_{jl}-c_{jl})}, & -\infty < c_{jl} < \beta_{jl} < d_{jl} < \infty,
\end{aligned}
\qquad (18)
$$

where $\mu_{1j}, \mu_{2j}, \mu_{3j}$ and $\sigma_{1j}, \sigma_{2j}, \sigma_{3j}$ are the hyper-parameters. The joint prior distribution of a_j, α_j, λ_j, and $\beta_j, j = 1, 2, \ldots, p$ is the product of their marginal prior densities, given by:

$$
\pi_3(\Theta) \propto \frac{1}{a_j \alpha_j \lambda_j \prod_{l=1}^{m}(d_{jl}-c_{jl})} \exp\left\{ -\frac{1}{2}\left(\left(\frac{\log a_j - \mu_{1j}}{\sigma_{1j}}\right)^2 + \left(\frac{\log \alpha_j - \mu_{2j}}{\sigma_{2j}}\right)^2 + \left(\frac{\log \lambda_j - \mu_{3j}}{\sigma_{3j}}\right)^2 \right) \right\}. \qquad (19)
$$

4.4. Posterior Analysis

The posterior probability distribution is obtained by combining past information with the observed sample using likelihood and prior distribution. Therefore, the joint posterior density of the random variables a_j, α_j, λ_j, and $\boldsymbol{\beta}_j, j = 1, 2, \ldots, p$, given the data, can be written as:

$$p(\Theta|\text{data}) = \frac{L(\text{data}|\Theta)\pi(\Theta)}{\int \int \cdots \int L(\text{data}|\Theta)\pi(\Theta)d\Theta}, \tag{20}$$

where $p(\Theta|\text{data})$ is the joint posterior density, $L(\text{data}|\Theta)$ is the likelihood function for the given observed data as in (8), and $\pi(\Theta)$ is the joint prior density which can be taken from (15), (17) and (19). Under the joint priors, the joint posterior densities are obtained as:

$$\pi_1(\Theta|\text{data}) = K_1 \prod_{j=1}^{p} \left[\prod_{i=1}^{n_j} \left(a_j(\alpha_j + \lambda_j t_i) t_i^{\alpha_j - 1} e^{\lambda_j t_i} + \boldsymbol{\beta}_j^\top \boldsymbol{x}_i \right) \right.$$
$$\left. \times a_j^{q_{1j}-1} \alpha_j^{q_{2j}-1} \lambda_j^{q_{3j}-1} \exp\left\{ -(r_{1j} a_j + r_{2j} \alpha_j + r_{3j} \lambda_j) \right\} \right] \tag{21}$$
$$\times \exp\left\{ -\sum_{i=1}^{n}\sum_{j=1}^{p} \left(a_j t_i^{\alpha_j} e^{\lambda_j t_i} + \boldsymbol{\beta}_j^\top \boldsymbol{x}_i t_i \right) \right\},$$

$$\pi_2(\Theta|\text{data}) = K_2 \prod_{j=1}^{p} \left[\prod_{i=1}^{n_j} \left(a_j(\alpha_j + \lambda_j t_i) t_i^{\alpha_j - 1} e^{\lambda_j t_i} + \boldsymbol{\beta}_j^\top \boldsymbol{x}_i \right) a_j^{k_{1j}-1} \alpha_j^{k_{2j}-1} \right.$$
$$\left. \times \lambda_j^{k_{3j}-1} \exp\left\{ -\left((\theta_{1j} a_j)^{k_{1j}} + (\theta_{2j} \alpha_j)^{k_{2j}} + (\theta_{3j} \lambda_j)^{k_{3j}} \right) \right\} \right] \tag{22}$$
$$\times \exp\left\{ -\sum_{i=1}^{n}\sum_{j=1}^{p} \left(a_j t_i^{\alpha_j} e^{\lambda_j t_i} + \boldsymbol{\beta}_j^\top \boldsymbol{x}_i t_i \right) \right\}.$$

$$\pi_3(\Theta|\text{data}) = K_3 \prod_{j=1}^{p} \left[\prod_{i=1}^{n_j} \left(a_j(\alpha_j + \lambda_j t_i) t_i^{\alpha_j - 1} e^{\lambda_j t_i} + \boldsymbol{\beta}_j^\top \boldsymbol{x}_i \right) \right.$$
$$\times \frac{1}{a_j \alpha_j \lambda_j} \exp\left\{ -\frac{1}{2}\left(\left(\frac{\log a_j - \mu_{1j}}{\sigma_{1j}}\right)^2 + \left(\frac{\log \alpha_j - \mu_{2j}}{\sigma_{2j}}\right)^2 \right.\right. \tag{23}$$
$$\left.\left. + \left(\frac{\log \lambda_j - \mu_{3j}}{\sigma_{3j}}\right)^2 \right) \right\} \right] \exp\left\{ -\sum_{i=1}^{n}\sum_{j=1}^{p} \left(a_j t_i^{\alpha_j} e^{\lambda_j t_i} + \boldsymbol{\beta}_j^\top \boldsymbol{x}_i t_i \right) \right\}.$$

where K_1, K_2, and K_3 are the normalizing constants or they are the denominator part in the right-hand side of Equation (20) according to each joint posterior distribution.

It is not possible to compute the integral in the denominator of (20) analytically under each considered prior due to the complex form of the likelihood function. Therefore, we cannot obtain the posterior density in closed form. Hence, in such a situation, the Markov Chain Monte Carlo (MCMC) method [32] can be used to approximate the integrals. Popularly used MCMC algorithms are the Gibbs sampling algorithm [33] and the Metropolis–Hastings (M–H) algorithm [34]. For the implementation of the Gibbs sampling algorithm, the full conditional distribution of each parameter is required. Therefore, in this situation, the M–H algorithm is preferable.

4.5. Loss Function

The selection of the loss function is vital in Bayesian analysis. We consider two different types of loss functions; namely, the squared error (symmetric) and LINEX (asymmetric) loss functions for a comprehensive comparison of Bayes estimates. The squared error loss function (SELF) for a parameter Θ_j is defined as:

$$L_1(\Theta_j, \hat{\Theta}_j) = (\Theta_j - \hat{\Theta}_j)^2.$$

Then, the Bayes estimate for parameter Θ_j under SELF can be obtained as the posterior means and calculated by:

$$\hat{\Theta}_j^{self} = \frac{1}{N-M} \sum_{l=M+1}^{N} [\Theta_j]_{\Theta_j = \Theta_j^{(l)}},$$

where $\Theta_j^{(l)}, l = 1, 2, \ldots, N$ are the MCMC random samples generated from the posterior distribution of Θ_j and M is the number of iterations used in the burn-in period.

However, we also consider the LINEX loss function (LLF) as an asymmetric loss function, which is given by:

$$L_2(\Theta_j, \hat{\Theta}_j) = e^{\rho(\hat{\Theta}_j - \Theta_j)} - \rho(\hat{\Theta}_j - \Theta_j) - 1, \quad \rho \neq 0.$$

Under LLF, the Bayes estimates of parameter Θ_j can be obtained as follows:

$$\hat{\Theta}_j^{llf} = -\frac{1}{\rho} \log \left(\frac{1}{N-M} \sum_{l=M+1}^{N} e^{-\rho[\Theta_j]_{\Theta_j = \Theta_j^{(l)}}} \right),$$

where ρ is the hyper parameter of the LLF and the magnitude of ρ reflects the degree of asymmetry. For $\rho > 0$, the LLF is quite asymmetric about 0 with overestimation being more serious than underestimation. The vice versa is true for $\rho < 0$. If ρ is close to zero, then the estimates under LLF are approximately equal to the estimates obtained under SELF. Hence, LLF is more applicable in lifetime modelling, for instance, an over-estimation of the survival function and failure rate function is usually much more serious than an under-estimation [35].

5. Interval Estimation

5.1. Asymptotic Confidence Interval

On the basis of the asymptotic property of MLE, we obtained the interval estimates of the unknown parameters in this subsection. The exact distribution of MLEs cannot be obtained because the MLEs of the unknown parameters are not in closed form. The sampling distribution of $\hat{\Theta}$ can be approximated by a $(2p + (p \times m))$ variate normal distribution with a mean, Θ, and a variance-covariance matrix, $\Sigma(\Theta)$, which is nothing but the inverse of the Fisher information matrix, $I(\Theta)$, given by:

$$I(\Theta) = E\left[-\frac{\partial^2 \ell(\Theta)}{\partial \Theta \partial \Theta^\top}\right]_{\Theta = \hat{\Theta}}.$$

The exact mathematical expressions for the above expectations are difficult to obtain; therefore, the observed Fisher information matrix $I_O(\Theta)$ can be used to approximate the Fisher information matrix, $I(\Theta)$, which is obtained by dropping the expectation operator, E, in $I(\Theta)$. The variance of MLEs of the unknown parameters, i.e., $\text{var}(\hat{\Theta})$, is the diagonal elements of the asymptotic variance-covariance matrix, $\Sigma(\hat{\Theta})$. Thus, for a given confidence level γ, a two-sided $100(1-\gamma)\%$ asymptotic confidence interval (ACI) for $\hat{\Theta}$ can be constructed as follows:

$$\left[\hat{\Theta} - z_{\gamma/2}\sqrt{\text{var}(\hat{\Theta})}, \hat{\Theta} + z_{\gamma/2}\sqrt{\text{var}(\hat{\Theta})}\right],$$

where $z_{\gamma/2}$ is the upper $\gamma/2$ quantile of the standard normal distribution. Furthermore, we also computed the two-sided $100(1-\gamma)\%$ confidence interval for the estimates of the cumulative CSH $\hat{H}_j(t;\hat{\Theta}_j,x)$, which is given by:

$$\left[\hat{H}_j(t;\hat{\Theta}_j,x) - z_{\gamma/2}\sqrt{\text{var}(\hat{H}_j(t;\hat{\Theta}_j,x))}, \hat{H}_j(t;\hat{\Theta}_j,x) + z_{\gamma/2}\sqrt{\text{var}(\hat{H}_j(t;\hat{\Theta}_j,x))}\right],$$

where the variance of the cumulative CSH $\text{var}(\hat{H}_j(t;\hat{\Theta}_j,x))$ is obtained by using the delta method as follows:

$$\text{var}(\hat{H}_j(t;\hat{\Theta}_j,x)) = g(\Theta_j)\Sigma(\hat{\Theta})g(\Theta_j)^\top,$$

$$\text{and } g(\Theta_j) = \left.\frac{\partial H_j(t;\Theta_j,x)}{\partial \Theta}\right|_{\Theta=\hat{\Theta}}.$$

5.2. Bayes Credible Interval

In the Bayesian approach, for a γ level of significance, the $(1-\gamma)$ interval estimate of a parameter Θ is a credible interval based on given data, which covers the parameter with $(1-\gamma)$ level of confidence. The $100(1-\gamma)\%$ Bayes credible interval (BCI) $[\Theta_L, \Theta_U]$ for Θ is obtained by setting Θ_L equal to the $\gamma/2\%$ quantile and Θ_U equal to the $(1-\gamma/2)\%$ quantile of $\Theta_l, l = 1, 2, \ldots, N-M$. Similarly, the same procedure is also adopted for obtaining the Bayes credible interval for $H_j(t;\Theta_j,x)$.

6. Simulation Study

We conducted a Monte Carlo simulation study to observe the finite sample behaviour of the proposed estimators of the unknown parameters and cumulative CSH functions. In this simulation study, the datasets were generated for various sample sizes such as $n = 100$, 200, and 400. For each sample size, we have calculated the average estimate (AVE) and the mean square error (MSE) for point estimates, and the average length (AVL) and coverage probability (CP) for ACI and BCI of a_j, α_j, β_j, and $H_j(t|x)$ over 500 replications.

For simplicity, we assumed two causes of failure, i.e., $j = 1, 2$, and one covariate, say x. The covariate x is generated using a Bernoulli random number for each sample with an equal probability of success and failure. Without loss of generality, we have arbitrarily taken the true value of the parameters as $a_1 = 0.5, \alpha_1 = 0.6, \lambda_1 = 0.2, \beta_{11} = 0.6, a_2 = 0.7, \alpha_2 = 0.5, \lambda_2 = 0.2$, and $\beta_{21} = 0.8$. We assume that λ_j is known for mathematical simplicity. The censored time D is generated from $U(0, d)$, where d is chosen in such a way that on average 20% observations are right censored. The survival time T is generated through an inverse transformation following the steps given in [36], Chapter 3. For each simulated survival time, the causes of failure are generated from a Binomial distribution with a probability of success of $\frac{h_1(t|x)}{h_1(t|x)+h_2(t|x)}$ for cause 1 and the failure outcome is considered as cause 2. The estimates of $H_j(t|x)$ for $j = 1, 2$ are obtained at $t = 0.8$ with covariates value $x = 0.6$.

The MLEs $\hat{a}_j, \hat{\alpha}_j$, and $\hat{\beta}_j$ of unknown parameters of the proposed model (4) do not have a closed-form solution. The score equations (10)–(13) are a system of multiple non-linear equations, which can be difficult to solve analytically. Therefore, the MLEs of the unknown parameters a_j, α_j, and β_j are obtained based on the log-likelihood function given in Equation (9) through the optim function in R software. In the optim function, to get the MLE of a_j, α_j, and β_j, we need to supply some initial values, say, $a_j^{(0)}, \alpha_j^{(0)}$, and $\beta_j^{(0)}$. Since we do not have any theoretical method to define the initial values in the literature, we arbitrarily tried multiple sets of initial values from the parametric space in order to eliminate the impact of initial values [37,38]. We considered the initial values that offered the maximum likelihood function value and showed the convergence code "0", indicating the successful completion of the optimization. The MLE $\hat{H}_j(t|x)$ of the cumulative CSH function $H_j(t|x)$ was obtained by the invariance property of the MLE. As we mentioned in Section 4.4, the joint posterior densities based on each considered prior have a complicated form and it is also difficult to obtain the conditional posterior densities of the unknown parameters. Therefore, we employed the MCMC procedure for generating random samples from joint posterior densities. For this purpose, we used the BUGS `software` via the R2OpenBUGS package in R `software` [39]. The inbuilt BUGS system determines which of the available MCMC algorithms could be applied to a particular problem. To implement MCMC algorithms, BUGS only requires the log-likelihood function and the prior distribution of the parameters. On the basis of the properties of posterior densities, the BUGS system chose the appropriate MCMC algorithms [39].

Furthermore, for computing the hyper-parameters for baseline informative priors, we utilized the empirical Bayes method by using the MLE. First, we generated 1000 random samples of size 100. Now, corresponding to each sample, we obtained the average MLE and the empirical variance of a_j and α_j and then compared them with the mean and variance of gamma, Weibull, and log-normal priors of the a_j and α_j. Calculated hyper-parameters of gamma, Weibull, and log-normal priors are given in Table 1. The hyper-parameter of LLF is fixed as $\rho = \pm 1.5$ and known as LLF1 and LLF2, respectively. The hyper-parameters c_{jl} and d_{jl} of the regression parameters are assumed to be 0 and 2, respectively.

Table 1. Hyper-parameters of the gamma, Weibull, and log-normal priors for baseline parameters of the modified Weibull CSAH model.

Priors	Hyper-Parameters
Gamma	$q_{11} = 11.48, r_{11} = 21.69, q_{21} = 25.60, r_{21} = 39.75, q_{12} = 2.06, r_{12} = 3.44,$ $q_{22} = 16.69, r_{22} = 22.09$
Weibull	$k_{11} = 3.78, \theta_{11} = 1.71, k_{21} = 5.87, \theta_{21} = 1.44, k_{12} = 1.46 \theta_{12} = 1.51,$ $k_{22} = 4.65, \theta_{22} = 1.21$
Log-normal	$\mu_{11} = -0.68, \sigma_{11} = 0.08, \mu_{21} = -0.46, \sigma_{21} = 0.04, \mu_{12} = -0.71 \sigma_{12} = 0.39,$ $\mu_{22} = -0.31, \sigma_{22} = 0.06$

We generated $N = 10{,}000$ Markov chains for each parameter, and the first $M = 4000$ samples were used in the burn-in period for reducing the effect of initial values. Furthermore, for minimizing the effect of the autocorrelation, every second equally spaced outcome was considered, i.e., thin = 2. By the visualization of the convergence diagnostics plots, it was observed that the chains converged nicely. Therefore, the last 6000 MCMC samples were used to obtain Bayes estimates of the unknown parameters and cumulative CSH functions under both loss functions. The numerical results are presented in Table 2. The Bayes estimates given in this table are denoted as B-self, B-llf1, and B-llf2, where B denotes the first letter of the priors considered in Section 4. For example, for gamma, B = G; for Weibull, B = W; and for log-normal, B = LN. Based on the findings given in these tables, the following observations were made.

From Table 2, it is very clear that the Bayes estimates are significantly better compared to the MLE. It is also observed that as the sample size increases, the MSEs decrease for MLE and Bayes estimates, which verifies the consistency property of all the estimators. Furthermore, we noticed that the AVLs for ACI and BCIs decreased and CPs maintain the nominal level (95%). It was also noted that the performance of the log-normal prior is relatively good when compared to the gamma and Weibull priors. However, in some cases, the gamma prior also performs well. The performance of MLE gets better as the sample size increases. Besides that, for large samples, for example, $n = 400$, in most of the cases the Bayes estimates dominated. It was also noted that the performance of the LINEX loss function at $\rho = 1.5$ was relatively good compared to SELF and LINEX $\rho = -1.5$ corresponding to each prior.

Table 2. Simulation results for parameter estimation of the modified Weibull cause-specific AH model under MLE and Bayes estimates.

			Cause 1				Cause 2			
n	Method		a_1	α_1	β_{11}	H_1	a_2	α_2	β_{21}	H_2
	True value		0.5	0.6	0.6	0.8012	0.7	0.5	0.8	1.1187
100	MLE	AVE	0.5350	0.6494	0.6175	0.8388	0.7567	0.5450	0.7582	1.1492
		MSE	0.0234	0.0231	0.1642	0.0315	0.0373	0.0075	0.2376	0.0492
	ACI	AVL	0.5672	0.4880	1.5375	0.7412	0.6583	0.3303	1.7849	1.0228
		CP	0.9520	0.9500	0.9480	0.9560	0.9340	0.9760	0.9300	0.9620
	G-self	AVE	0.5180	0.6381	0.7453	0.8847	0.7464	0.5848	0.8935	1.1967
		MSE	0.0050	0.0053	0.1063	0.0281	0.0231	0.0108	0.1135	0.0404
	G-llf1	AVE	0.5107	0.6326	0.6621	0.8650	0.7304	0.5804	0.7883	1.1711
		MSE	0.0047	0.0048	0.0758	0.0239	0.0206	0.0100	0.0934	0.0354
	G-llf2	AVE	0.5256	0.6438	0.8381	0.9055	0.7633	0.5892	1.0044	1.2233
		MSE	0.0056	0.0059	0.1532	0.0333	0.0264	0.0117	0.1515	0.0469
	G-BCI	AVL	0.3864	0.3366	1.2934	0.6311	0.5713	0.2978	1.4296	0.7206
		CP	0.9980	0.9880	0.9660	0.9580	0.9360	0.8800	0.9680	0.9360
	W-self	AVE	0.5281	0.6465	0.7368	0.8899	0.7495	0.5824	0.8896	1.1982
		MSE	0.0057	0.0057	0.1038	0.0291	0.0237	0.0115	0.1114	0.0404
	W-llf1	AVE	0.5206	0.6412	0.6534	0.8703	0.7332	0.5775	0.7843	1.1727
		MSE	0.0053	0.0052	0.0745	0.0247	0.0212	0.0106	0.0921	0.0354
	W-llf2	AVE	0.5357	0.6518	0.8304	0.9107	0.7667	0.5875	1.0008	1.2248
		MSE	0.0063	0.0063	0.1499	0.0346	0.0271	0.0125	0.1488	0.0470
	W-BCI	AVL	0.3901	0.3277	1.2960	0.6309	0.5757	0.3174	1.4310	0.7211
		CP	0.9900	0.9840	0.9640	0.9520	0.9380	0.8900	0.9780	0.9380
	LN-self	AVE	0.5137	0.6360	0.7476	0.8817	0.7346	0.5841	0.9036	1.1896
		MSE	0.0044	0.0053	0.1064	0.0274	0.0218	0.0103	0.1150	0.0389
	LN-llf1	AVE	0.5068	0.6303	0.6650	0.8622	0.7189	0.5800	0.7981	1.1663
		MSE	0.0043	0.0047	0.0760	0.0234	0.0197	0.0095	0.0932	0.0343
	LN-llf2	AVE	0.5210	0.6418	0.8397	0.9023	0.7513	0.5883	1.0141	1.2160
		MSE	0.0049	0.0060	0.1532	0.0324	0.0247	0.0111	0.1547	0.0450
	LN-BCI	AVL	0.3764	0.3384	1.2921	0.6272	0.5664	0.2888	1.4281	0.7169
		CP	0.9940	0.9920	0.9640	0.9580	0.9480	0.8800	0.9700	0.9400
200	MLE	AVE	0.5198	0.6268	0.5800	0.8084	0.7327	0.5363	0.7980	1.1454
		MSE	0.0112	0.0070	0.0922	0.0166	0.0151	0.0042	0.1146	0.0238
	ACI	AVL	0.3883	0.3256	1.0495	0.4873	0.4477	0.2291	1.2418	0.6946
		CP	0.9400	0.9740	0.9160	0.9260	0.9460	0.9520	0.9240	0.9680
	G-self	AVE	0.5131	0.6300	0.6498	0.8348	0.7317	0.5595	0.8780	1.1786
		MSE	0.0049	0.0036	0.0659	0.0150	0.0120	0.0058	0.0937	0.0240
	G-llf1	AVE	0.5084	0.6265	0.6034	0.8246	0.7231	0.5571	0.8110	1.1646
		MSE	0.0046	0.0033	0.0576	0.0139	0.0112	0.0055	0.0820	0.0218
	G-llf2	AVE	0.5180	0.6337	0.7002	0.8454	0.7406	0.5618	0.9481	1.1931
		MSE	0.0051	0.0039	0.0796	0.0164	0.0130	0.0061	0.1136	0.0266
	G-BCI	AVL	0.3106	0.2690	0.9754	0.4557	0.4197	0.2172	1.1653	0.5353
		CP	0.9760	0.9820	0.9520	0.9420	0.9440	0.8580	0.9440	0.9180
	W-self	AVE	0.5231	0.6394	0.6409	0.8396	0.7325	0.5566	0.8763	1.1790
		MSE	0.0056	0.0043	0.0651	0.0153	0.0123	0.0059	0.0939	0.0241
	W-llf1	AVE	0.5182	0.6358	0.5943	0.8293	0.7239	0.5540	0.8091	1.1649
		MSE	0.0053	0.0040	0.0575	0.0141	0.0114	0.0056	0.0824	0.0219
	W-llf2	AVE	0.5281	0.6429	0.6917	0.8502	0.7415	0.5591	0.9466	1.1935
		MSE	0.0059	0.0046	0.0780	0.0168	0.0133	0.0062	0.1137	0.0268
	W-BCI	AVL	0.3163	0.2687	0.9771	0.4566	0.4214	0.2266	1.1667	0.5357
		CP	0.9640	0.9660	0.9500	0.9340	0.9400	0.8720	0.9420	0.9220
	LN-self	AVE	0.5093	0.6271	0.6535	0.8330	0.7249	0.5595	0.8857	1.1753
		MSE	0.0044	0.0034	0.0657	0.0150	0.0115	0.0056	0.0949	0.0235
	LN-llf1	AVE	0.5047	0.6236	0.6072	0.8228	0.7164	0.5572	0.8187	1.1612
		MSE	0.0042	0.0032	0.0571	0.0139	0.0108	0.0053	0.0823	0.0214

Table 2. Cont.

n	Method		a_1	α_1	β_{11}	H_1	a_2	α_2	β_{21}	H_2
400	LN-llf2	AVE	0.5140	0.6307	0.7039	0.8437	0.7336	0.5617	0.9558	1.1897
		MSE	0.0046	0.0037	0.0796	0.0164	0.0124	0.0059	0.1158	0.0260
	LN-BCI	AVL	0.3048	0.2682	0.9753	0.4568	0.4164	0.2130	1.1664	0.5352
		CP	0.9800	0.9840	0.9520	0.9420	0.9520	0.8600	0.9380	0.9220
	MLE	AVE	0.5179	0.6215	0.5873	0.8106	0.7327	0.5364	0.7751	1.1346
		MSE	0.0071	0.0036	0.0436	0.0074	0.0090	0.0028	0.0705	0.0126
	ACI	AVL	0.2738	0.2262	0.7423	0.3420	0.3166	0.1615	0.8729	0.4866
		CP	0.9180	0.9640	0.9260	0.9480	0.9320	0.8880	0.8920	0.9640
	G-self	AVE	0.5146	0.6243	0.6265	0.8258	0.7300	0.5470	0.8309	1.1567
		MSE	0.0037	0.0025	0.0329	0.0071	0.0072	0.0034	0.0589	0.0123
	G-llf1	AVE	0.5117	0.6222	0.6009	0.8205	0.7254	0.5458	0.7942	1.1493
		MSE	0.0035	0.0024	0.0309	0.0067	0.0068	0.0032	0.0556	0.0115
	G-llf2	AVE	0.5176	0.6263	0.6532	0.8312	0.7347	0.5482	0.8689	1.1641
		MSE	0.0038	0.0026	0.0365	0.0075	0.0076	0.0035	0.0651	0.0132
	G-BCI	AVL	0.2434	0.2044	0.7277	0.3286	0.3057	0.1568	0.8685	0.3875
		CP	0.9620	0.9760	0.9520	0.9540	0.9340	0.8280	0.9180	0.9400
	W-self	AVE	0.5229	0.6322	0.6184	0.8294	0.7305	0.5452	0.8291	1.1565
		MSE	0.0041	0.0030	0.0328	0.0073	0.0074	0.0033	0.0587	0.0122
	W-llf1	AVE	0.5199	0.6301	0.5925	0.8241	0.7259	0.5440	0.7921	1.1491
		MSE	0.0040	0.0029	0.0311	0.0069	0.0070	0.0032	0.0556	0.0115
	W-llf2	AVE	0.5260	0.6343	0.6454	0.8349	0.7352	0.5465	0.8673	1.1640
		MSE	0.0043	0.0032	0.0361	0.0078	0.0078	0.0034	0.0648	0.0131
	W-BCI	AVL	0.2471	0.2068	0.7316	0.3304	0.3069	0.1603	0.8729	0.3884
		CP	0.9500	0.9600	0.9580	0.9580	0.9300	0.8380	0.9260	0.9380
	LN-self	AVE	0.5116	0.6223	0.6296	0.8244	0.7264	0.5471	0.8354	1.1551
		MSE	0.0034	0.0024	0.0327	0.0070	0.0070	0.0033	0.0591	0.0122
	LN-llf1	AVE	0.5087	0.6203	0.6040	0.8191	0.7219	0.5459	0.7984	1.1477
		MSE	0.0033	0.0023	0.0305	0.0066	0.0066	0.0032	0.0553	0.0115
	LN-llf2	AVE	0.5145	0.6244	0.6562	0.8298	0.7310	0.5483	0.8736	1.1626
		MSE	0.0036	0.0025	0.0364	0.0074	0.0074	0.0034	0.0657	0.0131
	LN-BCI	AVL	0.2407	0.2038	0.7275	0.3293	0.3045	0.1549	0.8732	0.3876
		CP	0.9700	0.9780	0.9560	0.9560	0.9340	0.8340	0.9280	0.9420

7. Illustrative Application

In this section, we used real data from a Mayo Clinic trial of primary biliary cirrhosis (PBC) of the liver conducted between 1974 and 1984 to demonstrate the applicability of the proposed model. This dataset is available in the *survival* package of R software. During these ten years, 312 patients were randomly assigned to receive D-penicillamine or placebo treatment from a total of 424 patients. Furthermore, the remaining 112 patients did not participate in the clinical trial but agreed to have their basic measurements taken and observed for survival. Six of those patients were not followed-up shortly after diagnosis, so these patients were removed from the study, resulting in $n = 418$ patients.

Among the $n = 418$ patients, 161 patients died, another 25 patients received a liver transplant, and 232 patients were not followed-up. Therefore, the competing risks model becomes reasonable for two competing outcome variables: liver transplant and death. The survival time is measured in days for all individuals. However, there are several covariates in the original data, such as treatment, sex, age, etc. For the analysis purpose, treatment is considered as a covariate. The baseline fitting summary of the data for death is reported in Table 3 and Figure 1. For more information on PBC data, one could refer to Therneau and Grambsch [40] and the application of competing risks on PBC data is available in the analysis of competing risks [41].

Table 3. Baseline parameter estimate and goodness of fit statistics for death.

Model	MLE	Log-Likelihood	AIC	BIC
MWD	$a = 0.0639, \alpha = 0.9986, \lambda = 0.0197$	−580.870	1167.74	1179.85
Weibull	Shape = 1.24, Scale = 12.67,	−584.0561	1172.11	1180.18
Log-normal	Meanlog = 2.341, Sdlog = 1.546	−585.9771	1175.95	1184.03
Burr XII	$a = 28.53 \; \alpha = 1.135, \lambda = 2.814$	−581.64	1169.28	1181.39

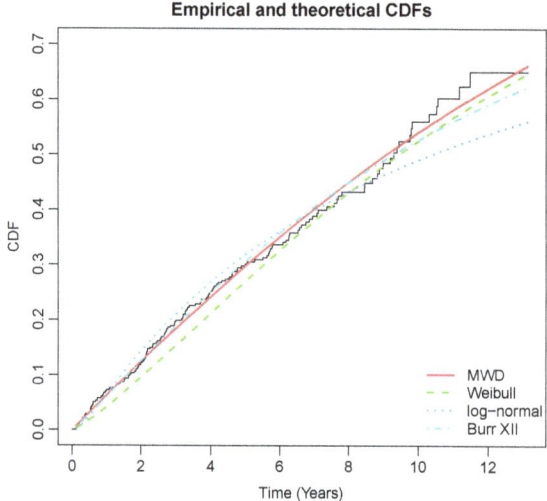

Figure 1. Fitted and empirical CDF plots of death for PBC data.

To transform survival time in terms of years, we divided it by 365, which yielded a median survival time 4.74 years. We also assumed that 106 patients who did not participate in the trial received the D-penicillamine treatment. Furthermore, we applied the proposed estimation methods to obtain the estimates of the unknown parameters and cumulative CSH functions. To choose unknown parameters for priors, we first tried several parameters and then chose the best one in terms of the convergence performance and computing time. Based on the results of this preliminary analysis, we decided to use the following parameters: $q_{1j} = q_{2j} = q_{3j} = 1.5, r_{1j} = r_{2j} = r_{3j} = 2.2$ (gamma prior); $k_{1j} = k_{2j} = k_{3j} = 2, \theta_{1j} = \theta_{2j} = \theta_{3j} = 0.71$ (Weibull prior); $\mu_{1j} = \mu_{2j} = \mu_{3j} = 0.1, \sigma_{1j} = \sigma_{2j} = \sigma_{3j} = 1$ (log-normal prior); and $c_{1j} = 0, d_{1j} = 1$ (uniform prior). The results of the estimates of the unknown parameters are presented in Table 4. We estimated the cumulative CSH functions using (5) based on the proposed estimators which are presented in Figures 2 and 3.

These plots indicate that the cumulative CSH rate for transplant patients is small compared to the same for the patients who experienced death. Figure 2 shows that the value of the cumulative CSH function due to transplant is small for the patients who received the placebo treatment. Similarly, the same is observed for the cumulative CSH rate due to death, see Figure 3. Moreover, the likelihood ratio test procedure was also used to test the significance of the treatment effect on transplant and death separately. The hypotheses of interest are $H_0 : \beta_{11} = 0$ against $H_1 : \beta_{11} \neq 0$ and $H_0 : \beta_{21} = 0$ against $H_1 : \beta_{21} \neq 0$. We calculated the likelihood ratio test statistics and corresponding p-values to be 5.44×10^{-06} and 1.02×10^{-03}. Hence, both the null hypothesis are rejected. This indicates that treatment had a significant effect on transplant and death.

Table 4. ML and Bayes parameter estimates of the modified Weibull CSAH model for transplant and death for the PBC data.

Method	Transplant				Death			
	a_1	α_1	λ_1	β_{11}	a_2	α_2	λ_2	β_{21}
MLE	0.0117	0.3038	0.1394	0.0026	0.0407	0.2946	0.2174	0.0286
MLE.SE	0.0054	0.9331	0.1965	0.0077	0.0101	0.0947	0.0353	0.0096
G-self	0.0062	0.9640	0.0852	0.0042	0.0600	0.8965	0.0443	0.0118
G-llf1	0.0062	0.8806	0.0827	0.0042	0.0599	0.8867	0.0439	0.0117
G-llf2	0.0062	1.0445	0.0878	0.0042	0.0601	0.9061	0.0447	0.0118
G.SE	0.0031	0.3312	0.0581	0.0030	0.0109	0.1136	0.0234	0.0079
W-self	0.0062	0.9681	0.0878	0.0040	0.0597	0.8828	0.0485	0.0118
W-llf1	0.0062	0.9057	0.0859	0.0040	0.0597	0.8737	0.0481	0.0117
W-llf2	0.0062	1.0295	0.0898	0.0040	0.0598	0.8919	0.0488	0.0118
W.SE	0.0030	0.2876	0.0510	0.0029	0.0109	0.1100	0.0219	0.0080
LN-self	0.0110	0.6324	0.1081	0.0036	0.0617	0.8262	0.0597	0.0118
LN-llf1	0.0110	0.5906	0.1066	0.0036	0.0616	0.8184	0.0594	0.0117
LN-llf2	0.0110	0.6756	0.1096	0.0036	0.0618	0.8339	0.0600	0.0118
LN.SE	0.0041	0.2384	0.0449	0.0027	0.0108	0.1018	0.0205	0.0080

SE: Standard error.

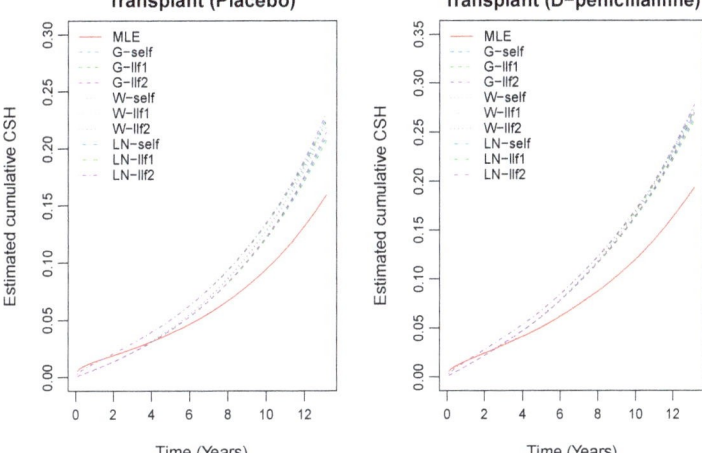

Figure 2. Estimated cumulative CSH for transplant based on the Bayes estimates for informative priors and MLE based on the PBC data.

To test the overall goodness of fit of the model (1) to the PBC data in competing risks framework, we used the Cox–Snell residual plot [42]. The Cox–Snell residual is defined as:

$$r_i = \hat{H}(t_i|x_i), \quad i = 1, 2, \ldots, n, \quad (24)$$

where $\hat{H}(t|x)$ is the estimator of cumulative CSH rate $H(t|x) = \sum_{j=1}^{2} H_j(t|x)$ and $j = 1, 2$ based on MLE for transplant and death, respectively. If the model holds, then these residuals should be a sample from a unit exponential distribution. Therefore, the hazard plot of residuals versus the Nelson–Aalen estimator of the cumulative hazard of the residuals will be a straight line with a slope equal to one. The residual plot of Figure 4 demonstrates a reasonable fit of the model (1). Readers are referred to Figures 12.6–12.9 of the book [42] for a reasonable fit.

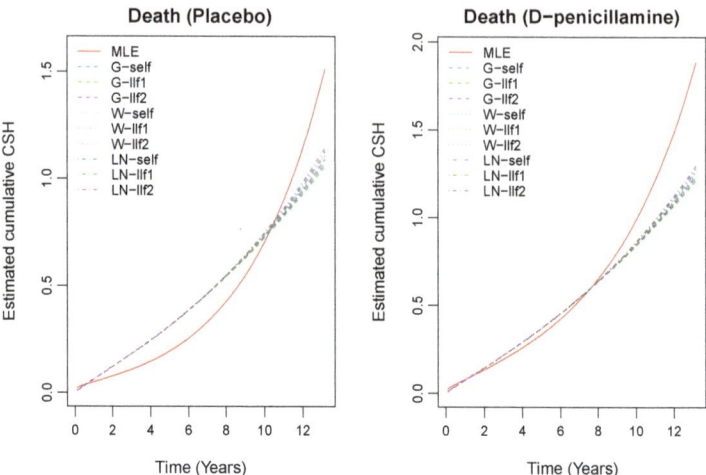

Figure 3. Estimated cumulative CSH for death based on the Bayes estimates for informative priors and MLE based on the PBC data.

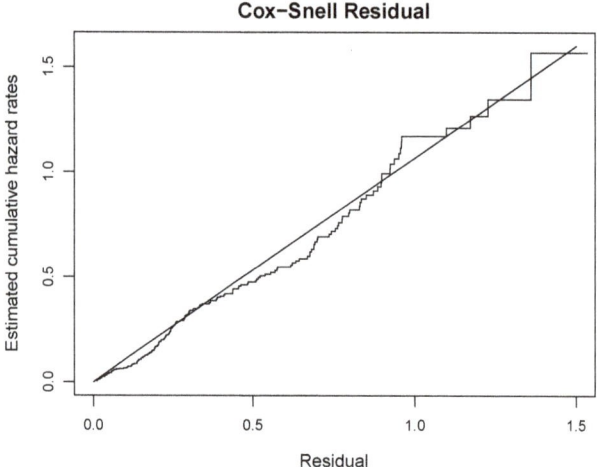

Figure 4. Plot of the Cox–Snell residual versus its estimates of cumulative hazard rate.

8. Conclusions

In this article, we propose a parametric cause-specific AH regression analysis, where the baseline CSH functions follow the MWD. The proposed AH model is a good alternative to the Cox PH model, and it is useful when excess risk is of concern. The estimation of the unknown parameters and cumulative CSH function is dealt with by ML and Bayes estimates. In addition to Bayes estimation, we propose three types of informative priors for baseline parameters, and uniform priors are considered for regression parameters. The simulation results show that the Bayes estimates based on each considered priors under the SELF and LLF dominate over MLE for a small sample size. Furthermore, across the priors, the choice of baseline log-normal priors gives better results with a smaller MSE and AVL. Moreover, selecting different priors and loss functions shows their applicability in the simulation study. We demonstrate the model utility with the PBC data. These data fit well with the model, and the covariate significantly affects transplant and death.

The proposed work can be extended for different censoring schemes such as interval, current status, and middle censoring schemes [7,9,18,42]. Furthermore, the situation of masking in competing risks analysis is widespread [43,44]. Therefore, the analysis of masked competing risks data using the proposed model seems to be an interesting attempt.

Determining the appropriate form of the prior is often difficult, historically affecting the widespread use of the Bayesian paradigm. According to [45], there is no hard and fast rule for selecting the best possible prior distribution to formulate the Bayes estimator. In this study, we considered an informative prior for the unknown parameters. However, a noninformative prior can be used when only limited or vague knowledge (a priori) about the parameters is available. The rationale for using noninformative prior distributions is often said to be *to let the data speak for themselves* so that inferences are unaffected by external information to the current data. Hence, all resulting inferences were completely objective rather than subjective. A commonly used noninformative prior in Bayesian analysis is Jeffrey's prior [46]. However, the half-t [47] distribution as a noninformative prior is also gaining attention of researchers. The proposed study can be extended for the noninformative priors which would be reported elsewhere.

Author Contributions: Conceptualization, H.R. and N.C.; methodology, H.R. and N.C.; validation, H.R, N.C. and T.E.; formal analysis, H.R.; investigation, H.R. and N.C.; resources, N.C. and T.E.; data curation, H.R.; writing—original draft preparation, H.R.; writing—review and editing, N.C., T.E. and M.P.; visualization, T.E. and M.P.; supervision, N.C. All authors have read and agreed to the published version of the manuscript.

Funding: This research received no external funding.

Informed Consent Statement: Not applicable.

Data Availability Statement: The PBC data used in this article is available in the *survival* package of R software by the name "pbc".

Acknowledgments: We thank to the two reviewers for their helpful and detailed comments that greatly improved the manuscript.

Conflicts of Interest: The authors declare no conflict of interest.

References

1. Cox, D.R. Regression models and life-tables. *J. R. Stat. Soc. Ser. Methodol.* **1972**, *34*, 187–220. [CrossRef]
2. Cox, D.R.; Oakes, D. *Analysis of Survival Data*; Chapman and Hall/CRC: London, UK, 1984.
3. Breslow, N.E.; Day, N.E. *Statistical Methods in Cancer Research*; International Agency for Research on Cancer: Lyon, France, 1987; Volume 2.
4. Aalen, O.O. A linear regression model for the analysis of life times. *Stat. Med.* **1989**, *8*, 907–925. [CrossRef]
5. Lin, D.; Ying, Z. Semiparametric analysis of the additive risk model. *Biometrika* **1994**, *81*, 61–71. [CrossRef]
6. Lin, D.; Ying, Z. Semiparametric analysis of general additive-multiplicative hazard models for counting processes. *Ann. Stat.* **1995**, *23*, 1712–1734. [CrossRef]
7. Kalbfleisch, J.D.; Prentice, R.L. *The Statistical Analysis of Failure Time Data*; John Wiley & Sons: Hoboken, NJ, USA, 2002; Volume 360.
8. Haller, B.; Schmidt, G.; Ulm, K. Applying competing risks regression models: An overview. *Lifetime Data Anal.* **2013**, *19*, 33–58. [CrossRef]
9. Lawless, J.F. *Statistical Models and Methods for Lifetime Data*; John Wiley & Sons: Hoboken, NJ, USA, 2003; Volume 362.
10. Pintilie, M. *Competing Risks: A Practical Perspective*; John Wiley & Sons: Chichester, UK, 2006; Volume 58,
11. Emura, T.; Shih, J.H.; Ha, I.D.; Wilke, R.A. Comparison of the marginal hazard model and the sub-distribution hazard model for competing risks under an assumed copula. *Stat. Methods Med. Res.* **2020**, *29*, 2307–2327. [CrossRef]
12. Meng, C.; Esserman, D.; Li, F.; Zhao, Y.; Blaha, O.; Lu, W.; Wang, Y.; Peduzzi, P.; Greene, E.J. Simulating time-to-event data subject to competing risks and clustering: A review and synthesis. *Stat. Methods Med. Res.* **2023**, *32*, 305–333. [CrossRef] [PubMed]
13. Zuo, Z.; Wang, L.; Lio, Y. Reliability estimation for dependent left-truncated and right-censored competing risks data with illustrations. *Energies* **2023**, *16*, 62. [CrossRef]
14. Jeong, J.H.; Fine, J.P. Parametric regression on cumulative incidence function. *Biostatistics* **2007**, *8*, 184–196. [CrossRef]
15. Anjana, S.; Sankaran, P. Parametric analysis of lifetime data with multiple causes of failure using cause specific reversed hazard rates. *Calcutta Stat. Assoc. Bull.* **2015**, *67*, 129–142. [CrossRef]

16. Lee, M. Parametric inference for quantile event times with adjustment for covariates on competing risks data. *J. Appl. Stat.* **2019**, *46*, 2128–2144. [CrossRef]
17. Lipowski, C.; Lo, S.; Shi, S.; Wilke, R.A. Competing risks regression with dependent multiple spells: Monte Carlo evidence and an application to maternity leave. *Jpn. J. Stat. Data Sci.* **2021**, *4*, 953–981. [CrossRef]
18. Rehman, H.; Chandra, N. Inferences on cumulative incidence function for middle censored survival data with Weibull regression. *Jpn. J. Stat. Data Sci.* **2022**, *5*, 65–86. [CrossRef]
19. Shen, Y.; Cheng, S. Confidence bands for cumulative incidence curves under the additive risk model. *Biometrics* **1999**, *55*, 1093–1100. [CrossRef] [PubMed]
20. Sun, J.; Sun, L.; Flournoy, N. Additive hazards model for competing risks analysis of the case-cohort design. *Commun. Stat. Theory Methods* **2004**, *33*, 351–366. [CrossRef]
21. Zhang, X.; Akcin, H.; Lim, H.J. Regression analysis of competing risks data via semi-parametric additive hazard model. *Stat. Methods Appl.* **2011**, *20*, 357–381. [CrossRef]
22. Li, W.; Xue, X.; Long, Y. An additive subdistribution hazard model for competing risks data. *Commun. Stat. Theory Methods* **2017**, *46*, 11667–11687. [CrossRef]
23. Sankaran, P.; Prasad, S. Additive risks regression model for middle censored exponentiated-exponential lifetime data. *Commun. Stat. Simul. Comput.* **2018**, *47*, 1963–1974. [CrossRef]
24. Lai, C.; Xie, M.; Murthy, D. A modified Weibull distribution. *IEEE Trans. Reliab.* **2003**, *52*, 33–37. [CrossRef]
25. Byrnes, J.M.; Lin, Y.J.; Tsai, T.R.; Lio, Y. Bayesian inference of $\delta = P(X<Y)$ for Burr type XII distribution based on progressively first failure-censored samples. *Mathematics* **2019**, *7*, 794.
26. Martz, H.F.; Waller, R. *Bayesian Reliability Analysis*; John Wiley & Sons: New York, NY, USA, 1982.
27. Ranjan, R.; Sen, R.; Upadhyay, S.K. Bayes analysis of some important lifetime models using MCMC based approaches when the observations are left truncated and right censored. *Reliab. Eng. Syst. Saf.* **2021**, *214*, 107747. [CrossRef]
28. Ng, H.K.T. Parameter estimation for a modified Weibull distribution, for progressively type-II censored samples. *IEEE Trans. Reliab.* **2005**, *54*, 374–380. [CrossRef]
29. Jiang, H.; Xie, M.; Tang, L. Markov chain Monte Carlo methods for parameter estimation of the modified Weibull distribution. *J. Appl. Stat.* **2008**, *35*, 647–658. [CrossRef]
30. Upadhyay, S.; Gupta, A. A Bayes analysis of modified Weibull distribution via Markov chain Monte Carlo simulation. *J. Stat. Comput. Simul.* **2010**, *80*, 241–254. [CrossRef]
31. Nelder, J.A.; Mead, R. A simplex method for function minimization. *Comput. J.* **1965**, *7*, 308–313. [CrossRef]
32. Robert, C.P.; Casella, G.; Casella, G. *Introducing Monte Carlo Methods with R*; Springer Science & Business Media: New York, NY, USA, 2010; Volume 18.
33. Geman, S.; Geman, D. Stochastic relaxation, Gibbs distributions, and the Bayesian restoration of images. *IEEE Trans. Pattern Anal. Mach. Intell.* **1984**, *PAMI-6*, 721–741. [CrossRef] [PubMed]
34. Hastings, W.K. Monte Carlo sampling methods using Markov chains and their applications. *Biometrika* **1970**, *57*, 97–109. [CrossRef]
35. Guure, C.B.; Ibrahim, N.A. Bayesian analysis of the survival function and failure rate of Weibull distribution with censored data. *Math. Probl. Eng.* **2012**, *2012*. [CrossRef]
36. Beyersmann, J.; Allignol, A.; Schumacher, M. *Competing Risks and Multistate Models with R*; Springer Science & Business Media: New York, NY, USA, 2012.
37. Knight, K. *Mathematical Statistics*; CRC Press: Boca Raton, FL, USA, 1999.
38. Dörre, A.; Huang, C.Y.; Tseng, Y.K.; Emura, T. Likelihood-based analysis of doubly-truncated data under the location-scale and AFT model. *Comput. Stat.* **2021**, *36*, 375–408. [CrossRef]
39. Lunn, D.; Jackson, C.; Best, N.; Spiegelhalter, D.; Thomas, A. *The BUGS Book: A Practical Introduction to Bayesian Analysis*; Chapman and Hall/CRC: Boca Raton, FL, USA, 2012.
40. Therneau, T.M.; Grambsch, P.M. *Modeling Survival Data: Extending the Cox Model*; Springer Science & Business Media: New York, NY, USA, 2000.
41. Lai, X.; Yau, K.K.; Liu, L. Competing risk model with bivariate random effects for clustered survival data. *Comput. Stat. Data Anal.* **2017**, *112*, 215–223. [CrossRef]
42. Klein, J.P.; Moeschberger, M.L. *Survival Analysis: Techniques for Censored and Truncated Data*; Springer: New York, NY, USA, 2003.
43. Fan, T.H.; Wang, Y.F.; Ju, S.K. A competing risks model with multiply censored reliability data under multivariate Weibull distributions. *IEEE Trans. Reliab.* **2019**, *68*, 462–475. [CrossRef]
44. Li, Y.; Ye, J. Analysis for partially accelerated dependent competing risks model with masked data based on copula function. *Commun. Stat. Simul. Comput.* **2022**, 1–17. [CrossRef]
45. Sinha, S. *Bayesian Estimation*; New Age International (P) Limited Publisher: New Delhi, India, 1998.

46. Jeffreys, H. *Theory of Probability*; Oxford University Press: London, UK, 1961.
47. Gelman, A. Prior distributions for variance parameters in hierarchical models (comment on article by Browne and Draper). *Bayesian Anal.* **2006**, *1*, 515–534. [CrossRef]

Disclaimer/Publisher's Note: The statements, opinions and data contained in all publications are solely those of the individual author(s) and contributor(s) and not of MDPI and/or the editor(s). MDPI and/or the editor(s) disclaim responsibility for any injury to people or property resulting from any ideas, methods, instructions or products referred to in the content.

Article

The Reliability of Stored Water Behind Dams Using the Multi-Component Stress-Strength System

Hanan Haj Ahmad [1,*], Dina A. Ramadan [2], Mahmoud M. M. Mansour [3] and Mohamed S. Aboshady [3]

1. Department of Basic Science, Preparatory Year Deanship, King Faisal University, Hofuf 31982, Al Ahsa, Saudi Arabia
2. Department of Mathematics, Faculty of Science, Mansoura University, Mansoura 35516, Egypt
3. Department of Basic Science, Faculty of Engineering, The British University in Egypt, El-Sherouk City P.O. Box 43, Egypt
* Correspondence: hhajahmed@kfu.edu.sa

Abstract: Dams are essential infrastructure for managing water resources and providing entry to clean water for human needs. However, the construction and maintenance of dams require careful consideration of their reliability and safety, specifically in the event of extreme weather conditions such as heavy rainfall or flooding. In this study, the stress-strength model provides a useful framework for evaluating the reliability of dams and their ability to cope with external stresses such as water pressure, earthquake activity, and erosion. The Shasta reservoir in the United States is a prime example of a dam that requires regular assessment of its reliability to guarantee the safety of communities and infrastructure. The Gumbel Type II distribution has been suggested as a suitable model for fitting the collected data on the stress and strength of the reservoir behind the Shasta dam. Both classical and Bayesian approaches have been used to estimate the reliability function under the multi-component stress-strength model, and Monte Carlo simulation has been employed for parameter estimation. In addition, some measures of goodness-of-fit are employed to examine the suitability of the suggested model.

Keywords: Gumbel Type II distribution; multi-component stress-strength model; maximum likelihood estimation; Bayesian estimation; Monte Carlo simulation; reliability analysis

1. Introduction

In reliability analysis, the study of the failure time of a component or a system is of great concern. Decision-makers in industry or governments encourage continuity in the enhancement of systems reliability since it measures the functioning of systems and predicts their outcomes in a better way. One of the main problems is estimating the parameters of the stress-strength function $R = P(Y < X)$, where Y is the stress and X is the strength, and both are considered random variables. Components or systems are subject to failure if their strength is less than the stress applied to them at any time.

Statistical inference of the stress-strength function has been studied by many authors. Several lifetime distributions were considered to fit the model under consideration, such as Birnbaum [1], Hanagal [2], Kotz et al. [3], Raqab et al. [4], Kundu and Raqab [5], Lio and Tsai [6], Nadar et al. [7], Rao and Kantam [8], Rao [9], Rao [10], Rao et al. [11], Kizilaslan and Nadar [12], Nadar and Kizilaslan [13], Dey et al. [14], and Wu [15]. For more recent works one may refer to [16–21].

A multi-component system, with k-independent and identically distributed (iid) strength components and one common stress, is in a functional state if at least s components are surviving at the same time, where $1 \leq s \leq k$, and this is known as an s-out-of-k: G system. Two examples of multi-component systems are: first, the suspension bridge is suspended by a k-vertical cable pair, this bridge will survive if at least s-vertical cable

pairs are functioning, i.e., not damaged. Second, the engine with six cylinders will work properly if at least four out of six cylinders are functioning.

Estimating the reliability of a system with the multi-component stress-strength model is of great importance and has many applications, see for example Ahmad et al. [22], who used the Power Lomax distribution under a progressive censoring scheme. Johari et al. [23] studied the reliability analysis of ground soil layers using the cross-correlation method. More reliability inference studies are presented in [24,25].

In this work, we consider the stress-strength model applied to reservoirs or artificial lakes behind dams. Dams are very important for providing water for different purposes during droughts such as drinking, cooking, washing, and irrigation, as well as producing hydroelectric power. They help in storing water in reservoirs during excess water flow and release it during times of low flow. Besides irrigation and other consumption purposes, water stored in these reservoirs is subject to other loss factors such as evaporation. We consider a model that is related to excessive drought times, and it is also claimed that in a specific region, if the stored water in a reservoir in August of the previous year is less than the water amount in the reservoir for at least two of the next four years, then no excessive drought will occur. In this model, X represents the strength and Y represents the stress.

In this study, we aim to estimate the stress-strength function's parameters $R_{s,k}$ which follow the Gumbel Type II model. This model was invented in 1958 by the German mathematician Emil Gumbel (1891–1911) and was useful for predicting the likelihood of climatic events such as annual flood flows (which is the case of this study), earthquakes, and other natural disasters. According to Abbas et al. [26], it has also been demonstrated to be sufficient for describing the component's life expectancy. In their book, Kotz and Nadarajah [27] investigated the Gumbel distribution with the aim of applying it to the analysis of datasets ranging from wind speed to flood data.

Several authors focused on the Gumbel Type II distribution in their research for its wide range of applications. For example, Nadarajah and Kotz [28] studied the Gumbel distribution's main properties. Feroze and Muhammad [29] performed Bayesian inference for the Gumbel Type II distribution under twice censored samples with different loss functions. Mansour and Aboshady [30] discussed different estimation methods using the Gumbel Type II distribution under the hybrid Type II censored scheme, they applied this model to study the performance of the insulating fluids for the breakdown voltages.

One of the basic motivations for using the Gumbel Type II distribution for modelling real data is its ability to keep the properties of a wide range of distributions, including the Weibull, Fréchet, and Gumbel distributions. This makes the Gumbel Type II distribution a flexible alternative for modelling data that are not compatible with some distributional forms. Another motivation for using the Gumbel Type II distribution is its ability to model both heavy-tailed and light-tailed distributions, as well as distributions that obtain positive or negative skewness. Moreover, the Gumbel Type II distribution is often used to model extreme events such as floods, hurricanes, and earthquakes, where accurate modelling of the distribution is essential for risk assessment and management. The Gumbel Type II distribution has been found to support a good fit for many extreme events, making it a preferable choice for modelling such events.

Even though several types of research have been performed on the statistical inference of the Gumbel Type II distribution, there is still a persistent need for more work in the field of multi-component stress-strength systems with Gumbel Type II distribution. In this study, we work on two goals: first, to find classical and Bayesian estimators of multi-component stress-strength functions and assess the estimators by providing a simulation study and applying suitable numerical techniques. Second, apply the new model to fit real data collected from reservoirs behind the Shasta dam.

The procedure for organizing the process of this work is schematically shown in the flowchart in Figure 1.

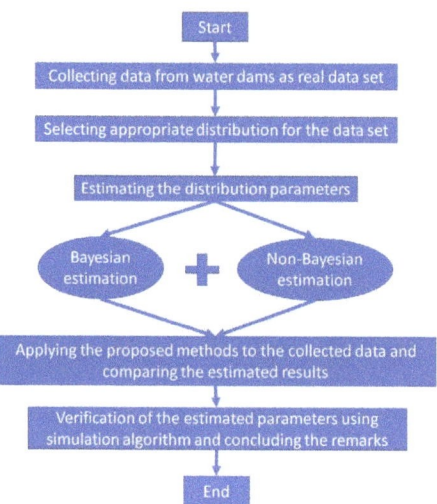

Figure 1. A flowchart indicating the research process.

2. Reliability Function

In this section, a closed form is obtained for the reliability function for a stress-strength model. Assuming the probability density function (PDF) and the CDF for the Gumbel Type II distribution, with a random variable X defined as,

$$f(x) = \alpha\beta x^{-(\alpha+1)} e^{-\beta x^{-\alpha}}, \; x > 0, \; \alpha, \beta > 0. \tag{1}$$

and

$$F(x) = e^{-\beta x^{-\alpha}}, \; x > 0, \; \alpha, \beta > 0, \tag{2}$$

and given the reliability function for a stress-strength model, that was defined by Bhattacharyya and Johnson [31], as

$$R_{s,k} = P[\text{at least } s \text{ of } (X_1, X_2, \ldots, X_k) \text{ exceed } Y] = \sum_{i=s}^{k} \binom{k}{i} \int_{-\infty}^{\infty} [1 - F(X)]^i [F(X)]^{k-i} dG(Y), \tag{3}$$

where $X_1, X_2, \ldots, X_k$ are iid random variables that follow the Gumbel Type II distribution with parameters α_1 and β_1 with cumulative distribution function (CDF) $F(X)$, and are affected by random stresses Y that follow the Gumbel Type II distribution with parameters α_2 and β_2 having CDF $G(Y)$. Substituting by the CDF in Equation (2) into $R_{s,k}$ defined in Equation (3), we obtain

$$R_{s,k} = \alpha_2 \beta_2 \sum_{i=s}^{k} \binom{k}{i} \int_{0}^{\infty} [1 - e^{-\beta_1 x^{-\alpha_1}}]^i [e^{-\beta_1 x^{-\alpha_1}}]^{k-i} x^{-(\alpha_2+1)} e^{-\beta_2 x^{-\alpha_2}} dx. \tag{4}$$

Let $u = x^{-\alpha_2}$ and substitute it into Equation (4) to obtain Equation (5)

$$R_{s,k} = \beta_2 \sum_{i=s}^{k} \binom{k}{i} \int_{0}^{\infty} [1 - e^{-\beta_1 u^{\frac{\alpha_1}{\alpha_2}}}]^i [e^{-\beta_1 u^{\frac{\alpha_1}{\alpha_2}}}]^{k-i} e^{-\beta_2 u} du. \tag{5}$$

By using the binomial expansion for $[1 - e^{-\beta_1 u^{\frac{\alpha_1}{\alpha_2}}}]$, we obtain

$$R_{s,k} = \beta_2 \sum_{i=s}^{k} \sum_{l=0}^{i} \binom{k}{i}\binom{i}{l}(-1)^l \int_0^\infty [e^{-\beta_1 u^{\frac{\alpha_1}{\alpha_2}}}]^{k-l} e^{-\beta_2 u} du. \tag{6}$$

Since the Maclaurin expansion for $[e^{-\beta_1 u^{\frac{\alpha_1}{\alpha_2}}}]^{k-l} = \sum_{r=0}^{\infty} \frac{(l-k)^r \beta_1^r u^{\frac{r\alpha_1}{\alpha_2}}}{r!}$, then Equation (6) is rewritten as

$$R_{s,k} = \beta_2 \sum_{i=s}^{k} \sum_{l=0}^{i} \sum_{r=0}^{\infty} \binom{k}{i}\binom{i}{l}(-1)^l \frac{(l-k)^r \beta_1^r}{r!} \int_0^\infty u^{\frac{r\alpha_1}{\alpha_2}} e^{-\beta_2 u} du. \tag{7}$$

Assuming $z = \beta_2 u$, Equation (7) is reduced to

$$R_{s,k} = \sum_{i=s}^{k} \sum_{l=0}^{i} \sum_{r=0}^{\infty} \binom{k}{i}\binom{i}{l}(-1)^l \frac{(l-k)^r \beta_1^r}{r!} \beta_2^{-\frac{r\alpha_1}{\alpha_2}} \Gamma\left(\frac{r\alpha_1}{\alpha_2} + 1\right). \tag{8}$$

3. Maximum-Likelihood Estimation

This section is devoted to deriving the maximum likelihood estimators (MLEs) for the reliability function's $R_{s,k}$ parameters. The basis for finding the estimators of the parameters is the log-likelihood functions, given the data. The MLEs have been used by many authors to derive the estimators of the parameters due to several advantages such as simplicity, unbiased for larger samples, and acquiring smaller variance. Furthermore, it can be developed for a large variety of other estimation methods. For more information on the likelihood theory, see Azzalini [32].

To find the MLEs of $R_{s,k}$, we start by obtaining the MLEs for the parameters α_1, α_2, β_1 and β_2. In this model, samples can be constructed as

$$\begin{pmatrix} X_{11} & X_{12} & \cdots & X_{1k} \\ X_{21} & X_{22} & \cdots & X_{2k} \\ \vdots & \vdots & \ddots & \vdots \\ X_{n1} & X_{n2} & \cdots & X_{nk} \end{pmatrix} \quad \text{and} \quad \begin{pmatrix} Y_1 \\ Y_2 \\ \vdots \\ Y_n \end{pmatrix}$$

Observed strength variables   Observed stress variables

Hence, the likelihood function for the observations can be written as

$$L(\alpha_1, \alpha_2, \beta_1, \beta_2) = \prod_{i=1}^{n} \left[\prod_{j=1}^{k} f(x_{i,j})\right] g(y_i), \tag{9}$$

where

$$f(x_{ij}) = \alpha_1 \beta_1 x_{ij}^{-(\alpha_1+1)} e^{-\beta_1 x_{ij}^{-\alpha_1}},$$

$$g(y_i) = \alpha_2 \beta_2 y_i^{-(\alpha_2+1)} e^{-\beta_2 y_i^{-\alpha_2}}.$$

Equation (9) can then be written as

$$L(\alpha_1, \alpha_2, \beta_1, \beta_2) = \alpha_1^{nk} \alpha_2^n \beta_1^{nk} \beta_2^n \left[\prod_{i=1}^{n}\prod_{j=1}^{k} x_{i,j}^{-\alpha_1-1}\right]\left[\prod_{i=1}^{n} y_i^{-\alpha_2-1}\right]\left[e^{-\beta_1 \sum_{i=1}^{n}\sum_{j=1}^{k} x_{i,j}^{-\alpha_1}}\right]\left[e^{-\beta_2 \sum_{i=1}^{n} y_i^{-\alpha_2}}\right]. \tag{10}$$

From Equation (10), the log-likelihood function can be derived as follows

$$\ell(\alpha_1, \alpha_2, \beta_1, \beta_2) = nk[\log(\alpha_1) + \log(\beta_1)] + n[\log(\alpha_2) + \log(\beta_2)] - (\alpha_1 + 1)\left[\sum_{i=1}^{n}\sum_{j=1}^{k}\log(x_{i,j})\right] \quad (11)$$

$$\times (\alpha_2 + 1)\left[\sum_{i=1}^{n}\log(y_i)\right] - \beta_1\left[\sum_{i=1}^{n}\sum_{j=1}^{k}x_{i,j}^{-\alpha_1}\right] - \beta_2\left[\sum_{i=1}^{n}y_i^{-\alpha_2}\right].$$

Computing the first partial derivatives for ℓ with respect to α_1, α_2, β_1 and β_2 and equating with zero will give the four equations below

$$\frac{nk}{\alpha_1} - \left[\sum_{i=1}^{n}\sum_{j=1}^{k}\log(x_{i,j})\right] + \beta_1\left[\sum_{i=1}^{n}\sum_{j=1}^{k}x_{i,j}^{-\alpha_1}\log(x_{i,j})\right] = 0, \quad (12)$$

$$\frac{n}{\alpha_2} - \left[\sum_{i=1}^{n}\log(y_i)\right] + \beta_2\left[\sum_{i=1}^{n}y_i^{-\alpha_2}\log(y_i)\right] = 0, \quad (13)$$

$$\frac{nk}{\beta_1} - \left[\sum_{i=1}^{n}\sum_{j=1}^{k}x_{i,j}^{-\alpha_1}\right] = 0, \quad (14)$$

$$\frac{n}{\beta_2} - \left[\sum_{i=1}^{n}y_i^{-\alpha_2}\right] = 0, \quad (15)$$

Straightforward from Equations (14) and (15), the estimators for β_1 and β_2 can be given as

$$\hat{\beta}_1 = \frac{nk}{\sum_{i=1}^{n}\sum_{j=1}^{k}x_{i,j}^{-\hat{\alpha}_1}} \quad \text{and} \quad \hat{\beta}_2 = \frac{n}{\sum_{i=1}^{n}y_i^{-\hat{\alpha}_2}} \quad (16)$$

Dragging the two estimates in Equation (16) into Equations (12) and (13), respectively, and solving will give estimates for α_1 and α_2, $\hat{\alpha}_1$ and $\hat{\alpha}_2$, respectively, and substituting by $\hat{\alpha}_1$, $\hat{\alpha}_2$, $\hat{\beta}_1$ and $\hat{\beta}_2$ in Equation (8), we obtain the MLE $\hat{R}_{s,k}$ as follows

$$\hat{R}_{s,k} = \sum_{i=s}^{k}\sum_{l=0}^{i}\sum_{r=0}^{\infty}\binom{k}{i}\binom{i}{l}(-1)^l\frac{(l-k)^r\hat{\beta}_1^r}{r!}\hat{\beta}_2^{-\frac{r\hat{\alpha}_1}{\hat{\alpha}_2}}\Gamma\left(\frac{r\hat{\alpha}_1}{\hat{\alpha}_2}+1\right). \quad (17)$$

Fisher Information Matrix

In this sub-section, the asymptotic confidence interval (ACI) for the reliability function will be derived using the Fisher information (FI) matrix. The concept of the FI matrix is based on the missing value principle which was introduced by Louis [33] and is defined as follows:

Observed information = Complete information − Missing information.

The asymptotic variance–covariance of the MLEs $\hat{\alpha}_1$, $\hat{\alpha}_2$, $\hat{\beta}_1$ and $\hat{\beta}_2$ are derived from the entries of the inverse matrix of the FI matrix $I_{ij} = E\{-[\partial^2\ell(\Phi)/\partial\phi_i\partial\phi_j]\}$, where $i,j = 1,2$ and $\Phi = (\phi_1, \phi_2, \phi_3, \phi_4) = (\alpha_1, \alpha_2, \beta_1, \beta_2)$. Unfortunately, obtaining an exact closed form for the previous expectations is very complicated. Hence, the observed FI matrix $\hat{I}_{ij} = \{-[\partial^2\ell(\Phi)/\partial\phi_i\partial\phi_j]\}_{\Phi=\hat{\Phi}}$. This is obtained by dropping the expectation operator E and using it to construct the confidence intervals for the unknown parameters.

The entries of the observed FI matrix are the second partial derivatives of the log-likelihood function, which is easily obtained. Therefore, the observed FI matrix is given by

$$\hat{I}(\hat{\alpha}_1,\hat{\alpha}_2,\hat{\beta}_1,\hat{\beta}_2) = \begin{pmatrix} -\frac{\partial^2 \ell}{\partial \alpha_1^2} & -\frac{\partial^2 \ell}{\partial \alpha_1 \partial \alpha_2} & -\frac{\partial^2 \ell}{\partial \alpha_1 \partial \beta_1} & -\frac{\partial^2 \ell}{\partial \alpha_1 \partial \beta_2} \\ -\frac{\partial^2 \ell}{\partial \alpha_2 \partial \alpha_1} & -\frac{\partial^2 \ell}{\partial \alpha_2^2} & -\frac{\partial^2 \ell}{\partial \alpha_2 \partial \beta_1} & -\frac{\partial^2 \ell}{\partial \alpha_2 \partial \beta_2} \\ -\frac{\partial^2 \ell}{\partial \beta_1 \partial \alpha_1} & -\frac{\partial^2 \ell}{\partial \beta_1 \partial \alpha_2} & -\frac{\partial^2 \ell}{\partial \beta_1^2} & -\frac{\partial^2 \ell}{\partial \beta_1 \partial \beta_2} \\ -\frac{\partial^2 \ell}{\partial \beta_2 \partial \alpha_1} & -\frac{\partial^2 \ell}{\partial \beta_2 \partial \alpha_2} & -\frac{\partial^2 \ell}{\partial \beta_2 \partial \beta_1} & -\frac{\partial^2 \ell}{\partial \beta_2^2} \end{pmatrix}_{(\alpha_1,\alpha_2,\beta_1,\beta_2)=(\hat{\alpha}_1,\hat{\alpha}_2,\hat{\beta}_1,\hat{\beta}_2)}, \quad (18)$$

By inverting the information matrix $\hat{I}(\alpha_1, \alpha_2, \beta_1, \beta_2)$, the approximate asymptotic variance–covariance matrix $[\hat{V}]$ for the MLEs can be obtained as:

$$[\hat{V}] = \hat{I}^{-1}(\hat{\alpha}_1,\hat{\alpha}_2,\hat{\beta}_1,\hat{\beta}_2) = \begin{pmatrix} Var(\hat{\alpha}_1) & cov(\hat{\alpha}_1,\hat{\alpha}_2) & cov(\hat{\alpha}_1,\hat{\beta}_1) & cov(\hat{\alpha}_1,\hat{\beta}_2) \\ cov(\hat{\alpha}_2,\hat{\alpha}_1) & Var(\hat{\alpha}_2) & cov(\hat{\alpha}_2,\hat{\beta}_1) & cov(\hat{\alpha}_2,\hat{\beta}_2) \\ cov(\hat{\beta}_1,\hat{\alpha}_1) & cov(\hat{\beta}_1,\hat{\alpha}_2) & Var(\hat{\beta}_1) & cov(\hat{\beta}_1,\hat{\beta}_2) \\ cov(\hat{\beta}_2,\hat{\alpha}_1) & cov(\hat{\beta}_2,\hat{\alpha}_2) & cov(\hat{\beta}_2,\hat{\beta}_1) & Var(\hat{\beta}_2) \end{pmatrix}. \quad (19)$$

Assuming some regularity conditions, $(\hat{\alpha}_1, \hat{\alpha}_2, \hat{\beta}_1, \hat{\beta}_2)$ will be approximately distributed as a multivariate normal distribution with mean $(\alpha_1, \alpha_2, \beta_1, \beta_2)$ and covariance matrix $I^{-1}(\alpha_1, \alpha_2, \beta_1, \beta_2)$, see Lawless [34]. Then, the $100(1-\gamma)\%$ two-sided confidence intervals of α_1, α_2, β_1 and β_2 can be given by

$$\hat{\alpha}_i \pm Z_{\frac{\gamma}{2}} \sqrt{Var(\hat{\alpha}_i)} \text{ and } \hat{\beta}_i \pm Z_{\frac{\gamma}{2}} \sqrt{Var(\hat{\beta}_i)} \quad (20)$$

where $Z_{\frac{\gamma}{2}}$ is the percentile of the standard normal distribution with a right-tail probability $\frac{\gamma}{2}$.

To construct the ACIs of the reliability function, $R_{s,k}$, it is necessary to compute its variance. The MLE of the $R_{s,k}$ is asymptotically normal with mean $\hat{R}_{s,k}$ and its corresponding asymptotic variance is given as

$$\hat{\sigma}^2_{R_{s,k}} = \sum_{i=1}^{4} \sum_{j=1}^{4} \frac{\partial R_{s,k}}{\partial \theta_i} \frac{\partial R_{s,k}}{\partial \theta_j} I_{ij}^{-1} \quad (21)$$

$$= \frac{\partial R_{s,k}}{\partial \alpha_1} \frac{\partial R_{s,k}}{\partial \alpha_1} I_{11}^{-1} + 2 \frac{\partial R_{s,k}}{\partial \alpha_1} \frac{\partial R_{s,k}}{\partial \beta_1} I_{13}^{-1} + \frac{\partial R_{s,k}}{\partial \alpha_2} \frac{\partial R_{s,k}}{\partial \alpha_2} I_{22}^{-1}$$

$$+ 2 \frac{\partial R_{s,k}}{\partial \alpha_2} \frac{\partial R_{s,k}}{\partial \beta_2} I_{24}^{-1} + \frac{\partial R_{s,k}}{\partial \beta_1} \frac{\partial R_{s,k}}{\partial \beta_1} I_{33}^{-1} + \frac{\partial R_{s,k}}{\partial \beta_2} \frac{\partial R_{s,k}}{\partial \beta_2} I_{44}^{-1}.$$

Then, the $100(1-\vartheta)\%$ two-sided confidence intervals of $R_{s,k}$ can be given by

$$\hat{R}_{s,k} \pm Z_{\frac{\vartheta}{2}} \sqrt{\hat{\sigma}^2_{R_{s,k}}} \quad (22)$$

4. Bayesian Estimation

Another method for obtaining the estimates for the distribution parameters and the reliability function is discussed in this section and is known as the Bayesian estimation. Before collecting and organizing the data, the joint prior distribution should be assumed, and what distinguishes this method is that the prior knowledge is merged in the solution steps. The Bayesian estimates for the four parameters α_1, α_2, β_1 and β_2 in addition to the reliability function $R_{s,k}$ is obtained under the squared error loss (SEL) function. First, the prior knowledge of the parameters α_1, α_2, β_1 and β_2 is assumed to follow gamma distribution as follows

$$\begin{aligned}\pi_1(\alpha_1) &= \alpha_1^{a_1-1} e^{-b_1 \alpha_1} &, \alpha_1 > 0, \\ \pi_2(\alpha_2) &= \alpha_2^{a_2-1} e^{-b_2 \alpha_2} &, \alpha_2 > 0, \\ \pi_3(\beta_1) &= \beta_1^{a_3-1} e^{-b_3 \beta_1} &, \beta_1 > 0, \\ \pi_4(\beta_2) &= \beta_2^{a_4-1} e^{-b_4 \beta_2} &, \beta_2 > 0, \end{aligned} \quad (23)$$

assuming that all the hyper-parameters a_i and b_i, $i = 1,2,3,4$ are known and non-negative. It can be noted that one reason for choosing this prior density is that Gamma prior is flexible in its nature with a non-informative domain, especially if the values of the hyper-parameters are assumed to be zero, for more details on selecting priors one may refer to Kundu and Howlader [35], Dey and Dey [36], and Dey [14].

Using the likelihood function in Equation (10) and the prior distribution for the parameters α_1, α_2, β_1 and β_2 assumed in the previous equations, the posterior distribution, denoted by $\pi^*(\alpha_1, \alpha_2, \beta_1, \beta_2 \mid \underline{x}, \underline{y})$, for these parameters can be derived as follows

$$\pi^*\left(\alpha_1, \alpha_2, \beta_1, \beta_2 \mid \underline{x}, \underline{y}\right) = \frac{\pi_1(\alpha_1)\,\pi_2(\alpha_2)\,\pi_3(\beta_1)\,\pi_4(\beta_2)\,L(\alpha_1,\alpha_2,\beta_1,\beta_2 \mid \underline{x},\underline{y})}{\int_0^\infty \int_0^\infty \int_0^\infty \int_0^\infty \pi_1(\alpha_1)\,\pi_2(\alpha_2)\,\pi_3(\beta_1)\,\pi_4(\beta_2)\,L(\alpha_1,\alpha_2,\beta_1,\beta_2 \mid \underline{x},\underline{y})\,d\alpha_1 d\alpha_2\,d\beta_1 d\beta_2}. \quad (24)$$

Given a parameter ϕ which is estimated by $\hat{\phi}$, the symmetric loss function SEL function assigns equal losses for both over- and under-estimations, which can be defined as

$$L(\phi, \hat{\phi}) = (\hat{\phi} - \phi)^2.$$

As a result, the Bayes estimate $g(\alpha_1, \alpha_2, \beta_1, \beta_2)$ under the SEL function can be written as

$$\hat{g}_{BS}\left(\alpha_1, \alpha_2, \beta_1, \beta_2 \mid \underline{x}, \underline{y}\right) = E_{\alpha_1,\alpha_2,\beta_1,\beta_2 \mid \underline{x},\underline{y}}\left(g(\alpha_1, \alpha_2, \beta_1, \beta_2)\right),$$

where

$$E_{\alpha_1,\alpha_2,\beta_1,\beta_2 \mid \underline{x},\underline{y}}(g(\alpha_1, \alpha_2, \beta_1, \beta_2)) = \frac{\int_0^\infty \int_0^\infty \int_0^\infty \int_0^\infty g(\alpha_1,\alpha_2,\beta_1,\beta_2)\pi_1(\alpha_1)\pi_2(\alpha_2)\pi_3(\beta_1)\pi_4(\beta_2)L(\alpha_1,\alpha_2,\beta_1,\beta_2 \mid \underline{x},\underline{y})\,d\alpha_1 d\alpha_2 d\beta_1 d\beta_2}{\int_0^\infty \int_0^\infty \int_0^\infty \int_0^\infty \pi_1(\alpha_1)\pi_2(\alpha_2)\pi_3(\beta_1)\pi_4(\beta_2)L(\alpha_1,\alpha_2,\beta_1,\beta_2 \mid \underline{x},\underline{y})\,d\alpha_1 d\alpha_2 d\beta_1 d\beta_2}. \quad (25)$$

The joint posterior density function of α_1, α_2, β_1 and β_2 can be obtained as follows

$$\pi^*(\alpha_1, \alpha_2, \beta_1, \beta_2 \mid \underline{x},\underline{y}) \propto \alpha_1^{nk+a_1-1} \alpha_2^{n+a_2-1} \beta_1^{nk+a_3-1} \beta_2^{n+a_4-1} e^{-b_1\alpha_1 - b_2\alpha_2 - b_3\beta_1 - b_4\beta_2} \\ \times \prod_{i=1}^n \prod_{j=1}^k x_{ij}^{-\alpha_1-1} \prod_{i=1}^n y_i^{-\alpha_2-1} e^{-\beta_1 \sum_{i=1}^n \sum_{j=1}^k x_{ij}^{-\alpha_1}} e^{-\beta_2 \sum_{i=1}^n y_i^{-\alpha_2}}. \quad (26)$$

The Bayesian estimate of $R_{s,k}$, under the SEL function, is the mean of the posterior function in Equation (25) and can be written as

$$\tilde{R}_{s,k} = \int_0^\infty \int_0^\infty \int_0^\infty \int_0^\infty R_{s,k} \pi^*\left(\alpha_1, \alpha_2, \beta_1, \beta_2 \mid \underline{x}, \underline{y}\right) d\alpha_1 d\alpha_2\,d\beta_1 d\beta_2. \quad (27)$$

It is clear that the integral in Equation (27) is difficult to be calculated analytically. Therefore, the Gibbs sampling method is used to obtain the Bayesian estimator for the reliability function $R_{s,k}$.

Gibbs Sampling

The Gibbs sampling method is a special case of the Monte Carlo Markov Chain (MCMC) and can be used to perform the Bayes estimate of $R_{s,k}$ numerically, in addition to the its related credible interval (CRI). The key idea in Gibbs sampling is to generate samples for the required parameters from the posterior conditional density function, given in Equation (26). Then, the posterior conditional density functions of α_1, α_2, β_1 and β_2 are given as

$$\pi_1^*\left(\alpha_1 \mid \alpha_2, \beta_1, \beta_2, \underline{x}, \underline{y}\right) \propto \alpha_1^{nk+a_1-1} e^{-b_1 \alpha_1} \prod_{i=1}^{n}\prod_{j=1}^{k} x_{ij}^{-\alpha_1-1} e^{-\beta_1 \sum_{i=1}^{n}\sum_{j=1}^{k} x_{ij}^{-\alpha_1}}, \tag{28}$$

$$\pi_2^*(\alpha_2 \mid \alpha_1, \beta_1, \beta_2, \underline{x}, \underline{y}) \propto \alpha_2^{n+a_2-1} e^{-b_2 \alpha_2} \prod_{i=1}^{n} y_i^{-\alpha_2-1} e^{-\beta_2 \sum_{i=1}^{n} y_i^{-\alpha_2}}, \tag{29}$$

$$\pi_3^*(\beta_1 \mid \alpha_1, \alpha_2, \beta_2, \underline{x}, \underline{y}) \propto \beta_1^{nk+a_3-1} e^{-b_3 \beta_1} e^{-\beta_1 \sum_{i=1}^{n}\sum_{j=1}^{k} x_{ij}^{-\alpha_1}}, \tag{30}$$

and

$$\pi_4^*(\beta_2 \mid \alpha_1, \alpha_2, \beta_1, \underline{x}, \underline{y}) \propto \beta_2^{n+a_4-1} e^{-b_4 \beta_2} e^{-\beta_2 \sum_{i=1}^{n} y_i^{-\alpha_2}}, \tag{31}$$

respectively. It is difficult to obtain the conditional density function of α_1, α_2, β_1 and β_2. Therefore, the Metropolis–Hasting (M–H) algorithm, proposed by Metropolis et al. [37], is applied using the normal proposal distribution for generating random samples from the posterior density of α_1, α_2, β_1 and β_2. The steps of Gibbs sampling are described as follows:

1. Start with initial guess $\left(\alpha_1^{(0)}, \alpha_2^{(0)}, \beta_1^{(0)}, \beta_2^{(0)}\right)$.
2. Set $l = 1$.
3. Using the following M–H algorithm, generate $\alpha_1^{(l)}, \alpha_2^{(l)}, \beta_1^{(l)}$ and $\beta_2^{(l)}$ from $\pi_1^*\left(\alpha_1^{(l)} \mid \alpha_2^{(l-1)}, \beta_1^{(l-1)}, \beta_2^{(l-1)}, \underline{x}, \underline{y}\right)$, $\pi_2^*\left(\alpha_2^{(l)} \mid \alpha_1^{(l)}, \beta_1^{(l-1)}, \beta_2^{(l-1)}, \underline{x}, \underline{y}\right)$, $\pi_3^*\left(\beta_1^{(l)} \mid \alpha_1^{(l)}, \alpha_2^{(l)}, \beta_2^{(l-1)}, \underline{x}, \underline{y}\right)$ and $\pi_4^*\left(\beta_2^{(l)} \mid \alpha_1^{(l)}, \alpha_2^{(l)}, \beta_1^{(l)}, \underline{x}, \underline{y}\right)$ with the normal proposal distributions

    $$N\left(\alpha_1^{(l-1)}, Var(\alpha_1)\right), N\left(\alpha_2^{(l-1)}, Var(\alpha_2)\right), N\left(\beta_1^{(l-1)}, Var(\beta_1)\right) \text{ and } N\left(\beta_2^{(l-1)}, Var(\beta_2)\right),$$

    where $Var(\alpha_1)$, $Var(\alpha_2)$, $Var(\beta_1)$ and $Var(\beta_2)$ can be obtained from the main diagonal in the inverse Fisher information matrix.
4. Generate a proposal α_1^* from $N\left(\alpha_1^{(l-1)}, Var(\alpha_1)\right)$, α_2^* from $N\left(\alpha_2^{(l-1)}, Var(\alpha_2)\right)$, β_1^* from $N\left(\beta_1^{(l-1)}, Var(\beta_1)\right)$ and β_2^* from $N\left(\beta_2^{(l-1)}, Var(\beta_2)\right)$.

    (i) Evaluate the acceptance probabilities

    $$\eta_{\alpha_1} = \min\left[1, \frac{\pi_1^*\left(\alpha_1^* \mid \alpha_2^{(l-1)}, \beta_1^{(l-1)}, \beta_2^{(l-1)}, \underline{x}, \underline{y}\right)}{\pi_1^*\left(\alpha_1^{(l)} \mid \alpha_2^{(l-1)}, \beta_1^{(l-1)}, \beta_2^{(l-1)}, \underline{x}, \underline{y}\right)}\right],$$

    $$\eta_{\alpha_2} = \min\left[1, \frac{\pi_2^*\left(\alpha_2^* \mid \alpha_1^{(l)}, \beta_1^{(l-1)}, \beta_2^{(l-1)}, \underline{x}, \underline{y}\right)}{\pi_2^*\left(\alpha_2^{(l)} \mid \alpha_1^{(l)}, \beta_1^{(l-1)}, \beta_2^{(l-1)}, \underline{x}, \underline{y}\right)}\right],$$

    $$\eta_{\beta_1} = \min\left[1, \frac{\pi_3^*\left(\beta_1^* \mid \alpha_1^{(l)}, \alpha_2^{(l)}, \beta_2^{(l-1)}, \underline{x}, \underline{y}\right)}{\pi_3^*\left(\beta_1^{(l)} \mid \alpha_1^{(l)}, \alpha_2^{(l)}, \beta_2^{(l-1)}, \underline{x}, \underline{y}\right)}\right],$$

    $$\eta_{\beta_2} = \min\left[1, \frac{\pi_4^*\left(\beta_2^* \mid \alpha_1^{(l)}, \alpha_2^{(l)}, \beta_1^{(l)}, \underline{x}, \underline{y}\right)}{\pi_4^*\left(\beta_2^{(l)} \mid \alpha_1^{(l)}, \alpha_2^{(l)}, \beta_1^{(l)}, \underline{x}, \underline{y}\right)}\right].$$

    (ii) Generate a u_1, u_2, u_3 and u_4 from a uniform $(0,1)$ distribution.
    (iii) If $u_1 < \eta_{\alpha_1}$, accept the proposal and set $\alpha_1^{(l)} = \alpha_1^*$, else set $\alpha_1^{(l)} = \alpha_1^{(l-1)}$.
    (iv) If $u_2 < \eta_{\alpha_2}$, accept the proposal and set $\alpha_2^{(l)} = \alpha_2^*$, else set $\alpha_2^{(l)} = \alpha_2^{(l-1)}$.
    (v) If $u_3 < \eta_{\beta_1}$, accept the proposal and set $\beta_1^{(l)} = \beta_1^*$, else set $\beta_1^{(l)} = \beta_1^{(l-1)}$.

(vi) If $u_4 < \eta_{\beta_2}$, accept the proposal and set $\beta_2^{(l)} = \beta_2^*$, else set $\beta_2^{(l)} = \beta_2^{(l-1)}$.

5. Compute $R_{s,k}^{(l)}$ at $(\alpha_1^{(l)}, \alpha_2^{(l)}, \beta_1^{(l)}, \beta_2^{(l)})$.
6. Set $l = l + 1$.
7. Repeat Steps $(3) - (6)$, N times and obtain $\alpha_1^{(l)}, \alpha_2^{(l)}, \beta_1^{(l)}, \beta_2^{(l)}$ and $R_{s,k}^{(l)}, l = 1, 2, \ldots, N$.
8. To compute the CRIs of $\alpha_1, \alpha_2, \beta_1, \beta_2$ and $R_{s,k}$, $\psi_k^{(l)}, k = 1, 2, 3, 4, 5$, $(\psi_1, \psi_2, \psi_3, \psi_4, \psi_5) = (\alpha_1, \alpha_2, \beta_1, \beta_2, R_{s,k})$ as $\psi_k^{(1)} < \psi_k^{(2)} \ldots < \psi_k^{(N)}$, then the $100(1 - \gamma)\%$ CRIs of ψ_k is

$$\left(\psi_{k(N \gamma/2)}, \psi_{k(N (1-\gamma/2))} \right).$$

The first M simulated variants are discarded in order to ensure convergence and remove the affection of initial value selection. Then the selected samples are $\psi_k^{(i)}, j = M+1, \ldots, N$, for sufficiently large N.

Based on the SEL function, the approximate Bayes estimates of ψ_k is given by

$$\hat{\psi}_k = \frac{1}{N - M} \sum_{j=M+1}^{N} \psi^{(j)}, k = 1, 2, 3, 4, 5.$$

5. Real Data Analysis

In this section, the reliability function is estimated using the MLE and Bayesian estimation methods, where the data under consideration are obtained for the water capacity in the Shasta reservoir in the United States. The view of Shasta Lake during the season of floods in addition to a general view of the Shasta dam are shown in Figure 2.

Figure 2. View of Shasta Lake during the season of floods and a plan view for the dam.

To consider the scenario of the excessive drought, we will focus on the total amount of water in the period from 1980 until 2019. Our claim is that an excessive drought occurs if the total amount of water in August in two years of the next four years is less than the amount of water filling the reservoir in December of the preceding years, otherwise, no excessive drought will occur. This problem was previously studied in different contexts, i.e., see Fatma [19] and Akram [16]. The source of the data is available in [38].

For computational simplicity, the water amount in the reservoir for any given month is divided by the total capacity of the reservoir and the data will then be as follows:

$$X = \begin{pmatrix} 0.5597 & 0.8112 & 0.8296 & 0.7262 \\ 0.7152 & 0.4637 & 0.3634 & 0.4637 \\ 0.2912 & 0.4141 & 0.7540 & 0.5381 \\ 0.7226 & 0.5612 & 0.8140 & 0.7552 \\ 0.5249 & 0.6060 & 0.7159 & 0.5295 \\ 0.7420 & 0.4688 & 0.3451 & 0.4253 \\ 0.7951 & 0.6139 & 0.4616 & 0.2948 \\ 0.6881 & 0.7967 & 0.5913 & 0.8037 \end{pmatrix} \text{ and } Y = \begin{pmatrix} 0.7009 \\ 0.5321 \\ 0.3572 \\ 0.7179 \\ 0.6395 \\ 0.8279 \\ 0.7665 \\ 0.3135 \end{pmatrix}$$

The first row of the observations in matrix X represents the storage amount of water (divided by the total capacity storage of the lake) in August 1980–1983, respectively, while the second row represents this in August 1985–1988, respectively, and so on, with a sample size of 32 observations. Whereas the amount of water in December 1984, 1989, up to 2019 is represented by matrix Y, with a size of 8 observations. It was found that both X and Y values are well-fitted to the Gumbel Type II distribution. The Gumbel Type II distribution was chosen primarily because of its suitability for predicting the possibility of climatic events such as annual flood flows (which is the case of this study), earthquakes, and other natural disasters. However, fitting outcomes for certain classical models, such as the log-normal distribution, are poor, with p-values of 1.57936×10^{-11} and 0.00194213 for the X and Y datasets, respectively. While for the Gumbel Type II distribution, the Kolmogorov–Smirnov (KS) distance for X with the estimated parameters is 0.178521 and the corresponding p-value is 0.230418. Furthermore, for Y, the KS distance with the estimated parameters is 0.263293 and the corresponding p-value is 0.550885. A comparison between the empirical distribution of the dataset and the survival function of the Gumbel Type II distribution is presented in Figure 3.

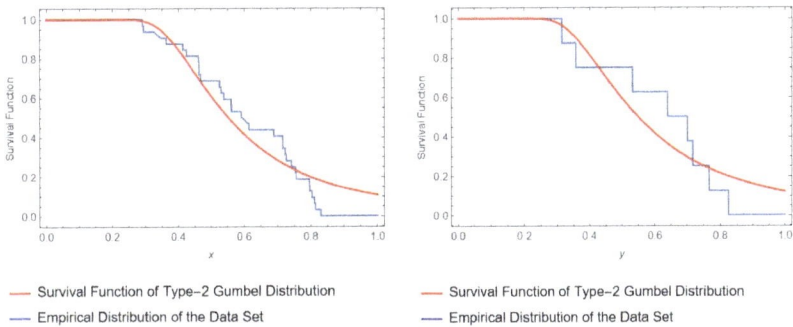

Figure 3. Empirical and fitted survival functions for the two datasets X and Y.

For the complete dataset, the MLEs for the parameters, α_1, α_2, β_1, and β_2, and the reliability function, in addition to the Bayesian estimation with respect to SEL function are displayed in Table 1.

Table 1. The point estimates for α_1, β_1, α_2, β_2 and R.

	α_1	β_1	α_2	β_2	$R_{2,4}$
MLE	0.303858	0.402204	0.00569851	238.391	0.00789931
Bayes	0.469386	0.393857	0.00850074	237.782	0.00824543

From Table 1, the estimated values are relatively close to each other, which indicates the good performance of the estimators. In addition, the two estimators for the reliability function $R_{2,4}$ seem to be very close and approximately equal to zero, indicating no excessive droughts in these periods. The convergence for the estimated parameters using the MCMC method with 1000 iterations is shown in Figure 4.

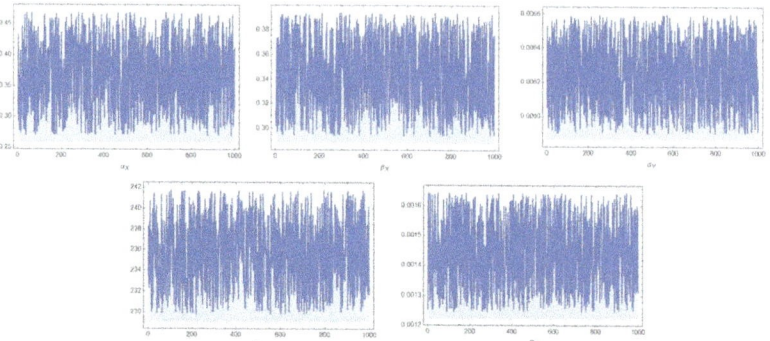

Figure 4. Convergence for the estimated parameters α_1, β_1, α_1, β_2 and R.

6. Simulation Study

A Monte Carlo simulation analysis is carried out in this section comparing the performance of the MLE and Bayesian estimates of the distribution's parameters α_1, β_1, α_2, and β_2 under various scenarios. The comparisons are made using the mean-squares-error (MSE) criterion. All computations are carried out in Mathematica 12, and all the results are obtained using 1000 Monte Carlo samples. We use various sample sizes (n) and (s,k) values in the simulation setup. Various parameter values are selected with different sample sizes (n) such as $n = 30$, 40, 50, 100, and 150 and α_1, β_1, α_2, and β_2 are assumed to be (0.2, 0.5, 0.05, and 200) and (0.3, 0.4, 0.05, and 200), respectively.

Tables 2 and 3 show that in most cases, the Bayesian estimators of the parameters have a large bias compared with the MLEs for small sample sizes. However, when the sample sizes grow larger, all of the estimators exhibit small biases. In terms of the MSE criterion, it is clear that as the sample size increases, the MSEs for the estimates of α_1, β_1, and α_2 decrease, as expected. However, it was noticed that the MSE for β_2 does not decrease as the sample size increases; hence, sometimes some values of MSE violate this pattern due to some causes such as the numerical solution of a certain number of non-linear simultaneous equations. It should be noted that informative priors improve the performance of Bayesian estimates in a reasonable way. As sample sizes grow larger, the MSE values for all estimators become nearly identical. To emphasize the performance of the proposed methods, another criterion is applied which is the coverage probability. The coverage probability indicates how many times a confidence interval contains the initial value of the estimated parameters through the number of simulated samples. In addition, the average interval lengths for both the ACIs and CRIs are calculated and tabulated in Tables 4 and 5. It is noted that for various values of α_1, β_1, α_2, and β_2, for n, s, and k, the CRIs perform better than the ACIs through the coverage probability and the average lengths of intervals.

Table 2. The MLE and Bayesian estimates for the parameters $(\alpha_1, \beta_1, \alpha_2, \beta_2) = (0.2, 0.5, 0.05, 200)$ with the associated MSE between parenthesis.

			MLE				Bayesian			
$(\alpha_1, \beta_1, \alpha_2, \beta_2)$	(s, k)	n	$\hat{\alpha}_1$	$\hat{\beta}_1$	$\hat{\alpha}_2$	$\hat{\beta}_2$	$\hat{\alpha}_1$	$\hat{\beta}_1$	$\hat{\alpha}_2$	$\hat{\beta}_2$
(0.2, 0.5, 0.05, 200)	(3, 5)	30	0.20146	0.50203	0.04999	199.837	0.1808	0.45054	0.04486	198.838
			(0.00017)	(0.00296)	(0.000)	(32.8054)	(0.0002)	(0.0034)	(0.000)	(33.0127)
		40	0.2014	0.50013	0.05001	199.969	0.18074	0.44884	0.04488	198.969
			(0.00013)	(0.00225)	(0.000)	(31.3774)	(0.00014)	(0.00271)	(0.000)	(33.9823)
		50	0.2011	0.50103	0.04998	199.897	0.18047	0.44964	0.04485	198.898
			(0.0001)	(0.00176)	(0.000)	(32.0521)	(0.00012)	(0.002)	(0.000)	(37.8047)
		100	0.20071	0.49831	0.04993	199.688	0.18012	0.4472	0.04481	198.689
			(0.00005)	(0.0009)	(0.000)	(31.9973)	(0.00005)	(0.00116)	(0.000)	(39.0693)
		150	0.20037	0.5002	0.04999	200.017	0.17982	0.4489	0.04486	199.017
			(0.00003)	(0.00059)	(0.000)	(33.7554)	(0.00004)	(0.00059)	(0.000)	(40.6417)
	(5, 5)	30	0.20222	0.49926	0.04997	199.657	0.18148	0.44805	0.04484	198.659
			(0.00017)	(0.00292)	(0.000)	(33.13)	(0.0002)	(0.00331)	(0.000)	(35.7178)
		40	0.20177	0.50036	0.04999	199.715	0.18107	0.44904	0.04486	198.716
			(0.00012)	(0.00205)	(0.000)	(32.5364)	(0.00013)	(0.00232)	(0.000)	(38.4116)
		50	0.20087	0.50181	0.04995	199.765	0.18027	0.45035	0.04483	198.767
			(0.0001)	(0.00176)	(0.000)	(34.8049)	(0.00012)	(0.00227)	(0.000)	(35.433)
		100	0.20051	0.5015	0.04999	199.824	0.17994	0.45006	0.04486	198.824
			(0.00005)	(0.00088)	(0.000)	(31.978)	(0.00005)	(0.00114)	(0.000)	(36.2068)
		150	0.20041	0.50021	0.05002	199.727	0.17986	0.44891	0.04489	198.728
			(0.00003)	(0.00058)	(0.000)	(32.943)	(0.00004)	(0.00058)	(0.000)	(34.9308)
	(5, 6)	30	0.20152	0.50146	0.05001	199.8	0.18085	0.45003	0.04488	198.801
			(0.00014)	(0.0022)	(0.000)	(32.295)	(0.00015)	(0.00232)	(0.000)	(33.4603)
		40	0.20155	0.50179	0.05005	199.89	0.18088	0.45032	0.04492	198.891
			(0.00011)	(0.0018)	(0.000)	(34.2618)	(0.00013)	(0.00204)	(0.000)	(34.2076)
		50	0.20141	0.49875	0.05	199.765	0.18075	0.44759	0.04487	198.766
			(0.00009)	(0.00149)	(0.000)	(30.8775)	(0.0001)	(0.00175)	(0.000)	(32.8875)
		100	0.20038	0.5005	0.04995	200.074	0.17983	0.44916	0.04483	199.074
			(0.00004)	(0.00067)	(0.000)	(31.4818)	(0.00005)	(0.00075)	(0.000)	(32.6242)
		150	0.20014	0.50009	0.04999	200.067	0.17962	0.4488	0.04486	199.067
			(0.00003)	(0.00052)	(0.000)	(33.1109)	(0.00004)	(0.00064)	(0.000)	(36.4121)

Table 3. The MLE and Bayesian estimates for the parameters $(\alpha_1, \beta_1, \alpha_2, \beta_2) = (0.3, 0.4, 0.05, 200)$ with the associated MSE between parenthesis.

			MLE				Bayesian			
$(\alpha_1, \beta_1, \alpha_2, \beta_2)$	(s, k)	n	$\hat{\alpha}_1$	$\hat{\beta}_1$	$\hat{\alpha}_2$	$\hat{\beta}_2$	$\hat{\alpha}_1$	$\hat{\beta}_1$	$\hat{\alpha}_2$	$\hat{\beta}_2$
(0.3, 0.4, 0.05, 200)	(3, 5)	30	0.3025	0.39763	0.05	199.822	0.27147	0.35685	0.04487	198.822
			(0.00036)	(0.00226)	(0.000)	(33.8999)	(0.00038)	(0.00234)	(0.000)	(40.3491)
		40	0.30229	0.39954	0.04984	199.835	0.27129	0.35856	0.04473	198.836
			(0.00026)	(0.0016)	(0.000)	(34.5172)	(0.00026)	(0.00166)	(0.000)	(35.5571)
		50	0.30102	0.40185	0.05003	199.753	0.27014	0.36064	0.0449	198.754
			(0.00021)	(0.00123)	(0.000)	(34.6565)	(0.00025)	(0.00138)	(0.000)	(42.4399)
		100	0.30021	0.40196	0.05007	200.059	0.26942	0.36074	0.04493	199.059
			(0.00012)	(0.0007)	(0.000)	(32.4818)	(0.00013)	(0.0007)	(0.000)	(32.5149)
		150	0.30078	0.39987	0.04999	199.555	0.26993	0.35886	0.04486	198.558
			(0.00007)	(0.00043)	(0.000)	(33.0983)	(0.00009)	(0.00052)	(0.000)	(38.4439)

Table 3. *Cont.*

$(\alpha_1, \beta_1, \alpha_2, \beta_2)$	(s, k)	n	MLE				Bayesian			
			$\hat{\alpha}_1$	$\hat{\beta}_1$	$\hat{\alpha}_2$	$\hat{\beta}_2$	$\hat{\alpha}_1$	$\hat{\beta}_1$	$\hat{\alpha}_2$	$\hat{\beta}_2$
	(5, 5)	30	0.30285	0.4029	0.04994	199.654	0.27179	0.36157	0.04482	198.656
			(0.00038)	(0.00225)	(0.000)	(33.433)	(0.00049)	(0.00238)	(0.000)	(40.4265)
		40	0.30167	0.40134	0.04994	200.091	0.27073	0.36017	0.04482	199.09
			(0.00026)	(0.00166)	(0.000)	(34.0351)	(0.00032)	(0.00196)	(0.000)	(33.7554)
		50	0.30159	0.40057	0.04993	200.15	0.27065	0.35949	0.04481	199.149
			(0.00022)	(0.00129)	(0.000)	(34.2804)	(0.00026)	(0.00164)	(0.000)	(43.0006)
		100	0.30051	0.40013	0.04995	199.983	0.26969	0.35909	0.04483	198.983
			(0.00011)	(0.00068)	(0.000)	(32.9482)	(0.00011)	(0.00069)	(0.000)	(33.3591)
		150	0.30005	0.40084	0.04996	199.626	0.26928	0.35973	0.04484	198.628
			(0.00007)	(0.00044)	(0.000)	(33.8825)	(0.00008)	(0.00051)	(0.000)	(35.5814)
	(5, 6)	30	0.30217	0.40028	0.04992	200.064	0.27118	0.35923	0.0448	199.063
			(0.00031)	(0.00158)	(0.000)	(33.822)	(0.0004)	(0.00236)	(0.000)	(36.4273)
		40	0.30233	0.39868	0.05001	199.671	0.27132	0.35779	0.04488	198.672
			(0.00025)	(0.00129)	(0.000)	(32.1462)	(0.0003)	(0.00168)	(0.000)	(37.4052)
		50	0.30195	0.39879	0.05	200.079	0.27098	0.35789	0.04487	199.079
			(0.0002)	(0.00109)	(0.000)	(33.8499)	(0.00021)	(0.00116)	(0.000)	(40.087)
		100	0.30038	0.40072	0.05001	199.938	0.26957	0.35962	0.04489	198.938
			(0.00009)	(0.00055)	(0.000)	(32.5754)	(0.00011)	(0.00064)	(0.000)	(36.7374)
		150	0.30054	0.40001	0.04998	200.075	0.26971	0.35899	0.04486	199.075
			(0.00006)	(0.00036)	(0.000)	(33.7145)	(0.00006)	(0.0004)	(0.000)	(38.2541)

Table 4. ACIs and CRIs for $(\alpha_1, \beta_1, \alpha_2, \beta_2) = (0.2, 0.5, 0.05, 200)$ with their corresponding coverage probabilities between parenthesis.

$(\alpha_1, \beta_1, \alpha_2, \beta_2)$	(s, k)	n	MLE				Bayesian			
			$\hat{\alpha}_1$	$\hat{\beta}_1$	$\hat{\alpha}_2$	$\hat{\beta}_2$	$\hat{\alpha}_1$	$\hat{\beta}_1$	$\hat{\alpha}_2$	$\hat{\beta}_2$
(0.2, 0.5, 0.05, 200)	(3, 5)	30	0.0507	0.2109	0.0281	567.508	0.0304	0.1265	0.0169	29.5104
			(0.95)	(0.951)	(1.000)	(1.000)	(0.9949)	(0.9951)	(0.995)	(0.995)
		40	0.0436	0.1833	0.0244	491.674	0.0261	0.11	0.0146	25.567
			(0.944)	(0.944)	(1.000)	(1.000)	(0.995)	(0.995)	(0.995)	(0.9949)
		50	0.0389	0.1643	0.0218	438.494	0.0233	0.0986	0.0131	22.8017
			(0.951)	(0.948)	(1.000)	(1.000)	(0.9951)	(0.9951)	(0.9951)	(0.9949)
		100	0.0275	0.1159	0.0153	308.949	0.0165	0.0695	0.0092	16.0653
			(0.954)	(0.935)	(1.000)	(1.000)	(0.9949)	(0.995)	(0.9949)	(0.995)
		150	0.0224	0.0948	0.0125	252.359	0.0134	0.0569	0.0075	13.1227
			(0.962)	(0.948)	(1.000)	(1.000)	(0.9949)	(0.9951)	(0.9949)	(0.995)
	(5, 5)	30	0.0506	0.2115	0.0283	570.071	0.0303	0.1269	0.017	29.6437
			(0.951)	(0.933)	(1.000)	(1.000)	(0.9949)	(0.995)	(0.9952)	(0.9949)
		40	0.0435	0.1839	0.0245	492.382	0.0261	0.1103	0.0147	25.6038
			(0.949)	(0.945)	(1.000)	(1.000)	(0.9949)	(0.9949)	(0.995)	(0.995)
		50	0.039	0.164	0.0218	439.355	0.0234	0.0984	0.0131	22.8464
			(0.964)	(0.956)	(1.000)	(1.000)	(0.995)	(0.9951)	(0.9949)	(0.9951)
		100	0.0274	0.1165	0.0154	309.768	0.0164	0.0699	0.0092	16.1079
			(0.954)	(0.941)	(1.000)	(1.000)	(0.995)	(0.995)	(0.9951)	(0.995)
		150	0.0224	0.0949	0.0125	252.428	0.0134	0.057	0.0075	13.1262
			(0.953)	(0.952)	(1.000)	(1.000)	(0.9951)	(0.9951)	(0.9951)	(0.995)

Table 4. Cont.

$(\alpha_1, \beta_1, \alpha_2, \beta_2)$	(s,k)	n	MLE				Bayesian			
			$\hat{\alpha}_1$	$\hat{\beta}_1$	$\hat{\alpha}_2$	$\hat{\beta}_2$	$\hat{\alpha}_1$	$\hat{\beta}_1$	$\hat{\alpha}_2$	$\hat{\beta}_2$
	(5, 6)	30	0.046	0.1931	0.0282	567.143	0.0276	0.1159	0.0169	29.4914
			(0.946)	(0.951)	(1.000)	(1.000)	(0.9951)	(0.995)	(0.995)	(0.995)
		40	0.0397	0.168	0.0245	493.172	0.0238	0.1008	0.0147	25.6449
			(0.945)	(0.951)	(1.000)	(1.000)	(0.9949)	(0.9952)	(0.995)	(0.995)
		50	0.0356	0.1499	0.0218	439.107	0.0213	0.09	0.0131	22.8335
			(0.938)	(0.941)	(1.000)	(1.000)	(0.9949)	(0.995)	(0.9951)	(0.9948)
		100	0.025	0.106	0.0153	308.724	0.015	0.0636	0.0092	16.0537
			(0.957)	(0.958)	(1.000)	(1.000)	(0.9951)	(0.9951)	(0.9949)	(0.9949)
		150	0.0204	0.0866	0.0125	251.642	0.0123	0.052	0.0075	13.0854
			(0.955)	(0.941)	(1.000)	(1.000)	(0.9949)	(0.9951)	(0.995)	(0.995)

Table 5. ACIs and CRIs for $(\alpha_1, \beta_1, \alpha_2, \beta_2) = (0.3, 0.4, 0.05, 200)$ with their corresponding coverage probabilities between parenthesis.

$(\alpha_1, \beta_1, \alpha_2, \beta_2)$	(s,k)	n	MLE				Bayesian			
			$\hat{\alpha}_1$	$\hat{\beta}_1$	$\hat{\alpha}_2$	$\hat{\beta}_2$	$\hat{\alpha}_1$	$\hat{\beta}_1$	$\hat{\alpha}_2$	$\hat{\beta}_2$
(0.3, 0.4, 0.05, 200)	(3, 5)	30	0.0759	0.1848	0.0283	571.737	0.0455	0.1109	0.017	29.7303
			(0.952)	(0.938)	(1.000)	(1.000)	(0.9951)	(0.995)	(0.995)	(0.995)
		40	0.0656	0.1594	0.0244	492.21	0.0394	0.0957	0.0147	25.5949
			(0.959)	(0.949)	(1.000)	(1.000)	(0.995)	(0.995)	(0.9951)	(0.9949)
		50	0.0582	0.1438	0.0217	437.88	0.0349	0.0863	0.013	22.7697
			(0.954)	(0.953)	(1.000)	(1.000)	(0.9948)	(0.9948)	(0.9951)	(0.995)
		100	0.0412	0.1013	0.0154	309.34	0.0247	0.0608	0.0092	16.0857
			(0.96)	(0.95)	(1.000)	(1.000)	(0.995)	(0.9951)	(0.9949)	(0.995)
		150	0.0335	0.0827	0.0125	251.705	0.0201	0.0496	0.0075	13.0887
			(0.946)	(0.946)	(1.000)	(1.000)	(0.995)	(0.995)	(0.995)	(0.9949)
	(5, 5)	30	0.0759	0.1844	0.0282	568.27	0.0456	0.1106	0.0169	29.55
			(0.94)	(0.95)	(1.000)	(1.000)	(0.995)	(0.995)	(0.9951)	(0.9952)
		40	0.0655	0.1599	0.0245	493.459	0.0393	0.0959	0.0147	25.6599
			(0.95)	(0.942)	(1.000)	(1.000)	(0.9951)	(0.9948)	(0.995)	(0.995)
		50	0.0584	0.1429	0.0218	438.597	0.035	0.0857	0.0131	22.807
			(0.947)	(0.94)	(1.000)	(1.000)	(0.9951)	(0.9951)	(0.9949)	(0.9949)
		100	0.0411	0.1015	0.0153	309.374	0.0247	0.0609	0.0092	16.0874
			(0.954)	(0.95)	(1.000)	(1.000)	(0.995)	(0.9951)	(0.9951)	(0.995)
		150	0.0336	0.0827	0.0125	252.025	0.0201	0.0496	0.0075	13.1053
			(0.953)	(0.964)	(1.000)	(1.000)	(0.9952)	(0.9951)	(0.995)	(0.9949)
	(5, 6)	30	0.0689	0.1689	0.0283	570.784	0.0413	0.1014	0.017	29.6808
			(0.956)	(0.945)	(1.000)	(1.000)	(0.995)	(0.9951)	(0.995)	(0.9951)
		40	0.0597	0.1463	0.0245	494.035	0.0358	0.0878	0.0147	25.6898
			(0.953)	(0.948)	(1.000)	(1.000)	(0.995)	(0.9951)	(0.995)	(0.995)
		50	0.0533	0.1305	0.0217	437.669	0.032	0.0783	0.013	22.7588
			(0.944)	(0.945)	(1.000)	(1.000)	(0.9951)	(0.995)	(0.995)	(0.9953)
		100	0.0376	0.0925	0.0153	308.903	0.0225	0.0555	0.0092	16.063
			(0.949)	(0.954)	(1.000)	(1.000)	(0.9951)	(0.9951)	(0.995)	(0.9949)
		150	0.0306	0.0756	0.0125	252.177	0.0184	0.0453	0.0075	13.1132
			(0.957)	(0.952)	(1.000)	(1.000)	(0.9951)	(0.9947)	(0.995)	(0.995)

7. Conclusions

In this study, the stress–strength model describing the amount of water held in a certain reservoir over time is modeled parametrically using the Gumbel Type II distribution. It introduces a mathematical procedure for obtaining a closed form for R. In addition to the Bayesian technique, the maximum likelihood estimation for the parameter R is carried out.

A simulation study is conducted to compare the effectiveness of the various approaches. The analysis revealed that the water in storage is sufficiently durable. In other words, since the value of R is constantly close to zero, droughts are unlikely to occur even when this amount of water is subjected to evaporation and consumption.

Author Contributions: Conceptualization, M.M.M.M. and M.S.A.; methodology, D.A.R., M.M.M.M., M.S.A. and H.H.A.; software, M.M.M.M.; validation, M.M.M.M., M.S.A. and D.A.R.; formal analysis, M.M.M.M., M.S.A. and D.A.R.; investigation, M.M.M.M., M.S.A. and D.A.R.; resources, M.M.M.M., M.S.A., H.H.A. and D.A.R.; data curation, M.M.M.M. and M.S.A.; writing—original draft preparation, M.M.M.M., M.S.A. and D.A.R.; writing—review and editing, H.H.A.; visualization, M.M.M.M. and M.S.A.; supervision, D.A.R.; project administration, M.M.M.M. and M.S.A.; funding acquisition, H.H.A. All authors have read and agreed to the published version of the manuscript.

Funding: This work was supported by the Deanship of Scientific Research, Vice Presidency for Graduate Studies and Scientific Research, King Faisal University, Saudi Arabia [GRANT No. 2241].

Data Availability Statement: All data are available in the manuscript.

Conflicts of Interest: The authors declare no conflict of interest.

References

1. Birnbaum, Z.W. On a use of Mann–Whitney statistics. *Proc. Third Berkley Symp. Math. Stat. Probab.* **1956**, *1*, 13–17.
2. Hanagal, D.D. Estimation of system reliability. *Stat. Pap.* **1999**, *40*, 99–106. [CrossRef]
3. Kotz, S.; Lumelskii, Y.; Pensky, M. *The Stress-Strength Model and Its Generalization: Theory and Applications*; World Scientific Publishing Company: Singapore, 2003.
4. Raqab, M.Z.; Madi, M.T.; Kundu, D. Estimation of $R = P(Y < X)$ for the 3-parameter generalized exponential distribution. *Commun. Stat.* **2008**, *37*, 2854–2864.
5. Kundu, D.; Raqab, M.Z. Estimation of $R = P(Y < X)$ for three parameter Weibull distribution. *Stat. Probab. Lett.* **2009**, *79*, 1839–1846.
6. Lio, Y.L.; Tsai, T.R. Estimation of $\delta = P(X < Y)$ for Burr XII distribution based on the progressively first failure-censored samples. *J. Appl. Stat.* **2012**, *39*, 309–322.
7. Nadar, M.; Kizilaslan, F.; Papadopoulos, A. Classical and Bayesian estimation of $P(Y < X)$ for Kumaraswamy's distribution. *J. Stat. Comput. Simul.* **2014**, *84*, 1505–1529.
8. Rao, G.S.; Kantam, R.R.L. Estimation of reliability in multi-component stress-strength model: Log-logistic distribution. *Electron. J. Appl. Stat. Anal.* **2010**, *3*, 75–84.
9. Rao, G.S. Estimation of reliability in multi-component stress-strength model based on Rayleigh distribution. *Prob. Stat. Forum.* **2012**, *5*, 155–161.
10. Rao, G.S. Estimation of reliability in multi-component stress-strength model based on inverse exponential distribution. *Int. J. Stat. Econ.* **2013**, *10*, 28–37.
11. Rao, G.S.; Kantam, R.R.L.; Rosaiah, K.; Reddy, J.P. Estimation of reliability in multi-component stress-strength model based on inverse Rayleigh distribution. *J. Stat. Appl. Probab.* **2013**, *2*, 261–267. [CrossRef]
12. Kizilaslan, F.; Nadar, M. Estimation of reliability in a multi-component stress-strength model based on a bivariate Kumaraswamy distribution. *Stat. Pap.* **2018**, *59*, 307–340. [CrossRef]
13. Nadar, M.; Kizilaslan, F. Estimation of reliability in a multi-component stress-strength model based on a Marshall–Olkin bivariate weibull Distribution. *IEEE Trans. Reliab.* **2016**, *65*, 370–380. [CrossRef]
14. Dey, S.; Singh, S.; Tripathi, Y.M.; Asgharzadeh, A. Estimation and prediction for a progressively censored generalized inverted exponential distribution. *Stat. Methodol.* **2016**, *32*, 185–202. [CrossRef]
15. Wu, X.Z. Implementing statistical fitting and reliability analysis for geotechnical engineering problems in R. *Georisk Assess. Manag. Risk Eng. Syst. Geohazards* **2017**, *11*, 173–188. [CrossRef]
16. Kohansal, A. On estimation of reliability in a multi-component stress-strength model for a Kumaraswamy distribution based on progressively censored sample. *Stat. Pap.* **2019**, *60*, 2185–2224. [CrossRef]
17. Xu, J.; Dang, C. A novel fractional moments-based maximum entropy method for high-dimensional reliability analysis. *Appl. Math. Model.* **2019**, *75*, 749–768. [CrossRef]
18. Zhang, X.; Low, Y.M.; Koh, C.G. Maximum entropy distribution with fractional moments for reliability analysis. *Struct. Saf.* **2020**, *83*, 101904. [CrossRef]
19. Akgul, F. Classical and Bayesian estimation of multi-component stress-strength reliability for exponentiated Pareto distribution. *Soft Comput.* **2021**, *25*, 9185–9197. [CrossRef]

20. Wang, Z.Z.; Goh, S.H. A maximum entropy method using fractional moments and deep learning for geotechnical reliability analysis. *Acta Geotech.* **2022**, *17*, 1147–1166. [CrossRef]
21. Wang, Z.Z.; Jiang, SH. Characterizing geotechnical site investigation data: A comparative study using a novel distribution model. *Acta Geotech.* **2022**. [CrossRef]
22. Ahmad, H.H.; Almetwally, E.M.; Ramadan, D.A. A comparative inference on reliability estimation for a multi-component stress-strength model under power Lomax distribution with applications. *AIMS Math.* **2022**, *7*, 18050–18079. [CrossRef]
23. Johari, A.; Vali, B.; Golkarfard, H. System reliability analysis of ground response based on peak ground acceleration considering soil layers cross-correlation. *Soil Dyn. Earthq. Eng.* **2021**, *141*, 106475. [CrossRef]
24. Johari A.; Rahmati, H. System reliability analysis of slopes based on the method of slices using sequential compounding method. *Comput. Geotech.* **2019**, *114*, 103116. [CrossRef]
25. Johari, A.; Hajivand, A.K.; Binesh, S. System reliability analysis of soil nail wall using random finite element method. *Bull. Eng. Geol. Environ.* **2020**, *79*, 2777–2798. [CrossRef]
26. Abbas, K.; Fu, J.; Tang, Y. Bayesian Estimation of Gumbel Type-II Distribution. *Data Sci. J.* **2013**, *12*, 33–46. [CrossRef]
27. Kotz, S.; Nadarajah, S. *Extreme Value Distributions: Theory and Applications*; Imperial College Press: London, UK, 2000.
28. Nadarajah, S.; Kotz, S. The exponentiated type distributions. *Acta Appl. Math.* **2006**, *92*, 97–111. [CrossRef]
29. Feroze, N.; Muahmmad, A. *Bayesian Analysis of Gumbel Type II Distribution under Censored Data*, 1st ed.; LAP LAMBERT Academic Publishing: Saarbruecken, Germany, 2014.
30. Mansour, M.M.; Aboshady, M.S. Assessing The Performance of Insulating Fluids Via Point of Statistical Inference View. *TWMS J. App. Eng. Math.* **2022**, *12*, 469–480.
31. Bhattacharyya, G.K.; Johnson, R.A. Estimation of reliability in a multi-component stress-strength model. *J. Am. Stat. Assoc.* **1974**, *69*, 966–970. [CrossRef]
32. Azzalini, A. *Statistical Inference Based on the Likelihood*, 1st ed.; Chapman and Hall/CRC: London, UK, 1996.
33. Louis, T.A. Finding the observed information matrix when using the EM algorithm. *J. R. Statist. Soc. B* **1982**, *44*, 226–233.
34. Lawless, J.F. *Statistical Models and Methods for Lifetime Data*, 2nd ed.; Wiley-Interscience: New York, NY, USA, 2002.
35. Kundu, D.; Howlader, H. Bayesian inference and prediction of the inverse Weibull distribution for Type-II censored data. *Comput. Stat. Data Anal.* **2010**, *54*, 1547–1558. [CrossRef]
36. Dey, S.; Dey, T. On progressively censored generalized inverted exponential distribution. *J. Appl. Stat.* **2014**, *41*, 2557–2576. [CrossRef]
37. Metropolis, N.; Rosenbluth, A.W.; Rosenbluth, M.N.; Teller, A.H. Equations of state calculations by fast computing machines. *J. Chem. Phys.* **1953**, *21*, 1087–1092. [CrossRef]
38. Available online: https://cdec.water.ca.gov/dynamicapp/QueryMonthly?s=SHA&end=1986-10&span=5years (accessed on 1 July 2021).

Disclaimer/Publisher's Note: The statements, opinions and data contained in all publications are solely those of the individual author(s) and contributor(s) and not of MDPI and/or the editor(s). MDPI and/or the editor(s) disclaim responsibility for any injury to people or property resulting from any ideas, methods, instructions or products referred to in the content.

Article

Reliability Analysis of Kavya Manoharan Kumaraswamy Distribution under Generalized Progressive Hybrid Data

Refah Alotaibi [1], Ehab M. Almetwally [2,3] and Hoda Rezk [4,*]

1. Department of Mathematical Sciences, College of Science, Princess Nourah bint Abdulrahman University, P.O. Box 84428, Riyadh 11671, Saudi Arabia; rmalotaibi@pnu.edu.sa
2. Department of Statistics, Faculty of Business Administration, Delta University for Science and Technology, Gamasa 11152, Egypt; ehab.metwaly@deltauniv.edu.eg or ehabxp_2009@hotmail.com
3. Department of Mathematical Statistics, Faculty of Graduate Studies for Statistical Research, Cairo University, Cairo 12613, Egypt
4. Department of Statistics, Al-Azhar University, Cairo 11751, Egypt
* Correspondence: hodaragab.55@azhar.edu.eg or hodaragab2009@yahoo.com

Abstract: Generalized progressive hybrid censoring approaches have been developed to reduce test time and cost. This paper investigates the difficulties associated with estimating the unobserved model parameters and the reliability time functions of the Kavya Manoharan Kumaraswamy (KMKu) distribution based on generalized type-II progressive hybrid censoring using classical and Bayesian estimation techniques. The frequentist estimators' normal approximations are also used to construct the appropriate estimated confidence intervals for the unknown parameter model. Under symmetrical squared error loss, independent gamma conjugate priors are used to produce the Bayesian estimators. The Bayesian estimators and associated highest posterior density intervals cannot be derived analytically since the joint likelihood function is provided in a complicated form. However, they may be evaluated using Monte Carlo Markov chain (MCMC) techniques. Out of all the censoring choices, the best one is selected using four optimality criteria.

Keywords: Kavya Manoharan Kumaraswamy distribution; progressive hybrid generalized type-II censoring; Bayesian and classical estimators; Metropolis–Hastings algorithm; MCMC techniques; optimal plan for progressive censoring

Citation: Alotaibi, R.; Almetwally, E.M.; Rezk, H. Reliability Analysis of Kavya Manoharan Kumaraswamy Distribution under Generalized Progressive Hybrid Data. *Symmetry* **2023**, *15*, 1671. https://doi.org/10.3390/sym15091671

Academic Editors: Arne Johannssen, Nataliya Chukhrova and Quanxin Zhu

Received: 25 July 2023
Revised: 19 August 2023
Accepted: 22 August 2023
Published: 30 August 2023

Copyright: © 2023 by the authors. Licensee MDPI, Basel, Switzerland. This article is an open access article distributed under the terms and conditions of the Creative Commons Attribution (CC BY) license (https://creativecommons.org/licenses/by/4.0/).

1. Introduction

The progressive type-II censoring (PCS-T2) method is the most popular scheme in reliability and survival analysis. Compared with the traditional type-II censoring method, it is better. Progressive censoring is advantageous in a variety of real-world applications, including business, medical research, and therapeutic settings. Up until the test's conclusion, it permits the removal of any remaining experimental units. Assume that n units are used in a life test and that it is not desirable to record every failure because of financial and time constraints. Consequently, only a portion of unit failures are seen. A sample like this is known as a censored sample. Assume that one of the units was accidentally damaged after the test started but before they all burned out. This unit needs to be taken out of the life test if the experiment is still going on. In this situation, a framework for analyzing this kind of data is provided by the progressive censoring scheme. A few examples of primary references are [1,2].

PCS-T2 has drawn a lot of attention in the literature as a very flexible censoring system (see [3] for further details). When testing n independent units at a time $T = 0$, the failure number to be noticed s and the progressive censored samples, $\underline{R} = (R_1, R_2, \ldots, R_s)$, where $n = \sum_{i=1}^{s} R_i + s$, are specified. When the initial failure is seen (suppose that $Y_{1:s:n}$), the other surviving units $n - 1$ are chosen at random, and R_1 of those units is disqualified from the test. Similarly, at the moment of the second failure (suppose that $Y_{2:s:n}$), R_2 of $n - R_1 - 2$

are selected at random and deleted from the test, and so on. At the time of the $s-th$ failure (suppose that $Y_{s:s:n}$), every survivor unit still present $R_s = n - s - \sum_{j=1}^{s-1} R_j$ is removed from the experiment.

Whenever the test units are particularly reliable, the major drawback of this censoring is that it could take longer to finish the progressively type-II hybrid censored samples (PHCS-T2). The authors of [4] proposed a progressive type-I hybrid censored strategy (PHCS-T1) as a remedy for this issue. This method combines PCS-T2 with conventional type-I censoring. Under PHCS-T1, the trial period is stopped at T, maximum likelihood estimators (MLEs) were not always available due to the fact that relatively a few failures might occur before time T in PHCS-T1. To resolve this issue, [5] presented the PHCS-T2 scheme. At $T^* = max(Y_{s:s:n}, T)$, the experiment comes to an end under PHCS-T2. It can take some time until such $s - th$ failures are really observed, despite the fact that PHCS-T2 promises a fixed number of failures.

It could take a while to gather the needed failures, even though the PHCS-T2 ensures an effective number of observable failures. Thus, [6] devised the generalized progressive type-II hybrid censoring (GPHC-T2). Assume that the thresholds $T_i, i = 1$, and 2, as well as the integer s, are preassigned in such a way that $0 < T_1 < T_2 < \infty$ and $1 < s < n$. c_1 and c_2 represent the overall number of failures up to periods T_1 and T_2, respectively. Then, at $Y_{1:s:n}$, R_1 of $n-1$ are arbitrarily excluded from the test, followed by R_2 of $n - R_1 - 2$, and so on.

The experiment is over, and all remaining units are deleted at $T^* = max(T_1, min(Y_{s:s:n}, T_2))$. If $Y_{s:n} < T_1$, failures are observed without any further withdrawals up until time T_1 (Case-I); if $T_1 < Y_{s:s:n} < T_2$, the test is terminated at time $Y_{s:s:n}$ (Case-II); or, if not, the test is terminated at time T_2 (Case-III). Keep in mind that the GPHCS-T2 modifies the PHCS-T2 by guaranteeing that the test is completed at the scheduled time T_2. T_2 demonstrates the longest period of time the researcher is willing to let the experiment continue. As a result, one of the following three data types will be visible to the experimenter:

$$\left(\underset{\sim}{Y}, \underset{\sim}{R} \right) = \begin{cases} Case\ I; \{[Y_{1:n}, R_1], \ldots, [Y_{s-1:s:n}, R_{s-1}], [Y_{s:s:n}, 0], \ldots, [Y_{c_1:n}, 0]\} \\ Case\ II; \{[Y_{1:s:n}, R_1], \ldots, [Y_{c_1:n}, R_{c_1}], [Y_{s-1:s:n}, R_{s-1}], \ldots, [Y_{s:s:n}, R_s]\} \\ Case\ III; \{[Y_{1:s:n}, R_1], \ldots, [Y_{c_1:n}, R_{c_1}], [Y_{c_2-1:n}, R_{c_2-1}], \ldots, [Y_{c_2:n}, R_{c_2}]\}. \end{cases}$$

Figure 1 indicates the cases of generalized type-II progressive hybrid sample as follows:

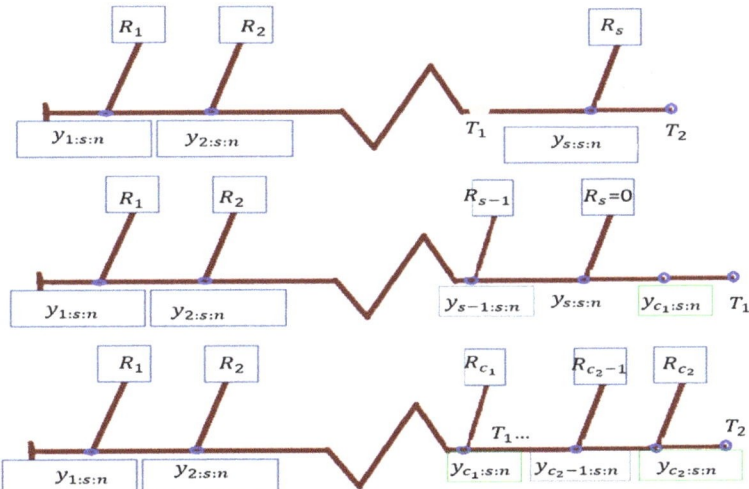

Figure 1. Generalized type-II progressive hybrid cases.

Assume that in a distribution with a cumulative distribution function (cdf) $F(.)$, and probability density function (pdf) $f(.)$, the variables $\underline{Y}$ and $\underline{R}$ represent the respective lifetimes. As a result, the GPHCS-T2 likelihood function is expressed as follows:

$$L_\varphi\left(\theta,\beta|\underline{y}\right) = C_\varphi \prod_{j=1}^{D_\varphi} f(Y_{j:s:n};\theta,\beta)\left[1-F(Y_{j:s:n};\theta,\beta)\right]^{R_j} \psi_\varphi(T_\tau;\theta,\beta), \quad (1)$$

where $\tau = 1, 2$, $\varphi = 1, 2, 3$, stand in for Case-I, Case-II, and Case-III, respectively, and $\psi_\varphi(.)$ is a combination form of dependability functions. Table 1 displays the GPHCS-T2 notations from Equation (1). Many censoring techniques can also be inferred as particular examples from Equation (1), including

Table 1. The notations of the GPHCS-T2.

φ	C_φ	D_φ	$\psi_\varphi(T_\tau;\beta)$	$R^*_{c_\tau+1}$
1	$\prod_{j=1}^{c_1}\sum_{i=j}^{s}(R_i+1)$	c_1	$[1-F(T_1)]^{R^*_{c_1+1}}$	$n-c_1-\sum_{i=1}^{s-1}R_i$
2	$\prod_{j=1}^{s}\sum_{i=j}^{s}(R_i+1)$	s	1	0
3	$\prod_{j=1}^{c_2}\sum_{i=j}^{s}(R_i+1)$	c_2	$[1-F(T_2)]^{R^*_{c_2+1}}$	$n-c_2-\sum_{i=1}^{c_2}R_i$

1. With T_1 setting to 0, use PHCS-T1.
2. $T_2 \to \infty$. by setting PHCS-T2.
3. You may do hybrid type-I censoring by setting $T_1 \to 0$, $R_j = 0$, $j = 1, 2, \ldots, s-1$, $R_s = n-s$.
4. $T_2 \to \infty$, $R_j = 0$, $j = 1, 2, \ldots, s-1$, $R_s = n-s$ can be used to do hybrid type-II censoring.
5. To do type-I censoring, set $T_1 = 0$, $s = 1$, $R_j = 0$, $j = 1, 2, \ldots, s-1$, $R_s = n-s$.
6. A type-II censored sample is produced by setting $T_1 = 0$, $T_2 \to \infty$, $s = 1$, $R_j = 0$, $j = 1, 2, \ldots, s-1$, $R_s = n-s$.

On the basis of GPHCS-T2, more studies have been conducted. For instance, Ref. [7] investigated the prediction issue of forthcoming Burr-XII distribution failure rates. The authors of [8] created the Weibull distribution with little data with an objective Bayesian analysis. The authors of [9] addressed the competing risks from exponential data, and [10] more recently examined both the point and interval estimations of the Burr-XII parameters. Last but not least, [11] addressed the Fréchet distribution's optimality under generalized censoring schemes. In this paper, the KMKu model under generalized censoring samples is studied. Where the KMKu model was initially proposed by [11]. Also, they found that the Kumaraswamy model's and KMKu shape forms in the pdf for different parameter values are comparable. It may be asymmetric, unimodal, increasing, or decreasing. In addition, the bathtub, U-shape, J-shape, or increasing shapes of the hazard rate function (hrf) for the KMKu model are all possible. But suppose that Y is the lifespan random variable of a test item adheres to the KMKu distribution, denoted by the notation $KMKu(\theta,\beta)$, where $\theta > 0, \beta > 0$ are the shape parameters. Therefore, it is supplied by its pdf, cdf, reliability function (RF), $R(.)$, and hrf, all represented by the letters $f(.)$, $F(.)$, and $h(.)$ accordingly:

$$f(y;\theta,\beta) = \frac{\theta\beta y^{\theta-1}}{e-1}\left(1-y^\theta\right)^{\beta-1} e^{(1-y^\theta)^\beta}, 0 < y < 1; \theta\beta > 0, \quad (2)$$

$$F(y;\theta,\beta) = \frac{e}{e-1}\left(1 - e^{-1}e^{(1-y^\theta)^\beta}\right), \quad (3)$$

$$R(y;\theta,\beta) = 1 - \frac{e}{e-1}\left(1 - e^{-1}e^{(1-y^\theta)^\beta}\right), \quad (4)$$

and
$$h(y;\theta,\beta) = \frac{\frac{\theta\beta y^{\theta-1}}{e-1}(1-y^\theta)^{\beta-1}}{1-e^{(1-y^\theta)^\beta}}. \tag{5}$$

Although the KMKu model has a lot of flexibility because of its different shapes of hrf and pdf, to our knowledge, no studies have yet been done under censorship. Particularly, the generalized type-II progressively hybrid censoring scheme has not produced any data for the new KMKu lifetime model's survival traits and model parameters. To fill this gap, the following are the objectives of this study: Firstly, the probability inference for any function of the unknown KMKu parameters, such as $R(t)$ or $h(t)$, is derived. The second objective is to derive independent gamma priors from the squared error (SE) loss and produce Bayes estimates for the same unknown parameters, employing the provided estimation procedures, such as classical and Bayesian approaches. The unknown parameters of the KMKu distribution are discovered using the approximation confidence intervals (ACIs) and highest posterior density (HPD) interval estimators. The acquired estimates are computed using the R programming language's "maxLik" and "coda" packages because the theoretical findings of θ and β obtained by the suggested estimation techniques cannot be represented in closed form. [12,13] offered these packages. Using four optimality criteria, the ultimate aim is to develop the most efficient progressively censored sample technique. The effectiveness of the different estimators is investigated using a Monte Carlo simulation with the entire sample size, which can be combined in a variety of ways, effective sample size, threshold timings, and progressively censored samples. We compare the average confidence lengths (ACLs), mean relative absolute biases (MRABs), and simulated root mean squared errors (RMSEs) of the derived estimators. The optimal censoring tactic should be chosen after evaluating how effectively the given techniques will function in practice. The remaining portions of this study are structured as follows: The maximum likelihood, Bayes inferences, and reliability functions of the unknown parameters are presented in Sections 2 and 3, respectively. The credible and asymptotic intervals are built into Section 4. Section 5 goes into depth about the results of the Monte Carlo simulation. The optimal methods for progressive censoring are discussed in Section 6. Two actual data sets are indicated in Section 7. Finally, the conclusion and discussion are given in Section 8.

2. Likelihood Estimation

Assume that the representation of a GPHCS-T2 sample of size c_2 taken from $KMKu(\theta,\beta)$ is $Y = ((Y_{1:s:n}, R_1), \ldots, (Y_{c_1:n}, R_{c_1}), \ldots, (Y_{c_2:n}, R_{c_2}))$. The probability function of GPHCS-T2 may be represented by substituting y_j for $y_{j:s:n}$ in Equation (1) and adding Equations (2) and (3); for more information, see [14].

$$L_\varphi(\theta,\beta|\underline{Y}) \propto \prod_{j=1}^{D_\varphi} \frac{\theta\beta y_j^{\theta-1}}{e-1}(1-y_j^\theta)^{\beta-1} e^{(1-y_j^\theta)^\beta}\left[1 - \frac{e}{e-1} + e^{-1}e^{(1-y_j^\theta)^\beta}\right]^{R_i} \psi_\varphi(T_\tau;\theta,\beta), \tag{6}$$

where

$$\psi_1(T_1;\theta,\beta) = \left(1 - \frac{e}{e-1}\left(1 - e^{-1}e^{(1-T_1^\theta)^\beta}\right)\right)^{R_{c_1}^*+1}, \psi_2(T_\tau;\theta,\beta) = 1 \text{ and } \psi_3(T_2;\theta,\beta) = \left(1 - \frac{e}{e-1}\left(1 - e^{-1}e^{(1-T_2^\theta)^\beta}\right)\right)^{R_{c_2}^*+1}.$$

The proper log-likelihood function for Equation (6) is $\ell_\varphi(.) \propto \ln L_\varphi(.)$ as follows:

$$\ell_\varphi(\theta,\beta|\underline{Y}) \propto D_\varphi \ln(\theta\beta) + (\theta-1)\sum_{j=1}^{D_\varphi} \ln(y_j) - D_\varphi \ln(e-1) + (\beta-1)\sum_{j=1}^{D_\varphi} \ln\left(1-y_j^\theta\right) + \beta\sum_{j=1}^{D_\varphi}(1-y_j^\theta) + R_i\sum_{j=1}^{D_\varphi} \ln\left[1 - \frac{e}{e-1} + e^{-1}e^{(1-y_j^\theta)^\beta}\right] + \gamma_\varphi(T_\tau;\theta,\beta), \tag{7}$$

where

$$\gamma_\varphi(T_1;\theta,\beta) = \left(R^*_{c_1+1}\right)\ln\left[1 - \tfrac{e}{e-1}\left(1 - e^{-1}e^{(1-T_1^\theta)^\beta}\right)\right], \gamma_2(T_\tau;\theta,\beta) = 1, \text{ and}$$
$$\gamma_3(T_2;\theta,\beta) = \left(R^*_{c_2+1}\right)\ln\left[1 - \tfrac{e}{e-1}\left(1 - e^{-1}e^{(1-T_2^\theta)^\beta}\right)\right].$$

By partially differentiating Equation (7) with reference to $\hat{\theta}$ and $\hat{\beta}$, the subsequent two findings are produced. After being equal to zero, likelihood equations must be simultaneously solved in order to create the MLEs.

$$\frac{\partial \ell_\varphi}{\partial \theta} = \frac{D_\varphi}{\theta} + \sum_{j=1}^{D_\varphi}\ln(y_j) - (\beta-1)\sum_{j=1}^{D_\varphi}\frac{y_j^\theta \ln(y_j)}{\left(1-y_j^\theta\right)} - \beta\sum_{j=1}^{D_\varphi} y_j^\theta \ln(y_j) - R_i\sum_{j=1}^{D_\varphi}\frac{e^{(1-y_j^\theta)^\beta} y_j^\theta \beta\left(1-y_j^\theta\right)^{\beta-1}\ln(y_j)}{e\left(1 - \frac{e}{e-1} + e^{-1}e^{(1-y_j^\theta)^\beta}\right)} + \frac{\partial \gamma_\varphi(T_\tau;\theta,\beta)}{\partial \theta}, \quad (8)$$

and

$$\frac{\partial \ell_\varphi}{\partial \beta} = \frac{D_\varphi}{\beta} + 2\sum_{j=1}^{D_\varphi}\ln\left(1-y_j^\theta\right) + R_i\sum_{j=1}^{D_\varphi}\frac{e^{(1-y_j^\theta)^\beta}\left(1-y_j^\theta\right)^\beta \ln\left(1-y_j^\theta\right)}{e\left(1 - \frac{e}{e-1} + e^{-1}e^{(1-y_j^\theta)^\beta}\right)} + \frac{\partial \gamma_\varphi(T_\tau;\theta,\beta)}{\partial \beta}, \quad (9)$$

where $\varphi = 1, 3$ and $\tau = 1, 2$, respectively, we have

$$\frac{\partial \gamma_\varphi(T_\tau;\theta,\beta)}{\partial \theta} = -\left(R^*_{c_\tau+1}\right)\frac{e^{(1-T_\tau^\theta)^\beta}\beta T_\tau^\theta \ln(T_\tau)}{\left[1 - \frac{e}{e-1} + e^{-1}e^{(1-T_\tau^\theta)^\beta}\right]}, \frac{\partial \gamma_\varphi(T_\tau;\theta,\beta)}{\partial \beta} = -\left(R^*_{c_\tau+1}\right)\frac{e^{(1-T_\tau^\theta)^\beta}\beta \ln\left(1-T_\tau^\theta\right)}{e\left[1 - \frac{e}{e-1} + e^{-1}e^{(1-T_\tau^\theta)^\beta}\right]}.$$

According to Equations (8) and (9), it is necessary to simultaneously satisfy a system of two nonlinear equations in order to derive the MLEs of θ and β in the KMKu model. As a result, for θ and β, there is not, and cannot be computed, an analytical closed-form solution. Thus, it may be estimated for each specific GPHCS-T2 data set using numerical techniques like the Newton-Raphson iterative method. When the estimates of θ and β are derived by replacing them with $\hat{\theta}$ and $\hat{\beta}$, the MLEs $\hat{R}(t)$ and $\hat{h}(t)$, respectively, may be easily computed.

3. Bayes Estimator

The HPD intervals for the Bayes estimators of θ, β, $R(t)$, and $h(t)$ are developed using the SE loss function. To do this, it is assumed that the KMKu parameters θ and β, respectively, have independent gamma priors of the forms $\omega(v_1, v_2)$ and $\omega(v_3, v_4)$.

The normal distribution can be a standard choice for data if the domain of that distribution is from $-\infty$ to ∞, and the beta distribution can be a standard choice for data if the domain of that distribution is from 0 to 1. Similarly, the gamma distribution can be a standard choice for non-negative continuous data if the domain of the gamma distribution is from 0 to ∞. This is one of the most important reasons, but there are other reasons as follows:

- We believe the main motivation for the gamma prior is usually to constrain the random variables to positive values.
- The gamma distribution is considered one of the most important and well-known statistical distributions because it is compatible with many engineering, mathematical, statistical, and medical applications.
- The gamma distribution is one of the most famous distributions that is used in mathematical solutions (integrations), especially when the data are from 0 to ∞.
- In previous studies, the gamma distribution was the most popular prior distribution and was associated with the best statistical results.

Gamma priors should be considered for a variety of reasons, including the fact that they are (1) adjustable, (2) offer diverse shapes based on parameter values, and (3) fairly basic and brief and might not generate a solution to a challenging estimation problem. Then, the combined previous density of θ and β is determined; for more details on this topic, see [15,16].

$$\pi(\theta,\beta) \propto \theta^{v_1-1}\beta^{v_3-1}e^{-(\theta v_2 + \beta v_4)} \quad (10)$$

If it is anticipated that for $i = 1, 2, 3, 4, v_i > 0$ are known. The joint posterior pdf of θ and β, Equations (6) and (10), when combined, results.

$$\pi_\varphi\left(\theta,\beta|\underline{y}\right) \propto \theta^{D_\varphi+v_1-1}\beta^{D_\varphi+v_3-1}e^{-(\theta v_2+\beta v_4)}\prod_{j=1}^{D_\varphi}\frac{\theta\beta y_j^{\theta-1}}{e-1}\left(1-y_j^\theta\right)^{\beta-1}e^{(1-y_j^\theta)^\beta}\left[1-\frac{e}{e-1}+e^{-1}e^{(1-y^\theta)^\beta}\right]^{R_i}\psi_\varphi(T_\tau;\theta,\beta) \qquad (11)$$

The Bayes estimate, $\tilde{\eta}(\theta,\beta)$, of θ and β respectively, under SE loss, $\eta(\theta,\beta)$ is what is meant by the posterior expectation of Equation (11), which is given.

$$\tilde{\eta}(\theta,\beta) = \int_0^\infty \int_0^\infty \eta(\theta,\beta)\pi_\varphi\left(\theta,\beta|\underline{y}\right)d\theta d\beta.$$

It is clear from Equation (11), that it is impossible to explicitly express the marginal pdfs of θ and β. In order to accomplish this, we recommend creating samples from Equation (11) utilizing Bayes MCMC methods to calculate the joint Bayes estimates and supplying their HPD intervals. The complete conditional pdfs of θ and β are provided for the MCMC sampler from Equation (11) to be performed as intended.

$$\pi_\varphi^\theta\left(\theta|\beta,\underline{y}\right) \propto \theta^{D_\varphi+v_1-1}e^{-\theta v_2}\prod_{j=1}^{D_\varphi}\frac{\theta\beta y_j^{\theta-1}}{e-1}\left(1-y_j^\theta\right)^{\beta-1}e^{(1-y_j^\theta)^\beta}\left[1-\frac{e}{e-1}+e^{-1}e^{(1-y^\theta)^\beta}\right]^{R_i}\psi_\varphi(T_\tau;\theta,\beta), \qquad (12)$$

and

$$\pi_\varphi^\beta\left(\beta|\theta,\underline{y}\right) \propto \beta^{D_\varphi+v_3-1}e^{-\beta v_4}\prod_{j=1}^{D_\varphi}\frac{\theta\beta y_j^{\theta-1}}{e-1}\left(1-y_j^\theta\right)^{\beta-1}e^{(1-y_j^\theta)^\beta}\left[1-\frac{e}{e-1}+e^{-1}e^{(1-y^\theta)^\beta}\right]^{R_i}\psi_\varphi(T_\tau;\theta,\beta). \qquad (13)$$

The Metropolis-Hastings (M-H) approach is considered to be the best solution to this problem because no analytical method exists to reduce the posterior pdfs of θ and β in Equations (12) and (13), respectively, to any known distribution (for further information, see [17,18]. The sampling method of the M-H algorithm is implemented according to:

First, establish the starting points, $\theta^{(0)} = \hat{\theta}$ and $\beta^{(0)} = \hat{\beta}$.
Set $S = 1$ after that.
Thirdly, from $N(\hat{\mu}_1,\hat{\sigma}_1)$ and $N(\hat{\mu}_2,\hat{\sigma}_2)$, respectively, create θ^* and β^*.
The fourth step: Obtaining $\varrho_\theta = min\left\{1,\frac{\pi_\varphi^\theta\left(\theta^*|\beta^{(s-1)};\underline{y}\right)}{\pi_\varphi^\theta\left(\theta^{(s-1)}|\beta^{(s-1)};\underline{y}\right)}\right\}$ and $\varrho_\beta = min\left\{1,\frac{\pi_\varphi^\beta\left(\beta^*|\theta^{(s)};\underline{y}\right)}{\pi_\varphi^\beta\left(\beta^{(s-1)}|\theta^{(s)};\underline{y}\right)}\right\}$.

Fifth, use the uniform $U(0,1)$ distribution to generate the samples u_1 and u_2.
Sixth: Set $\theta^{(S)} = \theta^*$ and $\beta^{(S)} = \beta^*$, respectively, if u_1 and u_2 are both smaller than ϱ_θ and ϱ_β, respectively. Set $\theta^{(S)} = \theta^{(S-1)}$ and $\beta^{(S)} = \beta^{(S-1)}$, correspondingly, if not.
Seventh: Establish that S equals S + 1.
Eighth: Repeating steps three through seven a number of times B will give you the values for $\theta^{(S)}$ and $\beta^{(S)}$ for $S = 1, 2, \ldots, B$.
Ninth: To calculate the RF in Equation (4) and hrf in Equation (5), use $\theta^{(S)}$ and $\beta^{(S)}$ for $S = 1, 2, \ldots, B$, respectively, for a given mission period $t > 0$.

$$R^{(S)}(t) = 1 - \frac{e}{e-1}\left(1 - e^{-1}e^{(1-y^{\theta^{(S)}})^{\beta^{(S)}}}\right), y > 0,$$

and

$$h^{(S)}(t) = \frac{\frac{\theta^{(S)}\beta^{(S)}y^{\theta^{(S)}-1}}{e-1}\left(1-y^{\theta^{(S)}}\right)^{\beta^{(S)}-1}}{1-e^{(1-y^{\theta^{(S)}})^{\beta^{(S)}}}}, y > 0.$$

The convergence of the MCMC sampler must be ensured, and starting, $\theta^{(0)}$ and $\beta^{(0)}$ values must be eliminated. The first simulated variants, let us say B_0, are removed as burn-ins. Therefore, using the remaining $B - B_0$ samples of $\theta, \beta, R(t)$, or $h(t)$, (let us suppose η), the Bayesian estimates are computed. On the basis of the SE loss function, the Bayes MCMC estimates of η are shown.

$$\tilde{\eta} = \frac{1}{B-B_0}\sum_{S=B_0+1}^{B}\eta^{(S)}$$

245

4. Interval Estimators

The HPD interval estimators in this section are based on acquired MCMC-simulated variations, as opposed to the approximative confidence estimators of θ, β, $R(t)$, or $h(t)$ that are based on observed Fisher information.

4.1. Asymptotic Intervals

To compute the ACIs for θ and β, the Fisher information matrix must first be inverted to produce the asymptotic variance-covariance (AVC) matrix. According to certain regularity criteria, $(\hat{\theta}, \hat{\beta})$ is nearly normal with a mean (θ, β) and variance $I^{-1}(\theta, \beta)$. In agreement with [19], we estimate $I^{-1}(\theta, \beta)$ by $I^{-1}(\hat{\theta}, \hat{\beta})$, replacing $\hat{\theta}$ and $\hat{\beta}$ for θ and β.

$$I^{-1}(\hat{\theta}, \hat{\beta}) = -\begin{bmatrix} a_{11} & a_{12} \\ a_{21} & a_{22} \end{bmatrix}^{-1} \qquad (14)$$

where

$$a_{11} = \frac{\partial^2 \ell_\varphi}{\partial \theta^2} = -\frac{D_\varphi}{\theta^2} - (\beta-1)\sum_{j=1}^{D_\varphi} \frac{y_j^\theta \ln(y_j)\left(1+\ln(y_j)\left(1-y_j^\theta\right)\right)}{\left(1-y_j^\theta\right)^2} - \beta \sum_{j=1}^{D_\varphi} y_j^\theta \left[\ln(y_j)\right]^2 + R_i \sum_{j=1}^{D_\varphi} \frac{\beta y_j^\theta (\ln(y_j))^2 e^{(1-y_j^\theta)^\beta}\left(1-y_j^\theta\right)^{\beta-1}\left(1+\beta y_j^\theta\left(1-y_j^\theta\right)^\beta + \frac{y_j^\theta(\beta-1)}{(1-y_j^\theta)}\right)}{e\left(1-\frac{e}{e-1}+e^{-1}e^{(1-y_j^\theta)^\beta}\right)^2} + \frac{\partial^2 \gamma_\varphi(T_\tau;\theta,\beta)}{\partial \theta^2} \qquad (15)$$

$$a_{12} = a_{21} = \frac{\partial^2 \ell_\varphi}{\partial \theta \partial \beta} = -\sum_{j=1}^{D_\varphi} \frac{y_j^\theta \ln(y_j)}{\left(1-y_j^\theta\right)} - \sum_{j=1}^{D_\varphi} y_j^\theta \ln(y_j) - R_i \sum_{j=1}^{D_\varphi} \frac{y_j^\theta \ln(y_j) e^{(1-y_j^\theta)^\beta}\left(1-y_j^\theta\right)^{\beta-1}\left(1+\beta\left(1-y_j^\theta\right)^\beta\left(\ln\left(1-y_j^\theta\right)\right) + \frac{\beta \ln\left(1-y_j^\theta\right)}{(1-y_j^\theta)}\right)}{e\left(1-\frac{e}{e-1}+e^{-1}e^{(1-y_j^\theta)^\beta}\right)^2} + \frac{\partial^2 \gamma_\varphi(T_\tau;\theta,\beta)}{\partial \theta \partial \beta}, \qquad (16)$$

$$a_{22} = \frac{\partial^2 \ell_\varphi}{\partial \beta^2} = -\frac{D_\varphi}{\beta^2} + R_i \sum_{j=1}^{D_\varphi} \frac{\left(\ln\left(1-y_j^\theta\right)\right)^2 e^{(1-y_j^\theta)^\beta}\left(\left(1-y_j^\theta\right)^\beta + \left(1-y_j^\theta\right)^{2\beta}\right)}{e\left(1-\frac{e}{e-1}+e^{-1}e^{(1-y_j^\theta)^\beta}\right)^2} + \frac{\partial^2 \gamma_\varphi(T_\tau;\theta,\beta)}{\partial \beta^2}, \qquad (17)$$

where

$$\frac{\partial^2 \gamma_\varphi(T_\tau;\theta,\beta)}{\partial \theta^2} = -\left(R^*_{c_\tau+1}\right) \frac{\beta \ln(T_\tau) T_\tau^\theta e^{(1-T_\tau^\theta)^\beta}\left(\left[1-\frac{e}{e-1}+e^{-1}e^{(1-T_\tau^\theta)^\beta}\right]\left(1-T_\tau^\theta\left(1-T_\tau^\theta\right)^{\beta-1}\right) + T_\tau^{2\theta} e^{-1}\beta\left(1-T_\tau^\theta\right)^{\beta-1}\right)}{\left[1-\frac{e}{e-1}+e^{-1}e^{(1-T_\tau^\theta)^\beta}\right]^2},$$

$$\frac{\partial^2 \gamma_\varphi(T_\tau;\theta,\beta)}{\partial \theta \partial \beta} = \frac{\left(R^*_{c_\tau+1}\right) e^{-1} e^{(1-T_\tau^\theta)^\beta}\left(1-T_\tau^\theta\right)^\beta \ln\left(1-T_\tau^\theta\right)}{\left[1-\frac{e}{e-1}\left(1-e^{-1}e^{(1-T_\tau^\theta)^\beta}\right)\right]},$$

and

$$\frac{\partial^2 \gamma_\varphi(T_\tau;\theta,\beta)}{\partial \beta^2} = \frac{-\left(R^*_{c_\tau+1}\right)\ln\left(1-T_\tau^\theta\right)e^{(1-T_\tau^\theta)^\beta}}{e\left[1-\frac{e}{e-1}+e^{-1}e^{(1-T_\tau^\theta)^\beta}\right]^2}$$

$$\left(\left[1-\frac{e}{e-1}+e^{-1}e^{(1-T_\tau^\theta)^\beta}\right]\left(1+\beta\left(1-T_\tau^\theta\right)^\beta \ln\left(1-T_\tau^\theta\right)\right) - \beta e^{-1}\left(1-T_\tau^\theta\right)^\beta \ln\left(1-T_\tau^\theta\right) e^{(1-T_\tau^\theta)^\beta}\right).$$

The two-sided $100(1-\gamma)\%$ ACIs are therefore given by $\hat{\theta} \pm Z_{\frac{\gamma}{2}}\sqrt{\hat{\sigma}_1^2}$ and $\hat{\beta} \pm Z_{\frac{\gamma}{2}}\sqrt{\hat{\sigma}_2^2}$, for θ and β, respectively, where $Z_{\frac{\gamma}{2}}$ stands for the top $\frac{\gamma}{2}$ percentage points of the standard normal distribution, $\hat{\sigma}_1^2$ and $\hat{\sigma}_2^2$ are the primary diagonal elements of

Equation (14). Furthermore, we employ the delta method to first establish the estimated variance of $\hat{R}(t)$ and $\hat{h}(t)$ (see [20]) before developing the ACIs of $R(t)$ and $h(t)$ as

$$\hat{\sigma}^2_{\hat{R}(t)} = \epsilon_R^T I^{-1}(\hat{\epsilon})\epsilon_R \text{ and } \hat{\sigma}^2_{\hat{h}(t)} = \epsilon_h^T I^{-1}(\hat{\epsilon})\epsilon_h,$$

where $\epsilon_R^T = \left[\frac{\partial R(t)}{\partial \theta} \quad \frac{\partial R(t)}{\partial \beta}\right]_{(\hat{\theta},\hat{\beta})}$, and $\epsilon_h^T = \left[\frac{\partial h(t)}{\partial \theta} \quad \frac{\partial h(t)}{\partial \beta}\right]_{(\hat{\theta},\hat{\beta})}$.

Then, $R(t)$ and $h(t)$ both have two-sided $100(1-\gamma)\%$ ACIs that are supplied by $\hat{R}(t) \pm Z_{\frac{\gamma}{2}}\sqrt{\hat{\sigma}_{\hat{R}(t)}^2}$ and $\hat{h}(t) \pm Z_{\frac{\gamma}{2}}\sqrt{\hat{\sigma}_{\hat{h}(t)}^2}$, respectively.

Adding bootstrapping techniques to improve estimators or create confidence intervals for θ, β, $R(t)$, or $h(t)$ is easy.

4.2. HPD Intervals

The method put forward by [21] is used to create $100(1-\gamma)\%$ HPD interval estimates of θ, β, $R(t)$, or $h(t)$. First, we assign numerical values to the MCMC samples of $\varepsilon^{(j)}$ for $j = B_0+1, B_0+2, \ldots, B$ as $\varepsilon_{(B_0+1)}, \varepsilon_{(B_0+2)}, \ldots, \varepsilon_{(B)}$ correspondingly. The discovery is that the $100(1-\gamma)\%$ two-sided HPD interval of ε is supplied by $\varepsilon_{(j^*)}, \varepsilon_{(j^*+(1-\varepsilon)(B-B_0))}$, where $j^* = B_0+1, B_0+2, \ldots, B$ is selected so that $\varepsilon_{(j^*+(1-\varepsilon)(B-B_0))} - \varepsilon_{(j^*)} = \min_{1 \le j \le \gamma \le (B-B_0)} \left\{\varepsilon_{(j+(1-\gamma)(B-B_0))} - \varepsilon_{(j)}\right\} \varepsilon_{(j^*)}, \varepsilon_{(j^*+(1-\gamma)(B-B_0))}$.

5. Optimal PCS-T2 Designs

The experimenter may want to pick the "best" censoring scheme out of a collection of all accessible censoring schemes in order to provide the most details about the unknown parameters under investigation, especially in the context of dependability. First, [1] examined the problem of deciding which censoring strategy is most appropriate under various circumstances. However, a number of optimality criteria, $R = (R_1, R_2, \ldots, R_s)$, where $\sum_{i=1}^{s} R_i$ have been proposed, and several assessments of the top censoring strategies have been made. The precise values of n (total test units), s (effective sample), and $T_i, i = 1, 2$ (ideal test thresholds) are picked in advance according to the accessibility of the units, the accessibility of the experimental settings, and cost factors (see [22]). A number of articles in the literature have addressed the topic of contrasting two (or more) different censoring techniques. For examples, see [23,24]. To help us choose the best censoring strategy, O_i, Table 2 offers a variety of widely used measures.

Table 2. Illustrations of numerous helpful censoring methods and best practices.

Criterion	Method
O_1	Maximize trace $[I_{2\times 2}(.)]$
O_2	Minimize trace $[I_{2\times 2}(.)]^{-1}$
O_3	Minimize det $[I_{2\times 2}(.)]^{-1}$
O_4	Minimize $Var[\log(\hat{t}_p)]$, $0 < p < 1$

It is advised that the observed Fisher information, $[I_{2\times 2}(.)]$ values for O_1, be maximized. For criterion O_2 and O_3, we also wish to reduce the determinant and trace of $[I_{2\times 2}(.)]^{-1}$. The best censoring strategy for multi-parameter distributions may be selected using scale-invariant criteria. While dealing with unknown multi-parameter distributions makes it more challenging to compare the two Fisher information matrices, dealing with single-parameter distributions allows for the use of scale-invariant criteria to compare a variety of criteria O_4. The logarithmic MLE of the $p-th$ quantile, $\log(\hat{t}_p)$, tends to have a variance that is minimized by the p-dependent criterion O_4. As a result, the logarithm of the KMKu distribution for time $\hat{t}_p$ may be calculated using

$$\log(\hat{t}_p) = \left\{1 - \left[\ln\left(e\left(1 - p\left(\frac{e-1}{e}\right)\right)\right)\right]^{\frac{1}{\beta}}\right\}^{\frac{1}{\theta}}, \quad 0 < p < 1,$$

By using the delta technique to solve for Equation (4), the estimate of the variance for the $log(\hat{t}_p)$ of the KMKu distribution is given as

$$Var(log(\hat{t}_p)) = [\nabla log(\hat{t}_p)]^T I_{2 \times 2}^{-1}(\hat{\theta}, \hat{\beta}) [\nabla log(\hat{t}_p)],$$

where

$$[\nabla log(\hat{t}_p)]^T = \left[\frac{\partial}{\partial \theta} log(\hat{t}_p), \frac{\partial}{\partial \beta} log(\hat{t}_p)\right]_{(\theta=\hat{\theta}, \beta=\hat{\beta})}$$

$$P(R_1 = \mathfrak{K}_1) = \binom{n-s}{\mathfrak{K}_1} r^{\mathfrak{K}_1} (1-r)^{n-s-\mathfrak{K}_1}.$$

while $i = 2, 3, \ldots, s-1$. The maximum value of the O_1 criterion and the lowest value of O_i, $i = 2, 3, 4$, correspond to the best censoring. On the other hand, the greatest value of the O_1 criterion and the lowest value of the O_i, $i = 2, 3, 4$ criterion correspond to the best censoring.

6. Simulation

Using different combinations of T_i; $i = 1, 2$ (threshold points), n (sample size), s (size of censored sample), and R (censored removal), Monte-Carlo (MC) simulations were carried out to assess the true performance of the acquired point and interval estimators of θ, β, $R(T)$, and $h(T)$. To establish this goal, for KMKu(1.4, 1.5), KMKu(1.4, 0.5), and KMKu(0.4, 0.5), we replicated the GPHCS-T2 mechanism 1000 times. Taking $(T_1, T_2) = (0.6, 0.85)$, two different choices of n and s were used as (n = 30, 50, 100), and the choices of s were used as (s = 20, 25) at n = 30, (s = 35, 45) at n = 50, and (s = 70, 90) at n = 100. At $T_1 = 0.6$, the true values of $R(T_1)$ and $h(T_1)$ were 0.4278 and 1.4899, respectively. At $T_2 = 0.85$, the true values of $R(T_2)$ and $h(T_2)$ were 0.2526 and 3.3106, respectively.

Additionally, by utilizing the binomial elimination distribution and taking into account different censoring schemes for each combination of s and n, the following is conducted: according to the following probability mass function, the number of units removed at each failure time is expected to follow a binomial distribution.

$$P(R_i = \mathfrak{K}_i | R_{i-1} = \mathfrak{K}_{i-1}, \ldots, R_1 = \mathfrak{K}_1) = \binom{n - s - \sum_{j=1}^{i-1} \mathfrak{K}_j}{\mathfrak{K}_i} r^{\mathfrak{K}_i} (1-r)^{n-s-\sum_{j=1}^{i} \mathfrak{K}_j}.$$

Additionally, assume that for any i, R_i is independent of X_i. In light of this, the likelihood function can be written as follows:

$$L(x_i, \beta, \theta, r) = L_1(x_i, \beta, \theta | R = \mathfrak{K}) P(R = \mathfrak{K}),$$

where

$$P(R = \mathfrak{K}) = P(R_1 = \mathfrak{K}_1, R_2 = \mathfrak{K}_2, \ldots, R_{s-1} = \mathfrak{K}_{s-1}) = P(R_{s-1} = \mathfrak{K}_{s-1} | R_{s-2} = \mathfrak{K}_{s-2}, \ldots, R_1 = \mathfrak{K}_1) \times P(R_{s-2} = \mathfrak{K}_{s-2} | R_{s-3} = \mathfrak{K}_{s-3}, \ldots, R_1 = \mathfrak{K}_1) \ldots P(R_2 = \mathfrak{K}_2 | R_1 = \mathfrak{K}_1) P(R_1 = \mathfrak{K}_1).$$

That is,

$$P(R = \mathfrak{K}) = \frac{(n-s)!}{(n - s - \sum_{i=1}^{s-1} \mathfrak{K}_i)! \prod_{i=1}^{s-1} \mathfrak{K}_i} r^{\sum_{i=1}^{s-1} \mathfrak{K}_i} (1-r)^{(s-1)(n-s) - \sum_{i=1}^{s-1}(s-i)\mathfrak{K}_i},$$

where the GPHCS-T2-based KMKu distribution's parameters do not affect the binomial parameter r (Independent). We chose the binomial parameter r with varied values of 0.3 and 0.8.

The MLEs and 95% ACI estimates of $\theta, \beta, R(t)$, and $h(t)$ were assessed after 1000 GPHCS-T2 samples had been gathered using R 4.2.2 programming software and the "maxLik" library. We simulated 12,000 MCMC samples and omitted the first 2000 iterations as burn-in to obtain the Bayes point estimates along with their HPD interval estimates of the same unknown parameters using the "coda" library in the R 4.2.2 programming language. The estimates and their variances were equated with the Fisher information matrix of θ and β to produce the ML estimator, which it denoted as elective hyper-parameters, and this was contributed by [25]. This process allowed for the extraction of the hyper-parameters of the informative priors.

Some observations from Tables 3–5 include

Table 3. Bias, MSE, WCI, and CP for parameters and reliability measures: $\beta = 1.4$, $\theta = 1.5$.

n	r	s			MLE					Bayesian		
				Bias	MSE	WACI	CP	Optimality		Bias	MSE	WCCI
30	0.3	20	β	0.3647	0.96096	3.5687	95.8%	O_1	0.862132	0.0495	0.03658	0.9815
			θ	0.3083	0.30741	1.8074	95.3%	O_2	0.050431	0.0652	0.0178	0.6268
			$R(0.6)$	−1.0730	0.01021	3.5687	95.8%	O_3	24.39956	−1.0929	0.00159	0.9815
			$H(0.6)$	2.6011	2.15503	1.8074	95.3%	O_4	0.397259	2.2794	0.15897	0.6268
			$R(0.85)$	−1.3190	0.00311	3.5687	95.8%			−1.3269	0.00026	0.9815
			$H(0.85)$	9.8905	28.98923	1.8074	95.3%			8.2579	1.30669	0.6268
		25	β	0.3133	0.68518	3.0049	96.0%	O_1	0.603238	0.0348	0.01182	0.6606
			θ	0.1931	0.20528	1.6075	95.7%	O_2	0.028622	0.0196	0.00163	0.4069
			$R(0.6)$	−1.0962	0.00644	3.0049	96.0%	O_3	29.16632	−1.1016	0.00050	0.6606
			$H(0.6)$	2.6177	1.64301	1.6075	95.7%	O_4	0.637278	2.2792	0.05406	0.4069
			$R(0.85)$	−1.3278	0.00190	3.0049	96.0%			−1.3295	0.00009	0.6606
			$H(0.85)$	9.6683	20.97684	1.6075	95.7%			8.1852	0.42306	0.4069
	0.8	20	β	0.4478	1.11270	3.7458	95.6%	O_1	0.897504	0.0686	0.04368	1.0098
			θ	0.2881	0.29977	1.8260	95.3%	O_2	0.054545	0.0541	0.00853	0.6131
			$R(0.6)$	−1.0925	0.00827	3.7458	95.6%	O_3	23.77178	−1.0994	0.00147	1.0098
			$H(0.6)$	2.7704	2.38574	1.8260	95.3%	O_4	0.410967	2.3269	0.17886	0.6131
			$R(0.85)$	−1.3285	0.00217	3.7458	95.6%			−1.3295	0.00025	1.0098
			$H(0.85)$	10.3764	33.31616	1.8260	95.3%			8.3746	1.53529	0.6131
		25	β	0.3005	0.65995	2.9601	96.2%	O_1	0.588428	0.0312	0.00897	0.6494
			θ	0.1892	0.20103	1.5942	95.3%	O_2	0.02822	0.0199	0.00162	0.4063
			$R(0.6)$	−1.0954	0.00634	2.9601	96.2%	O_3	28.83162	−1.1009	0.00041	0.6494
			$H(0.6)$	2.5961	1.54340	1.5942	95.3%	O_4	0.290327	2.2713	0.04112	0.4063
			$R(0.85)$	−1.3273	0.00191	2.9601	96.2%			−1.3293	0.00008	0.6494
			$H(0.85)$	9.5939	20.02147	1.5942	95.3%			8.1634	0.31889	0.4063
50	0.3	35	β	0.2321	0.33855	2.0926	95.2%	O_1	0.3524	0.0219	0.00682	0.2936
			θ	0.2206	0.16385	1.3310	94.8%	O_2	0.0109	0.0389	0.00404	0.1817
			$R(0.6)$	0.0150	0.00491	0.2684	94.9%	O_3	40.4391	0.0044	0.00056	0.0984
			$H(0.6)$	0.2660	0.86775	3.5013	95.4%	O_4	0.4010	0.0230	0.03428	0.7479
			$R(0.85)$	0.0019	0.00151	0.1522	95.8%			0.0005	0.00010	0.0418
			$H(0.85)$	1.2233	10.31472	11.6464	95.4%			0.1173	0.24180	1.8061
		45	β	0.1009	0.17989	1.6157	95.3%	O_1	0.2308	0.0127	0.00185	0.1390
			θ	0.0688	0.07292	1.0241	95.5%	O_2	0.0051	0.0080	0.00043	0.0697
			$R(0.6)$	0.0038	0.00306	0.2163	95.2%	O_3	52.6779	−0.0009	0.00013	0.0468
			$H(0.6)$	0.1237	0.55947	2.8931	95.4%	O_4	0.3850	0.0228	0.00944	0.3526
			$R(0.85)$	0.0023	0.00099	0.1228	95.9%			−0.0008	0.00002	0.0202
			$H(0.85)$	0.5401	5.79962	9.2044	95.3%			0.0729	0.06640	0.8489
	0.8	35	β	0.2292	0.33120	2.0704	95.7%	O_1	0.3413	0.0302	0.00762	0.2866
			θ	0.1710	0.13353	1.2666	94.8%	O_2	0.0103	0.0289	0.00277	0.1549
			$R(0.6)$	0.0043	0.00413	0.2516	94.5%	O_3	40.8715	0.0003	0.00049	0.0905
			$H(0.6)$	0.2984	0.88222	3.4929	95.3%	O_4	0.5510	0.0472	0.03668	0.6994
			$R(0.85)$	−0.0013	0.00132	0.1424	95.8%			−0.0010	0.00009	0.0382
			$H(0.85)$	1.2328	10.27127	11.6023	95.7%			0.1697	0.26968	1.7342
		45	β	0.1024	0.17088	1.6527	95.8%	O_1	0.2313	0.0132	0.00183	0.1361
			θ	0.0614	0.07091	1.0767	95.4%	O_2	0.0052	0.0077	0.00047	0.0735
			$R(0.6)$	0.0020	0.00301	0.2196	95.0%	O_3	52.8830	−0.0011	0.00013	0.0450
			$H(0.6)$	0.1288	0.55691	2.9153	95.4%	O_4	0.3953	0.0242	0.00934	0.3352
			$R(0.85)$	0.0018	0.00100	0.1240	95.6%			−0.0009	0.00002	0.0195
			$H(0.85)$	0.5493	5.70139	9.3735	95.9%			0.0762	0.06541	0.8280

249

Table 3. Cont.

n	r	s		MLE						Bayesian		
				Bias	MSE	WACI	CP	Optimality		Bias	MSE	WCCI
100	0.3	70	β	0.1428	0.13884	1.3498	95.3%	O_1	0.1469	0.0129	0.00257	0.1755
			θ	0.1269	0.06502	0.8674	95.3%	O_2	0.0020	0.0189	0.00121	0.1107
			$R(0.6)$	0.0045	0.00218	0.1823	94.6%	O_3	80.6294	0.0016	0.00021	0.0575
			$H(0.6)$	0.1901	0.40464	2.3807	95.0%	O_4	0.6115	0.0162	0.01332	0.4378
			$R(0.85)$	−0.0017	0.00065	0.0999	96.1%			−0.0001	0.00004	0.0249
			$H(0.85)$	0.7729	4.38212	7.6300	95.3%			0.0702	0.09184	1.0646
		90	β	0.0668	0.07946	1.0740	95.7%	O_1	0.1065	0.0062	0.00054	0.0852
			θ	0.0497	0.03711	0.7299	95.5%	O_2	0.0011	0.0045	0.00020	0.0495
			$R(0.6)$	0.0013	0.00162	0.1577	95.0%	O_3	102.5854	−0.0003	0.00005	0.0275
			$H(0.6)$	0.0898	0.25612	1.9533	94.7%	O_4	0.8814	0.0107	0.00299	0.2093
			$R(0.85)$	0.0000	0.00050	0.0880	95.0%			−0.0004	0.00001	0.0120
			$H(0.85)$	0.3625	2.56087	6.1131	95.6%			0.0351	0.01967	0.5192
	0.8	70	β	0.1309	0.13318	1.3361	95.4%	O_1	0.1442	0.0146	0.00261	0.1649
			θ	0.1046	0.06010	0.8696	94.9%	O_2	0.0020	0.0157	0.00107	0.1047
			$R(0.6)$	0.0020	0.00220	0.1838	94.7%	O_3	80.5925	0.0005	0.00021	0.0568
			$H(0.6)$	0.1803	0.40288	2.3868	95.0%	O_4	0.6090	0.0220	0.01361	0.4150
			$R(0.85)$	−0.0018	0.00065	0.1001	95.9%			−0.0005	0.00004	0.0241
			$H(0.85)$	0.7125	4.25301	7.5901	95.2%			0.0816	0.09367	1.0046
		90	β	0.0505	0.06859	1.0078	95.4%	O_1	0.1039	0.0057	0.00047	0.0761
			θ	0.0318	0.03404	0.7127	94.5%	O_2	0.0011	0.0036	0.00019	0.0488
			$R(0.6)$	0.0004	0.00155	0.1544	95.2%	O_3	103.7077	−0.0004	0.00005	0.0271
			$H(0.6)$	0.0682	0.23049	1.8638	95.7%	O_4	0.7099	0.0103	0.00266	0.1933
			$R(0.85)$	0.0003	0.00047	0.0853	95.4%			−0.0004	0.00001	0.0113
			$H(0.85)$	0.2743	2.23659	5.7659	95.4%			0.0327	0.01719	0.4665

Table 4. Bias, MSE, WCI and CP for parameters and Reliability measures: $\beta = 1.4$, $\theta = 0.5$.

n	r	s		MLE						Bayesian		
				Bias	MSE	WACI	CP	Optimality		Bias	MSE	WCCI
30	0.3	20	β	0.2883	0.66402	2.9892	95.1%	O_1	0.5529	0.0373	0.0172	0.9061
			θ	0.0923	0.03017	0.5771	96.5%	O_2	0.0045	0.0191	0.0010	0.2005
			$R(0.6)$	−1.3142	0.00273	2.9892	95.1%	O_3	156.4684	−1.3223	0.0002	0.9061
			$H(0.6)$	4.4198	3.85075	0.5771	96.5%	O_4	3.6685	3.8534	0.1199	0.2005
			$R(0.85)$	−1.3780	0.00051	2.9892	95.1%			−1.3834	0.0000	0.9061
			$H(0.85)$	11.2462	28.57208	0.5771	96.5%			9.6102	0.7761	0.2005
		25	β	0.2330	0.41596	2.3587	95.6%	O_1	0.3694	0.0242	0.0044	0.6032
			θ	0.0565	0.01912	0.4950	95.3%	O_2	0.0024	0.0058	0.0001	0.1311
			$R(0.6)$	−1.3222	0.00166	2.3587	95.6%	O_3	187.5492	−1.3244	0.0001	0.6032
			$H(0.6)$	4.3140	2.50974	0.4950	95.3%	O_4	4.2533	3.8249	0.0314	0.1311
			$R(0.85)$	−1.3812	0.00029	2.3587	95.6%			−1.3839	0.0000	0.6032
			$H(0.85)$	10.8980	18.07372	0.4950	95.3%			9.5259	0.2003	0.1311
	0.8	20	β	0.3112	0.59476	2.7674	95.4%	O_1	0.5183	0.0446	0.0176	0.9133
			θ	0.0862	0.02909	0.5773	95.3%	O_2	0.0042	0.0168	0.0009	0.1972
			$R(0.6)$	−1.3207	0.00218	2.7674	95.4%	O_3	156.8018	−1.3236	0.0002	0.9133
			$H(0.6)$	4.4902	3.51118	0.5773	95.3%	O_4	1.9839	3.8741	0.1242	0.1972
			$R(0.85)$	−1.3808	0.00036	2.7674	95.4%			−1.3838	0.0000	0.9133
			$H(0.85)$	11.4035	25.72157	0.5773	95.3%			9.6601	0.7988	0.1972
		25	β	0.2760	0.46980	2.4606	94.4%	O_1	0.3856	0.0304	0.0058	0.6125
			θ	0.0560	0.01951	0.5019	95.5%	O_2	0.0025	0.0054	0.0001	0.1304
			$R(0.6)$	−1.3254	0.00173	2.4606	94.4%	O_3	188.0939	−1.3251	0.0001	0.6125
			$H(0.6)$	4.4269	2.85414	0.5019	95.5%	O_4	10.4186	3.8416	0.0413	0.1304
			$R(0.85)$	−1.3822	0.00027	2.4606	94.4%			−1.3842	0.0000	0.6125
			$H(0.85)$	11.1889	20.49050	0.5019	95.5%			9.5678	0.2637	0.1304

Table 4. Cont.

n	r	s		Bias	MSE	WACI	CP	Optimality		Bias	MSE	WCCI
						MLE					Bayesian	
50	0.3	35	β	0.1928	0.26587	1.8755	95.3%	O_1	0.2300	0.0209	0.00625	0.2453
			θ	0.0636	0.01464	0.4038	95.4%	O_2	0.0010	0.0111	0.00034	0.0531
			$R(0.6)$	0.0022	0.00138	0.1454	96.0%	O_3	266.3510	0.0003	0.00009	0.0379
			$H(0.6)$	0.4533	1.64429	4.7044	95.0%	O_4	4.7886	0.0504	0.04467	0.6665
			$R(0.85)$	0.0017	0.00022	0.0583	95.2%			−0.0001	0.00001	0.0118
			$H(0.85)$	1.2631	11.59297	12.4008	95.4%			0.1365	0.28360	1.6561
		45	β	0.1025	0.15357	1.4834	95.2%	O_1	0.1528	0.0111	0.00136	0.1177
			θ	0.0252	0.00856	0.3492	95.8%	O_2	0.0005	0.0027	0.00005	0.0238
			$R(0.6)$	0.0010	0.00090	0.1177	95.9%	O_3	332.8660	−0.0007	0.00002	0.0179
			$H(0.6)$	0.2438	0.97587	3.7545	95.7%	O_4	9.7083	0.0284	0.00981	0.3228
			$R(0.85)$	0.0015	0.00015	0.0473	95.2%			−0.0003	0.00000	0.0057
			$H(0.85)$	0.6769	6.72601	9.8189	95.4%			0.0737	0.06177	0.7925
	0.8	35	β	0.2216	0.30042	1.9661	95.3%	O_1	0.2360	0.0286	0.00733	0.2601
			θ	0.0591	0.01448	0.4111	95.5%	O_2	0.0010	0.0097	0.00031	0.0514
			$R(0.6)$	−0.0014	0.00128	0.1404	95.7%	O_3	264.3238	−0.0009	0.00009	0.0380
			$H(0.6)$	0.5296	1.84331	4.9029	95.3%	O_4	6.8233	0.0715	0.05206	0.7134
			$R(0.85)$	0.0005	0.00020	0.0555	94.9%			−0.0004	0.00001	0.0117
			$H(0.85)$	1.4571	13.09846	12.9931	95.3%			0.1886	0.33239	1.7468
		45	β	0.1251	0.17500	1.5656	94.3%	O_1	0.1585	0.0147	0.00189	0.1420
			θ	0.0244	0.00782	0.3334	95.3%	O_2	0.0005	0.0023	0.00004	0.0228
			$R(0.6)$	−0.0008	0.00097	0.1224	96.3%	O_3	331.8112	−0.0011	0.00003	0.0200
			$H(0.6)$	0.3053	1.12358	3.9811	94.4%	O_4	3.4415	0.0380	0.01355	0.3838
			$R(0.85)$	0.0010	0.00015	0.0485	95.8%			−0.0004	0.00000	0.0064
			$H(0.85)$	0.8313	7.71142	10.3916	94.4%			0.0977	0.08563	0.9557
100	0.3	70	β	0.1020	0.10312	1.1941	96.0%	O_1	0.0930	0.0071	0.00176	0.1407
			θ	0.0390	0.00642	0.2745	95.2%	O_2	0.0002	0.0063	0.00013	0.0334
			$R(0.6)$	0.0012	0.00065	0.0997	94.9%	O_3	526.4983	0.0006	0.00003	0.0220
			$H(0.6)$	0.2402	0.65129	3.0217	95.9%	O_4	3.0162	0.0158	0.01276	0.3863
			$R(0.85)$	0.0007	0.00010	0.0386	95.3%			0.0001	0.00002	0.0070
			$H(0.85)$	0.6667	4.49884	7.8970	96.1%			0.0451	0.07991	0.9471
		90	β	0.0661	0.06870	0.9948	95.5%	O_1	0.0688	0.0055	0.00046	0.0784
			θ	0.0164	0.00369	0.2292	95.4%	O_2	0.0001	0.0014	0.00002	0.0160
			$R(0.6)$	−0.0005	0.00048	0.0858	95.7%	O_3	654.6192	−0.0003	0.00001	0.0117
			$H(0.6)$	0.1605	0.44507	2.5397	95.2%	O_4	6.7361	0.0139	0.00338	0.2125
			$R(0.85)$	0.0003	0.00007	0.0332	95.6%			−0.0001	0.00001	0.0038
			$H(0.85)$	0.4370	3.01381	6.5894	95.3%			0.0361	0.02109	0.5289
	0.8	70	β	0.1036	0.10480	1.2028	95.8%	O_1	0.0929	0.0115	0.00204	0.1556
			θ	0.0320	0.00609	0.2791	95.3%	O_2	0.0002	0.0050	0.00011	0.0339
			$R(0.6)$	−0.0002	0.00064	0.0994	95.7%	O_3	525.8864	−0.0002	0.00004	0.0232
			$H(0.6)$	0.2484	0.66914	3.0567	95.8%	O_4	4.7902	0.0283	0.01472	0.4259
			$R(0.85)$	0.0003	0.00009	0.0381	96.1%			−0.0002	0.00002	0.0073
			$H(0.85)$	0.6812	4.58927	7.9658	95.9%			0.0754	0.09250	1.0493
		90	β	0.0652	0.07266	1.0258	95.7%	O_1	0.0689	0.0060	0.00052	0.0794
			θ	0.0161	0.00373	0.2310	95.1%	O_2	0.0001	0.0013	0.00002	0.0161
			$R(0.6)$	−0.0001	0.00052	0.0894	94.8%	O_3	650.3684	−0.0004	0.00001	0.0124
			$H(0.6)$	0.1583	0.47338	2.6260	95.6%	O_4	6.4073	0.0153	0.00379	0.2188
			$R(0.85)$	0.0005	0.00008	0.0345	94.8%			−0.0002	0.00001	0.0040
			$H(0.85)$	0.4317	3.19473	6.8025	95.6%			0.0396	0.02362	0.5400

Table 5. Bias, MSE, WCI and CP for parameters and Reliability measures: $\beta = 0.4$, $\theta = 0.5$.

n	r	s		MLE						Bayesian		
				Bias	MSE	WACI	CP	Optimality		Bias	MSE	WCCI
30	0.3	20	β	0.0477	0.03572	0.7173	96.0%	O_1	0.0822	0.0069	0.0009	0.2488
			θ	0.1693	0.10228	1.0642	95.4%	O_2	0.0011	0.0454	0.0066	0.3352
			$R(0.6)$	0.0653	0.01134	0.7173	96.0%	O_3	0.0822	0.0392	0.0014	0.2488
			$H(0.6)$	1.0736	0.26208	1.0642	95.4%	O_4	0.0011	1.0039	0.0089	0.3352
			$R(0.85)$	−0.1242	0.00977	0.7173	96.0%			−0.1418	0.0008	0.2488
			$H(0.85)$	3.1086	1.57995	1.0642	95.4%			2.8625	0.0409	0.3352
		25	β	0.0420	0.02739	0.6279	95.8%	O_1	0.0591	0.0051	0.0003	0.1640
			θ	0.0938	0.05590	0.8511	94.9%	O_2	0.0006	0.0139	0.0009	0.2075
			$R(0.6)$	0.0413	0.00854	0.6279	95.8%	O_3	170.1243	0.0291	0.0003	0.1640
			$H(0.6)$	1.0797	0.21444	0.8511	94.9%	O_4	5.0156	1.0038	0.0029	0.2075
			$R(0.85)$	−0.1395	0.00729	0.6279	95.8%			−0.1478	0.0002	0.1640
			$H(0.85)$	3.0747	1.22571	0.8511	94.9%			2.8470	0.0134	0.2075
	0.8	20	β	0.0747	0.04126	0.7408	96.2%	O_1	0.0818	0.0116	0.0012	0.2625
			θ	0.1633	0.09437	1.0204	96.1%	O_2	0.0011	0.0378	0.0051	0.3251
			$R(0.6)$	0.0443	0.01003	0.7408	96.2%	O_3	131.1160	0.0330	0.0012	0.2625
			$H(0.6)$	1.1578	0.29506	1.0204	96.1%	O_4	3.2292	1.0197	0.0110	0.3251
			$R(0.85)$	−0.1436	0.00864	0.7408	96.2%			−0.1467	0.0007	0.2625
			$H(0.85)$	3.2918	1.79718	1.0204	96.1%			2.8933	0.0527	0.3251
		25	β	0.0589	0.02782	0.6120	95.7%	O_1	0.0592	0.0065	0.0003	0.1698
			θ	0.0991	0.04971	0.7834	95.8%	O_2	0.0006	0.0125	0.0006	0.2058
			$R(0.6)$	0.0296	0.00743	0.6120	95.7%	O_3	159.3168	0.0275	0.0003	0.1698
			$H(0.6)$	1.1330	0.21505	0.7834	95.8%	O_4	2.2242	1.0084	0.0034	0.2058
			$R(0.85)$	−0.1517	0.00618	0.6120	95.7%			−0.1491	0.0002	0.1698
			$H(0.85)$	3.1924	1.23457	0.7834	95.8%			2.8564	0.0157	0.2058
50	0.3	35	β	0.0369	0.01839	0.5118	95.6%	O_1	0.0387	0.0044	0.00032	0.0627
			θ	0.1055	0.04398	0.7108	95.9%	O_2	0.0002	0.0229	0.00165	0.1006
			$R(0.6)$	0.0183	0.00581	0.2903	95.5%	O_3	230.4277	0.0052	0.00044	0.0790
			$H(0.6)$	0.0795	0.14627	1.4672	95.2%	O_4	2.9344	0.0102	0.00326	0.2111
			$R(0.85)$	0.0086	0.00523	0.2817	95.6%			0.0021	0.00026	0.0627
			$H(0.85)$	0.2401	0.84128	3.4719	95.8%			0.0328	0.01498	0.4164
		45	β	0.0292	0.01287	0.4300	95.8%	O_1	0.0284	0.0031	0.00009	0.0311
			θ	0.0523	0.02265	0.5534	95.8%	O_2	0.0001	0.0065	0.00019	0.0406
			$R(0.6)$	0.0030	0.00414	0.2520	94.7%	O_3	287.7103	0.0000	0.00010	0.0390
			$H(0.6)$	0.0702	0.10813	1.2599	95.7%	O_4	3.0968	0.0088	0.00092	0.1034
			$R(0.85)$	−0.0003	0.00374	0.2397	94.6%			−0.0008	0.00006	0.0317
			$H(0.85)$	0.1885	0.59457	2.9324	95.7%			0.0220	0.00423	0.2099
	0.8	35	β	0.0451	0.01827	0.4997	95.6%	O_1	0.0375	0.0065	0.00039	0.0608
			θ	0.0916	0.03438	0.6323	95.2%	O_2	0.0002	0.0181	0.00104	0.0866
			$R(0.6)$	0.0071	0.00524	0.2826	95.7%	O_3	223.9769	0.0018	0.00038	0.0752
			$H(0.6)$	0.1093	0.14684	1.4405	95.6%	O_4	1.6721	0.0177	0.00378	0.2016
			$R(0.85)$	−0.0004	0.00484	0.2727	95.5%			−0.0005	0.00024	0.0604
			$H(0.85)$	0.2965	0.83295	3.3853	95.6%			0.0468	0.01780	0.4059
		45	β	0.0295	0.01341	0.4392	95.7%	O_1	0.0280	0.0034	0.00010	0.0323
			θ	0.0448	0.02086	0.5386	96.2%	O_2	0.0001	0.0054	0.00016	0.0383
			$R(0.6)$	0.0003	0.00415	0.2525	93.7%	O_3	288.9783	−0.0006	0.00009	0.0395
			$H(0.6)$	0.0723	0.11132	1.2774	96.0%	O_4	3.5188	0.0098	0.00097	0.1069
			$R(0.85)$	−0.0018	0.00383	0.2426	94.8%			0.0012	0.00006	0.0328
			$H(0.85)$	0.1896	0.61493	2.9842	95.8%			0.0236	0.00451	0.2164

Table 5. Cont.

n	r	s			MLE					Bayesian		
				Bias	MSE	WACI	CP	Optimality		Bias	MSE	WCCI
100	0.3	70	β	0.0267	0.00855	0.3473	95.7%	O_1	0.0171	0.0024	0.00012	0.0376
			θ	0.0690	0.01783	0.4484	95.0%	O_2	0.0000	0.0117	0.00043	0.0568
			$R(0.6)$	0.0090	0.00284	0.2061	95.8%	O_3	442.4535	0.0026	0.00016	0.0489
			$H(0.6)$	0.0645	0.07290	1.0283	95.1%	O_4	2.9947	0.0057	0.00125	0.1240
			$R(0.85)$	0.0020	0.00263	0.2008	95.7%			0.0010	0.00010	0.0387
			$H(0.85)$	0.1797	0.40180	2.3841	95.5%			0.0177	0.00568	0.2530
		90	β	0.0129	0.00536	0.2827	94.7%	O_1	0.0128	0.0013	0.00003	0.0181
			θ	0.0256	0.00907	0.3597	95.0%	O_2	0.0000	0.0029	0.00006	0.0233
			$R(0.6)$	0.0024	0.00205	0.1771	95.8%	O_3	572.9885	0.0000	0.00003	0.0222
			$H(0.6)$	0.0310	0.04803	0.8508	94.7%	O_4	2.3973	0.0038	0.00031	0.0595
			$R(0.85)$	0.0007	0.00187	0.1696	94.9%			−0.0003	0.00002	0.0179
			$H(0.85)$	0.0838	0.25437	1.9506	94.9%			0.0096	0.00137	0.1225
	0.8	70	β	0.0274	0.00795	0.3328	95.3%	O_1	0.0168	0.0034	0.00013	0.0392
			θ	0.0565	0.01500	0.4261	95.1%	O_2	0.0000	0.0098	0.00034	0.0558
			$R(0.6)$	0.0035	0.00280	0.2070	94.8%	O_3	441.2820	0.0011	0.00015	0.0484
			$H(0.6)$	0.0693	0.06869	0.9913	94.9%	O_4	3.2956	0.0092	0.00133	0.1304
			$R(0.85)$	−0.0016	0.00254	0.1976	95.5%			−0.0002	0.00010	0.0390
			$H(0.85)$	0.1834	0.37293	2.2845	94.9%			0.0243	0.00610	0.2614
		90	β	0.0109	0.00515	0.2782	95.1%	O_1	0.0127	0.0013	0.00003	0.0183
			θ	0.0212	0.00904	0.3635	95.5%	O_2	0.0000	0.0026	0.00005	0.0248
			$R(0.6)$	0.0022	0.00212	0.1802	95.2%	O_3	577.1218	0.0000	0.00003	0.0236
			$H(0.6)$	0.0253	0.04644	0.8393	94.9%	O_4	2.5652	0.0037	0.00028	0.0612
			$R(0.85)$	0.0011	0.00191	0.1712	94.9%			−0.0004	0.00002	0.0190
			$H(0.85)$	0.0693	0.24508	1.9224	94.9%			0.0092	0.00125	0.1231

- The key general finding is that the suggested values for θ, β, $R(t)$, and $h(t)$ performed well.
- All estimations of θ, β, $R(t)$, and $h(t)$ functioned satisfactorily as n(or s) grew.
- In most cases, the MSE, Bias, and WCI of all unknown parameters fell while their CPs grew as (T_1, T_2) increased.
- Due to the gamma information, the Bayes estimates of θ, β, $R(t)$, and $h(t)$ behaved more predictably than the other estimates. Regarding credible HPD intervals, the same statement might be made.
- When the parameter of binomial r was increased, the proposed estimates of θ, β, $R(t)$, and $h(t)$ performed better in most cases.

7. Application

The data set, which has been examined by [11], had 30 assessments of the tensile strength of polyester fibers. The following details are included in the data set: "0.023, 0.032, 0.054, 0.069, 0.081, 0.094, 0.105, 0.127, 0.148, 0.169, 0.188, 0.216, 0.255, 0.277, 0.311, 0.361, 0.376, 0.395, 0.432, 0.463, 0.481, 0.519, 0.529, 0.567, 0.642, 0.674, 0.752, 0.823, 0.887, 0.926". For data on the strength of polyester fibers, where the Kolmogorov-Smirnov distance is 0.0569 with a p-value of 0.9999, [11] explores the MLE of this model using several measures of goodness-of-fit. The Kolmogorov-Smirnov test findings showed that the KMKu distribution fits the data on polyester fiber strength.

Two GPHCS-T2 samples with s = 20 and 25 were produced from the tensile strength of polyester fibers data in order to explain the proposed estimation methodology. The binomial removal has been used to obtain the GPHCS-T2 samples with different parameters of p = 0.2, 0.5, and 0.8. Table 6 lists the computed $R(t)$ and $h(t)$ at t = 0.6 and 0.85 by maximum likelihood estimates (MLE) and Bayesian estimation, respectively, along with their standard error (SE). By repeating the MCMC sampler 12,000 times and disregarding the first 2000 times as burn-in, the Bayes estimates (with their SE) were evaluated using incorrect gamma priors and are also provided in Table 4 because there was no prior knowledge about the unknown KMKu parameters θ, and β from the given data set. In order to estimate unknown hyperparameters for the computational logic, elective hyperparameters were employed. In terms of the minimum standard error and interval width values, it is evident from Table 6 that the MCMC estimates of $\theta, \beta, R(t)$, and $h(t)$ performed better than the others.

Table 6. MLE and Bayesian estimation.

			MLE				Bayesian			
			Estimates	SE	R(0.6)	R(0.85)	Estimates	SE	R(0.6)	R(0.85)
s	p				H(0.6)	H(0.85)			H(0.6)	H(0.85)
20	0.2	β	0.8884	0.5264	0.3253	0.1189	0.9884	0.3296	0.3047	0.1017
		θ	1.0033	0.2514	2.7480	6.4884	1.0556	0.2365	2.9811	7.1010
	0.5	β	1.5376	0.5760	0.2111	0.0436	1.3577	0.3243	0.2505	0.0608
		θ	1.2293	0.2692	4.1919	10.4235	1.2399	0.1761	3.7759	9.3192
	0.8	β	1.5404	0.5751	0.2091	0.0431	1.6921	0.3877	0.1800	0.0324
		θ	1.2231	0.2677	4.2022	10.4439	1.2090	0.1681	4.5521	11.3874
25	0.2	β	1.4928	0.4925	0.1858	0.0392	1.5520	0.3081	0.1795	0.0360
		θ	1.0776	0.2203	4.1819	10.2139	1.0966	0.1464	4.3074	10.5745
	0.5	β	1.5231	0.5001	0.1884	0.0389	1.5572	0.3157	0.1811	0.0362
		θ	1.1143	0.2294	4.2299	10.3859	1.1085	0.1507	4.3121	10.6013
	0.8	β	1.5221	0.4996	0.1883	0.0389	1.4511	0.3053	0.2044	0.0451
		θ	1.1129	0.2293	4.2285	10.3804	1.1252	0.1523	4.0571	9.9345

Figures 2–4 were created to examine the maximum values of the estimators by profile likelihood as well as the existence and uniqueness of the log-likelihood function by contour plot with regard to different d and q options based on GPHCS-T2 samples with s = 20 and distinct p = 0.2, 0.5, and 0.8, respectively. Figure 5 clearly shows that the MCMC technique converged favorably and that the recommended size of the burn-in sample was adequate to completely nullify the impact of the recommended beginning values. Figure 5 demonstrates that the estimated estimates of θ and β were roughly symmetrical for each sample when s = 20.

Figures 6–8 were created to examine the maximum values of the estimators by profile likelihood as well as the existence and uniqueness of the log-likelihood function by contour plot with regard to different d and q options based on GPHCS-T2 samples with s = 25 and distinct p = 0.2, 0.5, and 0.8, respectively. Figure 9 clearly shows that the MCMC technique converged favorably and that the recommended size of the burn-in sample was adequate to completely nullify the impact of the recommended beginning values. Figure 9 demonstrates that the estimated estimates of θ and β were roughly symmetrical for each sample when s = 25.

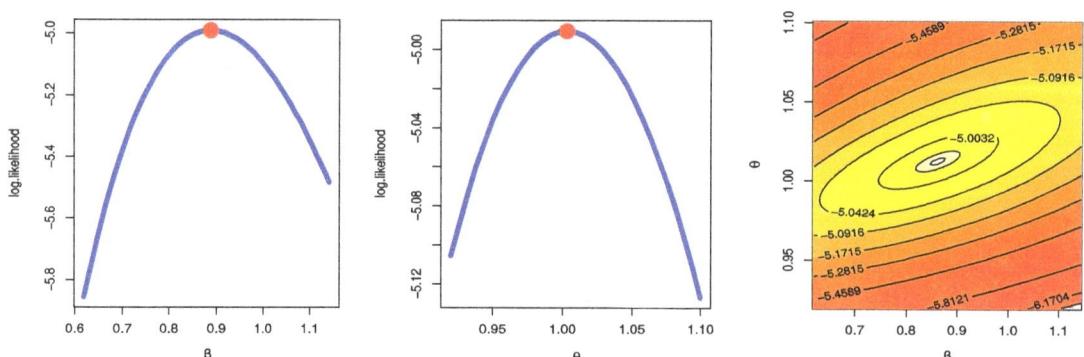

Figure 2. Profile likelihood and contour plot s = 20 p = 0.2.

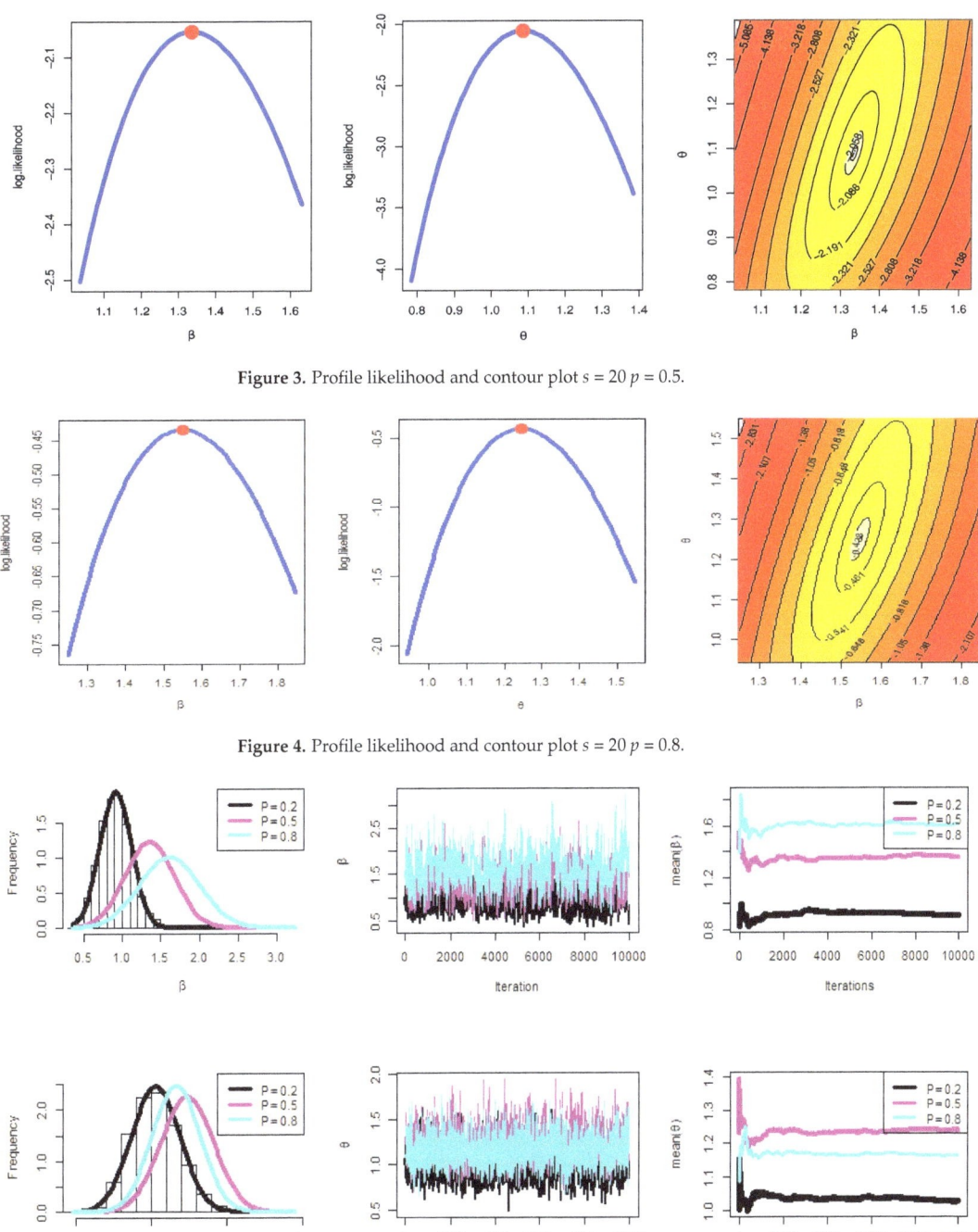

Figure 3. Profile likelihood and contour plot $s = 20$ $p = 0.5$.

Figure 4. Profile likelihood and contour plot $s = 20$ $p = 0.8$.

Figure 5. Bayesian checks when $s = 20$.

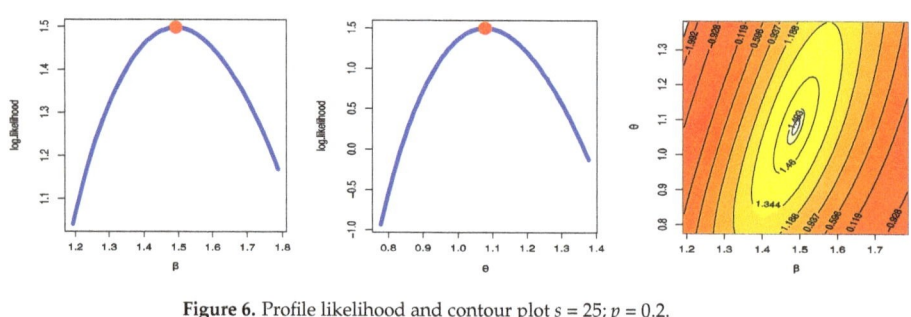

Figure 6. Profile likelihood and contour plot $s = 25$; $p = 0.2$.

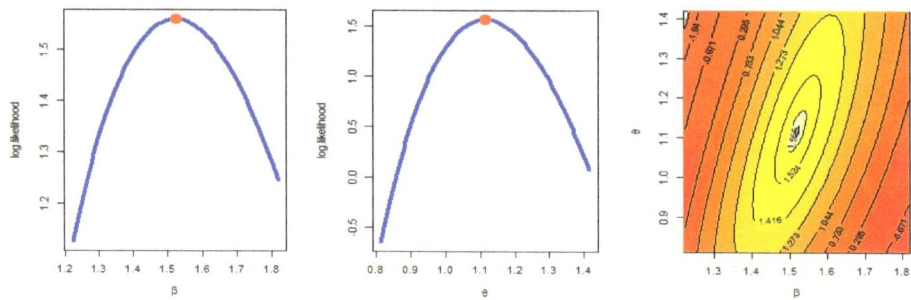

Figure 7. Profile likelihood and contour plot $s = 25$; $p = 0.5$.

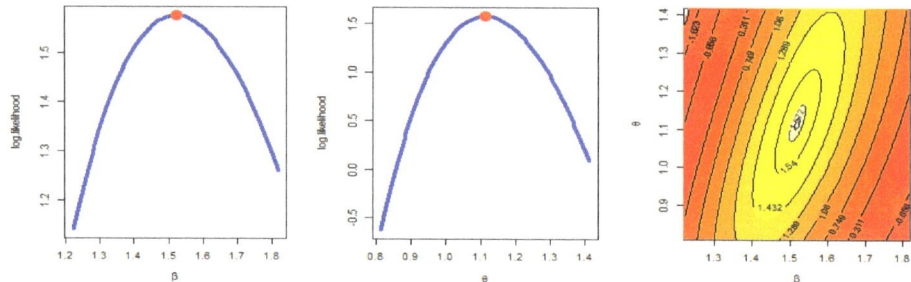

Figure 8. Profile likelihood and contour plot $s = 25$; $p = 0.8$.

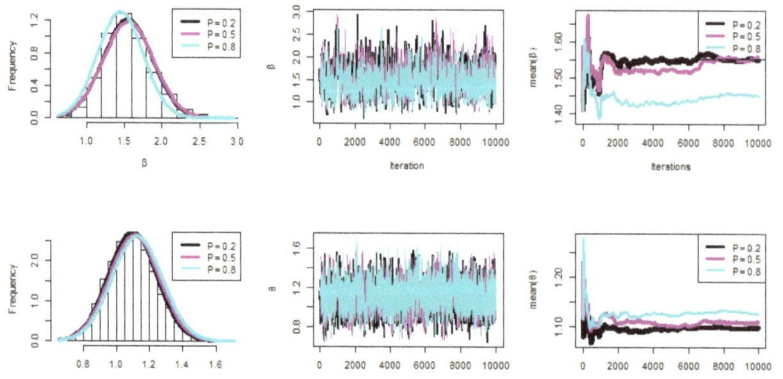

Figure 9. Bayesian checks when $s = 25$.

8. Conclusions and Discussion

This paper examines the reliability analysis of the unknown parameters, reliability, and hazard rate functions for the generalized type-II progressive hybrid censoring-based KMKu model. The "maxLik" package of the R programming language was used to compute the frequentist estimates with their asymptotic confidence intervals for the unknown parameters and any function of them. Since the likelihood function was produced in complex form, the posterior density function was obtained in nonlinear form. Consequently, the Bayesian estimates and the related HPD intervals were created using the Metropolis-Hastings technique and accounting for the squared error loss function. Numerous simulation experiments were run utilizing various total test unit choices, observed failure data, threshold times, and progressive censoring schemes in order to compare the behavior of the collected estimates. The outcomes demonstrated that the Bayes–MCMC strategy performed substantially better than the frequentist approach. Under generalized type-II progressive hybrid censoring, it was suggested to estimate the KMKu distribution's parameters, reliability, and hazard functions using the Bayesian MCMC paradigm. We believe that the technique and results described here will be helpful to reliability practitioners and that they will be used to inform future censoring tactics. The 30 assessments of the tensile strength of polyester fibers are used to demonstrate how the recommended strategies may be applied in real-world circumstances. The most important results can be summarized in the following points:

- The key general finding is that the suggested values for $\theta, \beta, R(t)$, and $h(t)$ performed well.
- All estimations of $\theta, \beta, R(t)$, and $h(t)$ functioned satisfactorily as n (or s) grew.
- In most cases, the MSE, Bias, and WCI of all unknown parameters fell while their CPs grew as (T_1, T_2) increased.
- Due to the gamma information, the Bayes estimates of $\theta, \beta, R(t)$, and $h(t)$ behaved more predictably than the other estimates. Regarding credible HPD intervals, the same statement might be made.
- In most cases, the proposed estimates of $\theta, \beta, R(t)$, and $h(t)$ performed better when the parameter of binomial r was increased.
- The MLE has a unique solution and a maximum value of log-likelihood.

Author Contributions: Conceptualization, R.A., E.M.A. and H.R.; methodology, R.A., E.M.A. and H.R.; writing—original draft preparation, R.A., E.M.A. and H.R.; writing—review and editing, R.A., E.M.A. and H.R. All the authors have the same contribution and agree to publish the manuscript in Symmetry Journal. All authors have read and agreed to the published version of the manuscript.

Funding: This research was funded by Princess Nourah bint Abdulrahman University Researchers Supporting Project number (PNURSP2023R50), Princess Nourah bint Abdulrahman University, Riyadh, Saudi Arabia.

Institutional Review Board Statement: Not applicable.

Informed Consent Statement: Not applicable.

Data Availability Statement: The data used to support the findings of this study are included within the article.

Acknowledgments: Princess Nourah bint Abdulrahman University Researchers Supporting Project number (PNURSP2023R50), Princess Nourah bint Abdulrahman University, Riyadh, Saudi Arabia.

Conflicts of Interest: The authors declare no conflict of interest.

References

1. Balakrishnan, N.; Aggarwala, R. *Progressive Censoring: Theory, Methods, and Applications*; Springer Science & Business Media: Berlin, Germany, 2000.
2. Balakrishnan, N. Progressive censoring methodology: An appraisal. *TEST* **2007**, *16*, 211–259. [CrossRef]
3. Balakrishnan, N.; Cramer, E. *The Art of Progressive Censoring*; Springer: New York, NY, USA, 2014.
4. Kundu, D.; Joarder, A. Analysis of Type-II progressively hybrid censored data. *Comput. Stat. Data Anal.* **2006**, *50*, 2509–2528. [CrossRef]
5. Childs, A.; Chandrasekar, B.; Balakrishnan, N. Exact likelihood inference for an exponential parameter under progressive hybrid censoring schemes. In *Statistical Models and Methods for Biomedical and Technical Systems*; Vonta, F., Nikulin, M., Limnios, N., Huber-Carol, C., Eds.; Birkhäuser: Boston, MA, USA, 2008; pp. 319–330.

6. Lee, K.; Sun, H.; Cho, Y. Exact likelihood inference of the exponential parameter under generalized Type II progressive hybrid censoring. *J. Korean Stat. Soc.* **2016**, *45*, 123–136. [CrossRef]
7. Ateya, S.; Mohammed, H. Prediction under Burr-XII distribution based on generalized Type-II progressive hybrid censoring scheme. *J. Egypt. Math. Soc.* **2018**, *26*, 491–508.
8. Seo, J.I. Objective Bayesian analysis for the Weibull distribution with partial information under the generalized Type-II progressive hybrid censoring scheme. *Commun. Stat.-Simul. Comput.* **2020**, *51*, 5157–5173. [CrossRef]
9. Cho, S.; Lee, K. Exact likelihood inference for a competing risks model with generalized Type-II progressive hybrid censored exponential data. *Symmetry* **2021**, *13*, 887. [CrossRef]
10. Nagy, M.; Bakr, M.E.; Alrasheedi, A.F. Analysis with applications of the generalized Type-II progressive hybrid censoring sample from Burr Type-XII model. *Math. Probl. Eng.* **2022**, *2022*, 1241303. [CrossRef]
11. Alotaibi, N.; Elbatal, I.; Shrahili, M.; Al-Moisheer, A.S.; Elgarhy, M.; Almetwally, E.M. Statistical Inference for the Kavya–Manoharan Kumaraswamy Model under Ranked Set Sampling with Applications. *Symmetry* **2023**, *15*, 587. [CrossRef]
12. Henningsen, A.; Toomet, O. maxlik: A package for maximum likelihood estimation in R. *Comput Stat.* **2011**, *26*, 443–458. [CrossRef]
13. Plummer, M.; Best, N.; Cowles, K.; Vines, K. CODA: Convergence diagnosis and output analysis for MCMC. *RNews* **2006**, *6*, 7–11.
14. Luo, C.; Shen, L.; Xu, A. Modelling and estimation of system reliability under dynamic operating environments and lifetime ordering constraints. *Reliab. Eng. Syst. Saf.* **2022**, *218*, 108136. [CrossRef]
15. Shirong, Z.; Ancha, X.; Yincai, T.; Lijuan, S. Fast Bayesian Inference of Reparameterized Gamma Process with Random Effects. *IEEE Trans. Reliab.* **2023**, 1–14. [CrossRef]
16. Zhuang, L.; Xu, A.; Wang, X.-L. A prognostic driven predictive maintenance framework based on Bayesian deep learning. *Reliab. Eng. Syst. Saf.* **2023**, *234*, 109181. [CrossRef]
17. Gelman, A.; Carlin, J.B.; Stern, H.S.; Rubin, D.B. *Bayesian Data Analysis*, 2nd ed.; Chapman and Hall/CRC: Boca Raton, FL, USA, 2004.
18. Lynch, S.M. *Introduction to Applied Bayesian Statistics and Estimation for Social Scientists*; Springer: New York, NY, USA, 2007.
19. Lawless, J.F. *Statistical Models and Methods for Lifetime Data*, 2nd ed.; John Wiley and Sons: Hoboken, NJ, USA, 1982.
20. Greene, W.H. *Econometric Analysis*, 4th ed.; Prentice-Hall: New York, NY, USA, 2000.
21. Chen, M.H.; Shao, Q.M. Monte Carlo estimation of Bayesian credible and HPD intervals. *J. Comput. Graph. Stat.* **1999**, *8*, 69–92.
22. Ng, H.K.T.; Chan, P.S.; Balakrishnan, N. Optimal progressive censoring plans for the Weibull distribution. *Technometrics* **2004**, *46*, 470–481. [CrossRef]
23. Pradhan, B.; Kundu, D. Inference and optimal censoring schemes for progressively censored Birnbaum–Saunders distribution. *J. Stat. Plan. Inference* **2013**, *143*, 1098–1108. [CrossRef]
24. Alotaibi, R.; Mutairi, A.; Almetwally, E.M.; Park, C.; Rezk, H. Optimal Design for a Bivariate Step-Stress Accelerated Life Test with Alpha Power Exponential Distribution Based on Type-I Progressive Censored Samples. *Symmetry* **2022**, *14*, 830. [CrossRef]
25. Dey, S.; Singh, S.; Tripathi, Y.M.; Asgharzadeh, A. Estimation and prediction for a progressively censored generalized inverted exponential distribution. *Stat. Methodol.* **2016**, *32*, 185–202.

Disclaimer/Publisher's Note: The statements, opinions and data contained in all publications are solely those of the individual author(s) and contributor(s) and not of MDPI and/or the editor(s). MDPI and/or the editor(s) disclaim responsibility for any injury to people or property resulting from any ideas, methods, instructions or products referred to in the content.

MDPI AG
Grosspeteranlage 5
4052 Basel
Switzerland
Tel.: +41 61 683 77 34

Symmetry Editorial Office
E-mail: symmetry@mdpi.com
www.mdpi.com/journal/symmetry

Disclaimer/Publisher's Note: The statements, opinions and data contained in all publications are solely those of the individual author(s) and contributor(s) and not of MDPI and/or the editor(s). MDPI and/or the editor(s) disclaim responsibility for any injury to people or property resulting from any ideas, methods, instructions or products referred to in the content.

www.ingramcontent.com/pod-product-compliance
Lightning Source LLC
LaVergne TN
LVHW070502100526
838202LV00014B/1770